ICE CREAM
AND
FROZEN DESSERTS

ICE CREAM
AND
FROZEN DESSERTS

A Commercial Guide to Production and Marketing

Malcolm Stogo

JOHN WILEY & SONS, INC.

New York   Chichester   Weinham   Brisbane   Singapore   Toronto

This book is printed on acid-free paper. ∞

Copyright © 1998 by John Wiley & Sons, Inc. All rights reserved.

Published simultaneously in Canada.

This publication is designed to provide accurate and authoritative information in regard to the
subject matter covered. It is sold with the understanding that the publisher is not engaged in
rendering legal, accounting, or other professional services. If legal advice or other expert
assistance is required, the services of a competent professional person should be sought.

Library of Congress Cataloging-in-Publication Data:
Stogo, Malcolm.
    Ice cream and frozen desserts : a commercial guide to production
and marketing / Malcolm Stogo.
        p.   cm.
    Includes bibliographical references and index.
    ISBN 0-471-15392-3 (cloth : alk. paper)
    1. Ice cream, ices, etc.   2. Frozen desserts industry.   I. Title.
TX795.S772   1997
641.8'62'068—DC21   97-11372

Printed in the United States of America.

20 19 18

CONTENTS

FOREWORD

Socrates once said, "There is only one good, knowledge, and one evil, igno-rance" This statement could guide us both in our lives and in our businesses. It is surely appropriate regarding the fun business of making and selling ice cream. In this book, *Ice Cream and Frozen Desserts: A Commercial Guide to Production and Marketing*, Malcolm Stogo brings his vast practical experience in frozen dessert retailing together with the "nuts and bolts" of manufacturing and mar-keting to provide the "knowledge" that is the one business "good."

I call the ice cream business the fun business. From more than fifty years in the fun business it is easy to recall the joy in countless eyes, young and old, an-ticipating the taste of that first bite of the scoop they have selected. The people we work with and compete with are all trying to satisfy that desire for the sweet cold taste of ice cream. To be sure, there is a large market for the low-priced commercial types of ice cream, and the products are good values, but there is also a growing market for premium products. Individual store operators have a wonderful opportunity to use their unique ideas to create unlimited selections of the best ice cream ever tasted. The fun business is hard work, requires dedica-tion, perseverance, and lots and lots of cleaning. While it shares many of the pit-falls of small businesses, the rewards can be great.

As individual ice cream operations grow, it is sometimes necessary to advance to larger and more efficient production systems. This text discusses continuous ice cream freezers and the equipment required to convert a batch freezing oper-ation to continuous production. The recipes section includes methods and the larger portions required for continuous freezing.

The benefit of Malcolm Stogo's years of dedication to quality ingredients and hardware and his patience in experimenting until he has the perfect formula— these make for a great reference and business guide.

Recipe for the fun business: 1 Cup of the "one good, knowledge," a cup of hard work, a cup of quality ingredients, and finally a cup of loving attention. Mix and freeze well and enjoy the best ice cream you have ever tasted.

Bill Lambert
General Manager (Retired)
AE Farms, Des Moines, Iowa

PREFACE

Is there any better treat than a frozen dessert, be it ice cream, sorbet, or gelato? I don't think so! What is it that makes nearly everyone, from child to adult, smile with anticipation when a dish of ice cream is placed in front of them. I think it's a combination of things, but the most important is that it just tastes great! Whether it's high fat, low fat, or no fat, there is nothing better than freshly made ice cream, sorbets, frozen yogurts, gelatos, and water ices.

Ice Cream and Frozen Desserts is all about how to produce, present, and sell high-quality, freshly made ice cream and other frozen desserts to the consuming public. Whether you're interested in producing ice cream on a large scale with a continuous freezer or operating an ice cream shop with a batch freezer, the topics and products covered can help you find success. While there are many areas of difference between large and small operations, common ground does exist, especially in the areas of ingredients, marketing, and sanitation. Written as an everyday tool for anyone actively involved in the production and marketing of ice cream, it includes something for everyone to learn and use.

This book is an outgrowth of my first, *Frozen Desserts: A Complete Retailer's Guide.* It includes the best of *Frozen Desserts* along with new material covering continuous freezing production methods and emphasizing marketing products to supermarkets. The emphasis on marketing is important because, as every sharp operator knows, if you can't make people aware of your products, they won't buy them. The expanded recipe section is the largest written source ever produced for commercial ice cream production. Each recipe has been written in an easy-to-use format that caters to either a small batch freezer producer or a large ice cream manufacturer.

Since the early 1970s, producing a high-quality frozen dessert has been a labor of love for me. I've been fortunate in being able to participate in the ice cream revival that captured the American public, and during the last ten years I have learned much from my consulting business with clients all over the world. One thing in particular that I have learned is that there is much in common wherever you go. Everyone tries hard to produce the best, whether it is here in the United States or in faraway places like Saudi Arabia, Australia, Iceland, South Africa, or the United Kingdom. Hopefully, I have been able to convey in this book what I have learned and experienced.

If there is one message I can offer you on how success is achieved in this industry, it is that it takes hard work, good common sense, and passion for what you are doing. Finally, you must be willing to listen and learn from others. This book is intended to prepare you for the challenge, help get you started, and keep you motivated and on the right track in a business that I have enjoyed so much. I hope you'll find my enthusiasm contagious!

Malcolm Stogo

ACKNOWLEDGMENTS

Writing this book has taught me that no matter how much one knows about making ice cream, there is always something new to learn. It's truly amazing that in the five years since I wrote my first book, *Frozen Desserts,* so much has changed and there is so much more to learn.

There are so many people to thank. Some were actively involved in the writing of this book, some were people I learned much from, and others were there to give me the support I needed over the years to pursue my dream of making great ice cream and helping others do the same.

But first and foremost is my wife, Barbara Landau Stogo. It is our partnership in marriage and business that has made it possible. I have said it before, and I will say it again. Barbara has instincts that are always right. When we produced our first commercial line of ice cream back in 1979, it was her creative idea to hand write the labels on our pint containers. Not only was that ice cream the best we ever produced, but it was that look that got people to try it. Trends come and trends go, but it was also her idea to make white chocolate ice cream way before anyone else in this industry even thought about it. It's been her partnership and her encouragement that has allowed me the freedom to be where I am today.

My parents, Philip and Rose Stogo, taught me at age eight what food was all about. Without that start, I wouldn't be writing this book today. My in-laws, Hyman and Lucy Landau, are simply wonderful. No matter the flavor or the product, they are always willing to taste, judge, and offer a solid opinion. My daughter, Emily, at the age of six cracked the eggs that were used in the first ice cream I ever produced and sold. I owe many thanks to Art and Betty Sherman for their friendship and seed money for my first independent ice cream business. Robert Shapiro, my partner at Ice Cream Extravaganza in New York City, taught me what vision is all about. When I think about vision, I think about Bobby.

Thank you Carol Robbins and Herb Wolff. Your book, *The Very Best Ice Cream and Where to Find It* inspired me to write my own.

I have been very lucky to have known two gentlemen who are no longer with us, Mac McCluskey of Emery Thompson and Chat Neilsen of Neilsen-Massey Vanillas. All I had to do was pick up the phone, and did I learn. Today, I am equally lucky to know and have learned from the following individuals: Steve Thompson of Emery Thompson, a one man booster of mine for many years; Fred Nickerson of Ramsey/Sias, from whom I have learned so much; Craig

Colonno of AE Farms—when it comes to ice cream mixes, go no farther than talking to Craig; Harold Barnes, who offered solid advice on learning the ropes of international consulting; Dennis Andes, the best graphic-arts ice cream person in the country; Tony Lana, Steve Boud, and Rocco Colafrancesco for filling me in on what's new in this industry.

A special thank you to my friend Ben Silloway, who gave me my first big consulting job at Haagen-Dazs. You gave me a free rein and a lot of what is in this book was learned from that experience. Also, a word of thanks to Donald and Carol Kalen and Esther and Mack Gould for listening to my ideas and responding with their honest advice, which I respect so very much. To Sally Lambert, her knowledge and inspiration to anyone who has ever met her is immeasurable. To Jerome Kuster, a very special young man with very special qualities, I thank you.

Education comes in many forms, so I thank the following magazines for helping me through the years to learn what this business is all about: *Dairy Foods Magazine, Dairy Field,* and *Restaurants & Institutions.*

Thank you to Bernice Pettinato of Beehive Productions. It was Berni who did such a great job editing my first book, *Frozen Desserts,* and oh how lucky I am to have had her editing skills on this book as well. Her eye for the right word, expression, or comma is golden in my eyes.

Special thanks to my editor at John Wiley & Sons, Claire Thompson for seeing something in "my idea" for this book, and to her assistant, Maria Colletti, for helping me through the trials and tribulations of putting all of this together. To David Sassian, thank you for shepherding this book to its conclusion.

Lastly, thank you to our Boots. Her input into this book has been immeasurable.

A VERY SPECIAL THANK YOU

I am proud to say that Bill Lambert is my friend and associate. He is also my mentor. Bill is the former general manager of AE Farms, the ice cream subsidiary of Anderson Erickson Dairy of Des Moines, Iowa. I met Bill a few years back when AE Farms was developing a product for one of my clients. From that experience has come a relationship that I cherish dearly.

Without a doubt, it's been Bill's knowledge and experience that I have tapped into during almost every phase of this book. Time and again I have asked Bill some of the silliest questions you can imagine, and his response has always been the same. To Bill there is a reason for every question asked, and he or she who doesn't ask is the fool. It's the only way to learn; and I thank him for simply listening and responding. How lucky I am.

Raised working in Lambert's Dairy, Des Moines, Iowa that was founded by his father in 1916, Bill has for the last forty-five years been involved in almost every phase of ice cream production. Ask any of his former employees or associates, and you will get the same answer. There is no one better. Thank you Bill.

ICE CREAM
AND
FROZEN DESSERTS

INTRODUCTION

HISTORY OF COMMERCIAL ICE CREAM IN THE UNITED STATES

The story of precisely when and where the confection we call "ice cream" originated is one full of *possibly, probably,* and *may have been.* It is said that the Romans used snow and ice for chilling beverages and foods, and that Marco Polo brought back from his travels in the Orient a recipe for water ices supposedly thousands of years old. Hints turn up here and there about various frozen concoctions appearing in royal courts of medieval England and France. The best guesses as to the origins of ice cream per se point to fifteenth- or sixteenth-century Europe (Dickson, 1978, p. 14).

An anonymous manuscript dated circa 1700, *L'Art de Faire des Glaces,* is the earliest significant writing on the preparation of ice cream and water ices (Dickson, 1978, p. 18). *The Art of Cookery Made Easy,* by Hannah Glass, was printed in London in 1747 and contained the following recipe:

To Make Ice Cream

Take two pewter basins, one larger than the other; the inward one must have a close cover, into which you are to put your cream, and mix it with raspberries, or whatever you like best, to give it a flavour and a colour. Sweeten it to your palate; then cover it close, and set it into the larger basin. Fill it with ice, and a handful of salt: let it stand in this ice three quarters of an hour, then uncover it and stir the cream well together: cover it close again, and let it stand half an hour longer, after that turn it into your plate. These things are made at the pewters.

From Private Glamour to Public Clamor

It is apparent, then, that ice cream did not originate in the United States, but certainly it was popularized and industrialized here. Its commercial origins in this country can be dated back to 1774. In the first recorded public mention of

1

ice cream, a caterer named Philip Lenzi announced in a New York newspaper that he had just arrived from London and was prepared to supply ice cream and other confections, on special order, to a limited clientele (IAICM, 1986, p. 6).

Just as European royalty had done, some of our early national leaders enjoyed ice cream in their own homes. Historical record has shown that George Washington clearly had a taste for ice cream and even purchased a "Cream Machine for Making Ice," as well as keeping "two pewter ice cream pots" at his Mount Vernon home (Dickson, 1978, pp. 22–23). Thomas Jefferson devised an eighteen-step process for its manufacture while he was in France. During Jefferson's presidency, the official White House hostess, the wife of Jefferson's secretary of state, was Dolley Madison. In this role she glamorized ice cream by serving it at state dinners.

Indeed, ice cream was constantly served as a dessert at the White House during the early days of our nation. Consequently, many of the first ice cream makers in this country learned their craft there. In 1832, one of the first retail ice cream businesses in Philadelphia was opened by Augustus Jackson, a former White House cook (Dickson, 1978, p. 24).

Equipment

The Freezer   Ice cream making was removed from the sole realm of the wealthy, who had servants to accomplish the difficult process, with the invention of the hand-cranked freezer. In 1846, a New Jersey woman, Nancy Johnson, devised what was "essentially a cumbersome version of the same home ice cream freezers" available today (Dickson, 1978, p. 25). In 1905, the Emery Thompson Machine & Supply Company invented the first batch ice cream freezer, then called brine freezers because of the solution used to develop cold refrigeration. By the early 1920s these freezers (see Figure I-1) were being used all over the world. The original design was so good that the modern version is the workhorse of many batch freezer operations worldwide.

The resurgence of the ice cream industry in the 1960s brought new life to the batch freezer. It has been so popular with new operators entering the industry in the 1990s that demand has constantly surpassed the manufacturers' supply. The used equipment market—batch freezers, soft serve machines, and ice cream dipping cases—has also become remarkably profitable.

The Scoop   The evolution of the ice cream scoop began around 1876, when a patent was given to William Clewell of Reading, Pennsylvania. The device was a tin and steel cone with a key release. By early 1900 there were at least twenty-two different patents for ice cream dippers. In 1914, Raymond B. Gilchrist patented what was probably the most successful, and certainly the most familiar, scoop for over twenty years. By 1935, a major change in scoop design was introduced by Sherman Kelley with the Zeroll dipper (Smith, 1986, pp. 144–145). Self-defrosting fluid in its handle allows ice cream to be rolled and instantly released. Many imitations of this practical and sanitary scoop are in use today.

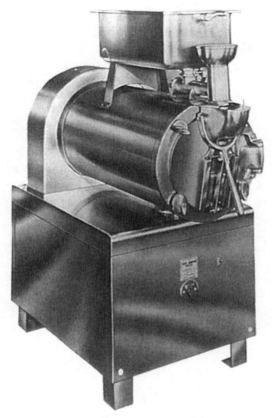

FIGURE I-1. Emery Thompson batch freezer (early 1920s).

In the 1920s, the "Handy Disher," was produced by the Mayer Manufacturing Corporation of Chicago. Instead of scoops, it serves slices of ice cream in three sizes: sixteen, eighteen, or twenty portions to the quart.

When ice cream production declined dramatically during the Depression era, many companies that produced scoops were forced to close or merge.

The Soda Fountain During the late 1850s, the soda fountain started to appear in different forms around Boston and Philadelphia. Eugene Roussel, a French immigrant to Philadelphia, sold soda mixed with syrup in his shop. Success led him to add more flavors of syrup, and he cultivated a larger market for carbonated water. In Lowell, Massachusetts, Gustavus D. Dows built the first ornate marble soda fountain (Dickson, 1978, p. 91). By the early 1900s, soda fountains became incredibly fancy works of art with many elaborate variations. Around 1903, the first fountain counter that allowed customers to watch ice cream creations being made right in front of their eyes was installed at the

Broad Street Pharmacy in Philadelphia (Dickson, 1978, p. 92). It was not long before every neighborhood druggist wanted a fountain counter, and many went into debt to have one constructed.

Product

The Ice Cream Soda   Robert Green is credited with the invention of the ice cream soda during the Franklin Institute Exposition in Philadelphia in 1874. He had a concession stand there selling fresh sweet cream, syrup, and carbonated water. During one extremely busy day, he ran out of cream so he melted ice cream as a substitute. Demand outpaced the time it took to melt the ice cream, so he simply plopped the ice cream into the soda and created an instant success.

The Ice Cream Cone   At the 1904 Louisiana Purchase Exposition, Ernest A. Hamri had a stand next to an ice cream booth. Mr. Hamri had come to Saint Louis from Damascus, Syria, in 1903, bringing with him the recipe for zalabia that originated in countries around the Persian Gulf. He sold the crisp, waferlike pastry, which was baked on a flat waffle iron, served with sugar or other sweets at his concession stand during the fair.

His stand was so close to the ice cream booth that he was able to watch with interest the activities of his fellow concessionaires. One day they ran out of dishes for their ice cream because of the terrific demand for the product. To be of help, Mr. Hamri quickly rolled one of his thin pastries into the shape of a cone or cornucopia. The cone hardened in a few seconds as it cooled. His neighboring vendor put ice cream in it and handed it to an eager customer. Thus the cone was on its way to becoming a great American institution.

While Hamri is generally acknowledged as the inventor of the cone, others have also claimed credit. In particular, Italo Marchiony had a patent issued to him for such a cone well before the Exposition opened. However, only at his death in 1954 did the public learn of his contribution because he never did anything during his lifetime to promote his product or take credit for it (Dickson, 1978, pp. 66–72).

No matter the originator, by 1924 a new industry had produced nearly 245 million cones.

The Banana Split   The first banana split is credited to David Strickler, a soda jerk working in Latrobe, Pennsylvania, at the Tassell Pharmacy in 1904. He was a great experimenter and had his own dish designed. His version, except for the price, is quite similar to the one sold today: three scoops of ice cream; a whole banana cut lengthwise; and chocolate, marshmallow, whipped cream, nuts, and plump cherry, all for ten cents.

The Eskimo Pie   The Eskimo Pie, one of the most profitable products ever created in the ice cream industry, was invented by C. K. Nelson of Omaha, Nebraska, in 1919. He experimented unsuccessfully for several years with the idea of dipping ice cream into chocolate, until he learned that cocoa butter enhances chocolate's clingability. The idea was perfected with the help of Russell Stover, then with the Graham Ice Cream Company in Omaha. By 1922, the partners were selling a million pies a day and Nelson was collecting royalties of $30,000 a week (Dickson, 1978, p. 74).

The product was so profitable that imitators were soon freely impinging on the patent, and Nelson and Stover were forced to spend huge amounts of money defending it. Stover eventually sold out to Nelson, who, in turn, later merged with the U.S. Foil Company, a subsidiary of R. S. Reynolds, known today as Reynold's Metals. The Eskimo Pie Corporation still has a large share of the market even though the Eskimo Pie patent was declared invalid in 1928.

The Good Humor Ice Cream Sucker Harry Burt, Sr., an ice cream parlor operator and confectioner in Youngstown, Ohio, learned of Nelson's chocolate-covered ice cream and tried his own hand at the product in 1920. His experience with lollipops, the Good Humor Sucker, provided the inspiration for adding wooden handles to the ice cream. He "liked the name 'Good Humor' because it expressed his belief that the humors of the mind were regulated by those of the palate" (Dickson, 1978, p. 77). This invention is responsible for the explosion of novelty ice cream confections found in supermarkets today.

The Popsicle In 1923, Frank Epperson, a northern Californian, patented the "Epsicle." The original idea came about by accident when Epperson was eleven years old. He had mixed some then-popular soda water powder and left it on the back porch overnight with a stirring stick in it. That night in 1905 the temperature dropped to a record low. The following morning young Frank discovered frozen soda water on a stick. Years later Epperson recognized the commercial value of his accidental invention, which at one tome became America's favorite refreshment treat, the "Popsicle." Over time, variations such as the Fudgsicle, Creamsicle, Dreamsicle, Sidewalk Sundae, and Cheerio were introduced, but none has surpassed the taste-tingling orange-flavored Popsicle in popularity.

The Frozen Drumstick The concept of commercially producing a chocolate nut sundae in a sugar cone originated with I. C. Parker, advertising manager in 1930 of Pangburn Candy and Ice Cream Company in Fort Worth, Texas. Parker hand-made one of the treats, took it home, and asked his wife, Jewel, what it looked like. She said, "It looks like a drumstick," meaning a chicken leg. Thus the name was registered and the item became known as the "Drumstick" (Aynes, 1986).

The cones were produced in quantity by placing them upright in wire baskets and hand-filling them with ice cream one at a time. They were then blast frozen, hand-dipped in a pan of chocolate syrup, immediately rolled in ground peanuts, and packaged in glassine bags for sale in retail outlets and drugstores.

Industry

Jacob Fussell has been credited with starting the first wholesale ice cream business in Baltimore around 1851. A successful milk dealer, he became a successful ice cream maker and soon opened additional plants in Washington, D.C., Boston, and New York. In the late 1800s the ice cream industry was producing 20 million quarts annually and the total investment was approximately $15 million. By 1950 the volume produced had increased a hundredfold.

It was not until the early 1900s, when mechanical and technical advances provided alternatives to the hand-cranked freezer, that the industry began to boom. Trade journals, such as *The Ice Cream Review* and *The Ice Cream Trade Journal*, were founded to supply the industry with news. Trade associations were organized not only to promote the industry, but to fight the constant flow of government regulations affecting it.

In the late 1800s, companies such as Hinton's of New England, and Breyer's and Abbott's of Philadelphia were just starting up. Allen and Mary Hinton produced ice cream on a small farm near Andover, Massachusetts. The ice cream was transported into town by horse and buggy, and eventually the Hintons sold their products from a huge barn. Their business grew until they both died in the early 1900s. While their business was a small one, they were certainly pioneers in the industry (Hinton, 1987).

In 1923, the largest manufacturer of ice cream in this country was The Breyer's Ice Cream Company of Philadelphia, and while no longer independent (Unilever), it is still one of the largest. The business started in 1853 when William Breyer made ice cream at home and sold it to his neighbors. Growth encouraged him to open a store, and by 1923 the Breyer's plant was producing more than 22 million quarts of ice cream a year. The butterfat was then 11½–12 percent.

At that time, some manufacturers used artificial flavorings, but Breyer's gave its dealers a sign to hang in their stores. This sign would become a famous trademark for the company. It read

> I pledge that Breyer's ice cream never contained adulterants, gums, gelatine, powders or fillers, extracts or artificial flavorings of any kind. Real cream, granulated sugar and pure flavorings are used to make Breyer's ice cream.—Henry W. Breyer, President.

Also in the early 1920s, the Good Humor Corporation (now owned by Unilever) was created by Harry Burt as an outlet for his creation, the Good Humor Ice Cream Sucker. Using his marketing skills, he outfitted a white truck with a set of bells from the family bobsled and dressed the driver in white. Within a short period of time, dozens of his trucks were jingling all over his hometown of Youngstown, Ohio. The company was eventually sold after Harry's death in 1926. The story of its subsequent success during the late twenties and early thirties is almost absurd, but true. Mobsters and Wall Street speculators became involved in the company and created plenty of front-page news. The publicity helped sales tremendously (Dickson, 1978, pp. 77–81). Good Humor, like the Fuller Brush man, became a distinctly American institution and remains so today.

Market Trends

Prohibition After a slow start in the late eighteenth century because of scattered availability, by the 1920s ice cream was being dispensed everywhere in America, "from the corner drugstore soda fountain to the Pullman car" (Dickson, 1978, p. 33). Companies like Reed's of Des Moines, Iowa (Figure I-2) were sprouting up all over the place and became very popular within their locales. Reed's was family owned and operated with every member having his own responsibilities. They produced their own ice cream from scratch and had stores dispensing it all over Iowa. Indeed, the era of prohibition provided the perfect opportunity for the burgeoning ice cream industry to fill the void created by the drying-out of America. The virtues of ice cream rather than beer were even extolled in a song introduced at the Pacific Ice Cream Manufacturers Convention

FIGURE I-2. The Reed family's ice cream operation. Pictured from left to right are Charles Hinkle, Jay Reed, and Bill Reed. (Photo courtesy of Dennis Reed, Des Moines, Iowa).

in 1920 (Dickson, 1978, pp. 33–34). To the tune of "Old Black Joe," it went like this:

> Gone are the days when father was a souse,
> Gone are the days of the weekly family rows,
> Gone from this land since prohibition's here—
> He brings a brick of ice cream home instead of beer.
> (Chorus)
> He's coming, he's coming, we can see him coming near—
> He brings a brick of ice cream home instead of beer.

The Depression Era   After the prosperity of the 1920s, the years of the Depression provided both high and low points for the ice cream industry. While consumption in general was increasing because of the newness of ice cream to the public, money for such a nonessential item became scarcer and scarcer. In fact, ice cream consumption decreased by half during the Depression. Industry leaders feared a continued decline when the Twenty-first Amendment was ratified in 1933 to repeal prohibition, making beer and liquor once more available to consumers.

Pre-World War II   By 1935 the sales decline stopped, thanks to the enthusiastic support of the trade association and journals. Hollywood certainly helped with movies like *Kid Millions,* starring Eddie Cantor and having a fantastic finale inside an ice cream factory. Beautiful women were seen carrying vanilla, chocolate, and strawberry ice cream to a mammoth freezer. The city of Baltimore declared a special "Ice Cream Week" (Dickson, 1978, p. 40). Good Humor ice cream trucks ranged through neighborhoods carrying all kinds of ice cream novelties. Every corner drugstore had a soda fountain dispensing unique versions of the ice cream soda, milk shake, and sundae. The ornate fountain at Schwab's Drugstore in Hollywood was written into so many movie scripts that Schwab's became a household name.

World War II   Even though World War II brought rationing, the momentum of ice cream's popularity was not brought to a halt. The short supply of certain ingredients as a result of rationing only inspired manufacturers to concoct new flavors using available ingredients.

   American servicemen were among the biggest boosters of the frozen confection. In 1945, for example, the navy commissioned a new ship with a $1-million ice cream parlor that was capable of producing 10 gallons of ice cream every 7 seconds (Dickson, 1978, pp. 47–48). When the war was over and the men came home, ice cream consumption skyrocketed, with more than 20 quarts of ice cream produced for each American in 1946 (Dickson, 1978, p. 50).

Postwar Change   By 1948 ice cream consumption had leveled off and the industry started to mature. When suburbia started to flourish in the late forties and early fifties, soda fountains in drugstores gave way to "bottled miracles and Revlon displays" (Dickson, 1978, p. 53). Living standards changed and modernized supermarkets, candy stores, and luncheonettes sprang up in suburban America, picking up the slack in ice cream sales.

But quality standards suffered under the demands of the supermarkets for more cheaply priced ice cream to give them an edge over their competitors. Many manufacturers reduced the butterfat content, started using stabilizers, and increased the air pumped into their products to combine low cost and high profits. Supermarkets began pushing and successfully selling their own private-label brands to price-conscious consumers.

For the general public, the choices for good quality ice cream became slim as small companies went out of business because they could not compete on price and profitability with the larger manufacturers. During this time ice cream was actually available for sixty-nine cents a half gallon. The changes of the 1950s brought declining sales and inferior products.

Resurgence and Innovation   The early 1960s saw a slow resurgence of ice cream operations with the arrival on the scene of Baskin Robbins, Dairy Queen, Carvel, Bresler's, and others. These companies concentrated on low-butterfat ice creams and many varieties of flavors to entice public interest. Once that interest was again piqued, a niche for high-quality ice cream was recreated.

In 1961, one of the first to respond to the new market was Reuben Mattus, a Bronx manufacturer who had been squeezed out of the supermarket business because of his company's small size. Rather than give up, he "created one of the richest, heaviest, and most expensive ice creams ever to come out of an ice cream plant" (Dickson, 1978, p. 57). He gave it a European name, Häagen-Dazs and marketed it with such flair that it became the fastest growing ice cream company of the sixties, seventies, and eighties. Today it is still considered the "creme de la creme" of ice creams distributed worldwide (Robbins and Wolff, 1982, p. 117).

His creation of and success with a superpremium product encouraged a new generation of ice cream makers to enter the industry with their own ice cream manufacturing plants, dairy shops, and small chains. Companies such as Ben & Jerry's, AE Farms, Bruhn's, Colombo, Dreyer's Grand Ice Cream, Hershey's, and Blue Bell became thriving businesses thanks to Mattus's idea that ice cream was special, and that there were consumers who wanted quality and were willing to pay for it.

The 1980s saw Italian gelato gain popularity, ices upgraded as a product called sorbet, novelties of every imaginable kind being produced, and ice cream sandwiches and bars becoming a gourmet's treat. The popularity of frozen desserts in the United States spread throughout the world. In the late seventies, ice cream consumption in Japan was almost zero. That country has now become one of the world's largest consumers. England, which always had a sleeping ice cream industry, is today having an ice cream renaissance. Other countries, such as Italy, Spain, and even Russia, are producing and selling as much ice cream as the United States, based on population.

The Novelty Market In the mid-1980s the dormant novelty frozen dessert market began to awaken, and between 1985 and 1988 almost 2,000 new novelty products hit the supermarket shelves. The spectacular growth registered sales gains of 35 percent between the years 1985 and 1987. By 1988, retail novelty sales had reached more than $1 billion, with demand outpacing supply for a number of years on products like the Dove and Häagen-Dazs chocolate bars. The Carnation Company's Bon Bon and the Dole Fruit Bars were also major hits for two years. However, trouble was on the horizon of the novelty market.

Competition became very fierce among the major players for both shelf space and a share of the market. As long as these players were willing to spend large sums of money on distribution, slotting allowances, research and development, and advertising, their product lines continued to grow. But increasing costs of getting products on the shelves were shrinking profit margins. The situation became a "frenzied auction" in which the grocery trade often sold shelf space to the highest bidder (Lieb, 1988). When retailers started using advanced computerized techniques to track product movement and profitability, the grocery trade was no longer dependent on manufacturers to fill shelf space. Companies became reluctant to establish new product lines and simply expanded what they already had or retreated from the market.

During the mid 1990s, however, novelty manufacturers began to concentrate their marketing efforts to children via exterior packaging, product design, and the placement of their products on the supermarket shelves (as low as possible). The strategy worked. Sales now have been better than ever (Dairy Foods, 1996).

Health Consciousness While the novelty market slowed down in the early 1990s, a new attitude swept through the country in general and the frozen dessert industry in particular. The public started a health kick. Suddenly, the terms *light* and *frozen yogurt* were in vogue. Consumers were looking for products that were low in cholesterol, fat, and calories. The search became a national obsession.

In response, frozen yogurt companies like TCBY, Freshens, and Penguins opened shops all over the country, one faster than the other. Beginning in 1988, every major dairy processor came out with a "light" product. Some products were called ice milk, others were called "lite," and still others, frozen yogurt. The names were really not important as long as the products were perceived to fit the consumer's idea of a healthful product.

The Market Today As a result of the changes in U.S. nutritional labeling laws, ice milk is now called reduced-fat ice cream. This name change has resulted in a 60 percent increase in sales in that category over 1994. Conversely, frozen yogurt sales are being squeezed because of the new laws, and sales of both lowfat and nonfat in the United States have actually declined 40 percent over 1994.

Sorbets are taking the United States by storm, posting an increase of 208 percent in 1996 over 1994 (IICA, 1997). Why did this happen? Because consumers have discovered something unique in sorbets: flavor, taste, and excellent body texture. Even more important, they are cholesterol free (except for chocolate) and fat free. Other trends include the entrance of ice cream cakes into the supermarket retail segment and a renewed strength in sales of novelties catering to children.

Today's market is also characterized by globalization. Increasing numbers of U.S. products are being exported throughout the world, and European-style products are entering the U.S. market. In Europe, the quality of ice cream has improved dramatically because of the influence of U.S. products. This is especially evident in the United Kingdom, France, Russia, and the Eastern bloc countries. In the Middle East, ice cream production is still primitive, but, with dairy processors extensively trying to mimic U.S. products, there are signs of real improvement taking place.

Conclusion

And so the industry has come full circle. The pure and natural ingredients used when ice cream was introduced in the United States and made in hand-cranked freezers are once again in demand by quality-conscious consumers. The waffle cone and novelty items so popular today were created long ago. Today's diners and old-fashioned ice cream parlors are copies of the originals from the 1940s. "What goes around, comes around."

Learn from the history. Where the industry goes from here is up to you.

THE LANGUAGE OF ICE CREAM PRODUCTION AND RETAILING

Formal Terminology

Ice cream is one of those things we encounter almost daily in our lives that we purchase, consume, and enjoy without thinking too much about the details that result in a product being made available to us. That lack of knowledge may surround a product with mystery, and the "secret" jargon of a particular industry even adds to that mystery. But the mystery lies only in not knowing. After all, even your mother's homecooking seemed mysterious until you tried your own hand at it. Certainly procedures will seem difficult and the terms hard to understand until you have been introduced to them and become familiar with their purposes and explanations.

So here is your introduction to the terms used in the everyday world of ice cream production. The ice cream industry is not a mystery; it is just another business than can be understood through common sense and familiarity.

Air: A term used in conjunction with *overrun.* Air is incorporated into ice cream by the whipping action of the dasher inside the barrel of the batch freezer.

Bisque: Ice cream that contains either macaroons or some other bakery product.

Bulk ice cream: Ice cream usually packed in a 2½- or 3-gallon paper or plastic tub that is purchased by retailers for resale to the consumer as individual servings.

Butterfat: An ingredient made from rich sweet cream. Egg-yolk solids and cocoa are sometimes included in calculating the percentage of butterfat in a product, but those ingredients should not be confused with the fat from the cream. The specific percentage of butterfat is a unique characteristic of various frozen desserts. The most frequently asked question in the industry is about the percentage of butterfat in the ice cream you are producing. *See* Ice cream.

Confectioners' sugar: A very fine sugar, also known as 10X, sometimes used in producing ices or sorbets. It will produce a smoother scooping product, but it will not make a sugar syrup solution.

Corn syrup: A liquid sweetener that provides a firm, heavy body to finished ice cream and that improves shelf life. It is considered an inexpensive substitute for sugar, but approximately twice as much corn syrup as sugar is needed to obtain the right taste. *See also* Sugar syrup.

Cream, heavy: Cream that has a butterfat content of 35 percent and that can be whipped into a thick froth.

Cream, light: Cream that has a butterfat content of 20 percent and that cannot be whipped into a thick froth.

Custard: A frozen dessert with eggs as the predominant ingredient in its base, making it similar to French ice cream. The term comes up frequently in discussions about making your own ice cream mix.

Dasher: The main part inside the barrel of a batch freezer. It agitates the ice cream mix into a partially frozen state with its two main components, the blades and the beater.

Egg yolks: An ingredient used in ice cream to produce richness and smoothness. Too much egg yolk inhibits the freezing process and should be avoided.

Egg-yolk solids: An emulsifier that improves the texture and body of the ice cream. It is also sometimes considered a sweetener.

Emulsifier: An additive used to create smoothly textured ice cream to facilitate scooping and to provide control during the various stages in manufacturing.

Flavorings: All the ingredients added to an ice cream mix to provide flavor. They can be fresh ingredients such as fruits and nuts, or packaged substances such as extracts and concentrates. All nonfresh flavoring substances are classified as category I (pure extracts), II (pure extracts with a synthetic component), or III (artificial flavors).

Freezer, batch: A piece of equipment that makes a single flavor and specified quantity of ice cream using measured flavorings and ice cream mix.

Freezer, continuous: Ice cream production equipment in which a continuous amount of ice cream mix is fed into one end of the freezing chamber with the partially frozen product coming out the other end.

Freezing point: The temperature at which ice cream mix will freeze, approximately 27–28 degrees Fahrenheit depending on the sugar content of the mix. Mix with a lower sugar content will freeze at a slightly higher temperature.

French ice cream: A rich version of ice cream that contains at least 1.4 percent egg-yolk solids. Most superpremium ice cream made today contains egg yolks.

Fructose: A white crystalline powder that is very sweet and is sometimes used as a substitute for sugar. Only half as much is needed. Some diabetics can use fructose on the advice of a doctor.

Gelato: Italian ice cream that is low in butterfat (5–10%) with intense flavor and usually served in a softer state than regular ice cream.

Granite: Made from the same ingredients as an ice, granite is a coarser version with ice crystals formed as part of the final product. *See also* Ices or sorbets; Italian water ice.

Hardening: The process during which ice cream freezes to at least −15 degrees Fahrenheit after the product has been drawn from either the continuous or batch freezer. This fast freezing process usually takes 8–12 hours in a one- or two-door blast freezer or walk-in freezer.

Ice cream: A frozen dessert made from dairy products with at least 10 percent butterfat, except for chocolate ice cream that requires only 8 percent butterfat. Federal standards require finished ice cream to weigh 4½ pounds per gallon. *See also* French ice cream; Philadelphia ice cream; Variegated ice cream.

Ice cream, premium: Any ice cream product that has at least 12 percent butterfat in the mix.

Ice cream, superpremium: Any ice cream product that has at least 14 percent butterfat in the mix.

Ice cream mix: An unfrozen prepared mix of cream, water, and sugar or other sweeteners. It can include egg-yolk and other solids.

Ice crystals: The frozen portion of water in the ice cream mix. They are formed when ice cream is exposed to air (either external or air pockets within the product itself) when out of the freezer or in a freezer that is above 0 degree Fahrenheit.

Ice milk: See Reduced-fat ice cream.

Ices or sorbets: All ices or sorbets are water-based and contain no butterfat, although some sorbets contain egg whites. Almost all ices are prepared with fruit. *See also* Granite: Italian water ice.

Italian water ice: A lightly sweetened product that is usually made with an extract flavoring (as opposed to American or French sorbet that some times uses pieces of fruit).

Locust bean gum: A stabilizer used in the production of sherbet and ices.

Neapolitan: A product having at least two flavors, usually fruit, in the same package.

Overrun: The increase in the volume amount of finished ice cream over the volume of mix used. It results from the amount of air whipped into the product during the freezing process.

Philadelphia ice cream: Ice cream usually having no eggs in the mix.

Reduced-fat ice cream: Previously called ice milk, a frozen product containing 2–7 percent butterfat.

Sherbet: A frozen product, sometimes confused with ices, made with fruits and containing 1–2 percent butterfat.

Skim milk: Milk having very little or no fat content that is widely used in commercial ice cream production because it is an inexpensive way to acquire the necessary milk solids.

Stabilizer: A substance added to an ice cream mix to produce smoothness and uniformity in the finished product and to enhance resistance to melting. It also reduces or retards the formation of ice crystals resulting from heat shock (changing of temperature from cold to hot and back to cold again) during storage.

Sugar syrup: A solution made from hot water and cane sugar that is used in making ices or sorbets. The ratio of water to sugar (usually 2 or 3 quarts water to 1 pound sugar) varies depending on the fruits used. *See also* Corn syrup.

Sweeteners: Any ingredients used to sweeten the unfrozen ice cream product; mainly sugar, fructose, honey, maple syrup, or a corn sweetener.

Variegated ice cream: An ice cream mixed with fudge or syrup to create a marbled effect in the finished product.

Yogurt, frozen: A creamy frozen dairy product that usually has fewer calories and lower sodium and cholesterol than regular ice cream. A 4-ounce serving has 100–120 calories and at least 2–4 grams of fat. Some frozen yogurts have no yogurt cultures in the product.

Yogurt, nonfat, frozen: Frozen yogurt that contains less than 0.5 percent fat.

Service Lingo and Slang—Yesterday and Today

When I was young I loved jimmies on my ice cream. I would ask for them when I was out of town with my parents and often no one knew what I was talking about. Imagine my surprise when I discovered that other people called them sprinkles! You have surely encountered similar situations. Things have different names in different locales and in different times. I have explored the world of ice cream lingo and present here words and phrases that may evoke memories, but that are primarily intended to promote recognition when you are on the serving side of the counter.

The All-American: The victory sundae of World War II, made with vanilla ice cream, marshmallow topping, maraschino cherries, and fresh blueberry topping.

Banana Split: A popular concoction ever since the late 1920s, made with a banana sliced lengthwise, three scoops of ice cream, and plenty of toppings served in a boat-shaped dish.

Belch water: A glass of seltzer.

Black Cow: A root beer soda with vanilla ice cream that was a real favorite of GIs during World War II.

The Broadway: Another GI favorite, with chocolate soda and coffee ice cream.

Burn It and Let It Swim: A float or soda.

Canary Island Special: A vanilla soda with chocolate ice cream.

Catawba Flip: Strictly a concoction of the past, consisting of chipped ice, egg, ice cream, and soda all mixed together.

Chicago: Pineapple soda, but sometimes the name for a pineapple sundae.

Chocolate soda: The all-time favorite ice cream soda, prepared with 2 ounces of chocolate syrup in a 16–20-ounce glass with soda water and one large scoop of ice cream, topped with whipped cream and a maraschino cherry.

Coff: Coffee or coffee ice cream.

Coffee Frappe: A New York special, prepared with 2 ounces of coffee syrup, one egg white, vanilla ice cream, soda water, and some shaved ice all mixed thoroughly and served in a 16-ounce glass.

Cow Juice: Milk.

Creamsicle: A frozen dessert product on a stick made with vanilla ice cream coated with orange ice or sherbet.

Dusty Miller: A chocolate sundae sprinkled with malted milk powder. (Also known as a Dusty Road.)

Eighty-Two: Two glasses of water.

Eskimo Pie: Invented in the 1920s by Christian Nelson, this 2-ounce stickless ice cream bar covered with chocolate was the rage of the era and is still popular today, being sold all over the world.

Fizz: Carbonated water.

Frozen custard: A soft ice cream product rich with eggs that is popular in the midwestern parts of the United States. Otherwise it has been replaced by a blander version called soft ice cream.

Go for a Walk: To take out.

Good Humor Bar: Chocolate-covered ice cream on a stick.

Hand-packed: A pint or quart of ice cream that has been packed by hand from the bulk ice cream tub in the dipping case. Hand-packed ice cream is considered fresher than a prepacked product.

Ice cream cone: Invented by Ernest A. Hamri, the first cones were baked on a flat waffle iron in Saint Louis in 1904. Most of the cones sold today are called "sugar cones" because of the sweetness of the cone. Variations include cake, waffle, and pretzel cones.

Ice cream sandwich: Either a round or square brick of ice cream sandwiched between two cookies of the same size.

Ice cream soda: A soda prepared with flavoring syrup, ice cream, and soda water.

Ice cream sundae: A creation developed in the late 1890s. It was originally called the "Soda-less Soda" because of laws prohibiting the sale of sodas on Sunday. Served in a tulip glass, this concoction usually consists of two scoops of ice cream, a fruit or hot fudge topping, fresh whipped cream, and a maraschino cherry.

In the Hay: Strawberry milk shake.

L.A.: A la mode.

Malted: A milk shake with one large tablespoon of malt powder added to the shake before mixing.

Milk shake: Served in a 16–20-ounce glass, this popular ice cream drink has been a favorite for more than sixty years. Two scoops of ice cream, 8 ounces of very cold milk, and 2 ounces of syrup are the main ingredients, which are then mixed thoroughly. A thick shake has less milk and more ice cream.

Mud: Chocolate ice cream.

No Cow: Without milk.

O.J.: Orange juice.

One on the City: Water.

Pink Stick: Strawberry ice cream cone.

Scoop: The tool used to scoop ice cream from the tub to a cone or cup.

Seltzer: A drink sometimes called "two cents plain," soda water, carbonated water, or club soda. It is created by mixing carbon dioxide gas with water.

Soda Jerk: A name derived from the constant action of the clerk in the neighborhood shop jerking the draft arm of the fountain. During the 1920s, the profession was considered respectable and, indeed, sometimes the soda jerk was called "the Professor."

Split One: A banana split.

Sprinkles: Confectionery bits sometimes called jimmies and available in different colors. They are a favorite with children.

Tortoni: A frozen dessert prepared with macaroons, rum, and ice cream.

Twist It, Choke It, and Make It Cackle: Chocolate malted with egg.

Waffle cone: An ice cream cone that is not as sweet as a sugar cone. It can be purchased or baked on the premises.

REFERENCES

Arbuckle, W. S. 1983. *Ice Cream Store Handbook.* Columbia, Mo.: Arbuckle & Co.
Arbuckle, W. S. 1986. *Ice Cream.* Fourth edition. Westport, Conn.: AVI.

Aynes, Dane. 1986. Historical portrait of Big Drum, Inc. *The Ice Screamer*, June, pp. 5–7.

Browsing through old catalogs (1926). 1983 reprint. *The Ice Screamer*, August, p. 12.

Centennial Celebration (1951). 1986 reprint. The ice cream review. *The Ice Screamer*, February, pp. 3–5.

Dairy Foods Special Research Report. 1996. *Dairy Foods*, August.

Dickson, Paul. 1978. *The Great American Ice Cream Book*. New York: Atheneum.

Eskimo Pie (1922, *The Soda Fountain Magazine*). 1982 reprint. A present-day ice cream romance. *The Ice Screamer*, October, pp. 9–11.

Harris, Eleanor (1940, *The Saturday Evening Post*). 1986 reprint. One of America's best known, most loved ice creams. *The Ice Screamer*, February, pp. 3–30.

Hinton, Mike. 1987 The story of Hinton's ice cream, Alice Hinton, 1939. *The Ice Screamer*, December, pp. 3–5.

IAICM. 1986. *The History of Ice Cream*. Washington, D.C.: International Association of Ice Cream Manufacturers (now International Ice Cream Association).

IICA. 1995, 1996, 1997. *The Latest Scoop*. Washington, D.C.: International Ice Cream Association.

Keeney, Philip G. 1989. Correspondence Course 102: Ice Cream Manufacture. Available from The Pennsylvania State University, University Park, Pa.

Lieb, Mary Ellen. 1988. Frozen novelty meltdown. *Dairy Foods*, May, pp. 34–36.

Marks, Ed. 1983. History of the ice cream cone. *The Ice Screamer*, August, pp. 3–5.

Marks, Ed. 1985. My fellow member, Marlo Perry. *The Ice Screamer*, August, p. 6.

Morse, Barbara White. 1985. John Gardiner Low and his original art tile soda fountain. *The Ice Screamer*, December, p. 4.

The pied pipers of ice cream (1977, *The Lipton Magazine*). 1983 reprint. *The Ice Screamer*, June, p. 5.

Popsicle Industries. (1973). 1983 reprint. A part of American history. *The Ice Screamer*, August, pp. 3–4.

Robbins, Carol T., and Herbert Wolff. 1982. *The Very Best Ice Cream and Where to Find It*. Boston: The Very Best Publishers. Also published in 1985 by Warner Books, New York.

Smith, Wayne (1982). 1986 reprint. Evolution of ice cream dippers. *The Ice Screamer*, April, pp. 3–4.

Smith, Wayne. 1986. *Ice Cream Dippers*. Walkersville, Md.: Wayne Smith.

PART

1

⬡⬡⬡⬡⬡⬡⬡⬡⬡⬡⬡⬡⬡⬡⬡⬡⬡⬡⬡⬡⬡⬡⬡⬡⬡⬡⬡⬡⬡

ICE CREAM
PRODUCTION

⬡⬡⬡⬡⬡⬡⬡⬡⬡⬡⬡⬡⬡⬡⬡⬡⬡⬡⬡⬡⬡⬡⬡⬡⬡⬡⬡⬡⬡⬡

1

⊠⊠⊠⊠⊠⊠⊠⊠⊠⊠⊠⊠⊠⊠⊠⊠⊠⊠⊠⊠⊠⊠⊠⊠⊠⊠

BATCH FREEZING PROCESS

To operate a retail ice cream business, you must either buy your ice cream from an ice cream manufacturer or produce it yourself. From a profit standpoint, if you believe your business can produce a volume in excess of $250,000 per year, making your own makes a lot of sense. With this volume, the payback in equipment costs will take about 15 months assuming your ingredient costs are approximately 16 percent, versus buying product from a manufacturer (25 percent) or middleman (a distributor who buys the product from the manufacturer at 31 percent). (See also "Deciding to Make or Buy the Product" in Chapter 8.) If you want to have personal pride in your product and to differentiate yourself from your competition, then you will choose to make your own product. Batch freezing enables you to do just that. It is one of three methods used to produce frozen dessert products. The other two are the continuous freezing method and the use of soft serve equipment. (See in Chapter 6 for a discussion of soft serve equipment.) Be it ice cream, frozen yogurt, gelato, Italian ices, or sorbets, batch freezing is the method of choice for most new companies entering this industry.

Nearly everyone I have encountered in the frozen dessert business started out with a batch freezer. Some ice cream makers eventually change to continuous freezing equipment, which is a more sophisticated system than batch freezing and requires a large capital outlay for setting up. Most large dairies, in particular, use only continuous freezing equipment, primarily because uniformity of product is assured. Other advantages of the continuous freezing method include less possibility of ice crystals forming and quick production time. Obviously, then, it is a method suited to large-scale production, but because it is so mechanical, it deters creativity.

The batch freezing process is well suited to the individual frozen dessert shop owner or small chain (three to five shops) for the following reasons:

- Batch freezing production equipment costs less than continuous freezing equipment.
- Using a batch freezer allows for constant taste testing and correction during production.
- The batch freezing process provides the flexibility for a small operation to create many flavors in a short period of time without spending lots of time setting up the production run, and while using only a small amount of mix. This flexibility is essential for the independent operator, hotel chef, or restaurant owner who values a quality product and who is aware of the time frame (30 minutes to produce versus a day to as long as a week to obtain from a manufacturer) and production costs.

While taste is, of course, subjective, praise for operations in the United States producing ice cream in batch freezers has come from sources such as *Time* (1981) and *People* (1984) magazines and the book, *The Very Best Ice Cream and Where to Find It* (Robbins and Wolff, 1985).

EQUIPMENT NEEDED

Constructing a batch freezer production facility requires between 300 and 800 square feet of production space. The following equipment is needed:

- *Batch freezer:* to produce the product.
- *Hardening cabinet (blast freezer):* to quickly freeze the product after extrusion from the batch freezer.
- *Freezer storage cabinet:* to store blast-frozen product hours after production.
- *Refrigerator:* to store ice cream mix and other perishable ingredients.
- *Three-compartment sink:* for overall cleaning of equipment, tubs, and so on.
- *Hand sink:* for washing hands.
- *Tables:* to use for missing ingredients before and after ice cream production and for decorating ice cream cakes and pies; stainless steel, six feet long (2).
- *Shelving:* for storing ingredient flavorings, tubs, and so on.
- *Blender and food processor:* for pureeing fruit, nuts, and other ingredients.
- *Plastic or cardboard tubs:* for use in packing ice cream produced in the batch freezer; 2½ or 3 gallon tubs and lids, either plastic or paper. (150).

- *Hot water boiler:* to provide enough hot water for overall cleaning purposes.
- *Scale:* to weigh ingredients.
- *Timer:* to time a batch of ice cream during production.
- *Miscellaneous:* spatulas, measuring and mixing bowls, wire sieves (strainer), refrigerator pen markers, flavor labels or stamps, and so on.

Batch Freezer

The original batch freezer, a vertical freezer using rock salt and ice to create a brine solution as a source of cold refrigeration, was in many ways similar to the ice cream freezers used at home today. Modern commercial batch freezers are horizontal and have copper tubing with cold freon surrounding the cylindrical chamber for refrigeration. The original freezers had wooden paddles for scraping the walls of the chamber. The stainless steel blades of today's freezers do the same job. But even with all of the improvements made since the 1950s, the main body of the batch freezer has remained basically the same. It is still the reliable workhorse of the industry.

The batch freezer is a relatively compact unit performing all the functions necessary to produce a quality product. It is used to make one batch at a time, hence the name. The process begins with ice cream mix being poured into the chamber at approximately 40 degrees Fahrenheit and ends 8–10 minutes later with a semifrozen product. The length of time depends on the water and butterfat content of the mix. Ice cream mix varies between 10 percent and 16 percent butterfat with the lower percentage mixes taking longer to freeze because of the higher water content. The temperature in the semifrozen state is usually 24–25 degrees Fahrenheit, which permits extrusion of the product into tubs for hardening.

The process itself is simple and the batch freezer is a simple machine to operate. You fill the freezing chamber with mix and flavoring ingredients, and set the time for freezing. It does not matter whether you are making butter pecan or strawberry ice cream. The machine takes the ingredients that are fed into it and freezes them to the consistency you want for extruding into a tub.

The batch freezer is a large machine. Depending on the manufacturer and model, it is at least 24 inches wide, 37 inches deep, and 51 inches high. Most batch freezers are belt driven and have a 3-horsepower compressor and an agitator motor that turns the dasher or beater inside the freezing chamber. Some come with wheels or have them as an option (which I highly recommend). Electrical requirements are usually single- or three-phase electrical current, 60-cycle, 220 power. When reading equipment literature you might see the number "3/60/220" or "3/60/208/230" to specify those electrical requirements. Most batch freezers are water cooled but air-cooled units are available and are found particularly in areas where the use of water is restricted.

The main parts of a batch freezer are as follows:

Dasher: a unit consisting of the scraper blades and beater that fits into the freezing chamber. It mixes the ingredients prior to freezing, agitates the ice cream mix during the freezing process, and constantly scrapes the mix off the sides of the chamber. After freezing, it helps extrude the product from the freezing chamber.

The blades should be sharpened and aligned by the manufacturer at least once before the spring season begins. They are the most important part of your machine and the part most subject to possible damage. The blades can be bent by

- Resting the dasher on them on the edge of a sink or table.
- Dropping the dasher to the floor.
- Having foreign matter, such as peach pits, hit them.
- Trying to help the discharge of product by sticking a spoon in the discharge gate.
- Starting the dasher against a frozen mass. If the product is frozen too stiff and the dasher has turned off because of overload, wait for the product to thaw before turning the dasher back on.

Many batch freezers are available today with two settings—high and low—to control the speed of the dasher, which in turn controls the overrun of the finished product.

Freezing chamber: the barrel or drum-shaped container surrounded by refrigerant. The ingredients are poured into the chamber for initial freezing.

Hopper: the stainless steel chute attached to the outside walls of the batch freezer through which the ingredients are poured. The hopper has a cover, which is a requirement of many local health departments, that prevents unwanted outside particles from entering the chamber. A large hopper is recommended for ease in adding large pieces of ingredients.

Handle: a level or arm that controls the extrusion of the product from the freezing chamber.

Spout: a tube or lip that projects from the freezing chamber through which the product is extruded.

Switches: on/off controls for the dasher and refrigeration. The batch freezer cannot be operated without first turning on the dasher switch. While in operation, turning off the dasher switch automatically turns off the refrigeration. The refrigeration switch can only be turned on after the dasher is already in operation.

Hardening Cabinet (Blast Freezer)

Once the product has been extruded from the batch freezer, it needs to be hardened. That is, the extruded product is at 24–25 degrees Fahrenheit and must be chilled quickly, within 8–10 hours, to between −15 and −30 degrees Fahrenheit. Hardening must be done quickly to prevent the finished product from containing ice crystals that result from melting and from being exposed to air.

A blast, or hardening, freezer accomplishes this final step of production. The desired temperature inside a blast freezer is between −25 and −45 degrees Fahrenheit. (Note that the temperature inside a *holding* freezer will be 0 to −25 degrees Fahrenheit.) A well-cared-for, uncrowded unit will harden ice cream in 8–12 hours.

To facilitate hardening, fill the freezer from the bottom up because the coldest air will be at the bottom. Whenever possible, do not stack the containers on top of one another because the cold air will not be able to circulate properly. Having wire racks inside a hardening room or blast freezer is highly recommended to allow air circulation and faster hardening.

Always check the doors to make sure they are closed tightly. Make this checking a habit for everyone in your establishment. A door left open or ajar will keep the ice cream from hardening or cause a meltdown. The refrigeration will also not work properly if the compressor vents are dirty and clogged or if the temperature in the room around the freezer is too high.

These freezers are similar to storage freezers in construction and capacity, but they are designed to hold temperatures down to −45 degrees Fahrenheit. Models are available with either one or two doors. Because of their many years of experience in making quality freezers, Kelvinator, Traulsen, and Masterbilt are excellent highly recommended blast freezers (see Table 1-1). The Kelvinator freezer (see Figure 1-1) features interior doors that give added insulation for keeping cold air inside the unit. Traulsen freezers are noted for their heavy-duty construction and durability.

Table 1-1. Blast, Flash, or Hardening Freezers

| Manufacturer | Model | Capacity | Dimensions (inches) | | | Electrical Requirements |
			Width	Depth	Height	
Kelvinator	VHC26	1 door	$38\frac{1}{8}$	$38\frac{3}{8}$	$84\frac{7}{16}$	$115/60/1$	$\frac{1}{2}$
Kelvinator	VHC48	2 door	57	39	85	$115/230/1$	$1\frac{1}{2}$
Traulsen	RIF 1-34HUT-BF	1 door	$48\frac{1}{2}$	$36\frac{15}{16}$	$89\frac{1}{2}$	$208/60/3$	2
Traulsen	RIF 2-34HUT-BF	2 door	78	$36\frac{15}{16}$	$89\frac{1}{2}$	$208/60/3$	2
Masterbilt	IHC-27	1 door	31	$35\frac{3}{4}$	82	$115/230/1$	1
Masterbilt	IHC-48	2 door	52	$35\frac{3}{4}$	82	$115/230/1$	$1\frac{1}{2}$

FIGURE 1-1. Klevinator Model HC48 flash freezer.

PREPRODUCTION CONSIDERATIONS

Quality Control

The determining factor that separates an outstanding operation from an ordinary one is quality control. To be successful today, an operation must be both good and different. There is no incentive for customers to seek you out if you do not provide something unique. That's one reason why quality is stressed throughout this book. Being quality-minded means working in a clean and sanitary environment and using the best ingredients and proper processing methods to produce a superior product. Being organized, using proven standardized written recipes, and instilling good work habits in your employees contribute greatly to obtaining and maintaining quality control.

Quality control means maintaining a particular level of consistency and you can achieve that consistency only by using precise procedures and following an exact recipe. You need a thorough understanding of how your equipment works and why certain ingredients are used and in what quantity. Take time to plan and test. After each test, write down your comments and the opinions of employees and friends. Then you will be able to refer to your notes when trying to decide which products and flavors you want on the menu. Using a timer is imperative. Get into the habit of doing so. Note the time for each batch because quality can fluctuate within a 1–3 minute time span. Do not allow your employees to guess when measuring the amount of ingredients used or the time allowed for production.

Maintaining quality control in production requires that

- Each new employee be trained to operate each piece of production equipment.
- All ingredients be handled in a manner consistent with the health department's policies regarding proper sanitary procedures.
- All ingredients be marked with the date received and with expiration dates after which they can no longer be used.
- The volume weight of each ice cream tub meets the operation's standard for acceptability.
- All products manufactured be taste-tasted to assure consistency of quality.
- Procedures established to guard against the overproduction of slow-moving flavors be strictly adhered to.
- Products being served from the dipping case be checked constantly for flavor, body, texture, and distribution of chips, nuts, and fruits within the tubs.

Good Purchasing Practices

Purchasing ingredients for a batch freezing operation is in some ways very different than purchasing for a large continuous freezing operation. In many cases, because of size minimums, the way ingredients are packed, and freight costs, a small ice cream manufacturer cannot obtain the same ingredients that a larger one could. For example, many manufacturers pack only in 5-gallon pails, and once the pail is opened it must be refrigerated. If an operation has limited refrigeration capabilities, the pail option is not a good one. For batch freezer operations, #10 cans usually packed six to a case are optimal because an operator can use only what is needed, one can at a time.

Knowing what to buy, who to buy it from, and at what price takes time to learn. Always ask for samples. Never buy a ingredient without first doing a taste test. Run small test batches of ingredients that you will be using to produce products, and compile a final list of the items you decide on. Help yourself by documenting the results of your tests and by maintaining good bookkeeping procedures and records. A purchase or suppliers journal listing each supplier's products, prices, quality, and quantity of packages makes purchasing ingredients and supplies an orderly function of everyday business.

When you set up your suppliers journal, list a backup supplier for every product in your inventory of ingredients. While you certainly want to be friendly with suppliers, you do have to let them know that the reasons you are buying from them are quality and service. Let them know that they need you as much as you need them. If you are perceived as a small-time operator, you are less likely to get preferential service. Emphasize to them that you insist on certain things, such as quality and service, and if they cannot meet your requirements, you will have to do business with someone else.

When choosing suppliers, rate them on the following characteristics:

- *Availability of quality ingredients:* Do they maintain an adequate inventory to service their clientele?
- *Price:* Are they competitive with other suppliers carrying similar products?
- *Service:* Can they answer your questions about their products and how you can use them in your business?
- *Packaging:* Will their products be shipped in clearly marked containers that will arrive in good condition?
- *Delivery:* Do they have a specific policy about delivery schedules that does not conflict with your business hours?
- *Payment:* Are their payment terms clear and can they be counted on to be understanding if problems arise?

What does all of this mean? Simply, it is important to know the makeup and size of your ingredients, to differentiate between the levels of quality in each, and to have a full understanding of pricing. By the end of your first season you will have learned that there are no bargains and that the price paid, in most cases, separates good quality from bad. Sometimes, though, a high-quality artificial ingredient will nearly duplicate the taste, texture, and color characteristics of its natural counterpart but will be much less expensive. The price you need to set on your product to be competitive in the marketplace will determine whether or not you can afford to use an expensive all-natural ingredient.

In some instances the difference in price between one level of quality and another is not substantial and for a few cents more per pound you might be able to buy a much higher grade. The small extra expense could mean the difference between producing a good product and an excellent one.

Standard Operating Procedures

Because vanilla is the most popular flavor you will produce and so you will need a large supply, a day's ice cream production should always begin with any vanilla-based flavors (see Chapter 13). After the vanillas are produced, you can proceed with the coffee, chocolate, fruit, and nut flavors. Regardless of which flavors you produce, your batch freezer must be cleaned between batches. However, chocolate can be produced after coffee without a clean-out if you are careful to extract as much of the finished coffee ice cream as you can.

Clean ice cream batches should be one of the first quality standards you strive for. A clean batch is one that has no flavor characteristic from the previous batch. It will be easier to maintain clean batches if you make it a practice to add most of the bulk ingredients (fruits, chocolate chips, nuts, cookie pieces, etc.) to the tubs as the finished ice cream is being drawn out of the batch freezer. For an even distribution of bulk ingredients throughout the tub, add them to the ice cream a little at a time as it is being extruded from the freezer.

Most experienced operators use this method because the finished product is so much better in quality than that of one in which all the ingredients, wet and dry, are poured directly into the batch freezer. If you add the ingredients directly into the batch freezer during the freezing process, the blades or dashers will break them up in to a pureed, mashed, or granulated mass. Adding bulk ingredients during extrusion is more difficult to master, but it will help you to produce clean batches as well as bring positive reactions from your customers who will enjoy, for example, biting into a large piece of chocolate or almond.

A compromise method is to add the bulk ingredients directly into the freezer at the very end of the batch, just before extruding the finished product. However, this method sometimes results in uneven distribution. You will need to have mastered the batch freezer before expecting good results with this method.

Most ice cream production equipment will make an excellent product if you know how to use it. Improper use of the batch freezer will create defects that produce icy, sandy, or fluffy finished products. When too much air is whipped into the product, the excessive overrun creates ice cream that is fluffy. This problem occurs because of the high speed of the dasher and the length of time the product remains in the chamber. In most cases, a fluffy product results from firm ice cream left in the batch freezer for 10 minutes or longer with the dasher still on. Drawing the ice cream out of the batch freezer takes time to learn, but the end result is better quality, higher yields, and improved profit margins.

One of the easiest ways to maintain a hands-on approach to quality control is constant tasting of your products. During the batch process, slowly open the extrusion door or place a spatula into the hopper to pick up some of the product. Under no circumstances should your hands touch the hopper opening or extrusion door during the batch process. The blades are sharp and you do not want to contaminate the product. Use clean spatulas at all times. You should know what your ingredients taste like before you use them and you should know what the product tastes like when it comes out of the batch freezer. Tasting should continue through all stages of freezing and storage.

You will find it comparatively easy to produce an excellent product once, but to repeat it again and again is another matter entirely. When testing batches of product, it is a good idea to record the exact ingredients and procedures as you go along. Then you will be able to make a consistent product simply by referring to your recipes. Most customers are aware of how a product should taste and come to expect the same taste with each purchase. Therefore, the use of ingredients and flavoring agents should not be altered from any basic recipe. Not only is the taste important, but also the color and appearance of the finished product, which are, of course, easily noticed. Customers know that too much color in the product usually means that artificial flavors or colors have been used. In creating a high-quality product, the color should be characteristic of the flavor. Intense flavor and color when done properly with a high butterfat ice cream mix is a desired characteristic of an upscale operation. Using only natural, or high-quality artificial, ingredients and following recipes closely will set the standards of quality that should be the benchmark of your operation.

Finally, because the texture and body composition of ice cream is determined by the quality and age of the ice cream mix, be sure your mix is fresh. Check the dates on the mix containers. Use a first-in, first-out rotation for the containers. Ice cream mix has a shelf life of approximately 21 days, after which it deteriorates and curdles. Curdled mix has a sour taste, and any attempt to salvage the mix will result in unhealthy and poor-quality products. Keep the mix properly refrigerated. Note the following:

- Mix received should be clearly marked showing date received.
- Mix should immediately be placed inside refrigerator or walk-in.
- Mix should be stored at 36–38 degrees Fahrenheit.
- If you are purchasing mix to be stored in a refrigerator, never have more than a 10 day supply of mix on hand at any one time.
- Any mix taken from storage for use in production, but not used, must be refrigerated at the end of each day.

If mix is purchased in a frozen state, the following procedures should be followed to ensure good sanitation and proper rotation:

- Mix received should be marked clearly showing the date received.
- Place all mix into the freezer on a first-in, first-out rotation basis.
- At the beginning of each week, determine how much is needed for that week, and then place that amount in the refrigerator. Ice cream mix needs at least 3 days in the refrigerator to defrost properly before use.

During the summer season, you should have on hand at least a 3-day supply of mix to cover any contingencies. At the beginning of each week, the plant manager should determine how much mix is required for your batch freezer production for the coming week. Based on your current inventory of mix on hand, order accordingly.

For more information on ice cream mixes, see Chapter 4.

OPERATING THE BATCH FREEZER

Before using the batch freezer, you should make sure you understand the mechanics of operating it. Carefully read the operating manual and feel free to ask any questions of the manufacturer's representative. Once you understand how to work the freezer, the next thing to do is make sure that the barrel or freezing chamber is spotlessly clean. Pour a gallon of warm water into the machine, run the dasher for 30 seconds, and empty the water. Examining the water will show if any particles are left in the machine or if it is clean. Repeat the warm water rinse until the water comes out clean. Next pour a cold water chlorine-based sanitizing solution (2 capfuls of bleach to 3 gallons of water, or follow manufacturer's recommendations for a similar solution) into the machine and run the dasher again for 30 seconds. Empty that solution and pour in a gallon of cold water for a final rinse. Smell the rinse water for any trace of chlorine and continue rinsing as necessary. After you have emptied the machine for the last time, you are ready to start the production run. (You will take the machine apart for cleaning at the end of the day, so this preliminary cleaning will turn up any leaks from not reassembling the parts properly the previous day.)

Planning a Day's Production Run

You should never begin a day's production run without a list of the flavors to be produced that day (see Figures 1-2 and 1-3). Being organized with a list will save time and money because you will avoid duplication and be able to operate in an efficient manner. You will be able to make sure that you have all the ingredients needed for the day's production, that frozen ingredients have been properly defrosted, and that the marinating process has been completed for the flavors requiring it (see Chapters 5, 13, and 15 for discussions of marinating). If anything is missing, or if emergencies arise, you will be able to make changes in the list and still operate efficiently.

The list should be arranged so that you can produce flavors in a sequence that will require little cleaning of the batch freezer during the day's run, except when switching from producing fruit flavors to nut or candy flavors, and from liquor to nonliquor flavors. (The rule of thumb is to avoid mixing one ingredient with another that might result in an objectionable taste.) You can minimize the cleaning required between batches by starting the day's run with vanilla-based flavors, then coffee, and finish with the chocolates. When extruding each flavor, be sure you remove as much of the product as possible as long as it is frozen and firm. Doing so will keep the flavors pure and prevent tastes from being interfered with.

After you have run through the vanilla, coffee, and chocolate flavors, you must clean the machine. Drain and discard the excess product left in the chamber. Then run 30-second warm and cold water rinses. When the water coming out of the chamber is clear, you can start the next batch. Once you have done this interim cleaning several times, you will understand the value of running

DAILY PRODUCTION LIST		
FLAVOR	SEQUENCE	NUMBER OF TUBS
French Vanilla		
Vanilla Chocolate Chip		
Vanilla Fudge		
Vanilla Oreo®		
Vanilla Chocolate-Almond		
Cherry Vanilla		
Strawberry		
Strawberry Cheesecake		
Banana		
Banana Nut Fudge		
Butter Pecan		
Pecan Praline		
Peanut Butter		
Coffee		
Coffee Chip		
Kahlua		
Mud Pie		
Mocha Chip		
Mocha Almond Fudge		
Chocolate		
Chocolate Choc.-Chip		
Chocolate Truffle		
Chocolate Choc.-Almond		
Chocolate Brownie		
Rocky Road		
Malted Vanilla		
Milky Way®		
Snickers®		
Heath Bar®		
Coconut		
Coconut Almond Joy®		
Rum Raisin		

FIGURE 1-2. A daily production list.

WEEKLY PRODUCTION LIST									
Flavor	M	T	W	T	F	S	S	Week	Month
French Vanilla									
Vanilla Chocolate Chip									
Vanilla Fudge									
Vanilla Oreo®									
Vanilla Chocolate-Almond									
Cherry Vanilla									
Strawberry									
Strawberry Cheesecake									
Banana									
Banana Nut Fudge									
Butter Pecan									
Pecan Praline									
Peanut Butter									
Coffee									
Coffee Chip									
Kahlua									
Mud Pie									
Mocha Chip									
Mocha Almond Fudge									
Chocolate									
Chocolate Choc.-Chip									
Chocolate Truffle									
Chocolate Choc.-Almond									
Chocolate Brownie									
Rocky Road									
Malted Vanilla									
Milky Way®									
Snickers®									
Heath Bar®									
Coconut									
Coconut Almond Joy®									
Rum Raisin									

FIGURE 1-3. A weekly production list.

flavors in sequence. It takes a lot of experience operating the batch freezer to learn to run flavor sequences without much interruption for cleaning. However, the amount of time saved in a small and busy operation is invaluable.

After the interim cleaning, you are ready to run the nut and candy flavors as a group. Then it is necessary to clean the freezer again. Finally, you are ready to run the fruit flavors as a group. Remember that any flavors made with liquor or mint require a separate cleaning after each batch because of the strong flavors.

Running a Batch

For a 20-quart batch freezer, you will need 2½ gallons of ice cream mix (5 gallons for a 40-quart freezer). When pouring the mix into a batch freezer, be sure to remove all the liquid from the container. Shake the container before opening it because sweeteners tend to settle to the bottom. Otherwise the quality of the mix will be reduced because the finished product will have an uneven sweetness. It is also a good idea to drain one container into another to get every drop of mix. By doing so you can save nearly half a gallon of mix during an average day's production.

Then follow your recipes closely, pouring the other initial ingredients into the chamber. Turn on the dasher to run for a minute or so to completely stir all the ingredients, after which you turn on the refrigeration and continue with the batch as per the recipe you are using. Learning and understanding the recipes is not difficult when you work with them daily. The hard part is always remembering the little things that have to be done.

When pouring the mix and ingredients into the freezer at the beginning of the batch, fill the chamber to half of its volume capacity. Filling up more than half will decrease the overrun of the finished product and possibly affect the quality.

It takes 8–10 minutes to run a batch of finished ice cream. Some flavors, such as those with nuts, will take less time than a plain vanilla-based product, so you have to watch closely during the last 2 minutes of processing. It is best to set your timer at 7 minutes so you will be alerted to the approaching end of the batch time. However, the first flavor of the day always takes at least 2 minutes longer to complete than any other run because the chamber is not cold enough at the start.

Overrun

Overrun is the increase in the volume of finished ice cream over the volume of mix used. It results from the amount of air whipped into the product during the freezing process by the action of the dasher. Overrun, which is measured in percentages, can be controlled in a batch freezer operation in the following three ways:

1. It can be lowered by filling the freezer chamber to more than half its volume capacity.

2. It can be lowered by letting the refrigerant run slightly longer than the 8–10 minutes usually required for running a batch.

3. It can be lowered or raised by changing the speed of the dasher. A low speed will produce overrun of 20–49 percent, while a high speed will produce 50–100 percent overrun. Anything higher than 50 percent is considered high overrun, while anything lower is low overrun.

Too much air will dissipate flavor and produce a product fluffy in texture and light in weight. However, the flavor can be enhanced. Most commercial ice cream for dipping stores, restaurants, hotels, and foodservice facilities will have an overrun of 75–100 percent because of the high yield, which makes it cheaper to produce.

A low-overrun batch can be dense and heavy, resulting in a more expensive product. Superpremium ice cream from dairies is a low-overrun product, as are pints, quarts, and novelties packed directly from the batch freezer. Low-overrun ice cream requires less flavoring and has a creamy texture. Fruit and nut flavors require a low overrun to allow the flavors to stand out. You need to be careful when producing nut flavors in particular. Because of the oil content, they can overprocess easily in a low-overrun cycle. Oil breaks down the cream, thus forcing out the air that has been pumped into the product during the freezing cycle. Nuts should be added in the middle or at the end of the batch cycle to prevent coagulation. Coagulation is a curdling or clotting process that occurs when nuts absorb moisture. A dense, chalky taste results. Use roasted nuts whenever possible because they are less apt to absorb moisture.

Extrusion

When the batch reaches the desired consistency after the 8–10 minutes running time, extrude the finished ice cream as soon as possible. It should not take longer than 3–5 minutes to empty the freezer chamber. First, turn off the refrigerant switch to prevent the product from freezing as a solid block inside the chamber. Most batch freezers have an automatic refrigerant shut-off if you accidentally turn off the dasher before the refrigerant. But be careful. If you shut off the refrigerant too soon, the finished ice cream will not harden properly, ice crystals will form in the tubs, and proper overrun will not be achieved. If the refrigerant remains on too long, overprocessed ice cream will result. It is the worst ice cream you can produce because it is too dense and unscoopable, and, with no air in the finished product, it will be coarse.

Be organized for the extrusion or it can end up taking 10 minutes or more to perform, and the results could be watery or overprocessed. Sometimes it is advisable to keep the refrigerant on slightly longer than usual to keep the overrun within the desired range, but you must be careful when doing so.

Have your out-of-batch ingredients on hand and, if necessary, another person to help pour them into the freezer or the tubs. Make sure the tubs and pans are dry and cool before using them because any water mixed with the ice cream will form ice crystals. With a piece of masking tape, mark the tubs with the name of the flavor and date.

Years ago, almost all dairy manufacturers of ice cream used either stainless steel tubs or paperboard cartons. Since the 1970s, plastic containers have become the preference of independent ice cream operators. Stainless steel containers corrode and get bent out of shape. They are hard to find now, are expensive, and look unappealing when worn out. The Ropak Corporation produces an excellent line of plastic containers, the Quality-Pak (Figure 1-4). These containers are made of freezer-grade resins specifically formulated for the dairy industry in general and for frozen dessert products in particular. They come with snap-on lids to inhibit crystallization and oxidation and maintain freshness and quality. Paperboard containers are difficult to handle. They are not reusable, cause refuse problems, and are difficult to scrape because of the thinness of the paperboard. Constant scooping and scraping makes cuts in the paperboard. On the other hand, the smooth walls and bottoms of the Ropak container eliminate waste and increase the number of scoops per container. These containers fit all major dipping cabinets and come in 1½-, 2½-, and 3-gallon sizes. If you have a space problem and still want to offer as many flavors as possible, the Negus Square Pak container (see Figure 1-5) is an excellent choice.

FIGURE 1-4. Ropak Corporation plastic containers, 1½- and 3-gallon sizes.

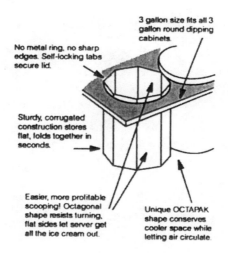

3 gallon size fits all 3 gallon round dipping cabinets.

No metal ring, no sharp edges. Self-locking tabs secure lid.

Sturdy, corrugated construction stores flat, folds together in seconds.

Easier, more profitable scooping! Octagonal shape resists turning, flat sides let server get all the ice cream out.

Unique OCTAPAK shape conserves cooler space while letting air circulate.

Dimensions

2½ gal. -	ID	-9-1/8″ x 6-3/8″ x 10″
	OD	-9-3/4″ x 7″ x 10-1/2″
3 gal. -	ID	-8-1/8″ x 8-1/8″ x 10″
	OD	-8-3/4″ x 8-3/4″ x 10-1/2″
3½ gal. -	ID	-8-7/8″ x 9″ x 9-3/4″
	OD	-9-1/2″ x 9-1/2″ x 10-1/2″

FIGURE 1-5. Negus Corporation Octapak and Square Pak containers.

If you are going to pack pints or novelties for individual sale, do so only after the batch freezer has been emptied and all of the finished product has been put into the blast freezer. Many operators make the mistake of letting their finished product sit on the counter to melt while they move on to pint loading or making novelties, or try to decide what to do next. Do not jeopardize the quality of your finished product by being disorganized. If you do not want to pack your pints manually, Tindall Packaging's Model 890 semiautomatic filling machine (see Figure 1-6) is a very versatile alternative. This machine can pack units up to a half-gallon.

Cleaning the Batch Freezer

As previously mentioned, you should assemble the dasher into the barrel and clean once with sanitizing solution and once with plain cold water at the beginning of each day. Then, after the day's production run is complete, empty any excess mix out of the batch freezer and store it in the refrigerator for the next day's run. (Likewise, refrigerate the mix drippings if not used in the last run.)

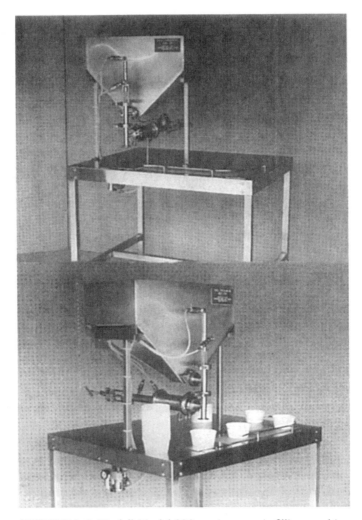

FIGURE 1-6. Tindall Model 890 semiautomatic filling machine.

Then use the following procedure for cleanup:

1. Rinse the chamber with warm water until all the excess ingredients are cleaned out.
2. Open the chamber, remove the entire dasher assembly, and clean all the parts with the same chlorine-based sanitizing solution that was used for the pre-use cleaning procedure.
3. Pour a cold sanitizing solution into the chamber as the last function before the cleaning is complete.

4. Wipe all other parts of the batch freezer with a liquid dishwashing detergent and rinse with a hot water chlorine-based sanitizing solution.
5. Use a sanitizing test kit to check for any bacteria in the freezer chamber.
6. Put a sanitary lubricant, such as Petro-Gel manufactured by the McGlaughlin Oil Company or Lubri-Film from Haynes, on all the movable parts. The sanitary white grease should be used on all stainless steel parts and will extend the life of your equipment.

Get into the habit of keeping your batch freezer as clean as it was the day you bought it.

STORING THE PRODUCT

Ice particles and icing result for the most part from slow hardening or poor storage of the finished product. Poor storage practices include having too much product in the hardening cabinets, which prevents cold air from circulating properly, and not properly caring for the cabinets themselves. If the compressors are not working properly, a warmer temperature inside the cabinets results.

Ice is formed by water, warm temperatures, and exposure to air. Failure to store the product immediately after it has been removed from the batch freezer will result in melting that promotes icing during hardening. There is less chance of ice forming in products made with a high-butterfat mix because of the increased percentages of fat, sugar, and other solids.

Ice crystals will also form in the product as it sits in the dipping case, where there is a strong possibility for temperature changes throughout the day. Also, once in the case, it is exposed to air and loses some of its creaminess and flavor. Be sure to examine the product periodically for texture, color, and appearance. Look for meltdowns along the edges of the tubs that occur when the product has been removed from the dipping case or if there has been a drastic change in temperature.

Ice cream with a sandy or gritty texture is caused by improper freezing in the blast or hardening cabinets at temperatures above −10 degrees Fahrenheit. Ice cream stored for long periods of time in either a storage freezer or dipping case will also tend to become sandy. So be sure to rotate your products, particularly in the storage freezers. But try not to move them back and forth between the dipping case and storage freezer because the subsequent softening and rehardening will break down the product and allow ice crystals and bacteria to form.

BATCH FREEZER EQUIPMENT MANUFACTURERS

When just starting up, try not to let pricing be the determining factor in your choice of equipment suppliers. It's important to initiate relationships with manufacturers, and being informed about them and their equipment helps cultivate good relationships. A good supplier is interested in seeing you succeed, and will help you if needed and answer any questions you might have. Your suppliers can share ideas for improving your operation and they can let you know about new equipment on the market. Take advantage of this help during your learning period.

Most important, being on good terms with suppliers can improve the service you get from them. That improved service is worth a lot of money over a period of time, but is especially critical in the beginning stages of your operation.

In the United States, there are four major manufacturers of batch freezers. All but the Emery Thompson Company specialize in soft-serve machines, which are similar in principle to batch freezers. Regardless of manufacturer, any of today's batch freezers will produce good ice cream. (It is the other variables—ingredients, knowledge, desire—that make a difference.)

Emery Thompson

Considered by many in the industry to manufacture the best batch freezer in the world, the Emery Thompson Company is the oldest maker of batch freezers. Indeed, you can travel to some of the most out of the way places in the world and find one of their batch freezers in operation. They are real workhorses, not sophisticated pieces of equipment. All of the main parts except the dasher blades are made of stainless steel, which is stronger than plastic, so fewer repairs will be needed. They are easy to operate and to clean. Some people even consider the purchase of an Emery Thompson batch freezer an investment because of the resale value. The support service for new operators given by the company is excellent, and for this reason it is rare to find someone who has a complaint about an Emery Thompson batch freezer.

The company manufactures three basic models that are classified by size of production. Model 10NW is a 10-quart finished product, horizontal batch freezer measuring 23½ inches wide by 32½ inches deep by 53 inches high. It is water cooled. This unit is used to make ice cream or sorbets mainly in restaurants or in small shop operations. It can produce 12–15 gallons an hour.

Model 20NW can produce 20-quart batches with a 25–30 gallon per-hour capacity. It measures 23½ inches wide by 37 inches deep by 49 inches high and is water cooled. This unit comes with a standard high-speed dasher or is available with two speeds for producing low-overrun products. Since 1965, this model in particular has been a mainstay for the small shop operator and hotel chef. It has tremendous resale value.

Model 40BLT (Figure 1-7) produces 40 quarts of finished product per batch and has a 50-gallon per-hour capacity. Measuring 27 inches wide by 54 inches deep by 49 inches high, it is also water cooled. This unit is available with a standard high-speed dasher or with two speeds for low-overrun production. It is used mainly for water ice and large-scale ice cream production, especially by small, multistore chains.

One major advantage of all three models is an extrusion level that opens the

FIGURE 1-7. Emery Thompson Model 40-BLT batch freezer.

spout very quickly, allowing the product to be released from the freezer chamber in a matter of minutes.

Coldelite

Coldelite, the American subsidiary of Carpigiani an Italian manufacturer of soft serve machines and batch freezers, is preferred by many in the industry who want to make an Italian gelato-style product because of the low-overrun produced by the Coldelite batch freezers. All of their batch freezers deliver a finished product with a 55–65 percent overrun, which is far denser than most commercial economy-grade ice creams having a 100 percent overrun. Coldelite's low-speed dasher assembly and motor is specifically designed to produce a low-overrun finished product. This feature is especially advantageous for operators manufacturing not only gelato, but sorbets, and a superpremium ice cream.

Coldelite batch freezers come with an attached preset timer that can be set for a specific batch time once the dasher and refrigeration are both turned on for the production mode. A buzzer will sound when it is time to remove the finished product. They also feature a cold faucet near the top of the hopper to facilitate cleaning.

One unique feature of the freezer is a one-piece beater with three attached blades. Each blade gently floats a thin film of frozen product onto the cylinder wall, creating a very smoothly textured product that allows for maximum extraction. Maximum extraction will permit you to move from one flavor to the next with minimal or no cleaning of the chamber between batches.

Coldelite manufactures four basic models ranging in size and function from a small model strictly for restaurant use to their largest unit used in small commercial plants.

Model LB-100 is a countertop unit that produces a hundred 4-ounce servings or 4½ gallons of finished product per hour. It is used in restaurants and by caterers to produce fresh, high-quality products in a small space. It measures 14½ inches wide by 22 inches deep by 26 inches high and is air cooled. It comes with a preset timer attachment.

Model LB-250 is a small floor model measuring 24 inches wide by 24½ inches deep by 50½ inches high. It is water cooled and has a cylinder capacity of 9 quarts. Producing up to 9½ gallons of finished product per hour, it is used primarily in restaurants and small shops.

The most popular unit made by Coldelite is model LB-500, used in restaurants and hotels, and by independent shop owners. It can manufacture 19 gallons of product per hour with a cylinder capacity of 18 quarts. Measuring 24

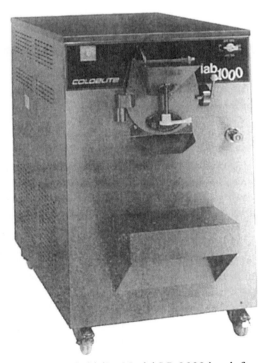

FIGURE 1-8. Coldelite Model LB-1000 batch freezer.

inches wide by 31½ inches deep by 50½ inches high, it is available as either air or water cooled.

Model LB-1000 (See Figure 1-8) is a large batch freezer suited for a small production plant for multistore operations. This unit has a cylinder capacity of 38 quarts and can produce 40 gallons of product per hour. It is available as either air or water cooled and measures 31 inches wide by 44 inches deep by 50½ inches high.

The Coldelite units are expensive batch freezers and have the disadvantage of using plastic parts in many of the important areas of the batch freezer. These parts, including the dasher blade and extrusion lever, tend to wear out and need to be replaced.

Taylor

Taylor, the largest manufacturer of soft serve machines in the world, has a service record and distributor support system that are easily among the best in the industry. The company makes an excellent batch freezer that is engineered to produce a smooth high- or low-overrun ice cream or sorbet. Its two most popular models are the 104 and 220.

Model 104 (Figure 1-9) is a tabletop unit that can take 2 quarts of mix per batch and has only one speed that produces a high-overrun product of 80–100 percent. It has a cylinder capacity of 3 quarts and can produce 12 quarts per hour. It comes only air cooled and measures 16³⁄₁₆ inches wide by 26¹³⁄₁₆ inches

FIGURE 1-9. Taylor Model 104 tabletop batch freezer.

deep by 21⅜ inches high. This unit is ideal for restaurants making small signature ice cream desserts daily.

Model 220 (Figure 1-10) has a 20-quart mix capacity and produces approximately 15–20 gallons an hour. It comes either air or water cooled and measures 18⁷⁄₁₆ inches wide by 40½ inches deep by 56½ inches high.

These batch freezers have hoppers that allow for easy access when pouring in mix, and special 5-inch spouts for adding other ingredients to the chambers. In addition to a manual timer with a buzzer, Taylor batch freezers also have a special red dial light that is separate from the timer and lights up automatically when the product is in a refrigeration cycle. Another advantage of these batch freezers is a high-speed beater that operates for extruding the finished product.

Electro-Freeze

Another large manufacturer of soft serve equipment, Electro-Freeze sells under its own name a batch freezer built by the Emery Thompson Company. This ma-

FIGURE 1-10. Taylor Model 220 batch freezer.

chine is reasonably priced and has a good service-support system because of the excellent distributor network maintained by Electro Freeze. Their units are made of heavy-duty stainless steel and have large hoppers and extruder spouts. Two basic models, differing in the overrun percentages produced, are available.

Model FT1 has only one speed and is for high overruns of 70–100 percent. This water-cooled unit has a cylinder capacity of 20 quarts and produces approximately 60 gallons an hour. It measures 23½ inches wide by 31½ inches deep by 51 inches high.

Model FT2 is a water-cooled floor model having two speeds to produce either high (70–100 percent) or low (15–30 percent) overruns. With a 20-quart cylinder capacity, it can produce about 45 gallons an hour on low speed, and 60 on high. It also measures 23½ inches wide by 31½ inches deep by 51 inches high.

REFERENCE

Robbins, Carol T., and Herbert Wolff. 1985. *The Very Best Ice Cream and Where to Find It.* New York: Warner Books.

2

CONTINUOUS FREEZING PROCESS

The continuous freezing process consisting of the continuous freezing production and packaging line and the hardening room or tunnel (see Figure 2-1) was first patented in 1913, and by the mid 1930s its use was fairly widespread throughout the industry. It allows for large-scale production of ice cream and

FIGURE 2-1. Typical layout of a large ice cream plant for the production of various types of ice cream. (From *Tetra Pak Dairy Processing Handbook;* courtesy of Tetra Pak Hoyer, Pleasant Prairie, Wisconsin, and Lund, Sweden.)

Key
A: Raw material storage
B. Dissolving of ingredients and mixing
    1. Mixing unit
    2. Plate heat exchanger
    3. Mixing tanks (at least two for continuous processing)
C: Pasteurization, homogenization, and fat standardization of the mix
    4. Plate heat exchanger
    5. Homogenizer
    6. Tank for AMF or vegetable fat
D: Production area

7. Aging/storage tanks	15. Return conveyor for empty trays
8. Continuous freezers	16. Tray tunnel extruder
9. Bar freezer	17. Chocolate enrobing unit
10. Wrapping and stacking unit	18. Cooling tunnel
11. Cartoning unit	19. Wrapping unit
12. Cup/cone filler	20. Cartoning unit
13. Hardening tunnel	21. Cold storage
14. Cartoning line	

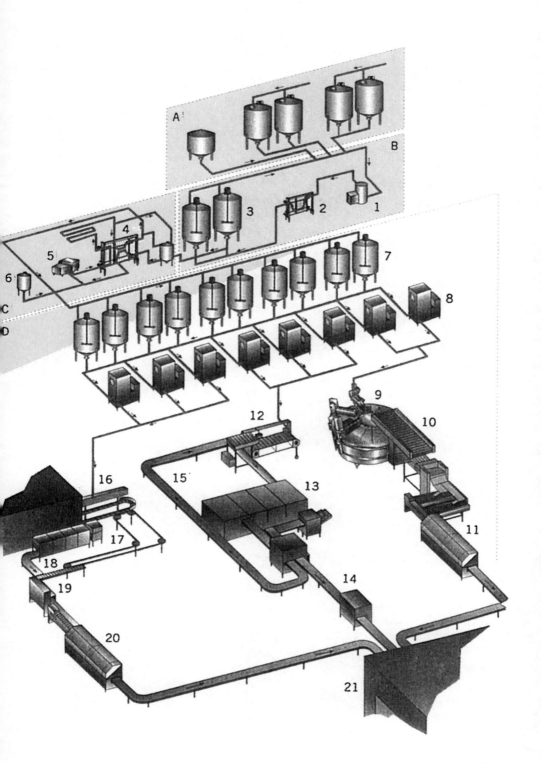

other frozen dessert products. The threshold mark for considering producing frozen dessert products using the continuous freezer method over the batch method is 40 gallons per hour (150 liters). The following are the major points a manufacturer will consider in connection with the continuous freezing method.

- *Uniformity of product:* On a gallon-per-gallon basis, there is more uniformity on each finished product produced because of the quantity of the production run. (At least forty times larger than any single flavor production run in a batch freezer).
- *Labor vs. skill:* Batch freezers require constant filling and emptying. On the other hand, continuous freezing is a more sophisticated and involved process, which means the personnel involved have more responsibility and must be better skilled to operate the equipment.
- *Production level:* Continuous freezing allows for more production on a per hour basis and avoids the stops needed to fill and empty a batch freezer.
- *Flexibility:* Continuous freezers can be connected to different processing machines to produce pints, quarts, half gallons, cups, cones, ice cream cakes and so on, while batch production is really only suitable for direct bulk containers.
- *Overrun:* It is much easier to adjust and control overrun on a continuous freezer.
- *Sanitation:* A continuous freezer can be easily sanitized through a cleaning-in-place (CIP) system.

CONTINUOUS ICE CREAM PRODUCTION LINE

Learning how to produce ice cream on a large scale is not difficult, but for the operator in charge, exact measurement of ingredients, practice, and patience are essential. Figure 2-2 provides an overview of the process via the production line's components.

Making the Ice Cream

The major function of the continuous freezing process is to produce a semi-frozen finished ice cream product using ice cream mix and various other ingredients. This is accomplished by freezing a portion of the water in the mix by lowering its temperature while incorporating air into the product.

Continuous Freezing Function The process starts after the ice cream mix has been produced (see chapter 4) and stored for at least 4 hours at a temperature of 32–41 degrees Fahrenheit under continuous gentle agitation, or purchased from a manufacturer. At this point, a metered amount of mix is pumped from the storage tank to the flavor tank. This is accomplished by opening the outlet

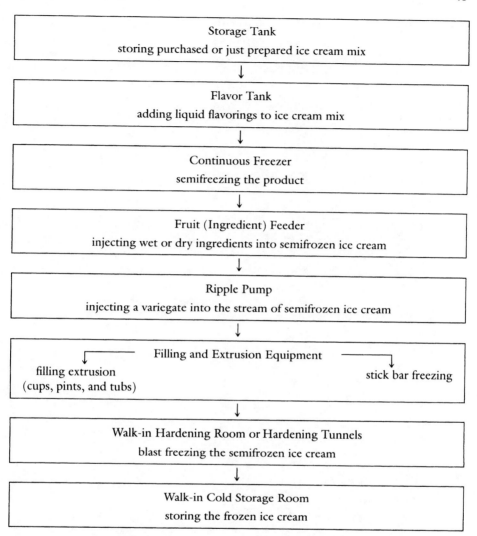

FIGURE 2-2. The continuous ice cream production line.

valve of the storage tank and letting the proper amount of ice cream mix flow out. Next, depending on the ice cream product to be produced, any additional liquid flavorings (vanilla extract, fruit extracts, etc.) are poured into the flavor tank and combined thoroughly with the ice cream mix. The mix is then pumped to the inlet of the continuous freezer.

The speed, viscosity (stiffness), and overrun settings need to be set according to the continuous freezer being used, following closely the manufacturers recommendations. Once the mix has entered the freezing chamber and air has been incorporated, it then passes through the chamber under agitation and partially becomes frozen.

Ingredient or Fruit Feeder Function   A fruit or ingredient feeder is a separate unit in the continuous freezing production line for the specific purpose of injecting one or more wet or dry ingredients into a flowing stream of ice cream. It is used for producing flavors other than straight vanilla or chocolate. As the ice cream leaves the continuous freezer, it is piped through the fruit feeder (ingredient feeder) where an auger-feed system uniformly deposits the ingredients into or onto the passing stream of ice cream, then passing it through a gentle blender to assure even distribution of the particles.

Ripple Pump (Variegator) Function   If a marble or ripple effect is desired in the product, a variegate sauce is injected by means of a ripple pump. The sauce is poured into 5- or 10- gallon tanks that are mounted above a sanitary variable-speed positive pump. It is then pumped through a nozzle that adds a stream of the variegate into the flow of ice cream, thus causing a marbled effect. The variegating nozzle can be a single or multiple tube, and some systems allow for rotation of the nozzle as it feeds the sauce, resulting in a more varied effect.

The ice cream is then piped to the next stage in the process, which will be either filling (tubs, pints, etc.) extrusion or molding (see Chapter 6).

Packaging the Product

Semifrozen ice cream is piped from the continuous freezing production line for packaging into either bulk or retail containers as close to the continuous freezing line as possible. Filling all semifrozen products requires a device that provides a bottom-up filling system. The ice cream is so firm that without such a system there will be voids in the container resulting in a short fill. Bulk containers are usually filled with a float. The float is a disk about the same diameter as the bulk container being filled, with a pipe in the center of the disk. This disk and pipe are hung over a slightly smaller pipe in which the finished product is being delivered. As the ice cream fills the tub, it floats the disk upward until the operator slides the filled container out and a new one in.

Whatever packaging equipment is used, the following functions are very important:

- *Continuous accurate fill:* The volume weight of ice cream must correspond to the weight listed on the label.
- *Avoidance of air pockets:* If the flow of product into the container is not consistent, air pockets will occur throughout the container.
- *Temperature of the product:* If the product is not frozen enough (too soft), there will be a drastic variation in the fill weight and crystallization will occur.

- *Closure of the lid:* Most filling machines have a mechanism that automatically attaches a lid to a container. Personnel along the packaging line should watch closely to make sure the lid is fastened tightly to the container.

Bulk Packaging Of all the dairy products, packaging for retail pint, quart, and half-gallon ice cream products is probably the most market driven. Decisions as to size and style of the package are based almost entirely on marketing forces. For example, consumers prefer to serve ice cream from round containers, and they like to view the product through a window. Similarly, convenience, impulse buying, and, in many cases, price are determining factors usually at the point of purchase (where a consumer is standing directly in front of the freezer deciding what to purchase). During the summer selling season in particular, half-gallon store-branded packages are sold by supermarkets as price leaders.

Bulk packaging of ice cream is usually in round or square paperboard cartons, about 75 percent of the market, or in round plastic 2½- or 3-gallon tubs like the ones produced by the Ropak Corporation. Plastic packaging, about 25 percent of the market, for freezer use is made up of HDPE resin material. So, environmental concerns could be another factor in a dairy's choice of packaging material for ice cream. Philosophically, paper has the advantage of being made from renewable resources, while plastic is an oil-based product. However, plastic is far ahead in the recycling derby with organized programs in place for collecting and sorting containers. Companies like Anderson Erickson are leading the way in recycling plastic. They have made a commitment to HDPE recycling by not only taking an active part in the process, but in investing in a recycled resin manufacturer and helping to raise $1 million for its start-up. AE's motivation seems quite simple: To do the right thing by seeing less of its plastic packaging end up in the landfill. If this pays a dividend in dollars or in community goodwill, so be it. Paper, on the otherhand, is still pretty much a throwaway product.

For round paper containers, producers have the option of running preformed containers or producing straight-sided containers from blanks. In the latter case, because packages are formed as needed, processors benefit from reduced warehousing, material handling, and shipping costs. Another benefit is the ability to produce a range of sizes, pints to half-gallons for example, on the same forming machine. Forming machines can produce oval, square, and rectangular containers as well as conventional round shapes. The forming of paperboard containers is done either on a single spindle conveyer or on a manual single spindle. Using a single spindle conveyer, the operator uses a single-spindle can former to build the tub. When done manually, the operator sets up each tub by hand.

Tamper-Evident Packaging Tamper-evident packing systems, which indicate obviously that someone has opened a package, have become universal throughout the food industry. Because of having to deal with one crisis of tampering after another, suppliers reluctantly went into tamper-evident systems. Today, suppliers now look at such packaging as a competitive advantage. Suppliers want to know that their packages have not been tampered with and consumers want to know that the package they have purchased has never been opened.

Newer systems focus on strips or rings that must be torn from the container before the lid can be removed. These systems are more suitable for consumers than internal seals because tampering will be evident in the store before the product is purchased and brought home for opening. Following are two tamper-evident systems that work very well:

- *Tear strip:* A major improvement has been the Flex Guard, a tear strip that is part of the lid. Developed by the Sweetheart Cup Company, this system locks the lid, which contains a tear strip, onto the container. The strip is easy to open, but unlike other tamper-resistant devices such as bands or seals, once removed its absence on the package at the point of purchase is a sure sign that tampering has occurred or was attempted.
- *Breakaway ring:* Secur-a-Tear has been developed by Cardinal Packaging for 5-quart ice cream containers. The system works by applying the breakaway plastic ring to an empty container. After the pail has been filled, the lid is placed on the container and locked into the ring. It is then impossible to remove the lid without breaking the ring.

Blast Freezing the Semifrozen Ice Cream

The final step in the manufacture of ice cream is blast freezing the product by placing it in a walk-in freezer or freeze tunnel to harden. Blast freezing takes the semifrozen dessert product from a temperature of approximately 26 degrees Fahrenheit to −25 to −40 degrees Fahrenheit in approximately 8–12 hours in a hardening room. Most modern ice cream production plants now use hardening tunnels for blast freezing in 50 percent less time (3 hours) than that of a walk-in hardening room.

The following factors must be considered when blast freezing a product:

- *Size of package:* It can take as little as 1 hour to blast freeze a 4-ounce package to 8–12 hours to freeze a 2½ gallon bulk container. Ice cream will freeze slightly faster in a plastic container than a paper container.
- *Temperature:* The colder the room, the faster the hardening. Hardening room temperature should be between −20 degrees Fahrenheit to −40 degrees Fahrenheit. Constant movement into the room from the production floor or carelessly leaving the hardening room door ajar or open will dramatically affect freezing room temperature.
- *Air circulation:* Air flow inside the room is very important and will shorten the hardening process by almost half the time over still air. Also, if too many containers are stored in the room on top of one another or too close together, freezing time will be dramatically slowed down and quality of the product will be affected.

- *Section of the room:* Ice cream will harden faster when placed along the walls. The center of the room is the warmest spot.
- *Temperature of the product entering the hardening room:* The more quickly the product moves from the production and packaging line to the hardening room, the better the blast freezing process will be, resulting in a smoother textured product.
- *Composition of mix and percentage of overrun:* The higher the fat content, the longer the product will take to freeze. Likewise, the higher the overrun, the longer it will take to freeze.

CONTINUOUS ICE CREAM FREEZER EQUIPMENT

Due to advancements in ice cream production technology, today's continuous freezers are self-contained units that can be operated either manually or semi-manually, or that are totally computerized with automatic start-up, freeze-up guard, and overrun control systems. They can come with either one, two, or three barrels and are capable of producing between 100 and 1,200 gallons of ice cream per hour with a 100 percent overrun. Many units have a 0–100 percent overrun flexibility that is adjustable at the control panel.

The main parts of a continuous freezer are as follows:

Freezing cylinder or barrel: depending on the specific size unit or manufacturer, ice cream mix is pumped through the cylinder so that air can be whipped into the mix. Longer and smaller in diameter than that of a batch freezer, it is made of stainless steel, with a hard interior chromium plate that ensures a smooth and uniform consistency to the product being produced.

Dasher: a long stainless steel piece that has blades mounted on it to scrape the semifrozen ice cream as it gets firmer from the inside wall of the cylinder toward the front.

Freon compressor: the refrigerating unit.

Air/mix pump: usually situated on front panel of the unit, its purpose is to pump air into the ice cream mix before it reaches the freezing cylinder.

Control panel: regardless of the unit used, all continuous freezers manufactured today have some sort of manual, semiautomatic, or totally computerized control panel for automating all operational functions so that viscosity and overrun can be controlled.

CIP connection: all units have some kind of clamp-type connection to a CIP unit to ensure maximum sanitation.

Continuous Freezer Manufacturers

Continuous freezers are manufactured worldwide by five major companies that have the capability of not only manufacturing excellent equipment, but of supplying technical support and repair when needed. Regardless of the manufacturer, any of today's continuous freezers will produce excellent ice cream when used properly.

Hoyer Based in both Lake Geneva, Wisconsin, and Højbjerg, Denmark, Hoyer is a unit of the Alfa Laval Company specializing in the production of industrial processing equipment for the ice cream industry. Founded in 1948 in Arnus, Denmark, Hoyer equipment is now found throughout the world. Besides producing a full range of state-of-the-art production equipment, Hoyer provides its customers with assistance for new product development and design of production systems, and a staff of technicians who can provide installation and repair support services anywhere in the world.

Hoyer's continuous freezers are divided into two distinct groups, the KF and Gelmark series (see Table 2-1). Hoyer's KF series provides ice cream manufacturers with a wide choice of high quality continuous freezers that meet different capacity and automation requirements. The KF1150, 1200, and 1200E freezers are available in three different models, all of which have the same basic elements: a flooded cooling system and a nickel cylinder and dasher. Each model is equipped with different types of control systems as follows:

- *N-model:* manually controlled freezer with push-button control of the main motor start, refrigeration, and pumps. Overrun control is accomplished by controlling the cylinder via an air back pressure valve.
- *X-model:* equipped with an advanced control system that includes automatic start-up, freeze-up guard, and an overrun control system.
- *XC-model:* fully computerized with automatic control of all main parameters and display of all necessary data including mix and ice cream tempera-

Table 2-1. Hoyer Continuous Freezers

Model	Maximum Capacity (liters per hour)	Maximum Capacity (U.S. gallons per hour)
KF300W	300	80
KF1150	1,000	260
KF1200	2,000	530
KF1200E	3,000	800
Gelmark 80	80	20
Gelmark 160	160	40
Gelmark 300	300	80
Gelmark 750	750	200
Gelmark 1100	1,100	300

tures and volumes, air flow, ammonia supply, and so on. Disruptions are also displayed.

Hoyer also produces as part of the KF series a model KF300W. It is a continuous freezer with a built-in freon refrigeration plant.

The Gelmark series of continuous freezers is for the small-to-medium size ice cream manufacturer. Gelmark freezers, while manually operated, are equipped with a self-contained freon refrigeration unit and designed for easy installation. They require connection to water and electricity only. The vertical freezing cylinder with its hard chromium-plated surface provides extremely efficient freezing. Ice cream mix and air intake are metered by a piston pump, while the frozen ice cream is discharged from the cylinder by means of a constant-pressure valve. The unit is operated by a control panel and has a hot gas defrosting system that provides accurate regulation of viscosity as well as automatic freeze-up protection. Computerized models of these units are also available.

Cherry Burrell   Backed by more than 120 years of tradition, Cherry Burrell is the only manufacturer of continuous freezers that is based in the United States. A worldwide organization that continues to embrace the spirit of innovation and customer service, Cherry Burrell's Voigt line of continuous freezers are excellent pieces of equipment for high-volume ice cream production.

The Voigt Premier Automatic Series models (Figure 2-3) are totally computerized. A single product selection adjusts the Voigt freezer to your desired set points for capacity, overrun, viscosity, mix-flow rates, and ingredient incorporation. You can even toggle between English or metric units. With an easy to read screen control, the operator using the Voigt automatic freezer can select the set points for each of the above, and then the Voigt freezer will continually adjust the viscosity, overrun, and mix flow rate. Easy to install, the Voigt freezer is prewired. It even has a built-in modem for remote troubleshooting.

The Voigt Premier Manual Freezer is an economical, low capacity freezer that is highly accurate and straightforward to use. It handles ice cream and other frozen desserts with ease, and is available in three models for production capacities of 150–400 gallons per hour at 100 percent overrun. All three models have manual controls, 10–150 percent overrun flexibility, and specially designed dashers for optimum crystalline structure. They come prewired with self-contained electricals and pneumatics for fast, simple installation, and have an exclusive sanitary air booster package.

APV Crepaco   Long recognized as a leader in developing equipment and systems to make ice cream, APV Crepaco of Rosemont, Illinois, manufactures a complete line of continuous freezers and accessory production equipment that makes it a one-stop shopping source.

APV supplies freezers for every production need, from simple to sophisticated (see Table 2-2). Its WS series represents the top of the line in high-technology freezers. Designed to give the operator more control of the production

FIGURE 2-3. Cherry Burrel Voigt Series P continuous freezer.

Table 2-2. APV Continuous Freezers

Model	Maximum Capacity (liters per hour)	Maximum Capacity (U.S. gallons per hour)
WS 06	1,000	260
WS 08	1,500	400
WS 12	2,300	600
WS 15	3,000	800
MF 50	100	27
MF 75	160	42
MF 100	430	111
MF 200	550	145

process, the WS series offers a choice of manual, semiautomatic, and fully automatic models (Figure 2-4). The semiautomatic and fully automatic models feature APV Crepaco's proven Viscotrol system. Viscotrol maintains constant ice cream viscosity whether it is stiff and dry for extrusions or soft and flowable for mold filling. This feature helps maintain filler accuracy and extrusion portion control. The differences between the three basic designs are as follows:

Manual Control

Positive displacement rotary lobe pumps with rubber covered rotors and CIP bypass covers

All-electric variable frequency pump drives

TEFC dasher motor

FIGURE 2-4. APV series of continuous freezers, models WS-06, -08, -12, and -15). (Side panel removed to show better view of freezer.)

Panel mounted switches for dasher, pumps, bypass covers, and hot gas control

Adjustable cylinder pressure

Adjustable overrun control from 0–150 percent

Stall monitor for freeze-up prevention

Semiautomatic Control

Electronic controllers for overrun and Viscotrol

Control and display of cylinder pressure

Airmass flow meter for overrun control from 0–150 percent

Cylinder vent valve

Mix and ice cream temperature display

Adjustable cylinder pressure

Fully Automatic Control

Industrial video display unit (screen) with program logic controller (PLC) for automatic control of all freezer functions

Control settings memory for up to sixty products

Precise control and monitoring capability for viscosity, overrun, capacity and cylinder pressure

Instant readout for all key process functions

Alarms and diagnostic messages

Product temperature control for mold filling

On all the models, variations in overrun control are virtually eliminated through the use of a product discharge pump. This feature effectively isolates the freezing cylinder from downstream pressures often encountered in extrusion applications. A variable ratio pump system, developed by APV, enables production of low- and high-overrun (from 0–159 percent) products at a constant cylinder pressure set by the operator. The WS series also offers two types of dashers: types 30 and 80. Type 30 is the standard open dasher while type 80 allows for special applications requiring stiffer drier-appearing ice cream at a given temperature.

APV units are made of all stainless steel parts including all frame components, side panels, doors, and even the refrigeration jacket. Internal piping is also stainless steel. The overrun is controlled through a microprocessor using a mass air flow controller that maintains exacting deviation limits, enabling maximum accuracy at the filling machine molding and extrusion systems. Low temperature specially equipped WS models are also available that are designed to produce conventionally frozen ice cream from 22 degrees Fahrenheit to extrusion temperatures as low as 14 degrees Fahrenheit.

For small-scale laboratory and production uses, APV produces its MF series of fully contained units with built-in refrigeration condenser units. They are easy to install and operate.

Gram A leader in the manufacture of ice cream production equipment for many years, Gram from Denmark is recognized for its simple and functional equipment that has a reputation for never breaking down. Its continuous freezers come in five basic designs (Table 2-3) based on 100 percent overrun and all include the following basic features:

- *User-friendly design structure:* built of stainless steel with large removable side panels for easy access. The cladding has nonhorizontal surfaces to minimize the accumulation of water and product remnants. The smooth surfaces of all their models provide better hygiene and facilitate cleaning. The operation terminal is rinse-water proof and placed in the cladding. The cladding is also provided with a drip nose and is generally manufactured without contact to other surfaces. It is easily removed by means of a key. No screws are employed. Easy access is provided to all components when the cladding is dismounted.
- *Pressure injection:* overrun control is effected by connecting the external air system to the freezer at a minimum pressure of 75 psi. The air is passed through a fine filter to a manually adjusted air proportioning valve at the freezing cylinder.
- *Scrapers (dashers):* two types of scraper shafts are available to produce various textures and viscosities of ice cream and other frozen novelties. One is an open type scraper for several uses and one is a closed type for low-temperature ice cream.
- *Programmed computer production:* the advanced control panels are easy to use and can interface and exchange data with other production units (fruit feeder, etc.), freezer units, and a factory network. It can store up to ninety-nine individual product programs. All programs are monitored in terms of parameters that include cylinder and outlet pressure, overrun, and any drop in mix flow or air flow.
- *Patented built-in aerator:* ensures top quality ice cream. The aerator facilitates production of ice bars and stiff ice cream with high overrun, improved texture, high melt resistance, and large quantities of air bubbles and crystals.

Table 2-3. Gram Continuous Freezers

Model	Maximum Capacity (liters per hour)	Maximum Capacity (U.S. gallons per hour)
FCF-4	500	124
FCF-8	1,000	250
FCF-14	2,100	540
FCF-18	3,000	750
FCF-50	4,000	1,000

Technogel   For many years, the Italian manufacturer Technogel has been one of the most innovative producers of ice cream machinery. Its success stems from an emphasis on high technology, good quality materials, and continuous innovation both in the absolute reliability of its products and in the after-scale service to its customers.

Technogel designs, manufactures, and sells the widest available range of continuous ice cream production equipment specifically suited to the needs of its customers. The main features of all their continuous freezing equipment are

- Hard-chrome-plated pure nickel barrel
- Open dasher with eccentric shaft and stainless steel blades
- Watertight control panel with digital ammeter
- CIP inlet
- Mechanical speed variator and piston speed indicator
- Overrun adjustment valve
- Barrel pressure gauge and high/low pressure gauges for refrigeration circuit
- Hot gas valve
- Removable rear flange
- Refrigeration gas Freon R22

Technogel produces a small range of self-contained continuous freezers that are designed to combine high performance and up-to-date technology with simple operation and maintenance, its 100, 150, and 300 models. These freezers can produce extruded and molded ice cream and can be connected to automatic production lines. The performance of the machines is extremely flexible thus enabling the production of either high-overrun (up to 100 percent) or low-overrun ice cream. The units have attachments for CIP system hook-up. A unique feature is the placement of the rear flange or barrel, which is located externally to the cylinder and can be quickly disassembled for cleaning and servicing. As are all of their continuous freezers, these units are equipped with a digital ammeter that automatically controls the stop–restart of the compressor according to the ice cream hardness, thus preventing any possible accidental freeze-up in the dasher.

Designed for medium-size ice cream producers, their single-flavor, double-barrel models 600/2 and 800/2 produce up to 600 and 800 liters of ice cream at 100 percent overrun. The main feature of these two units is the pump assembly, which includes two pistons pumps with alternate movement driven by a mechanical motovariator. The two barrels have independent refrigeration units and separate controls. The hot gas control works on the second barrel.

PMS Company   PMS has been a leader in both remanufactured and new ice cream production and novelty stick equipment for more than 30 years both in the United States and throughout the world. It is the exclusive U.S. agent for

Table 2-4. PMS Sidam Continuous Freezers

Model	Maximum Capacity (liters per hour)	Maximum Capacity (U.S. gallons per hour)
KF 450	2,400	600
KF 300	1,600	400
KF 150	800	200

Technogel and Sidam as well as other manufacturers of industrial ice cream production equipment.

PMS's three models of the Sidam KF series of continuous ice cream freezers (new; see Table 2-4) has been specifically developed to produce premium stick and stickless novelties. This series comes either in one, two, or three barrels. These freezers are prewired self-contained units with a control panel that will allow even the most inexperienced freezer operator to work efficiently and confidently. All movable parts are stainless steel and hard chrome plated.

FRUIT OR INGREDIENT FEEDER MANUFACTURERS

Because fruit and ingredient feeders (Figures 2-5 and 2-6) must work in close conjunction with the production capacity of a continuous freezer, they are available in many different size configurations as listed in Table 2-5.

RIPPLE PUMP EQUIPMENT MANUFACTURERS

A ripple pump is a separate unit attached to the continuous freezing production line that injects a metered amount of variegating sauce into a stream of semi-frozen ice cream. PMS specializes in the manufacture of ripple pumps and nozzles. Their units are built of stainless steel with ¾ hp motor. The hopper holds 6 gallons of sauce and the nozzles (one or two flavors) have the capacity to inject sauces into ice cream for an hourly capacity of up to 2,400 gallons. Other recommended companies that manufacture ripple pumps are Gram, Technogel, and Hoyer.

PACKAGING EQUIPMENT MANUFACTURERS

Most filling equipment manufacturers offer a comprehensive range of fillers for ice cream, frozen yogurt, and sorbets to meet virtually any packaging requirement.

FIGURE 2-5. APV ingredient feeder, Model SE 600 HR.

Fillers are available for ice cream packaging in bulk (2½–3 gallon containers, half-gallon, quart, and pint) and single-serving units (3½–4 ounces). Having the right packaging equipment in your plant results in tremendous saving in labor costs and employee efficiency.

The following packaging equipment manufacturers produce fillers for carton or round containers in either paper or plastic.

Autoprod

Autoprod produces many different kinds of fillers for the dairy industry. This company has an excellent worldwide reputation for no-nonsense equipment that never breaks down. Its units include the following:

Versa-Pak Rotary Ice Cream Filling Capping System (RO-A7 IC). Specifically designed for plain, fruit, nut, and candy ice cream products, this system fills 3-

FIGURE 2-6. Cherry Burrell Model HCIF high capacity ingredient feeder.

ounce, dual or single pint, quart, and half gallon containers. Production is 3,600 units per hour, or 7,200 units per hour in dual mode. The unit has a no-drip, positive cutoff valve for accurate filling and fills a variety of paper or plastic containers. Cup diameter changeover takes 15 minutes or less. Optional features are available for CIP and SIP (sterilize-in-place) cleaning. (See Figure 2-7.)

Versa Pak Rotary Fill/Seal/Cap System (Model RO-A7 HS). This unit is similar to the RO-A7 IC system, but is specifically designed for heat sealing from rollstock. Die cutting takes place directly over the container.

Rotary Tamper-Evident Filler/Sealer (Model RO-AI). Ideal for small continuous freezer operations, this unit fills up to 16 ounces (pint containers). Production is up to 3,000 units per hour. It has no-drip nozzles to ensure clean seal flanges.

Rotary Portion Control Fill/Seal and Fill/Cap System (Model 1000). This unit is a very functional filler for small continuous freezer operations. It fills up to 16 ounces (pint) and has a production capability of up to 1,680 units per hour. It has no-drip nozzles and can heat seal pre-die-cut lids.

Table 2-5. Fruit or Ingredient Feeder Equipment

| | | Hoppers | | Production Capacity |
| | | Number of | Size (gallons) | (gallons) |
Manufacturer	Model			
Technogel	LCPF	1	8	300
Technogel	HCPF	1	13	900
Technogel	HCPF-2	2	13	1,800
Technogel	FF10	1	8	425
Technogel	FF30	1	13	1,250
Cherry Burrell	HCIF	1	20	2,400
APV	S-410	1	7	1,000
APV	S-420	1	14	2,000
APV	S-430	1	14	2,700
APV	SE-600 HR	1	25	3,400
APV	MF-20 or 30	1	20	2,700
Hoyer	FF4000	1	25	2,400
Hoyer	FF1200	1	5	900
Gram	NF-400	1	8	250
Gram	NFD-5000	1	29	1,250

Rotary Portion Control Fill/Seal and Fill/Cap System (Model 2000). Filling containers up to 10 ounces, this unit is otherwise similar to the model 1000. Production is up to 1,200 units per hour.

Fast-Pack Tamper-Evident Fill/Seal Cap System (Model FP 1X3TE). This stainless steel high-volume unit is capable of running up to six filling production lines. While producing tamper-evident seals from roll film or foil from rollstock, it can fill up to 3,000 containers per hour on each line for a total of 18,000 units per hour when all six lines are being utilized. Its no-drip nozzles ensure clean seal flanges, and it has advanced CIP and SIP cleaning. It also has lidding capabilities for snap-on reclosable lids.

APV Crepaco

APV offers a comprehensive range of fillers for ice cream and other frozen desserts to meet virtually any packaging requirement, from individual portion cups and cones, to small bulk containers, cartons, and tubs, to large institutional and restaurant-size tubs. Its carton fillers include the following models:

Technohoy Cart-O-Fil. This machine provides in-line carton erection, hot-melt gluing, filling, and closing. With the flexibility to handle various sizes of rectangular glued cartons, its production ranges from 1,300 to 6,600 units per hour, depending on the size of carton.

FIGURE 2-7. Autoprod Versa Pak VP RO-A7 IC filling machine.

Model 588 Hot Melt Carton Filler. Made especially for tamper-evident packaging, this model erects, hot-melt glues, and fills cartons on one compact machine.

Model 558 Hot Melt Carton Filler. A smaller, lower-speed version of the Cart-O-Fill system, this unit is designed to fill fully glued-sealed, tamper-evident cartons.

Model 456 (Anderson) Round Ice Cream Carton Filler. This compact, high-speed ice cream filling system is designed to fill and cap up to 3,600 round half-gallon and quart containers per hour. The system has a high-speed conveyer with a unique spinner capper for advancing the lids to a vertical capping chute. An optional special filler nozzle is available for two or three variegated products, and a vibratory feeder places fruits and nuts onto the product prior to capping.

APV container fillers can handle various sizes and styles, from straight-walled or nested round containers to tubs, and from cups to cones. This line of equipment includes the following units:

RUF-Filler. The Technohoy RUF utilizes either an eight- or ten-segment rotary table revolving around a rigid center column to which a variety of dispensing, filling, and lidding (including heat seal) components are mounted. This flexible filling system allows the production of a wide variety of products from cups and cones to large bulk containers. Production depends on the size of unit filled, but its capability ranges from 1,500 to 9,000 units per hour.

Ventura. An extremely flexible filling machine, the Technohoy Ventura is available with more than forty different dispensing, filling, and lidding accessories to produce an unlimited variety of products. It is available in several multilane configurations for high output requirements. Production, depending on style and size of the unit filled, from 6,000 to 25,000 units per hour.

Model 456 Round, Straight-Walled Container Filler. This model is a compact, high-speed rotary filler using a Microfill volumetric principal to fill and lid round, straight-walled containers. Production, depending on style and size of the unit filled, is up to 3,600 units per hour.

Model 456N Round, Nested Container Filler. For round, nested containers, this is a versatile dispensing, filling, and lidding system. The Microfill volumetric fill principle coupled with the optional container supply magazine and large capacity lid supply/orientater means a minimum of operator attention. Production, depending on style and size of unit filled, is up to 3,600 units per hour.

DF-Line. Designed for perfect, uncomplicated filling operations for large squat bulk-type containers, the production of this model, depending on style and size of unit filled, is up to 1,800 units per hour.

Gram

Gram's extensive experience with dairy products and packaging puts it in the unique position of being able to offer a varied product line of fillers or custom-built units to meet the individual needs of its customers. Some of its models are listed as follows:

Model CE93. This modern space-saving filling unit can be supplied with a PLC control. Its capacity range is from 3,000 to 7,200 cones or cups per hour.

Model FAC 8 Bulk and Cake Filler. This unit is available in three different designs, with or without electronic cam switching. It has a capacity range of 1,920 pints and 7,200 3-ounce containers per hour, and up to 900 per hour for bulk packaging from 1 to 6 quarts (1½ gallons). This unit comes with a pint inserter, extrusion filler, vacuum lid inserter, roller device for pressing on snap-on lids, and date marking equipment.

In Line Filler (ILF 15, 4 and 16 wide, 6 wide). Because of its advanced PLC, this unit has a capacity range of between 7,200 and 22,500 cups or cones per hour. It comes with a cone inserter and sleeve aligner and lidder. This model is built to allow quick and easy switching of product lines.

T.D. Sawvel

Sawvel's equipment is ideally suited for the small ice cream manufacturer. All of its fillers utilize a volumetric bottom-up filling to give a consistent fill every time. The filling begins at the bottom of container to assure fill without air pockets or cavities. Its line includes the following models:

Model 110. Designed for continuous flow or multiple batch freezer operations, this unit will fill 3-ounce cups to 32-ounce quart containers at up to 1,800 units per hour. It is built of stainless steel with special tooling available for ice cream cones and has a 15-gallon hopper with a date marker. It is designed so the operator can load containers, lids, and product from the same area while packing containers.

Model 120S. This unit is ideal for round ½-gallon paper containers and is available for single or dual line production. It can fill up to 3,600 units per hour. In addition to bottom-up volumetric fill, it features automatic lidding capabilities. A single or double flavor variegator is available as an optional accessory.

Model 130. An automatic rotary ice cream filler for 1- or 2-quart straight-wall paper containers, this model has an automatic infeed and outfeed conveyor with programmable limit switch controls. It can fill up to 3,600 units per hour. In addition to bottom-up volumetric fill, it features automatic lidding capabilities. Optional accessories include single or double flavor variegators, a lid unscrambler, and a top dresser for dry or wet products.

Model 1000. This is a versatile compact unit for filling tubs from 1 to 3 gallons in size. It can fill up to 600 3-gallon tubs per hour. Optional product spinners are available to provide more uniform filling. This model makes it easy to change from filling one product to another.

Model 702. This unit is an automatic 3-gallon filler with a capacity of up to 800 3-gallon tubs per hour, with an infeed conveyer and an air-driven revel (thick sauce) variegator for single or dual flavors. It has lid spinners with a capacity for sixty lids and a 180-degree tub rotation for no-mess lidding.

Tindall

Tindall's specialty is in the production of medium-price fillers that are easy to operate and very functional. Most of its units come with an optional variegator to inject a ribbon of sauce into the container. Its models include the following:

Model 135 Bulk Can Filler. Built of stainless steel, this unit can easily be moved in and out of production areas. It fills 2½- and 3-gallon tubs with production up to 30 tubs per minute or 1,800 tubs per hour. The automatic lidder holds approximately fifty lids.

Model 136 Bulk Can Filler. This model fills all bulk tubs from 1 to 3 gallons in size. Its production is approximately 1,800 tubes per hour, and the automatic lidder holds fifty lids.

CIP CLEANING UNIT

You cannot operate a continuous freezing production line without a cleaning in place (CIP) system because all production equipment that comes into contact with any ingredient involved in the process of producing ice cream must be cleaned immediately after use. A CIP system is a separate unit that is equipped with a high-pressure centrifugal pump to ensure efficient washing of the plant using a solution of lukewarm water and nonfoaming detergent. The major benefit of having a CIP system is to eliminate the task of manually dismantling and cleaning each piece of equipment that has been in contact with an ingredient.

The hardware consists of a suitably sized tank (about 60–80 gallons), a high capacity stainless steel shell and tube heater, a variable speed sanitary pump, and a variety of chemicals pumps to supply the necessary materials to the system, as well as the control and recording units.

For the purpose of this discussion, following is a brief description of how a CIP operation works with pumps being used to clean out the mix tanks supplying ice cream mix to the ice cream plant:

1. Pump dispenses a tap water rinse.
2. Another pump delivers a washing solution of an alkaline type (with chlorine).
3. A second tap-water rinse follows.
4. Another pump dispenses a tap-water rinse with an acid sanitizer.

The CIP unit controls and records the quantities of water and solution, temperatures, times, pressure, velocities, and chemical concentrations. A typical CIP unit usually has a fail-safe system that shuts the unit down if the parameters of a particular program are not met as the system operates.

Hoyer (Figure 2-8), APV Crepaco, Brink's Ecolab, Sani-Matic, and Damrow Equipment all manufacture CIP units in a variety of sizes and configurations.

WALK-IN REFRIGERATION

Because of its versatility, reasonable cost, and storage efficiency, walk-in refrigeration is the most commonly used for continuous freezing operations. Mechanically cooled units, a refrigerator operates at 38–42 degrees Fahrenheit (3.5–5.6 degrees Celsius), while a freezer keeps the product below 32 degrees Fahrenheit (0 degrees Celsius).

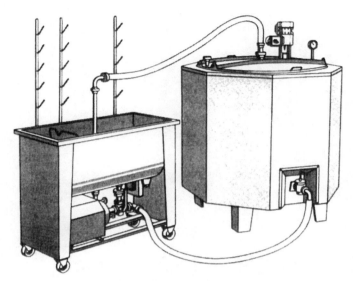

FIGURE 2-8. CIP system from Hoyer with connection to an aging vat.

When producing, blast freezing, and storing ice cream, there are basically two kinds of walk-in freezers: hardening rooms and storage rooms. A hardening room is a large walk-in freezer that maintains a temperature of −20 degrees Fahrenheit to −40 degrees Fahrenheit. The refrigerant used to obtain such low temperature is either ammonia or Freon. To maintain proper blast freezing temperatures, the entrance to the room should not be direct, but rather through the walk-in storage freezer or refrigerator. The three major design considerations for constructing a hardening room are

1. A well insulated wall and door structure to maintain freezing temperature.
2. Proper internal air circulation.
3. Adequate refrigeration (compressors) for the temperature desired and for the size of the room being constructed.

After the ice cream has been hardened, it should be transferred to a walk-in storage freezer awaiting shipment to retail outlets. The temperature of the walk-in storage freezer should be between −10 degrees Fahrenheit and −20 degrees Fahrenheit.

Since personnel have to continually move back and forth between hardening and storage freezer rooms, it is very important that they have adequate insulated clothing (see Figure 2-9) to protect them from the extreme cold temperatures of each room.

Currently, the two primary methods for specifying and installing walk-in refrigerators and freezers are as preengineered or prefabricated, and as customized

FIGURE 2-9. Refrigiwear −50 degree Fahrenheit outerwear clothing.

built-in models. The prefabricated walk-in is usually constructed from a series of 4-inch (10-cm) thick manufactured modular panels. Each panel is constructed with urethane insulation material that is foamed into place between two sheets of metal, such as galvanized steel, painted galvanized steel, aluminum (embossed or plain), painted aluminum, or 18-, 20-, or 22-gauge steel. These panels are attached to each other (with a variety of latches and bolts) to form the outer walls, ceiling, partitions, and floor (optional) of the unit. They are available in many combinations of heights, lengths, and widths.

The specification of a prefabricated walk-in using the manufacturer's standard modular panels produces a unit that is "normal" in size. The standard widths, lengths, and heights are determined by each manufacturer. For a small ice cream manufacturing operation, a walk-in might be 8 feet 4 inches wide by 19 feet 6 inches deep.

A large ice cream manufacturer usually requires the construction of a built-in refrigerator or freezer. These units are usually constructed of Styrofoam walls, floors, and ceiling that are protected with structural glazed tile walls, quarry tile floors, and aluminum or stainless steel ceilings. Large built-in refrigerators may also be constructed of fiberglass panels laid over the insulation. A built-in unit has the advantage of lasting many years under conditions of heavy use, but the disadvantage is cost and the difficulty of moving or enlarging the unit.

Walk-in refrigerators and freezers are usually specified with either self-contained (top or side mounted) or remote refrigeration systems. The self-contained units are usually hidden on top of the walk-ins by closure panels, but sufficient air space must be available for keeping air-cooled units from building up heat in the space above the walk-in. If the large air mass in the space above the false ceiling is insufficient for removing the heat of the compressor, additional ventilation will be necessary. Remote refrigeration units can be located some distance away, but the further the distance, the greater the heat (efficiency) loss. Remote refrigeration has the advantage of keeping noise and heat away from the production area. Refrigeration can be either air cooled or water cooled depending on environmental conditions and utility availability.

The refrigeration system is usually rated by the horsepower of the motor and the BTUH (British thermal units per hour). Most walk-in refrigeration is connected to a 115-volt, 208-volt, or 460/480-volt power source. The efficiency of the refrigeration equipment will be determined in part by

- The amount of insulation
- The number of doors and frequency of opening them
- The efficiency of air flow within the cavity
- The distance between the compressor and evaporator
- The degree of cleanliness of the compressor (air cooled)
- The temperature of incoming water to the compressor (water cooled)
- Refrigerant level in the refrigeration system
- The condition and method of sealing the doors

Walk-in refrigeration must be provided within easy access of the ice cream production line. Common accessories and features that may be added to the walk-in specifications include

- Ramps for units not level with the floor
- Locks for doors
- Thermoplastic strip curtains to reduce loss of refrigeration when door is open
- Air vent to relieve pressure when doors are opened or closed
- Window doors for placing packaged ice cream in the walk-in without the necessity of walking in
- Outdoor, protected refrigeration systems
- Freezer alarm systems that activate when temperatures rise to a certain level
- Roof caps for walk-ins located outdoors

The first line of defense against changing temperature fluctuations for walk-in refrigeration is a well constructed, easy-to-access door and curtain. Doors come in either vertical sliding, horizontal sliding, or sectional overhead. Insulated traffic doors that separate one area of your production facility from another offer additional protection. This protection is important because it keeps heat isolated. All doors should have a quiet opening and closing feel to them and should be built of galvanized steel. Curtains add a secondary protection against temperature fluctuations and are highly recommended for every entrance to a walk-in refrigerator or freezer.

Because the refrigeration equipment will be working 24 hours a day, it is wise to do everything possible to reduce the loss of energy by using the best equipment possible. Refrigeration is not the place to cut corners or to omit energy-saving accessories. Heat recovery from water-cooled refrigeration systems is easy to engineer and will bring a quick return on the investment.

HARDENING TUNNEL SYSTEMS

Advancements in freezing technology have made hardening tunnels a practical and efficient way to blast freeze product in a relatively short time, eliminating the need for huge walk-in hardening rooms. Today, most large ice cream manufacturers use either a spiral hardening tunnel or in-line tray tunnel to blast freeze their frozen dessert products. A hardening tunnel can freeze a pint product in 3–4 hours at a temperature of −30 degrees Fahrenheit to −50 degrees Fahrenheit. Smaller packages can be blast frozen in less than 1 hour.

Spiral Tunnels

A continuous-air blast freezing system, the spiral freezer (Figure 2-10) distributes uniform air flow across all tiers of the spiral. The horizontal flow path en-

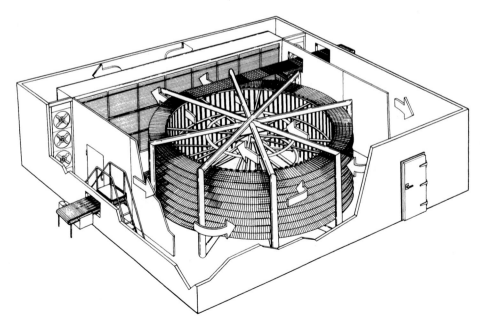

FIGURE 2-10. Northfield spiral system freezing tunnel.

sures an immediate and sustained freezing action without disturbing the products. Inside this unit is a conveyer that starts at floor level and gradually winds around in an upward spiral motion.

The freezer components of this system include the following:

Spiral conveyer: constructed of heavy-duty stainless-steel members. All metal-to-metal contact surfaces are capped with polyethylene to extend life and ensure sanitation.

Fans and coils: the finned heat exchange surface is constructed of aluminum and is designed with the following features:

- Wide graduated fins are spaced so as to minimize blockage from frost build-up
- Low temperature rise through freezer for rapid efficient freezing
- Water and/or hot-gas defrost is usually available
- Large face area to extend operating time between defrosts
- Shallow coil depth for maximum heat exchange efficiency and ease of cleaning

Airflow baffling: constructed of stainless steel. Baffles ensure cold air constantly to ice cream containers without air by-pass. The baffle arrangement provides easy access for cleanup and maintenance without removal of baffle panels.

Insulated enclosure with floor: most units feature 5 inches of foam-in-place insulation with rugged full overlap doors having heated jambs to prevent freeze-ups, and shrouded infeed and outfeed openings to minimize infiltration of plant air and exfiltration of freezer air. The floor system is designed to prevent buckling under freezer/defrost cycles. Floors are stainless steel construction and are sloped for easy drainage.

Controls: usually prewired. Conveyer belt speed is controlled by a solid-state AC variabie frequency inverter with fixed speed by-pass control. Safety shut-off probes and emergency stops are located strategically throughout the system. When an unsafe operating condition is detected, an alarm sounds and the "Spiral View" window illuminates the fault. Diagnostic meters include run time per hour, cage motor and tension motor amp, air temperature read-out, belt speed, and product dwell time (amount of time needed to blast freeze a semifrozen ice cream product to a completely frozen state).

Compressor (s): includes a microprocessor-controlled screw compressor with motor and starter, accumulator, receiver and evaporative condenser.

Refrigerant: usually ammonia.

APV Ice Cream, Gram Equipment of America, InTec Inc., Northfield Freezing Systems, and Tetra Pak Hoyer all manufacture spiral tunnels that are customized to match the freezing capabilities of the ice cream manufacturer's needs.

In-line Tray Tunnels

Tray tunnels are designed to air blast freeze a wide variety of products (ice cream cakes, bars, cups, etc.) in cardboard containers, wire baskets, or trays. A fully automatic, continuous in-line tray tunnel receives product from the end of a processing line and, after freezing it, delivers the product ready for transfer into the storage freezer.

Gram's in-line tunnel system model BT (highly recommended) consists of an endless conveyer system with replaceable stainless steel trays. It is available in a variety of designs, with different shapes and trays to ensure maximum output. A built-in lubrication system combined with a special guard system eliminates the need for any lubricant in the freezing area.

REFERENCES

Arbuckle, W.S. 1983. *Ice Cream*. Fourth edition. Westport, Conn. AVI.
Birchfield, John C. 1988. *Design and Layout of Foodservice Facilities*. New York: Van Nostrand Reinhold.

3

SANITARY CONDITIONS

Consumers who buy your products do so because they find them great tasting and enjoyable. They assume those products to be safe for consumption as well. To have the best quality products that will ensure repeat purchases, it is not enough to simply rely on quality ingredients. You have to start with good sanitation. You must

- Actively promote hygienic practices by personnel.
- Plan for and maintain a sanitary working environment.
- Constantly monitor your product for contamination.

With these goals in mind, every ice cream manufacturing operation should consider adopting a mission statement like the following as a reminder to uphold the highest principles of sanitation:

STATEMENT OF SANITARY QUALITY

To ensure the highest quality of our products, we pledge to:

Operate clean and sanitary facilities that meet high standards of integrity in the protection of the products produced.

Comply with or exceed all national, state, and local public health laws relative to sanitation dairy production, processing, and distribution.

Prevent unsanitary conditions before it becomes necessary to correct them.

HYGIENIC PERSONNEL

The fundamental factor in producing a healthy quality ice cream product is the hygiene of personnel. Every person associated with dairy products should be hygienic minded and constantly observant of sanitary details. Hygienic personnel have a desire to employ only healthful practices and habits, and to make a determined effort to correct errors in hygienic behavior. They are conscientious about their physical health, especially about being free from contagious diseases. A medical examination should be required once a year.

Hygienic habits include innumerable personal details such as the following:

- Hands and nails should be clean.
- Hands should be washed before touching dairy products or clean utensils, especially after touching unsterile cans, shaking hands with anyone, coughing against the hand, wiping the nose, scratching, visits to the toilet, and so on.
- Unsanitary practices such as coughing in or near the equipment or spitting on the floor should be avoided.
- Plastic gloves should be worn at all times during the production phase.
- A net or cap should be worn to prevent loose hair from contaminating the product or equipment.
- Clean fresh clothes should be worn every day.
- Wounds or sores should be bandaged to prevent any possible contact with the equipment or product.

Adequate refrigeration, proper operating routines, and correct washing and sanitizing of all equipment cannot ensure a healthy environment if personal hygiene is lax. It is up to management to make sure that the plant has modern up-to-date sanitary equipment and procedures in place that employees can use on a daily basis. Likewise, the people involved in production must take responsibility for lessening the possibility of the spread of communicable diseases and maintaining a bacteria-free product.

A SANITARY WORK ENVIRONMENT

Facility Planning and Design

When planning an ice cream production facility, it is critically important that every decision be made with plant sanitation in mind. If this approach is taken, it will then be possible to create and implement sanitation procedures that can be followed without deviation by everyone within the plant.

During the plant design phase, the following should be considered to insure good sanitation:

- All interior surfaces should be smooth and free of scratches and grooves, particularly surfaces in contact with the product.

- Floors should have a slightly abrasive surface to prevent slipping on wet areas.
- Surfaces (floors specifically) should be sloped to provide quick drainage.
- All connecting walls must have cleanable surfaces and curved corners at connecting points.
- All equipment surfaces should be accessible and easy to take apart for cleaning.
- Equipment mounted on the floor should allow for uniform scrubbing around and under it.
- Construction materials must be moistureproof and free of odors that can be absorbed by dairy products.
- Tin-coated metal equipment should be frequently inspected for scratches or chips; metal can dissolve in products, causing undesirable flavors.
- Adequate light and ventilation is extremely important (pay special attention to it during the design process). Also, all lighting must have plastic covers that protect the area from glass and broken bulbs.
- Operations should be separated. Unpasteurized or raw products must be stored in rooms apart from equipment to avoid equipment contamination or accidental mixing with pasteurized products.
- Separate facilities must be available for products that absorb obvious odors coming from washrooms, storage rooms, boilers, refrigeration compressors, restrooms, and so on.
- Hot and cold running water must be conveniently located and the supply unrestricted.
- Floor drains are essential for each room and must be located for complete drainage, leaving no puddles. They should be out of traffic lanes but be accessible for cleaning.
- Every room should have a basin equipped with a mixed faucet for hot and cold water for washing hands, liquid soap, cleaning agents, a drinking fountain, and single-service paper towels.
- Shelving is needed for proper storage. Health departments prefer wire racks because they are adjustable and easy to clean, and they allow air to circulate. Use these racks for storing all dry ingredients. Position the containers so that those purchased first are used first, thus lessening the possibility of contamination and bacterial growth.
- All containers of ingredients must be stored a minimum of 6 inches above the floor and protected from splash and other contamination, specifically by roaches and rodents.
- All of the floors and walls in the production room should be tiled. Where walls and floor meet, the surfaces should be rounded to allow proper cleaning. The tile should be resistant to water and dairy products and should have a good reputation for holding up under heavy traffic around the equipment.

Plant Self-Inspection

Why should an ice cream manufacturer conduct internal inspections? Whether you are a small batch freezer operation or a large dairy, there are a number of reasons. Among them are

- Product quality
- Compliance with the current good manufacturing practices (GMPs)
- Maintenance of good sanitary practices
- Having written accurate records of inspections
- Assuring that the facility is safe to the workers
- Assuring the production of safe frozen dessert products. This point is required under the provisions of the federal Pure Food, Drug, and Cosmetic Act. It is also the cornerstone of any HACCP (hazard analysis critical control point) program.

Keys to the Program   A self-inspection is aimed at evaluating sanitary practices and uses GMPs as guidelines. It is a very effective means of determining unsafe practices that might result in product adulteration and of evaluating management's commitment to proper food handling.

The first key is to have someone on staff who is capable of conducting such inspections, and there are three ways you can go about accomplishing this:

1. Having someone already on staff who has knowledge of what is required to conduct a sanitation inspection.
2. Hiring an outside expert to provide proper education to a member of your staff.
3. Simply appointing someone. This is only recommended if there is a commitment on the company's part to educate that person.

The inspectors or sanitarians must have a basic knowledge and understanding of a number of different areas. These include:

Plant operations and protocols. These include all standard operating procedures for production, cleanup, and maintenance. They should have access to all manuals and how your workers are trained.

Current good manufacturing practices. GMPs are the basis of all sanitary inspections. They are categorized as "should" and "shall." *Should* means a practice that is mandatory, and *shall* means it is recommended for consideration as part of normal operating procedure.

Pest control protocols or practices. Many companies employ outside sources to control pests. The inspector should work with these individuals to learn why they do what they do and to assure your company that these outside services are going their job.

Local, state, and federal regulations. Inspectors should familiarize themselves with all regulations that affect their operation. They should know the agencies and outside inspectors and work with them instead of trying to outsmart them. The agencies usually win in the end.

Labor issues. If your plant is a union shop, get the members' cooperation to make any changes and improvements. Simply make them your ally in this effort.

Another key is documentation. There are many ways the evaluation can be recorded. They are as follows:

- *Checklists:* a written form designed specifically for your plant. Usually, answers to questions are in the form of "yes" or "no" to whether there is compliance to established practices and procedures, or a number scale showing compliance to same.
- *A notebook:* used to write down observations, both good or bad, that can then be written up in more detail at a later date.
- *National Food Processors Association Sanitation Report Form:* used by many sanitarians, the form grades a plant by two criteria. The first is a numerical grade ranging from 1 for the lowest to 4 for the highest. It employs pluses and minuses to enhance this range. The second criteria is called the "p Factor" that ranges from 0 to 1.0. This inspector's determination of the probability that an FDA investigator will have adverse findings. The higher the "p Factor," the greater the chance of adverse findings.

The final key to self-inspection is the most important. It is management support. Without it, no program can succeed.

Preparing to Inspect   How do you go about preparing for an inspection? That really depends on the inspection. There are two kinds of inspections; routine and detailed. *Routine* is just that, routine. It may be conducted on a daily or weekly basis and may be as simple as walking through the warehouse or production facility to just look at what is going on. It may involve the use of a checklist and be targeted as assuring yourself the pest control agent has checked all the traps or that cleanup was conducted as it was designed.

A *detailed* inspection is designed to take a comprehensive look at the facility's overall compliance with the company's GMPs, to determine if any potential unsafe situations are developing, and to determine if there are any situations that may result in a compromised product. This kind of inspection should examine a plant from top to bottom. It is this kind of inspection that most FDA investigators will do when they come to your plant. Before conducting such an inspection, do not announce your intentions. If people learn that they are going to be inspected, they start to clean up or change their habits. The objective of the inspection is to view normal operations and recommend changes, if changes are in order.

Whether for a routine or a detailed inspection, there are certain tools that the inspector should carry during an inspection:

Notebook to record comments, violations, and/or approval of specific areas inspected.

Flashlight with unbreakable lens.

Black Light to test for rodent urine.

Whirl-Pak bags or plastic petri dishes for sample collection.

Copies of Pertinent Regulations to show the employees who sometimes do not believe what you tell them.

Reporting and Correcting   Once the inspection is completed, the inspector should sit down with plant staff and review the observations made. This exit interview should be a summation of the overall plant condition, highlighting major concerns that should be addressed immediately.

Then a detailed report based on observations is prepared. The report should incorporate the following:

- *Observations.* All suspect and potential adulteration of sanitary issues should be described.
- *Degree of concern.* So that issues of most concern are addressed first, a grading system for observations should be established.
- *Recommendations.* Recommendations for addressing each area of concern should be made in language that is easily understood by all employees.
- *Time lines.* An area on the reporting form should be provided for time lines to allow those responsible a reasonable amount of time to make corrective changes in areas specified.

GENERAL SANITATION PROCEDURES

Receiving Ingredients and Supplies

Inspect all incoming ingredients, product packaging supplies, single-service items, laundry, and so on, including pallets, for evidence of any kind of pest infestation or contamination. Frozen or refrigerated items should be handled first. Get them to proper storage immediately. When receiving ingredients or supplies, either reject or discard the following:

- Out-of-condition, outdated, damaged, leaking, contaminated, or soiled products.
- Items that *may* have been contaminated by water, condensation, pests, or previous cargo on the truck.
- Refrigerated dairy ingredients warmer than 45 degrees Fahrenheit (7.2 de-

grees Celsius) and frozen ingredients warmer than 0 degrees Fahrenheit (−17.8 degrees Celsius). (If a recording thermometer is mounted in the truck, check to see the temperature history of the load.)

- Pails, totes, or canned ingredients that are leaking, badly dented, or pitted with rust, or that have swollen puffy ends.

Storing Ingredients, Supplies, and Product

All ingredients and finished product ice cream tubs should be either placed off the floor on shelves or on wooden pallets. This requirement applies to any area in the facility, including the main plant area, walk-in refrigerator, and walk-in freezer. Store all dry and refrigerated items in regular storage areas that are clean and tidy as follows:

- In an orderly manner, at least 6 inches off the floor, on clean shelves, dollies, racks, or pallets.
- Arranged in the proper order for FIFO (first-in, first-out) item rotation. Place newest items at bottom or in back of older items.
- In a manner to avoid cross-contamination. Items that might leak or drip must be stored below other items.
- In clean, covered, labeled containers if items have been removed from original containers.

Do not store any items in the following areas:

- Under or near possible sources of contamination, such as sewer lines (grease traps), water lines, or refrigeration lines, or where there is accumulated condensation or evidence of leakage.
- In toilet rooms, vestibules, garbage rooms, salvage areas, or mechanical equipment rooms.
- Directly on the floor or against the wall.
- In overcrowded conditions.

Dry Storage Dry storage means any product, ingredient, or supply item that does not have to be refrigerated, such as the following:

Ingredient containers: keep sealed until used. When using only a portion of a bag or container of an ingredient, close the bag or container securely or transfer the contents of opened bags or boxes of ingredients to clean, sanitized, covered, labeled, approved plastic or metal containers.

Clean utensils, packaging, and single-service supplies: store under the same sanitary conditions as for ingredients. Check all partial packages of either packaging materials or ingredients to be sure they are properly sealed.

Cleaners and sanitizers: DO NOT store above or close to ingredients, packaging supplies, single-service items, or product contact items.

Insecticides: store these and other toxins in a separate area locked away from cleaners and sanitizers. DO NOT store them above or close to ingredients, packaging supplies, single-service items, or product contact items

Be sure to frequently check critical products for signs of pest infestation. Insects many be tiny and difficult to see. Also, leave a space of at least 18 inches (the "whiteline") between stacks of product and between stacks and walls if storage is for more than 30 days.

Controlled-Temperature Storage In any controlled-temperature environment, fixed temperature procedures must be in place so employees are aware that proper refrigeration is being maintained in the plant. This is accomplished by constantly checking the outside temperature gauges to ensure that the refrigeration systems are working as required.

Frozen items (0 degrees Fahrenheit or below): check freezer temperature frequently, at least twice daily, to ensure that items such as chocolate chips or chunks, nuts, and frozen fruit are being stored properly.

Refrigerated items (40 degrees Fahrenheit, or below): check refrigerator temperature frequently, at least twice daily, to ensure that items such as ice cream mix, pasteurized whole or pureed fruit, fresh fruit, fudge, and caramel purees are being stored properly.

Proper Cleaning of Equipment

All equipment in the ice cream production facility, whether it is a batch or continuous freezing operation, must be cleaned daily; washed, rinsed, and dried well. If it is not, sterilizing and sanitizing it later on is meaningless. Equally important is inspecting equipment for wear, rust, leaks, loss of tinned surface, and other signs of deterioration.

In general, any piece of equipment in the facility must be cleaned in the following manner:

Washing
- Wash all equipment with lukewarm (80–110 degrees Fahrenheit) water to remove milk remnants.
- Soaking may be necessary when the milk or mix has been allowed to dry.

Rinsing
- Rinse thoroughly and then follow by vigorous scrubbing with a stiff-bristled brush (sanitize brush after each use) and hot water (115–120 degrees Fahrenheit) containing a washing powder (cleaning agent), not soap.

- The outside of the equipment also should receive the same careful washing treatment. When the surface has been scrubbed to a high polish with a washing solution, it should be rinsed again with clean, warm water (100–110 degrees Fahrenheit) to remove the thin film of the washing solution.
- Finish cleaning with the use of a sanitizing solution or bleach.

Drying

- Drying using heat or ventilation, the last step in cleaning, reduces deterioration and corrosion, and inhibits growth of organisms. Never use a cloth or towel to dry a piece of equipment because it only recontaminates the equipment.
- Drying can be eliminated when the equipment is to be immediately refilled with a dairy product.

Sterilizing/Sanitizing

- To sanitize, use water that has been heated to 170 degrees Fahrenheit for at least 10 minutes.
- To sterilize, use steam at 240 degrees Fahrenheit for 15 minutes.

Scheduling Sanitation Procedures

Both during and at the end of each day, the following cleaning procedure should be strictly enforced:

1. When you are finished using a particular ingredient, put it back where it belongs.
2. All containers containing ingredients should be closed tight and wiped down clean so that no ingredients are on the outside of the container.
3. Use a disposable sanitized wipe for cleaning surfaces that do not come into contact with the product; for example, the front doors of any refrigeration equipment.
4. Sweep and mop the floor using clean hot water. Be sure to rinse the mop thoroughly after each use.
5. Wash all utensils and containers with clean hot water in one sink and a sanitizing solution in the other. Do not allow for such items to accumulate. Keep the sink area clean all day.
6. Clean all equipment such as blenders, scale, and so on with a clean hot water disposable wipe.
7. Pick up and clean floor mats with hot clean water.
8. Make sure the water bucket used for washing the floors is emptied, cleaned, rinsed, and sanitized.
9. Frequently remove all trash and garbage from the plant area.

A completed product that has been frozen and stored must be checked from time to time to make sure its bacteriological characteristics conform to health department standards. Weekly examinations should be made for bacteria count, flavor, body and texture, color, and appearance. Packages should be clean, neat, and properly labeled. Any products not meeting company and health department standards should be discarded.

SANITATION FOR BATCH FREEZER OPERATIONS

Batch freezer ice cream production can take place either in the back room of a retail frozen dessert shop, in a restaurant kitchen, or in a separate manufacturing facility. Whatever the facility, this room or area must be treated according to the highest sanitary standards. While it is virtually impossible to produce bacteria-free products in such environments, products can be safe for consumption if they have a low enough bacteria count, which can be achieved only through rigorous and unceasing sanitary practices.

Along with your architect, design the necessary production space with sanitation in mind. Do not let it be an afterthought because once constructed, changes will be difficult to make.

You will need a minimum of 200–300 square feet of space to produce ice cream in a batch-freezer operation. This space is suitable for production for at least two retail stores. Less space will compromise quality and create bad sanitary conditions primarily because refrigeration needs breathing space to operate properly. The problem will become more severe as your business grows and you need more ingredients on hand to support that growth, thus shrinking your available storage space. Plan for these contingencies at the design stage.

Use rubber floor mats near the sinks and batch freezer to help avoid accidents. In many states, floor drains are required in food-production areas, and, in any case, one should be placed near the batch freezer to allow for proper drainage of water. The drains also help make cleanup easier. To prevent food particles from falling into or getting embedded in any areas behind or alongside the equipment, there should be no rough edges or crevices anywhere.

The room or area should be properly ventilated either with windows, air conditioning, or an exhaust system to remove the hot air resulting from the refrigeration units that are constantly running. Consider air conditioning for cooling in the summer. Without proper ventilation, sanitary conditions will be difficult to maintain because the buildup of hot air from the ambient temperature and from refrigeration compressors in the production area will be conducive to roach, rodent, or bacterial problems.

Cleaning Ice Cream Tubs and Utensils

A three-compartment sink is required in batch freezing production area to completely wash, rinse, and dry tubs and utensils. A well-designed sink will have the following components:

- A drainboard for soiled utensils
- A prerinse hose
- A detergent dispenser
- A drainboard for clean utensils
- A storage rack (a separate piece of equipment) above the sink for clean utensils and tubs

The following procedure is recommended:

Sink 1: Wash and scrub with a stiff-bristled brush all tubs and utensils with hot (115–120 degrees Fahrenheit) water using a cleaning agent (not soap) to remove milk remnants.

Sink 2: Fill the sink with a warm water for rinsing all tubs and utensils.

Sink 3: Fill the sink with a sanitizing solution. Follow the manufacturer's recommended usage level for the sanitizer used. Rinse all tubs and utensils in this solution, and let them air dry on the sink countertop.

Cleaning the Batch Freezer

After the day's production run is complete, each of the following procedures should be carried out to ensure that the batch freezer is thoroughly cleaned and sanitized.

1. At the beginning of each day, place the dasher into the barrel. Clean first with sanitizing solution and then with cold water.
2. At the end of each day, rinse the chamber with lukewarm water until all the excess ingredients are cleaned out.
3. Open the chamber, remove the entire dasher assembly, and clean all the parts using a sanitized sponge with the same kind of chlorine-based sanitizing solution that was used for the preuse cleaning procedure.
4. Pour a cold sanitizing solution into the chamber as the last function before the cleaning is complete. This is done using a modified rinse method. Prepare a sterile rinse solution following the manufacturer's recommendations in 100-milliliter quantities per 9.46 liter capacity of the batch freezer barrel. With the outlet valve of the barrel closed, pour the sterile rinse into the inlet. Operate the scraper for 2 minutes and collect a sample through the outlet valve in a sterile bottle.
5. Use a sanitizing kit to check the sample for any bacteria in the freezer chamber.
6. Wipe all other parts of the batch freezer with liquid dishwashing detergent and rinse thoroughly with a hot water chlorine-based sanitizing solution. Make sure there are no film marks left on the batch freezer from the detergent.
7. Place a sanitary lubricant (Haynes or Petro Gel) on all the movable parts.

Weekly Cleaning Procedures

At the end of the each week, the following steps should be taken to ensure proper sanitary conditions.

1. Take all containers off the shelves, and clean the shelves thoroughly using a disposable sponge with a sanitizing solution.
2. Wipe down all walls with an abrasive cleaner.
3. Clean all floor drains with an abrasive cleaner.
4. Clean and then remove all equipment from the tables. Next, clean the tables with a sanitizing solution.
5. Clean the floors with a chlorine-based cleaner, and then repeat with clean hot water.
6. Soak the mop in a chlorine-based solution overnight to remove any odors.
7. Wash with a cleaning agent all trash containers in the plant on the last day of the week.

Monthly Cleaning Procedures

Preferably on a monthly basis, but quarterly at least, you should thoroughly conduct a major cleaning of the production plant, including the following:

1. Remove all tubs from the blast freezers, and clean the freezer thoroughly by removing all the shelves and cleaning them and the walls of the freezer with both a sanitizing solution and clean hot water.
2. Take all ingredient containers out of the walk-in refrigerator and clean the floors and walls thoroughly with a sanitizing solution and clean hot water.
3. Sweep all floors in both the walk-in refrigerator and freezer.

CIP FOR THE CONTINUOUS FREEZING PRODUCTION LINE

You cannot operate a continuous freezing production line without a cleaning in place (CIP) system (see in Chapter 2). It has to be the cornerstone of operating your plant. All production equipment that comes into contact with any ingredient involved in the process of producing ice cream mix and finished ice cream must be cleaned immediately after use. Having a CIP system in place eliminates the task of dismantling each piece of equipment. Of course, CIP effectiveness depends on the equipment used and its proper installation, and the temperature, speed, and circulation of the cleaning agents used.

For a CIP unit to work properly, consider the following:

- Sufficient size and capacity of the unit
- Detergents that are compatible with the unit

- Proper power connections to ensure temperature and velocity of the solution used

CIP Procedure

The steps listed, once implemented on a daily basis, will ensure that good sanitary practices are being followed.

1. Turn on the CIP unit and run clear water (100 degrees Fahrenheit) through the system to all connected equipment. This water should then be disposed of by way of a grease trap.
2. Turn on the centrifugal pump to circulate the cleaning solution containing sufficient acid (phosphoric and hydroxyacetic) to give 0.15–0.6 percent acidity, at 150–160 degrees Fahrenheit and 5–7.5 feet per second velocity for 20–30 minutes. Next, rapidly drain the system of this cleaning solution.
3. Rinse the system with water at 145 degrees Fahrenheit for 5–7 minutes.
4. Flush for 20–30 minutes with 150–160 degree Fahrenheit water containing 1–1.25 pounds of alkali detergent for each 10 gallons of water.
5. Rinse with cold water until equipment is cool.

CLEANING AND SANITIZING AGENTS

Whether you clean manually or have a CIP unit, properly using the right cleaning and sanitizing agent is important for achieving clean working environment. Do not use any cleaning agents that contain soap as this will leave a surface film that is difficult to rinse away. Certain alkalis, such as sodium hydroxide should not be used because they cause corrosion on metallic surfaces.

Make sure the water you use does not contain any appreciable amount of calcium or magnesium. Water containing these substances is classified as hard water. Hard water leaves a deposit of "milk stone" on the surface of the equipment. If the source of your water is classified this way, it can be altered by adding a water softening agent (such as pyrophosphate or metasilicate).

A sanitizer is a chemical agent that is applied in a separate operation after cleaning. Sanitizers destroy both disease-causing and harmless bacteria. The effectiveness of the sanitizer weakens as it contacts more and more dish and equipment surfaces, so the solution should be changed whenever it falls below the required strength. Use of a sanitizing kit with color codes lets you know if the solution is still effective. For mixing with a chemical, a water temperature of at least 75 degrees Fahrenheit is needed.

Sanitizing agents work best under strict temperature and time controls. Heat penetrates and facilitates drying of equipment. Low temperatures and short times do not adequately sanitize or dry equipment. Chemical agents only work effectively for sanitizing under the following conditions:

- When equipment surfaces are completely clean.

- When the chemical agents are in contact with the surfaces to be sanitized for the required time.
- When the active chemical used is sufficiently concentrated.

Volatile chemical sanitizers must be used (and stored) at lower temperatures than are used for cleaning. When used at 110 degrees Fahrenheit or higher, there is a rapid loss of concentration. There are however, many advantages to using sanitizing agents at lower temperatures.

- Equipment undergoes less strain due to expansion and contraction as with high-temperature sanitizing. This is an important consideration when cleaning freezers and pumps.
- Low-temperature sanitizing encourages the flushing out of equipment just before use, removing any dust that may have entered the equipment.

The disadvantages to lower temperature sanitizing are that it seldom leaves the equipment dry and thus encourages corrosion.

Only four types of sanitizing agents have pleasing odors; all others produce aromas objectionable in dairy products.

- *Hypochlorides (sodium hypochloride):* work fast, but quickly lose strength and are slightly corrosive. The solution should contain no less than 50 parts available chlorine per million parts solution in contact with surface a minimum of 15 seconds.
- *Chloramines:* are less rapid in action, lose strength less quickly, and are less corrosive than hypochlorides. The solution should contain no less than 50 parts available chlorine per million parts solution in contact with surface a minimum of 1 minute.
- *Quaternary ammonium compounds:* less effective sanitizers, they are odorless, nontoxic, and noncorrosive. They are, however, extremely effective on clean surfaces and are less influenced by water hardness or softness.
- *Soaps, calcium, and magnesium:* less effective than any of the above. When correctly formulated, these compounds work at 220 parts per million or more, at pH levels of 5.0 or higher, and at 75 degrees Fahrenheit or higher in contact with the surface at least 30 seconds.

EFFECTIVE BACTERIAL CONTROL

Effective bacterial control promotes health protection, product popularity, quality, and lower spoilage loss. Because of advanced technology in ice cream mix and freezing production equipment, there is no reason why ice cream manufacturers cannot meet the recommendations concerning bacterial control. If proper cleaning and sanitizing of all production equipment is conducted daily, there is little or no chance of nonsporing bacteria occurring because pasteurization kills practically all of it. While pasteurization does kill coliform bacteria, carelessness and employees untrained in the handling and cleaning of production equipment is regarded as the greatest potential source of contaminating microorganisms in packaged ice cream.

A high bacteria count can be caused by any of the following:

• High count in raw materials
• Ineffective processing methods
• Ineffective sanitizing methods
• Carelessness
• Prolonged storage of ingredients and ice cream mix

All frozen dairy desserts are tested during production by conducting standard plate count (SPC) and coliform counts on the finished product. Standards for the coliform count are almost uniformly 10 per gram of both pasteurized ingredients and the finished ice cream product. There are no standards for the SPC, but most health authorities set a maximum of 50,000 per gram.

In the past, it was routine policy for product samples to be picked up and sent to an outside laboratory. By the time the results were ready they were irrelevant, the product having left the plant long ago and perhaps already bought and consumed. Now, to save time, ice cream manufacturers perform many types of routine testing at their own on-site laboratories or at sites close to the production because of increased state and federal regulations and the testing needed to support HACCP programs. The proliferation of convenient, computer-driven instruments enables this more vigorous brand of quality control. That they can yield reliable results to even minimally trained operators is a dramatic improvement in recent times. For example, a new rapid laboratory test for coliform and standard plate counts using 3M's Petrifilm Series 2000 Plates offers an alternative to traditional agar plate micro-testing. This technology enables us to reduce the time needed to see bacteria colonies. Instead of waiting 24 hours to obtain results of coliform colony counts with agar plating, Petrifilm 2000 begins yielding results after 4 hours of incubation. Presumptive coliform colonies begin to appear at 6 hours of incubation, and confirmed colonies after 8 hours. Catastrophic coliform contamination may be apparent after only 4 hours. Because samples are placed directly on the film, several steps are eliminated in the extensive preparation of agar petri dishes, thus saving more time.

REFERENCES

Arbuckle, W. S. 1986. *Ice Cream*. Fourth edition. Westport, Conn.: AVI.

Birchfield, John C. 1988. *Design and Layout of Foodservice Facilities*. New York: Van Nostrand Reinhold.

Blumenthal, Michael M., and Robert F. Stier. 1993. Plant self inspection. *Dairy, Food and Environmental Sanitation*, September, pp. 549–553.

Darrah, Robert. Dairy Quality and Safety Committee Plant Section. In *Pocket Guide to Dairy Sanitation*. Des Moines, Ia.: IAMFES.

Flickinger, Bruce. 1995. Defining and designing the modern QC laboratory. *Food Quality Magazine*, September, pp. 33–38.

Gorski Donna. 1996. Efficient labs. *Dairy Foods Magazine*, June, pp. H–K.

Marshall, Robert T. 1992. *Standard Methods for the Examination of Dairy Products*. Sixteenth edition. Washington, DC: American Public Health Association.

Pennsylvania State University. 1990. *Ice Cream Manufacture, Plant Sanitation*. Course 102, Lesson 12, pp. 1–8.

4

⊠⊠⊠⊠⊠⊠⊠⊠⊠⊠⊠⊠⊠⊠⊠⊠⊠⊠⊠⊠⊠⊠⊠⊠⊠

ICE CREAM MIX PRODUCTION

Making ice cream is no different than preparing any other food product; the end product is only as good as the effort and ingredients that go into it. To produce quality ice cream requires a quality ice cream mix.

For the preparation of a basic ice cream mix, you first need to consider the use of bulk or canned ingredients and whether pasteurization should be high-temperature short-time (HTST) or batch. There are four combinations of these two considerations, and the choice of approach depends primarily on the size of your operation.

1. *Bulk ingredients and continuous HTST pasteurization:* used primarily by plants processing more than 1 million gallons of mix per year.
2. *Canned ingredients and HTST pasteurization:* used by medium-size plants producing 250,000–1,000,000 gallons of mix per year.
3. *Bulk ingredients and batch pasteurization:* a low-cost ingredient method also used by medium-size plants producing 250,000–1,000,000 gallons of mix per year.
4. *Canned ingredients and batch pasteurization:* used primarily by plants processing fewer than 250,000 gallons of mix per year. Equipment costs for this method are the least of the four methods mentioned.

Regardless of the process used, a mix production operation (Figure 4-1) involves

1. Selecting the ingredients
2. Figuring the mix formula

3. Mixing the ingredients
4. Pasteurizing
5. Homogenizing
6. Cooling
7. Storing the mix properly

INGREDIENTS

Nearly all ice cream produced today has as its basic ingredient a prepared ice cream mix. This mix includes dairy ingredients (cream and milk), sugar or other sweeteners, and stabilizers. Some also include egg-yolk and other solids such as MSNF (milk solids not fat). All of these ingredients have a specific purpose, and each is used proportionally depending on the percentage of butterfat used.

Dairy Ingredients

Milk, the major ingredient, is composed of water, fat (referred to as milkfat or butterfat), and MSNF (e.g., lactose, protein, and minerals). The butterfat is the major source of fat in an ice cream mix and is derived for the most part from fresh sweet cream. The amount of butterfat used determines how rich the ice cream will be. The richest commercial ice cream in the United States has a butterfat content of approximately 16 percent. A 14 percent butterfat ice cream is considered a premium product, while an economy product has a butterfat content of 12 percent.

Cream, a concentrated source of butterfat, is separated from whole milk and may contain 20–40 percent butterfat. It is found only in milk in the form of tiny globules held in suspension in the state of emulsion.

MSNF from sources other than the milk and cream used is sometimes added to supply the amount needed for a specific formula. These sources include skim-milk or whole-milk powder, condensed skim or whole milk, and sweetened condensed skim or whole milk. Whey solids are sometimes used as a cost-reducing method for a portion of the MSNF called for in a formula. The legal limit for whey solids replacement is 25 percent of the total MSNF in the mix.

The butterfat and MSNF components of milk contribute to the flavor of frozen dairy desserts, with the MSNF having only an indirect effect. The proteins help give a smooth texture and body. The lactose (milk sugar, found only in milk) adds to the sweetness, which is primarily provided by adding sugars. Using too much MSNF or whey solids will result in flavor problems usually described as "cooked" or "powdery," and may also cause a sandy condition in the finished ice cream due to lactose crystallization.

Egg yolks are used mainly to add flavor, body, and whipping ability. Egg-yolk solids are a required ingredient in French-style ice cream.

Sweeteners

Sugars used in ice cream mix production are called either sweetening agents or simply sweeteners. Their main purpose is to bring out the full flavor of the ice cream mix by sweetening the dairy ingredients and other flavors, such as fruits, to enhance consumer acceptance. The total amount of sweetener used in an ice cream mix varies depending on the butterfat content, but it is usually about 12–17 percent.

The primary sweetening agents are *sugar* and *corn syrup solids.* Sugar is used mainly to increase or decrease the sweetness of the finished product, but it also depresses the freezing point. Sucrose (cane or beet sugar) is the most widely accepted source of sugar used in the manufacture of ice cream mix. Liquid fructose (found in fruit juices and honey), costing about a third as much as sugar, is being used in economy ice cream products. The amount of fructose that can be used is limited because it depresses the freezing point much more than does sucrose, resulting in a mix that can be difficult to freeze and keep hard.

Corn syrup solids are only about a third as sweet as sugar, so they can be used for a 2 : 1 or 3 : 1 replacement of sugars. By increasing the total solids of the mix, a smoother texture, better body, and better keeping quality of the finished product results. The improved processing of corn syrup solids has completely eliminated the grain or cereal flavor once regarded as a defect in ice creams containing these solids. The low cost of corn syrup solids (compared to butterfat or MSNF) makes this addition quite popular; however, the amount that can be used is limited to about one-third of the total sweetener solids. Larger proportions may make the finished product too heavy, stringy, and gummy.

Stabilizers and Emulsifiers

Stabilizers have the ability to form gel structures in water or to combine with water as "water of hydration." (Water of hydration means the mixing of water with another compound.) They are used in small amounts (0.1–0.5 percent) in ice cream mix to provide product uniformity and smoothness in body and texture by reducing ice crystallization and melting. When the temperature of ice cream rises, some ice crystals melt; conversely, when the temperature drops, water is refrozen into ice crystals. Temperature fluctuations thus result in textural changes. Stabilizers absorb or hold some of the water freed by melting, thereby preventing the formation of large ice crystals when refreezing occurs.

Most stabilizers are of natural origin, but some are chemically modified natural products such as propylene glycolalginate and sodium carboxymethyl cellulose, which are polysaccharides from botanical sources. Some typical stabilizers are *gelatin, sodium alginate, locust bean gum, guar gum, zanthan gum,* and *carrageenans.*

Gelatin is an animal protein extracted from either bone or animal hide (bovine or porcine). It is characterized as either acid process (pig skins and ossein) or alkaline process (ossein and cattle hides). In general, gelatin improves the overrun of mixes, adds viscosity and a creamy texture, and slows meltdown.

Sodium alginate is extracted from different species of brown seaweed. It is a vegetable stabilizer that improves whipping ability and leaves a cleaner mouth-feel than animal-derived products. It produces favorable results with HTST mix processing.

Locust bean gum is grown in Cyprus and imported from Europe. It con-tributes to the viscosity of the mix and promotes overrun, slows down melting, and produces a slightly less sticky texture than guar gum.

Guar gum is an inexpensive food-grade polymer that is readily soluble in cold mixes and has a low flavor content, fast hydration (mixes well with water), and high viscosity. Its major drawback is that usage levels exceeding manufacturers' recommendations result in a very stringy product.

Zanthan gum is produced by bacterial biosynthesis. It is used essentially to supply considerable viscosity at low concentrations, and often with other hydro-colloids (locust bean gum, guar gum, and carageenan) to solve problems related to the low viscosity of ice cream mixes.

Carrageenans are extracted from seaweeds and are used to prevent ice cream mix separating. They are excellent for forming transparent water gels, are avail-able in both cold- and hot-water soluble types, have no off flavor, and have low usage levels that make them economical.

Emulsifiers help unlike substances, such as butterfat and water, combine in order to produce a drier, stiffer, and smoother product. The most common emulsifiers used in ice cream mix production are *lecithin, mono-* and *diglycerides,* and *polysorbates.* Lecithin is found in foods such as eggs and milk and is com-mercially prepared from soy beans. A good example of the use of lecithin is in French-style or custard ice creams that have an abundance of egg yolks in them. Mono- and diglycerides are also made from soy beans. Polysorbates, however, are not a natural ingredient. So even though they are very effective and inexpen-sive, they are considered less desirable than other emulsifiers because of claims of unhealthful side effects.

Suppliers provide many combinations of stabilizers and emulsifiers for specific applications. The types needed vary greatly depending on the mix composition and finished product description, for example, for hard versus soft ice cream mixes. Therefore, providing the supplier with a finished product description (premium, economy, low-fat, frozen yogurt, etc.) and the basic formula (indicating the ingre-dients to be used) is essential for obtaining the proper stabilizer combination.

MIX FORMULAS

The importance of producing a quality ice cream mix can not be overstated. Without a good mix, you simply cannot produce good ice cream. In calculating the right formula for a frozen desert mix, you must

- Consider the percentage of butterfat to be used and the desired body and texture.

- Decide on the size of the batch.
- Determine the availability and cost of the ingredients.

Mix Formula Software Program

At most dairies today, computers are used extensively to develop and calculate mix formulas through a process call *linear programming*. Taking into consideration all the variables, the program figures the ingredients needed and calculates both the unit and total cost of the mix batch produced based on the amount of gallons produced. While the use of computers has made calculating mix formulas easier, a human error in supplying information to the computer will, of course, result in an incorrect formula. Therefore, care must be taken to ensure that all information is accurate and that unit ingredient costs are up-to-date.

One company, Midwest Controls, has developed an excellent software program called "MixCalc" to calculate ice cream mix formulas. Specifically, the program calculates quantities of ingredients for each batch of product. At the beginning of the operation, the operator enters the product code, batch size, and the percentage of fat and MSNF in the cream, condensed milk, and any other dairy ingredients. The software then calculates the quantities of all the ingredients needed based on the formula of the product, which has already been entered into the program. These quantities remain in the program until the operator changes them, for example, if he or she switches to another silo of cream with a different fat or MSNF content, or if the product changes. The quantities are entered into a programmable logic controller (PLC). To make a batch the operator initiates the operation and the PLC meters the cream, condensed milk, and other liquid ingredients into one of the batch tanks. The PLC also tells the operator the name and quantity of dry ingredients that must be added by hand.

In addition to the calculations, MixCalc can also do the following:

- Maintain a running summary of the quantities of ingredients that have been used over any interval of time.
- Maintain a record of every ingredient used in every batch in case problems arise.
- Controls all the mixing of both liquid and dry ingredients through a PLC.

Manually Calculating Ice Cream Mix Formulas

There is no question that manually calculating an ice cream mix formula is difficult. For many years the manual method was the only way to do the job, so operators learned how to do it. While computers are used extensively today to do the calculating, it is still a good learning experience for an operator to know how it is done manually, especially if there is a glitch in the computer causing a crash or a bug in the software program itself. Following is an example of a 12-percent butterfat ice cream formula done manually.

⊠ 12% BUTTERFAT ICE CREAM MIX FORMULA

Batch size: 110 gallons
Pounds per gallon finished mix: 9.2328 pounds
Pounds per mix batch: 1,000 pounds

Mix Composition

1. Butterfat   12%
2. MSNF (milk solids not fat)   11%
3. Cane sugar solids   12%
4. Regular corn syrup solids   5%
5. Egg–yolk solids   .5%
6. Stabilizer (dry weight)   .2%
   Total solids   40.70%

Dairy Ingredients Specifications

Cream #1   40.00% fat
Milk #1   3.50% fat

Quantities to Be Used

	Weight in Pounds
Cream #1	256
Milk #1	505
Skim Powder	55
36 DE Corn Syrup	50
Egg Yolks	12.5
Liquid Sugar	120
Stabilizer	2
Total Batch Weight	1,000.5 pounds

All formulas were calculated the same way, for example, as that for 12-percent butterfat ice cream milk, which is explained as follows:

1. Calculation of single source ingredients; Multiply the percentages of each by 1,000 pounds.

Sugar	.12 × 1,000 =	120 pounds
Corn syrup solids	.05 × 1,000 =	50 pounds
Egg yolk solids	.005 × 1,000 =	5 pounds

   (Frozen egg yolks are 40% solids so we need 12.5 pounds to get 5 pounds of egg yolk solids)

2. Calculation of amount of cream, milk, and skim milk powder: This calculation requires several steps because nonfat milk is present in all three re-

maining items and butterfat is included in two of them. Start by adding all known amounts needed.

Sugar	120	pounds
Corn syrup solids	50	pounds
Egg yolks	12.5	pounds
Stabilizer	2	pounds
Total	184.5	pounds

Subtract the 184.5 pounds of known items from the 1,000 pound total batch resulting in 815.5 pounds of milk, cream, and skim powder remaining to be calculated.

3. Calculation of skim milk powder: 100% minus the sum total of the following:

Butterfat	12%
Sugar	12%
Corn syrup solids MSNF	5%
Egg yolk source	0.5%
Stabilizer	0.2%
Total	29.7%

Total derived is 70.3% (100 − 29.7). This is the percentage of the formula that must contain all of the MSNF (called serums). The percentage of MSNF in normal skim milk is 8.8%. If the 70.3% were skim milk, it would contain $.703 \times .088 = .061864 = 6.1864\%$ MSNF. The formula requires 11%, so there is a shortage of 4.8136% (11.0 − 6.1864) that must come from the skim milk powder. The skim milk powder is 3% moisture or 97% solids, which means that average serum (8.8%) that the excess milk solids can contribute is 88.2% (97 − 8.8%).

Divide the shortage of milk solids by amount of excess milk solids the skim powder can provide.

$$4.8164\% \div 88.2\% \times 100 = 5.46$$

Multiplying by 100 gets the pounds per 100 weight of formula. Since the total formula weight is 1,000 pounds, we need 54.6 pounds of skim milk powder ($4.8164\% \div 88.2\% \times 1,000 = 54.6$). Subtracting the 54.6 pounds of skim milk powder from the 815.5 pounds makes the total of 760.9 pounds remaining that can be milk and/or cream and must contain 120 pounds of fat needed for the 12% required in formula.

4. Calculation of milk and cream: We now know that the calculation of milk and cream must be the 760.9 pounds to maintain the 12% mix formula. To make the calculation to arrive at the poundage of milk and cream, we use a reliable dairy math system called "Pearson's Square." First determine the needed fat test of the mixture by dividing the 120 pounds of fat

needed by the 760.9 pounds of the total blend, which equals 15.77%. To conduct this calculation, draw a square as shown in Figure 4-2.

In the center, enter the needed fat test (15.77%). In the upper left corner of the fat test, place the fat percentage (3.5%). In the lower left corner, place the fat percentage of cream (40%). Subtract the smaller from the larger diagonally (i.e., 40.00 − 15.77 = 24.23) and place the results in the right-hand corners. This indicates that 24.23 parts of milk and 12.27 parts of cream will make 36.50 parts of a mixture that tests 15.77% butterfat.

Converting this to percentages (12.27 ÷ 36.50 × 100 = 33.616) indicates that 33.616% of the 706.9 pounds of milk and cream is 256 pounds of cream, and the remaining is 505 pounds of milk.

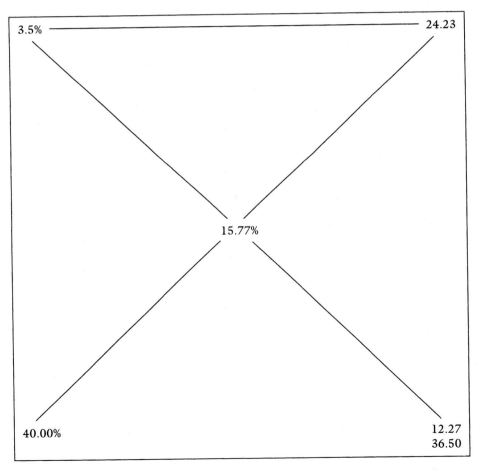

FIGURE 4-1. Pearson's Square for manually calculating milk and cream poundage.

Table 4-1. Milk Solids Calculation Proof

Pounds	Items	Butterfat	MSNF	Sugar	Corn Syrup	Egg Yolk	Stabilizer
505	Milk (3.5%)	18	44				
256	Cream (40%)	102	13				
55	Skim powder		53				
120	Sugar			120			
50	Corn syrup				50		
12.5	Egg yolk					5	
2	Stabilizer						2
1,000.5	Totals	120	110	120	50	5	2
	Percent	12%	11%	12%	5%	.5%	.2%

5. To proof the calculations: Each ingredient is entered in a table as shown in Table 4-1. Note the following concerning the milk, cream, and skim powder:

> *Milk:* multiplying the amount of pounds of milk (505) by fat in the milk (3.5%) equals 18. Multiplying amount of pounds by the percentage of MSNF (8.8%) in the whole milk equals 44.
>
> *Cream:* multiplying the amount of pounds of cream (256) by fat in the cream (40%) equals 102. Multiplying amount of pounds of cream (256) by the percentage of MSNF (.05%) in the cream (40%) equals 13.
>
> *Skim powder:* multiplying 55 pounds of MSNF (explained earlier is 3% moisture) by 97% equals 53.

Each of the totals of individual components divided by the size of the batch (1,000 pounds) equals the percentage, which is equal to the formula, proving our calculations are correct.

MIXING THE INGREDIENTS

The first, and most important, step in beginning the mixing process is the accurate measurement of the raw materials before loading them into the batching tank. The two best measuring systems are load cells or a metering and scale system. A load cell is a metal electronic device that weighs wet or dry ingredients by deflection as the ingredient touches the metal. A metering and scale system is one in which all the liquid ingredients are measured by meters and the dry ingredients are weighed on a scale.

To perform the mixing you will need a batch mixer and a pasteurizing vat. The size of the equipment used depends on the volume of business and production methods. Piping from the batch tank to the funnel pump and return must be large enough for continuous flow. Dry ingredients are added to the batch mixer through a funnel pump (or blender adequate in size and power). A two-way shut-off valve, installed just below the funnel hopper in the vertical pipeline prevents air from entering the mix when the funnel hopper in the vertical pipeline has been emptied. All liquid ingredients are either poured into the mixing vat from a container or pumped in from a storage tank.

The process is started by combining all of the liquid and dry ingredients needed and then pouring them into a large stainless steel vat in the following manner:

1. Place the required amount of milk in the batch or process tank and start the agitator.
2. Open the outlet valve of the batch tank for the piping that goes to the funnel blending pump and returns to the tank.
3. Start the funnel blending pump as the milk passes through the T below the funnel.
4. Open the valve at the bottom of the funnel and slowly pour the dry ingredients into the funnel, feeding the dry materials carefully so they do not accumulate in the funnel. To prevent the stabilizer from balling up, mix it with at least ten times its weight in dry sugar before pouring it into the funnel.
5. Turn on the vat to agitate the ingredients.
6. Add the remaining ingredients (cream and egg yolks) to the batch. It is important not to include the cream before the blending because excessive pumping my cause churning on the butterfat and make further processing more difficult.

The batch of mix is now ready to be processed.

PASTEURIZATION

In the United States, pasteurization is required for all finished dairy products (with the exception of a few certified farms that are allowed to sell raw milk) to eliminate disease-producing bacteria. Heat is used to kill the bacteria. Any manufacturer thinking about producing a frozen dairy product must acquire a full understanding of the following:

- Federal, state, and local regulations
- Maximum allowable bacterial counts of ingredients, even when followed by pasteurization
- Time and temperature requirements for the pasteurization process
- Maximum allowable bacterial counts of the finished product, which vary according to the type of frozen dessert

- Requirements for freezing the production on the premises where it is pasteurized

Details for all of the topics listed can be found by contacting your state's department of agriculture and obtaining the code that affects the manufacture of frozen desserts.

Equipment

There are two common types of pasteurizing vats: the spray vat or the pressure wall processor. The pasteurizing vats should be located close to the batch mixer. Some plants recess the vat into the floor to facilitate dumping of materials; some prefer a dump tank and pump to fill the vat.

Processes

Pasteurization is done by either the batch or the continuous method. In batch pasteurization, the mix is heated in the pasteurizing vat before homogenization and cooling. Batch pasteurization requires a minimum temperature of 160 degrees Fahrenheit for at least 30 minutes. When considering this method, you should make sure that the equipment has the capacity to meet high demands in summer without expensive overtime. In the average plant, a batch mixer and pasteurizer may be combined; in larger plants, they are separate.

The continuous method, called high-temperature short-time (HTST), is the industry's preferred method for pasteurization because of the following:

- It saves time, labor, and space savings over batch systems.
- It has increased capacity over batch systems.
- It can regenerate between hot and cold mix for savings in fuel and refrigeration. (Regeneration is the process in which the cool mix, which is being heated, is then used as a cooling medium for the hot mix coming from the homogenizer.)

Using the HTST method, the system continuously pasteurizes, homogenizes, and cools the mix product as long as raw material is supplied. The method requires a temperature of 175 degrees Fahrenheit for no less than 30 seconds. Its main advantage is its efficiency and the resulting reduction in costs of heating and cooling by as much as 80 percent or more.

For ice cream mixes, the U.S. Public Health Administration has established 175 degrees Fahrenheit for 25 seconds as the minimum time–temperature combination for HTST pasteurization, and 155–165 degrees Fahrenheit for a period of 30 minutes for the batch method.

After pasteurization is complete, the mix is then pumped to the homogenizer.

HOMOGENIZATION

The ice cream is homogenized to prevent fat separation, improve the body and texture of the finished products, and prevent churning of the fat during the freezing process. Moreover, homogenization makes possible the use of such optional ingredients as butter, plastic cream (concentrated butterfat), frozen cream, and butter oil when fresh ingredients are not available or are considered too expensive.

The homogenizing unit has a positive piston type pump that pulls hot mix from the pasteurizer and forces it through a narrow opening under great pressure and velocity. Stainless steel pistons push the product through the homogenizing valves to assure uniform small particles.

This process is accomplished with either a single- or two-stage valve system. Most ice cream mix homogenization is done by a two-stage method with the actual homogenizing or breaking up of fat globules occurring in the first stage under high pressure. In the second stage, the pressure is much lower and any clumps of small globules resulting from the high pressure treatment will be dissipated. The result of proper homogenization is that the fat globules are reduced to 2 microns or less in size, increasing their surface and thereby making the product taste richer.

In a single-stage system, the pressure is usually somewhat lower (around 1,750 psi) than in the two stage system (2,000 psi total with settings of 1,500 psi on the first stage and 500 on the second.) The single-stage operation is more common in milk operations.

The choice of equipment size depends on the dairy's production and the size of the pasteurizer. A 300-gallon pasteurizer needs at least a 250-gallon-per-hour homogenizer since the homogenizer must be able to handle the total amount of mix available in one hour or less. The homogenizing unit should be located close to the pasteurizer to facilitate drawing the mix through a short sanitary pipe and forcing it over the cooler.

Accurate valves and pressure gauges are important. Homogenization pressures are determined by desired viscosity, mix composition and stability, temperatures, and the kind of homogenizer unit used. The pressure gauge should be steady. Failure of a gauge to respond to adjustment may indicate a plugged line, slipping of the belt, worn valve, or packing under the valve.

COOLING

After pasteurization and homogenization is completed, the mix must be cooled immediately to 40 degrees Fahrenheit or less to preserve the bacterial quality and fresh taste. Cooling is done by pumping the mix over a cooler or through plate-type or swept surface heat exchangers. Water is the cooling medium in the upper two-thirds of the cooler, and direct expansion in the lower third. The mix comes in contact with the coolest water as it flows over the cooler if the water enters the tubes at the bottom and discharges at the top.

If the mix is cooled and stored for 12–24 hours, its viscosity will be increased. Some think this produces a better mix, but many believe a mix that is cooled fast and used immediately is more fluid resulting in better whipping and freezing. Most plants do not age the mix before use.

Most HTST pasteurizing systems use a plate system for heat exchange functions. Tubular coolers are usually a tube within a tube, with product in one tube and the cooling material in the other tube surrounding the product. Other tube types might be a shell and tube with the product going through many small tubes and the cooling material circulated in the large shell.

STORING THE MIX

After cooling, the mix should be stored in refrigerated tanks or drawn off into 10-gallon cans and placed in a cold room (40 degrees Fahrenheit or lower). Storage tanks may be refrigerated by any system that maintains 40 degrees Fahrenheit or lower. Such a system may include circulated refrigerated water or glycol solution, or direct expansion systems of ammonia or freon. Storage tanks with automatic and accurate temperature and agitator controls will allow the operator to use the mix when it is most convenient.

At this point, the mix is ready for immediate freezing, but can be aged or stored for several days. Aging for 12 hours or more does provide a small measure of increased viscosity but it is not noticeable if the mix is agitated frequently.

After the appropriate storage time, the mix production process is complete and you can begin the ice cream freezing process.

ICE CREAM MIX EQUIPMENT MANUFACTURERS

The following two manufacturers sell equipment to meet almost any dairy processor requirement for ice cream mix production.

Alfa-Laval Hoyer

Hoyer offers a complete range of mix processing equipment from small self-contained pilots plants to specially designed mix plants (Mixmark) capable of producing many hundreds of gallons of mix per hour (see Table 4-2).

The Mixmark self-contained mix unit is ideally suited to meet the mix processing requirements of small- to medium-capacity producers. Mixmark units are equipped with all the components necessary for mixing, pasteurizing, and homogenizing. Mounted on a stainless steel base, the Mixmark unit is ready for immediate production after connection to the utilities.

For larger mix capacities Hoyer designs complete mix plants that include all stages of mix processing from liquid and solids intake, to weighing and batching, mixing, homogenization, pasteurization, and aging/storage.

Table 4-2. Alfa-Laval Hoyer Mix Processing Equipment

Model	Typical Maximum Capacity[a] (liters per hour)	Typical Maximum Capacity[a] (U.S. gallons per hour)
Pilot Plant	50	14
Mixmark 150	150	40
Mixmark 250	250	70
Mixmark 500	500	130
Mixmark 1000	1,000	260

[a]Actual capacity will depend on mix formulation and production conditions.

APV Crepaco

From initial mix plant concept, to flow diagrams, to final specifications and designs, APV's engineers will assist dairy processors in setting up a completely new mix plant or in extending the capacity of an existing plant. APV also offers a series of standard mix plants for smaller capacity mix requirements for either batch or continuous batch systems. They are as follows:

Model Micro-Mix Type 150 and 300. These two models are for producing mix at 150 and 300 liters per hour. Designed for batch pasteurization, they are completely self-contained and pre-wired, resulting in quick installation on site. Only the connection of water and electricity is required.

Model Mini-Mixi. Comprised of two models for mix production of 200 and 500 liters per hour, this unit is designed for HTST pasteurization. Both models are partly skid-mounted and include prepiping and prewiring, resulting in a very short installation on site. These units, however, are not available in the United States.

Model Medi-Mix. Comprised of two models for mix production of 300 and 800 liters per hour, this unit is designed for HTST pasteurization. Both models are partly skid-mounted and include prepiping and prewiring, resulting in a very short installation on site. These units, however, are available in the United States.

Model Maxi-Mix. Comprised of three models for mix production of 1,500, 2,500, and 5,000 liters per hour, this unit is designed for HTST pasteurization. It is recommended mainly for experienced mix producers starting up or extending at the Maxi capacity range. These units are available in the United States.

REFERENCE

Mans, Jack. 1994. Humboldt Creamery Association, ice cream powerhouse. *Dairy Foods Magazine*, September, p. 95.

5 ⊠⊠⊠⊠⊠⊠⊠⊠⊠⊠⊠⊠⊠⊠⊠⊠⊠⊠⊠⊠⊠

FLAVOR INGREDIENTS

You cannot make a high-quality frozen dessert product without using high-quality ingredients; and it will not matter to your business what ingredients you use if the flavors you produce are not what the buying public is looking for. Listen to your customers, read everything that is available on current trends in the industry, and watch people's eating habits. The popularity in the late 1980s of frozen yogurt and so-called lowfat products was unanticipated by many in the business who were left behind in the market because of their lack of awareness. We are now going through a similar life cycle with sorbets, and only consumer-oriented producers are going to benefit from the surge of demand for sorbets that is now taking place in the industry. Similarly, today's consumers are sensitive to nutrition and how it affects their health. Everyone is looking for sugar and fat substitutes. To be successful, the products you market must focus on what the consumer wants.

Among the characteristics by which consumers will judge your frozen dessert products, taste will be a major factor. Eating one of your products will elicit an impulse reaction, either good or bad. How your products taste is influenced not only by their butterfat content, but also by the flavorings you use. When aiming for a particular quality, you will need to seriously consider the use of artificial versus natural flavorings. For example, using only a 14-percent mix with all-natural flavorings will produce a product superior to one made from a 16-percent mix with artificial ingredients.

Flavoring ingredients are divided into the following three categories:

Category I:	Pure or natural extracts (used for premium and superpremium products)
Category II:	Pure extracts combined with some artificial flavor (used for premium and economy products)
Category III:	Completely artificial flavors (used for most economy products)

An *extract* must contain at least 35 percent alcohol by volume, and anything containing less is called a *flavor*. The alcohol used for extracting and holding the flavoring matter in suspension permits a higher concentration of flavoring matter in an extract than in a flavor.

Modern technology has made artificial flavors available in virtually unlimited quantities at low cost. They are used mainly in fruit, liquor, liqueur, and candy-flavored products. If not used properly, artificial flavorings can result in poor-quality products. Their overuse can result in products that taste harsh, overpowering, and objectionable. They are especially used by companies to create an intense flavor profile that sometimes can be difficult to accomplish with a natural flavor, such as peach.

Natural flavors and extracts, although costly and limited in supply, are preferred by today's consumers for almost all food products. The use of natural vanilla is especially popular. In most cases, the delicate, mild flavors imparted by natural flavoring materials assure little danger of overflavoring even at high concentrations. Thus the use of natural flavorings and extracts can be unrestricted and dictated by your own preference.

Most of the frozen dessert industry uses category II ingredients because of price considerations. Those in the business of producing premium or super-premium products will use category I ingredients, and will use more of them per product than other operators.

VANILLA

Vanilla is the favorite ice cream flavor among U.S. consumers. Just taking a whiff from a bottle of pure vanilla extract can send the olfactory system into euphoria. The Aztecs and the Europeans once considered the vanilla bean to be a powerful aphrodisiac.

More than 75 percent of all ice cream produced contains vanilla flavoring in some form, derived from either the vanilla bean or the extract from the bean. If you had a product with and without vanilla, people would perceive the one with vanilla as sweeter. The marriage of vanilla and chocolate has been a successful one dating back to the 1500s when Montezuma welcomed Cortes to Mexico with a vanilla-cocoa beverage. Vanilla softens or rounds out harsh, bitter notes in most chocolate ice cream applications. It is also often used to enhance fruit ice cream flavors. As a background flavor, vanilla rounds out the fruit flavor and takes off some of the tart edges. Vanilla is the single most important flavoring ingredient used in the production of ice cream.

Sources of Supply

Vanilla originated in Mexico. It comes from vanilla pods, the fruit of the Tlilxochitl vine, the orchid *Vanilla fragrans*. This plant is now also grown in the

Bourbon Islands (of which Madagascar is one), Indonesia, and Tahiti. Just as wine grapes vary by region and harvest, vanilla beans vary by strain, climate, soil, time of harvest, and curing practices. The Mexican and Bourbon vanilla beans are superior in flavor to the Tahitian beans. However, the supply from Mexico is limited because of labor costs and the use of most land there for oil fields.

The finest of the Bourbon vanilla beans come from Madagascar, the fourth-largest island in the world. Bourbon growers vine ripen their beans to yield higher levels of betaglucosidase, gluco vanillin, and other flavor precursors. Indonesian growers pick their beans prematurely. Instead of slow curing in the sun as practiced in Madagascar and Mexico, a 3–4 month process that draws the maximum flavor from each bean, Indonesians often cure beans in a few weeks over wood or kerosene fires. Early harvesting and fire-curing create a vanilla bean with flavor and aroma characteristics that are sharp, smoky, and woody. Compared to the Bourbon and Mexican vanilla, the flavor of the Indonesian bean is also a little weaker. Tahitian beans produce an extract that has a more aromatic flavor than the Bourbon and Mexican vanilla, with a bit of harshness to it.

Curing the Beans

Vanilla beans are produced from a vanilla flower. Each successfully fertilized blossom produces a pod that grows to 6–9 inches long in about 6 weeks. The characteristic vanilla flavor and aroma are not present in the green pods. It is within the last weeks of growth that the most important flavoring components develop. The yellowish green pods begin to turn more yellow at their tips 6–9 months after pollination, indicating readiness for harvest. After the pods are harvested, they are cured to develop the flavor of the vanilla beans.

The curing process of Mexico, the Bourbon Islands, Tonga, and Tahiti are fairly similar, except for the initial step that begins the enzymatic reaction. In Mexico, the vanilla beans are first wrapped in blankets and then in straw mats, and placed in ovens for 24–48 hours. In the Bourbon Islands, Tonga, and Tahiti, the beans are instead first immersed for a short time in hot water. Then they are spread out in the sun for up to 8 hours to absorb heat, becoming so hot they almost burn the workers hands as they are turned and spread out (Nielsen, 1985). Late in the afternoon they are gathered and wrapped in blankets and straw mats, placed in large wooden boxes and allowed to sweat overnight. This process is done over and over again until, based on the experience of the curer, they are properly cured. The beans are then stored on racks in holding rooms to further develop and mellow the flavor. Overall, the curing takes 3–6 months, and about 5 pounds of green, uncured beans are required to make 1 pound of properly cured beans.

In most areas, once the vanilla beans have been cured, they are graded according to moisture content and quality, then sorted according to length and bundled with string into bunches of 60–100 beans.

Extracting the Flavoring

Once the beans are received by the vanilla manufacturer, the flavoring matter must be extracted from them. Alcohol is necessary to remove the flavoring matter from the vanilla beans. Most manufacturers recirculate alcohol and water over the beans under varying degrees of heat and pressure. Nielsen-Massey, the vanilla manufacturer recommended in this book for all recipes, uses an entirely different system. Under precise temperature control, they extract the delicate flavoring matter from the vanilla beans at 72 degrees Fahrenheit using specially constructed stainless steel extractors. After the beans are loaded into an extractor (a large vat), a series of menstruums (solutions of alcohol and water) are continually recirculated over and through the beans by use of pumps. This process takes a number of weeks to complete, rather than days for processes using heat. The finished vanilla is then filtered into a holding tank to await bottling.

Classifications

Vanilla extracts are described by the term *fold,* which refers to the amount of concentrated vanilla in the extract. As established by the U.S. Food and Drug Administration, 13.35 ounces of vanilla beans are used to make a gallon of one-fold vanilla extract, while 26.7 ounces of beans are used for a gallon of two-fold vanilla. The advantage of using two-fold pure vanilla over a single fold is a concentration of flavor that, if used properly, results in less expense in the long run.

The categories of vanilla flavorings are (I) pure vanilla, (II) vanilla-vanillin blend, and (III) imitation vanilla. Pure vanilla (I) is derived from an extraction process involving the vanilla beans and alcohol. Imitation vanilla (III) is composed primarily of USP vanillin (an artificial version of the principal flavoring component of vanilla) and/or ethyl vanillin. Many other ingredients, synthetic and natural from substances other than vanilla beans, can be used to make imitation vanilla. Many flavoring essences make up the well-rounded pure vanilla flavor, and scientists and flavor chemists have not yet been able to truly duplicate that flavor. Imitation vanilla is not recommended in the production of ice cream because, if used improperly, it results in a harsh unnatural flavor easily detected in the finished product.

A vanilla-vanillin blend (II) is the combination of pure vanilla and vanillin, with not less than half the flavor derived from vanilla beans. Artificial vanillin is made from lignin contained in sulfite waste pulp liquor, a by-product of papermaking, derived from coniferous trees. Adding 1 ounce of vanillin to a fold of pure vanilla produces a two-fold vanilla-vanillin blend, which is less expensive to make and use than pure vanilla.

The categories of vanilla flavoring ingredients are reflected on ice cream cartons as "Vanilla Ice Cream" when flavored with pure vanilla, "Vanilla-Flavored Ice Cream" when flavored with a vanilla-vanillin blend, and "Artificially Flavored" when imitation vanilla is used.

Usage

To bring out the full flavor of the components of ice cream, some dairies use vanilla beans to make their own vanilla, but most use extracts. The amount of vanilla used depends to a large extent on the butterfat and sugar content of the ice cream mix used. The lower the butterfat and sugar content, the more vanilla will be needed. With a 10–14-percent butterfat content, a Madagascar Bourbon works very well. At the 14–16-percent fat level, the fat tends to mask the vanilla flavor, so a blend of Bourbon and Indonesian is more effective. This blend delivers an initial impact of vanilla in the front of the mouth, followed by the Bourbon in the back of the mouth. In general, you have to use 50 percent more vanilla flavor in low- or no-fat systems in order to produce the best tasting products. When alternative sweeteners are used, you must alter the type of vanilla used in the formulation. This is especially true in a sugar-free ice cream mix versus a sucrose-based mix. You need to evaluate the sugar-free base independently.

For use in the production of fruit-flavored frozen yogurts, a combination of Madagascar Bourbon and Tahitian pure vanilla is recommended. Each of the flavor components in this special blend has its individual attributes: Pure Madagascar vanilla is described as a sweet, creamy, woody and mellow flavor, and Tahitian pure vanilla is described as floral, sweet, and fruity. When combined, the resulting vanilla extract has a sweet, fruity, and creamy flavor. The Madagascar Bourbon vanilla smoothes and mellows the acidic bite of the yogurt, while the Tahitian vanilla component lifts and enhances the fruit flavor.

All of the recipes in this book use two-fold pure vanilla extract, sometimes called double-strength, manufactured by the Nielsen-Massey Company.

CHOCOLATE

Chocolate ice cream is second only to vanilla in popularity. Demand for it has increased since the mid-1980s, when consumers developed a passion for chocolate in everything from candies to baked goods.

Sources of Supply

Chocolate originates from the fruit of the cocoa tree, the cacao bean, which undergoes much processing before it can finally be used. Cocoa trees, *Theobroma cacao,* grow in Central America and other tropical regions such as the East Indies and the African Gold Coast. The young plants need the ample shade provided by the tropical forests. Most trees bear fruit within 4 years of planting and continue to yield cocoa beans for an average of 40 years.

The two basic varieties of cocoa are Criollo and Forastero, with the latter being the major source of the world's cocoa. The Criollo variety is found mainly in Ecuador and Venezuela. Criollo trees tend to produce a smaller yield, only about 10 percent of the world's crop, and ripen later than other varieties. The seeds are of a finer quality and have a mild aroma. They are used in the production of high-quality chocolate or for blending with other varieties.

Processing

After picking, the cocoa beans are cleaned, sorted, and shipped to a processing plant. There they are cleaned again and roasted to remove moisture and to bring out the flavor and aroma of the chocolate. They are then cooled quickly and crushed to separate the shells from the nibs, which are the seed parts used to make chocolate and cocoa. The nibs are then milled between heavy stone grinders, and the heat from the friction of milling produces a liquid. This pure bitter-chocolate liquid is generically called chocolate liquor that can be sold as bitter baking chocolate or processed into cocoa.

Cocoa is made from the liquor by subjecting it to high pressure in hydraulic presses. This process removes a large amount of the cocoa butter and leaves a hard, dry cake that normally contains 22 percent fat. This cake is put through a milling process to produce natural sifted cocoa.

Dutch-process cocoa is made the same way except the beans are treated with an alkali during roasting. This treatment makes the cocoa more soluble, gives it a darker color, and brings out a finer chocolate flavor. Because alkali counteracts the acid taste normally found in natural cocoa, ice cream operators consider Dutch cocoa the best product to use in making chocolate ice cream.

Usage

For flavoring ice cream, cocoa is considered a more concentrated ingredient than chocolate liquor. Cocoa contains a larger percentage of real chocolate flavor and less of the tasteless fat than does the liquor.

Cocoa used in ice cream production is generally available in two versions defined by fat content:

- 22–24-percent fat, a very high fat cocoa used mainly for the production of premium to superpremium ice cream that adds excellent body to the finished product.
- 10–12-percent fat, a lower fat cocoa used to flavor 10-percent, 12-percent and 14-percent butterfat chocolate ice creams, richer in flavor but lacking the full body texture of the 22–24-percent cocoa.

In most cases, because there is at least 15 percent sugar in the ice cream mix, it is not necessary to add sugar to the cocoa mixture for use in either a continuous freezing operation or a batch freezer. Industry standards and many recipes in other books call for additional sugar, but if a bittersweet chocolate ice cream is preferred, do not add any sugar. If a less bittersweet flavor is desired, add sugar at the ratio of 4–8 ounces sugar to each pound of cocoa. Consider consumer preferences when deciding whether or not to add sugar.

All of the chocolate recipes in this book, unless otherwise stated, use a Dutch process 22–24-percent fat cocoa. For dairies using continuous freezing ice cream equipment, the cocoa is blended into the mix operation before actual ice cream production takes place. For batch freezer operations, approximately 2 pounds of cocoa is used with 2½ gallons of ice cream mix. Remember that when cocoa is mixed with water, the water has to be nearly boiling to create a loose paste or syrup. Always mix the cocoa paste or syrup with at least 1 gallon of ice cream mix in the batch freezer for at least 10 minutes to properly dissolve the cocoa mixture. The reason I recommend using a Dutch-process cocoa is because it provides an excellent flavor and a dark brown color for your ice cream.

All of the chocolate ice cream recipes in this book were tested using a 22–24-percent cocoa from Van Leer Chocolate of Jersey City, New Jersey, but there are other U.S. manufacturers that make excellent cocoa for use in ice cream production. I consider any of the cocoas listed in Table 5-1 among the best. For strong chocolate flavor, Forbes 289 chocolate flavor base (Double Dark), although not a cocoa, is also highly recommended.

Chocolate Chips

The chocolate chip or flake you choose to use can make the difference between simply good ice cream and great ice cream. These products come in different sizes and varieties, so sampling them before you start production is essential. Call or write to the companies listed in Table 5-2 for samples. Chips and flakes are either cocoa-based or a blend of cocoa and chocolate liquor. They are available in liquid and solid form. The liquid versions are added to the ice cream during the freezing process to form irregularly sized pieces. Recently, the "soft chip" has become very popular for a flavor using a chocolate chip. Van Leer Chocolate has been a forerunner in this new chocolate technology and their dark and white soft chunks are extremely popular. Because soft chunks have a lower melting point, they stay soft in ice cream and melt instantly in your mouth releasing a full rich chocolate flavor.

Table 5-1. U.S. Manufacturers of Cocoa

Company	Product Number	Product Name or Description
Van Leer	9000	22–24% Premium cocoa
Van Leer	9003	10–12% Cocoa
Johnston	31204	Cokay (35) Pure
Johnston	31209	D.G. Cocoa
Ambrosia	Rotterdam	22–24% Fat
Ambrosia	Royale	22–24% Fat

Table 5-2. U.S. Manufacturers of Chocolate Chip and Flakes

Company	Product Number	Product Name or Description
Forbes Company	Flake type	Chocolate Chips
Ambrosia	Liquid	Chocolate Chips
Ambrosia	Chokets	Chocolate chips, solid
Van Leer	6100	Soft Dark Chunks (large)
Van Leer	6116	Soft Dark Chunks (small)
Van Leer	6105	Soft White Chunks
Van Leer	222	Chocolate Liquor
Masterson	31207	Chokay Liquor Chip
Masterson	31194	Soft Chunk
Guernsey Dell	24-3873	Imported Chocolate Flake
Guernsey Dell	24-4223	Thick Choco Flake

CANDY-BASED PRODUCTS

While vanilla and chocolate remain the most popular flavors, ice cream varieties containing various candy-base inclusions now makeup a sizable portion of the market. This growth has enabled product designers to flex their creativity by developing varieties that taste almost like eating Heath, Milky Way, Almond Joy, and Snickers candy bars, or cookies like Oreos, Hydrox, and graham crackers. Most of the credit for this idea belongs to the small independent ice cream operators of the 1970s and 1980s.

Most of the companies that manufacture these candies and cookies have now caught up with the craze. Some, like Leaf, Inc. of Forest Lake, Illinois, have actually been promoting the use of their candy bars (Heath Bar) in ice cream production. You can purchase broken or bite-size pieces in bulk form from most manufacturers.

As part of the candy inclusion technology that is sweeping the ice cream industry, one company, Van Leer/Gertrude Hawk of Dunmore, Pennsylvania, has created what it calls mini-melt technology used to produce candy ice cream cones and cups consisting of an outer chocolate shell surrounding a fruit-flavored or chocolate interior. When consumed, the shell melts leaving the fruit or chocolate taste to linger momentarily. Because of the low melt point of the chocolate, these ingredients are shipped and kept in a frozen state until they are used for ice cream production.

The following manufacturers make candy and cookie products that you should consider using in your ice cream. See the Appendix for complete addresses.

Leaf, Inc.: Heath Bars
Sunshine Biscuits: Hydrox cookies
M&M Mars: M&Ms® (plain and peanut), Milky Way® Bars, Snickers®

Hershey Chocolate USA: Reese's Pieces, Almond Joy, and Mounds bars

Nabisco: Oreo cookies, Graham Crackers, Ginger Snaps, Chips Ahoy, Nutter Butter peanut butter cookies

Nestle: Raisinets, Butterfinger, Rainbow Morsels, Nestles Buncha Crunch, Goobers peanuts, Nestle Crunch bars, Chunky pieces, Alpine White pieces

Pecan Deluxe: Pecan Pralines, Milky Way pieces (Candy Bar Blend), and Chocolate Truffles

Van Leer/Gertrude Hawk: Cherry, banana, orange, and caramel ice cream cones; vanilla cashew, truffle butter pecan, and Swiss mocha cups

All of these items, and others, can be purchased directly from the manufacturers or from wholesalers.

A number of factors come into play when working with candy-based inclusions. You need to define the target market and decide what contribution the inclusion gives to the product. A large percentage of all candy-based and cookie ice cream flavors have been aimed at children, teenagers, and so-called yuppies. For example, in the 1990s the incredible popularity of cookie-dough ice cream was due almost entirely to consumption by children and teenagers.

Designing ice cream flavors that include candy and cookie ingredients is no different than designing any other flavors. You need to base the product on how it should look and taste. Because ice cream with candy- or cookie-based inclusions promotes a value-added image, the inclusions should appear in high contrast to the ice cream itself. With chunk-type pieces, this often means that bigger is better. Ideally, the consumer should find a piece of the inclusion in every bite, or at least several per scoop.

NUTS

Many popular flavors of ice cream contain nuts and, of course, nuts can be used as wet or dry toppings as well. Because of their popularity and versatility, the nut industry caters to the ice cream industry by coming up with new flavors and ideas and by providing nut products in different sizes. In particular, the peanut, pecan, and walnut marketing board associations (see Appendix) promote new nut flavors on a fairly regular basis through their newsletters.

Nuts contain protein and fat. Their flavor is derived from the oils in them. The most popular nuts used in the ice cream industry are pecans, almonds, walnuts, and peanuts. Table 5-3 lists some of the various nut products available. They are used primarily as nutmeats, pastes, or extracts, all of which should be refrigerated or stored in a cool, dry place to prevent them from getting rancid. Pistachios, almonds, and hazelnuts should be purchased already blanched with the outer skins removed. Nuts added to ice cream need to be coated with some kind of barrier or they become soggy or rancid. This can be done by oil roasting the nuts or by using an actual coating of chocolate or praline. Most operators

Table 5-3. Various Nutmeats

Company	Product Number	Product Name or Description
Walnuts		
A. L. Bazzini	—	Light halves
or	—	Light pieces
Westcott Nut	—	Light halves and pieces
	—	Light syrupers pieces
	—	Light baker pieces
Guernsey Dell	03-4089	Yogurt walnuts
	04-4628	Walnut fudge pieces
Peanuts		
Boyer Brothers	5510/8997	Smooth peanut curl
	7993/8998	Crunchy peanut curl
	8203/8223	All natural smooth
Guernsey Dell	02-3210	Peanut brittle peanuts
	03-3955	Choco Fudge Peanuts
	01-2018	Peanut butter crunch
	04-4700	Peanut butter bites
	24-4639	Peanut/Choco Flakes
	24-4640	Peanut butter flakes
	06-6507	Peanut butter swirl
	05-5458	Background syrup
Superior Nut	—	Liquid peanut variegate
Peanut Corporation of America	—	Many varieties and sizes
Pecans		
Pecan Deluxe	01-001-45	Pecan Krisp Supreme
	01-004-45	Pecan Crunch Supreme
	02-001-40	Praline Pecan Supreme
	02-103-40	Panned praline pecans
	08-001-50	Praline base
	08-002-50	Butter pecan base
	07-005-50	Pecan Pie Ribbon
Virginia Dare	—	Pecan background flavor
	—	Pecan emulsion
Limpert Brothers	5020	Butter pecan base
Guernsey Dell	02-3240	Large praline pieces
	02-3285	Medium praline pieces
	03-4217	Coated sugar pecans
	05-5500	Praline syrup
Almonds		
Guernsey Dell	02-3017	Praline almonds
	03-3595	Large Choco Almonds
	24-3900	White Choco Almond Chunks
	24-4220	Imported flake with almonds
Paramount Farms	—	Many varieties and sizes
Westcott Nut	—	Many varieties and sizes

purchase their nutmeats already roasted, with little or no salt added. I prefer my nuts this way because I believe salt hinders the production freezing process and contributes the melting effect in the dipping case. For a strong visual appeal to the customer, use large pieces of nutmeats, both in the product and as a garnish or topping.

Most nut flavors of ice cream are prepared using a nut flavor-base in liquid (an extract) or paste form. A combination of the base and nutmeats during the freezing process creates the final flavor of the ice cream. Nuts can also be added to the fruit feeder in a continuous freezing operation, directly into the batch freezer during processing, or by hand to the tubs during extrusion. Since you will get different results with each method, you should use different sizes of nut products depending on the method chosen. In a batch freezer operation, add the nuts to the freezer during processing, and use only halves or large pieces because the dasher blades will cut them apart. Use syruper (a particular small-size category) or small pieces when adding the nuts by hand as the finished product is being extruded. Small pieces added during processing will be granulated by the dasher blades.

Walnuts

Walnuts are rich in food value. They are a good source of several vitamins, including thiamine, vitamin B, and folacin. They are naturally low in sodium and contribute substantial amounts of dietary fiber. They contain no cholesterol and are high in unsaturated fats. According to the Walnut Marketing Board, walnuts have been recognized as the oldest food from trees known to humankind. Records indicate their use as far back as about 7000 B.C. Considered food for the gods in the early days of the Roman empire, walnuts were named *Juglans regia* in honor of the god Jupiter. Today they are commonly called "English" walnuts after the English merchant marines whose ships transported walnuts around the world. In the United States, California's mild climate and deep fertile soils provide ideal growing conditions for the English walnut. California walnuts comprise 98 percent of the U.S. commercial crop and two-thirds of the world's trade. The four major varieties of walnuts are the Hartley, Franquetts, Payne, and Eureka.

Walnuts are harvested from late August to early November. After harvesting, they are hulled, washed, mechanically dehydrated, and separated by size and color. Once purchased, they should be kept in refrigerated storage (32–38 degrees Fahrenheit and 65 percent relative humidity) to maintain their freshness. As an ingredient for ice cream, most operators prefer large, light-colored halves and pieces or regular small syruper pieces. Either of these forms can also be used for toppings. If sandiness appears, soak or boil walnuts in a simple syrup solution and drain them prior to use for optimal appearance in ice cream products. Use 10 pounds of sugar to 1 gallon of water for an excellent syrup solution. Raw walnuts can be roasted at 375 degrees Fahrenheit for approximately 10 minutes. Usage level in ice cream production is approximately 7 percent.

Walnuts are popular in a number of different ice cream flavors from across the globe, particularly in Europe and the Middle East. Spumoni, an Italian ice cream with candied fruit and chopped walnuts, Kulfi Ruh Giulab, an Indian ice cream with rose essence and walnuts, Azuuki Bean, and walnut-flavored ice cream are just some examples.

Walnuts add a slightly bitter taste that contrasts well with the sweetness of ice cream. They also make excellent ice cream toppings. Alone or as part of a topping (like maple walnut fudge), walnuts add the body and mouthfeel consumers look for in upscale, premium ice creams. Walnuts also make an excellent coating for ice cream bars. Just dip the bars in chocolate and coat them with walnuts (either granulated or small pieces) for a unique crunch.

Peanuts

Americans have had a long love-affair with the peanut in all its forms. According to the Georgia Peanut Commission (Tifton, Georgia), more than 4 million pounds are consumed daily, with children literally growing up on peanut butter sandwiches. Providing "nutrition in a nutshell" (Georgia Peanut Commission), a peanut contains 26 grams of protein along with many of the essential B vitamins and polyunsaturated Fats. Peanuts are also low in sodium and are cholesterol free.

Peanuts grown in the United States are harvested in August, September, and October. They should be kept under refrigeration to prevent them from becoming rancid. India and China produce over half the world's peanut production, so it is safe to assume that any flavor made with peanuts in that part of the world is very popular.

Because they are available in so many forms, peanuts are a useful and flexible ingredient. Raw peanuts come in the shell, shelled with red skins remaining, or shelled with skins removed. They can be roasted in the shell or shelled and then dry roasted. The roasting process is accomplished by hot air or vacuum pressure. The vacuum-pressure method forces salt through the shell, and a subsequent hot-air roasting leaves the salt residue inside the shell. Other than peanut butter, peanut products for commercial ice cream production range in size from ground to large shelled pieces.

Peanut butter is made from roasted peanuts ground with salt, with or without sweetener and emulsifier added. By U.S. law, peanut butter must contain 90 percent peanuts. The Superior Nut Company of Cambridge, Massachusetts, produces an excellent liquid peanut butter that flows at room temperature. This base, packed in 5- or 55-gallon drums, is for variegating the sauce into the ice cream during processing and comes either as a smooth curl or crunchy in texture. (A smooth curl is a variegated product that is similar to a thick sauce). It can be swirled into the ice cream in a batch freezer operation by hand using a spatula as the ice cream is extruded into the tubs. In a continuous freezing operation, this peanut butter variegate will create a terrific trail as a contrast to the base flavor. Guernsey Dell, of Chicago, Illinois, also specializes in peanut butter bases as well as all kinds of coated and uncoated peanut products. Other companies such as Limpert Brothers of Vineland, New Jersey, and Pecan Deluxe of Dallas, Texas, manufacture similar products that come in 5-gallon pails or #10 cans, which hold 3 quarts (96 ounces) of liquid product.

Pecans

With more than 80 percent of the world's pecan crop being produced in the United States, it is no wonder they are so popular here. You can drive through the South and find pecans for sale in all varieties and shapes at every roadside restaurant or gift shop. Hundreds of varieties are harvested during the season, which starts in October and ends the following March.

Pecans contain mostly unsaturated fatty acids, are low in sodium, and contain no cholesterol. Their full flavor is easily brought out in almost any ice cream flavor produced. Pecan praline and butter pecan ice cream rank high on the consumer's list of favorites.

Pecans come finely granulated or in either halves or pieces. To insure freshness, store below 41 degrees Fahrenheit and protect them from moisture, light, heat, and oxygen. Because they easily absorb other odors, they should also be stored separately, when possible, or with nonodorous products. Once opened, vacuum-packed nuts should be used as quickly as possible and stored under refrigeration.

To ensure a nice show of pecans in your finished product, use fancy large pecan halves for either continuous or batch freezer operations. SNA, Navarro Pecan Company, Tracey Lucky, and Young Pecan Company all offer a large variety of sizes and shapes.

Almonds

Almonds are low in fat and come in varieties ranging from raw, blanched, and roasted to chocolate covered. They have become increasingly popular since the introduction of such flavors of ice cream as Vanilla Chocolate Almond and Chocolate Chocolate Almond by the Haagen-Dazs Company. You might choose to use roasted slivers or chopped (diced) pieces for making regular almond-flavored ice cream, and large pieces to provide the full nut taste when using chocolate-coated almonds.

Pralines

Originally popular only in the southern parts of the United States, pralines have become increasingly popular since the late 1980s, both throughout the United States and in the Middle East. A praline is an oil-roasted nut that is coated in sugar, which will dissolve in the ice cream over an extended period of time. The most popular praline nut is the pecan, but almonds and cashews also make a terrific praline product.

Both Pecan DeLuxe, Dallas, Texas, and Guernsey Dell, Chicago, Illinois, produce a variety of sizes of praline nuts.

Other Nuts

Other nuts such as hazelnuts, pistachios, and macadamias provide a special appeal in superpremium ice cream products that attract consumers willing to spend more. Because these nuts are so expensive, care should be taken in their handling and storage, as well as in their precise usage in recipes. In particular, hazelnut pastes from Pregel (Grande Isle) and Monte Bianco (Colavita), both Italian based manufacturers, are outstanding products to use for a flavor base in ice cream production.

FRUITS

There is no question that especially in the summer time, any ice cream flavor made with fruit, especially fresh fruit, will sell. Taken as a whole, fruit flavors are the largest category of flavors you will produce. Strawberry ice cream has always ranked third in popularity after vanilla and chocolate. Because of the availability of fresh fruits during the summer season other popular flavors include banana (although good bananas are available year round), raspberry, cherry, and peach.

Fruit flavorings come in four basic forms: the fruit itself, fruit puree, fruit variegates, and fruit extracts. Extracts can be either natural or artificial. Fruits are available as fresh, frozen, or processed.

Fresh and Frozen Fruit

For the best-quality frozen dessert, fresh fruit is preferable, but is expensive when not in season and is time consuming to prepare for the production run. However, anything fresh appeals to the buying public, so the use of fresh or frozen fruit (uncooked) whenever possible is worth considering.

Fresh fruit can be used in an ice cream mix only after the fruit has been washed, peeled and pitted when necessary, cut up, and marinated with sugar to produce a fruit syrup. Marinating the fruit takes at least 12 hours, so it has to be prepared for production use a day in advance. The syrup imparts the full flavor of the fruit to the ice cream more effectively than does the fruit by itself. It also breaks down the fruit so icing does not occur during the production run. Depending on the fruit used, either citric acid or lemon juice solutions can be used at the rate of 5 ounces to each 100 pounds of the batch to bring out both a more balanced fruit flavor and to smooth out any excess sweetness that sometimes camouflages the natural flavor. For example, strawberries harvested in the summer close to where they will be purchased and consumed are naturally sweeter than those harvested in the winter from distant places, such as Mexico and California, and then shipped across the United States for sale. The sweetness of other fruits can also vary at different times of year, and also due to weather and travel conditions.

For the marinating process, mix 2–7 pounds of fruit with 1 pound of sugar, depending on the natural sweetness of the fruit being used. The best mixture for marinating all fruits, fresh or frozen, is one part puree and one part pieces. Some suggested ratios for fruit to sugar are

Apples,	7 : 1
Strawberries,	3 : 1
Raspberries,	4 : 1
Peaches,	2½ : 1
Cherries,	3 : 1

That ratio will also vary depending on the percentage of butterfat in your ice cream mix. For example, a 16-percent butterfat mix will require less sugar in the fruit syrup than a lower butterfat mix will. The fruit–sugar ratio is vital because without an adequate amount of sugar in the fruit mixture, the pieces of fruit in the ice cream will impart an icy texture that consumers find objectionable.

Remember, too, that sweetening is a matter of taste, so adjust your recipes according to customer feedback on the matter.

Like fresh fruits, frozen fruits also require marinating with sugar but you will need to remember that most already have 10 percent sugar in them. These fruits are cheaper and easier to use than fresh, but the taste of a fresh fruit is far superior to anything frozen. When frozen fruit is used, you will get the best results by considering the following:

- To best preserve flavor and texture, defrost slowly.
- Defrost in a refrigerator or walk-in box.
- Defrosting may take 24–30 hours for a 30-pound box or 5-gallon pail.
- Most properly thawed fruits will return to their original freshness.
- Never refreeze thawed fruit.
- To accelerate thawing of syrup packs only, thaw at room temperature or run cool water over the container tin container or plastic bag.
- Thawed fruit should be used within two hours if stored at room temperature, or immediately place in refrigerator to maintain sanitary health considerations.
- Cover thawed fruit tightly to preserve its color and flavor.
- Once thawed fruit is refrigerated, make sure you use it within two days.

Most frozen fruit is packed in either 5-gallon pails or 20–30 pound cases, either whole IQF (individually quick frozen), broken pieces, or sliced. Once received it should be stored immediately in a freezer. A large variety of frozen fruit can be purchased from most foodservice distributors, but I highly recommend Dot Foods of Mt. Sterling, Illinois, Global Trading of Greenville, South Carolina, and Clermont Fruit Packers of Clermont, Oregon.

The total weight of the marinated fruit mixture used should not exceed 25 percent of the weight of the finished product. For example, if you use 3 pounds of strawberries and 1 pound of sugar, you will have 4 pounds of marinated fruit. That quantity must be used with 12 pounds of ice cream mix to result in 16 pounds of product (that is, 4 is 25% of 16, and 12 is the remaining 75%).

Lastly, remember that most superpremium fruit-flavored frozen desserts are slightly overflavored because that is what consumers want, given the success of the category.

Processed Fruit

Fruit that is heated or cooked is being used increasingly by ice cream producers worldwide because of health concerns regarding bacteria in fruit not handled properly during the harvesting, picking, and washing process prior to shipment to dairy processors. Processed fruit comes three ways: whole, sliced, or pureed (see Table 5-4). It is packed in either #10 cans, 5- or 55-gallon pails, or totes (55-gallon plastic container with an attached extrusion connection that can feed fruit directly into the fruit feeder). A leading fruit supplier of totes is Ramsey/Sias of Breckville, Ohio. Whole or sliced fruit is processed and packed either solid or dry pack. The solid pack is designed for those ice cream formulations requiring some juice and syrup for additional flavor (approximate ratio of

Table 5-4. Processed-Fruit Suppliers

Company	Product Number	Product Name or Description
Strawberries		
Limpert Brothers	3453	Dew Fresh Strawberries, chunks dry packed
Star Kay White	—	Strawberry pieces, shredded
Pre Gel	—	Concentrated strawberry flavor
Ramsey	4841	Combo Pack Strawberries
Guernsey Dell	06-6662	Strawberry variegate
Raspberries		
Ramsey	4081	Seedless raspberry puree
Guernsey Dell	06-6593	Raspberry Revel, variegate for tart flavor
Star Kay White	—	Raspberry, puree and seedless
	—	Black raspberry, puree
Limpert Brothers	3090	Red raspberry puree
	3070	Black raspberry puree
Peaches		
Limpert Brothers	3340	Peach cubes, stabilized
Pre Gel	—	Peach concentrate
Guernsey Dell	06-6088	Peach chunks and background
Ramsey	4035	Peaches chunks

fruit to juice is 36 parts fruit, 14 parts juice). The dry pack is designed for those ice cream formulations requiring only fruit.

Puree Flavor Bases   Pureeing is putting whole fruit through a blending process to make a liquid substance. Sugar and/or corn syrup is then added to the product to bring out the full flavor of the fruit. Depending on the fruit (e.g., peach or blueberry), sometimes a fruit extract is added to the puree to boost the flavor impact. The product is then packed for sale to an ice cream manufacturer.

For a product designer, a puree's primary function is to add fruit solids (creating fruit body texture to the ice cream mix) to the ice cream flavor being produced. Purees do not add as much flavor as an extract or concentrated flavor base, but they help make the flavor well rounded.

When using a puree, make sure it is agitated properly with the ice cream mix in the flavor tank, prior to production. Each flavor has its own particular usage level, so it is important to sample some of the combined flavor before production begins.

Variegating Sauces   Variegates are often used instead of or in addition to pieces. A variegating sauce is a thick syrup that is used to create a marble affect in the hardened ice cream. In the finished ice cream, variegates appear as a ribbon. In addition to fruit sauces, caramels, marshmallows, chocolate, fudge, and butterscotch are commonly used for variegating.

Variegates are added to the semisoft ice cream in a continuous freezing operation through the variegator (ripple pump). To obtain the desired textural characteristics in the finished product and for proper flow through the pump, the variegate must not be too thick or thin. In a batch freezer operation, variegates are hand-swirled into the tubs as the ice cream is being extruded. Do not add a variegate into the hopper of the batch freezer because the dasher churns the ice cream too much to hold the variegate in place, resulting in a blended product with unintended color and flavor. If you line the tubs with the variegating sauce before the extrusion takes place, you can create a marbled effect as the product is being extruded. This marbling is accomplished by swirling the variegate off the walls of the tubs with a spatula as the ice cream is being extruded.

Guernsey Dell of Chicago, Illinois, Ramsey/Sias of Cleveland, Ohio, and Star Kay White of Congers, New York, all produce outstanding variegates of all sorts.

Kinds of Fruits

Strawberry   The strawberry, the fruit of the plants of the genus *Fragaria,* has a particular and unique structure. The seeds, which unlike those of other fruits are on the outside, are the true fruits of the plant. The inside of the fruit has a fleshy "berry" fiber to it. The fiber or flesh is particularly flavorful and bodied so that when used for ice cream production, it is easy to get the true flavor of strawberry in the finished hardened product.

There are now hundreds of varieties of strawberries. They exhibit great diversity of size and flavor; but one thing is certain, strawberries are best used when fully ripe. Strawberries from the Northwest (Washington and Oregon) have the best overall flavor of any U.S. strawberry. Their fiber content is excellent with the only negative aspect being its off color of less red (more purple and blue). Strawberries from California have excellent color, but they have more water content, less fiber, and are not as flavorful as the berries from Washington and Oregon.

Fresh or frozen strawberries (unsugared) should be purchased and used whole. They need not be mashed, sliced, or heated to enhance their flavor during marinating. Using a 3:1 ratio of fruit to sugar will give a balance of sweet and tart flavor that can be adjusted based on the butterfat of the ice cream mix. Use less sugar with higher butterfat percentages.

If frozen (4 parts fruit to 1 part sugar) strawberries are used, they should be fully defrosted first. Once defrosted, let them sit for 6–8 hours to allow the marinating to take full effect. Then drain off the juice. Some of the juice (25% of what is left) can be used for flavoring the batch, but be careful not to use more because juice is mostly water and you do not want to create ice (crystallization) in your finished product.

Because of improved flavor technology, many ice cream producers are now heavily using processed strawberries. For a batch of ice cream using 2½ gallons of ice cream mix, about 3 quarts of processed strawberries will produce an excellent-tasting product. I highly recommend the processed strawberries available from Ramsey/Sias, Star Kay White, Limpert Brothers, Pre Gel, and Monte Bianco (see Table 5-4).

Raspberry   The raspberry, *Rubus ideas* and other *Rubus* species, grows wild in the cooler regions of the northern hemisphere, and in some southern parts. The first people known to have cultivated raspberries were the ancient Greeks, who are said to have called the fruit "idaeus" because it grew thickly on the slopes of Mount Ida, as it still does. Raspberries can be either red or black. Both are excellent fruits used for ice cream production.

For at least 6 months of the year, the high cost of fresh raspberries limits their use by many large operators. Raspberries have a strong, full-bodied flavor, but must be pureed to remove all or at least 85 percent of the seeds. Because raspberries contain more water, more sugar is used than for other fruits to inhibit icing. Frozen raspberries are readily available and less expensive than fresh, and they are acceptable for use in frozen dessert production. Processed raspberries tend to be too sweet and should be used only when mixed with either fresh or frozen fruit to improve the flavor. If you must use processed raspberries, the products of the companies listed in Table 5-4 are recommended.

Peach   The Freestone Peach, *Prunus persica,* is one of the world's favorite fruits. With early origins in Asia Minor or Persia, the freestone peach is a descendant of the wild almond, which still grows in that region.

Successfully producing a peach-flavored ice cream is difficult. Only fully ripened yellow peaches have any flavor and because peaches are a water-based fruit, icing occurs easily. Proper flavoring can be achieved by using a natural peach extract in conjunction with the marinated (at least 12 hours) peach pulp mixture. The skins should not be removed because they substantially increase flavor.

Frozen peaches are now being used increasingly by ice cream manufacturers and they are in demand year round. They are shipped two ways, either IQF— dipped in a vitamin C bath to preserve freshness and color, without sulfites—or packaged in plastic pouches with syrup (combination of puree and sugar syrup). Frozen peaches come either in halves, sliced, diced, or irregular cuts. Wawona Frozen Foods of Clovis, California, is a recommended processor of frozen peach products, and both the Virginia Dare Company, of Brooklyn, New York, and the David Michael Company, of Philadelphia, Pennsylvania, manufacture excellent natural peach extracts. If processed peaches have to be used, Table 5-4 lists recommended suppliers.

Cherry   The Montmorency cherry is considered the best fresh cherry for ice cream production. A 3:1 ratio of fruit to sugar plus a natural extract will produce a good flavor. The cherries need not be mashed or pureed because of their good body structure. During either a continuous or batch freezer operation the cherries will maintain their integral character throughout the freezing process. Since fresh cherries are considered mildly flavored, you will need to use more of them.

Cherries are available in a frozen state as wholes, halves, sliced, or mixed diced. Processed cherries from Limpert Brothers and Ramsey/Sias are recommended and come in many varieties, including Burgandy, Bordeaux, and black. They are either dry packed or stabilized in a syrup solution.

Banana   Bananas are a wonderful summer addition for any type of ice cream or sorbet production. It is a remarkable fruit. More bananas are consumed than perhaps any other kind of fruit in the world.

The banana plant, of the genus *Musa,* is a strange growth that looks like a palm tree, but is not a tree at all. It is a perennial herb that grows a new trunk every year, and dies back to its roots after it has flowered and fruited. Bananas are basically an easy fruit to use in ice cream production if one major consideration is controlled, that being the ripening process. A banana totally yellow, almost rotten, is the best banana to use. The riper the banana, the more flavor in the fruit.

Fresh bananas can be pureed and dispersed directly into the flavor tank in a continuous freezing operation, or poured directly into the batch freezer. The blades of the batch freezer will puree them instantly. Processed bananas are available from a number of manufacturers like Chiquita Brands of Cincinnati, Ohio. Their banana puree comes in cans, pails, and drums with no sugar added.

Blueberry In the past, blueberries have been a neglected fruit in ice cream production. That status is now quickly changing because there has been a major commercial cultivation of the fruit since the mid-1980s, taking it from the wild into the commercial world for many areas of food production.

It is a small bluish fruit of various scrubby (lowbush) and bushy (high bush) plants of the genus *Vaccinium*. Wild blueberries are found wherever suitable conditions (acid soil and enough moisture at all seasons) exist. Most commercially cultivated blueberries are grown in North America.

They have a sweet-tart flavor that when balanced properly in ice cream production creates a smooth creamy delicious texture in the finished product. A list of the available packers of cultivated blueberries in a frozen state is available from MBG Marketing Group, The New Jersey Blueberry Industry Advisory Council, The British Columbia Blueberry Co-op Association, and The Oregon and Washington Blueberry Commissions (see Appendix).

Other Fruits Fresh or frozen pineapple, kiwi, cranberries, mangoes, dates, and apricots can all be used successfully in ice cream production. They are full bodied and have the bulk and texture characteristics for proper freezing with ice cream mix.

When it comes to tropical fruits, the mango is a rising star. In sorbet production, mango, kiwi, passion fruit, and guava are all getting a lot of attention from manufacturers because they are perceived as being both refreshing and healthy. In addition, combining exotic tropical flavors with more familiar flavors such as strawberry (strawberry-kiwi) has become an effective strategy for broadening their appeal.

BAKERY MIX-INS

Like candy-based ice cream products, bakery mix-ins now play a similar role in the development of new ice cream flavors. Because of a company called Bel Foods of Dublin, California (now part of Guernsey Bel of Chicago, Illinois), this flavor ingredient category is becoming enormously popular with ice cream manufacturers. The employees at Bel Foods start with the original product, be it cheesecake (plain, raspberry or strawberry), brownies, or tiramisu, and figure out how to convert it to an ingredient that can be processed by an ice cream manufacturer. They have produced a large variety of bakery mix-in ingredients that are applicable for use in nonfat, low-fat, and no-sugar-added ice cream products.

Bakery mix-in ingredients are shipped frozen and must be kept frozen until they are ready to be used. They are injected directly into the hopper in the batch freezer or dispersed through the fruit feeder in a continuous freezing operation.

CHOOSING AN INGREDIENT SUPPLIER

Not only are the kind and quality of the ingredients themselves important, but the care that is taken in their manufacture and shipping is also critical. Choose only suppliers with reputations for an overall concern for their products. Ingredient suppliers such as Ramsey/Sias of Cleveland, Ohio; Star Kay White of Congers, New York; Nielsen-Massey Vanillas of Waukegan, Illinois; Van Leer Chocolate of Jersey City, New Jersey; and Guernsey Dell of Chicago, Illinois, have standards of quality in conducting their businesses that make them leaders in their respective fields. For example, to avoid heat damage, they ship their products only in refrigerated trucks, and they will refuse a sale if they feel their products will be handled or used improperly. They simply refuse to sacrifice quality just to make a sale.

Certainly, choosing an ingredient supplier requires trial and error and a lot of learning on your part. Ice cream manufacturers such as AE Farms of Des Moines and Ben & Jerry are excellent examples of companies who care very much about the ingredients they use. They nurture relationships with their suppliers to ensure the best quality and freshness of the ingredients they use. A good example of this nurturing, and specifically quality assurance involves Ben & Jerry's production of Georgia Peach ice cream. They use only ripe peaches, pitted and with sugar added at the farm. The peaches are then shipped to their production facility in Vermont. For weeks on end, nonstop, they produce their Georgia Peach ice cream for only as long as the peaches are in season. This way of production is not the easiest, but it certainly produces the best tasting peach ice cream you have ever eaten.

Efforts like that are really worth it because controlled purchasing is the most important preproduction function of any ice cream production operation. It takes a lot of energy and planning, but without controlled purchasing you could soon run into financial trouble, end up producing poor quality products, and conceivably go out of business. Likewise you will find that taking the time to learn about suppliers and their products will help foster good relationships with them. Such relationships are invaluable because suppliers can teach you about how to use certain ingredients and advise you of trends in the industry.

Today's trends include the use of fresh, natural ingredients, used in large pieces so consumers can see what they are getting. As a general rule, do not keep excessive inventory of ingredients on hand. The longer a product sits in storage and the more it is handled, the more its flavor and freshness will dissipate. It will also lose its basic properties that affect the texture and appearance of the finished product.

Dealing with an established ingredient manufacturer will give you a choice of ingredients for a particular flavor. As much as possible, buy direct from a manufacturer to obtain the best prices. Many manufacturers do not require large quantity purchases, particularly if they are located in your vicinity. Freight costs are a major factor in pricing, so you should educate yourself on what is available locally. You might be able to purchase high-quality ingredients locally for the same price as a lesser grade from elsewhere. Buying direct will also usually get you a fresher product than buying from a distributor.

Use a distributor only when your storage is limited or price minimums make it impossible to buy direct. However, a distributor does provide the advantage of being able to choose from a variety of ingredients from different manufacturers, and working with a distributor knowledgeable in the industry can be a valuable asset.

Whether you buy direct or from a distributor, be sure to ask for samples from a range of quality for each ingredient. Then you can choose the quality and price you prefer. Taste the samples and run small batches of product to see how they compare to the manufacturer's claims. You will also get an idea of how your own sense of taste compares to the manufacturer's rating of its own products. You will quickly learn to rely on common sense and your own taste buds. The sampling and experimenting will give you a good understanding of the ingredients and help determine your own standards of quality.

PURCHASING

Evaluating Purchasing Needs

At the beginning of each new season, evaluate your needs and order accordingly. Keep an adequate supply of ingredients you use constantly, such as vanilla extract, cocoa, chocolate chips, and different varieties of nuts and processed fruits. Then you will not run out of product at the height of the season. If you do not produce your own ice cream mix, then you should keep a 5-day inventory on hand because dairies run out of mix at least once during every season due to heavy demand.

Buying in advance and in quantity gives you leverage for volume discounts. It may not always be possible to purchase that way, but it is worth the try because the extra 10 percent discount is bottom-line profit.

Ordering

Do not pick up the telephone to order supplies until you know exactly what you want. Having preprinted order sheets for each supplier will make ordering easier. The sheets should list every item you could possibly need so that all you have to do is check off the items needed.

Do not let suppliers substitute items unless you are told about it and approve in advance. Suppliers will frequently use the excuse that they did not want you to run out of an item, so they substituted a different quality or manufacturer. Tell them that doing so is unacceptable to you so that they know they cannot take advantage of you. If you use substitutes, you'll end up with an inconsistent product and a subsequent loss of business.

Receiving and Storage

Plan orders with each supplier so that delivery times are set in advance (because everyone wants morning deliveries). If you know that your ice cream mix delivery is going to arrive on a Monday afternoon, make sure your Friday order includes extra cases of mix to start production on Monday morning.

When your order arrives, check the invoice as follows before the delivery person leaves:

1. Check the amount received against what is recorded on the invoice and on your purchase order.
2. Always check for weight, quantity, freshness, and the overall condition of the package. In particular, ice cream mix should be checked for expiration dates usually marked on the top of the container.
3. If there is a shortage, note it on the invoice and have the delivery person acknowledge the shortage in writing. Complaining about a shortage after the delivery person has left is not a good business practice because most suppliers are reluctant to give a credit after the fact.
4. Make sure the prices on the invoice are correct. Mistakes, honest or otherwise, do occur. Careless, unorganized operators do not notice them at all and have only themselves to blame either for the extra effort involved in correcting the errors or for potential losses.

If you fail to properly store your purchases in refrigerated or properly ventilated dry storage areas, you defeat the purpose of buying high-quality ingredients. An organized storage system should be considered during the design of your establishment because inadequate storage leads to a dirty environment and wasted ingredients. Date all containers the day you receive them. All frozen or refrigerated items must be stored immediately. Especially be sure to store ice cream mix in proper rotation according to its expiration dates so that you use the oldest containers first.

REFERENCES

Arbuckle, W. S. 1986. *Ice Cream*. Fourth edition. Westport, Conn.: AVI.

Brandt, Laura. 1996. The creation and use of vanilla. *Food Product Design*, March, pp. 70–87.

Davidson, Alan. 1991. *Fruit, A Connoisseur's Guide and Cookbook*. New York: Simon & Schuster.

Hegenbart, Scott. 1994. Harvesting the benefits of fruit-containing ingredients. *Food Product Design*, December, pp. 25–46.

Ingredient Technology Application. 1996. Two desserts in one. *Dairy Foods Magazine*, January, p. 50.

Kuhn, Mary Ellen. 1995. Flavor forecast: Anything goes! *Food Processing*, August, p. 30.

Kuntz, Lynn. 1994. Ice cream inclusions: Deep freeze delights. *Food Product Design*, July, pp. 50–64.

Lind, Peter. 1993, Ben & Jerry's: Beyond specifications and price. *Dairy Foods Magazine*, May, p. 54.

Nielsen, Chat, Jr. 1985. *The Story of Vanilla*. Waukegan, Il.: Nielsen-Massey Vanillas.

McWard, Christine. 1995. Going nuts. *Baking Buyer*, September, p. 23.

6

⌗⌗⌗⌗⌗⌗⌗⌗⌗⌗⌗⌗⌗⌗⌗⌗⌗⌗⌗⌗⌗⌗⌗⌗⌗⌗⌗⌗⌗

ICE CREAM NOVELTIES

Ice cream produced and sold in the United States is considered the ninth largest product category in most supermarkets, and ice cream novelties are a big part of that category. The term "novelty" means something unique. As it relates to ice cream, we mean any single-serve portion-controlled product. Worldwide, especially in Europe, ice cream novelties enjoy an even a bigger market. You name it, every size, shape, and flavor are being offered: from ice cream and frozen yogurt to sorbets and nonfat products.

Today, creativity in this product area is boundless. If it has not already been created, produced and sold, it probably will be soon. Many have been successful, some have failed. But what is really important to the ice cream manufacturers is protecting shelf space. Protect your turf, confuse the market. That is the game, and for the big ice cream manufacturers it seems to be very successful. Ice cream novelties are no longer a fad, but a serious stable business. More than anything else, however, value, innovation, and brand development are the keys to getting a novelty into a freezer case, and staying there.

- *Value.* Give consumers value, and you will get their money. That is the main reason that multipacks are successful. Parents with young children look for products they can use everyday, and a six or eight multipack fits the bill. They offer significant savings over the same product purchased individually. To drive the segment even further, bonus packs promote value using words like "8 Cups, 2 Free" or "12 Pops for the Price of 10."

- *Innovation.* Is there a more creative, fast-paced dairy category than frozen novelties? I do not think so. What makes the segment so intriguing and appealing is that products come and go, so there is always something new. Being able to offer products that can not be duplicated, improves the sales chances a manufacturer has with a retailer. Just looking at the supermarkets shelves where one-third of all the space is taken up by novelties, it seems as if there is no end in sight.

- *Brand Identity.* The most successful ice cream novelties are the ones with strong brand identity and outstanding graphics on the package. Simply put, consumers recognize brand names. Research and in-store data confirm that consumers are product and flavor loyal, and that a primary reason for forgoing a purchase is the unavailability of a desired product or flavor.

SPECIAL CONCERNS

Consumers' Perceptions

Consumer demand drives the novelty market through two distinct buying groups. Females age 35–54 and children age 7–13. Today's consumers are bipolar in their purchasing patterns—most either treat themselves to high-fat, indulgent ice cream novelties or partake of products with pared down fat and calories. For the most part, a consumer's impulse decision to buy or not depends on choosing a particular product or flavor. Consumers essentially perceive novelties to be a warm-weather treat and mainly purchase them for the following reasons:

- *Convenience.* A novelty is a single serving of a product, and that is the biggest reason consumers purchase novelties—no fuss instant gratification. Convenience also means the place where consumers purchase their products, usually at supermarkets with neighborhood convenience stores being close behind.
- *Dessert.* It is considered a dessert, so it can be indulgent and satisfy an impulse urge.
- *Snack.* It can easily replace a cookie, jello, cup yogurt, or pudding. As an afternoon treat especially for children when they come home from school.
- *Household Staples.* "Someone in my household asked for it" is a common reason why ice cream novelties are purchased. Some frozen treats, notably water ice pops, fudge bars, and fruit-juice bars, are grocery list staples. "I always buy it" is among the top three reasons for purchasing each of these three items.
- *Portion Control.* Novelties have an inherent advantage, a built-in limitation that many other treat foods do not. They are portion controlled, which is a great marketing tool for promoting the segment to attract weight-watching consumers.
- *Price.* Because parents treat novelties as a staple that they need to have in their freezer at all times, price is a major driving force especially for any boxed (four or six to a box) novelty product geared toward children.

Children's Novelties There is no question that the largest growing segment of the ice cream novelty market is products geared toward children. Research over the years has found that children take a very active role in determining what they eat beginning at age 10. At this age, they also become more adventuresome in the products and flavors they like. It is a key age that ice cream marketers use for designing packaging. Under the age of ten, children like easy-to-eat shapes and portion size products. They do not like mixed flavors and hybrid products such as cake and ice cream novelties. They prefer inclusions they can "relate to," inclusions that are "part of their world" such as cookie dough, cookie pieces, and chocolate, as opposed to fruit bits and pieces.

Most children like the following:

- Flavors that are basic (vanilla, chocolate, and orange) and candylike flavors, with color.
- Products that are similar across types. For example, strawberry frozen yogurt must resemble strawberry ice cream.
- Sprinkles, especially mixed colors.
- Wrapped ice cream cones, usually packed four to a box, and juice bars, usually packed six to eight to a box. Ice cream cones are a terrific dessert item, particularly after a dinner meal on a hot summer day. The best-selling flavors are vanilla ice cream cones with either caramel or fudge swirled into the cone and sprinkles on top. Other popular flavors are any with a chocolate coating and either peanuts or sprinkles on top of the coating.
- Juice bars for snacks. Give the product a funny name, have colorful packaging, and offer different sizes and shapes (animal and Disney characters), and you will have a winner on your hands. They are low in calories and they can be sucked, something kids love to do. The most popular flavors are orange and any wild flavor and color like grape.
- Ice cream sandwiches. In fact, they are the second largest category behind ice cream bars in the novelty category. The most popular flavor is a chocolate wafer with vanilla ice cream.

Most children identify their mother as the primary purchaser in the family, putting the parent in the role of both purchaser and "gatekeeper." Therefore, ice cream novelty products intended for children have to have appeal to parents as well. Marketing to kids can have lasting benefits for an ice cream manufacturer because early exposure to specific products may result in long-term brand loyalty. The secret: understand what children want and what the gatekeepers will buy for them.

Adult Novelties The adult ice cream novelty market is geared toward products at both ends of the fat spectrum: high fat ice cream bars and bon bons that satisfy craving, and fat-free and cholesterol-free novelty products such as frozen yogurt bars, sandwiches, juice bars (high in real fruit content), and sorbet bars. This segment is growing mainly because of convenience and diet concerns. The increased availability in the late 1990s of sorbets packaged in pints and individually wrapped juice bars have dramatically helped this segment grow. Sorbet juice bars either by themselves or mixed with nonfat frozen yogurt are very appealing to consumers watching their calorie or fat intake.

Licensing When it comes to ice cream novelties, the name game works. Basically, it works like this: Take a popular national brand, apply it to a customized product, and watch sales grow. The concept is called *brand expansion*. It all started with the introduction of Jell-O Pudding Pops in 1979. The Jell-O brand, of course, had no previous affiliation with the frozen novelty business, but that did not matter. Sales soared, and the concept of brand extension in the frozen desserts category was off and running.

Candy bar brands like Milky Way, Snickers, and Three Musketeers obviously attach well to ice cream novelties mainly because the ice cream products taste like the candy bars. For children's products, licensing of cartoon characters has been incredibly successful. Characters such as Looney Tunes under license from Warner Brothers and the Disney Mickey's Parade lines have been instant successes.

Packaging

Not Just Containers Because multipack box packaging is the dominant element used for packaging the ice cream novelties sold in supermarkets and club stores, it is extremely important that this package convey a clear message to the consumer. The individual elements that convey this message are as follows:

- *Product visibility:* use a photograph of the product.
- *Product signage:* should be colorful and concise.
- *Nutritional information:* should include specifics such as "cholesterol-free" or "fat-free" in answer to the simple questions that consumers usually have. If your product has a distinct plus to it, you should exploit it in dramatic form, but make sure what you are saying is the absolute truth.
- *Size of package:* be aware that regardless of the specific novelty, consumers are most likely to buy them in multipacks of six or twelve.
- *Individual-wrap packaging:* "foil-type" or "plastic-type" are preferred. Paper wraps are perceived as being easiest to open, while plastic-type wraps are viewed as best for not leaking. Consumers say foil-type wraps are best for not sticking to the product, and for conveying a premium message and preserving freshness.

Packaging Costs Since all ice cream novelties are single-serve products, paper packaging costs are of great concern to manufacturers. Each novelty has to be separately wrapped and then boxed for sale as either three, four, or six to a pack. Only in convenience stores are novelties sold individually, thus eliminating the need for an exterior package.

One way manufacturers are cutting paper costs is through the use of high-barrier white polypropylene (PP) film with process-print graphics instead of single-serve chipboard boxes. One pound of PP film has the same surface area as two pounds of paper wrap, resulting in a 50 percent savings in material costs.

Merchandising

Most consumers are at the mercy of the supermarket's buyer and stocking system to offer their favorite ice cream products. In particular, novelties are even more prone to unavailability than other ice cream products such as pints, quarts, and half gallons because of the large variety of novelty products and flavors. Until recently, space allotment for novelties has always been whatever space is left over after pints, quarts, and half gallons have filled the supermarket freezer shelves.

If you want to ensure success in the ice cream novelty business, then you must have an in-store merchandising plan in place at the time of a new products introduction. Garnering shelf space is a constant war that manufacturers have with supermarket frozen dessert buyers. Buyers simply pit ice cream novelty manufacturers against one another. Whoever pays the most for shelf space gets preferential treatment. Buyers usually makes a conscious decision either in January or February of each year of what new products they will feature and what slow-moving products will be removed from the shelves, so having an in-store merchandising plan in place is critically important. In-store merchandising encompasses the following:

- *Graphics:* Eye-catching color graphics on the outside of novelty cartons.
- *FSI (frequency single insert) advertising:* featured ads coupled with coupons. Money spent on feature ads helps get the attention of retailer and consumer alike.
- *Stand-alone display freezers:* enable manufacturers to feature their own products with display advertising. They also help trip consumers' awareness as they cruise the supermarket aisles.
- *Point-of-sale materials:* Novelties are often an impulse decision, so strong point-of-sale materials, such as mobiles and cling-ons (signs attached on the outsides of supermarket freezer doors), are more important than ever.

ICE CREAM NOVELTY PRODUCTION

Modern ice cream production technology has been instrumental in the growth success of the novelty market since the late 1970s. Today, machinery can produce portion-control products in nearly every shape and size, such as coated and uncoated bars, cups, fancy funny face and character bars, and ice cream sandwiches. But the human element, of course, is still critical in the production of ice cream novelties. All plant personnel must have knowledge of what ingredients are used, how the equipment operates, and planning a day's production. Particularly, once the production line is in operation, control of the rate of freezing, stick insertion, portion control, and extraction from the molds are areas that must be constantly watched.

Methods

Ice cream novelties are produced either on a vitaline or brine system, or through a extrusion system. Using the vitaline system, semifrozen ice cream is poured into molds that are placed inside a brine tank to freeze the product at −20 degrees Fahrenheit. The extrusion method enables a manufacturer to produce unusual types of novelties that are impossible to produce on a vitaline system.

Using the extrusion method, the ice cream must be frozen to a certain stiffness so that it retains its form between the time it is extruded until it enters a hardening tunnel. The ice cream is drawn from the continuous freezer at 20–22 degrees Fahrenheit. The external contour of the slice can be almost any desired shape and is determined by the shape of the extrusion nozzle. Complex extrusions utilizing more than one flavor or color can be produced from multiflavor extrusion nozzles supplied by more than one continuous freezer barrel. By placing different extrusion devises inside each other, faces with eyes, noses, and mouths can be formed, as well as other intricate designs.

Semisolid ice cream is drawn either vertically or horizontally. As the stiff extruded ice cream flows through the extrusion nozzle, portions of appropriate size are cut off by an electrically heated wire. In vertical extrusion, the flat portion of the ice cream slice falls precisely onto a continuous row of stainless steel supporting plates fastened to a conveyer chain, which carries the portions into the hardening tunnel for rapid freezing. The temperature in the hardening tunnel is usually in the range of −45 degrees Fahrenheit to −50 degrees Fahrenheit. A 10 percent ice cream butterfat mix with 85–100 percent overrun is the most commonly used.

Chocolate Coatings

More than one-third of all ice cream novelties produced have some kind of exterior chocolate coating. In particular, a combination of vanilla ice cream and dark chocolate coating has been a popular seller since the 1940s. The coating used should have a true chocolate flavor, melt readily in the mouth (melting point of 75 degrees Fahrenheit) without a waxy feel, solidify rapidly with minimal drip during application, adhere well to the ice cream, and form a thin layer that resists cracking or breaking during handling.

The usual composition of coatings for frozen desserts is vegetable fat, cocoa, sugar, milk (including skim milk and buttermilk), lecithin, and flavors. Coatings should be heated to a temperature of 95–105 degrees Fahrenheit before they are used during production of any ice cream novelty.

There are several factors that must be considered during any coating application:

- *Temperature of the coating.* The higher the temperature, the less coating is required. Take note that if the coating is too hot, it will melt the ice cream.
- *Temperature of the ice cream.* The colder the ice cream, the warmer the coating must be to obtain the necessary thickness of the coating adhering to the product.
- *Overrun.* Ice cream products that have a high overrun promote melting at the outer surface. The resulting action is a bleeding effect between the ice cream and the coating.
- *Coating solidification.* The higher the coating temperature, the longer it will take for the coating to solidify to the product.

ICE CREAM NOVELTY EQUIPMENT MANUFACTURERS

The following companies produce a varied selection of both vitaline and extruded ice cream novelty production equipment.

APV Crepaco

Promcoline Concept APV developed the Promcoline system to meet the specific requirements of individual novelty manufacturers. The system includes the following:

Extrusion Station. From the freezer, the ice cream mix is accepted by the APV Crepaco extrusion system designed for plain ice cream as well as for products full of inclusions.

Ingredient Decorating Positions. Between extrusion onto the stainless steel band and the hardening tunnel are the ingredient feeding stations that allow a whole range of decorated products to be produced. Caramel extrusion and nut dispensing and depositing units are also available.

Main Hardening Tunnel. All tunnels in Promcoline have stainless-steel components for easy cleaning procedures. Promcoline tunnels allow for the expansion and contraction that takes place during operation and cleaning.

Air Handling Units. Housed within the hardening tunnels are the most advanced air handling units in the business. They operate in balanced pairs to maximize longitudinal air flow above and beneath the band, yet at the same time offer maximum access for maintenance and cleaning.

Enrobing Aftercooler. Promcoline places much importance on chocolate enrobing and comes with an aftercooler that sets the chocolate properly.

Wrapper. From the aftercooler, the multiline wrapper takes over to provide a packaging solution for a high-capacity plant.

Glacier EXCEL Extrusion System For many years the Glacier system has been synonymous with high-quality ice cream extrusion of bars, cups, cones, and logs. The system includes a complete range of production equipment such as extruders, fillers, chocolate and juice dipping stations, enrobers, and wrappers. The system can also interface with off-line fillers and other forming equipment. There are three different versions of this system depending on the product size, product type, production volume, and process requirements.

The main features of the system are large product plates, a lubrication-free main conveyer chain, a unique worktable with open stainless steel profile for easy washing, a main hardening conveyer, an insulated tunnel enclosure, and a varied range of vertical and horizontal extruders and cutting systems. For lower capacity requirements, a single lane product handling system is available. It can handle bars, cones, and sandwiches.

Technohoy LOG-LINE Extrusion Line The LOG-LINE is used for horizontal extrusion of log-type ice cream products. Its capacity is forty-five strokes (logs) per minute. The line can be designed for an infinite amount of custom made applications. Either layered or round products can be extruded and decorated with either ice cream or dry ingredients. LOG-LINE is equipped with pneumatic automation controlled by a program logic controller (PLC). This guarantees production flexibility and avoids unnecessary time and labor requirements. A chocolate enrober as well as an ingredient feeder can be connected to the Technohoy LOG-LINE.

Gram

The European company Gram has vast experience in producing both manual and automatic novelty extruders and fillers.

Ice Cream and Water Ice Filler, Type 06 For the small and medium size manufacturer of novelties, the Type 06 unit is Gram's most popular novelty filler. It consists of an open hopper for the supply of filling matter and a round housing with a rotary cylinder drum provided with bores and filling pistons. The arm with pusher rods and the cylinder drum are connected with a hydraulic combined lifting-rotating cylinder so that the functions can be carried out. The filling volume is determined by the size of the bore and the piston length. The volume filler can be equipped with various nozzle plates to allow special ratios of flavors and filling material in the ice bars.

In-Line Filler Gram's in-line filler has a capacity ranging from 7,200 to 22,500 cups or cones per hour. Built of stainless steel, the unit has an advanced PLC control that is simple to operate and a high degree of flexibility for quick and easy switching of product lines.

Automatic Rotary Novelty Freezers Gram produces a range of freezers that are all self-contained, each with its own integral brine plant. The only connections necessary are for power and refrigeration. The effective water/steam high-speed washer and sterilizer of the unit keeps the machine clean and fully sterilized without dismantling, resulting in a considerable reduction in lost production time for this process. The units are available in 6-wide, 8-wide or 12-wide designs, depending on the size of cups used.

Multilane Wrapper The Gram type HSW wrapper can wrap any frozen product produced on an automatic novelty freezer. The multilane arrangement of the unit in connection with its electric/hydraulic operation aims at securing a low working speed and a steady performance. Because of this method of wrapping production, damages to the product are minimized. By replacing guide rollers and folding mechanisms, the machine can be arranged for wrapping different designs.

Using this system, the products are wrapped, the wrappings are heat sealed, and the individual pieces are cut off and deposited on the conveyer without coming into contact with any machine component or human hands. The wrapping encompasses two sections: a paper feeder and the wrap section proper with a conveyor belt. The HSW wrapper can be supplied for operation with both paper and foil, and it can be provided with "picture-in-place" (PIP) equipment so that a "whole print" (i.e., package is covered in one print area as opposed to separate print areas) is found on the individual wrapping.

Single-Lane Wrapper By far, its single-lane unit is Gram's most popular novelty wrapper. It operates by way of a conveyor belt whereby the product is placed directly in the paper web for sealing lengthwise and crosswise, and for cutting off. The paper reels are placed on the wrapping section proper, and cold-sealing, hot-sealing, or polyethylene film can be used.

REFERENCES

Arbuckle, W.S. 1986. *Ice Cream.* Fourth edition. Westport, Conn.: AVI.
Dairy Foods Special Research Report. 1995. *Dairy Foods,* October.
Dairy Foods Special Research Report. 1996. *Dairy Foods,* August.
Doeff, Gail. 1995. Masters of the ice cream universe. *Dairy Foods,* January, pp. 64–69.
Dreyer, Jerry. 1994. Stick to the basics when marketing novelties. *Dairy Foods,* May, p. 20.
Gorski, Donna. 1995. Sandwich celebration. *Dairy Foods,* February, p. 26.
Gorski, Donna. 1995. Kit tested, parent approved. *Dairy Foods,* March, p. 43.
Reiter, Jeff. 1993. Packages of the year. *Dairy Foods,* January, p. 38.
Reiter, Jeff. 1993. A license to chill. *Dairy Foods,* June, p. 34.

7 ◻◻◻◻◻◻◻◻◻◻◻◻◻◻◻◻◻◻◻◻◻◻◻◻◻◻◻◻◻◻◻

BRINGING PRODUCT TO MARKET

Making a product is one thing, getting it to market, and eventually to the ulti-mate consumer is something else altogether. Unless you are going to operate your own retail frozen dessert business (see Part 2), your product is most likely to reach the consumer via a supermarket. It is no longer sufficient simply to make the product, put it onto a supermarket freezer shelf, wait for it to leave, and then replenish the shelf. Those days are simply gone, forever.

SETTING UP A STRATEGY

In the volatile world of ice cream supermarket distribution, the ice cream freezer case is a tumultuous place. Even for the best of the best, whether you are Häa-gen-Dazs or Ben & Jerry's, retailers care only about one thing: whether your product will sell. For a long time now, supermarket retail freezer space has been cramped, and no product, regardless of how great it might be, will have a place unless it is promoted. That means it takes a lot of marketing and merchandising support to push it out and into the customers hands. Of course being a Häa-gen-Dazs or a Ben & Jerry's does help, especially if you are willing to pay a slot-ting fee (see later in this chapter).

Years ago having an effective in-store merchandising program mainly meant creating clever aisle and freezer shelf displays and devising eye-catching point-of-sale materials. Those things are still important, but for the savvy marketer, in-store merchandising options have become much more sophisticated and varied, and the need for a carefully conceived merchandising strategy is more critical than ever.

Coming up with new products is always a calculated risk. With a new prod-

138

uct, no matter how good it tastes or how fantastic the package looks, or even if it meets consumers demand, there is no such thing as a "sure" thing. But there are strategies to make product introduction less of a gamble. The companies that succeed are those that identify an unfulfilled niche, research it carefully, and plan all aspects of new product launches, product development, packaging, and sales support.

Since planning is such an integral part of launching a new product, it makes sense that coordination takes place between the developers (R&D people) of the product and the marketing people who are going to market it. Following are some useful hints to help prevent new product failure.

- *Clearly define the product.* Without a comprehensive definition of the product, execution from concept to launch will go awry.
- *Identify needs and wants.* Talk to and listen to customers. You will find that it is easier for consumers to pinpoint what they do not want, rather than what they do.
- *Create leverageable attributes.* Building leverageable attributes, such as convenient sizes of packages and chunky inclusions (chips, nuts, pieces of fruit, etc.) into the product that differentiate and communicate its superiority will yield competitive advantages.
- *Realize that speed is not everything.* Problems take longer to fix once the product is in the marketplace. Proper execution is essential in establishing and maintaining the product's dominance.
- *Utilize all available resources.* Allocate both internal and external resources prudently to maximize output and minimize bottom-line cost.
- *Develop a brand plan.* Define the product's objective. Conduct a visual audit of the retail marketplace to evaluate competitive communication practices.
- *Properly position the product.* Positioning refers to the physical placement of a product line in a retail environment. Proper positioning requires matching a product's characteristics (such as quality level and pricing) with the appropriate sales outlet. For example, an expensive premium product would not do well in price-conscious surroundings. In addition, proper positioning means identifying and communicating the benefits that set the product apart from the crowd.
- *Choose a unique name.* Consumers gravitate toward names that are memorable, recognizable, and synonymous with quality or value. Even with all other packaging elements in place, if the name does not have appeal, consumers will not buy the product.
- *Dress the brand for success.* Design a unique trade appearance by combining color, graphics, nomenclature, and type style, size, and shape to project an overall look or impression.
- *Keep up the image.* To build long-term brand equity, set production and marketing standards that can be adhered to and enforced from the highest level within the operation. Brand image is the company's most valuable asset.

Over the years, the best testing grounds for new ice cream products have been in retail frozen dessert shops. Smart ice cream manufacturers monitor retail trends before even thinking about developing a new flavor or product. If a new ice cream flavor or new product works well in this retail environment, you can bet that it will also work well in a packaged form via a pint or half gallon. In a few days or weeks of an introduction of a new product, if repeat sales occurs, you know the product has a chance. If a customer purchases a new product two or three times within 30–45 days of first trying the product, you can be fairly confident that a positive trend is occurring.

Ice cream manufacturers compete for the same shelf space and for a piece of every consumer dollar spent for frozen desserts. Some, lacking widespread name recognition, rely on "local flavor" to help them succeed. That is, they develop a reputation for quality and service within their own locale. But operations come and go and even superior products can get overlooked by the public. So to ensure long-term success, whether you are a manufacturer or a retailer, you need to know a few things about how consumers think and what you can do to keep them coming back.

UNDERSTANDING CONSUMER BEHAVIOR

One of the most perplexing problems confronting manufacturers looking for a competitive edge is trying to understand why consumers behave the way they do. If you can reach some level of understanding in that area, you will be able to market and sell your products successfully.

Marketing techniques based on knowledge of consumer behavior have helped to broaden the industry in general, making frozen desserts more than just an impulse treat for a hot summer's night. Studying the needs and wants of human beings will enable you to determine how best to satisfy the consumer and thus assure your company a share of the frozen dessert market. Inattention to consumer behavior can be costly in the business arena. For example, in the early 1980s many dairy companies were not paying close attention to consumer behavior and failed to react quickly enough to the craze for superpremium ice cream. From 1982 through 1987, sales of superpremium ice cream increased by 104 percent, compared with only a 32 percent gain for other quality levels. By 1988, superpremium ice cream represented 12 percent of overall ice cream sales in dollar terms, compared with 4.7 percent in 1980 (*Wall Street Journal*, Dec. 21, 1988, p. B1). Likewise, during the diet-conscious late 1980s, frozen yogurt became popular and many dairy companies and chains were again slow to react. They simply did not understand the human behavior involved and were not flexible enough in their thinking to adapt to the inclinations of the buying public. The late 1990s show a similar trend with the tremendous increase in popularity of sorbets. Ice cream manufacturers who pay attention will be able to react appropriately to garner market share.

Sources of Information

Being in business means coming into contact with consumers everyday. That contact will give you the opportunity to study human behavior and see how it influences the frozen dessert business. It is critical to keep in close contact with the habits of the consuming public. Then when their tastes shift, you will be ready to respond. Get answers to the following questions and you will have a good understanding of what you need to do to continually market your products successfully.

- Do the customers like my products? Do they tell me what they do not like as well as what they do like? Getting honest answers about dislikes is especially invaluable for fine tuning your improvements.
- What other frozen desserts in general do my customers like and where do they get them? Having this information will help you understand the consumer's wants.
- Do I cater to different categories of customers and understand the behavioral traits of each? For example, having contests for children and asking them what new flavors they might like will make them feel important. In the area of frozen dessert novelties, catering to children will capture the business of many parents.

Remember that it is important to communicate with your customers any way you can. That means sampling programs in supermarkets, posting 800 telephone numbers on your packages for consumer comments, and watching very closely the consistency of repeat sales.

During any sampling program in a supermarket, write down suggestions and comments from your customers. People like to talk and give their opinions about almost anything. If you accumulate these comments, you may see patterns and habits that can help you in your business. This especially true in a small operation where interaction with customers comes into play more often and can be reacted to faster than in a large organization.

Manufacturers in particular should listen closely to their ingredient and packaging suppliers for useful information on flavor and product trends. They should make good use of what is offered by them in way of any marketing ideas point-of-purchase (POP) materials, and branded flavor carton packaging. Flavor ingredient companies such as Guernsey Dell, Pecan Deluxe, and Ramsey/Sias supply illustrations of ingredients to their customers for use on half-gallon packaging for supermarket sales.

Today, marketing information and ideas are abundantly available in magazines such as *Prepared Foods, Frozen Foods, Dairy Foods,* and *Dairy Field*, and at trade shows held by associations such as the International Dairy Foods Association and by suppliers. Seminars run by the Ice Cream University of Scarsdale, New York, and the books it publishes offer the most current and practical knowledge anyone can get on producing and marketing frozen desserts. Also,

The Latest Scoop, published yearly by the International Ice Cream Association is a valuable tool on what product categories are selling and what are not.

Consumer Decision Making

Understanding all the factors that influence a consumer's decision-making process takes time and effort. You have to be acutely aware of what entices a consumer to purchase a product. That awareness is critical to your success. It will enable you to understand customers and react quickly to changes in their habits.

A consumer's decision-making process begins with need arousal. Thousands of different stimuli can trigger the awareness of a need. Once the need has been raised to a conscious level, the consumer needs information before making a decision about how to satisfy that need. "What do I want?" Sometimes a person wants the instant gratification of a cup of rich ice cream. At other times that same person might feel the need to be diet conscious and choose a nonfat frozen yogurt or sorbet instead. After deciding what he or she wants, the next question is, "Where can I get it?" If you know consumers are asking themselves these questions and anticipate the answers to these, you can market your products effectively.

After gathering the information, the consumer evaluates the choices available. Reasons for one choice over another are compared and assigned a personal level of importance, and the decision is made. If you have done your marketing job well, your product will be the one chosen.

Accessing Consumer Satisfaction

Your ability to access consumer satisfaction can have a direct and almost immediate impact on the sales volume of your operation. To be beneficial, you need to continually monitor consumer satisfaction and use that information to plan and refocus your marketing efforts.

Consumers voice their comments in various ways: directly to you by way of the 800 telephone number on your package, to the employees of a retail operation, and to their friends and families. You can gather information and measure consumer satisfaction by encouraging oral interaction. You can also utilize comment cards.

Comment cards are useful, but they generally will not reflect the opinion of the vast majority of your customers. They are primarily used by the highly motivated customer who has something either very negative or very positive to say. They are usually placed inside a product's package. Comments are also transmitted to the manufacturer by way of an 800 telephone number printed on the package or container. However, surveys have shown that management response to resolving complaints on comment cards can produce positive results. More than 71 percent of all complainants are likely to tell others when their complaint was resolved by management. Likewise, more than 73 percent will tell others when their complaints were not resolved. As such, comment cards enable you to present a positive marketing ploy by showing that you care enough about what your customers think to provide a way for their opinions to be expressed.

Train your sales force to ask for comments from supermarket employees, the people who stock your products on the freezer shelves. Most will respond with some kind of comment, or simply say "everything is OK." If there is something wrong, whether you ask or not, the supermarket will eventually let you know. A dissatisfied customer (supermarket) will be more vocal in responding by stating what is wrong with your products, especially a new product introduction. Not responding to the negative situation immediately can only result in negative word-of-mouth advertising. Resolve the problem as soon as possible by offering the supermarket a replacement product, or an allowance to help promote it.

For operations that have a hotline (an 800 telephone number), the most effective way to deal with consumers is to immediately identify and respond to the problem in an manner that will satisfy the consumer. In most cases, the manufacturer's customer service representative will listen to the complaint and offer to send some kind of free coupon with a value close to the amount claimed by the consumer. And once you have actually gotten your product onto a supermarket's freezer shelf, you will have another source of information. All of the mass market chains have adopted a system called Efficient Consumer Response, which essentially acts as an electronic and automatic reorder system connected to check-out scanners. This system tells the chain how products are performing on a daily basis, and it is now a major tool used to get and keep supermarket freezer shelf space. Manufacturers are now using this information to monitor new product introductions and pricing so they can react promptly to the marketplace with changes in flavor profile, packaging and, pricing.

MERCHANDISING YOUR PRODUCTS

In the frozen dessert arena, there is no room for duplicate products. An ice cream retail product must offer something special to the consumer; it must have a unique selling point. Whether it is the product itself, the message on the package, the size of the package, or even the price, it all comes down to delivering something the consumer wants and, it is hoped, cannot get from your competitor.

A product concept is obviously only as good as the product being marketed. Of course, short-term results can be achieved for inferior products by using hyped-up promotion, but repeat long-term business can be assured only by providing a quality product. On the other hand, it is a misconception to think that a high-quality product will sell itself. If the public is unaware of its existence or of its quality characteristics, a product is doomed to failure So, how do you let the public know about the unique selling points of your products? The answer lies in merchandising, in providing your product with the capability of promoting itself through the astute use of branding, packaging, and pricing.

The Importance of Branding

Make no bones about it, branding works. It adds value to all kinds of products, and ice cream products are no exception. If a brand has a good reputation, a consumer will feel comfortable about trying a new product in that brand's line. Also, since people are afraid of what is going into their food products, they tend to trust a branded product over ones they do not know.

For a newcomer to become a successful brand, it goes without saying that a high-quality product is essential. The key is to make the consumer aware of the product and its attributes, to communicate information. In-store promotions work extremely well for the newcomer. And now, with the existence of the Internet, it is possible to offer all kinds of information about the company and its products, including nutritional information, recipes, and so on. A good example is Ben & Jerry's website, a world of knowledge generated right from the keyboard of the consumer's computer. Ben & Jerry's believes consumer awareness has increased brand loyalty.

Packaging

It may not be the most important thing—the product is—but the package is the first thing the customer sees. It is the first step in a product's sale. Even for repeat sales, if the customer does not remember the name, there is a good chance that he or she will recognize the package.

There's an old saying, "Don't judge a book by it's cover," but when making purchase decisions, consumers have little to go on other than the product's package. Therefore, marketers have learned that creative, colorful packaging that demands a second look is one of the most important marketing tools a product can have on its side.

Since ice cream packaging has always been evolutionary rather than revolutionary, packages must continually be focused as an effective marketing vehicle for today's consumer. Accordingly, new materials, labeling laws, and configurations, as well as vastly improved printing methods, have produced an endless array of new containers and graphics in the freezer case to meet today's needs.

Design   Every product line, new or overhauled, must convey a consistent simple message to the consumer. Without it, the line is sure to be doomed. Likewise, if your product packaging does not draw eye contact from the customer, then there is something wrong with the package. It is that clear and simple. Keep in mind the following points:

- *Brand Identity*. Recognize that package design is a critical part of a brand's identity. Do not assume the public knows who you are.
- *Message*. Do not make the package confusing. Be concise, and know what you want to say. Remember, everything on the package falls into various categories of information and levels of importance, but not every word is

"important." What is important on the package is your logo, name, product flavor (written and in pictorial form), and one or two of the product's health attributes, shown prominently.

- *Product Recognition.* Consumers see and purchase with their eyes. Product identification on the package must be bold. The graphics used must be able to communicate the quality and benefits of the product inside.
- *Brand Vision.* Communicate the brand vision, what it is that you want your brand to convey to consumers, with your package designer.
- *Consumer Preferences.* Stay in touch with the consumer.
- *Looking Ahead.* Stay ahead of the times. Know when to change your look. Ten years is about the longest period of time that a packaging style or theme will remain fresh.

Because children play such a major role in influencing a parent's purchase, products geared toward children should have package designs that appeal specifically to them. Kids love characters, so designs should be broadly broadcast to them with brightly colored backgrounds to maximize in-store impact.

And regardless of the targeted age group, color is a powerful tool. Packages need to be recognized, and one way to do that is through the use of colors. One thing you should never do is use colors that every other ice cream manufacturer is using. If you do, your package will dissolve into the crowd. Note the following psychological factors of color:

- Green is a warm and friendly color, and conveys a message of "good-for-you" regarding health, so you see more and more lowfat and nonfat frozen dessert products using this color in the supermarket.
- White generally signifies low in calories.
- Clear plastic or absence of color signifies purity.
- Gold or silver signifies upscale or premium.
- Yellow, orange and red are action colors that attract children and teenagers.
- Black and metallic are considered slick, modern colors.

Finally, packaging must be convenient for the retailer and, ultimately, for the consumer. If the manufacturer has an oversized package, the retailer must reconfigure an entire shelf to fit it in. For example, if the clearance on the shelf is set for half-gallon square box packaging, a round half-gallon package will bump into the lip and make restocking difficult.

Printing   The ice cream industry has come a long way with high-quality flexographic printing, a method of direct rotary printing using flexible rubber or photopolymer printing plates and fast-drying solvent or water-based inks. Chromaflex Pro has been developed by Sealright or Overland Park, Missouri. It is a newer type of flexography that uses process art (printing from a series of two or more halftone plates to produce intermediate colors and shades from yellow, megenta, cyan, and black) for the reproduction of continuous-tone images, such as illustrations or color transparencies and photographs. Another high-quality printing process is Ultra-Flex, which allows for near-perfect photographic printing on paper containers. Other container companies with quality printing capabilities are Airlite of Omaha, Nebraska, and Gen Pak of Toronto, Canada (See Figure 7-1).

There is no question that high-quality printing gives value to the product. When consumers look inside a freezer case, the sharply printed package stands out. Even if they are not familiar with the product or have never heard about it, they may pick it up anyway just because their eyes will be drawn to it.

FIGURE 7-1. GenPak ice cream plastic containers and lids (pints and quarts).

Product Labeling and the 1990 NLEA

With the growing awareness of nutrition and health considerations in food selection, "health-friendly" labels are becoming increasingly critical for a product's success. More and more consumers are reading labels. The 1990 Nutrition Labeling and Education Act (NLEA) drastically changed the packaging industry by putting into law the requirement that manufacturers properly inform consumers of the contents and nutritional elements of their products. Dealing with NLEA has now become a normal part of business, whether you are a small or big manufacturer. For small manufacturers, the process has been more difficult and challenging because they do not have the money or staff to deal with changing labels over and over again. So to make it work to their advantage, many have looked at relabeling as an opportunity to upgrade the entire look of their packaging as well. Being in compliance with the NLEA has meant huge changes for ice cream manufacturers across the board. Some changed their label nutrient label claims, while others reformatted products.

It is important that ice cream manufacturers understand the impact labels have had on consumers, and how labels and ingredient statements influence purchase decisions. One thing is certain, consumers are tired of health claims on packages that do not meet their expectations once the product has been purchased and consumed. Most consumers do read the nutrition labels for one reason or another. Even more important is that shoppers from more affluent households or those with family members on a medically restricted diet are always more likely to read labels.

Figure 7-2 is a sample of an NLEA-compliant nutritional label declaration for a premium ice cream (14-percent butterfat) pint package produced by the Anderson Erickson Dairy, Des Moines, Iowa. The following list is an item-by-item breakdown of that label.

Serving Size: expressed in common household units followed by the metric equivalent in grams or milliliters.

Servings per Container: expressed in whole numbers. For products that contain 2–5 servings per container, the number of servings may be expressed in half-serving increments. The use of the terms "approximately" or "about" are allowed to designate the number of servings per container if the number is not a whole number.

Amount per Serving: the amount of calories per serving and amount of calories from fat.

Calories: expressed as the number of calories per serving in 5-calorie increments up to 50 calories, and 10-calorie increments above 50 calories. Foods with fewer than 5 calories may be labeled as having 0 calories.

Calories from Fat: expressed in the same increments as described for calories. Foods with less than a half gram of fat per serving may express this value as zero. However, the phrase, "Not a significant source of calories from fat"

Nutrition Facts

Serving Size 1/2 Cup (102 GRAMS)
Servings Per Container 4

Amount Per Serving		
Calories 240	Calories from Fat 130	
	% Daily Values *	
Total Fat 15g		22%
Saturated Fat 9g		45%
Cholesterol 55g		18%
Sodium 55g		2%
Total Carbohydrate 23g		8%
Dietary Fiber 0g		0%
Sugars 23g		
Protein 4g		
Vitamin A 10%	Vitamin C 0%	
Calcium 10%	Iron 0%	

*Percent Daily Values are based on a 2,000
calorie diet. Your daily values may be higher
or lower depending on your calorie needs:

	Calorie: 2,000	2,500
Total fat	Less than 65g	80g
Sat fat	Less than 20g	25g
Cholesterol	Less than 300mg	300mg
Sodium	Less than 2,400mg	2,400mg
Total Carbohydrate	300g	375g
Dietary Fiber	25g	30g

Calories per gram
Fat 9 - Carbohydrate 4 - Protein 4

FIGURE 7-2. Sample nutritional statement for a pint container of 14-percent butterfat ice cream. (Courtesy of Anderson Erickson Dairy, Des Moines, Iowa.)

must appear below the line following the iron declaration. Calories from fat can be calculated by multiplying the grams of fat per serving by 9.

Total Fat: a statement of the number of grams of fat per serving expressed in half-gram increments below 3 grams of fat per serving and in 1-gram increments above that level. Foods with less than a half gram of fat per serving may be labeled as zero.

Saturated Fat: the number of grams of saturated fatty acids per serving in half-gram increments. Foods with less than a half gram of saturated fat per serving may be declared zero saturated fat if no claims for fat or cholesterol are made.

Cholesterol: expressed in milligrams of cholesterol per serving in 5-milligram increments. Foods with fewer than 2 milligrams per serving may express the cholesterol content as zero if no claims are made regarding fat, fatty acids, or cholesterol. If the food does not normally contain cholesterol, the statement "Not a significant source of cholesterol" shall be placed below the line following the iron declaration.

Sodium: expressed as milligrams of sodium per serving. Fewer than 5 milligrams per serving can be labeled as zero, while values above that figure must appear in 5-milligram increments up to 140 milligrams, and 10-milligram increments above that figure. The daily value for sodium is fewer than 2,400 milligrams.

Total Carbohydrate: states the number of grams of carbohydrate per serving expressed to the nearest gram. If the serving contains less than 1 gram, the term "Less than 1 g" may be used. Foods with less than a half gram may be labeled as zero.

Dietary Fiber: the number of grams of total dietary fiber contained in each serving portion of food expressed to the nearest gram.

Sugars: must be expressed in grams per serving to the nearest gram. Foods containing less than a half gram may be declared zero. If the food contains less than 1 gram of sugar, the statement, "Not a significant source of sugar" shall be placed below the line following the iron declaration.

Protein: expressed to the nearest gram per serving.

Vitamin A: expressed as a percentage of the recommended daily intake of 500 IU.

Vitamin C: expressed as the percentage of the recommended daily intake of 60 milligrams contained in a serving of the product.

Calcium: expressed as the percentage of the recommended daily intake of 1,000 milligrams contained in a serving of the product.

Iron: expressed as the percentage of the recommended daily intake of 18 milligrams contained in a serving of the product.

Daily Value Basis: the asterisked statement explaining the basis for the Daily Values listed in the top portion of the label. The Daily Values are now calculated on a 2,000 calorie per day basis.

Calories per Gram: a statement of the number of calories per gram of fat, carbohydrate, and protein in the product.

Pricing

There is no such thing as a standard for pricing supermarket ice cream packaged goods. What is known and accepted is that by the time a product reaches the consumer, it is likely to sell for between double and triple the routine production cost. That means that retailers, distributors, and other players eventually earn most of the spread between the production cost and the ultimate selling price to the consumer. In most instances, the retailer will mark up the product by 35–100 percent more than the price for which it was purchased. While the retailer is marking up the product, the distributor is working on a margin, not a mark-up. These two words, "margin" and "mark-up" do not mean the same thing. Margin is the percentage of the selling price that the gross profit is, while mark-up is the percentage of the cost that the gross profit is. Most distributors work on margins of 20–30 percent of the price at which they sell a product to a retailer.

Extremely critical is the calculation of how these terms determine the end price. For example:

Ice Cream Pint

Manufacturer's cost	$.65 cents, a mark-up of 85%, a margin of 45%
Sold to a distributor from manufacturer	$1.20, a margin of 25%
Retailer purchases from distributor	$1.60, a margin of 30%
Consumer's cost	$2.29

It is particularly important for the manufacturer to know these costs and profit margins in advance, because the manufacturer must make sure its cost is in a pricing range that will enable everyone handling the product (distributor and retailer) to feel comfortable knowing that they will be able to make a profit. With this information, the manufacturer can plan for a cost-efficient introduction of a new product. Equally important, this analysis helps the marketing people to do a better job of bringing the product to the marketplace more competitively against a similar brand's product.

GAINING PRODUCT EXPOSURE

You have an idea, your people are excited about it, and you have completed your product development work. Through consumer research, you know the public is inclined to like the type of product you will be launching. Now the questions are:

- How do we get it to market?
- How do we get consumers excited about it?
- How do we get initial product exposure for it?

These are questions marketing people deal with every day, and the answers are simply that they must make sure the product's marketing plan is understood and implemented. Besides developing all the needed packaging, point-of-purchase, and advertising plans, there are several effective ways to get initial exposure:

- Plan to have a media blitz that incorporates sending out press releases and samples to food critics of every newspaper, magazine, television/radio station in your selling area.

- Bring product samples to supermarket managers and the heads of their freezer department in every supermarket in your selling area.
- Introduce the new product at trade shows. Trade shows are a wonderful opportunity to get exposure. You are able to sample and introduce the product to a lot of people in a very short amount of time, and you will get an instant response as to whether the product is good or bad. Trade shows can be great confidence builders for any new product.

Trade Shows

Presenting, demonstrating, and sampling a product at a trade show can be an excellent means of exposure. The first time you exhibit can be daunting, but, like setting sail in unfamiliar waters, it is often the only way to find new territory. Imagine an adventure that could:

- Give you a better understanding of how good your products are.
- In a short period of time, enable you to meet a vast number of people (brokers, distributors, supermarket buyers) interested in purchasing your products.

To effectively exhibit in a trade show, you need to develop a trade show marketing plan. This plan is not an operational plan that outlines all the show's logistical details. It is not about how much electrical wiring you need, the color of your carpeting, or how many people you need to staff the show. Instead, the trade show marketing plan is about big-picture thinking. For example, you need to think about how trade shows fit within the corporate strategy. If your brand is under a large corporate umbrella, make sure that it does not get lost at a trade show where the corporate logo physically overshadows the booth. Allow specific kiosk space within the booth so the brand can stand on its own, and have the personnel available who are knowledgeable enough to explain to potential supermarket store buyers exactly what the product is and what it can do in relation to sales in the marketplace.

Consider also that today business communication between companies is faster than ever, but to a large extent the human touch is gone. Computers, the telephone, faxing, E-mail and the Internet control how people talk to each other and how business is conducted. The trade show, however, allows you to get in touch with actual human beings. In a sense it is networking at its best. Having that viewpoint when planning a trade show emphasizes its capability for allowing your personnel to meet and talk in person to those who otherwise are just voices on the other end of the telephone line.

And if your company does business on a worldwide basis, make sure you plan your trade show booth to promote this strategy. Encourage your staff to spend time with foreign visitors explaining to them your product line and how you can do business with them. If you have a large overseas distributor network, bring them to the trade show to help represent your company. Their addition to your booth will reinforce your international corporate strategy in a big way.

Mission Statement   The first thing you should do as you develop your trade show marketing plan is to define your objectives (e.g., getting as much company and product awareness and exposure as possible within the confines of the trade show booth) in a simple but comprehensive mission statement. This is especially important for a new company just getting off the ground. Having the mission statement in place will enable you to refer back to it for a reality check. Following is a example of one:

> The long-term objectives of the trade show program are to support new product introductions and increase market penetration for existing products by promoting to targeted audiences and generating qualified sales.

Market Analysis: The Overview   Doing a market analysis will help you define what is going on in the market and how your product or product lines are likely to be received at the show. This is especially important if you are exhibiting a number of lines within the same trade show space.

Self- and Competitor Analysis   If you seriously conduct an analysis to find out your strengths and weaknesses as compared to your competition, then you can use that information to get the most out of the money spent to set up a trade show exhibit. Ask yourself the following questions:

- Who are our competitors?
- Which of them exhibit in the same kind of shows that we do?
- How does their size space compare to ours?
- How does our exhibit space differ from theirs?
- How do show attendees react to our exhibit space?
- Are our employees who work these shows customer friendly?
- What single strength do our competitors have over us at trade shows?
- What is our goals at these shows? Do we want to create awareness for our products or do we want to just sell products right off the floor?

The answers will enable you to focus on what your trade show marketing plan has to accomplish.

Developing the Trade Show Strategy   After you have identified your objectives, spend time thinking about translating the objectives into strategies for the trade show function. If you are a national company, consider the following:

- Use national shows to gain broad awareness and recruit distributors.
- Use regional shows to establish relationships and gain credibility.

- Place product in the exhibits of strategic partners all around the hall.
- Have both sales and product development personnel staffing the booths.
- Promote shows aggressively, using familiar advertising themes that people connect with you.
- Implement a comprehensive lead follow-up program.

The lead follow-up program is probably the most important function and one that is often overlooked. What is the point of spending all your money and personnel time at trade shows if you do not follow up on the leads generated? Equally important is the time spread between the end of the show and the time a lead is contacted or provided with samples. The shorter the spread, the more you will get out of the lead.

Resources Required By including an estimate of the resources required in your trade show marketing plan, you clearly explain what you need to implement the strategies and plans you have made. Such a listing gives you an opportunity to gain buy-in for your needs right from the start, which is one of the major benefits of creating the plan in the first place.

Conclusion Whether you are an exhibitor or visitor, trade shows offer big and small companies alike the opportunity to learn what is happening in the industry. To a newcomer, they can be mindboggling, but the benefit of the learning experience cannot be overstated. Every industry magazine lists upcoming trade shows well in advance of the events. Plan to attend as many as possible.

Brokers and Distributors

As is the case with many other food products, ice cream distribution is dependent on the size of the manufacturer. The larger the organization, the more likely it will be to do its own distribution, called DSD (direct store distribution). The theory behind DSD is to be as close to the consumer as possible. That means delivering direct to a supermarket with the driver placing the product directly onto the assigned space inside the freezer compartment. This approach allows the company to know firsthand what is and what is not selling. Also, a good driver will get to know the freezer manager, which helps incredibly in keeping good relations with the supermarket. Another function of DSD is carrying products from small manufacturers who do not have a distribution system in place, thus filling the truck to capacity and enabling small manufacturers to get into a supermarket by means of a "piggyback ride" instead of trying to find a distributor.

While most major ice cream manufacturers do distribute their own products in the big metropolitan areas, the large majority of distribution is eventually handled by distributors. While some distributors will also sell and market products, their main function is to take and deliver orders from the retailers they serve. Therefore, a product typically needs to have earned some level of demand before a distributor is likely to take it on.

For a small manufacturer, finding a distributor is difficult. The only real way to connect with a distributor and create interest is to show them that you have a product that sells. That usually means distributing your own products until you have built up a customer base that, it is hoped, will spark someone's interest. It is like handing a distributor a silver platter of goodies, your customer list. The most important thing to distributors is how much money can be made handling your product line. With your customer list in their hands, they know they will make money from the start.

Another way of attracting a distributor is through trade shows. If you exhibit in a show, brokers and distributors come to you, but the hard part is consummating the deal after the show to turn interest into reality. At the trade show, have a sign that announces "Distributor's Inquiries Welcomed."

Food brokers can also be major players in the marketing process. While they neither purchase nor distribute products, brokers act as manufacturers representatives to retailers and distributors within a predetermined area. A broker is paid through a sales commission earned from the manufacturer. Typically, these commissions range from 10 percent to 15 percent on continuing direct sales to a supermarket, and closer to 5 percent on sales to distributors. The biggest drawback for most new ice cream manufacturers dealing with brokers is that early sales are not likely to generate commissions high enough to support the broker's efforts. Most brokers and distributors will ask for exclusive territorial rights to represent a manufacturer's product.

DEALING WITH THE SUPERMARKET ENVIRONMENT

Doing business today is a lot different than it was even as little as 5 or 10 years ago. Changing lifestyles along with a vast disparity in buying patterns between families and single consumers have drastically affected how products are presented, packaged, and purchased. Competition between supermarket chains is very aggressive, and the appearance of club stores has forced traditional retailers to become more price conscious than ever.

So, once you have gotten your product onto a supermarket freezer shelf, what can you do to ensure its salability within that environment? There are many ways, but one in particular deserves special mention here: fostering a relationship between the delivery driver and the supermarket. If you, as the manufacturer, are supportive of the job the delivery driver does, you can be assured that the driver will attend to the freezer section in which your product is placed with care and concern. After all, it is the driver who is going to be filling up the freezer shelf with new product, removing damaged packages, and cleaning up the shelf to make it look presentable. And such a driver will be in a good position to keep you informed about what is happening with your product, through both personal observation and feedback from store personnel.

Product Display

Aside from attention-grabbing packaging to entice impulse purchases and maintaining a consistently high-quality product to encourage repeat purchases, keep in mind that stocking and displays are key to increased sales. There is a science to product positioning, often referred to as shelf planning or slotting. Marketers say that anything below 18 inches from the floor is dead space. Products displayed there simply do not get noticed, and people are reluctant to bend down to reach an item. Try to have your pints and half-gallons displayed at adult eye-level in the freezer case. Novelties intended to appeal to children should be at the lowest level for easy viewing.

And, while some people may call it bribery even though it is legal, you should be aware of the existence of slotting fees. These are amounts of money paid by manufacturers for the right to stock products on supermarkets' shelves. The term "slot" originated when computers were first used to develop a slot for the product in the warehouse. It was so expensive to put the information into the computer that the supermarkets began charging a fee for this work. Many manufacturers blame slotting for both driving up the prices of products already on the shelves and keeping products on the shelves even though they are not selling.

Just getting your product onto the shelf and in the best position is not the end of the story. The condition of the freezer also plays an important role in affecting sales. Freezers are expensive to purchase and operate and they are difficult to maintain. So you need to be vigilant to make sure you get good visual presentation of your product. If the freezer is not maintained just right, glass misting, condensation, frost, and freeze-over can occur, obscuring even the most eye-catching packaging. Also, retailers tend to put too much product on the shelves. A typical freezer may be designed to hold forty facings, but the freezer manager may try to put in fifty. The freezer becomes cluttered and everything is not properly faced-up. As a result, the customer cannot see what is inside without rummaging through the case, adding to the chaos. Ultimately, sales are affected.

When problems like this exist, it is up to the delivery driver to address them with the freezer department manager. If the relationship is a good one, there should be no problem getting results. So, be supportive of your delivery drivers, because they are an integral part of the success of your products' sales.

"Pop" Your Way To More Sales

Want to sell more ice cream products to supermarket chains and specialty grocers? One way to do it is through "point-of-purchase" (POP) displays. Here are a few tips to steer you in the right direction.

Separate your product's shelf display from the competition. Use attractive branded freezer plastic shelf separation sleeves to have a break point between different branded products.

Provide information about your product. Even if not read on site, product information is essential in establishing consumer confidence in your product. It can easily be placed next to or on the freezer case.

Promote "demand merchandise." Products that sell the most should be promoted the most. This is done effectively with attractive aisle or static cling signs touting selection. These signs stand out and offer a visual draw from the customer to the freezer door. Promoting a bad product will be a waste of money because the public is not stupid, and it will eventually backfire on the manufacturer.

Take advantage of traffic patterns. Position your POP to make full use of customer traffic patterns. Try to get a supermarket to position your own branded freezer near the checkout counter. The closer you are to the cash register, the more sales you will get. You would be surprised how much money customers will spend for anything near the register line.

Promote through the eye. Use eye-catching signs on the POP display. There are many innovative merchandising pieces you can use to attract attention, from freezer clings and shelf talkers, (a promotional device that fits in the molding or price rail of a shelf) to suction-cup danglers. Much of the problem with current POP displays is that they simply are not visible from far enough away. This may be due to poor positioning where the customer's line of sight is blocked by other merchandise. More often, the problem is that the signage is not attractive or bright enough.

Highlight specials. Use POPs to promote a special price offering for your products. Price promotions at specific times of the year are effective, especially during major holidays. The key to price promotions is to entice trial. While this strategy can be expensive, the rewards are worth it, especially if the product truly tastes great. It will invite repeat business. (Keep in mind, though, that if your product is not up to snuff, a price promotion can work against you in that the customer will never purchase your product again.) A price special merits its own POP display, not something altered to meet an immediate need.

Sample, Sample, and Sample Some More

Time has proven that point-of-sale sampling with the manufacturer present tends to be the most effective means of selling a new product in any given retail outlet. Doing tastings is also helpful to a manufacturer's understanding of who the ultimate customers are and what they want in a product. The product used for sampling is typically at the manufacturer's rather than at the retailer's expense. It will educate the consumer about who you are and what you are offering. It is not the retailer's job to promote, it is yours. It is the manufacturer who has to get the product into the customer's mouth, and the best way to do that is through sampling.

Ice cream demonstrations (demo) do have some pitfalls. Unless the customer is going directly home, he or she will not be affected by an impulse buying opportunity. Most people wait until they are done shopping to go to the ice cream freezer because they do not want their ice cream to melt. So it is hard to judge the success of a ice cream demo by daily sales volume. Ultimately, what you want to do is to plant a seed that may come to fruition at another time or place.

If you demo your products every weekend, you will see sales jump. Park the sampler in front of the freezer case in which your products can be found. Offer a special deal on your products during the demo ("Buy One, Get One Free" works especially well).

Supermarket Employees

Another boost for sales can come about when supermarket employees like a product enough to personally recommend it to customers. Where such recommendations actually occur, a new product is almost assured of enjoying some initial sales. It is strongly advised that both the manufacturer and distributor of a product get to know these employees on a first-name basis. That one-on-one contact is worth as much as the dollars spent on media advertising.

PITFALLS TO AVOID

In today's marketplace, most ice cream manufacturers develop products and flavors with only two things in mind: to expand market share or to protect what they already have. In developing a new product or flavor, manufacturers should never fall in love with the idea so easily as to end up losing sight of what they were really trying to accomplish in the first place, that is, to get the product introduced, priced right, and accepted by the public.

By placing close attention to the following common pitfalls, you can find the path of least resistance to bring a new product to market.

- *Overlooking Weak Signals.* Though they may be just a small blip on your screen, subtle signals for concern should not be ignored or rationalized too readily in the early product distribution stage. Listen very carefully to what freezer managers have to say about your product. They know better than anybody what is selling at any given time.
- *Overreliance on Market Research.* Both manufacturers and retailers rely too much on market research and not enough on common sense. What sells in New York might not sell as well in Des Moines. Marketing people tend to look at numbers as a whole and forget the importance of regional tastes.
- *Overpricing.* To a large extent, the size of the package dictates its price. This is especially true with single-serve products such as novelties. When a product becomes a luxury, and not a regular purchase, you are in trouble. Manufacturers in particular tend to think that their products are worth

more than what the public is willing to spend, resulting in unrealistic pricing right down the line to the ultimate consumer.

- *Unrealistic Optimism.* Do not get too excited during a launch. Success can only be gauged during the second, third, and fourth reordering cycles.

REFERENCES

Anderson, Peggy. 1996. New product roulette, there's no sure thing. *Dairy Foods*, October, pp. 60–68.

Chadbourne, Brian. 1996. 10 Lessons learned the hard way. *Prepared Foods Magazine*, January, p. 25.

Doeff, Gail. 1996. Reach out and grab someone. *Dairy Foods*, April, pp. 74–76.

Gerson, Vicki. 1993. Packages that pop. *Dairy Field*, January, pp. 46–50.

Gorski, Donna. 1994. Packaging trends. *Dairy Foods*, January, pp. 66–69.

Gorski, Donna. 1996. NLEA, one year later. *Dairy Foods*, May, pp. 31–32.

Keebner, Kami. 1993. Package wonders. *Dairy Field*, November, pp. 46–51.

Kuhn, Mary Ellen. 1996. In-store marketing innovation. *Food Processing*, April, pp. 26–28.

Leighton, Peter. 1994. Working your freezer for better sales. *Health Foods Business*, July, p. 29.

Lewis, Robert C., and Susan V. Morris. nd. The positive side of guest complaints. *The Cornell Hotel and Restaurant Association Quarterly*, vol. 27, no. 4, p. 14.

Mans, Jack. 1993. Tuning the package at both ends. *Dairy Foods*, January, pp. 58–59.

Mans, Jack. 1996. All packages great and small. *Dairy Foods*, January, pp. 72–76.

Mans, Jack. 1996. Keep it running. *Dairy Foods*, April, pp. 72–79.

Morrow, Paula. 1996. Destination Known. Mapping out an exhibit marketing plan: A three-step approach. *Exhibitor*, October, pp. 22–27.

Perry, Philip M. 1995. How to "POP" your way to more sales. *Health Food Business*, September, pp. 68–70.

Plant Operations Application. 1994. *Dairy Foods*, January, pp. 74–76.

Reiter, Jeff, 1993. Green crusader. *Dairy Foods*, July, pp. 67–69.

Slagle, Jake Denzer. 1995. To market, To market. *Food Distribution Magazine*, February, pp. 19–44.

Starr, Peter, and Sara Starr. 1996. Frozen foods: Determining their profitability. *Health Food Business*, February, pp. 28–32.

A RETAIL FROZEN DESSERT BUSINESS

⊠⊠⊠⊠⊠⊠⊠⊠⊠⊠⊠⊠⊠⊠⊠⊠⊠⊠⊠⊠⊠⊠⊠⊠

8

⊠⊠⊠⊠⊠⊠⊠⊠⊠⊠⊠⊠⊠⊠⊠⊠⊠⊠⊠⊠⊠⊠⊠⊠

OPENING A
RETAIL FROZEN
DESSERT BUSINESS

Why would anyone want to own and operate a business, let alone a retail frozen dessert business? Certainly there are as many reasons as there are owners, but some of the most obvious include making a profit, achieving a sense of accomplishment, and being your own boss. Regardless of the reasons, owning and operating any kind of business is a challenge, and it can be enjoyable too.

CHOOSING THE RETAIL FROZEN DESSERT BUSINESS

The introduction of superpremium ice cream in the mid-1970s, and its enthusiastic acceptance by consumers, revived the ice cream industry in general and the ice cream retail dipping shop in particular. Today, both the industry and the shops are as vibrant as ever. While the demand today is different than that of the 1970s, consumers still want products that are high quality and innovative, whether they range from the high fat ice creams to no fat, no cholesterol fruit sorbets.

A retail frozen dessert shop is a niche business. It will provide you with the opportunity to use your creativity and imagination in preparing new products and flavors, which can be personally satisfying if you are so inclined. At the same time, you are offering products that can instantly satisfy a customer's craving, and so you are making other people happy as well. And because so many people have a sweet tooth to be satisfied, there is good potential for profit in the business. The variation in the industry spawned by changing tastes and health consciousness of consumers has created an atmosphere of growth and opportunity.

Ice cream and other frozen desserts are not complex products. Building a new store or expanding to a second or third location is not nearly as difficult as, for example, constructing and operating a restaurant or a restaurant chain. An ice cream store today includes many products usually centered around ice cream, sorbet, and frozen yogurt, the leading sellers in the business. When people ask me why I chose selling ice cream over, for example, operating a restaurant, I simply tell them it is more fun, causes fewer headaches, and has no grease.

The advantages of being in the retail frozen dessert business includes the following:

- For a small frozen dessert business that makes it own products, there is a faster return on investment over a shorter period of time, because being both the producer and seller of a product allows for a higher profit margin.
- Once you are into retailing your own products, it is easier to break into wholesale to increase sales and garner market share because capital requirements are then next to nothing.
- It is a people-oriented business, so you can enjoy working with the public.

The disadvantages include:

- It is labor intensive and good help can be hard to find.
- Most retail businesses have long hours and are open 7 days a week, 12 months a year.
- There is usually a lot of responsibility for a single proprietor.
- It is a people-oriented business, and you might not have the personality for dealing with customers on a daily basis.

It may sound silly, but without an initial dream and the passion to pursue it, none of us who have been around for awhile would have had that first store. But as important as dreams are, there is reality to contend with. Simply put, have passion for the idea, but don't fall in love with the dream. Consider your dreams as a general concept. Be willing to change and adapt to fit the market. And, most important, take your time and do your research properly. If you have the dream of opening a retail frozen dessert shop, the following questions must be addressed early on in your research:

- Where do you want the store located?
- What size should it be?
- How are you going to work the store? Are you going to be present to manage the store yourself or just be an absentee owner? (I have rarely seen a successful ice cream store that was run by absentee owner.)
- What is the profit potential?

Considering Business Conditions

A concept will work only if business conditions related to your specific choices are conducive for success. One advantage of any frozen dessert business is that sales are good in recessions as well as in prosperous economic times. People crave sweets and are often impulsive in satisfying that craving regardless of economic conditions. Ice cream and other frozen desserts contain sugar and are not high-priced products. The cost of an ice cream cone is not something people spend a lot of time thinking about. On the other hand, during recessions people will think twice about spending $75 for a dinner for two.

Business conditions and the market you are trying to reach go hand in hand, however. You would be foolish to market a high-priced product in an economically depressed community. Every product has a price barrier and you must make sure not to go beyond that limit for your intended market.

Asking suppliers in the industry how operations similar to yours are doing is a good idea, as well as asking other merchants and manufacturers themselves.

Because consumers think of ice cream and frozen desserts as warm weather treats, the notion is that business is best during the summer. While this notion is generally true, it is inaccurate to assume that warm weather itself stimulates the most business. In the United States, warm weather states do no more business than do states in the northeast and north central parts of the country (IICA, 1995, p. 18).

However, areas where the weather is cyclical are excellent places for frozen dessert operations. The change from cold to warm weather does bring people out for impulse buying. Periods of constantly hot weather, as in Florida or Texas, result in strong sales in supermarkets but weak sales in dip shops. Statistics show that May through August are prime months for shop sales in the northeast, while February, March, November, December, and January are good sales months in the south (IICA, 1995, p. 23).

You should note that seasonal business is usually good from an employee-hiring standpoint because it is difficult to get student help (which is low cost) during the winter or school months.

The timing of your opening can play a major role in your success or failure. The best time of year to open a retail business is February or early March, just before the spring selling season and just after the slowest sales months of the year (December and January) (IICA, 1995, p. 23). Most new operations take at least three full months of construction for building or renovating, and almost every new retail business is late opening for one reason or another. So, planning is extremely important to allow for contingencies. You should figure on beginning construction in September or October of the year preceding your planned opening.

Refining the Idea

Every operation begins with an idea, a concept, a mental image, and even a dream. Ideas take time to evolve, sometimes months or years, and the process will take many paths. In most cases, original thoughts will be dramatically different from the final version.

Visit as many ice cream manufacturers and retail shops as you can. Trips to different parts of the country, and even throughout the world, will turn up many variations of your own idea and will be worth the time and effort. Do not be intimidated by your lack of knowledge. Ask questions of people in the business. They will generally answer if they feel you are not a threat to their own business. Be honest with them and you will be amazed at the help you will receive. Best of all, this advice is free.

Trade shows (gatherings of suppliers to display their wares) can be gold mines of information. The people at these shows will be happy to answer your questions. They know that some day you might be one of their customers. Go to these shows and gather as much information as you can. Major dairy trade journals, such as, *Dairy Foods, Dairy Field, The National Dipper*, and *SDI* (Scandinavian Dairy Information) include lists of all regional, national, and international trade shows. You can also ask any potential supplier for recommendations about which shows are worthwhile.

In case you are thinking about taking over an existing business, you should be aware of the pros and cons of such a move. The most significant advantage of doing so is in knowing what you are getting. You will be able to examine existing sales and expense records and determine if a profit is being made. On the other hand, if the business has been run down, you may need to invest a considerable amount of money for repairs and renovations. The biggest disadvantage in buying such an operation is that it is always more difficult to rebuild an image than to develop a new one.

Deciding to Make or Buy the Product

Whether or not you are going to make your own ice cream is a decision that will influence the path your concept takes. The subject is complex and the ramifications of operating a business based on either option requires that you understand what it takes to operate each. The best thing to do is visit ice cream manufacturers and retail shops that are run both ways and take a good look at the differences and similarities of each.

If you decide to make your own product, you will have to prepare a product list of what you want to sell. (Selecting products and flavors to make is one of the most enjoyable aspects of the business because of the research involved, such as traveling to other dairies, ice cream manufacturers, and retail shops for taste-testing.) The quality of your own products is usually superior to a ready-made product, and the costs are less in many cases. Most frozen dairy desserts have a large profit margin. The costs of ingredients and ice cream mix and the percentage of air pumped into the finished product (overrun) vary, depending on the quality level of your product. Buying a finished product from a dairy is more expensive for a shop owner because of the dairy's overhead, delivery costs, advertising expenses, and profit margin.

At first look, then, it would seem that the main reason for making your own product is profit. But years of experience have shown me that the real reason is having control over the quality of the product. You share what you sell with the public. If your goals are long term, you should seriously consider making your own product instead of selling someone else's. You can make the best ice cream in town for the same cost as purchasing the cheapest ice cream from a dairy.

You should not be intimidated by the fear of failure or by a lack of knowledge. Certainly, there are difficulties at the start and costs are high because of having to buy equipment and ingredients. You will need help in learning how to use the equipment and in developing flavor recipes, but getting such help is not as difficult as it may seem. Equipment manufacturers, ingredient and mix companies, consultants, seminars, and books can get you started on the right path.

So why would anyone choose to sell someone else's finished product? For many, an ice cream shop is operated as a secondary source of income, with absentee ownership, as a franchise of a major chain. Other attractions for buying a finished product include knowing beforehand the cost of a uniform product and a low labor factor for the daily operation of the business. Also fear of the unknown and not fully understanding the real costs and opportunities involved keeps many people from making their own products.

Can My Shop Support the Investment of Purchasing Ice Cream Production Equipment?

If you expect your first store to do more than $200,000 a year in sales, purchasing a batch freezer and making your own product will save you an amount equivalent to 10–15 percent of ingredient costs (see the following section on the costs of making your own ice cream). Based on a sales volume of $200,000, the costs for purchasing a finished product from an established ice cream manufacturer will be 28–35 percent of sales, depending on the butterfat content and quality of the product purchased. Using a 30-percent cost factor for purchasing a finished product versus 18 percent for producing your own, a savings of $24,000 a year (without allowing for the labor costs) may be possible.

To make your own products on a small scale, you need a batch ice cream freezer, a blast freezer, a large table, and approximately 150–250 square feet of additional space in your shop. (If you are making frozen desserts for a restaurant operation, even less space is needed.) Batch freezers are the equipment that actually makes the product and they are manufactured in sizes with capacity to produce 10, 20, or 40 quarts at a time. They come with either one or two speeds. Depending on the manufacturer, a single speed can be used for high or low overrun. Two-speed machines are capable of accomplishing both and are recommended for flexibility in producing various qualities. Blast freezers are used to maintain temperatures of −25 degrees Fahrenheit and are available in either single- or double-door models. Installing a walk-in freezer is an option for larger operations. For more details about equipment, see Chapters 1 and 2.

What about Ingredient Costs? By totaling the ingredient and labor costs of producing your own ice cream and comparing those costs to the selling price of the product, you can establish a food cost percentage. A single ice cream cone selling for $1.50 will have a cost of 35 cents based on a final cost of $5.00 per gallon to produce the ice cream (see the example following), or a 19–21 percent food cost for the retailer. If the ice cream is purchased from a distributor and not produced by the retailer, the cost increases to 25–33 percent. The 6–12 percent difference is due to the distributor's profit mark-up and delivery charges. That difference is considerable and it is magnified with increased volume. For example, on a business grossing $400,000, the food cost of producing your own is approximately $80,000 as compared with about $120,000 for purchasing a finished product. When you consider the depreciation of the production equipment, the profits on making your own become even larger.

The fact is, a high-quality ice cream can be produced at the same cost as purchasing a finished product of lower quality. In terms of butterfat, a 16-percent butterfat ice cream can be produced for the same cost as buying a 12-percent finished product. The cost of a single batch of 5 gallons of finished product at 100-percent overrun can be figured as follows:

French Vanilla Ice Cream

Ice cream mix, 16% butterfat, 2½ gallons	$15.75
Vanilla extract, two-fold, 4 ounces	2.40
Egg base, 16 ounces	1.25
Labor	3.50
Overhead	1.00
Amortization of equipment	1.00
Total	$24.90

This cost breaks down to about $5.00 a gallon for producing a high-quality 16-percent butterfat product versus buying an economy grade 12-percent product from a dairy for about the same price.

The construction of a production room, and the total cost of purchasing the initial inventory of ingredients and equipment will add about $35,000 to the price of setting up your retail operation. The cost of a batch freezer ranges from $12,500 for a very small 20-quart model to at least $18,500 for a large 40-quart machine. Figure $1,000 for electrical and plumbing work to install the machine. Plan on at least $4,500 for one double-door blast freezer, $2,500 for one double-door storage freezer, and $2,000 for one two-door refrigerator. A 6-foot table and wire racks are needed for work areas and storage. The initial purchase of ingredients and other start-up supplies will run at least $4,000. And there are always some miscellaneous costs.

An average business doing in excess of $200,000 a year will recoup this initial investment in approximately 18 months or two summer seasons.

A PLAN OF ACTION

Devising a plan of action is very important. It will enable you to think clearly and avoid many of the most common start-up mistakes entrepreneurs usually make.

1. *Rushing into business.* Take your time. If a decision is right today, it should be right two months from now.

2. *Picking a second-best location.* Do not settle for a location because it is cheaper in rent. The retail ice cream shop business is an impulse business. You need to be where there is traffic, and a secondary location usually means less traffic. Do your homework. It is the most important decision you will have to make.

3. *Spending no time surveying your potential location.* You must spend at least two weeks surveying your potential location. That means standing in front of it and watching people walk and drive by. Who are your neighbors? Will they help or hinder your future business? You simply cannot guess about being comfortable with the site.

4. *Writing a business plan just to raise money.* Most business plans are written to raise money, which, in my opinion, is the wrong reason. I constantly tell people to write their business plans to answer the most important question of all: Do they have passion for their idea? Writing the plan will also force you to learn about every aspect of this new proposed business venture. If your passion is solid, then the plan will ultimately convey that message.

5. *Falling in love with your idea.* Yes, you need to initially fall in love with your idea, but what is important is what is left after the romance is gone.

6. *Hiring an outsider to write your business plan.* You can have someone advise you, but you must write the plan yourself. Anyone else has all to gain, and nothing to lose.

7. *Being undercapitalized.* Undercapitalization dooms most new businesses in the first two years of operation. It will cost approximately $100–125 per square foot to build a retail frozen dessert store with new equipment.

8. *Spending all your cash before your first season is even over.* An extension of undercapitalization, having a shortage of operating cash is a surefire road to disaster. Remember, after the summer ends, there will still be bills to pay, especially rent and taxes.

9. *Ignoring the competition.* Most new entrepreneurs think they are better than the competition, and so can ignore them. This is a very big mistake!

10. *Inflating sales projections.* Be realistic in what sales projections are possible to achieve, especially during the first two years. Be conservative in your thinking. It is better to overachieve, than underachieve.

A Market Survey

If you decide to pursue the idea of a frozen dessert business, you will need to conduct a market survey. A market survey is an objective analysis of a particular site and its surroundings with regard to the feasibility of locating a business there. You will not get financing from a bank or any other lending institution without it.

You should have another person conduct the survey with you because objectivity is extremely important; personal emotions must not enter into it.

Many diverse details, such as competition, location traffic flow, and economic activity, must be considered. When conducting a market survey, get answers for the following questions:

Location: Does your idea make sense for the location you are seeking; that is, does it provide enough exposure to the public? Can the operation be open year round or must be seasonal? Is there room for expansion? (This point is particularly important if you plan to go into wholesale manufacturing at a later time.)

Competition: Is there any other frozen dessert competition (shop, cafe, gourmet shop, restaurant) in the area?

Access: Will your customers be able to find you? How far will they have to travel to reach you? Is there sufficient parking in a lot or on the street? Do enough people pass by your location to provide a potential customer base?

Population: Is there a large enough population in the area to support the business?

Economic conditions: Is the area stable or growing? (If neither, discount it as a potential site.) Is your concept compatible with the income level of the area? (Obviously, an upscale business will fail in a low-income area.)

Zoning regulations and taxes: Is the area restrictive for a retail or manufacturing business?

Record your observations in writing. Take many pictures. The notes and photos will become invaluable in helping your concept to take a concrete shape. Make a drawing, no matter how rough, of what you think your place of business should look like.

Then ask yourself another series of questions:

- Shall I have a retail operation, or could I survive as only a wholesale or manufacturing operation?
- Shall I sell only ice cream or frozen yogurt, or shall I have a full-line frozen dessert shop?

- Shall I serve other food as well?
- Do I really want to be in the frozen dessert business?

Talk about your thoughts with family and friends. Their objectivity combined with the answers you have already gathered will help to give your concept direction.

A Pro Forma Statement

Whether you already have or will need to acquire the capital to start the business, you will need to prepare a business plan or a pro forma statement (see Figure 8-1) to help you determine if your idea has merit and to make the financial decisions necessary to proceed with your concept.

Such a statement is a projection of sales, expenses, and cash flow over a certain period of time, usually a year or two, and should be formulated with the help of an accountant. You should remember, though, that it is only a calculated analysis of anticipated revenue and expenses, and that future events can render the entire analysis worthless. However, such a guide is an absolute necessity and cannot be ignored simply because of future uncertainties.

It is difficult to project sales for a new operation, but accurate projections can be made for certain expenses, such as rent and insurance. Other expenses such as utilities, payroll, taxes, and the cost of dairy and other supplies will run close to the industry averages. Therefore, it is easier to arrive at a pro forma statement by determining expenses than by anticipating sales. Then you will know what sales are required to sustain an operation with the costs you have specified, which will give you an idea of the chances for your success.

You need to be aware that cash flow is the single most important criterion in the first year in determining the rent you can afford to pay. Cash flow is the amount of money kept in reserve for both anticipated and unanticipated needs. It is accumulated by using part of the paid-in capital raised when the business is organized and through the actual revenues taken in by the business.

In a new business, part of the capital raised should be set aside for emergencies. You also need to keep in mind that rent will be a major expense and you should plan to have enough cash reserve to cover the rent for three or four months. As part of your proposed plan, you will want to project construction costs. An architect or contractor can help. The projections can be detailed or simply figured on a per-square-foot basis.

By preparing a projected cash flow, sales projection, and construction budget, you will be well armed to seek financing and will have something to compare to when the operation is actually started.

XYZ SHOP

Pro Forma Statement for the Year 19XX

	Jan.	Feb.	Mar.	Apr.	May
NET SALES					
Cost of Sales					
Food Costs					
Paper Costs					
Total Costs					
GROSS PROFIT					
OPERATING EXPENSES					
Employee Labor					
Manager Labor					
Payroll Taxes					
Travel					
Advertising					
Linen					
Supplies					
Repairs					
Office Expense					
Cash Over/Short					
Miscellaneous					
FIXED EXPENSES					
Rent					
Insurance					
Legal & Accounting					
Taxes & Licensing					
Other					
OPERATING PROFIT					
Depreciation					
NET PROFIT					

FIGURE 8-1. Sample pro forma statement.

June	July	Aug.	Sept.	Oct.	Nov.	Dec.	TOTAL

START-UP FINANCING

Regardless of how talented or successful you might have been in the past, you cannot start a new business venture without capital, that is, money. Raising capital can be difficult and traumatic, but it is done every day by people who use sound, practical business sense. You need to know that there are two basic forms of capital: equity and debt. Equity capital is that which you or your partners provide and stand to lose if the business fails. Debt capital is borrowed and must be paid back to the lenders whether the business succeeds or fails.

Sources of Equity Capital

Equity capital can be obtained from the following sources:

Life savings: The easiest capital to raise is your own money, in the form of bank savings, securities, or real estate.

Live insurance policies: The cash value of whole life insurance policies can be borrowed against at low interest rates. The larger and older the policy, the more cash value there is available. The exact sum is easily obtained by calling your insurance company.

Home mortgage: If you consider mortgaging your home or other property, be very careful because you may lose them if the business fails. If you are already paying a mortgage, you could consider refinancing, especially if you've been paying on the mortgage for some time or if the property has substantially appreciated in value. Refinancing will provide you with additional funds, but your new mortgage payments could be higher than before if interest rates have gone up or if you borrow a larger amount.

Partnerships: Going into business with a partner who contributes his or her own equity is a common practice. The advantages outweigh the disadvantages by a large margin, but you should be aware of some specific difficulties. Many partnerships fail because of uneven work responsibilities, jealousy, personality conflicts, and insufficient revenue to support two equal partners working actively in the business.

Family and personal friends: Parents and friends are usually willing to lend money and do so without expectations of immediate return. Problems can arise when the business runs into rough times and your lenders start to worry about getting their money back. Because of the possibility for ill will and strained relationships, it is best to avoid these sources unless all else fails.

Sources of Debt Capital

There are many sources from which funds can be borrowed, and with a good credit rating, debt capital is readily available.

Banks: The best sources for debt capital are banks, but they have a reputation for being very conservative when it comes to lending money for new small- or medium-size businesses.

Bank loans have the virtue of simplicity: An institution gives you money and you promise to pay it back with interest. Since you must pay back the lender whether your business is a success of failure, the entire risk is on your shoulders. You will need to convince the bank's loan officers of your ability to repay the loan. The four most important things you must accomplish in your dealings with the bank are as follows:

1. Drafting an honest, readable, and convincible business plan.
2. Showing your passion and "tooting your own horn." This is no time for modesty. As long as you are honest, do not be shy about touting your talent, drive, and expertise. Every loan officer learns early on that management strength can make or break a business.
3. Explaining how you will use the money. Obvious? Maybe, but you would be surprised at how many applicants ask a bank for a loan but cannot precisely explain how they will spend it.
4. Proving your repayment potential. The first thing a banker learns in "Lending 101" is that the borrower must be able to pay back the loan. Think about it. Hard. If you cannot convince the lender your business can generate sufficient cash flow to repay the loan, the process is over.

The procedure is not easy, but the results are worth it. Provide a complete financial statement of your net worth. You will also have to provide a resume, a pro forma statement, and any other information that will help obtain loan approval. Bankers focus on the numbers and your ability to repay; they may not understand the potential of your new business.

Loan officers will almost insist with a new loan application that some kind of collateral (some valuable property) be put up as security to back the loan. If you do not keep up with the payments, the lender can grab the collateral and sell it to collect what you owe. A lender may want a second mortgage on your home, a security interest in your mutual funds, or the equipment or inventory of your business.

If you cannot obtain a loan on your own merits, consider a cosigner who will guarantee repayment to the bank if you should default. Naturally, it is not easy to find people willing to take on such a responsibility, but friends and relatives might be more willing to be loan cosigners than to actually lend you money.

If you are refused a loan, always ask for the reasons because you have the right to know. That information will tell you what you need to do to get approval the next time you try for a loan.

Present owner: An owner will often finance the sale of a business or property, particularly if he or she has had difficulty making the sale. The terms of owner financing are similar to those of a mortgage. In most cases, the owner will want a down payment of 10–30 percent, with the balance in monthly payments. Sometimes a balloon payment, a large lump sum agreed to by both parties at the end of a set period, is incorporated into the terms.

Small Business Administration: The SBA is an agency of the federal government set up to assist small businesses. However, SBA loans are difficult to get and the process can be frustrating. In most cases, the agency acts as a cosigner for a commercial loan with a private lender, such as a bank. Only when a private lending source will not approve a loan will the SMB become a direct lender, and those cases are rare. You can apply only after two banks refuse you and you have to supply the SBA with letters from the banks stating the refusal. You will have to also provide the same information as required by a bank. You will have to wait 6–8 weeks for processing. Always try other means of financing during the wait.

Finance companies: There are many finance companies willing to make loans for new ventures, and they are not as conservative as commercial banks. However, they do charge higher interest rates, which is their biggest disadvantage, and the maturity of the loan is usually shorter than those from a bank. In many cases they will want collateral as a guarantee of repayment, usually the equity in your home or some other property.

Other sources: Insurance companies, small business investment companies, and venture capital companies or individuals are other potential sources for debt capital. These sources take a long time to process applications and are usually more difficult to succeed with than the other sources listed. However, if all else fails, try them.

For help with other than major capital, there are other useful sources that can be easier to deal with than all of the previously mentioned conventional sources. They include leasing, long-term pay outs to purveyors, and borrowing or purchasing equipment from suppliers who have a primary interest in your success with their products.

Precautions for Borrowing   Regardless of what method you use to obtain capital, take the following precautions before finalizing any application:

- Shop around for the best terms.
- Try to get a loan commitment before you negotiate the purchase of the business to give you an idea of where you stand when it comes to financing.
- Get all loan commitments in writing.
- Show the loan papers to an attorney or accountant.
- Be reasonably sure you will have the resources to repay the loan without penalty.
- Make sure you know in advance what the net proceeds of the loan will be. Frequently, the interest is automatically prepaid to the lender at the beginning of the loan, not during the life of the loan.

THE SPACE

Location

You have heard it before and I am sure you will hear it again and again. Location, location, location. It is probably the most important decision you will have to make once you have crossed the line from thinking about your dream to turning it into a reality. People already in a retail business will tell you again and again about its importance. It is one of the major factors determining success or failure. Finding the right location takes time, hard work, and luck (being in the right place at the right time).

The main factors to consider when evaluating a possible location are

- *Competition:* Frozen desserts are impulse items. Customers will go to the closest place to buy an ice cream cone, frequently without regard to quality. You must realistically evaluate the surrounding competition.
- *Traffic density:* Enough people must pass by to provide a potential customer base, whether the community be residential or commercial. The location must be accessible to foot and car traffic. A location with cheaper rent but less traffic will not help you succeed.
- *Zoning:* Various areas have specific zoning laws that differ in their definitions and interpretations. Make sure the regulations of the area in which you are interested will allow you to conduct your business in a normal fashion.
- *Neighborhood profile:* The best location for the average shop is a residential community with abundant street traffic and parking. Most neighborhoods have a primary shopping area. If that area is viable, you will have day and evening business and you will probably have to carry a varied product mix.
- *Expenses:* The rent and utilities must be within your budget.
- *Professional opinion:* It is important to consider the opinion of established commercial real estate people regarding your concept and potential location.

You should use real estate agents to help you look for a location. They can do the initial hunting, but make sure they know what you want. Let them know that you are not interested in a so-called bargain. If you are interested in leasing, tell them you want a fair rent and a lease agreement with suitable use-clause structure (see later in "Leasing Agreements," item 5). Before the search is over, these factors may put you at odds with your agent and you might have to acquire a different one. But remember, you, not they, will be making the payments.

Whether buying or leasing, the frontage of the location is a key feature. The wider the store front, the more desirable it is. A long narrow store usually lacks adequate aisle space and counters wide enough to display the product. Merchandising is difficult when customers have a hard time seeing the product. Do not consider a location that has less than 15 feet of frontage.

This rationale is explained as follows: Looking into the space from the front door, starting from either the left or right side, the following space is needed for adequate retailing:

   3 feet for placement of the back-bar counter and equipment
   3–4 feet for adequate aisle space for employees to work behind the counter
   3 feet for placement of the ice cream dipping case
   4 feet for aisle space for customers being served and viewing the store

Without a doubt, a corner location is the most desirable. It usually allows for two window fronts providing added exposure for your product and operation.

Leasing Space

Do not purchase business property unless you have a strong desire to do so or you are offered very flexible purchasing and financing terms. Buying a business property ties up capital that is usually needed to operate the business. Buying could force you to spend even more capital on improvements that a landlord might do anyway. It is better to lease for the sake of cash flow.

Simply put, leasing is the right to use a particular item, land, building, or store for a specific period of time and payment as set forth in a lease agreement. Leasing differs from purchasing a property in that you do not obtain title to the leased property. It is an alternative to purchasing if your funds are limited, you want to be in a mall, you do not want a long-term commitment, and nothing is available for purchase.

The advantages of leasing are

- It does not require an immediate large outlay of cash for a down payment and you need not seek mortgage financing.
- It stipulates a fixed rent for a specific period of time, with no fluctuations for that period due to taxes, increased insurance, or building repairs. In fact, repairs are usually done by the landlord.
- It provides flexibility in that you can leave if you want to when the lease period is up.

The disadvantages are

- If the landlord refuses to extend a new lease, your investment in your business could be in danger.
- After the current lease expires, the new rental figure could be increased to the point of forcing you to relocate.
- There is always the uncertainty of new terms in a new lease.
- Repairs to your premises could be slow and some leases stipulate that improvements and repairs be done at the tenant's expense.

The more prime the location, the more you will pay per square foot for space, so you should lease only the space you absolutely need. You cannot consider taking extra space for future expansion. Rent is a key factor for your success in the first year. On the average, the rent for an ice cream shop should not exceed 10–12 percent of the estimated gross sales. For example, a shop grossing $300,000 sales per year should pay a rent of about $2,500 per month. In a mall operation, the rent should include all common and advertising charges even though the lease will state a per-square-foot charge separately from common charges. Common charges are the financial obligations of each tenant in a shared environment and include the costs of advertising, utilities, maintenance, and any increases in real estate taxes. Before agreeing to a lease specifying common charges, make sure you fully understand what they are, including the maximum amounts you will have to pay under the provisions of the lease.

Leasing in Malls   Ice cream sales are low-ticket items; that is, you need to sell a lot of $1.25–$1.50 portions (high volume) just to cover the overhead, let alone make a profit. Because of traffic density, mall locations have become ideal areas for most frozen dessert chains. The high rent is acceptable if daily traffic flow can be guaranteed. A good concept will get its share of the sales dollar if the mall location is right, the business is managed well, and the price of the product is affordable.

When investigating a mall location, ask other merchants about stores that are available or soon will be. Contact the leasing agents of major mall developers. A new or existing mall location takes at least 2 years to finalize, and "key" money is now the norm in acquiring one. Key money, also known as a tenant construction fee, is simply paying for the right to acquire the site. The right to acquire a prime food court location in a mall will often cost $50,000 or more.

Leasing Agreements   Once it is apparent that you are interested in renting a particular place, pressure will be put on you to sign a lease. You will have to be forceful but fair with the real estate agents. Tell them what you can afford to pay and how long a lease you want. If you act anxious to take the space, they might take advantage of your eagerness and, to get a higher commission, ask for more than you can afford.

And if it seems that simply finding the right space is difficult, negotiating the terms of a lease can be traumatic. I recommend using the experience of an attorney who specializes in commercial real estate. While it is your responsibility to negotiate the business terms, the attorney will negotiate the legal terms. You should be sure you understand all of the following points:

1. *An exact description of what is to be leased,* that is, the shop premises and the physical extent of the lease line. In a mall, there are many common landlord corridors or passageways where the public walks or congregates before entering your premises. Your financial responsibility extends only to the lease line, not beyond.

2. *The monthly rent.* Can it be increased? How? Is it possible to negotiate a lower rent during the beginning period of the lease that will result in better cash flow for the business?

3. *Items included in the rent.* Are utilities included? What is *not* included?

4. *The term of the lease.* A long lease with a fixed rent is most desirable from a cash flow standpoint, and it increases the resale value of your business. The next-best situation is to have options to renew.

5. *Use clauses.* Most leases have a use clause that stipulates what you can or cannot sell on your tenant premises. You should try to have this clause be as general as possible on your behalf, and as restrictive as possible in how the landlord will rent to other tenants that might be in competition with you. An example of the language you should try to get into your lease agreement is as follows:

> The landlord will not enter into any lease agreement with anyone else that infringes on the tenant's exclusive right to sell ice cream and other frozen desserts in the said mall for the entire period covering this lease.

For the most part, potential tenants do not view use clauses to be important until the landlord decides to rent to someone else who might compete with them. Without the protection of the preceding wording of a use clause, what do you do? Where is your protection? Do not let it specify that you can sell only "ice cream" and nothing else. Mall landlords especially will try to limit you to selling either ice cream or frozen yogurt, but not both. Even though it was the original intention of a shop owner to sell just one product, very few operations stick with only one product. If you can get the word "food" into the use clause, do it. It might be crucial in determining the direction of your business after you have been operating for a while.

6. *Maintenance.* Who pays for maintenance? Does it include items such as plumbing, heating, wiring, painting, and other general repairs?

7. *Leasehold improvements.* Who pays for them and who gets to keep them after the lease is up?

8. *Advertising.* Can you hang a sign?

9. *Local laws.* Is the landlord in conformance? If he or she is not, can you be let out of the lease?

10. *Insurance.* How much fire and liability insurance must be carried by the tenant?

11. *Right to sublet.* It is very important to have this right included in the terms of the lease if you want to sell the business or leave the premises before the lease term is up.

12. *Termination clause.* What are your rights?

13. *Catastrophe.* What happens to your lease in case of a catastrophe?

14. *Right to sell.* Do you have the right to sell your business? Be careful of the wording regarding this point.

To be successful in your endeavor, you need to understand these points and know exactly what is being negotiated for you.

There is usually a time lapse from the date you sign the lease to the day you open. So, you should try to negotiate a rent-free period to cover that lapse, particularly in a mall setting because of severe design criteria. This period will become important should you find yourself behind schedule in construction or renovations. A fair landlord will allow for it since it is in his or her best interest for you to succeed.

CONSTRUCTION

You have purchased your property or signed a lease and now you are ready to build or remodel. If you are leasing you need to know that most leases commence with the signing of the agreement, or shortly thereafter. You will have to start paying rent immediately, unless you have negotiated a rent-free period in your lease agreement. If you are purchasing the property and entering into a mortgage situation, try to have the property closing as close as possible to the beginning of the actual construction. Ask the bank to delay the start of mortgage payments until you open the business, a concession that is possible to obtain if you explain the situation to your banker in a businesslike and rational manner.

Because you want to keep rent payments before opening the operation to a minimum, you should prepare for construction even before signing the lease. For example, if you are considering a mall location, make sure you know whether union or nonunion construction labor is allowed. Nonunion labor is usually less expensive and less restrictive regarding work hours than union labor. However, most new construction in large mall developments is done with union labor. Knowing which situation you will be involved in will prepare you for the costs involved.

It is at this point that you must objectively decide what you are capable of and willing to do yourself and what will require outside assistance. Be realistic about your available time and skill limitations. Most people entering a business for the first time are quite unaware of the costs involved in retail construction. Architects, contractors, and equipment manufacturers will all give you estimates and advice as long as you promise to consider them for the project if you sign a lease. Equipment manufacturers sometimes even help design your shop, with, of course, emphasis on their equipment. (But a good designer can use their layout as a basis for a plan.) Take advantage of this free advice because the dollar value is considerable.

Be sure to set a specific date for your opening and discuss it with your architect, contractor, and anyone else involved. Make sure it is realistic and plan everything around that date. Having a deadline puts pressure on everyone to perform.

Retail Design and Construction Tips

We all know that attractive, well-kept, and sanitary surroundings affect not only the quality of the product served therein but also the morale and attitude of the staff and the appeal of the establishment as a whole. That is a given. How to achieve this environment is something else all together. First of all, hiring an architect/designer and contractor familiar with the construction of food establishment is very important. They will know the building codes and government regulations. In addition to teaching you how to operate and maintain your equipment, equipment manufacturers can also help you set up the safeguards necessary for good sanitary conditions. They know which equipment does and does not meet the requirements of the board of health.

While the following is not an all-inclusive design and construction list, it will certainly give you an understanding of some important criteria you should consider.

- Depending on the type of business and the seating capacity of the establishment, specific sinks and bathroom facilities are required. In some situations a single-compartment hand sink is sufficient, and in others, two- or three-compartment sinks are required. Being in the dairy or restaurant food production business, you will probably be required to have a three-compartment sink (size of sink compartment depends on the largest piece of equipment that needs to be cleaned in that sink), depending on the state in which you are located.

- The floors should be properly constructed, smooth, nonabsorbent, and maintained in good condition. Cracks, breaks, and worn spots can hold dirt, food soil, and bacteria. Building finishes such as glazed and ceramic tile on the walls are desirable because they are easily cleaned and are damage resistant. Cement-block walls are less expensive but will turn brown if exposed to heat. Painted surfaces will get chipped when equipment is moved around. Quarry tile is the industry standard floor finish because it stands up to wear, is grease resistant, and is less slippery when wet than other floor finishes. Carpeting is not recommended because it retains liquids, thereby providing food for harmful microorganisms.

- Properly installed floor drains are necessary in any area where water is flushed for cleaning, or to receive discharges of water or other fluid waste from equipment. They are especially important in areas such as the production room where pressure spray methods for cleaning equipment are used.

- Walls and ceilings must be cleaned periodically, so they should be constructed of smooth, nonabsorbent materials such as glazed or ceramic tile, or cement block with epoxy paint. They should also be light colored as an aid to locating dirt and facilitating cleaning.

- Proper lighting is necessary not only for customer comfort product presentation, but also to enable your employees to see the areas of the shop that need cleaning. Insufficient cleaning can result in a buildup of dirt and food soil. Good lighting is also necessary for the correct preparation and handling of the products and for the proper cleaning and sanitizing of equipment and utensils.

- Street clothes and personal belongings can contaminate food, equipment, and food preparation surfaces. Therefore, an easily cleanable room separate from all food preparation areas should be designated for changing and storing clothes and for storing other personal belongings. Lockers should be provided. Toilet and lavatory facilities should be available in this room so that employees can be reminded to wash their hands before starting work. Locker room facilities are a requirement of the United States Public Health Service, and this rule is uniformly enforced by most local health departments.
- Wall-hung equipment that eliminates the need for legs and equipment racks with a minimum number of legs makes cleaning the floor easier.
- Built-in garbage areas facilitate disposal of trash and garbage.

Remember, your facility will have to be approved by a health inspector before you are allowed to open, so make sanitary conditions a design priority right from the start.

Hiring an Architect

After the lease is signed, it is time to hire an architect. Select an architect carefully because of the complexity of the process of designing, bidding, and supervising the construction of your new operation. Choose someone with experience in projects similar to yours. Visit places they have worked on and ask those owners about the quality of work, the cost of the project, and adherence to the budget.

Agree upon a schedule for working drawings and have the contract reflect dates for payments. Insist that the architect understand your concept. Your shop should not be a copy of someone else's design and decor. Neither should the architect get carried away in areas of design where execution would be difficult and costly. You set the construction budget and by now you should know many of the construction and equipment costs. Use that information when reviewing drawings presented to you. Time is money, and being able to properly execute drawings into construction will save you both.

Hiring a Contractor

After you have approved all the plans, they are sent out for bids. The architect is responsible for getting the bids, evaluating them, and choosing a contractor with your approval. The main reason for getting bids is to ensure an honest construction price and to find out how your budget compares to reality. If the bids are too high, you have to make changes in your plans.

Choose a contractor who has done construction in the retail food business. Ask for references and check them. Make sure the contractor is not so busy that your job is just one of many, because your job might get short shrift, causing you to delay your opening. The agreement should include a performance-and-completion clause tied into the payment schedule. Like any business person, every contractor understands money, especially if a large portion of the contract is for employee labor.

The contract should be reviewed by your attorney to project your interests regarding the following matters:

1. How are construction costs outlined in the contract? Who authorizes and approves any extras once construction begins—you, the architect, or the contractor?

2. Do all parties agree on a completion date? A written agreement will give you some leverage in getting the contractor to complete the work on time.

3. Who is financially responsible for delays? A penalty clause should be inserted if the price you have agreed to is tied to a completion clause that the contractor approved.

4. How is overtime paid and who approves it? You should insist that the contract specify your written approval in advance for all overtime.

5. What percentage of the fee is held back for work not completed by the opening date? To cover all contingencies, 10 percent is common.

6. What are the legal responsibilities of the contractor? What are his obligations to perform? The contractor's obligation to perform his best efforts according to detailed working drawings and in a set time frame is the paramount feature of any construction contract. The contract should read that all construction work be of acceptable standards as per the bid specifications.

Once the agreement has been signed, work along with the contractor and make changes in the plans as needed. Inspect the work periodically and let the contractor know how you feel about it. When construction is completed, make a thorough inspection. Write down every problem and find out when it will be fixed. Your agreement specifies that money will be held back until your list of problems has been taken care of. Every reputable contractor goes through this process, so you need not worry about your insistence. If the contractor wants to be able to use you as a reference, he or she will make sure you are satisfied with the job.

EQUIPMENT REQUIREMENTS

While cost is important, the first priority in any equipment purchase should be to acquire exactly what is needed. The amount of equipment needed to merchandise and dispense your products depends on the size of the operation and the different product items on the menu. But for all operators, new or expanding, the need for information about the necessary equipment is the same.

Much time and money can be saved and many problems avoided by doing some research before making any decisions to buy. Realistic needs and budgets can be met only by finding the answers to these questions:

- Who do I go to for advice?
- What do I need?
- What model should I buy?
- How much should I spend?
- Should I buy new or used?
- Should I lease or buy?

Make a list of the equipment you will need and note the electrical requirement for each. Give the list to your architect or contractor to avoid the common problem of inadequate electrical capacity in retail construction.

General Considerations

Refrigerant and Other Local Health Board Requirements Regardless of the equipment you intend on purchasing or from whom, make sure it is NSF (National Sanitation Foundation) and UL (Underwriters Laboratories) approved. Such approval is a requirement of almost all local health departments in the United States.

Because of the new Federal Clean Air Act of 1993, it is critically important that whatever refrigeration equipment is purchased, the correct refrigerant is installed. For many years. chlorofluorocarbons (CFCs) have been used in commercial refrigeration products. Scientific evidence suggests that CFCs released into the atmosphere are one cause of ozone depletion and, because of the ozone layer protects the Earth from ultraviolet radiation, global warming.

The federal statute requires all manufacturers to switch to R404A or R402B, both CFC-free refrigerants. Since the availability of R404A is currently limited because of needed design modifications to compressors, R402B is presently the refrigerant of choice because it stills works with existing equipment in the marketplace. R402B can be used as a short-term solution until 2020.

New Versus Used The obvious reason for buying used equipment is cost. In most cases, you can expect to save 40–60% or more for used dipping cases, soft serve machines, batch freezers, blast freezers, and storage freezers. But unless you are very astute about foodservice equipment, buying used can be costly. An unastute person will have no idea how old a compressor is, its condition, and whether there are leaks in the refrigerant. Morever, most old refrigeration equipment is not energy efficient resulting in forfeiting any savings gained by buying used equipment. Also, any equipment that has electronic or mechanical sophistication, such as cash registers, ice machines, and batch freezers that are computer controlled should always be purchased new because computer chips malfunction under heavy use and often need to be replaced. There is nothing worse than having a cash register fail to operate, especially on a weekend when speed of service is critically important and you cannot find a repairperson to fix your cash register.

Leasing Versus Buying   There is a growing trend for leasing equipment such as batch freezers, blast freezers, and other major equipment needed to furnish a new start-up business.

The advantages of leasing are

- For a new business, leasing dramatically decreases the amount of funds needed up front to purchase a piece of equipment.
- Lower down payment requirements. Most lease contracts require little or no down payment.
- More flexibility on monthly payment requirements.
- Keeping bank lines open. Most banks maintain a credit limit for each borrower. If you finance an equipment purchase with a bank loan, it may count against your total credit availability.

The advantages of buying are

- Lower interest rates. The discrepancy between lease rates and borrowing rates can be substantial.
- Ability to depreciate the value of the asset.
- Control of the asset. As owner of the asset, you have control in a purchase. This provides more flexibility if you decide to sell the asset before the finance term expires.

Even with the increasing trend in leased equipment, the majority of major equipment acquisitions are still made through outright purchases. However, as with most business decisions, the determining factor usually comes down to money.

American Dipping Cases

The most important piece of equipment in your shop for dispensing product to your customers is the dipping case. Today, dipping cases are classified as either European or American. Over the years, few changes have been made to the interior or exterior design or refrigeration units of American dipping cases, which are well built and durable. Exceptions are the new Kelvinator curved and straight front glass dipping cabinet. They are reasonably priced (less than half the cost of a similar sized European unit) when compared to the European dipping cases. These curved glass cabinets are highly recommended, and are very close in visual appeal to their European counterparts.

American dipping cabinets are easily serviced because of the design and the large domestic commercial-refrigeration support system. Most units have excellent Copeland compressors. The predominant refrigeration system in these units has a no-clog radiant shell condenser whereby the condenser coils are fastened to the inside of the outer cabinet wall. The outer walls actually get warm when the cabinet is running. Dissipating heat in this way eliminates the need for a finned compressor in the compressor compartment.

Although, for the most part, American cases lack visual appeal and most have narrow countertops, the large selection available makes it relatively easy to find a size and price to fit any need and budget. You should choose a unit that is well lighted and has a shiny stainless steel finish for visual appeal. Make sure the pivoting flip has a solid steel frame with a heavy gasket hinge holding the glass or plastic doors. The unit should have a floor drain to facilitate defrosting (which should be done weekly). Heavy-duty plastic pads in the bottom of the cabinet help to prevent damage if a tub is accidentally dropped into it. Plastic (available from Futura of Long Island City, New York) or stainless steel flavor signs are also advantageous. If available, consider a locking system for the doors.

Every manufacturer offers some kind of dipperwell and a can-clamp mounting system that supports the tubs of ice cream and keeps them from spinning while you are dipping. These clamps are easily installed inside the walls of the cabinet in threaded mounting holes already in place.

Particularly in heavy-volume locations where cases are not in public view, some operators forgo the can-clamp system to maximize use of space and ease of operation. To keep the tubs from moving around, these operators use a tool called a Container Retainer manufactured by Stevens Design of Seminole, Florida. This handy stainless steel tool totally secures and aligns tubs with little effort and time.

Today, most dipping cases are enclosed inside the front counters of the store for a more uniform appearance. If you do so, make sure the compressor system can be reached easily for servicing. The grills should be removable for easy access to the vents that should be cleaned weekly for efficient operation of the unit.

There are four recommended American manufacturers of dipping cases: Kelvinator, McCray, Master-Bilt, and Hussmann (see Table 8-1).

Kelvinator Kelvinator is one of the largest and most respected manufacturers of refrigeration equipment for the ice cream industry. As previously mentioned, their curved glass dipping cases are the newest pieces of ice cream dipping cabinets to be manufactured in the United States. They are models CKDC 27, 47, 67, and 87. These illuminated visually appealing dipping cabinets in either curved or straight front glass are fabulous when you consider their cost versus purchasing a European style dipping cabinet (see the following section) with similar features. Although slightly more expensive than a conventional dipping

Table 8-1. *American-Style Dipping Cases*

Model	Size (length in ft)	No. of Tubs		Dimensions (inches)			Electrical Requirements	HP
		Display	Storage	Length	Depth	Height		
Kelvinator								
KDC-47	4	8	4	$46\frac{1}{2}$	$26\frac{11}{16}$	$50\frac{11}{16}$	115/60/1	$\frac{1}{3}$
KDC-67	6	12	8	67	$26\frac{11}{16}$	$50\frac{11}{16}$	115/60/1	$\frac{1}{2}$
KDC-87	8	16	12	88	$26\frac{11}{16}$	$50\frac{11}{16}$	115/60/1	$\frac{3}{4}$
CKDC-27	2	4	2	$25\frac{3}{4}$	$26\frac{11}{16}$	$50\frac{11}{16}$	115/60/1	$\frac{1}{3}$
CKDC-47	4	8	4	$46\frac{1}{2}$	$26\frac{11}{16}$	$50\frac{11}{16}$	115/60/1	$\frac{1}{3}$
CKDC-67	6	12	8	67	$26\frac{11}{16}$	$50\frac{11}{16}$	115/60/1	$\frac{1}{2}$
CKDC-77	8	16	12	88	$26\frac{11}{16}$	$50\frac{11}{16}$	115/60/1	$\frac{3}{4}$
McCray								
IC-8	4	8	4	49	$27\frac{1}{2}$	$50\frac{1}{2}$	115/60/1	$\frac{1}{2}$
IC-16	8	16	12	93	$27\frac{1}{2}$	$50\frac{1}{2}$	115/60/1	$\frac{3}{4}$
Master-Bilt								
DD-46	4	8	4	$47\frac{3}{4}$	$27\frac{3}{4}$	50	115/60/1	$\frac{1}{2}$
DD-66	6	12	8	$69\frac{1}{8}$	$27\frac{3}{4}$	50	115/60/1	$\frac{1}{2}$
DD-88	8	16	8	$90\frac{5}{8}$	$27\frac{3}{4}$	50	115/60/1	$\frac{3}{4}$
Hussmann								
DC-8	4	8	4	$45\frac{5}{8}$	$25\frac{13}{16}$	$51\frac{1}{4}$	115/60/1	$\frac{1}{3}$
DC-12	6	12	8	$47\frac{5}{16}$	$25\frac{13}{16}$	$51\frac{1}{4}$	115/60/1	$\frac{1}{2}$
DC-16	8	16	12	$87\frac{7}{16}$	$25\frac{13}{16}$	$51\frac{1}{4}$	115/60/1	$\frac{3}{4}$

cabinet, any smart ice cream retainer will understand their appeal to the consuming public viewing your frozen desserts.

Kelvinator dipping cases (see Table 8-1 and Figure 8-2) come in stainless steel cabinets that are available in a choice of solid-color or wood-grain finishes for the front. The units have good interior lighting and picture windows for good product viewing. They come with a drip tray having at least two built-in dipperwell mounts and a good can clamp. The long-lasting and easily serviced compressor has an excellent warranty. The disadvantages of the Kelvinator cases are a narrow top shelf for display and a manual defrost system.

McCray McCray's dipping cases feature a large 12-inch countertop for display and an excellent Copeland compressor. The outer structure is stainless steel and the glass front is made of tempered glass. The interior lighting consists of full-length fluorescent tubes.

Master-Bilt One of the manufacturers that makes a 6-foot unit displaying twelve tubs, Master-Bilt makes durable and reasonably priced dipping cases. They feature excellent interior lighting and a good can-clamp system. The outer structure and countertop are made of stainless steel.

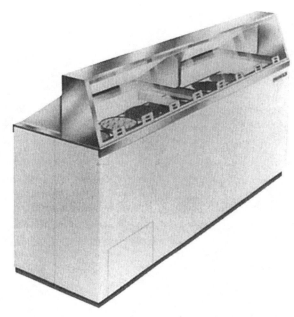

FIGURE 8-2. Kelvinator Model KDC-87 dipping cabinet. (White Consolidated Industries, Kelvinator Division)

Hussmann The Hussmann Company has a long history of manufacturing quality equipment for the dairy and food industries. Their dipping cases are finished in a gleaming white baked-on acrylic enamel on both the interior and exterior. The condenser unit is at the back for ease of servicing. The top serving shelf is stainless steel and an optional, easy-to-use canholder tray unit that requires no adjustments at the time of purchase is available. A lock kit for the lid is also available.

European Dipping Cases

Frozen dessert purchases are frequently made on impulse and it is well known that impulse items sell better when they are creatively and attractively displayed. With lots of glass and shiny stainless steel, the upscale European dipping cases are perfect examples of selling by visual appeal. These cases offer optimal product display in oblong pans for easy viewing by customers. By maximizing use of space, European cases can display one-third more product than comparably sized American cases using round tubs.

Constant circulation of cold air throughout the case provides a uniform temperature that inhibits the ice cream from melting regardless of where any particular flavor is placed. American cases do not have this capability and so require certain flavors to be positioned in cold spots.

Some of the finest European dipping cases are available from the Italian equipment manufacturers, COF, distributed in the United States by Coldelite (see Figures 8-3 and 8-4), and ISA (see Figures 8-5 and 8-6). Both manufacturers' units are attractively designed with an overstructure of shiny stainless steel and tempered glass. Screws allow the front glass to swivel for cleaning both sides of the glass. All units come with a dipperwell. Models are available in different length sizes to maximize product display. The smaller units hold up to twelve oblong pans, while the larger ones can hold up to twenty-four. The forced cold-air ventilation system is frost-free and newer models are available with an automatic defrosting cycle.

Dipping Case Accessories

Once you have purchased a dipping case, you will soon learn that there are many tricks of trade that must be utilized so that the case works to its fullest ca-

FIGURE 8-3. COF (distributed by Coldelite) Model Quasar nine-hole dipping cabinet.

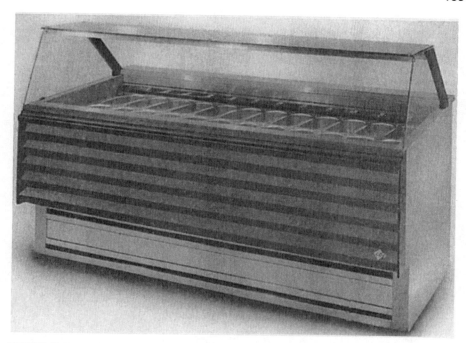

FIGURE 8-4. COF (distributed by Coldelite) Model Naxos twenty-four-hole dipping cabinet.

pacity. The following are two recommended accessories you should consider for your dipping cases:

> *Can holding systems.* A piece of equipment made of either plastic or metal, or a combination of both, a can holding system should do two things. Its main purpose is to hold the ice cream tub in place while scooping, thus completely eliminating a common complaint of owners: tub movement while scooping. It also enables the employee to use a proper scooping technique to ensure portion control. T.J.'s Racks is a recommended supplier of can holding systems.
>
> *Flavor signs.* Attractive, distinctive flavor signs inside the dipping case are a must. Too often owners either fail to address this issue or they place poorly made or handwritten signs to let customers know what they are selling. Futura of Long Island City has a variety of different designs and sizes from which to choose.

Storage Freezers and Refrigerators

The proper storage of ice cream at temperatures from 0 to -25 degrees Fahrenheit is critical in the everyday operation of a business. Because you will need to

FIGURE 8-5. ISA Model Isetta 7 display cabinet holds seven oblong pans.

store a product for up to 3 weeks without affecting its quality, you must be sure to have adequate facilities. Your needs can be accommodated by either walk-in (see Chapter 2, "Walk-In Refrigeration") or upright units.

Storage freezers and refrigerators are usually specified for either self-contained (top or side mounted) or remote refrigeration systems. The refrigeration systems are available as either air- or water-cooled models, depending on environmental conditions and utility availability. The self-contained units are commonly hidden on top of walk-in models by closure panels, but sufficient air space must be available for keeping air-cooled units from overheating. Remote systems can be located some distance away from the storage unit, but the further the distance, the greater the heat (efficiency) loss. Remote refrigeration has the advantage of keeping noise and heat away from either the front of the shop or production area.

Maintain all refrigeration equipment in peak operating order, especially during the summer months to keep the compressors from overworking. Blow out the condenser coils frequently and have the refrigeration equipment checked every spring by a refrigeration service company.

Most of today's units have preset automatic defrosting cycles that need to be watched to make sure the cycles are not operating during peak business hours when the doors are constantly open. You will need to read the equipment manual if you want to change the cycle.

FIGURE 8-6. ISA Model CV8 display cabinet holds eight round tubs.

The three main manufacturers of upright storage freezers are Kelvinator, Master-Bilt, and Traulsen (see Table 8-2). Kelvinator manufactures one- and two-door models with a top-mount condensing system. The doors are self-closing to minimize loss of cold air. Both models have an automatic defrost cycle that maintains a constant interior temperature. They have removable shelves and are easy to clean. Because Kelvinator is such a large manufacturer of refrigeration equipment, getting service is fairly easy almost anywhere in the United States.

Like their blast freezers, Master-Bilt's storage freezers are very sturdy (22-gauge steel exterior), easy to maintain, and very well insulated. Since interior insulation is important for holding ice cream for an extended time (up to 1 month), Master-Bilt units are highly recommended.

Traulsen manufactures top-of-the-line equipment and is preferred by many in the foodservice industry. Their stainless steel units are well insulated to hold the interior temperature and are easily serviced by commercial refrigeration companies.

Table 8-2. **Storage Freezers**

Model	Storage Capacity (3-gal. cans)	Dimensions (inches)			Electrical Requirements
		Width	Height	Depth	
Kelvinator					
VSL26 1 door	26	$32\frac{5}{8}$	84	$35\frac{3}{8}$	115/230/1
VSL50 2 door	50	$58\frac{5}{8}$	84	$35\frac{3}{8}$	115/230/1
Traulsen					
RLT-1-32WUT 1 door	26	$29\frac{7}{8}$	$84\frac{1}{4}$	$34\frac{15}{16}$	115/230/1
RLT-2-32WUT 2 door	50	58	84	$34\frac{15}{16}$	115/230/1
Master-Bilt					
TUF 27	26	31	$82\frac{1}{2}$	$35\frac{3}{4}$	115/230/1
TUF 48	50	52	$82\frac{1}{2}$	$35\frac{3}{4}$	115/230/1

Ice Cream Merchandisers

Because sales of frozen dessert products tend to be seasonal (that is, more impulse buying is done in the warmer months), shop operators have had to think of ways to expand business during the slow periods. Consequently, merchandising products for take-out has become a big business. Ice cream cakes, pints, quarts, and novelties are products well suited for take-out business. You can

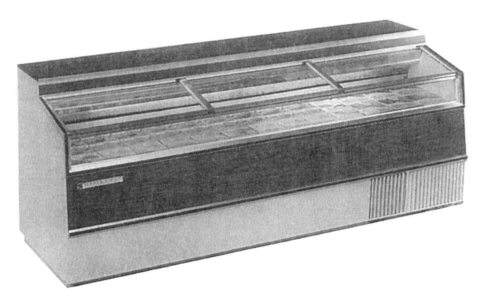

FIGURE 8-7. Master-Bilt Model GT horizontal display merchandiser, available in five sizes.

make these products yourself or buy them from an outside distributor. Either way, you will need display cabinets to show customers what is available.

Merchandising cabinets can be either horizontal or vertical, and can be either floor or countertop models. They should all have glass fronts or tops to provide product visibility. Glass sliding doors are easy to use and clean. It is recommended that they all be reach-in units so customers can help themselves to their purchases.

Both Kelvinator and Master-Bilt manufacture horizontal (see Figure 8-7) and vertical (see Figure 8-8) models in at least four different sizes that are durable and eye appealing (see Table 8-3). Vertical cabinets have recently become preferable. They hold more product in a limited space than do horizontal models. However, they are not recommended for displaying individually packed

FIGURE 8-8. Master-Bilt Model TLG vertical display merchandiser, available in three sizes.

Table 8-3. Merchandising Cases

Manufacturer	Model	Capacity (cubic feet)	Width	Height	Depth	Electrical Requirements	HP
Horizontal							
Kelvinator	MCT-4½	12.8	58⅞	43¹¹⁄₁₆	36	115/60/1	⅓
Kelvinator	MCT-6	18.8	76⅞	43¹¹⁄₁₆	36	115/60/1	½
Kelvinator	MCT-7	22.8	88⅞	43¹¹⁄₁₆	36	115/60/1	¾
Kelvinator	MCT-8	26.8	100⅞	43¹¹⁄₁₆	36	115/60/1	¾
Master-Bilt	GT-40	10.0	48⅜	38	31¾	115/60/1	½
Master-Bilt	GT-50	13.5	60⅛	38	31¾	115/60/1	½
Master-Bilt	GT-60	17.4	72	38	31¾	115/60/1	½
Master-Bilt	GT-80	25.5	95⅝	38	31¾	115/60/1	¾
Master-Bilt	GT-100	32.0	119	38	31¾	115/60/1	1
Vertical							
Kelvinator	VGL26	24.8	32⅝	84	35⅛	115/60/1	⅓
Kelvinator	VGL48	43.3	52	84	35⅛	115/60/1	½
Master-Bilt*	BMG27	25.3	31	78½	36	115/60/1	1
Master-Bilt	BMG52	48.7	56	78½	34½	115/60/1	1½
Master-Bilt	BMG80	75.0	85	78½	34½	115/60/1	1½
Countertop							
Silver King	SK-CTM	1.6	31	21	16½	115/60/1 3.1A	⅙
Silver King	SKCTM-D1	1.6	24	21	20¾	115/60/1 3.1A	⅙

*All Master-Bilt vertical cabinets are also available in BLG models providing a lower temperature than the BMG models. Having a bottom-mounted condenser system, the BLG models have the same dimensions as the BMG series.

novelties or ice cream cakes that are meant to be viewed from the top of the package rather than from the side.

Horizontal cabinets are definitely recommended for displaying pint and ice cream cake packages that are to be seen from the top. These cabinets allow for the entire inside to be used for storage of products (as opposed to vertical cabinets that need wire or plastic racks to support the products), provide well-lit product visibility, and have usable countertop shelf space that is a valuable feature for merchandising nonrefrigerated products. For countertop merchandising, the Silver King Company of Minneapolis, Minnesota, manufactures a line of display cases, called Frozen Treats (see Table 8-3) to promote impulse buying of novelty items on your main counter or near your cash register. These units are made of heavy-duty stainless steel and have a Plexiglas lid that is easily removed for filling and dispensing. Model SK-CTM, which sits on the counter, is available with exteriors in either white textured vinyl or Presidential Walnut Woodgrain vinyl. Model SKCTM-D1 is intended to be recessed into the counter and features a suspended cabinet for a trim appearance with maximum product visibility. Big Apple Refrigeration, Yonkers, New York, is the exclusive distributor of a European line of countertop freezers called Caravell that serve the same purpose (see Figure 8-9).

Ice Cream Cake Display Cases

If you plan to do a serious business in ice cream cakes, you will need a cake case. The public likes to see what it is getting, especially when buying something for a special occasion, as ice cream cakes would be. Unlike merchandising units that are mostly self-service for customers buying packaged products, cake cases are specifically designed to showcase individual products using a spacious shelf arrangement and glass front to allow customer viewing.

The cake cases available today are attractive and allow plenty of space for diversity. The Kelvinator and Master-Bilt cases are similar in construction (see Table 8-4). Each has a three-shelf system inside the case that has sufficient space to display a large variety of products in different shapes and sizes. Both cases are recommended for use in dipping shops, bakeries, or gourmet food shops.

FIGURE 8-9. Master-Bilt Caravelle Model CIF-23 countertop display freezer.

Table 8-4. Ice Cream Cake Cases

Manufacturer	Model	Capacity (cubic feet)	Width	Height	Depth	Electrical Requirements
				Dimensions (inches)		
Kelvinator	FPD-5	18.0	60	50	$29\frac{3}{4}$	115/60/1
Master-Bilt	FIP-50	17.6	60	50	31	115/60/1
Federal	CGIC-485c		48	50	36	115/60/1
Federal	CGIC-605c		60	50	36	115/60/1

Combination Freezer and Flavor Rail

A combination freezer and flavor rail unit (see Table 8-5 and Figure 8-10) is ideal for any restaurant, hotel, foodservice, or ice cream store operation that has a back counter long enough to hold the equipment. This unit is a storage freezer with a flavor rail attached on the top back part of the unit that usually faces the wall where the unit is placed. The flavor rail holds in place all the dispensers for syrups and toppings used for making a variety of milk shakes, floats, and elaborate sundaes. It comes with jars that are usually plastic with stainless steel syrup pumps.

Back-Bar Dipping Cabinets

Back-bar dipping cabinets are often used in restaurants and ice cream shops for back-counter dipping needs and storage. They are available in sizes to fit almost any space requirements. Kelvinator (see Figure 8-11), Master-Bilt, and the C. Nelson Manufacturing Company all manufacture similar units in sizes from 5.4 to 31.5 cubic-foot capacity (see Table 8-6).

Table 8-5. Combination Freezer-Flavor Rail Units

Manufacturer	Model	Capacity (cubic feet)	Width	Height	Depth	Electrical Requirements
				Dimensions (inches)		
Kelvinator	8-FR	18.6	$54\frac{1}{8}$	$47\frac{7}{16}$	$30\frac{5}{8}$	115/60/1
Master-Bilt	FLR60*	12.5	43	38	$30\frac{1}{8}$	115/60/1
Master-Bilt	FLR80†	16.8	54	38	$30\frac{1}{8}$	115/60/1

*5-opening topping rail.

†10-opening topping rail.

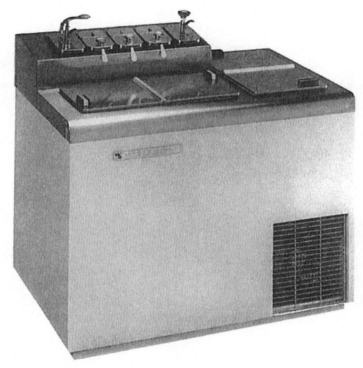

FIGURE 8-10. Master-Bilt Model FLR combination freezer and flavor rail, available in two sizes.

Refrigerator/Freezer Bases

Many businesses have limited space for storage of dry goods and for refrigeration. Smart operators will utilize every square foot of undercounter space for refrigeration. While the capacity of individual refrigerator/freezer bases may not be very large, they will increase refrigeration capacity in areas close to employees working the front counters. Such units are available in worktop as well as undercounter models. Beverage Air of Spartansburg, South Carolina, is a recommended supplier (see Table 8-7).

Accessory Equipment

Whether your business is a dipping shop, restaurant, or any other kind of food-service operation that is to include frozen desserts, you will need to plan for accessory equipment in addition to the major items previously discussed. Any good restaurant equipment supply distributor can provide catalogs and other literature that should help you in making decisions. Listed next are most of the pieces you will have to consider.

FIGURE 8-11. Kelvinator Model 8DF back-bar dipping cabinet.

Hot Fudge Machine A hot fudge machine is an obvious necessity. Most either come with a ladle or are pump driven. Portion control is easily obtained with a pump machine, but using a ladle is more eye-appealing from a merchandising viewpoint and more likely to evoke a positive response from a customer.

Most machines come with one or two wells, are constructed of stainless steel, and provide a maximum of 1-ounce portions using either the ladle or a single stroke of the pump. Some have lighted fronts to promote hot fudge, a recommended feature.

Many companies manufacture these machines, but I recommend Server Products of Menomonee Falls, Wisconsin. Their machines have adjustable thermostats and are well constructed. They can pump directly from a #10 tin, which saves time because you do not have to pour the contents from the tin into another container, and are portion controlled. Specifically, I recommend the single model LFSP #81300, which is pump driven, or the Twin FSP #81230 that has two wells. Model Twin FS #81220 comes with two wells, but the fudge is ladle-served rather than pumped.

Free-Standing Serving Rails Free-standing syrup and topping rails are designed to sit on a countertop rather than as a part of the dipping cabinet freezer. They come in different sizes and combinations for ladling or pump-driven dispensing. The most popular sizes have two, three, or four wells. You will need to specify the combinations you want. Again, I recommend the Server company's

Table 8-6. Back-Bar Dipping Cabinets

Manufacturer	Model	Capacity (cubic feet)	Dimensions (inches)			No. of Holes
			Width	Height	Depth	
Master-Bilt	DC4S	10.9	54	$32\frac{5}{8}$	$21\frac{1}{8}$	4
Master-Bilt	DC4D	7.6	$30\frac{5}{8}$	$32\frac{5}{8}$.	$30\frac{1}{8}$	4D
Master-Bilt	DC6D	12.5	43	$32\frac{5}{8}$	$30\frac{1}{8}$	6D
Master-Bilt	DC8D	16	54	$32\frac{5}{8}$	$30\frac{1}{8}$	8D
Master-Bilt	DC10D	21	$66\frac{5}{8}$	$32\frac{5}{8}$	$30\frac{1}{8}$	10D
Master-Bilt	DC12D	28.9	$84\frac{5}{8}$	$32\frac{5}{8}$	$30\frac{1}{8}$	12D
Kelvinator	2SF	5.4	$32\frac{1}{8}$	$32\frac{9}{16}$	$20\frac{15}{16}$	2
Kelvinator	4SF	11.3	$55\frac{11}{16}$	$32\frac{9}{16}$	$20\frac{15}{16}$	4
Kelvinator	4DF	9.1	$30\frac{5}{8}$	$32\frac{9}{16}$	$30\frac{9}{16}$	4D
Kelvinator	6DF	14.1	$43\frac{11}{16}$	$32\frac{9}{16}$	$30\frac{9}{16}$	6D
Kelvinator	8DF	18.6	$54\frac{3}{16}$	$32\frac{9}{16}$	$30\frac{19}{16}$	8D
Kelvinator	10DF	23.6	$66\frac{5}{8}$	$32\frac{9}{16}$	$30\frac{9}{16}$	10D
Kelvinator	14DF	31.5	$89\frac{1}{8}$	$32\frac{9}{16}$	$30\frac{9}{16}$	4D
Nelson	BS-2	5.3	$32\frac{1}{4}$	$20\frac{1}{4}$	$32\frac{3}{4}$	2
Nelson	BS-4	10.4	$53\frac{1}{4}$	$20\frac{1}{4}$	$32\frac{3}{4}$	4
Nelson	BD-6	13	$43\frac{1}{4}$	$30\frac{3}{8}$	$32\frac{3}{4}$	6D
Nelson	BD-10	22.8	$68\frac{3}{4}$	$30\frac{3}{8}$	$32\frac{3}{4}$	10D
Nelson	BD-12	27.9	$81\frac{1}{2}$	$30\frac{3}{8}$	$32\frac{3}{4}$	12D

Notes: Electrical requirements for all three manufacturers are 115/60/1. The letter D by the hole category signifies a double row of holes.

Table 8-7. Beverage Air Refrigerator/Freezer Bases

Model	Dimensions (inches)			Electrical Requirements	HP
	Width	Height	Depth		
Refrigerated Worktops					
WTR27	27	27	$39\frac{1}{2}$	115/60/1	$\frac{1}{6}$
WTR48	48	27	$39\frac{1}{2}$	115/60/1	$\frac{1}{5}$
WTR60	60	27	$39\frac{1}{2}$	115/60/1	$\frac{1}{4}$
Freezer Worktops					
WTF27	27	27	$39\frac{1}{2}$	115/60/1	$\frac{1}{4}$
WTF48	48	27	$39\frac{1}{2}$	115/60/1	$\frac{1}{3}$

Notes: Undercounter models are the same except that the outside height is $34\frac{1}{2}$ inches instead of $39\frac{1}{2}$ inches.

products, particularly models SR4 #82820 with four wells, SR3 #82860 with three wells, and SR2 #82900 with two wells.

Drink and Milk-Shake Mixers and Dispensers   The design of mixers used to prepare milk shakes, smoothies and other frozen drinks has changed dramatically as improvements have been made to the motors that run these machines. Mixers are now capable of blending up to 3 quarts of liquid at a time. They are available with high and low speeds and a pulse switch. They all come with heavy-duty motors, each removable for servicing and cleaning, for each spindle. Some drink mixers even come with an agitator speed for mixing drinks (such as smoothies) with ice.

Mixers are available with either one or three heads with separate motors controlling each. Individual heads can be removed for service, repair, and cleaning, and the remaining heads can still be operated. The machines operate on three speeds that give the spindle maximum mixing flexibility, and they can be operated with a paper cup adapter to eliminate sloppy handling.

Hamilton Beach (see Figures 8-12 and 8-13), Vita Mix, and Waring manufacture excellent mixers (see Table 8-8). For preparing smoothies or blending

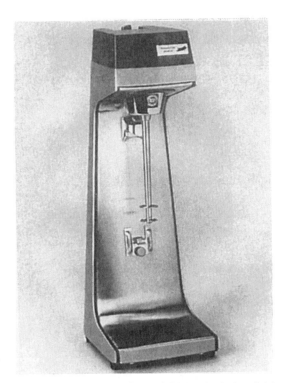

FIGURE 8-12. Hamilton Beach Model 936 single-head drink mixer.

FIGURE 8-13. Hamilton Beach Model 950 triple-head drink mixer.

Table 8-8. *Drink and Milk-Shake Mixers*

Manufacturer	Model	Capacity (no. of heads)	Dimensions (inches)			Electrical Requirements
			Width	Height	Depth	
Hamilton Beach	936	1	$6\frac{9}{16}$	7	$19\frac{7}{16}$	120V
Hamilton Beach	950	3	$16\frac{3}{8}$	$8\frac{1}{8}$	20	120 V
Hamilton Beach	94900	1	10	$7\frac{1}{2}$	26	120 V
Waring	DMC 20	1	$17\frac{1}{2}$	7	$18\frac{1}{4}$	120 V
Waring	DMC 200	3	$14\frac{1}{2}$	8	$19\frac{1}{2}$	120 V
Vita Mix	748	1	$7\frac{1}{4}$	$8\frac{3}{4}$	20	120 V

mix-in candies and frozen fruits with either soft or hard ice cream, the Hamilton Beach "The Big Chill," model 94900, is an excellent unit. It has two speeds that operate very well with its heavy duty motor.

Taylor Products makes the best soft serve shake dispensers that money can buy. Using one of their shakemasters, you can dispense a completely finished shake flavor with one simple movement of the self-closing handle. You can eliminate measuring, mixing, and blending time at the counter. An exclusive solid-state thermistor control has the most sensitive temperature probe in the industry. With product at a constant temperature, the unit's freezer will have to run less and thus require less energy. Taylor manufactures more than ten different models of shakemasters, from tabletop to large, high-volume foodservice models. I recommend model 452. It is a single-flavor unit that has a 20-quart mix reservoir. It measures 18 7/16 inches wide by 31 inches deep by 57 1/4 inches high and operates on either three-phase, 20-amp service, or single-phase, 30-amp service.

Whipped-Cream Mixers   There is nothing better than topping an ice cream sundae with fresh whipped cream. There is simply no comparison in taste between fresh and commercially prepared whipped cream. Any innovative operator who makes the effort to serve fresh whipped cream will ensure happy and satisfied customers.

Coldelite, a manufacturer of soft serve machines, makes two different models of "Kwik-Whippers" (#KW-77 and #KW-50) that produce fresh whipped topping at a rate of 40 and 30 gallons per hour. The topping will hold its peak for 24 hours under refrigeration and has an overrun yield of 4 to 1. The machine is a portable self-contained unit that is easy to use (just pour in liquid heavy cream and press a button) and to clean. Model #KW-77 (see Figure 8-14) measures 13 inches wide, 14 5/8 inches deep, and 19 inches high, and its electrical requirements are 115 volts, 60 amps, single phase (115/60/1).

Perfect for small ice cream shops, ISI North America manufactures a hand-held cream whipper that produces fresh whipped cream. The unit uses an N_2O whipper charger for set-up and recharging when necessary.

Ice Cream Scoops   Obviously, you can not dispense ice cream without a scoop. While there have been many variations of this nineteenth-century invention throughout the years, the basic designs are still in use today.

One of these designs is the spring scoop, and I highly recommend the one made by Hamilton Beach Company (Figure 8-15), available in nine different sizes. Its ease of operation makes it easy for a beginner to learn to scoop ice cream. It also facilitates portion control. However, the spring attachments do eventually break.

The Zeroll Company of Toledo, Ohio, manufactures another kind of scoop (Figure 8-16) that is the easiest scoop in use today. Unlike the spring scoop, it has no moving (and consequently breakable) parts, making it the ultimate in durability, practicality, and simplicity. Instead, it has a nontoxic defrosting fluid

FIGURE 8-14. Coldelite whipped cream mixer Model KW-77.

encased in the handle that responds to the warmth of the hand to instantly release even the hardest ice cream. Also, instead of squeezing and compressing the product, this scoop rolls the ice cream into a ball, which allows 10–20 percent more servings per gallon. The recommended scoop for a 4-ounce portion of ice cream is the Zeroll 1010 or 1020.

Zeroll also manufactures a Zerolon scoop that was developed to overcome the problems related to hard, over-chlorinated, or high mineral content water by protecting against corrosion and discoloring.

Comparisons of the Hamilton Beach and Zeroll scoops are given in Table 8-9.

The Zeroll Company also produces an ice cream blade (spade) called an "Ice Cream Machine" (model 1065-1065C). It also contains a self-defrosting fluid in the handle that allows for instant release of the ice cream. The flat blade is well suited to scraping the sides of a tub and for packing even layers into take-out pints and quarts.

FIGURE 8-15. The spring scoop manufactured by Hamilton Beach.

SIGNAGE

When you were doing the initial planning you should have been taking pictures of the operations you visited. Now you can refer to those photos for samples of logos and menu signage and for help with planning and laying out the signs for your own operation. Do not leave this task for the last minute or you will have sloppy signage, or none at all, for the opening. You should even post a sign during construction to let the public know you are coming.

The architect frequently takes on the responsibility for designing and bidding out the work on the logo and interior menu signage. You should use a sign manufacturer, like Futura of Long Island City, New York, that produces a large percentage of its work for the ice cream industry.

FIGURE 8-16. The Zeroll Scoop, manufactured by the Zeroll Company.

Table 8-9. *Zeroll and Hamilton Beach Ice Cream Scoops*

Manufacturer	Model	Size (oz.)	Approx. Scoops per Gallon
Zeroll	1010	4	18
Zeroll	1012	3	24
Zeroll	1016	$2\frac{1}{2}$	29
Zeroll	1020	2	36
Zeroll	1024	$1\frac{1}{2}$	48
Zeroll	1030	1	72
Hamilton Beach	67-12	3	24
Hamilton Beach	67-16	$2\frac{1}{2}$	29
Hamilton Beach	67-20	2	36
Hamilton Beach	67-24	$1\frac{1}{2}$	48
Hamilton Beach	67-30	1	72

Note: Model numbers for Zerolon scoops are the same as for Zeroll scoops except that they end in "ZT."

A Logo

A logo is your identifying symbol. It is one of the most important elements of your advertising campaign and so deserves careful consideration. It should be simple, descriptive, and eye-catching. The key to the use of a logo is repetition so that the public becomes familiar with it. It is also a good idea to develop a phrase or slogan to accompany the logo. If your customers like your products, they will remember the slogan, and vice versa.

A Name

The name of your operation is a reflection of its personality and conveys, in a general sense, its theme. Like your logo, it should be simple and descriptive. If you have trouble coming up with a name, ask your architect or graphic designer for ideas. They are usually in tune with that sort of thing and enjoy the opportunity to provide suggestions.

Keep an open mind and be alert because ideas are all around you. I called my first restaurant "Someplace Different" for two reasons. The first was because I overheard a group of business people talking about where to have lunch. Having tired of their usual place, someone suggested that they go to someplace different. The second reason was because my restaurant was totally different from any other place in the area at the time.

In creating the name for what became the largest single grossing ice cream operation in the United States, Ice Cream Extravaganza, a later operation of mine, we wanted to convey the message that our establishment was a place where our customers' eyes could focus on every imaginable ice cream product and flavor available in one setting. People told us over and over again that a visit with us was really an extravaganza. The name Ice Cream Extravaganza worked well for us.

Menu Signage

After the quality of your products and the service you give your customers, the next most important element in the operation is its menu signage. It presents a list of your offerings in a descriptive, interesting, and stimulating manner. It is your calling card, introduces your products, and represents your image. Well-planned menu signage will attract customers even in your absence and will be your best selling tool if you are working with inexperienced or uncaring employees.

You will spend a lot of money on menu signage, so you should consider it carefully. Menus can be large modules hanging on the walls or they can be lists positioned close to the products being sold. They should be set in large, simple type that is easy to read and looks neat. Keeping the copy simple will translate into higher sales because the customer will not get confused and will be able to make a decision fairly quickly. Contrasting colors will also help the customer focus on the items.

Wherever possible, use large (24 × 30 inches) photographs showing your products in a setting that differs from the printed menu.

THE FIRST CREW

One of the biggest challenges in operating your own business is finding competent employees. In general, the food industry has a reputation for unprofessional standards relating to personnel. It has been an industry of long hours, low pay, and poor working conditions attracting mostly unskilled labor. Only recently have university programs been developed for the high-level education of students interested in careers in the food industry. As an individual owner/operator, you can make a different by taking a serious interest in hiring and training and in treating your employees well.

Do not make hiring a low priority. Do not wait until the last minute to hire employees or you will find yourself without enough employees on opening day to handle the business coming in through the front door.

Job Descriptions

Prepare a written job description for every position you are going to have available. It will help clarify what you are looking for in an employee and thus help you conduct a proper interview. You can even give the description to applicants so there will be no misunderstandings about the job. It will also help eliminate duplication of functions.

Shop Manual

You should have a manual describing the details of your operation. A good manual will accomplish the following:

- Explain the philosophy of the owner
- Describe job functions
- Define the standards for employee work habits and conduct
- Give detailed directions for how products are prepared and served (see Chapter 10)
- Provide answers for almost any question imaginable about the operation

Specifically, it should explain what employees can expect in the way of pay raises, benefits, work schedules, and opportunities for advancement. It should cover every facet of the operation, including how products are dispensed to customers, employee relations, handling the cash register, opening and closing procedures, and keeping the shop clean. In addition, it should include step-by-step directions for making sundaes, milk shakes, and ice cream sodas, and describe in detail how ice cream is scooped, cared for, and handled.

Associations and companies such as the International Ice Cream Association and Kelvinator have published manuals for the ice cream industry that are invaluable references when drafting your own custom manual.

Hiring for the Opening

As soon as you start advertising the opening of your business, people will apply for jobs. Having an orderly hiring procedure will lead to a smoother opening for your business. Note the following suggestions:

1. Put a "Help Wanted" sign in the front window.
2. Purchase employee applications from any stationery or business supply store. Do not use scraps of paper to record employee applications.
3. Have all applicants fill out the forms. The completed forms will give you basic information and an idea of what an applicant is like. The neatness of the handwriting and the effort put into filling out the form will give many clues about the person's compatibility with your operation.
4. Conduct a short interview. Look for applicants who smile and know how to say "please" and "thank you." Chewing gum or smoking during the interview shows poor manners, so do not hire applicants who do either. Be sure to write down your impressions on the application.
5. About 3 weeks before the shop opens, review the applications, pull out the ones that impressed you favorably, and call those individuals back for a follow-up interview.
6. During the second interview, look for individuals who express a willingness to work hard, an enjoyment of being around frozen desserts, and a liking for work in a retail environment. They should present a good attitude and appearance, possess an intellectual aptitude for the work, and, if possible, have experience in a similar business. Ask for references and be sure to check them.
7. Be friendly with the applicants. Tell them what you will expect from them and why working in your establishment will be a pleasant experience.
8. Clearly state the probable hours and salary of the position, and any other benefits you are offering. Be competitive but fair. Explain about performance evaluations for future pay increases and about opportunities for growth.
9. Once you have decided whether or not to hire an applicant, let him or her know immediately.
10. Save the applications of anyone you liked but were unable to hire because of the limited number of jobs available. You never know when you will have an opening.

Since the shop will probably be open 7 days a week, you will need enough employees to cover at least fourteen, and possibly up to twenty-one, shifts depending on the number of hours in a shift. (See the next section, "Other Pre-opening Considerations," for a discussion of hours of operation). You will need at least two managers to open and close, because without adequate management you will be opening and closing by yourself. Do not be shortsighted, because you could end up being mentally and physically exhausted before the shop is 3 months old.

During the first few weeks of business, it is a good idea to have more employees working than are actually needed. While having more employees will add to your payroll costs, those costs will be offset in the long run because the first customers will be served well and will be likely to return after such a good experience. First impressions are the most important ones and you have worked too hard to come this far only to end up with unhappy customers. Also, you have no idea who is going to work well and who is not.

Pay a fair wage and set shifts at no longer than 6–7 hours a day, 5 days a week. Employees will be constantly on their feet and long shifts are draining, resulting in burnt-out employees. Allow for at least one short break and lunch or dinner during the shift. To be sure you are in compliance with all local and state labor laws concerning breaks, length of shifts, and so on, contact the appropriate authorities for guidance and any written materials on the subjects.

Keep in mind that the less turnover of employees there is, the more efficient your operation will be.

Summer Employees

During the summer selling season you will need a lot of employees to work in your shop. Luckily, both high school and college students will be looking for jobs. Take advantage of their availability, but do it in a way that not only helps you, but them too. Every person applying for a job will tell you how much they want to work, their availability, and so on. What they will not usually tell you is when they are going to quit at the end of the summer, and that is your dilemma. What generally happens is that in early August, your employees start telling you they are going on a vacation with their parents, they have to go back to school the last week in August, and so on.

By this time you are stuck. You start saying to yourself, "How am I going to operate the business the last two weeks in August and the first week in September?" The answer is simple. Develop a bonus system, and make it part of the hiring process. Offer all summer employees a certain amount of extra money (bonus) for each week worked during the summer, but only paid to employees who work the whole summer selling season. The bonus (say, $25 for each week worked) is paid to them with their last paycheck at the end of the summer. What this accomplishes is your upfront notice to potential employees that you only want employees who will work the whole summer, not just a part of it.

Training

The week before your shop opens, bring in all the future employees for a training course. There are at least three good reasons for doing so:

1. They have to learn what your business is all about, including the physical layout of the premises.
2. They have to learn the daily operations.
3. If they learn the proper procedures at the beginning, you will save money in the long run and not be embarrassed serving the first customers.

The best time for this training is at night after the construction people have left for the day. You should emphasize how to scoop and serve your product (see Chapter 10). Scooping is important because it can cause a loss of profits when not done properly and because it is something the customers will watch closely. To the customer there is a direct correlation between the size of an ice cream cone, for example, and its price. They need to see that they are getting their money's worth, and you need to guard against overscooping that cuts into your profit margin.

Teach the employees how to make sundaes, milk shakes, and ice cream sodas. Stress the importance of presenting a visually appealing product and emphasize that sloppiness is unacceptable.

Set a standard for employee attire. Have shirts, hats, and aprons made up with your logo on them, require or provide uniforms, or make sure your employees come to work in clean attire that is all of the same kind and color. The appearance of the employees is as important to customers as the quality of your products is.

Customers will come to your shop for fresh-dipped ice cream portions. But no matter how good the product, if the portions are not prepared and served properly and pleasantly, customers will not come back. Teach your employees to acknowledge a customer's presence with a smile and "Can I help you?" Make sure that every order is prepared according to your established formula and that its presentation is neat and visually appealing. Instruct your employees on proper service procedures and emphasize the use of courtesy, cordiality, and *cleanliness*.

Explain the rules of your establishment and insist that they be followed. See Chapter 9 for additional discussion of employees.

OTHER PREOPENING CONSIDERATIONS

Permits and Inspections

Regardless of where the operation is located, you will have to apply for licenses for construction and operation. These usually fall under the jurisdiction of the local board of health. Let the contractor apply for all building permits. He is familiar with the process and knows how to get the papers properly filed. But you yourself should apply for the health permit to operate as soon as your lease has been signed and executed. If your architect has completed the proper drawings, the application is strictly a paperwork process and should not delay the opening of your business. However, if either the architect or the contractor has not followed the required health codes, you will find yourself in trouble.

An inspection of the completed facility prior to opening is usually required by the board of health. The situation is one of pay now or later. If the contractor bent a rule to save you some money, you will simply spend it in fines later on. Improper construction might not be discovered by a board of health inspector prior to opening, but it will probably turn up during the annual or semiannual inspections.

Insist that your contractor follow the working drawings and that proper seams along the floor and walls are closed with metal, plastic, or rubber trim. Caulking should be used wherever applicable. Health inspectors like to see good finishing touches since they reflect on your seriousness in operating a clean establishment.

Operational Details

For any new business, the first month of operation can be chaotic if enough planning is not done prior to opening. Most new owners wait until the last moment to plan their daily operations. To avoid that pitfall and save yourself aggravation, be sure to take care of the following details well before opening day.

Hours of Operation When deciding on your hours of operation, there are five major issues to consider:

> *Clientele:* At what times of the day or evening will people patronize your establishment? What are the prime shopping hours in the area you are located?
> *Profitability:* When will the volume of traffic be the greatest? What, if any, days or hours should you be closed?
> *Labor:* Can you find a sufficient number of employees to staff the operation?
> *Preparation time:* How much time is needed before opening each day to prepare for the day's work?
> *You:* Can you function properly if your business is open 7 days a week? (Many owners underestimate the demands on their time and overestimate their ability to cope.)

Most frozen dessert operations do the major portion of their business at night and during the weekend. Covering these times and days should be your main concern. It is likely that you will make some initial mistakes in setting the hours of operation. If you try to be consistent, give serious thought to changes, and advertise changes well in advance of instituting them, things should go smoothly. Always remember, nothing is more irritating than going some place expecting it to be open and finding it closed.

You should be prepared to seriously analyze the hours of operation after your first major selling season.

Having a Telephone   It is important to have a telephone and a listing in the telephone directory for two reasons. First, the listing lets customers know you are in business and that you can be reached to answer questions. Second, you will need to use it yourself to check on the operation when you are not there, to order supplies, to contact repair services, and so on.

Planning the Grand Opening

Take the time to make a plan for the grand opening. Write down a schedule listing what you have to do and what others are responsible for.

Draw excitement and mystique to the opening. Get a local newspaper to write about it. Consider the following for your grand opening plan:

- *Purpose of the campaign:* Write down a clear-cut statement about what you want to accomplish. Launching the campaign has the sole purpose of promoting the opening of your new business.
- *Intended audience:* Whom are you trying to reach? You should try to reach the widest market within a narrow geographical area that can result in a positive initial response and build toward repeat business.
- *Cost of the campaign:* Certainly a key consideration, you need to set a budget that will not hurt your cash flow. You should not spend all of your advertising money at once. You might need some for later promotions or for the business in general.
- *Promotions for the grand opening:* To build repeat business, you have to start by getting customers in for the first time. To entice the public to come and see you, "2 for 1," "Buy One Get One Free" and "50 cents off" coupons and "free" promotions are short-term vehicles for getting short-term results.
- *Length of the campaign:* In most cases, a short opening promotion of about a month will give the best results. After a month the promotion loses its dramatic appeal.
- *Measuring results:* It is always important to know if your campaign is getting results. Save redeemed coupons on a daily basis and figure their percentage of sales or customer counts. If the redeemed coupons for the opening promotion equal 5–10 percent of sales, you have done extremely well with your campaign.

Finishing Touches

As careful as you might be in planning for every contingency, there is always something that is overlooked when a new business begins operations. The following list will help you anticipate some of the items frequently overlooked or forgotten. Be sure to review it at least a few days before the grand opening.

- *Equipment on hand:* Do you have cash registers and know how to work them? Do you have all the necessary equipment such as the hot fudge dispenser and the blender for making milk shakes? Do you have fire extinguishers?
- *Functioning of equipment:* Does the hot water boiler work properly? Does the air conditioning work properly? Is the telephone installed? Do you have sufficient outside lighting? Is it on an automatic timer? Has refrigeration (dipping cases, storage freezer, blast freezer, and refrigerators) been run for several days?
- *Product:* Are ingredients on hand? Have you made enough ice cream for at least 3 business days? Have you posted the menu?
- *Employees:* Have you hired and trained employees? Do you have uniforms for employees? Do you have extra employees for the first few weeks?
- *Cleanliness:* Do you have all health permits? Have you hired a sanitation company to remove daily trash?
- *Opening:* Have you set a date for the opening and advertised it in the front window? Have you planned a promotion?

Once everything checks out, take a deep breath, treat yourself to a special dinner, and get a good night's sleep before the opening because it might be the last one you will get for a while. Then you will be ready to realize your dream!

REFERENCES

Arbuckle, W.S. 1983. *Ice Cream Store Handbook.* Columbia, Mo.: Arbuckle Co.

Arbuckle, W. S. 1986. *Ice Cream.* Fourth edition. Westport, Conn.: AVI.

Birchfield, John C. 1988. *Design and Layout of Foodservice Facilities.* New York: Van Nostrand Reinhold.

Broome, J. Tol, Jr. 1994. Money, the Art of the Loan. *Restaurant hospitality* (January), pp. 54–55.

Chiffriller, T. F., Jr. 1982. *Successful Restaurant Operation.* New York: Van Nostrand Reinhold.

IICA. 1995. *The Latest Scoop.* Washington, D.C.: International Ice Cream Association.

Khan, Mahmood. 1987. *Foodservice Operations.* New York: Van Nostrand Reinhold.

Liederman, David, and Alex Taylor. 1989. *Running Through Walls.* Chicago: Contemporary Books.

Reid, Robert D. 1989. *Hospitality Marketing Management.* Second edition. New York: Van Nostrand Reinhold.

Restaurant Security Newsletter. 1994. *Restaurants & Institutions,* February, pp. 121–124.

Robbins, Carol T., and Herbert Wolff. 1985. *The Very Best Ice Cream and Where to Find It.* New York: Warner Books.

Sklarow, Val. 1995. Preparing to open your specialty coffee store. *Food Distribution Magazine*, April, pp. 48–49.

Steingold, Fred. 1996. Raising money for your business. *Health Foods Business*, March, pp. 69–70.

Wells, Danny. 1995. Opening a new store the right way. *Health Food Business*, February, p. 19.

9 ⌧⌧⌧⌧⌧⌧⌧⌧⌧⌧⌧⌧⌧⌧⌧⌧⌧⌧⌧⌧⌧⌧⌧⌧

OPERATING A FROZEN DESSERT RETAIL ESTABLISHMENT

Operating any retail business is demanding. It requires your money, your time, and all the effort and attention you can give it. Whether your business is new or firmly established, an informed approach to its operation will help ensure success.

EMPLOYEES

The employees are the heart of any business. They represent you and your store to the public and thus they can make you successful or doom you to failure. As discussed in Chapter 8, the image of employees in, and of, the food industry is a poor one. The industry attracts mostly unskilled labor because of its record of poor working conditions, long hours, and low pay. If you want to attract and keep competent, reliable people, you will have to be prepared to deal with them accordingly.

Owner–Employee Relations

People are an integral part of a retail business. Whether they are customers or employees, how you treat them eventually becomes part of the personality of your operation. Because frozen dessert shops are usually small as compared with most retail businesses, that personality will be highly visible and will have a direct bearing on your success.

Working with Young Employees To a large extent, most ice cream shops are manned by young employees scooping their hearts out, all summer long. If you treat them like children, they will act like children. Treat them with respect and give them responsibility. Then, they will have an incentive for taking a personal interest in the shop's success. And when they perform their jobs well, praise them. Praise goes a long way towards making a good employee a better one.

Certainly you should be friendly with your employees, but do not try to become friends with them. You need to maintain a certain distance as an authority figure to be able to conduct business in a serious manner. The best you can do for them is to teach respect, primarily by example, and help them take on responsibility in a positive fashion. If you use the following three R's to motivate your employees, you will be well on your way to having a successful relationship with them.

1. *Respect.* Treating your staff like human beings not like machines. The way you treat your employees is how they will treat your customers.
2. *Recognition.* A pat on the back is only a few vertebrae up from a kick in the "you know what," but a pat will take you a lot further than a kick. Make it a substantial pat, one that shows sincere interest and awareness on your part.
3. *Rewards.* In addition to recognition, do not overlook rewards. They do not have to be big, just something concrete to let your employees know you appreciate them. Examples of rewards that have an immediate impact are a dinner for two at a nice restaurant in your area, a free pass to an amusement park, or tickets to an up-coming musical concert or major league sports event.

Remember, in addition to fostering a good relationship with your employees, following these three R's will help keep them from going to the competition.

Working Conditions Serving ice cream is a labor-intensive business. Your employees must be on their feet all the time. Their hands will be constantly sticky and will get sore from scooping ice cream. Show your employees that you care about their work environment as much as you care about the public areas of your shop by keeping their work environment clean, neat, painted, and generally well maintained. You could also provide the following as inducements to keeping good help:

- Air conditioning, not only in the front of your shop, but also in the back work areas where ice cream production takes place
- Uniforms that are comfortable as well as attractive
- Rubber mats on the floors to relieve the pressure of standing all day long
- Proper tools and utensils to aid job performance
- Locker and washroom facilities for changing clothes and resting during breaks

If employees are unhappy with the job, they can do many things to make their employers unhappy. They can call in sick frequently, waste time on the job, and look for any excuse to use the telephone. They can treat customers rudely and eventually quit, or you will have to fire them. Of course, it is impossible to keep everyone happy all the time, but if your basic principles for operating the business are fair and considerate, you can build a positive relationship with your employees.

Staff Meetings Regular meetings provide an opportunity for discussion about the shop and its operation. They should be held in the shop and should not be longer than an hour, for which time your employees should be paid. You should always have an agenda. Ask employees to come with questions and ideas for discussion. Allowing employees to be part of the decision-making process contributes to a team attitude that will help your business.

It is important to be constructive in these sessions. Praise those who deserve it and state general complaints as needed. However, complaints with a specific employee should not be brought up at these meetings but should be dealt with privately. Encourage employees to air their complaints as well.

Hiring and Training

The basics for hiring and training are presented in Chapter 8 ("The First Crew"), and if you start out on the right foot, you will have a better chance at keeping your operation running. Review the sections about job descriptions and a shop manual, and pay particular attention to suggestions for an orderly hiring procedure.

When you reach the point where you have to add or replace employees, be prepared for a disruption of the normal workflow of the shop. New employees usually start out being slow and sloppy, and they rarely understand the shop's prices. Consequently, good training sessions are imperative for maintaining consistent standards. It is a good idea to have new employees work in the shop for at least two sessions alongside regular employees, but not be counted as part of the work crew for those days.

Assign one of your employees with good work habits to be a mentor for the new employee and use this buddy system for at least the first week that the new employee is on the job. You want to avoid at all costs having a new employee form bad habits. This system will also help keep trainees from feeling bewildered and discouraged because there will always be someone around of whom they can ask questions.

Be sure to give new employees their own copy of the shop manual (see Chapter 8, "The First Crew"). Don't hesitate to tell new employees when they are doing a good job or when they are doing something incorrectly. You should be able to tell within the first 2 weeks if a new employee is going to work well.

Potential Problems

In return for offering a job to a prospective employee, you should expect from that person honesty, courtesy, and some degree of concern about your business. But ours is not an ideal world, so you will have to take some precautions to protect yourself from less-than-ideal employees.

Stealing and Pilferage   Employee thieves come from all walks of life and all income ranges, and they work in every type of business, including yours. They usually have two things in common: first, they have been placed in positions where they have an opportunity to steal. And second, they do not seem any different from their honest counterparts—who comprise a majority of any work force—that is, until they get caught. The actions of these dishonest employees usually end up astonishing their employers, employers just like you.

Your own presence will be the biggest deterrent to employee stealing and pilferage, but you will not be on the premises every hour of operation. You cannot stop employees from trying to steal, but you can make it difficult for them to succeed.

A good cash register (see discussion under "Keeping Track of Cash") with exact controls built into it and daily report sheets (see Figure 9-1) that are recorded properly and reviewed by you constantly will make it difficult to steal. Do not be fooled by daily cash reports that show overages from the register. Overages are usually a sign that something is wrong. In many cases an overage means that an employee is trying to steal cash but has not been fast enough in removing the money from the register. The attempt is made by ringing up an amount lower than what is collected from the customer. The money is put into the register and the employee will try to remove it some time during the day. Sometimes the employee gets confused and loses track of how much was put into the register or for some reason (such as someone is watching) cannot get the money out. The result is an overage on the report sheet.

Never allow too much money to accumulate in the cash register. To reduce the temptation for stealing, money should be removed periodically and deposited in a safe or in a drop safe.

Not only money is involved in stealing. Overscooping ice cream to friends, giving out free ice cream without permission, or taking ice cream home without permission are other forms of stealing. Taking inventories not only acts as a physical deterrent to pilferage but is also a psychological one. You can keep track of what items are being used by taking monthly, or more frequent, inventories. When employees see you taking inventory, they know you are concerned and watchful.

Employees who pay unusual attention to certain records, exhibit sudden wealth, are constantly watching the cash register, or begin taking excessive time off from work merit your attention.

Overscooping   Overscooping ice cream to customers can quickly cut into your profit margin. In general, it is a incessant battle with which you will have to live.

This is not to say you cannot exert some control over the problem. Teach your employees to scoop properly and constantly remind them what a serving should look like. Be sure to purchase the right scoops for the job (see Chapter 10).

SECURITY AND EMERGENCY PROCEDURES

Near the shop telephone you should post your home phone number and a list of the telephone numbers of the police, fire, and ambulance departments. On the wall should be a poster describing how to use the Heimlich Maneuver for helping choking victims, and the topic should be covered in detail in your shop manual. Every employee should know where the fire extinguisher is located and how it is used. Your managers, in particular, should be trained in handling emergency situations. They will be able to handle some problems on their own, but a robbery or a customer who becomes impossible to handle will require police assistance. In those cases, the manager should call the police first, then you. In any case, until help arrives, instruct your employees to do the following:

- Approach an argumentative person with a friendly, relaxed body style and language.
- Keep your voice calm and level. Attempt to maintain eye contact.
- Communicate the issue. Focus on the facts—that they (employees) are enforcing store policy, not an opinion or a personal issue.

Good security procedures should be set in place for all contingencies. Employees should never count money at the cash register in front of your customers. All doors other than the front one should be secured at all times. No one but employees should be allowed behind the counter.

When the shop has been closed for the day, no one should be allowed in for any reason. The closing procedures should be posted for all to see and should be strictly adhered to. Before leaving the shop, check all freezer and refrigerator doors to make sure they are closed securely. The safe and all doors should be checked to make sure they are locked.

Everyone on the last shift should leave at the same time. After the front door has been locked, a second employee should check the door. This procedure will keep the manager from wondering about the door all the way home and then returning to check on it.

KEEPING TRACK OF CASH

Because it is time consuming and can be complicated, many business owners are lax in keeping proper records about how the business is operating. It always seems that there are too many things to do in a day without having to get into extra paperwork. But keeping track of every cent coming into and going out of the shop will give you an insight into every facet of the operation.

If you cannot keep track of daily receipts in an orderly fashion, you are simply inviting employees to steal. You will also find it difficult to determine whether or not you are making a profit, and a serious cashflow problem could result. You will not be able to tell what money is yours and what belongs to the government. For example, many small businesses never separate their daily cash receipts from the sales tax they collect, and that is a very bad habit. They end up being unprepared at tax reporting time and ultimately are assessed late charges and penalties for not paying or for late filing. The business finds it difficult to catch up with the expense, the effect accumulates, and the business fails.

How can you keep the proper records to avoid such problems? Either hire an accountant or do the work yourself. It really is not difficult for the small-business owner to "keep the books." A number of manuals or computer software systems, all easy to use, can be found in any good office supply outlet.

The Cash Register

A well-designed cash register can provide information, protection, service, and convenience. Every retailer is vulnerable to losses from carelessness, laziness, indifference, forgetfulness, and temptation. And, if you are an absentee owner, you are particularly vulnerable. A good cash register will reduce errors, display the amount of change due on a transaction, and set controls that limit your cashier's authority, as well as make people who handle cash accountable.

Maybe the most important benefit you can realize from an electronic cash register is pricing accuracy. Preset price keys end the need to enter a price, speeding registrations and assuring accuracy. You simply label separate keys for each of your menu items. Then you can register items as fast as you can press the correct keys. Presets guarantee accuracy as well as provide sales counts for each item. Most registers can also be programmed to automatically add your state and local taxes. Tax computation is needed for speed, accuracy, and tax records.

Today's registers can also print sales analyses of products sold by the hour, day, month, or year. Your register should have a lighted screen to clearly show that a sale was actually rung up and to show the amount. The transaction should be visible to the customer as well to the cashier.

Enforce the following register practices to minimize bookkeeping problems:

- Ring up sales immediately.
- Over- or under-rings should be immediately brought to the attention of the manager on duty.
- Keep the register drawer closed except when making change.
- Place bills on the register ledge or on the top of the drawer while making change.

- Put change directly into the hands of the customer.
- Lock the register if, for any reason, it is going to be left unattended during business hours.
- Allow only the manager on duty to remove money from the register.
- Remove all cash from the register each night and then leave the drawer open while the shop is closed.

Handling Cash from Customer to Register

Handling cash sales and the use of the register should be clearly thought out by every employer, and the rules should be set down in the shop manual. While not appropriate for booth or table service, the following is a recommended procedure for handling an over-the-counter sale to a customer:

1. Immediately after the customer is served, payment is requested from the customer. The employee serving the customer is not to serve another customer until payment has been collected.
2. If only one item is ordered, the employee should inform the customer of the amount of the sale. The employee should count the amount given by the customer and if it is exact, acknowledge it, and say "thank you."
3. If more than one item is ordered, the employee should ring up the different products on the cash register and then inform the customer of the total owed. When the money is received, the employee should repeat to the customer the amount received.
4. The employee should then return to the register, punch in the amount tendered, and lay the money on the cash register ledge or on top of the drawer after it opens. The employee should then take out the customer's change, put the amount tendered into the drawer, and close the drawer.
5. The employee should then return to the customer with any change, repeat to the customer the total amount of the transaction, count out the change to the customer, put it in his or her hand, and say "thank you." For example, "That was six out of twenty dollars so your change is fourteen dollars—ten, eleven, twelve, thirteen, fourteen. Thank you!"

Many employers instruct their employees to put twenty-dollar bills under the tray in the register's drawer for safekeeping. Doing so also necessitates an extra step for the employee, which will usually be remembered if a customer should claim to having given a twenty-dollar bill instead of a ten.

Instruct employees to close the drawer at the completion of each sale. It should never be left open and should not be opened without the approval of the manager for any reason other than a sale.

Personal and travelers' checks should be approved by the manager with proper identification required of the customer.

Be sure to establish procedures for handling mistakes, or over-rings, made in ringing up sales. The total amount of the over-ring should be written on a piece of paper and approved by the manager or employee in charge. The paper is then placed in the drawer of the cash register.

The Cash Register Fund

For proper cash control and operating efficiency, it is recommended that cash in the register be kept at the lowest level necessary for running the business on a daily basis. Establish a specific amount of money, no larger than $50 to $100, to start each business day. So you will not have to disrupt the operation by having to go to the bank, or elsewhere for change, include enough variety of bills and coins to make change for the first sales of the day. Always have enough change in reserve to take care of other daily or weekend needs as well. Having a reserve is particularly important on Fridays to anticipate needs for the weekends when the banks are closed.

A good example of an opening register fund is as follows:

Change:	2 rolls of pennies	$ 1.00
	2 rolls of nickels	4.00
	2 rolls of dimes	10.00
	1 roll of quarters	10.00
		25.00
Bills:	30 singles	30.00
	2 fives	10.00
	1 ten	10.00
		50.00
Total:		$75.00

Handling End-of-Shift Cash Receipts

Once the cash is in the register, the next step is to make sure the total of the register tape equals the cash, checks, and vouchers in the drawer. With many registers, you can get a total of sales on the shift by "Z-ing out," that is, by putting the register key into the "Z" slot on the register. Then count the money in the drawer and deduct the starting cash. The total should equal the "Z" reading. Use a daily report sheet (see Figure 9-1) to record the totals and the money collected. This sheet will be your daily record of receipts and expenditures out of the register.

After the daily receipts are removed from the register, they need to be safeguarded until a bank deposit can be made. Many shops have a two-compartment safe for this purpose. The top part of the safe is opened by the employee who places the receipts into a slot that drops the money down into the bottom

CASH REGISTER REPORT

Initials _____   Date _____ AM or PM

Bank $ _____

Cash
   Coins   _____
   Singles   _____
   Fives   _____
   Tens   _____
   Twenties   _____
   Fifties   _____
TOTAL CASH   _____

Checks or Travelers' Checks

_____   _____

_____   _____

_____   _____

TOTAL CHECKS   _____

Petty Cash

_____   _____

_____   _____

_____   _____

TOTAL PETTY CASH   _____

TOTAL CASH   _____

LESS: BANK   _____

GRAND CASH TOTAL   _____

TOTAL PER CASH REGISTER–Z-TAPE READING   _____

  Less: Overring _____

  Adjusted Tape Reading   _____

CASH OVER or UNDER PER READING   _____

FIGURE 9-1. Sample cash register form.

part of the safe. Usually only the owner and manager have the combination to the bottom part. The employee has the combination only to the top part.

Some owners take the money home, but it is wiser to use the night depository at your bank. Choose a bank convenient to your business location, because it will be easier to make deposits (and obtain needed change).

Cash Disbursements

A cash disbursement takes place whenever you make payment for something by either cash or check. In a small business, cash disbursements are limited to two categories: general expenses and payroll. Always make disbursements by check, except for petty cash needs, as an element of control and as a permanent record of the payment. A petty cash fund may be kept on the premises and should not exceed $100. When the cash is nearly used up, replenish it by writing a check for the amount needed to restore the fund to the original amount. You can also remove money from the day's cash receipts if you write a receipt or voucher for the amount removed.

To set up your own general account you will need either a bank checking account and some columnar paper, or a commercial bookkeeping system, such as the one by Safeguard Business Systems Inc., available from your local stationery store. A commercial system is recommended over the do-it-yourself type for two reasons. First, considerable time is saved by not having to write information on the check and stub, and then in the journal. Second, the opportunity for errors is greatly reduced by eliminating the need to transfer numbers.

Keeping an accurate and up-to-date checkbook will tell you at a glance how your money is being spent and what your cashflow situation is. It provides the basis for you or your accountant to do proper record keeping.

Payroll Records

You need to maintain accurate payroll records to ensure that employees are paid properly and for other legal reasons. These include your responsibility to the federal, state, and local governments to withhold payroll taxes and to submit quarterly reports of such withholding from your employees' pay. You can figure the withholding amounts and fill out the reports yourself, or you can hire a payroll or accounting firm to do the work. You simply furnish the employee's name, address, social security number, rate of pay, and the hours worked, and the outside firm takes care of the rest. Using such firms is a common practice and one well worth considering.

Being lax about payroll records invites employee abuse of time cards or sheets, and then you will not know how many hours they worked or how long they took on breaks. A time card system or payroll work sheets are an absolute necessity for any business. Your employees will have to punch in on a time clock or write down the times for beginning and ending the day and any breaks they make take. Failure of an employee to comply with the system forces you to use arbitrary times for them that they might dispute. It is then the employee's responsibility to prove his or her case. Avoid these situations by stressing the importance of punching in and out from the first day that an employee starts work.

Monthly Operating Statement

To truly monitor the financial aspect of your business, you should compile an operating statement as an analytical tool. Constant referral to such a statement will let you know when to raise prices, reduce payroll, or reduce portion sizes. An operating statement is similar to a pro forma statement (see "A Plan of Action" in Chapter 8), but uses actual figures instead of estimates.

To create a factual operating statement, the following data are required:

- *Daily sales figures.* Each day's sales should be recorded in the sales journal. Sales should be broken down by categories, with a separate column for sales tax.
- *Inventory figures* (see below). On the last day of every month, an inventory should be taken of all products and ingredients. Amounts should be entered in the inventory book next to the price paid for each item. The value of the item is then computed and a total value figured for the entire inventory.
- *Cost of sales.* This category is critical in the operating statement because it will give you a true picture of the amount of ingredients used and product sold during the month. The cost of sales is computed as follows:

Opening inventory	$1,000.00
Monthly purchases	+ 500.00
Total	$1,500.00
Ending inventory	− 900.00
Cost of goods sold	$ 600.00

- *Operating expenses.* Operating expenses are those directly related to sales: payroll, utilities, linen service, trash collection, office expense, repairs and maintenance, and advertising. They should be watched closely as they do not always fluctuate in the same direction as sales. This situation is apparent during the change of seasons, such as winter to spring or summer to fall.
- *Occupancy expenses.* Rent, insurance, taxes, depreciation, and leasing expenses are occupancy expenses that must be met whether or not you are operating. They do not fluctuate from month to month.
- *Other miscellaneous expenses.* This category encompasses expenses that occur infrequently and are not considered major items in conducting the business.

After you have compiled the figures for all these categories, compute the percentages by category by dividing each expense by the monthly sales figure.

These percentages will point out trouble spots and areas in the operation needing improvement, especially when the percentages are compared on a monthly and yearly basis.

Product Costs

Cost management is the foundation of a successful retail establishment. Without understanding cost management, your chances of economic survival are greatly reduced.

Part of the record-keeping process is knowing the product costs of every item on your menu. Food cost management is understanding and controlling costs. It involves a complete knowledge of proper purchasing procedures, food handling and preparation, and labor utilization. All of these elements must be considered in determining the true cost of product. As shown in Figure 9-2, all products either bought or produced by your establishment should be costed out to figure the true cost per serving of a product. You will then be able to arrive at a selling price by multiplying the cost per serving by a percentage of profit.

When choosing products to feature in your establishment, you will need to strike a balance between food cost and aesthetic appeal to determine portion sizes. Aesthetic appeal refers to how the product looks. If the portion looks skimpy, make it larger, and vice versa. If you cannot balance the cost and visual appeal, do not handle the product. You do not want to hurt your image by making portions smaller or prices higher.

Purchasing   Purchasing the right item at the right price is the first requirement for obtaining a realistic product cost. If the quality is poor or the wrong item

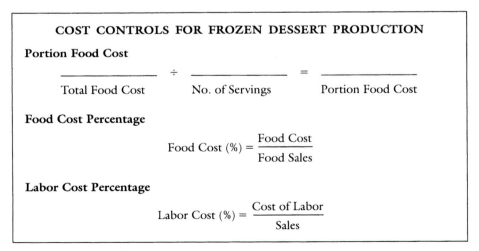

FIGURE 9-2. Sample worksheet for figuring cost controls for frozen dessert production.

purchased, waste will result and the actual purchase cost will be increased. When the cost becomes too high, you will have a difficult time making a profit.

During the peak months of business it is difficult to keep up with changes in product costs. Only when keeping track of your costs will you notice if a manufacturer increases the price of an ingredient. Having that information will show you the need to switch to a different manufacturer if you so desire. Many operators unwittingly absorb such increases without changing prices to the customer until they realize, sometimes after 3–6 months, that their profit margins have decreased, or even disappeared. (Operators also voluntarily absorb increases for a short period of time until they see if a price increase is permanent.)

To help keep track of product costs, purchase or design a suppliers journal having a separate sheet for each of your suppliers. List every product you buy from that supplier, along with the supplier's numbers and prices, and notes about the quality and the amount of product per package. (Knowing how the product is packed makes it easier to compare prices with another supplier.) (See also "Purchasing," in Chapter 5.)

Percentage of Costs to Sales   Figuring the percentage of costs to sales is a another key activity for keeping track of and managing cash. Knowing product costs allows you to figure any percentage you desire. If the percentage works out too low because of the prices you are setting, or if you need high prices to get a reasonable percentage, then at least you know immediately that there is a problem.

Controlling Product Costs   The best way to control product costs is to use standardized recipes and controlled production methods. Standardized recipes produce the following results:

- *Consistency of product.* If your customers can depend on the same characteristics and quality each time they purchase your product, they will be more likely to return. Because repeat business can mean the differences between success and failure, no operation can afford to take a chance on having an inconsistent product.
- *Exact portion cost.* Knowing exactly what a product costs enables you to set a fair price (see Figure 9-3).
- *Known yield.* This information (see Figure 9-4) enables you to set up proper production schedules.
- *Reduction of overproduction.* When you know the yield in advance, you eliminate overproduction.

Inventories   Keeping track of inventory is an essential part of any operation, large or small. You cannot prepare an accurate profit and loss statement without conducting an inventory first. The task can be made easier by using forms similar to those shown as Figures 9-5 and 9-6. Taking monthly or more frequent

RECIPE COST SHEET

Flavor _____

Recipe Yield _____

Date Product Made _____

Manufacturer	Ingredients	Amount of Ingredients	Unit Cost	Total Cost
			Total Cost _____	

FIGURE 9-3. Sample worksheet for figuring recipe costs.

inventories will help you figure product costs and keep tabs on what is being used, as well as provide a psychological deterrent to pilferage by employees.

Other Expenses

Rent You should plan on having enough cash flow to cover 3–4 months of rent payments. It is also a good idea to have a separate rent account in which you keep a certain amount of your daily sales to cover the monthly payment. The major causes for lack of funds to cover the rent are poor bookkeeping, poor purchasing, and simply taking too much money out of the business.

DIPPING YIELD

Sales   ÷ Cans Used = Dipping Yield

Monday	_____	_____	_____
Tuesday	_____	_____	_____
Wednesday	_____	_____	_____
Thursday	_____	_____	_____
Friday	_____	_____	_____
Saturday	_____	_____	_____
Sunday	_____	_____	_____

Sales Column = Total amount of ice cream sales for the day.

Cans Used = Ice cream inventory should be taken every morning before you open for business and every evening before you close. The formula is as follows:

Example

Morning Inventory	= 20½ tubs
Add: Ice Cream Produced That Day	= 10 tubs
Total Ice Cream Available	= 30½ tubs
Minus: Ending Inventory	= 24½ tubs
Usage That Day	= 6 tubs

Dipping Yield = Dividing the dollar amount of your ice cream sales by the number of cans used will give the dipping yield per can in dollars.

FIGURE 9-4. Sample worksheet for figuring dipping yield.

Rent is usually a fixed cost, except in mall situations where an override usually breaks in at some point. Override is additional rent due based on a fixed percentage of the portion of yearly gross sales that exceeds a certain amount as predetermined in your lease. For example, a lease states that any income over $300,000 is subject to a 10-percent override. If yearly gross sales total $500,000, the override is paid on $200,000. It is calculated by multiplying $200,000 by 10 percent, with the result that an additional $20,000 in rent is due.

In exchange for other favorable lease terms, landlords will argue for overrides by stating that they want to share in your success since they helped you attain it. Overrides are mutually agreed upon by all parties involved and are based on the break-even profit for the business. Obviously, the whole issue of overrides is a complicated one and deserves much thought.

ICE CREAM INVENTORY

WEEK ENDING ————

Flavor	Beginning Inventory	Tubs Produced	Tubs Used	Ending Inventory	Price Per Tub	Extension
French Vanilla						
Vanilla Choc. Chip						
Vanilla Fudge						
Vanilla Oreo®						
Vanilla Choc.-Almond						
Cherry Vanilla						
Strawberry						
Strawberry Cheesecake						
Banana						
Banana Nut Fudge						
Butter Pecan						
Pecan Praline						
Peanut Butter						
Coffee						
Coffee Chip						
Kahlua						
Mud Pie						
Mocha Chip						
Mocha Almond Fudge						
Chocolate						
Chocolate Choc.-Chip						
Chocolate Truffle						
Chocolate Choc.-Almond						
Chocolate Brownie						
Rocky Road						
Malted Vanilla						
Milky Way®						
Snickers®						
Heath Bar®						
Coconut						
Coconut Almond Joy®						
Rum Raisin						

INVENTORY				
				Date _____
Unit Size	Item	Quantity	Unit Price	Amount
			BALANCE FORWARD	6,125.00
	ICE CREAM			
2½ gal	Chocolate	2	16.00	32.00
2½	Oreo	6	15.00	80.00
2½	Strawberry	3	15.00	45.00
2½	Banana	1	15.00	15.00
2½	Chocolate Chip	2	15.00	30.00
2½	Vanilla	4	16.00	64.00
	CONES			
200 box	Sugar	6	7.00	42.00
400 box	Waffle	8	15.00	120.00
			TOTAL (PAGE)	6,553.00

FIGURE 9-6. Sample monthly inventory sheet.

Insurance To protect your investment of time and money in the business, you must have the proper insurance coverage. You should not even give a thought to not having any coverage or even to skimping on it. Whether you own or rent the property housing the operation, it is wise to have coverage in the areas listed below. In fact, a lease will probably require these coverages.

- *Fire and extended coverage:* for losses due to fire, vandalism, and malicious mischief. In most cases, you must insure up to 80 percent of the value of the property and equipment in your establishment.
- *Comprehensive liability:* for general and product liability. *General* liability covers injury to a person other than an employee inside your premises.

FIGURE 9-5. Sample weekly ice cream inventory sheet.

Most leases also require some amount of liability coverage to protect the landlord from third party suits. *Products* liability covers illness resulting from consumption of your products.

- *Theft insurance:* covers any theft inside your establishment, either by your employees or by outsiders.
- *Business interruption insurance:* reimburses you for loss when the operation is closed down through no fault of your own (by fire, for example). You should consider this coverage particularly if the lease requires rent payments whether you are able to open for business or not.

There are other types of insurance you might consider, such as auto liability, umbrella policies, fidelity bonds, medical insurance, and key man insurance. Auto liability insurance will cover bodily injury and property damage caused by a vehicle owned by the business. Umbrella policies provide additional coverage for excess liability. Fidelity bonds cover dishonesty by employees. Medical insurance, generally a group plan, is not a business requirement, but a benefit for employees. Key man insurance is life insurance on the key person or persons in the company, with the corporation listed as beneficiary. The corporation can use the proceeds, for example, to purchase the stock of the deceased individual.

Workers' Compensation   If your employees are injured or become ill because of their job, you must provide workers' compensation. Every state has a statute covering workers' compensation and these statutes have provisions for a Workers' Compensation Board for administration and arbitration. Employers are required to cover each employee with a workers' compensation insurance policy that can be purchased through a state-operated insurance fund or through a private insurance carrier. This insurance is considered a payroll expense for the employer, not the employee.

SANITARY CONDITIONS IN A RETAIL ICE CREAM SHOP

No matter how much you want quality to be the cornerstone of your operation, you will never have it without good sanitary conditions first. Achieving and maintaining good sanitary conditions requires perseverance and hard work. You cannot overemphasize to your employees the importance of operating a clean establishment for attracting customers and, ultimately, for having a successful business. Remember that employees working all day become oblivious to the environment and honestly will not notice things your customers will see instantly.

The day you open for business or, in the case of a change of ownership, the day you take possession of the business is the time to begin the daily process for maintaining sanitary standards. When buying an existing business or preparing for the grand opening after construction is completed, one of the first priorities most new owners have is a thorough cleaning of the premises. It usually takes hard work over many hours, but it is rarely an impossible task. The process of cleaning also gives you the opportunity to set the tone for the sanitary standards you want to maintain.

In many states, the health department now requires that at least one person from a food establishment take a food handling course. I strongly recommend that you and your manager take such a course. It will give you a thorough knowledge of basic food sanitation and help you operate a cleaner establishment. You will also then be able to teach your employees how to serve customers from a sanitation standpoint. You will be told about these courses when you apply for your department of health permit to operate a retail food establishment; you may even be forced to pay for the course when paying for the permit. You will also probably be given a time limit to complete the course.

The world around us is filled with dirt, litter, and pollution, and the public is constantly reminding us that they are concerned. Make your shop an oasis of quality and cleanliness and you will be assured of repeat business.

Sanitary Service Procedures

Serving ice cream and related products in a sanitary manner requires that you and your employees follow these basic procedures:

- An employee should never touch a food item directly. Always use napkins and/or food tissue paper to pick up a cone or any other food product.
- The dipperwells should be operating with running water and all dippers and spades should be inside the dipperwells when not in use.
- Pick up plastic spoons by the handles, and containers by the bottoms.
- All surfaces inside the dipping case should be kept clean constantly.
- Use only clean disposable cloths, paper towels, or Handi-Wipes for cleaning.
- When using a glass cleaner, spray away from all food products or spray directly into the towel.
- Clean all syrup and hot fudge machines daily.
- Use a utensil to dispense all dry toppings.
- Clean the ice machine bin daily to prevent bacteria from forming on the bottom of the bin.
- Keep all milk containers on ice or refrigerated when in use at the front counter.
- Never allow customers to directly touch any food products that they have not purchased.
- Food products within the customer's reach must be protected by a sneeze guard, a barrier made of glass, plastic, or stainless steel to protect the food from contamination by the public.
- Immediately clean up all spills, especially on the floor.
- Do not allow trash containers in the front of the store to overflow. Such carelessness is a clear sign of a dirty shop.

Establishing a Routine

Keeping good sanitary conditions requires opening and closing procedures during which 90 percent of the shop is cleaned. Once in practice, these routines are not difficult to maintain.

To leave no room for mistakes, put the procedures in writing and post them on the wall where everyone can see them. When opening the shop it is important to do the following:

1. Turn on all lights to be used that day. Good lighting improves the work environment.
2. Check for all refrigeration to be working properly.
3. Turn on the water for all dipperwells and put clean dippers and spades into the wells.
4. Refill all empty ice cream tubs.
5. Fill in any other supplies to be used that day.
6. Make sure the shop was properly cleaned the night before and immediately clean any areas needing attention.
7. Fill the ice bin.
8. Take a last look around the shop for overall cleanliness and appearance and then open for business.

Closing the shop is more difficult than opening. Cleaning any shop late at night is not an easy task. People are tired after a hard day's work and are anxious to leave. A manager will frequently find that a good cleaning for closing turns out to be not so good in the light of the next day, so it is important to have a closing procedure to follow to ensure proper cleaning. Again, write down and post the following:

1. Scrape down all ice cream tubs.
2. Clean the inside of the dipping cases.
3. Cover all ice cream tubs.
4. Remove all dippers and spades from the dipperwells and clean both the utensils and the wells. Use hot water to remove any bacteria that might form inside the pipes of the wells.
5. Remove all utensils from the topping bins and clean both the utensils and the bowls. Cover all toppings.
6. Clean all equipment in front of the store with a sanitizing solution, including soft serve, hot fudge, and milk shake machines. The manufacturers' manuals will describe in detail how to maintain and clean each machine.
7. Cover all exposed food products.
8. Refrigerate any products on the counter that were used during the day.
9. Clean all counters, floors, and walls.

10. If plastic tubs are used, make sure all dirty tubs are cleaned and sanitized.

11. Empty all garbage cans and insert new trash bags.

12. Restock all paper supplies.

13. Clean the bathroom.

14. Check all refrigeration units and make sure the doors are closed.

15. Clean the three-compartment sink.

16. Wash the floor at the front of the shop.

Keeping an establishment clean is not just a twice-a-day chore. Shops without set cleaning routines tend to accumulate dust and dirt in crevices, which eventually leads to roach and rodent problems. There is no such thing as too much cleaning.

Ice cream shops differ from other retail food establishments because of the heavy use of refrigeration, freezers, and soft serve equipment. All equipment in the front of the shop should be defrosted and cleaned. Special attention must be paid to the dipping cases where spilled ice cream, nuts, and chips become caked onto the case. Failure to defrost the cases allows ice to accumulate on the walls and eventually ice particles will drop into the ice cream itself, causing icing of the product.

Everyday Care of the Ice Cream Dipping Cabinet Without an ice cream dipping case that functions properly all day, everyday, you cannot operate your business and serve your customers properly. Keeping the doors closed on the dipping case will prevent excess air from entering and changing the composition of the ice cream. It is also important to institute a procedure for regular defrosting. The interior temperature should be 6–8 degrees Fahrenheit and should be constantly monitored with a thermometer. Position of the product in the case is another key factor in maintaining its quality. Because of sugar content and firmness of the finished product, certain areas of the case are not good for some flavors. Those flavors using ingredients such as coconut, cocoa, liquor, honey, and marshmallow have a high sugar content and need the coldest spots in the dipping case, which are the dipping holes over the compressor. The next coldest holes are the outside corners of the dipping case.

At the end of each day, the following cleaning functions should be done:

1. Using an ice cream spade, scrape down ice cream from sides of tubs. Be sure to clean spade between flavors and remove any pieces of ice cream from other tubs.

2. Cover tubs with lids.

3. Pick up ice cream balls and loose ice cream from bottom of freezer.

4. Thoroughly wash freezer: top door (inside and out, use brushes to clean hinges and around rubber gaskets), front and side.

5. Drain water from dipper well. Clean dipperwell with hot sudsy water. Take parts to the three-compartment sink to be washed. Put a drop of bleach in drain. Rinse with hot water.
6. Wipe as much of wall behind freezer as you can reach.
7. Use stainless steel cleaner to clean all stainless steel areas.

Covering each tub at night will keep the freezing temperature constant, exclude outside air, and inhibit ice crystals from forming inside the product. (Likewise, when taking an ice cream scoop from the dipperwell to serve a customer, shake the scoop to remove excess water that would form ice crystals on contact with the product.)

Roach and Rodent Control

Sanitary measures, such as daily cleaning, prompt garbage disposal, and proper food storage, must be followed diligently for successful roach and rodent control. A dirty environment with garbage and rubbish available simply invites the vermin.

Roaches are the most common insects that will be attracted to your establishment. They infest any area where there is food, especially kitchens, storage areas, washrooms, and basements. They can live in any place that is warm and has food and water available.

Rodents such as rats and mice thrive wherever ample food and shelter are provided. They travel inside walls and can enter a room through the slightest opening, so make sure your shop's construction is tight. Rodent-proofing your establishment consists chiefly of adequate refuse storage, collection, and disposal practices. Garbage containers should be rust resistant, watertight, and easy to clean. They should also have tightly fitting lids and sufficient capacity to hold garbage until pickup. Refuse collections should be thorough and frequent enough to prevent the accumulation of garbage outside the container and of boxes and cartons.

Plan to have an exterminator come to the shop at least twice a month, as required by the laws of most local health departments.

Personal Hygiene

Personal hygiene is a subject of great importance in the foodservice industry. First, it affects the general health of everyone working in a particular establishment. Good hygiene promotes good health, and healthy employees are alert and not likely to make the kinds of mistakes that can lead to contamination of the food. Second, good personal hygiene lessens the possibility of the spread of communicable diseases among the employees and customers alike.

Personal hygiene in the food industry refers to a group of work-related habits that should be automatic for all employees. Those habits include not only the obvious practices of washing hands thoroughly after using the washroom or sneezing, but also getting the proper amount of sleep, staying home when sick, and wearing clean clothes. There are certain basic rules that should be enforced at all times.

- Employees should come to work not only looking clean, but being clean.
- A head covering must be worn while working in the shop. Hair, a transmitter of bacteria, falling into the product is a major problem.
- Fingernails should be kept short and clean so that bacteria does not form under them.
- Any employee who sneezes should immediately go to the hand sink and wash his or her hands. Customers are very conscious of employees' personal hygiene.
- A toilet facility must be made available for all employees and a sign saying "Employees Must Wash Their Hands After Using The Toilet" must be posted in the facility. Liquid soap and either hand towels or hot air dryers must be provided.
- Uniforms should be made available to every employee, and there is no excuse for an employee to come to work in a dirty uniform. It is your responsibility to make more than one uniform available. Street clothing should never be considered as a uniform under any condition.
- Employees should not be permitted to smoke inside the shop while working. It is unsanitary and frowned upon by customers.
- A sick employee should not come to work and one who gets sick on the job should be sent home. Sick employees are carriers of bacteria.
- Immediately clean, disinfect, and bandage any cuts or sore on fingers, hands, and arms to prevent bacteria from infections from being transferred to the food.

Adequate refrigeration, proper operating routines, correct washing and sanitizing of all equipment, and control of insects and rodents are not sufficient alone to ensure a healthy environment. You could still have disease transference in your operation if an employee forgets or neglects the simple and common-sense rules of personal hygiene. Such an employee could eventually mar the favorable image of any establishment and substantially lower the customer base.

REFERENCES

Arbuckle, W. S. 1983. *Ice Cream Store Handbook.* Columbia, Mo.: Arbuckle & Co.
Arbuckle, W. S. 1986. *Ice Cream.* Fourth edition. Westport, Conn.: AVI.
Chiffriller, T. F., Jr. 1982. *Successful Restaurant Operation.* New York: Van Nostrand Reinhold.
Kahn, Mahmood. 1987. *Foodservice Operations.* New York: Van Nostrand Reinhold.

Nicodemus, Wade R., and Treva M. Richardson. 1981. *Sanitation for Foodservice Workers*. New York: Van Nostrand Reinhold.

NICYRA, 1996. The Sunday School Newsletter. *NICYRA Bulletin*, March, pp. 1–4.

Reid, Robert D. 1989. *Hospitality Marketing Management*. Second edition. New York: Van Nostrand Reinhold.

Sansoon, Michael. 1995. Fired up. *Restaurant Hospitality,* February, pp. 53–64.

Spangler, Leah. 1995. Promote the one you're with. *Restaurant Hospitality,* January, p. 24.

10

SERVING THE CUSTOMER

Your frozen dessert operation is like a theater. Your service counter or the tables at which your customers sit are the stage. Your products are the props and your employees, the actors. This setting allows you to present your products and cater to the desires of your customers, the audience. By being a director sensitive to the audience's needs and wants, you will be able to focus your entire marketing effort on the goal of satisfying your audience. Eventually, all of your hard work will result in repeat business and success.

As a major part of their marketing efforts, creative operators take great care not only in producing high-quality products, but also in presenting and serving them in a professional and dynamic manner. Setting and enforcing standards for doing so will provide a competitive edge in giving your operation that special flair sure to attract customers.

How a product looks is very important for success in selling it. Customers like to look around in an establishment and they enjoy watching orders being prepared. There is no point in your spending a lot of money to produce well-made products and then take no interest in how those products are perceived by the buying public. Your efforts will be wasted if your employees do not care how the products are prepared and served. To be able to train your employees effectively and efficiently, you will need to decide on standards of preparation and service and include that information in the shop manual (see "The First Crew" in Chapter 8) for easy reference.

Customers come to your shop for one thing, to purchase your delicious ice cream and frozen yogurt either alone in a cone or dish or as part of your sundaes, milk shakes, smoothies, and other concoctions you have created to entice them. As part of the purchasing experience, they want to be served courteously and quickly. When making decisions about your standards, put yourself in the customer's place and you will not go wrong.

SCOOPING

The scooping of ice cream and sorbet represents a high percentage of your customers' orders. Using proper scooping techniques is important both for customer satisfaction and for maintaining your profit margin.

Overscooping is the fastest way to reduce the profits of an operation. And once a customer has received an overscooped portion, it will be remembered as the standard against which future purchases will be measured. Employees should be constantly reminded what a proper single scoop of ice cream should look like and how much it should weigh. The standard weight in the industry for a single scoop is 4 ounces. Serving a 3-ounce scoop with a 1-ounce cap will make the serving seem larger than it is.

Underscooping will be just as bad for your business as overscooping. Your customers will feel cheated, word will get around, and you will have a difficult time overcoming a reputation for shortchanging customers. Under no circumstances should your customers receive less than they deserve. Have your employees constantly practice scooping and weigh their practice scoops. To properly serve your customers a single 4-ounce portion of ice cream, you should use portion-control equipment such as the Zeroll model 1010 scoop. To avoid having ice crystals form on the serving, take the scoop from the dipperwell and tap it against the side to remove excess water.

Scooping by the Ounce

One way to eliminate under- or overscooping is to price a serving by actual weight. You will need a portion-control scale that can accommodate a cone, by means of a coneholder attachment, as well as a cup. Place on your menu board the per ounce cost of your product.

The following is a good example of how this system works with a cost per ounce of 40 cents:

- Customer orders 4 ounces of ice cream served in a cup or cone.
- Employee proceeds to scoop what looks like 4 ounces into the cup or cone.
- Employee then places the cup or cone on a portion-control weight scale, which indicates that the serving weighs 4½ ounces.
- Customer is told the weight and price of the serving ($1.80).
- Customer is then told the serving is a half ounce over.
- If the customer wants only 4 ounces, the employee then removes the extra half ounce from the serving.

STANDARDS FOR SPECIFIC ITEMS

If you want to be successful selling ice cream that maintains its fresh-dipped texture and fresh flavor, you need to treat your product properly and dip it correctly. Following are descriptions of established industry practices for preparing and serving the basic products offered by frozen dessert operations. Use them to help you decide on the standards appropriate for your own operation. Such standards will make it easier for you to obtain personnel efficiency and provide better-looking portions resulting in more satisfied customers.

Ice Cream Cones

The ice cream cone is by far the biggest seller in any ice cream operation, so the importance of serving one well cannot be overemphasized. Portion control is critical, as already discussed. You need to balance the customer's desire for a large portion and your desire to make a profit.

Serving a 4–4½ ounce portion will satisfy both requirements and can be accomplished with one large scoop topped by a smaller one. Both the Zeroll model 1010 and the Hamilton Beach model 67-12 scoops will produce 4-ounce portions in a single scoop. If two scoops equaling 4 ounces are desired on a cone, use the Zeroll model 1024 or the Hamilton Beach model 67-24 scoop.

The following steps should be taken to properly dip an ice cream cone:

1. Remove the scoop from dipperwell and tap it lightly on a sponge pad to remove water. Failure to remove the water results in ice crystals in your product, which look bad and taste worse.

2. Start to scoop close to the can wall, cutting about a half inch down into the ice cream. Scoop in a circular pattern from the outside of the container toward the middle.

3. When the scoop is full, turn it over so the bowl faces up and cut off the portion by drawing the scooper lightly across the surface of the ice cream. Never cut off the portion by pressing the scoop against the side of the container. That action compresses the ice cream so the portion looks smaller than it actually is.

4. Scoop the next portion where the last one left off. Continue in the same circular pattern so that one layer of ice cream is removed at a time and the level goes down evenly. No ice cream should be left stuck to the sides of the container.

The ice cream should then be pressed into the cone so it will not fall off and create an unhappy experience necessitating your serving the customer all over again. Use quality cones and always wrap a napkin around each cone if they are not prewrapped around the bottom. Train your employees to ask customers if they would like a dry or wet topping to increase unit sales (see "Employee Involvement" in Chapter 11).

Portions

Single: 4–4½ ounces of ice cream
Double: two large scoops equaling 7–8 ounces of ice cream

Preparation and Presentation   If not prewrapped, wrap a napkin or food tissue paper around the cone and gently push the ice cream down into the cone. Try to present round scoops instead of small ones by scraping around the walls of the ice cream tub with the scoop. Then ask the customer if he or she would like a topping, such as sprinkles or granulated peanuts. If the order is "to go," wrap wax paper around the entire cone and put it into a bag.

Cups

A customer purchasing ice cream in a cup presents the perfect opportunity to practice suggestive selling. Use a cup slightly larger than is needed for the ice cream portion to allow room for toppings. Ask your customers if they would like a wet or dry topping and point out your display of toppings, which should be in a prominent location. The larger the topping counter, the more you will sell. Remember, toppings can increase a unit purchase by 25 percent or more.

Portions

Single: 4–4½ ounces of ice cream in a 5–ounce cup
Double: 7–8 ounces of ice cream in a 9–ounce cup

Preparation and Presentation   Scoop the ice cream and gently press it into the cup. Do not push it down or it will look like there is less than there is supposed to be. Then ask the customer if he or she would like a topping. If the topping is dry, simply turn the cup upside down into the dry topping bowl. For wet toppings, use a 1-ounce spoon or ladle to distribute the topping over the ice cream. If a pump is used, set the portion to 1 ounce. Instruct your employees to use their common sense to tell whether an adequate amount of topping is being served. Too much is always better than not enough (but do not let them go overboard).

Supply a napkin and a spoon with each serving. If the order is "to go," put a lid on the cup and place it into a bag with the napkin and spoon.

Ice Cream Sundaes

A terrific-looking sundae will practically sell itself. Customers enjoy deciding on what kind to order and watching their orders being made. Employees usually enjoy making sundaes. For maximum sales of ice cream sundaes, encourage your employees to be creative and take care in preparing them. Use signage with large photographs and clearly written explanations for effective merchandising of this product.

Portions

Small: 4–4½ ounces of ice cream in a 9-ounce cup
1½ ounces of any dry or wet topping
whipped cream
large maraschino cherry with stem

Large: 7–8 ounces of ice cream in a 12–16-ounce cup
1½-ounce portions of any two dry or wet toppings
whipped cream
large maraschino cherry with stem

Preparation and Presentation   Gently place the ice cream into the cup and pour the dry or wet topping over it. Dispense the whipped cream by starting from the wall of the cup and working toward the center using a circular motion and spiraling upward. Be generous with the whipped cream. Place the maraschino cherry on top of the whipped cream and serve with a napkin and spoon. Ask customers if they would like a glass of water with the sundae. It is a nice touch to ask them before they ask you.

If the sundae is "to go," put a cover on the cup and put it in a bag with the napkin and spoon.

Some Fabulous-Looking Sundaes

Peanut Cup Surprise: In a large sundae cup, place three 4-ounce scoops of vanilla ice cream with 2 ounces of hot fudge topping. Sprinkle with salted Spanish peanuts and garnish with bite-size Reese's Peanut Butter Cups.

Black Forest Sundae: Place a 3-inch square prepared brownie in a dessert dish or press into a sundae cup. Add two 4-ounce scoops of vanilla ice cream and ⅓ cup of cherry topping. Garnish with whipped cream and a maraschino stem cherry.

Pineapple Coconut Delight: Into a twin sundae dish, place one dip of chocolate ice cream into each hole. Over one scoop of ice cream, place 1 ounce of crushed pineapple, over the other, some sliced bananas. In between the two molds of ice cream, place a spoon of marshmallow topping. Sprinkle shredded coconut over the marshmallow, and top with a pineapple cube.

Pints and Quarts

Building a pint and quart take-out business will dramatically increase your sales during the winter and carry over into the summer. In-store advertising will encourage customers to purchase take-out products if they feel they are getting value and flavor that they cannot buy anywhere else. You will need a separate take-out freezer positioned in a visible area of your operation. Keep the freezer well stocked and clean at all times. Record the production of take-out products on inventory sheets and have your employees check the stock in the freezer against these sheets daily.

Your prepacked products must be attractively packaged and priced no higher than similar items available at your local supermarket or competing shop. The differences between prepacked and hand-packed products are price, freshness, and the method of packing. A prepacked container is filled directly from the batch freezer. Compared to products hand-packed at the time of purchase, the prepacked container is priced lower, not as fresh, and easier to pack. It is also lighter and less dense than hand-packed because of the air pumped into it during production. Without sophisticated filling machines, it is difficult to pack 16 ounces of the soft extruded product into a pint container.

Portions

Pint: 15–15½ ounces of ice cream in a 16-ounce container
Quart: 30–31 ounces of ice cream in a 32-ounce container

Preparation and Presentation   For hand-packed purchases, use a spade to put the ice cream into the container. Push down on the ice cream with the back of the spade and keep adding to it until the container is full. Smooth over the top of the ice cream. If the flavor is one with nuts or chips in it, it is a nice touch to use some of them from the topping counter to sprinkle on top of the ice cream. Cover the ice cream with a piece of waxed paper before closing the container with the lid. Place the purchase in a bag with some napkins and spoons.

Prepacked products are packed directly from a batch freezer or soft serve machine, blast frozen for 8 hours or more, and then put into a self-service display freezer. The containers should be attractive and easily identified, including a description of the product and the price. When a purchase is made, place the container in a bag with some napkins and spoons. (See Chapter 12, "Soft Serve Products," for more details.)

Egg Creams

If nostalgia appeals to you, having egg cream on your menu is a must. Just the name alone reminds people of the "good old days." It is a refreshing drink, but if you cannot make it properly, you would be better off not offering it. People will remember the taste, and repeat business can only be guaranteed when the egg cream is made well.

Because syrup is so important to the success of an egg cream, more is better than less.

Single-Portion Measurements

1 ounce of whole milk
2 ounces of chocolate or vanilla syrup
7 ounces of seltzer

Preparation and Presentation Pour the syrup, then the milk, and then half of the seltzer into the glass and mix well. Continue mixing and add the rest of the seltzer with a splash of syrup until the seltzer reaches the top of the glass. Serve with a napkin and a straw.

Banana Splits

In 1892, the United Fruit Company began importing bananas to the United States, and the rest, as they say, is history. Manufacturers soon created an elongated sundae dish just to handle the fruit. Its popularity was assured by the fact that the two (or more) scoops of ice cream remained separate rather than on top of one another, allowing two or more different sauces and toppings.

Like ice cream sundaes, banana splits practically sell themselves when the customers see attractive photographs or actual orders being prepared within their view. Let your employees be creative with this old-time favorite and use plenty of whipped cream for effect.

Single-Portion Measurements

1 ripe banana (make sure it is not overripe)
3 small scoops (2–2½ ounces each) of any flavor(s) of ice cream
1-ounce portions of any three different dry or wet toppings
whipped cream
1 large maraschino cherry with stem

Preparation and Presentation Slice the banana in half lengthwise and place each half on opposite sides inside a banana-boat dish. Place the three scoops of ice cream in the dish between the slices of banana. Leave a little space between each scoop. Pour each topping in the spaces and slightly over the ice cream. Dispense the whipped cream by starting from the sides of the dish and working around toward the center, spiraling upward. Place the maraschino cherry on top of the whipped cream and serve with a napkin and spoon. As an extra courtesy, provide a glass of water or seltzer with the banana split.

If the order is "to go," prepare the banana split in the manner described but use a paper or plastic banana boat dish with an attached lid. Gently place the order in a bag along with a napkin and spoon.

One Fabulous-Looking Banana Split

I'm Sailing Away with My Own Banana Boat Split: Slice pound cake to fit in the bottom of a banana split dish. Top cake with two 4-ounce scoops of vanilla ice cream and one 4-ounce scoop of chocolate ice cream. Slice a banana in half and press halves against the sides of ice cream. Drizzle with chocolate and strawberry toppings. Garnish with whipped cream, maraschino cherry, and waffle cookies as the "sails."

Ice Cream Sodas

Ice cream sodas have long been a mainstay of the neighborhood ice cream store. A resurgence of nostalgia from the 1950s has brought increased demand for them.

A good ice cream soda must be served in a tall glass with plenty of flavor in the soda to go along with the ice cream.

Single-Portion Measurements

9 ounces of seltzer
2½–3 ounces of syrup
1 ounce of milk
5–6 ounces of ice cream

Preparation and Presentation Pour the 3 ounces of seltzer into a tall 20-ounce paper or plastic container. Mix the syrup with the seltzer and add the milk. Place 5 to 6 ounces of ice cream (two 2½–3 ounce scoops) into the container and then put in the rest of the seltzer. Stir slowly and add a drop more of the syrup for more flavor. Remember, lack of flavor in a soda will be noticed quickly. Serve with a napkin, spoon, and straw. Adding a little whipped cream on top is an attractive touch.

If the order is "to go," put a lid on the container and gently place it in a bag along with a spoon and napkin.

A Bit of Nostalgia, A Few Old Time Favorites

The Black Cow: Into a soda glass put 1½ ounces root beer syrup. Add 1 spoon whipped cream or ice cream and blend. Add fine stream of carbonated water until glass is ¾ full. Float into the carbonated mixture two 1½-ounce scoops vanilla ice cream. If glass is not full, finish filling with coarse stream carbonated water. Top with whipped cream.

The Broadway: Into a soda glass put 1½ ounces chocolate syrup. Add 1 spoon whipped cream or ice cream and blend. Add fine stream of carbonated water until glass is ¾ full. Float into the carbonated mixture two 1½-ounce scoops coffee ice cream. If glass is not full, finish filling with coarse stream carbonated water. Top with whipped cream.

Milk Shakes and Malteds

Milk shakes have always been popular, and if you build a reputation for making a good one, you will be assured of repeat business.

To be good, a milk shake does not have to be extremely thick, but one that is thin from too much milk will be rejected by customers. Like the ice cream soda, make sure there is plenty of flavor from the syrup used. A real old-fashioned milk shake is made with partially frozen milk. Try it.

Single-Portion Measurements

6–7 ounces of ice cream
1½ ounces of syrup, plus 2 ounces of malt powder for malteds
7–8 ounces of milk

Preparation and Presentation Pour half the milk into a regular size (28-ounce) metal tumbler and add the syrup and ice cream. Attach the tumbler to a mixer and mix for 30 seconds. Then add the rest of the milk and run the mixer for another minute. Pour the finished shake into a 16-ounce glass and serve with a napkin and straw. If all of the milk shake does not fit into the glass, offer the leftover to the customer.

For malteds, add the malt powder during the first 30 seconds of mixing.

If the order is "to go," put a lid on the container and gently place it in a bag along with a napkin and straw.

A Couple of Totally Outrageous Shakes

Calypso Cobbler: In a milk shake mixer, place and mix together 4 ounces each of milk and apricot nectar, 2 ounces of pineapple juice, ½ teaspoon vanilla extract and two scoops of vanilla ice cream. Blend well, pour into tall glass, and top with coconut and orange slice.

Double Chocolate Almond Delight: In a milk shake mixer, place and mix together 5 ounces of milk, one scoop each of vanilla and chocolate ice cream, 1 ounce each chocolate syrup and sliced almonds, and ¼ teaspoon almond extract. Blend well, pour into tall glass, and top with whipped cream and sliced almonds.

Smoothies

A smoothie is a refreshing lowfat blended drink. Use your imagination to create as many flavors as you desire, but you will find that customers love the idea of a creating their own customized drinks. Most smoothies are prepared with either orange, pineapple, or apple juice. Bananas are used in most smoothies to create a creamier texture to the prepared drink.

16 Ounce Serving Without Ice

5 ounces of frozen fruit (includes a third of a banana)
5 ounces of juice
6 ounces of ice cream, frozen yogurt, sherbet, or sorbet

Preparation and Presentation Pour frozen fruit (including banana), juice, and either ice cream, frozen yogurt, sherbet, or sorbet into a regular size (28-ounce) metal tumbler or blender canister. Attach the tumbler to a mixer and mix for 30 seconds. Pour the finished smoothie into a 16-ounce container and serve with a napkin and straw.

If the order is "to go," put a lid on the container and gently place it in a bag along with a napkin and straw.

24 Ounce Serving With Ice   Using ice creates a colder, more granita-type texture to the smoothie drink.

6 ounces of frozen fruit (includes a third of a banana)
6 ounces of juice
6 ounces of ice cream, frozen yogurt, sherbet, or sorbet
6 ounces of ice

Preparation and Presentation   Pour frozen fruit (including banana), juice, ice, and either ice cream, frozen yogurt, sherbet, or sorbet into a regular size (28-ounce) metal tumbler or blender canister. Attach the tumble to a mixer and mix for 30 seconds. Pour the finished smoothie into a 16-ounce container and serve with a napkin and straw.

If the order is "to go," put a lid on the container and gently place it in a bag along with a napkin and straw.

Some Very Cool, Very Refreshing Smoothies

Strawberry Paradise: Pour 4 ounces of frozen strawberries (including a third of a banana), 3 ounces of orange juice, 2 ounces of ice, and 4 ounces of ice cream into a regular size (28-ounce) metal tumbler or blender canister. Attach the tumbler to a mixer and mix for 30 seconds.

Peach Smash: Pour 4 ounces of frozen peaches (including a third of a banana), 5 ounces of peach nectar, 2 ounces of ice, and 4 ounces of peach sorbet into a regular size (28-ounce) metal tumbler or blender canister. Attach the tumbler to a mixer and mix for 30 seconds.

Blueberry Passion: Pour 4 ounces of frozen blueberries (including a third of a banana), 5 ounces of orange juice, 2 ounces of ice, and 4 ounces of vanilla nonfat frozen yogurt into a regular size (28-ounce) metal tumbler or blender canister. Attach the tumbler to a mixer and mix for 30 seconds.

Ice Cream Coffee Drinks

Most Americans already drink their coffee with milk. But just think what you could do for coffee and dessert sales if you upped the ante by serving coffee with ice cream. If plain old cappuccino commands a premium, then the same beverage topped with ice cream is a gold mine. Try out a few of the following with your customers:

Mocha Frappe: Combine ¾ cup of strong coffee, 2 tablespoons of cocoa powder, and two 4-ounce scoops of vanilla or chocolate ice cream in a blender until smooth. Finish with 1 small scoop coffee ice cream and whipped cream. Garnish with shaved chocolate or chocolate-covered espresso beans.

Cafe Au Lait: Combine 1 cup of double-strength coffee and ⅛ teaspoon of ground cinnamon. Next, blend two 4-ounce scoops of vanilla or chocolate ice cream with coffee in a blender until smooth. Garnish with whipped cream and a cinnamon stick.

Coffee Brickle Ice Cream: Blend four 4-ounce scoops of vanilla ice cream with 1 teaspoon of instant coffee powder and 1 tablespoon of hot water until smooth. Top with almond liqueur, whipped cream, toasted slivered almonds, and almond brickle chips.

Caramel Coffee Ripple: Blend four 4-ounce scoops of vanilla ice cream with 1 ounce of caramel topping and 1 ounce of coffee liqueur until smooth. Blend in cold, strong coffee to taste. Top with whipped cream and drizzle with caramel topping.

ICE CREAM CAKES AND PIES

Besides just scooping ice cream, being in the ice cream business has many other rewards. One of them is selling a beautifully decorated ice cream cake or pie to a customer, and watching them leave your shop with a smile of satisfaction and anticipation. Even better, you might see them coming back again and again for another cake or pie as a repeat customer.

Selling ice cream cakes and pies can sometimes make the difference between success and failure in an ice cream shop. By putting in the effort and promoting the products, they can amount to 25–35 percent of your business. Equally important, these products can be sold year-round. You can even increase your operation's efficiency by using employees to make ice cream cakes during otherwise slow periods.

A new store will easily sell ice cream cakes at first because everyone will want to try one. This opportunity is your "first shot" at impressing customers with your quality and creativeness. Ice cream cakes can generate tremendous repeat business from satisfied customers, so make the best of your "first shot." The necessity of an attractive product cannot be overemphasized. The more attractive you make them, the more ice cream cakes you will sell.

Potential Markets

Most ice cream cakes are sold for birthdays, with a special emphasis on children's cakes. Display a wide assortment of children's cakes to take advantage of parents' impulse buying. Be creative when making these cakes. Purchase cake pans of all sizes, shapes, and characters. Children love a cake featuring a favorite Disney or cartoon character.

The busiest days for ice cream cakes are Valentine's Day, Mother's Day, and

Father's Day, respectively. Be sure to produce appropriate theme cakes for those days.

Producing and selling ice cream cakes for restaurants, caterers, and other foodservice facilities has become a new role for ice cream shop operators. In particular, a large market has developed for a "celebration cake" in the foodservice industry. This small cake serves two or four people and is intended for couples out for dinner to celebrate a birthday or anniversary. Restaurants and other foodservice facilities store these cakes in their freezers until needed. Foodservice personnel remove the cake from the freezer when dinner is ordered and by the time dinner is over, the cake is just the right consistency for serving with a candle or other trimmings.

Equipment, Supplies, and Ingredients

Your finished desserts are only as good as the ingredients that go into them and the equipment used to make them. Just as the artist needs the right brushes, the ice cream entrepreneur needs the right tools and equipment to produce a professional-looking product to compete in the world of take-home desserts.

Equipment and Supplies   To have a successful ice cream cake business you will need a variety of equipment and supplies, the most important of which is a cake merchandising freezer. Manufacturers such as Kelvinator, Master-Bilt, McCray, and Federal make well-lighted, attractive ice cream cases (see "Ice Cream Cake Cases" in Chapter 8). These cases allow for prominent display of different sizes of cakes in a single unit, thus showcasing the products for effective merchandising. The curved-glass unit from Federal Industries is highly recommended because of the way the cakes are displayed in the unit. The cakes simply seem to pop out at the customers.

Cake decorators, as artists, use certain equipment to achieve desired results. Often, elaborate decorations can be made from simple tools and a knowledge of their use. Any good artist will have a basic knowledge of the tools and materials required for the job. Without the proper tools, you will get unprofessional results, regardless of your creativity. Companies such as the Catalog Sales Division Company of Greenwood, Indiana; Parrish's of Los Angeles, California; Wilton of Woodridge, Illinois; and A. Panza & Sons of Edison, New Jersey, manufacture and distribute complete lines of ice cream cake equipment and tools. In addition, the Luck's Company of Tacoma, Washington, makes incredible ready-to-use, edible decorations of Disney characters, animals, and so on that have revolutionized the cake decorating industry.

The following is a basic list of everything you will need to produce a complete line of ice cream cakes:

Round cake pans. Metal cake pans with a removable bottom plate are recommended over "springform" pans. There is no spring to break, and the frozen ice cream cake can be removed from the pan in a few seconds. You will need various sizes of 3-inch deep round pans: 6 inch (4), 8 inch (2), 9 inch (2), and 10 inch (1).

Loaf pan for making bar cakes (4 inches by 8 inches).

Cake boards, which are white corrugated cardboard rounds (cake circles) that come in a variety of sizes and should be the supporting base of every ice cream cake you make. If the sides of the cake are unfrosted or only coated with cookie crumbs, the board should be the same size as the diameter of the cake. If the cake is frosted and decorated with a border, the cake board should be up to 2 inches larger than the pan.

Spatulas. A small offset metal spatula with a narrow 4-inch blade and a wooden handle is best for frosting a cake. When smoothing the top of the cake, a metal spatula with a longer handle is recommended.

Turntable. A heavy metal turntable that can support large size ice cream cakes without tipping is recommended. It should be at least 12 inches across and 4 inches high to allow it to turn easily, thus expediting the frosting and decorating processes.

Cake boxes in various sizes to correspond to the size of the cake board or pie.

Cake comb for doing fancy designs on the surface of the frosting. A cake comb is shaped like a triangle with a different size pattern on each side.

Plastic squeeze bottles for "drizzling" desserts with chocolate or other sauce. Each bottle holds at least 8 ounces with an opening large enough for easy filling.

Funnel for filling plastic bottles with various sauces.

Pastry brushes. A 1-inch pastry brush is used to remove crumbs from the surface of a cake, or to brush or glaze over fresh fruit for garnishing desserts.

Doilies in various sizes for displaying cakes and pies. The doily should be larger than the diameter of the dessert so it is visible.

Cake pedestals for displaying desserts in a display freezer. Do not use glass.

Small plastic bags with zipper seal that can be used for drizzling. Fill bag half full with chocolate coating or variegate. Cut a tiny opening in corner, then squeeze.

Pastry bags. Acrylic-coated vinyl bags are recommended because they are washable and reusable. A variety of 12-, 18-, and 24-inch pastry bags are recommended. The larger size bags are used exclusively for frosting cakes with nondairy whipped topping.

Couplers. A coupler or "coupling set" is a two-piece system used to attach a decorating tip to a pastry bag. It allows you to change tips in seconds by keeping the tip outside of the bag. The outer ring and base makes up one coupling set.

Rose nails, or flower nails, are decorating tools onto which you pipe a full rose or other flower.

Decorating tips. Keep a variety in stock for doing almost any decoration. The following sizes and quantities are recommended:

(2) tip #2	(2) tip #9	(4) tip #32
(4) tip #3	(2) tip #15	(6) tip #104
(2) tip #6	(2) tip #18	(2) tip #352
(2) tip #2-E	(2) tip #2D	(2) tip #827
(2) tip #200 (icing tip)		

Tip cleaning brushes for keeping tips clean.

You can purchase these supplies from the manufacturers previously mentioned or listed in the Appendix, or from most ice cream supply distributors and candy-making supply stores.

Cake Decorating Ingredients   The most beautiful ice cream cake or pie in the world will not bring a customer back for repeat business if the cake does not taste great. And you cannot have a great-tasting product without using high-quality ingredients. It is as simple as that. The following is a list of the basic ingredients you will need:

Food colors, which are available in paste or liquid. Water-based colors can be used to color buttercreme, nondairy topping, and ice cream. Oil-based candy colors can be used to tint white chocolate coating a rainbow of pastel colors.

Pink	Egg yellow	Green (emerald and leaf)
Orange	Red	Brown
Violet	Black	Royal blue
Lemon yellow		

White decorating icing or Buttercreme for making borders, flowers, and so on.

Nondairy whipped topping to use instead of real whipped cream because its shelf life is limited and once frozen, it will start to deteriorate very quickly in flavor and appearance. Nondairy whipped topping can be used for both frosting and decorating and is available in both liquid or powder.

Piping gel for writing on cakes and doing glasslike decorations. It is available in clear or precolored.

Chocolate coatings that are sometimes called bar coatings or dipped chocolate. They are wonderful for creating designs and decorations such as chocolate curls, chocolate shavings, chocolate drizzles, and chocolate dipped fruits and nuts.

Cookie crumbs, which are available in chocolate (Oreo or Hydrox), graham cracker, and granola. They are wonderful for use as the base for a cake or as a coating on the side.

Chocolate fudge. Any topping fudge that you use in your shop is suitable for cakes and pies.

Pie shells. Available from many commercial bakery or foodservice ingredient suppliers, they come in either chocolate or graham cracker.

Cake decorating requires a mixture of the proper tools, creative artistry, and cake-writing ability. It is not difficult. It is a learned skill, rather than an inborn artistic talent. With knowledge, the correct tools, and an abundance of practice, you, too, can create your own line of beautiful frozen desserts made with your signature ice cream flavors.

Ice Cream Cake and Pie Recipes

Now comes the best part, actually making your own ice cream cakes and pies. Because they are purchased primarily for some special occasion, you should take care in making sure that each is unique and special. An ice cream cake is easiest to produce using freshly made ice cream straight from the batch freezer or soft serve machine. The cake is molded inside a pan, frozen solid (8 hours or overnight), then removed from the pan and decorated. The following recipes are basic, but once you get the hang of things, the possibilities are endless.

Basic Ice Cream Pie Formula Every one loves pie—especially a creamy ice cream pie with all the gooey, yummy toppings! You will be glad to know that pies are easy and quick to make.

Ingredients

1	Pie crust, 9-inch, frozen (approximately 6 oz.)
24 oz.	Ice cream or frozen yogurt
4 oz.	Nondairy whipped topping
1–2 oz.	Decoration (drizzles, nuts, chocolate shavings, etc.)

Preparation

1. Weigh ice cream filling.
2. Using a white rubber spatula, carefully mound ice cream into pie crust, mounding most of the filling in the center.
3. Place pie on a turntable. Using a small offset spatula, spread ice cream into crust, making sure there are no air pockets. Form ice cream into a slightly mounded dome shape, with highest point in center of pie and sloping downwards to edges of crust. Top edges of crust should be visible.
4. Smooth surface with offset spatula, making sure the dome shape is uniform all around the pie.
5. Freeze pie until firm, several hours or overnight.
6. Place frozen pie on a turntable.
7. Using an 18-inch pastry bag and large star tip, make rosettes around edge of pie with whipped topping.
8. Garnish pie as desired.

Makes one 9-inch pie, approximately 36 ounces, that serves 8.

Basic Ice Cream Cake Formula   Ice cream cakes can be round, square, rectangular, or even heart-shaped, and they do not even have to include cake! You may choose to make a "cake" with a cookie crust instead of using a layer of cake. You may even use a brownie, or make your creation an all-ice cream "cake". An ice cream cake can be frosted and decorated just like a bakery-style cake. It can also have a crunchy graham cracker crust and be side-crumbed with more graham cracker crumbs like a real cheesecake.

Your customers will enjoy selecting a cake from a variety of flavors, shapes, sizes, and styles. Giving them a choice is important. Have fun!

Preparation of Base

Most operations produce ice cream cakes using a cake or crumb crust bottom. Consumers prefer a cake bottom, but, in reality, unless the cake is fresh, you will end up with a cake that is stiff, rubbery, and has no taste. A crumb crust bottom is just as attractive, has a nice crispy taste that works well with ice cream, and is not difficult to prepare.

> *Cake base:* Use either vanilla or chocolate sheet cake. Place pan face up. With a knife cut the shape to fit pan and place the cake inside the pan.
>
> *Cookie crumb base:* The type of crumb base used is totally dependent on the flavor of ice cream you will be using. Oreo or Hydrox crumbs work well with any vanilla- or chocolate-based ice creams, and the graham and granola works best with fruit flavored ice creams. You need the crumbs, margarine, and sometimes sugar to assemble the base. The following portions are based on producing a 9-inch round cake using 7½ ounces of prepared crumbs:

Oreo or Hydrox fine crumbs:	87% crumbs, 13% margarine
Graham	66% graham meal, 30.5% margarine, 3.5% sugar
Gingersnap:	82.5% gingersnap meal, 17.5% margarine
Granola:	84% granola meal, 16% margarine

Over low heat, melt the margarine, mix in sugar as needed, and then combine all ingredients.

Ingredients

1   Cake base (choose a cake layer, cookie crust layer, or brownie)
*   Fudge layer (or variegate), optional
*   Ice cream filling (preferably in soft stage)
*   Frosting (nondairy whipped topping, softened ice cream, buttercreme, etc.)
*   Garnish/decoration of your choice

The (*) indicates that the amount needed depends on the size of the pan and the height of the cake.

Preparation

1. Prepare cake base. Place in bottom of pan. If a crumb crust is used, it must be pressed firmly and evenly into bottom of pan. (Freeze crust before filling if cookie crumb crust is used.)

2. Apply fudge layer (if desired) directly on top of base. Spread to an even layer using a small offset spatula.

3. Fill pan to desired height with semifrozen ice cream. Smooth top to make an even layer, using offset spatula. A variegate can be added at this time. Layer it along with the ice cream, then lightly swirl the variegate and ice cream together with a small paring knife or metal skewer.

4. Freeze cake until firm, 8 hours or overnight.

5. Unmold cake from pan by carefully wiping sides of pan with a warm wet towel. Push bottom of cake up, releasing cake from sides of pan. Briefly freeze unmolded cake to set ice cream.

6. Place cake on appropriate size cake board. Crumb-coat sides of cake or frost with nondairy whipped topping. Decorate as desired.

Decorating Decorating an ice cream cake or pie is truly a lot of fun and, creatively, very rewarding. The customer's first impression of your cake and pie products will be when they are first thinking about ordering one of your finished creations, so take your time to do it right. That means a neatly frosted cake, borders that are uniform and professional, and decorations that are attractive, tasteful, and appropriate.

Using a spatula, spread the frosting over the top and sides of the cake, starting with the top. The use a cake comb to remove excess frosting and give your cake a smooth finished look. Fill a pastry bag with frosting. Starting from the top of the bag, push down and twist the bag until the frosting is down in the tip. Add designs to the frosted cake as follows:

- *Star:* Hold pastry bag straight up, with tip ¼ inch from surface. Apply pressure to bag until a star forms on the surface.
- *Zigzag:* Hold pastry bag in horizontal or flat position, with tip very close to surface of cake. Apply pressure to bag moving your hand from left to right with slight up and down motion.
- *Shell:* Hold pastry bag at 45-degree angle with tip 1¼ inches from surface of cake. Squeeze bag to release contents as shell builds. Gradually ease pressure to form "tail" moving 1¼ inches along surface. Stop pressure after tail is made. Continue to make shells starting at point of the previous shell.

Writing on the Cake or Pie Fill a writing gun (tip #3) or bag using piping gel or fudge to add a message and other details. Hold the gun angled slightly towards you. Moving your arm as you write will help the letters flow smoothly. Support the tip with opposite index finger. Touch the surface of cake or pie with the tip and apply pressure to make a small dot on surface. Lift slightly as you apply even pressure to form each letter. To stop a letter, touch surface lightly with tip and squeeze another small dot, then pull away.

REFERENCES

Arbuckle, A. S. 1983. *Ice Cream Store Handbook*. Columbia, Mo.: Arbuckle & Company, Inc.

Chiffriller, T. F., Jr. 1982. *Successful Restaurant Operation*. New York: Van Nostrand Reinhold.

Dairy Management Inc., American Dairy Association. 1996. *The Ice Cream Premium*. Brownsdale, Minn.: ADA.

Dairy Management Inc., American Dairy Association. 1996. *Shake Yourself a Winner, America's Moost Delicious Milk Shakes*. Brownsdale, Minn.: ADA.

Dickson, Paul. 1978. *The Great American Ice Cream Book*. New York: Atheneum.

International Ice Cream Association. 1993. *Let's Sell and Serve Ice Cream for Fun and Profit*. Washington, D.C.

Mariani, John. 1996. Banana splits. *Restaurant Hospitality*, March, p. 84.

Stogo, Malcolm, and Lisa Tanner. 1995. *Ice Cream Cakes*. Scarsdale, N.Y.: Malcolm Stogo Associates.

11

⊠⊠⊠⊠⊠⊠⊠⊠⊠⊠⊠⊠⊠⊠⊠⊠⊠⊠⊠⊠⊠⊠⊠⊠

MARKETING THE RETAIL FROZEN DESSERT SHOP

The marketing of a retail frozen dessert shop, that is, the overall advertising of the business (as opposed to merchandising a product or product line) is a personal thing. In most instances, it reflects the personality of the owner, which, it is hoped, translates down to the employees. In a sense, it is the playing out of your dream. Once the shop's lease is signed, that dream will slowly evolve into the real thing. If you can get your customers to fall in love with the dream, you will have a real winner on your hands.

Whatever ice cream products you are selling, consumers must know that their impulses to buy your products will be satisfied quickly and pleasantly. Make sure your products are fresh and appealing by constantly tasting them yourself. Train your employees to say "thank you" and "please come again." Caring about the individual will ensure repeat business. For example, if you serve soft frozen yogurt in two flavors and a customer wants half a portion of one flavor and half of the other, be willing to accommodate. Being inflexible will hurt your business in the long run. When a customer leaves your premises, and thanks either you or your employees, you know you are on the right track.

How you answer the following questions will give you a better grasp of how well thought out your marketing effort is, and most important, how it will be perceived by your customers:

- Are you producing and selling products that customers want?
- Is your business setting simple enough for the customer to understand what you are offering for sale?

- Does your establishment have a comfortable and inviting atmosphere?
- Is the menu signage understandable and easy to read?
- Does your price structure encourage or discourage sales?
- Are your employees trained to welcome and serve your customers?

It is not reasonable to think today that you can rent space, buy equipment, post signs, provide a product, and wait for customers to show up to consider yourself in business. How to market your new business and merchandise your products to potential customers is something you have to seriously think about even before you are actually open for business. That means developing marketing and advertising plans ready to go, plans based on understanding the customer's needs.

A marketing plan encompasses many things, each a small part of the whole. The key areas on which to focus your marketing plans are your products and their pricing, your employees, and your shop's visual environment.

THE PRODUCTS

Your product mix should be interrelated but varied enough so customers have choices that satisfy the needs of the entire family. A product line that matches the tastes, preferences, and expectations of your target market will result in a successful operation.

- Are your products unique? Most people go into business because they think they have an idea or product that is unique; something a customer could not get from the competition down the street. Part of your marketing plan examines how to convey that message.
- Do you encourage innovation in your product mix (the variety of products you offer for sale) and do you encourage customers to try new items?
- Does the actual experience of purchasing your product compare favorably with the consumer's perceptions prior to the purchase? Postconsumption feelings can tell you a lot about your product and operation. If the ice cream cone did not taste as good as was anticipated or as remembered from a previous purchase, you have some work to do.

Seeing the Products

If it cannot be seen, it will not be sold, and that is the plain and simple truth (see "Visual Appeal," later in this chapter). Follow these guidelines for getting your products "to the eye of the customer."

- *Let the public see the product close up.* The key to product promotion is to get the product as close to the customer as possible. Dipping cases, particularly the Coldelite Italian COF and the Kelvinator curved glass models (see Chapter 8), provide a good way to display wares.

- *Utilize counter space.* Create a visual interaction between the customer and product. Construct attractive topping bars that fit on the counter close to the dipping cases and right in front of the customer. Attractive displays tell the public you care about your operation and want their business.
- *Install attractive sneeze guards.* Wherever possible, install attractive sneeze guards on the front counter to increase the amount of space available for merchandising secondary products, such as toppings and cones. Even though the main purpose of the sneeze guard is to protect the product from the customer, it will also provide display space.
- *Utilize attractive surroundings around any equipment and fixtures to place products that are pleasing to the eye.* Products should blend with the surroundings but have enough contrast to be distinctive. When done well, customers are likely to notice and purchase secondary products, such as waffle cones, placed in their view.

Whatever product is displayed, it should look so appealing as to be irresistible. When everything looks tempting, customers will eventually purchase something and, in many cases, something more than they had intended.

Sampling the Products

Let customers sample your products. Whet their appetites by offering samples as they look over your wares. By offering a taste, you force a reaction. A quality product always stands out in a taste test and a consistent sampling program will contribute greatly to creating positive personal interactions. Samples are merchandising at its cheapest and, in many ways, its best.

The purpose of a sampling program is to educate customers about your products and to initiate sales. Sampling is also helpful when introducing new products or flavors. Purchase spoons to be used exclusively for sampling and provide samples whenever a customer desires a taste. Encourage sampling by doing the following:

1. When customers enter your shop, say "hello" and after a few moments, ask if they need help.
2. Regardless of the response, ask if they would like to taste a specific flavor. If they seem undecided, offer a sample of a new or unusual flavor, something they would be unlikely to do on their own.
3. If they respond favorably to the sample, ask if they would like to make a purchase of the product.
4. If they say "no," ask if they'd like another sample and this time let them pick the flavor.

By this point, you will usually have negotiated a sale. After the purchase is made and while the customer is beginning to eat the product, inquire whether he or she is enjoying it.

Secondary Products

Years ago, ice cream shops were one-product oriented. It was unheard of to sell anything but the ice cream itself along with sugar cones, hot fudge, rainbow and chocolate sprinkles, and granulated peanuts. Today's high rents and other overhead expenses have forced owners into thinking of new ways to increase their business. Many have introduced new product categories such as smoothies and espresso bars, while others have introduced secondary products that have a direct connection with the basic item being sold.

In the ice cream business, smoothies, espresso and cappuccino, toppings, mix-ins, and waffle cones aggressively marketed to the impulse buyer have all helped to increase unit sales by 20–50 percent. Handwritten signs or suppliers' posters do not constitute aggressive marketing. Innovative topping bars, cone stands, creative signage and display, and other devices pleasing to the eye will attract customers to secondary products. Let the public see what you have to offer; make sure secondary products are on the front counters. Being able to watch purchases being made is a big attraction. Have a product look so tempting that it is irresistible, and price will automatically become a lesser issue.

Be innovative. Do not be afraid to take chances. Not every new idea will work, but some will. If you understand that every customer is important to your business and try to maximize every sale, you will see how secondary products can boost your gross income without a large capital investment.

Waffle Cones and Bowls Waffle cones and bowls started as a fad in the United States in the early 1980s, but have become a staple for the majority of ice cream and frozen yogurt operations. They have provided an opportunity to offer customers something out of the ordinary. Being a high mark-up item, they also provide a comfortable profit, increasing unit sales by 25–35 percent.

These oversized cones and unique bowls not only sell themselves when displayed on front counters in attractive holders, but make it easier to sell the dry toppings that are becoming increasingly popular profit-generating items. What could be more appealing than such a neat and tasty container for your favorite ice cream covered with a luscious topping or two? Nothing, except maybe dipping the cone or bowl in chocolate (which I invented in my shop at the South Street Seaport in New York City [Robbins, 1986]).

There are no significant capital investment costs involved in handling waffle cones or bowls, so the risk is minimal. You can buy them premade or buy the mix and make them yourself. The advantages of premade cones and bowls include

- No investment in equipment or labor to produce them. They are thus a bottom-line profit center.

- Ample daily supply versus baking them one at a time throughout the day.
- A variety of sizes, ranging from small to jumbo, and uniformity within sizes.
- High-quality taste and long shelf life.

The advantages of making them on your premises include

- An aroma generated during baking that will entice customers to your shop.
- The visual attraction of the showmanship involved in the baking process.
- Freshness and high-quality taste.
- Versatility in that different shapes can be made when baking.
- A final cost that is about the same as the premade product.

Toppings Until the 1980s, toppings consisted mainly of sprinkles, hot fudge, granulated peanuts, and whipped cream. With the resurgence of frozen yogurt, a wide variety of toppings has become popular. Operators knew they would not last long simply selling four flavors of frozen yogurt daily. They needed something else, an extra attraction. So toppings have become an integral part of the frozen dessert business, accounting for up to a 50-percent gross profit margin because of their low wholesale cost. And that is why they are so heavily merchandised today.

When customers enter your shop, they are already in the mood to treat themselves. By offering an appetizing selection of toppings in an attractive way, you make it easy to maximize your sale. Topping bars today include everything from fruits, to nuts, to candy pieces, in addition to the traditional syrups and sauces. Nabisco, Hershey, Nestle, Leaf, M&M Mars, and other manufacturers of cookies and candies have recently made it easier for the operator to obtain pre-crushed products in bulk quantities for use in topping bars and blended desserts. The larger the variety, the more attracted to the topping bar customers will be and the more toppings you will sell (Arthur, 1988).

You can take advantage of many of the ingredients you already have on hand for ice cream production as well as create additional sales simply by utilizing existing counter space for a topping counter. Most shops have two dipping cases and the space between them is the best area for a topping bar, which requires only a flat surface at least 48 inches wide and 30 inches deep. To house the toppings, you can buy a drop-in stainless steel unit, such as those manufactured by Delfield Corporation of Mt. Pleasant, Michigan, or you can construct your own by using glass or metal bowls. You should handle twelve to twenty-four toppings. They will increase your unit sales and contribute to the attractiveness of your shop.

The keys to a successful topping operation include the following:

- Keep the topping bar filled all the time.
- Either have all the toppings labeled separately or have a framed sign on top of the sneeze guard explaining each one and its price.
- Keep the topping bar spotlessly clean all day.
- Put spoons in each container for a uniform appearance.

- Train employees to encourage customers to purchase toppings by specifically pointing out the wonderful array of choices and asking the customer if he or she would like some.

When a customer enters your shop and approaches the counter, it will probably take only a little encouragement to produce a larger sale than the customer originally intended. At a price of 25–50 cents per topping, the average unit sale can be increased by 25 percent or more.

Smoothies and Other Blended Desserts Thanks to the Dairy Queen Company and the introduction of their dessert product called "The Blizzard," and the increasing popularity of smoothies, blended desserts have become big business. Very refreshing and healthful, fruit smoothies can be marketed as either a beverage or a dessert (see Chapter 10), depending on the time of day. They are made from fresh or frozen fruit, fruit juices, and ice. Ice is used specifically to create a colder more granita-type drink. A Blizzard is simply a soft-serve product blended with crushed cookies or candies.

Part of the success of blended desserts can be attributed to the hundreds of combinations that can be produced using ice cream, frozen yogurt, and sorbets in combination with frozen fruits, cookies, and candies. Also, the dessert can be made right in front of the customer's eyes, making the purchase exciting as well as satisfying. Best of all, from the operator's viewpoint, blended desserts have a 45-percent profit margin over the cost of a basic serving of ice cream.

Three major companies make the machines used to produce the Blizzard-type drink. Flurry International, of Cleveland, Ohio, produces machines featuring a power mixing spoon and what it calls a "mix-thru" disposable cup collar. The mixing spoon, cup collar, and the cup itself are all disposable. The system enables an operator to mix and serve the product in the same container. This revolutionary blending concept is completely sanitary and prevents cross-over blending of flavors. The machine has a fast blending time of 5–10 seconds and is completely portioned controlled. It comes with a 2-year warranty and measures 10 inches wide by 9 inches deep by 24 inches wide.

Electro-Freeze's Model HDM 50 is a high-speed unit that mixes candies, fruits, and cookies in both hard and soft ice cream as well as in frozen yogurt. It is ideal for heavy production use and measures $9\frac{1}{8}$ inches wide by $9\frac{1}{4}$ inches deep by $23\frac{3}{4}$ inches high.

The Arctic Swirl, manufactured by Swirl Freeze of Salt Lake City, Utah, is another powerful blender that blends hard and soft ice cream and frozen yogurt. Model B is 12 inches wide, $26\frac{1}{4}$ inches deep, and $30\frac{5}{8}$ inches high.

PRICING

It is true that people will pay a higher price for a quality product, but there is a limit and consumers are constantly making purchasing decisions based on price as well as on quality. Proper merchandising makes price a less-important factor in such decision making. A fabulous-looking ice cream sundae will sell on impulse. Attractive signage will distract consumers from prices. But dirty surroundings and sloppy presentation will make customers resistant to any price.

Use your employees and signage to educate the consumer to the value of your products. Provide pleasant service and note the following guidelines to help make price a minor issue in the daily operation of your business:

- Make sure your employees know the price of every item on your menu. They should not be confused when a customer asks how much something costs. Give each employee his or her own copy of the shop handbook, which includes prices and descriptions of how products are made and presented (see Chapter 10).
- Make your products look glamorous and present them in a stylish fashion. You will be rewarded with high unit sales and repeat business.
- Keep your counters and displays clean and attractive so the customers can focus on the products, not on the prices.
- Do not try to fool your customers by using prices ending in 99 cents. Today's consumer will not be taken in by that strategy.
- Be straightforward. If you are going to charge extra for something, use an attractive sign to explain why.

Suggestive selling, attractive products and surroundings, pleasant and prompt service, and excellent signage all reduce the effect of how consumers view prices. Having a sale or using coupons usually elicits a favorable response from the public. If they perceive a bargain, they will take advantage of it. In a shop where prices are normally high, a sale will be seen as a big bargain and will bring good results. Promoting special sales during the winter months is a must for repeat business and keeps your operation active all year round.

EMPLOYEE INVOLVEMENT

Consumers must know that their impulses to buy an ice cream cone or a cup of frozen yogurt will be satisfied quickly and pleasantly, and you rely on your employees to provide that satisfaction. Employees are the backbone of your business. You cannot function without them. Accordingly, any marketing program must consider the role they play and allow for their involvement in every aspect of merchandising. When employees pack pints, for example, and take care to give the customers their money's worth, the result is a positive experience. A customer can think, "They take care in serving me," and you get repeat business. And that's the goal of merchandising. Employees must know the name of every flavor and its ingredients. They must know how to prepare and present ice cream sodas, milk shakes, sundaes, and so on (see "The First Crew" in Chapter

8 and "Employees" in Chapter 9). They must be trained to say "hello," "please," and "thank you," and to use suggestive selling.

Suggestive Selling

Suggestive selling means simply encouraging a customer to purchase a product in a sincere manner to produce a positive experience. Train your employees never to be forceful or curt and to be sure to welcome all customers. Simply saying "Good afternoon, may I help you?" will put customers at ease and make them more receptive to any suggestions you might make. For example, suppose a customer orders an ice cream cone. When your employee puts the ice cream on the cone, he or she should ask if the customer would like sprinkles or any other topping added. By making the suggestion, the employee has sparked a thought in the customer's mind that a topping would be a good addition. Most of the time the customer agrees to the idea, appreciates the time spent on him or her, and makes the purchase.

Employee awareness of cake making and ice cream production also helps with your overall marketing plan. When employees tell customers that the ice cream is made on the premises and explain how it is done, they give customers a better appreciation of your products.

Handling Customer Complaints

You cannot have outstanding customer service without a plan for handling customer complaints. The problem of poor service can be avoided if you let your employees know exactly how you expect them to treat customers. Spell out your expectations in the shop manual (see "The First Crew" in Chapter 8). Special attention must be paid to the development of people skills when training all personnel. First-class treatment can turn an average ice cream purchase into a memorable and positive experience. It has been shown (Reid, 1989) that a guest in a hotel will tell, on average, twelve other individuals about any problems that might have occurred during a stay. While a frozen dessert establishment obviously differs from a hotel, the fact remains that a dissatisfied customer will tell friends and relatives about an dissatisfaction.

Should you become aware of a particular service problem, deal with it immediately, preferably in person, but at least by telephone or letter. The first response should be an immediate apology. The customer must be made to believe that the company takes the complaint seriously and is willing to take action to resolve it. You should not present a defensive attitude. Keep in mind that your only goal is to make the customer happy. Respond to his or her comments in a rational, understanding way. Offer a free purchase, an immediate refund, or ask for suggestions about solving the problem. Common sense will determine the appropriate response for the moment. Frequently, a simple, sincere apology is sufficient.

VISUAL APPEAL

Next to an appropriately priced high-quality product, your shop's visual appeal is the key to attracting customers and encouraging repeat business. Therefore, the importance of visual appeal cannot be overemphasized. Whatever equipment and accessories you buy must be constructed and positioned in your shop so as to showcase your products and influence customers to make a purchase. If you have thought out how customers will enter your shop, where they will end up to place an order, and how they will make their way to that destination, you will have made a good start toward understanding how to approach your shop's visual environment.

Lighting

Having a well-lighted, uncluttered shop makes an appealing setting. The customers must feel that they are being wooed and invited to enter your shop and focus on what they want. Its importance cannot be emphasized enough. This includes both outside and interior lighting. Outside lighting attracts and draws customers to you. Interior lighting highlights your products and helps showcase the interior look of the shop.

Cleanliness

A dirty shop is something people will always remember and talk about. Eventually your business will suffer in the long run because of the negative word-of-mouth advertising. The best solution is to keep your operation spotlessly clean. (See Chapter 3 and "Sanitary Conditions in a Retail Ice Cream Shop" in Chapter 9.) Make sure spills are attended to immediately and that all serving utensils and dishware are immaculate. Should a customer complain about anything being dirty, respond immediately with an apology and replace the offending glass or silverware (or clean up any mess). To let your customers know you are interested in how they feel about your establishment, as they leave the premises, inquire as to whether they found everything satisfactory. Your efforts will be appreciated.

Equipment

American manufacturers have for years produced the same equipment in basically the same styles. Owners and operators of frozen dessert establishments have generally not demanded new and innovative equipment to sell their products because they have not thought of the marketing aspects of equipment. In Europe, however, the importance of style and merchandising (see Chapter 8) has not been overlooked. Europeans have long been designing equipment that is not only functional but also attractive to create awareness in the buying public.

Travel and the importation of goods has begun to influence even the ice cream industry in the United States. European refrigeration can be seen more frequently in supermarkets and gourmet shops. Italian manufacturers have been forerunners in producing ice cream freezers designed to visually promote products by displaying them at eye level. In contrast, most American freezers used in ice cream shops require constant looking down into the cases to see the product. The one exception is the curved glass dipping cabinet manufactured by Kelvinator.

Every ice cream shop needs equipment and how that equipment can be utilized for marketing the products should be a primary concern for any operator looking for success. (For specifications and additional details about equipment, see also Chapter 8).

Dipping Cases Built for the simple purpose of dispensing ice cream, dipping cases, especially American models, were never designed to be attractive. They are functional and sturdy, having a good compressor and requiring little repair.

To maximize the merchandising aspect of these workhorses, make sure the ice cream is properly displayed. At the beginning of each day, make sure each flavor is decorated on top. As the tubs are emptied, repeat the procedure. As it is used, the ice cream should be scraped down along the walls of the tub and smoothed out. Never scrape the remains of one tub onto the top of a new one. Wait until the new tub is one-quarter used and then add any leftovers.

If you think such effort is a waste of time, go visit other shops. See how they display products in their dipping cases. If they look good, it is probably because of an appealing presentation. And that is what merchandising is all about, making products appealing to the consumer. European equipment manufacturers, especially in Italians (see Chapter 8), have focused on appealing to consumers by creating dramatic environments for frozen dessert products. European display cases are well lighted, built with shiny stainless steel, and are structurally attractive. American cases are well lighted but the outer structural steel is not as shiny. Where American dipping cases hold conventional round tubs, Italian cases use rectangular steel pans that allow for one-third more ice cream to be displayed. The rectangular pans were designed with merchandising in mind. They can be stacked closely together to present a mass of product that is visually appealing simply because of its mass. But the Italian shop operators do not rely on mass alone. They make a special effort to present their products as works of art by constantly decorating the tops of the pans with fresh fruit.

The American philosophy in dipping cases has been a matter of function over form. The emphasis has been on how well the equipment works and how much it costs. The importance of customer perception has been overlooked. If you decide to purchase an American dipping case, ask about adjustments that can be made to help market your products. For example, find out if the compressor can be raised off the floor and the counter holding the ice cream built up so that the display level is higher for better visual appeal. Most dipping cases have only 8-inch wide countertops that limit merchandising capabilities. Consider purchasing one with a larger top, preferably 10–14 inches (like the McCray models). Then you will be able to display more secondary products.

Ice Cream Cake Display Cases Ice cream cake cases are generally designed to provide for merchandising inside and on top of them. The countertop is usually wide and should be utilized to display an attractively framed sign describing the varieties and sizes of cakes available. You should include some comments about why your cakes are special. The countertop can also be used to display secondary products.

The front of the case is glass, so be sure to display cakes that will impress customers with a look of freshness and style. Identify each cake separately with its description, size, and price. Do not detract from the display by putting boxed cakes in the case. Cakes boxed and already sold awaiting pickup should be stored in a backroom freezer.

Take-out Freezer Cases Take-out freezers are usually vertical cases with one or two doors or horizontal models that provide the customer with self-service products (See "Ice Cream Merchandisers" in Chapter 8). Each style has advantages, but space requirements will usually dictate your choice.

Take-out sales can be a business in itself. Utilizing your batch freezer and soft serve dispensing unit will enable you to sell take-out products all year long. Stock a large variety of products, such as pints, quarts, half-gallons, ice cream sandwiches, cakes, and other novelties. Neatly and clearly label packages with your logo and the price and description of the product. Having the logo on the containers will create name recognition and provide free advertising, two big pluses in creating a market for your product line. If the line is well received, name remembrance will make a positive contribution to repeat purchases. Make sure your prices are competitive if you want to do a large volume of business.

Signage and Graphics

Whereas a repeat customer has previous experience to rely on, a new customer in particular must be able to make eye contact with your products and have access to clear, concise signage in order to make a decision.

Design Poorly handwritten signs convey an attitude of carelessness and disinterest on the part of an operator and can have only a negative impact on a potential customer. Clear, striking signage and pictures are marketing tools that create interest and provide information. Careful planning and attention to design principles are required to make your printed displays successful (see Chapter 8). Food courts at malls are good places to look for ideas about signage.

Your graphics, menu, and board displaying the menu should satisfy four major objectives to be advantageous to your operation.

1. The menu should target the market you are trying to reach. It should convey that the needs and wants of the consumer are your top priority. In simple and concise language, the menu should clearly emphasize the items and flavors available to appeal to customer choice.

2. Signage and graphics should reflect the image of your operation. If you want to appeal to children, then the menu or sign board should have a fun and lighthearted design. The signboard is one of the first things a customer looks at when entering the premises, so it is important that it projects a positive image consistent with your environment.

3. Printed displays should influence the customer to make a certain kind of purchase. Popular items like single-dip cones, toppings, and specialty items should be highlighted either in special categories or on the first or second lines of menu boards. Prominently positioning add-ons and other secondary products will boost your chances of increasing unit sales.

4. Pictures and signs should express to the public why you are different from the competition. The menu in particular can be used to feature signature items that are sold exclusively by you. These items, such as fancy sundaes, waffle cones dipped in chocolate, and special flavors no one else has, must be outstanding in quality and priced to sell. You should promote them heavily and give them prominent positions on your menu.

By paying close attention to detail when designing your signage and graphics, you can avoid the following common mistakes:

- Sign boards that are too small to accommodate all your menu items. Overcrowding is visually unappealing.
- Menus lacking distinctive and descriptive selling copy to communicate to the customer. Consumers want to clearly understand what they will be getting for their money.
- Item descriptions that are too long. More than two lines of copy for any one item deters customer interest. Be concise.
- Type that is too small to be read easily. The resulting confusion turns people away.
- Handwritten notes attached to the menu or sign boards. These look shabby and rarely help sales.

Signs should be large and have bright colors so that a customer standing 15 feet away can clearly see the menu boards. Whatever colors you use, make sure they are compatible with the overall scheme of your shop. Whites and light shades communicate a clean, bright character and make smaller spaces appear larger. Using one basic color will let products stand out. Pastels present a soft and delicate feeling, while bright colors stimulate strong emotions. Dark colors tend to make small spaces feel confining and should be used only in conjunction with a strong decorating theme.

Using various colors can offer endless combinations in contrast and coordination. Color contrasting offers the opportunity to showcase different parts of your shop. You can direct the customer's eye to a point of contrast. Coordination can be used effectively as well. If red is predominant in your scheme, use a red sign or red menu listings to carry on the color scheme and promote visual continuity.

Use large, color photo transparencies, available from outlets such as the Great American Stock of Rio Rancho, New Mexico, to show consumers precisely what they will be getting for their money. These pictures can create powerful first impressions. They establish an image of your operation in the minds of consumers and stimulate a desire for a specific product. The photographs should be as realistic as possible. Your objective is to provide pictures that a customer can point to and say "I want that!"

Placement   The area behind the front counter at slightly above eye level (about 6 feet) is the best place to hang interior signage. Customers can easily see the menu boards and make their decisions quickly. The front counter itself is an excellent place to display framed signage. Small signs (10 inches by 12 inches) can list menu prices or describe your shop and its products. Design such signs to make the customers feel as if they are being spoken to directly. But remember to position such signage and any secondary products so that they do not present a barrier between the customer and your employees.

Signage in an attractive setting in your front window will encourage the public to enter your shop. The window serves many purposes, but its main use is to identify the shop name to the public. An image related to the products (a fancy ice cream cone, for example) should be displayed in or painted on the window. People love to window-shop and an attractive storefront will draw their attention.

Once identification has been accomplished, you will want to let people know about specific products that are being offered for sale. Limit merchandising in the front window to concise signage introducing new products or sales promotions, one at a time. More than two signs in any window blocks the view and creates a cluttered appearance, especially when the signs are grouped closely together. Before placing any sign in the window, be sure you have a definite purpose for its being there. Pick one spot for the signs and rotate the introductions for specific time periods to maximize their merchandising value. Window displays can be powerful marketing tools, so take advantage of them.

MARKETING IN YOUR NEIGHBORHOOD

Years ago, product quality, good service, and a clean inviting appearance were the primary elements necessary to operate a retail frozen dessert shop. Today these aspects are merely the basic requirements for getting into the game. Ultimately, the success of any dessert retail business is the human connection the store makes with the community it serves. A good way to make that connection is through involvement in neighborhood activities that provide excellent opportunities for off-premises promotions as well. Indeed, an active neighborhood store marketing program can accomplish three key goals for both new and established shops. It can

- Bring in new customers
- Increase the frequency of purchases among your present customers
- Increase the average check size per customer

The keys to a successful neighborhood store marketing program are

- *Networking.* Building business relationships through networking (talking to as many people as possible) builds business, and no activity is more important in community involvement than networking.
- *Potential profit for both parties.* Both the neighborhood organization (school, church, business, etc.) and your business must benefit from any kind of promotion that is staged. At the end of the promotion, if either party thought the promotion was not worthwhile, then future promotions with that party will not be possible.
- *A good relationship with your employees.* Since they will generally live in the neighborhood, they are your entrance to their schools, churches, athletic events, fairs, and festivals.

Neighborhood Marketing Targets and Ideas

The following list encompasses a wide spectrum of organizations and groups within a community, but is by no means all inclusive. These suggestions are intended to get you thinking in the right direction.

Apartment Complexes: Get to know the manager of every apartment complex in your area. Find out the rules of the complex and try to gain permission to give all new residents a copy of your take out menu and coupons.

Athletic Event Tie-In: There are several ways to tie in with athletic events. You can operate a concession, donate food, or even sponsor a team. You may be able to promote your shop through a banner or by paying for the team's T-shirt or some form of athletic sponsorship.

Area Schools: Schools offer many opportunities. You can provide or sell food for class parties, fairs, carnivals, and dances. At the high school level you can obtain recognition through your support of the sports teams, band, clubs, and student organizations. Key people to contact are the principal, head coaches, and student body advisors.

Churches and Synagogues: Both of these groups need to raise money for their own activities, so offering them a monetary deal with a promotion helps the group and yourself. Two of the best deals are discounting gift certificates and donating product they can sell.

Colleges: Begin by approaching fraternities and sororities concerning social functions and fund-raising activities. Talk with dorm officers and the officers of campus clubs and organizations.

Youth Groups: Scout troops and local recreation departments are important sources for sales and new customers.

Charity Events: You can donate ice cream, or ran a concession selling ice cream and give the event a percentage of sales.

Planning

Planning is all about information, and the more information you gather about your immediate trading area, the better prepared you will be when planning your off-premises promotions. The knowledge gained from the following will greatly increase your chance for success:

Competitive surveys. Find out your competition's role in the community and what groups and activities you can target.

Preparing a budget. Set a budget for how much you can afford to spend on off-premises promotions for the whole year. Then break it down on both a seasonal and individual promotion basis. These figures will help you plan for the future as well as evaluate events after the fact.

Analyzing your shop's strengths and weaknesses. Determine what you are doing right and wrong. Stick with the strengths and do not repeat activities that turned out less well than you had expected.

To help you decide whether or not a particular promotion will benefit you, be realistic in answering the following questions:

- What are your projected sales for the season?
- What percentage of sales can reasonably be attained with each promotion? How much should be spent to achieve that goal?
- Can you afford to implement all of your promotions?
- What is the goal of each promotion within your plan? Are you looking for a direct sales benefit or are you just trying to create an image within the community?

Making Contact

Off-premise promotions provide a temporary outlet for the sale of your shop's products away from your actual shop location. Personal contact is the most effective method of explaining the benefits of having your products sold at an event or site. A large percentage of business and clubs can be reached through a letter campaign. It is the simplest method for advertising your shop and generating awareness. Create a letter similar to the sample shown as Figure 11-1.

Dear _____ :

As the owner of (your location) I would like to personally invite you to make us a part of your organization's next meeting or event. Our products make for a great time no matter the event. Having [your shop's name] at your charity event or fund-raisers is a great way to attract people and raise funds for your group.

I will call you in the next few days to explain my special discounts for group parties or orders. We cater parties and functions of all types and sizes.

If you are planning an event for your organization, I think you will find that (your name) will please every one in your group.

Sincerely,

Your name
Shop address
Phone number

FIGURE 11-1. Sample letter advertising interest in off-premises promotions.

Follow-up is important. Allow for enough time for the letter to have reached its destination, with a day or two for the idea to be considered. Then make sure you place a telephone call and ask for an appointment to discuss a potential promotion or the possibility of working together in the future.

Implementation

Realize that employee enthusiasm is critical to the success of an off-premises promotion. Offer incentives and contests with each promotion. Delegate responsibility to ensure employee involvement. Outline specific tasks that need to be done by each employee for the various promotions.

And be aware that neighborhood store marketing is a process, not just a one shot deal. It takes at least two successful promotions with a group to build a strong relationship. Once that foundation is secured, the potential for growth is incredibly enhanced.

Analyzing Your Results

Evaluate every activity or promotion you do. The first season you begin an active campaign will be the toughest. Once you have involved your shop in a number of activities, it will be easier to determine which events will result in the objectives you desire. For example, you offer the boy scout club in your area a gift certificate promotion. The gift certificates have a retail value of $15. The boy scout club sells them for $10 each. For each one sold, the scouts remit back to you $8 and keep $2 for themselves. The scouts sell the gift certificates for 1 month and the actual promotion has a 6-month expiration date. When the promotion is over, you do the following analysis:

- Were the objectives met? Yes, we got an organization to join us in a promotion during the spring break from school. The scouts sold lots of gift certificates. They made some money and we got some new customers. Hopefully, they will become repeat customers as well.
- Did the promotion pay out? Yes, the scouts sold $5,000 worth of gift certificates. We got to keep $4,000 and they made $1,000.
- Were there any unexpected positive benefits? Yes, all of the boy scouts in the group became regular customers of the ice cream shop.
- Were there any unexpected negative results? Yes, gift certificates kept turning up a year after the promotion, but were honored anyway.
- Do you plan to run the event again, and if so, what improvements would you make? Yes, but we would run the promotion over the Christmas holidays with additional specific coupons attached to the gift certificates just for kids to redeem themselves as an added bonus.

After each promotion, then, ask yourself the following questions:

- Were the objectives met?
- Did the promotion pay out?
- Were there any unexpected positive benefits?
- Were there any unexpected negative results?
- Do you plan to run the event again, and if so, what improvements would you make?

MOBILE MERCHANDISING

There is plenty of potential for selling frozen desserts in environments other than dip shops. You can consider being mobile and going out doors directly to customers instead of waiting for them to come to you. Taking products to the public is not a new idea. Since the 1940s, street vendors have parlayed small capital investments into successful enterprises selling every kind of food product imaginable. While most of the initial growth in outdoor sales has been in the general foodservice industry, the frozen dairy dessert has been quick to catch up.

Carts

Mobile carts allow you to "put your merchandise where your market is." This concept, says Nancy McCain (1988), marketing manager of Carts of Colorado, is an ideal sales tool because of low maintenance costs, low overhead, and ease of use, all resulting in a high unit-profit margin. Ice cream and other frozen desserts are frequently bought on impulse. Carts make your products immediately available for satisfying consumers' impulses, as well as providing a stimulus for those impulses. Appealing graphics on the awning, umbrella, or sides of a cart will enhance your image and attract attention.

Mobile vending is a relatively inexpensive means for expanding your market by taking your product to the consuming public and by being in many places at the same time. You can be out daily on a routine basis, and you can also market your wares to the captive audiences at parades, sporting events, and carnivals.

Licenses and the Board of Health   Before purchasing a cart, check with the local department of licenses and inspections to see if any special licenses are required for conducting business outdoors from a cart. Many localities have specific regulations concerning particular streets and locations, how many vendors can solicit at a given time, and so on.

You will also need the approval of your local board of health, which will issue certificates that must be displayed prominently on each cart. To make sure that you comply with local ordinances, it is highly advisable that you discuss them with the local inspector, especially if you plan to purchase a used cart. Many older carts do not meet current health standards regarding dipperwells and cold running water. The following items are important for passing inspection by the board of health:

- Overall cleanliness.
- Dipperwells with continuous running water.
- Scoop holders inside the freezer compartment.
- Dual hot- and cold-water sinks and a wastewater tank if any food besides ice cream is sold. The wastewater tank must be at least 15 percent larger than the freshwater sink.
- Stainless steel work surfaces for all preparation and serving areas.
- Freezer plates covered with the same metal as the freezer's interior, preferably aluminum or stainless steel.

Size and Design   Carts come in different sizes and designs depending on the application the user has in mind, but there are basically two types available: pushcart and trailer-pushcart. As the name indicates, a pushcart is moved to a selling location by being pushed there, or by being loaded onto another vehicle for transport. Once at the site, it is easily maneuvered to any particular spot. Pushcarts usually come with three wheels, a disadvantage on rough surfaces that make the carts unstable and hard to push. Trailer-pushcarts are more easily transported to the vending site by towing. They thus require a strong steel frame that is an integral part of the cart, and a fully independent suspension system. To be easily pushed at the site, the trailer-pushcart must be lightweight and have two front and two rear wheels as well as a removable hitch.

Ice cream dipperwell carts range in sizes capable of holding from eight to twenty-two 3-gallon tubs in one or more freezer sections. Regardless of type, capacity, model, or manufacturer, choose a low cart, no higher than 42 inches. Taller carts are difficult to maneuver and work from. They are unappealing to consumers, especially children, who like to see what you are doing when you serve them.

Construction Carts require a small capital investment and low maintenance costs. Their low overhead and ease of use will result in a higher unit-profit margin for your products. The rapid growth in doing business by carts has prompted the need for improved cart design. Consequently, better-quality carts are being manufactured.

When considering the purchase of a cart, you should look for the following qualities:

- The use of durable, lightweight materials such as aluminum or fiberglass.
- Consistent workmanship by a manufacturer from cart to cart and evidence that close attention has been paid to the finishing details.
- Uniform, uninterrupted insulation that completely surrounds the product-load space to maintain temperature and quality. Polyurethane is most often used and recommended.
- A good refrigeration system. Combined with insulation, it is the most important factor in determining the quality of an ice cream vending cart. Ask a manufacturer what temperature its freezer will hold.

You should also evaluate the availability of parts and service. Likewise consider the cost of a base package and what options you will absolutely need. Standard equipment should include a freezer designed for serving dipped ice cream or novelties, stainless steel serving counters, pneumatic wheels, and handle bars for pushing. Options include plug-in cables for refrigeration units, locks on the wheels, storage/trash boxes, umbrellas, and dipperwells. More elaborate models can have sinks with hot and cold running water, refrigerated topping sections, and creative lighting systems. But because it pushes and maneuvers easily over most surfaces, the workhorse in the business is still the lightweight, well-built, low-priced dipperwell pushcart that will hold eight 3-gallon tubs.

Refrigeration However, if a vending cart does not maintain your product's quality by keeping it cold and unmelted, all of the advantages of taking your product to the consumers are negated. Several variables directly affect holdover time, which is the length of time that a refrigerated cart can maintain proper product temperature.

- *Amount of product.* Overloading inhibits air circulation inside the cart and raises the temperature of the interior freezing compartment.

- *Location of the cart.* If the cart does not have an umbrella or awning, intense sunlight will make it more difficult to hold the interior temperature.
- *Quality of the insulation.* If polyurethane is not used, holdover time will be reduced.
- *Type and capacity of refrigeration.*

There are three basic refrigeration systems available for mobile vending carts, and the better the system, the higher its cost.

1. *Dry ice:* the simplest refrigeration system, but consider the expense of replacing it daily and the fact that dry ice can be hard to find. You also have to be careful where you place it. Improper use can result in an ice cream product being too hard.
2. *Slug system:* more sophisticated and cheaper in the long run than dry ice. The refreezable slugs (plastic containers holding a freon refrigerant, similar to those available for picnic ice chests) provide refrigeration, but they have to be constantly refrozen. And, like dry ice, slugs make it difficult to maintain an even temperature.
3. *Holdover plate and compressor system:* far superior to the use of dry ice or slugs in that it provides reliable, uniform refrigeration at 10 degrees Fahrenheit. Holdover plates containing eutectic (easily freezable) solutions have compressor-charged refrigerant lines running through them. Individual plates are thoroughly and uniformly frozen by plugging the system into AC power. Doing so for 6–8 hours (pull-down time) will provide 12–14 hours of refrigeration (holdover time).

Manufacturers of Mobile Carts   As for any purchase, choosing a cart manufacturer willing to help you choose the right cart for your needs is an important consideration. Its products should be reliable and not require continuous and costly repairs and maintenance. I highly recommend the quality products of Carts of Colorado, All Star Carts (formerly Westrock) Corporation, Workman Cycles, and Hackney Brothers Body Company (see Table 11-1).

Carts of Colorado designs custom units and distributes a full line of carts used extensively in the retail of all frozen dessert products. Sizes available range from single-door models holding eight 3-gallon tubs to large units that support a 4-foot long dipping cabinet. One of their more attractive carts, their model CC2USS, comes with an umbrella and houses a soft serve freezer. Model CC3S is in their Competitor Series used exclusively for novelties. Model CC3D is for dipping ice cream and comes with a dipperwell with cold running water, a sink, a 22-gallon water tank, and a 28-gallon waste tank. Model CC2USS is a soft serve cart that can accommodate any standard soft serve equipment. It has a 5.7 cubic foot refrigeration, dry storage, and a six-pan condiment unit for toppings.

All Star Carts (formerly Westrock) Corporation invented the first mechanically refrigerated ice cream vending cart. Their model 510 (Figure 11-2) is a

Table 11-1. **Mobile Carts**

Model	Capacity		Dimensions (inches)		
	Cubic Feet	Items	Width	Depth	Height
Carts of Colorado					
CC3S	5.5	Novelties	$16\frac{1}{2}$	$38\frac{1}{2}$	$28\frac{1}{2}$
CC3D	Custom	8 Tubs	$46\frac{1}{2}$	$33\frac{3}{4}$	$26\frac{1}{4}$
CC3	8.87	Novelties	27	38	28
CC2USS	Custom	Soft serve	$71\frac{1}{2}$	$32\frac{3}{4}$	$36\frac{1}{2}$
All Star Carts					
501	10	8 Tubs	24	56	57
515	10	8 Tubs	24	41	32
520	18	18 Tubs	75	69	63
503	6	8 Tubs	30	25	42
505	10	10 Tubs	41	24	42
Hackney Brothers					
62	6.2	300–350 Novelties	51	30	38
83	8.3	400–450 Novelties	57	$34\frac{1}{8}$	$36\frac{1}{2}$
97	9.7	500–550 Novelties	65	$34\frac{1}{8}$	$38\frac{1}{2}$
108	10.8	600–650 Novelties	$62\frac{1}{2}$	32	$47\frac{7}{8}$

FIGURE 11-2. All Star Carts (formerly Westrock) Company Model 501.

mechanically operated pushcart with a dipperwell section that has adjustable continuous running water and fresh- and wastewater tanks. Models 505 (Figure 11-3) and 515 are novelty carts that have bicycle wheels. Models 520 (Figure 11-4) and 520T have two freezers that hold eighteen 3-gallon tubs, a topping rail and hot fudge unit, cone box storage, and a lockable cash drawer. The dipperwells on these units have continuous running water. The units also come with dual sinks for hot and cold running water that are large enough for washing hands and utensils, as well as wastewater tanks. In addition to their complete line of carts, they manufacture freezer bodies that fit into or on a van or truck.

Hackney Brothers manufactures a sleek line of mobile carts in many sizes, but only for selling novelty items because they lack dipperwells. Models 62, 83, 97, and 108 have refrigeration systems requiring overnight connection to a 115-volt source and come with 15-foot plug-in cables. They all have a freon-evaporator plate/compressor system with interior polyurethane insulation, umbrella-support tubes, and large (20-inch) bicycle wheels. Umbrellas, heavy-duty vinyl storage covers, and a dipperwell attachment are available at extra cost.

Workman Cycles, America's oldest bicycle manufacturer features a complete reasonably priced selection of ice cream tricycles and pushcarts. The model VICT ice cream tricycle features classic front load design and a stainless steel insulated dry ice cabinet.

FIGURE 11-3. All Star Carts (formerly Westrock) Company Model 505, a novelty cart with bicycle wheels.

FIGURE 11-4. All Star Carts (formerly Westrock) Company Model 520, a double freezer cart with its own dipperwell.

ISA makes an attractive, sleek gelato cart that is perfect for use as part of an outdoor cafe operation because it requires an electrical connection to function. Its interior display area can hold up to ten pans of product. The unit has a temperature control, defrosting system, large stainless steel work counter, canopy, and lighting for display.

Vans and Concession Trailers

For serving large groups of people or to provide a greater variety of products, consider a van or concession trailer. Their large size (compared with a pushcart) allows more than one employee at a time to serve the public, thus increasing your business capability, especially during peak lunch periods. Be aware that such vehicles will require commercial license plates.

The ice cream van is a self-propelled shop on wheels. It can be moved quickly from one location to another in response to customer demand. The Custom Sales and Service Company, of Hammonton, New Jersey, is one manufacturer of these that I recommend. Their "Lickety Split" unit comes on a heavy-duty GMC chassis with a 12-foot body having a pink, gray, and white exterior with hot pink graphics that will attract both children and adults. It features soft serve and slush machines, a soda system, complete topping rail, storage freezers, dipperwells with running water, and many other shop components.

A concession trailer will allow you to conduct a large daily business at fairs, carnivals, flea markets, parades, sporting events, and the like. All Star Carts (formerly Westrock) Corporation, of Bayshore, New York, makes an enclosed ice cream vending trailer, Model 525T, that I can recommend. It has a tubular steel frame with full independent suspension and a baked aluminum interior and exterior. The unit has two sides that fold up to expose two freezers holding a total of twenty-five 3-gallon tubs. Each freezer has its own dipperwell and continuous running water. A third freezer comes with a built-in topping rail that holds five different toppings, a double-boiler hot fudge machine, and a chocolate syrup pump holder mounted into a stainless steel countertop with a dual-compartment sink with hot and cold running water. The serving height from the countertop to the ground is 42 inches. The unit also has interior fluorescent lights, lockable sides and door, storage space above the serving area, and fresh- and wastewater tanks. All the freezers have holding-plate systems with mechanical refrigeration that eliminates the need for dry ice.

Hints for Mobile Merchandising

Becoming mobile is smart business. It allows for rapid expansion with few restrictions and little expense when compared with stationary operations. Consider the following:

- Use "guerrilla" marketing. Beat your competition to the punch by getting to the right traffic-dense locations first.
- Take advantage of the lower overhead to reduce selling prices and make your products aggressively competitive.
- Give free balloons with each sale.
- Cover your mobile units with graphic advertising that promotes your product's image.
- To attract children (who in turn attract parents), have special for them and add bells to your units.
- Take advantage of the public exposure to test new products.
- Offer your employees a commission pay scale to operate a mobile unit. That will give them an incentive to be creative and increase sales.
- Advertise your units as available for special catering events such as birthday parties or grand openings of other businesses.

REFERENCES

Chiffriller, T. F., Jr. 1982. *Successful Restaurant Operation.* New York: Van Nostrand Reinhold.

Kenny, Kathleen. 1982. Soft serve signature specials. *Restaurant Business,* pp. 1–8.

Kronard, Stephen. 1989. Taking it to the streets. *Dairy Field,* p. 25.

Kuhn, Mary Ellen. 1996. In-store marketing innovation. *Food Processing,* April, pp. 26–28.

Leighton, Peter. 1994. Working your freezer for better sales. *Health Foods Business,* July, p. 29.

Lewis, Robert C., and Susan V. Morris. nd. The positive side of guest complaints. *The Cornell Hotel and Restaurant Association Quarterly,* vol. 27, no. 4, p. 14.

Pegler, Martin M. 1989. *Successful Food Merchandising and Display.* New York: Retail Reporting Corporation.

Reid, Robert D. 1989. *Hospitality Marketing Management.* Second edition. New York: Van Nostrand Reinhold.

Robbins, Carol. 1986. N.Y. Ice cream extravaganza. *Dairy Foods,* vol. 87, no. 7 (July), pp. 53–60.

Star, Peter, and Sara Star. 1994. Nice on ice: How to fill your freezer. *Health Food Business,* December, pp. 28–34.

12

⊠⊠⊠⊠⊠⊠⊠⊠⊠⊠⊠⊠⊠⊠⊠⊠⊠⊠⊠⊠⊠⊠⊠⊠⊠⊠

SELLING SOFT
SERVE PRODUCTS

While hard ice cream has been the dominant frozen dessert product produced worldwide for many years, other frozen dessert products have their niche, and in many countries are more popular than ice cream. Soft serve products have been available in one form or another for more than 60 years (Arbuckle, 1983, p. 36), with soft ice cream and frozen custard in particular enjoying wide popularity since the 1950s. The American marketplace has recently seen the introduction of a number of other dairy and nondairy soft serve products, such as frozen yogurt, sorbets, and smoothies.

As the name implies, soft serve products are not hardened, and it is their soft, creamy texture that the public finds so appealing. They are easy to consume, thus providing instant gratification. They are especially easy to lick, a characteristic particularly enjoyed by children, who make up 50 percent of the customer base for soft serve products. Such products also lend themselves to decreased labor costs, as evidenced by growing numbers of consumers willing to serve themselves from soft serve freezers in supermarkets and convenience stores and restaurants (Racord, 1988).

Other than the investment in the equipment, handling soft serve products is a relatively low-cost operation. The equipment takes up little space and is easy to operate. The products increase profit margins and are self-promoting when the machinery is in the public view. Two major categories of soft serve products, low-fat and nonfat soft ice cream and frozen yogurt, attained amazing sales growth during the late 1980s because of intense consumer interest in diet and health. As a result, anyone seriously considering a frozen dessert business cannot ignore some form of soft serve product either as a main item or on a dessert menu.

SOFT ICE CREAM

Background

During the 1930s, soft ice cream was popular in neighborhood drug and candy stores, but immediately after World War II the soft ice cream and frozen custard market really blossomed (Arbuckle, 1983, p. 36). The flight to suburbia during that period resulted in frozen custard stands (Dairy Queen, for example) appearing along highways and on street corners all over the United States.

Then interest in soft ice cream began to decline and reached a low point during the mid-1980s when premium ice cream became the public's new center of attention. But thanks to such innovations as blended desserts, consumer interest in soft ice cream has been revitalized. With the introduction of its Blizzard products in the late 1980s, Dairy Queen became a billion-dollar retail company.

Whereas vanilla and chocolate were the only flavors sold up until about 1987, strawberry, coffee, and banana have arrived, and the demand is growing for even more flavors. Some shop operators create their own flavors from the basic vanilla for use in multiple soft serve machines.

Composition

The term *soft ice cream* is basically a trade name, and the product is sometimes called frozen custard. The difference between soft ice cream and frozen custard is the egg-yolk content. By federal law, frozen custard must contain 1.4 percent egg-yolk solids by weight. Both products have a fat content of 3–10 percent, with industry standards leaning toward the 6–10 percent range. Soft ice cream does have lower butterfat than the hard product, but it can be difficult for the consumer to tell because the soft state allows full flavor. Be aware that the lower the fat content of the mix, the higher the tendency of the finished product to be icy, coarse, and weak in flavor. These unfavorable characteristics are especially evident in products made with mixes containing less than 4 percent butterfat, where water is the predominant ingredient.

In addition to the butterfat, soft ice cream consists of 11–14 percent milk solids, 12–15 percent sugar, 0.25–0.6 percent stabilizers and emulsifiers, and 30–35 percent total solids. To avoid a finished product that is coarse, icy, and weak, soft ice cream needs a higher milk-solid content than is normally required for hard ice cream to offset the lower butterfat content of the mix.

Stiffness and dryness of the mix is extremely important for getting a smooth, creamy finished product from the soft serve freezer. Those characteristics are achieved in two ways:

1. By reducing the sugar content of the mix by 2–3 percent of that used for a hard ice cream product.

2. By reducing the freezing point for drawing out the product to 10–22 degrees Fahrenheit. This lower temperature not only produces a stiffer product, but makes it immediately suitable for serving to the public.

Because the softness of the product allows the sweet taste to come through, less sugar is required for soft ice cream than for hard, in which the additional chilling in the blast freezer dissipates the sweetness of the sugar. Stiffness and dryness are also enhanced by the use of emulsifiers that retard meltdown.

SOFT FROZEN YOGURT

Background

What began as a fad in the early 1970s has now become an established niche in the frozen dessert marketplace: frozen yogurt, produced and sold both as a soft serve product as well as hardpack. After its explosion onto the industry scene and its initial burst of success, frozen yogurt faded from the scene in the late 1970s because of problems with its sour taste and its being gummy, icy, and not very creamy.

Those problems have since been overcome and the 1980s health-consciousness of consumers has spurred the demand for frozen yogurt, particularly the nonfat variety. To the surprise of those in the foodservice industry, it is successful not only as a meal item, but also as a dessert item. When you consider its dual role, you can understand the excitement generated by frozen yogurt. It is just what the dairy industry in general and owners of restaurants, cafes, gourmet shops, and independent shops in particular were looking for to increase sales during lunch hours and the slow winter months. Its acceptance and popularity have pushed frozen yogurt into a full-service, year-round, any-time-of-day industry of its own.

Defining Frozen Yogurt

While there is no question that the interest in frozen yogurt has passed the stage of being a fad, there are still some questions about the identity of this product.

- Is frozen yogurt a true yogurt product?
- How much yogurt should be in frozen yogurt?

The general public does not have the slightest idea what the product is other than that it tastes good and implies healthfulness. Frozen yogurt is perceived as being synonymous with nutrition and more healthful than ice cream. If you consider only the calorie and fat content, then frozen yogurt is more healthful. However, its sugar content is about the same as an ice cream.

Yogurt, by definition, is a fermented dairy product including live cultures of two bacteria (*Lactobacillus bulgaricus* and *Streptococcus thermophilus*). The milk is cultured after pasteurization, and these bacteria multiply and react with lactose (milk sugar) to produce lactic acid and other compounds. They affect the flavor of the finished yogurt product, making it tart and imbuing the yogurt with other flavor characteristics that establish the unique "cultured" flavor profiles. These organisms continue to live in the mix and finished products even after the freezing process.

The resulting sour taste does not appeal to everyone, so some manufacturers of frozen yogurt products focus on the taste issue instead of the culture issue because it is difficult to use tart-tasting cultures and still make a product sweet enough to satisfy consumers. The flavoring problem is particularly acute for nonfat yogurt products, especially chocolate flavors. Frozen yogurt is generally flavored with flavor extracts, usually at the rate of 1 ounce per gallon of mix. Flavor extracts are used because they are inexpensive. For the best possible flavor, however, use a fruit puree, which has more body than an extract. Fruit purees cost more, and are used only by more upscale manufacturers who regard cost as secondary to flavor and quality.

EQUIPMENT

The popularity of soft serve products such as frozen yogurt has made it easier for operators of restaurants, gourmet shops, and independent ice cream shops to consider the purchase of a soft serve machine. Previously the cost seemed prohibitive to have a machine just for selling soft ice cream. While it is true that the equipment is expensive (starting at $6,000 for a countertop unit and $10,000 for a floor-standing model), soft serve freezers can accommodate many uses. Entire businesses can be centered around the frozen yogurt and nondairy soft desserts (as well as novelties and ice cream cakes for the take-out market) that these freezers can produce.

In general, soft serve machines are available in many sizes and capacities, as floor models or countertop units, in single-flavor or two-flavor twist units. A twist unit is desirable for soft ice cream or frozen yogurt because a third flavor can be created in the machine. A two-flavor machine with a twist has three compressors to allow for independent operation by flavor. The third compressor is used strictly for overnight or slow periods.

Most come in 220-volt, single- or three-phase electrical configurations, and as either air- or water-cooled units. Water-cooled units are preferable because they remove heat from the room by flushing it down the drain. Air-cooled units produce heat that must be ventilated out through the ceiling or a window.

Soft serve freezers are similar to batch freezers in operation in that the liquid product mix is fed into the freezing chamber and the mixture freezes on contact with the cylinder wall, creating fine crystals. A rotating beater, or auger, in the cylinder scrapes the frozen product from the wall, producing a smooth, creamy frozen product. The mix pump, beater/auger, and freezing actions are automatic and continuously produce the frozen product.

Most soft serve freezers are computer-controlled; that is, computer boards monitor the internal temperature and product thickness and turn the beaters off and on in response to those readings. Most of the inner parts are plastic for easy replacement and ready availability. While they are not as costly as stainless steel, they do break more often and will cause downtime if service is not available.

There are two basic types of soft-serve freezers, pressurized and gravity-fed. All soft serve products can be easily run in either machine. Neither machine allows for any solid ingredients to be added through the hopper.

- *Pressurized (pump)* freezers have systems that use a pump to force the mix into the barrel. In a pressurized freezer, the ratio of air and liquid mix is adjustable. Blending air into the liquid product expands its volume (overrun) and increases its yield. Because of the pressure of the pump, these machines allow for more overrun (about 20–30 percent) than do gravity-fed machines.
- *Gravity-fed* freezers are the simplest to operate and the easiest to clean and maintain. Liquid mix is refrigerated in a mix tank located directly above the freezing cylinder. Gravity allows the mix to flow into the cylinder through a metering orifice at the base of the mix-feed or gravity-feed tube. As mix enters the cylinder, air simultaneously enters the top of the tube. The air and mix are blended by the rotating action of the beater/auger. The ratio of air and mix is not controllable, causing the yield of the finished product (overrun) to fluctuate between 35 percent and 50 percent, depending on how often the freezer is used.

Keep in mind that controlling overrun is a multifaceted concern. Too little air and the product will be too cold to enjoy, taste heavy, and have a weak flavor; too much air results in dissipation of flavor and a product that is too fluffy and less creamy. With just the right amount of air, the texture reaches an optimal level where the flavor can be fully appreciated. Overrun also affects perceived value. As overrun increases, the size of the portion increases, and larger portions are generally perceived to be of greater value than smaller portions.

Making Choices

Visiting shops using equipment similar to what you have in mind and enlisting the help of equipment manufacturers can make your decision on purchasing equipment easier. When choosing a soft-serve equipment manufacturer, consider the following important factors:

Warranty: Try to find out from other equipment owners how well the manufacturers stand behind their equipment, and for how long. Make sure the compressor is warranted. Most soft serve equipment comes with a 5-year warranty on the compressor and a 90-day to 1-year warranty covering the costs of labor.

Service network: Having an authorized service company in your area is an absolute necessity for handling equipment emergencies.

Parts availability: Having parts available from either the manufacturer or the service company on a 24-hour basis is essential. Getting machinery fixed as quickly as possible is crucial to your operation, especially during periods of heavy volume.

Standard features and options: Compare prices and features. You will find some manufacturers more expensive than others, and then the decision rests with the best service record.

Once you have decided on a manufacturer, you can focus on a specific piece of equipment. Ask yourself the following questions:

- Do I want a countertop or floor model? Space determines your answer. If you have the space, choose the floor model. It costs more than a countertop unit, but the extra capacity of the hopper and chamber barrel will be advantages in the long run.
- How will my employees operate and maintain the freezer? Consider a gravity-fed freezer because it has fewer parts and thus is easier to use and clean.
- How heavily will the unit be used? For heavy-duty use, choose a pump-style freezer. It dispenses product faster than a pressurized unit.

Manufacturers

All of the manufacturers listed in Table 12-1 make excellent equipment and are highly recommended. For ease of operation and strong service support, Taylor Freezer equipment is unsurpassed (see Figure 12-1). Their Model 152 is frequently used in gourmet shops and restaurants for single-product, single-flavor use. Model 168 is recommended where space requirements are critical. The difference between models 754 and 8756 is in the freezer volume; Model 8756 has a large capacity freezer and two large pump reservoirs for high volume use (see Figures 12-2 and 12-3).

Coldelite freezers utilize advanced technology and are used in soft serve facilities throughout the world. Floor Model 8202 is their highest volume freezer, and Model 253G/P (gravity or pressurized) is a medium-size machine also used for high volume (see Figure 12-4). Their countertop Model UC 1131G/P (gravity or pressurized) is a high-performance compact unit (see Figure 12-5).

Electro-Freeze has an excellent reputation for their pump machines (higher overrun), specifically Model 30TFN.

Emery Thompson has developed a frozen custard machine, model number FC-500, similar to a continuous freezer in that it dispenses finished product within 15 seconds from the time the mix enters the cylinder chamber. It produces a denser, smoother, and colder product (in degrees) than that produced in a soft serve machine. The unit has enough cylinder capacity to produce 11

Table 12-1. Soft Serve Equipment Manufacturers

Model	Number of Flavors	Cylinder (quarts)	Hopper	Width	Depth	Height	Electrical Requirements
Taylor							
162 (C)	2 + T	(2) 1.5	(2) 8.5 qt	29	24	$28\frac{1}{2}$	220,20A
152 (C)	1	(2) 1.5	(2) 8.5 qt	$17\frac{15}{16}$	$27\frac{1}{2}$	28	115, 20A
754 (F)	2 + T	(2) 3.4	(2) 20 qt	$26\frac{7}{16}$	33	$57\frac{1}{4}$	220, 30A
168 (F)	2 + T	(2) 1.5	(2) 8 qt	20	24	$51\frac{1}{2}$	220, 20A
8756 (F)	2 + T	(2) 3.4	(2) 10 gal	$26\frac{7}{16}$	$39\frac{1}{8}$	$68\frac{1}{4}$	220, 30A
Coldelite							
UC-711 (G/P)	1	1.5	2 gal	18	33	$28\frac{1}{8}$	115, 30A
UF-213P	2 + T	5	(2) 5 gal	22	34	61	208/230
UF-213G	2 + T	5	(2) 5 gal	22	34	61	208/230
UC-113G/P (C)	2 + T	(2) 1.5	(2) 2 gal	17	$25\frac{1}{2}$	$32\frac{1}{2}$	230, 30A
UF-253G (F)	2 + T	(2) 2	(2) 5 gal	22	34	56	208/230
UF-8202 (F)	2 + T	(2) 4	(2) 10 gal	30	$41\frac{1}{2}$	57	208/230
UF-253G/P (F)	1	2	10 gal	22	34	56	208/230
Electro-Freeze							
30TFN (F)	2+T	(2) 2	(2) 5 gal	26	36	58	208/230
30T-CMT (F)	2+T	(2) 2	(2) 5 gal	26	$36\frac{1}{2}$	$68\frac{1}{8}$	208/230

Notes: C = countertop model; F = floor model; G = gravity-fed; P = pressurized; T = twist.

FIGURE 12-1. Taylor Model 162 countertop soft serve machine, with two flavors and a twist.

gallons of finished product per hour. It measures 17½ inches wide by 43 inches deep by 73½ inches high and its electrical requirements are 1/60/230 or 3/60/208/230.

Daily Maintenance and Care

Regardless of machine or manufacturer, all soft serve equipment must be taken apart and cleaned daily. In addition to using common sense regarding the care of your units, daily cleaning is a requirement of most boards of health. Failure to do so will allow bacteria to contaminate the mix, a serious problem when working with any dairy product. Adhere to the following procedures to ensure sanitary conditions in your operation:

1. Turn off the refrigeration to the freezing cylinder.
2. Turn on the beaters and extrude any remaining product.

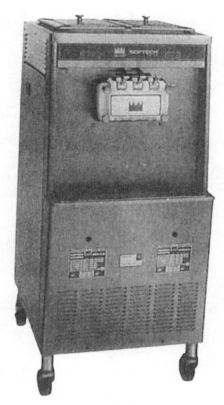

FIGURE 12-2. Taylor Model 754 gravity-fed soft serve machine, with two flavors and a twist.

FIGURE 12-3. Taylor Model 8756 pump soft serve machine, with two flavors and a twist.

3. Rinse the freezer cylinder with 2 quarts of cold water.
4. Prepare a 2-gallon sanitizing solution, following the manufacturer's recommendations for proper strength.
5. Remove both the hopper cover and mix tube assembly.
6. Fill the mix hopper with 1 gallon of the sanitizing solution.
7. Using a brush, clean around the mix hopper and feed tube.
8. Run the beaters for 30–60 seconds and then draw out the solution.
9. Remove and disassemble the freezer door and clean all the parts with the sanitizing solution.
10. Inspect the inside of the cylinder to make sure it is thoroughly clean.
11. Rinse all parts thoroughly with cold water.
12. Lubricate the seals and valves with a gel such as Petro Gel, manufactured by the McGlaughlin Oil Company of Columbus, Ohio.

FIGURE 12-4. Coldelite Model UC-253 G/P gravity-fed or pressurized soft serve machine with two flavors and a twist.

13. Reassemble all parts and run a sanitizing solution through the machine.

Note the following problem areas that can be avoided with proper care:

• *Freeze-ups* caused by too little product in the barrel.
• *Runny product* caused by dull scraper blades, kinks in water hoses (for water-cooled units), or not enough airflow space (for air-cooled machines) around the units.
• *Milkstone (hard-water deposits) in rubber gaskets and o-rings* can be avoided by using a water-softening agent and by changing rings and gaskets every 90 days.
• *Off taste,* an indication that harmful bacteria is present, can be avoided by proper cleaning and sanitizing.

FIGURE 12-5. Coldelite Model UC-1131 G/P gravity-fed or pressurized countertop soft serve machine with two flavors and a twist.

MARKETING SOFT SERVE PRODUCTS

Advanced production technology has made it possible to create soft serve products that are smooth and rich in taste. To maintain the successful appeal of this product category, manufacturers and foodservice operators will have to continually provide new flavors and products, and plan strong marketing programs to support the basic product. Marketing soft serve products (ice cream and frozen yogurt) is in many ways similar to marketing any other frozen dessert product because the same basic principles apply. The following suggestions will help you to launch the product or expand existing business:

- Use posters and banners to announce the new product, especially in the front window.
- Advertise in local newspapers.
- In the shop, use large (24 inches by 30 inches) attractive photographs of frozen yogurt by itself or as a meal alternative (as opposed to a dessert).

- Display point-of-purchase materials near the front door or counter.
- Distribute nutritional literature about the new product(s), especially listing the calorie count. You could contact local diet and fitness establishments in particular.
- Give out lots of samples during the introductory period and ask your distributor for free product, or at least a discount, during this time.
- Give out free samples of your product at nonprofit functions.
- Always list available flavors on a flavor board near the freezers.
- Conduct a direct-mail campaign to the residents in your community. It is very effective for promoting repeat business.
- Set up a demonstration booth right in front of your business (see "Demos" later in this chapter). It will attract customers and give you an audience for introducing the new product.
- Use coupons (see the next section).
- Use "Frequency Cards," cards that can be marked or punched after a purchase and redeemed for a bonus after a certain number of purchases. They work well for shops that do a heavy lunch business.

Be especially aware that that the sales base for soft serve products can be broadened by offering them as alternatives to hard ice cream, as a meal substitute or dessert in food operations, or as additions to a dessert operation.

Coupons

For most consumers, coupons are an essential part of the shopping experience because they feel they are getting a bargain when they use coupons. The foodservice industry has not ignored such a powerful motivating tool, and neither should you. Coupons can stimulate business during slow periods and bring in customers who might not otherwise come to your establishment. They build product awareness and give immediate results. If you take the time to plan a coupon program for precise content and duration, coupons can be money-makers.

For a coupon to be successful, it must have a meaningful value to motivate the consumer to use it. Discount coupons offering "2 for 1" deals or "cents off" work well by providing a monetary motivation. Coupon books, highly recommended for short promotions, are also effective motivators because using them is like playing a game. The consumer continually has to decide "Which coupon should I use now?" When using coupon booklets, note the following hints:

- Do not have expiration dates on the coupons. You want the customer to use all of the coupons and that might not be possible within a limited amount of time. Remember, each time a customer redeems a coupon, he or she is becoming more aware of what you have to offer.

- The book should be designed to offer something to all age groups, especially children. Children are usually accompanied by their parents when making a purchase, so you have the opportunity to make two or more sales from one.
- Any coupons you design should offer real value to enhance the probability of redemption. The more coupons that are redeemed, the more customer volume you will have. Increased volume translates into increased profits, not only during the time of the promotion but with increased repeat business.

Demos

One of the best marketing programs for introducing a new soft serve product and educating consumers about its merits is the in-store demonstration, or demo. No printed advertising can compare to the effectiveness of the one-on-one exchange between the demonstrator and the consumer tasting a product while being told of its value. A successful demo program requires three key ingredients:

1. A quality product, one that consumers can relate to, taste, and give an immediate reaction to.
2. A well-prepared and imaginative presentation in an attractive booth.
3. Well-trained and enthusiastic demonstrators.

Whether you use your own employees or hire outside demonstrators, you must be certain they are knowledgeable about your products and motivated to deal with consumers. You should also consider doing demonstrations yourself. There is no better way to instill consumer confidence in a product than personal contact with the actual individual behind the name (for example, Dave Thomas of Wendy's).

Product Enticements

Today's challenging market environment requires aggressive and innovative merchandising to achieve a competitive edge. Smart shop operators will take advantage of everything they have on hand to promote their basic products, including related products. When you think in terms of each customer as a profit center, these related products not only help sell the basics, but also increase unit sales as well. Waffle cones, topping bars, and blended desserts are perfectly suited as secondary products that can be used for merchandising your soft serve products (see especially "Secondary Products" in Chapter 11).

If you are in the soft serve business, there are two areas in particular that can easily boost your profit margin: milk shakes and take-out products. Milk shakes go with food. They are extremely popular in mall food courts during lunchtime. When you add shakes to your menu, you increase sales and check averages. A 16-ounce shake is priced from $1.75 and up and has nearly a 50-percent profit margin.

Take-out products are a natural extension of your business. The successful franchise operations of companies such as Carvel and Dairy Queen have proven the appeal and profitability of take-out items. In most cases, the mark-up on take-out desserts is 50–100 percent, and little capital investment is needed to produce all kinds of novelties, pints, and cakes. Using the soft serve machine you already own, the only extras required are plain bar sticks, wrappers, a blast freezer, and capable employees. While it is labor-intensive to make products for take-out, most of the work is done during off-peak hours, thus maximizing personnel. For display purposes you will need a vertical or horizontal freezer (see "Ice Cream Merchandisers" in Chapter 8 and the "Visual Appeal" section in Chapter 11). Remember that consumers are price-conscious, so check your competition before setting prices for take-out products.

SERVING SOFT SERVE PRODUCTS

Soft serve products can be sold as a dessert item in the same way that you would offer hard ice cream to the buying public. Not only is it possible to serve a cone or cup, you can also offer toppings or create a variety of sundaes, shakes, and smoothies.

Basic Items

For soft frozen yogurt in particular, the product as either a lunch time or dinner alternative, either by itself or with toppings, can greatly expand your selection of menu items. To take advantage of this opportunity, you must first have in your establishment an attractive topping bar in a visually prominent location. To cover both entree and dessert items, topping offerings should include

Fruits: apple, apricots, avocado, banana, blueberries, cantaloupes, cherries (sweet black or Bordeaux halves), coconut, cranberries, dates, honeydew melon, mandarin oranges, mangoes, nectarines, papaya, peaches, pears, pineapple, pink grapefruit, raisins, raspberries, spiced apple, strawberries, and watermelon.

Cookies, cereal (pieces or crushed): ginger snaps, graham crackers, granola, and wheat germ.

Candies: chocolate chips, pieces of popular candy bars (such as Snickers and Heath Bars), peppermint patties or sticks.

Nuts (whole, pieces, or crushed): almonds, cashews, peanuts, pecans, praline nuts, and walnuts.

Vegetables: grated carrots, bean sprouts, cauliflower and broccoli florets, green pepper rings, and so on as salad accompaniments.

Miscellaneous: carob, sunflower seeds, and croutons.

All soft serve products sold in a cup with or without toppings will be the largest selling item in an ice cream dessert shop. The cup should be graphically attractive and functional, with a large opening to accommodate toppings. For example, the Solo F5DB or Sweetheart T-305 cup accommodates a single serving of 5 ounces of soft serve product with or without toppings. A double portion is approximately 7 ounces served in a larger cup, similar to the Solo TS9 or the Sweetheart S-308. Sweetheart's VS512 cup will hold approximately 9 ounces of soft serve product for a triple serving.

Until the 1970s the wafer cone, such as those manufactured by Sweetheart, Ace, Novelty, and Cream Cone, was the predominant cone used for soft serve. However, this cone is slowly being replaced by waffle cones, similar to the ones made by Aga (Danish Cones of Miami Florida). The waffle cone not only tastes good, but its opening at the top is about 2½ inches in diameter, which is larger than that of a wafer cone and is well suited to serving soft serve products with a topping or two. It costs more than a wafer cone, but the functional advantages along with its looks and taste make the waffle cone an appealing item.

Other ways that soft serve can be served include shakes made of 7 ounces of soft serve and approximately 9 ounces of either whole, low-fat, or skim milk, and malts that are the same as shakes with the addition of 2 tablespoons of malt powder.

You can also prepare single-portion sundaes by using 5 ounces of soft serve and one topping or double portions using 7 ounces of soft serve and two toppings. Both sizes are served covered with whipped cream and topped with a cherry.

Specialty Sundaes

Just as for hard-pack ice cream sundaes, let your imagination go and create your own soft serve specialties. Offer them in conjunction with the following sundaes that have proven successful with consumers.

The Beachcomber: vanilla soft serve ice cream or frozen yogurt surrounded and topped with strawberries, bananas, granola, honey, and walnuts.

The Tropical Paradise: vanilla soft serve ice cream or frozen yogurt surrounded and topped with pineapple, coconut, and bananas.

Summer Paradise: a single serving of either lemon, vanilla, or strawberry soft serve ice cream or frozen yogurt surrounded and topped with oranges, pineapple, bananas, and dates.

Fruit Salad Supreme: any fruit-flavored soft serve ice cream or frozen yogurt surrounded and topped with fresh fruit salad, whipped cream, and a cherry.

Bananaberry Split: three small servings of any flavors of soft serve ice cream or frozen yogurt placed in a bowl between the two halves of a banana split lengthwise and topped with any two berry toppings, whipped cream, and a cherry.

Hot Fudge Sundae: any flavor soft serve ice cream or frozen yogurt covered with hot fudge, one topping, whipped cream, and a cherry.

Almond Fudge Sundae: a single portion of chocolate soft serve ice cream or frozen yogurt covered with hot fudge, fluffy marshmallow creme, and sliced almonds, and topped with whipped cream and a cherry.

Brownie Sundae: a chocolate brownie topped with soft serve vanilla ice cream or frozen yogurt and surrounded by hot fudge, with whipped cream, walnuts, and cherry over all.

Nutrition Plus (a frozen yogurt specialty): any flavor frozen yogurt surrounded and topped with granola, toasted coconut, sunflower seeds, and raisins.

Soft Serve Beverages

The following beverages are made by blending soft serve ice cream or frozen yogurt with fresh fruit juices. They are creamy and refreshing.

Sodas Prepare all of the following in 16-ounce cups:

Key West Flip: Pour 7 ounces of orange juice and add a single serving of vanilla soft serve ice cream or frozen yogurt. Top with sliced strawberries and bananas.

The Hawaiian: Pour 7 ounces of pineapple juice and add a single serving of soft serve vanilla ice cream or frozen yogurt. Top with coconut and pineapple (chunks or crushed)

All-American Chocolate Soda: Thoroughly mix 2 ounces of chocolate syrup with 7 ounces of seltzer. Add a single serving of either vanilla or chocolate soft serve ice cream or frozen yogurt.

Blended Juice Smoothies These delightful drinks differ from milk shakes in their use of juice instead of milk. They are very refreshing and healthful. Using a blender, mix together all the ingredients in 16-ounce cups. Sherbet can be used in place of the use of frozen yogurt.

Papaya: 6 ounces of papaya juice, ½ ounce of pineapple chunks, half a banana, and 4 ounces of vanilla frozen yogurt.

Apple: 6 ounces of apple juice or cider, half a banana, a dash of cinnamon, half an apple cut into chunks, and 4 ounces of either soft serve vanilla or apple ice cream or frozen yogurt.

Piña Colada: 6 ounces of vanilla soft serve ice cream or frozen yogurt, 1 ounce of shredded coconut, and 8 ounces of pineapple juice.

Strawberry: 6 ounces of strawberry soft serve ice cream or frozen yogurt, half a banana, and 8 ounces of either orange or pineapple juice.

Blueberry: 6 ounces of blueberry frozen yogurt, half a banana, and 8 ounces of orange juice.

Cranberry: 6 ounces of vanilla soft serve ice cream or frozen yogurt, half a banana, and 8 ounces of cranberry juice.

Pineapple: 6 ounces of vanilla frozen yogurt, 1½ ounces of pineapple chunks and 8 ounces of pineapple juice.

Berry: 6 ounces of vanilla frozen yogurt, half a banana, 2 ounces of strawberries, 2 ounces of blueberries, and 6 ounces of orange juice.

Milk Shakes To maintain your customers' perception of soft serve ice cream and frozen yogurt as a healthy and nutritious product, use low-fat or skim milk rather than whole milk for all your soft serve milk shakes. Using a blender, mix together all the ingredients in 16-ounce cups.

Vanilla: 6 ounces of vanilla soft serve ice cream or frozen yogurt, 8 ounces of either whole, low-fat, or skim milk, and 2 ounces of vanilla syrup.

Strawberry: 6 ounces of strawberry soft serve ice cream or frozen yogurt, 2 ounces of sliced strawberries, and 8 ounces of either whole, low-fat, or skim milk.

Tropical: 4 ounces of vanilla frozen yogurt, 2 ounces of strawberries, 2 ounces blueberries, half a banana, and 6 ounces of either whole, low-fat, or skim milk.

REFERENCES

Arbuckle, W. S. 1983. *Ice Cream Store Handbook.* Columbia, Mo.: Arbuckle & Co.

Arbuckle, W. S. 1986. *Ice Cream.* Fourth edition. Westport, Conn.: AVI Publishing.

Cianci, Maria. 1986. Creamy concoctions. *Restaurant Business,* April, pp. 1–7.

Durocher, Joseph. 1996. Soft cash to cold cash. *Restaurant Business,* March, pp. 128–130.

Kenny, Kathleen M. 1982. Soft serve signature specials. *Restaurant Business,* March, pp. 1–7.

Lieb, Mary Ellen. 1988. Facing the facts of life. *Dairy Foods,* vol. 89, no. 2 (February), pp. 35–40.

Racord, Anent. 1988. Mix'n profits. *Convenience Store Management,* September, pp. 72–76.

Stube, Christine. 1989. All things compared. *Dairy Foods,* vol. 90, no. 3 (March), pp. 33–40.

What's wrong with the soft serve machine? 1996. *Restaurant & Institutions,* May, p. 26.

FROZEN DESSERT RECIPES

⊠⊠⊠⊠⊠⊠⊠⊠⊠⊠⊠⊠⊠⊠⊠⊠⊠⊠⊠⊠⊠⊠⊠⊠⊠⊠⊠⊠⊠⊠⊠⊠

13 ⬚⬚⬚⬚⬚⬚⬚⬚⬚⬚⬚⬚⬚⬚⬚⬚⬚⬚⬚⬚⬚⬚⬚⬚

ICE CREAM RECIPES

If you are committed to producing a quality ice cream product, you will need to decide on which flavors to produce. The number of flavors you can create is limited only by your imagination. Whatever flavors you choose, make sure that the list is uniquely your own and that all the flavors will sell equally well.

This chapter provides recipes for many of today's most popular flavors. They have been designed to guide you along with step-by-step instructions on each flavor's preparation using either the batch or continuous freezing method. But remember, it takes quality ingredients, time, and effort to produce good results.

To some people in the industry, ice cream making is an art, and to others it is a science. To me, it is pure art. I dream, I create, and I dream again. You can, and should, do the same because creativity and the pleasure it brings to you and your customers will be the foundation of your success.

HOW TO USE THESE RECIPES

The left side of each recipe lists the usage levels of all ingredients needed for a batch recipe, while the right side lists the same for the continuous method. The usage levels of all the flavorings (fruit purees and extracts) and other ingredients (cocoa, chocolate, nuts, and fruit feeder particulates) are based on the use of a 16-percent butterfat ice cream mix. Pure vanilla extract is used in every recipe because it brings out the full flavor of every ingredient used. (I recommend a two-fold Madagascar Bourbon from Nielsen Massey).

When using these recipes, the important points regarding each method are as follows:

Batch Freezing Method
- The basis for each recipe is 2½ gallons of ice cream mix.
- The time to produce a normal batch of ice cream is 8–10 minutes.

- The batch freezer must be sanitized at the beginning and end of each day.
- A 60-minute timer is highly recommended to time each batch.
- Use preset measuring containers (plastic) to measure out ingredients.
- Keep the area around the batch freezer clean during production.
- To avoid slipping due to spills from dairy products, place a rubber floor mat in front of the batch freezer.
- Plan in advance what you are going to produce each day.
- To avoid crystallization, immediately place all ice cream produced into a blast freezer.
- Sharpening metal dasher blades at least once a year will allow you to operate the batch freezer on a continuous 8–10 minute production cycle and give you a textured finished product.

Remember, many variables can change the quality of the finished product. Improper use of the batch freezer can cause overprocessing, resulting in dense, unscoopable, and unedible ice cream. Using too much or even too little of any particular ingredient will cause an imbalance in the product's flavor. A good example is the use of egg base in French vanilla. Too much will make the finished product eggy or chewy, as well as soggy in the dipping case. Too little will not meet the federal requirement that the finished product must be 1.4 percent egg-yolk solids by weight to be called French Vanilla, and will result in a product lacking the characteristic egg taste.

Continuous Freezing Method
- The basis for each recipe is 100 gallons of ice cream mix.
- To convert a batch recipe to use for continuous freezing production, multiply all ingredients by 40.
- All fruits used, unless otherwise noted, are processed fruits (cooked), ready for immediate use.
- If frozen fruit is used, it must be marinated with sugar regardless of whether sugar has already been added by the manufacturer. However, before you start marinating, make sure you know how much sugar has already been added.
- Wherever possible, all recipes are measured in gallons because, for the most part, all fruit and variegates are packed in 5-gallon pails.
- Make sure any excess juice is drained from fruits poured into the fruit feeder.

THE RECIPES

Many ice cream manufacturers have a two-tier pricing structure to separate regular flavors from the more expensive superpremium or upscale flavors being offered. To the right of each ice cream recipe title I have indicated a category that distinguishes each flavor by uniqueness, ingredient costs, and production time. "Regular" recipes are for the traditional or old-fashioned flavors produced for the mass market. "Superpremium" recipes are for the expensive flavors produced for upscale operations, supermarkets, gourmet shops, hotels, and restaurants. Many retailers charge an extra 25 cents per scoop for the superpremium flavors.

The Vanillas

Vanilla ice cream is the most difficult flavor to produce. Because it is so pure, it takes a lot of time and patience to get it right. It might not be your favorite flavor, but without a good vanilla product, you will never be able to produce other quality flavors that are based on your recipe for vanilla.

It does not matter what fancy flavors you create, critics will always taste your vanilla first, so you must master the basics before you can hope to expand your flavor selection. Use only natural ingredients and pure vanilla extract (see "Flavorings" in Chapter 5) for a foundation of producing only the best.

Because vanilla is usually the first flavor made for a day's production, the freezing process will take a little longer than for subsequent flavors.

▨ FRENCH VANILLA   Regular

The use of pasteurized egg yolks or an egg base creates the richest of all vanilla flavors, French vanilla. The 1982 Code of Federal Regulations requires that the egg content in the mix be at least 1.4 percent of the total volume to be classified as French vanilla. Because French vanilla is the benchmark by which others have judged my flavor base, I am always very careful about how this flavor turns out. Make sure to follow the recipe exactly as stated.

Batch		Continuous
2½ gallons	16% ice cream mix*	100 gallons
4 ounces	two-fold vanilla extract	5 quarts
13 ounces	pasteurized egg yolks*	33 pounds

*Note: If you are unable to purchase frozen pasteurized egg yolks, a good substitute is egg base, manufactured by Limpert Brothers of Vineland, New Jersey, and other companies in the United States. The usage level for a 2½-gallon batch of ice cream for egg base meeting the federal standard (1.4 percent) for a French-styled ice cream is 32 ounces. If the ice cream mix used already has the required amount of egg-yolk solids in the mix, it is not necessary to add any additional egg yolks.

Batch Freezing Method

If your ice cream mix does not contain egg yolks, you will have to add 24 ounces of egg base instead of the 16 ounces listed in the ingredients list. Pour all ingredients into batch freezer. Turn on dasher and refrigeration and begin batch. When extruding finished product from the batch freezer, make sure it is firm, not soft. A good test is to use a thermometer to measure the temperature of the semifrozen ice cream. When temperature reaches approximately 23–24 degrees Fahrenheit for a high overrun product, turn off refrigeration. If you are producing a low overrun product, then a temperature of 22–23 degrees Fahrenheit is required. Another way of telling if batch is completed is to look inside the opening at the top of the chamber for peaks and valleys in the finished product. The product should be firm, not liquid.

When batch is complete, turn off refrigeration and extrude finished product.

Batch time: 9–11 minutes if it is the first batch of the day. Otherwise, batch time is 8–10 minutes.

Continuous Freezing Method

Before you start the continuous freezing of this flavor, make sure the sanitizing solution or the previous flavor of mix has been pushed through the freezer. Open the outlet valve of the mix storage tank and let the proper amount of ice cream mix flow into the flavor tank. Pour the vanilla extract and pasteurized egg yolks into the flavor tank and mix all the ingredients together. The mix is then pumped to the inlet of the continuous freezer. Set the speed, viscosity (stiffness), and overrun settings according to the manufacturer's recommendations. Start the continuous freezing process. As the ice cream leaves the continuous freezer, it is then piped to the next stage in the process, which is either filling (tubs, pints, etc.), extrusion, or molding.

⊠ PHILADELPHIA VANILLA   Regular

Philadelphia has always been noted for both its great ice cream and its old-fashioned ice cream parlors. Philadelphia vanilla is made without egg yolks—strictly cream and vanilla extract. Many older ice cream operators prefer this flavor over French vanilla because it is creamier and not camouflaged by the taste of egg yolks.

Batch		Continuous
2½ gallons	16% ice cream mix	100 gallons
4 ounces	two-fold vanilla extract	5 quarts

Batch Freezing Method

Pour ice cream mix and vanilla extract into batch freezer. Turn on dasher and refrigeration and begin the batch. The finished product will look very white because egg yolks have been omitted.

When batch is complete, turn off refrigeration and extrude finished product.

Batch time: 8–10 minutes.

Continuous Freezing Method

Before you start the continuous freezing of this flavor, make sure the sanitizing solution or the previous flavor of mix has been pushed through the freezer. Open the outlet valve of the mix storage tank and let the proper amount of ice cream mix flow into the flavor tank. Pour the vanilla extract into the flavor tank and mix the ingredients together. The mix is then pumped to the inlet of the continuous freezer. Set the speed, viscosity (stiffness), and overrun settings according to the manufacturers' recommendations. Start the continuous freezing process. As the ice cream leaves the continuous freezer, it is then piped to the next stage in the process, which is either filling (tubs, pints, etc.), extrusion, or molding.

⊠ DANISH SWEET CREAM   Regular

A favorite flavor in Denmark, Danish Sweet Cream is very rich and very pure; it is simply cream.

An associate of mine, Maureen Pratt, who owned the famous Mother Buckets ice cream shop in Greenwich Village, New York, during the early 1970s, made this flavor by accident. She was making French vanilla and forgot to put the vanilla extract and the egg base into the batch freezer. When she had completed the batch, she realized that she had made a mistake. The product looked very white and had the taste of heavy cream. It was delicious and refreshing, so she put it into her dipping case and called it Sweet Cream. Everyone loved the flavor, and it became the benchmark of her operation.

Batch
		Continuous
2½ gallons	16% ice cream mix	100 gallons
½ gallon	heavy cream	20 gallons

Batch Freezing Method

Pour ice cream mix and heavy cream into batch freezer. Turn on dasher and refrigeration. When batch is complete, turn off refrigeration and extrude finished product.

Batch time: 8–10 minutes. It is as simple as that.

Continuous Freezing Method

Before you start the continuous freezing of this flavor, make sure the sanitizing solution or the previous flavor of mix has been pushed through the freezer. Open the outlet valve of the mix storage tank and let the proper amount of ice cream mix flow into the flavor tank. The mix is then pumped to the inlet of the continuous freezer. Set the speed, viscosity (stiffness), and overrun settings according to the manufacturer's recommendations. Start the continuous freezing process. As the ice cream leaves the continuous freezer, it is then piped to the next stage in the process, which is either filling (tubs, pints, etc.), extrusion, or molding.

⊠ VANILLA CHOCOLATE CHIP   Regular

A favorite old-fashioned flavor that is very popular with children. Large chips are used so that the customers can see and taste the chocolate. These chips are sometimes called flakes or chunks.

Batch		Continuous
2½ gallons	16% ice cream mix	100 gallons
4 ounces	two-fold vanilla extract	5 quarts
2 pounds	large chocolate chips	80 pounds

Batch Freezing Method

Pour all ingredients except chocolate chips into batch freezer. Turn on dasher and refrigeration. Add ½ pound of chips at beginning and ½ pound at very end of run. When batch is complete, turn off refrigeration and swirl remaining 1 pound of chips into tubs as ice cream is being extruded from batch freezer.

Batch time: 8–10 minutes.

Continuous Freezing Method

Before you start the continuous freezing of this flavor, make sure the sanitizing solution or the previous flavor of mix has been pushed through the freezer. Pour the chocolate chips into the fruit feeder and adjust the controls to the appropriate setting. Open the outlet valve of the aging tank and let the proper amount of ice cream mix flow into the flavor tank. Next, pour the vanilla extract into the flavor tank. The mix is then pumped to the inlet of the continuous freezer. Set the speed, viscosity (stiffness), and overrun settings according to the manufacturer's recommendations. Start the continuous freezing process. As the ice cream leaves the continuous freezer, it is then piped through the fruit feeder (ingredient feeder) so that the chocolate chips can be discharged and mixed with the ice cream that has already become semifrozen. The ice cream is then piped to the next stage in the process, which is either filling (tubs, pints, etc.), extrusion, or molding.

⊠ VANILLA FUDGE   Regular

A favorite among traditional ice cream lovers, but vanilla fudge is difficult to prepare without proper planning. On the commercial market, you will see different varieties and qualities of vanilla fudge. For a superior flavor in a batch freezing operation, use a quality hot fudge, not a variegate or weave. A variegate is a thick syrup that is formulated for fudges, marshmallows, and fruits. Variegates are used mostly in continuous freezer equipment to create a marbled effect in hardened ice cream. Variegates are thinner in texture and are not really satisfactory for use in batch freezers.

Batch		Continuous
2½ gallons	16% ice cream mix	100 gallons
4 ounces	two-fold vanilla extract	5 quarts
4½ pounds	hot fudge	
	fudge variegate	180 pounds

Batch Freezing Method

Pour all ingredients except hot fudge into batch freezer. Turn on dasher and refrigeration. Heat fudge in a fudge warmer or double boiler until it loosens up and becomes creamy, but not too hot. Using a spatula, paint inner linings of tubs with fudge. Do not put any fudge into batch freezer. It will not hold its body, but instead will immediately start to blend with the cream and turn it brown.

When batch is complete, turn off refrigeration and, as finished ice cream is being extruded, use your spatula to scrape fudge off of inner lining of tubs and swirl it around in the ice cream. Keep scraping fudge until all of it is off. Add more as needed. Remember, you want your customers to be able to see lots of fudge in the tubs.

Using a spatula, decorate tops of tubs with some of the fudge.

Batch time: 8–10 minutes.

Continuous Freezing Method

Before you start the continuous freezing of this flavor, make sure the sanitizing solution or the previous flavor of mix has been pushed through the freezer. Pour the chilled (40 degrees Fahrenheit) fudge variegate into the ripple pump supply tank and adjust speed to inject at the rate as prescribed in the formula, or approximately 10–14 percent of the weight of the ice cream mix. Open the outlet valve of the aging tank and let the proper amount of ice cream mix flow into the flavor tank. Next, pour the vanilla extract into the flavor tank. The mix is then pumped to the inlet of the continuous freezer. Set the speed, viscosity (stiffness), and overrun settings according to the manufacturer's recommendations. Start the continuous freezing process. As the ice cream leaves the continuous freezer, it is then piped through the ripple injection unit so that the fudge variegating sauce can be injected into the stream of ice cream that has already become semifrozen. The ice cream is then piped to the next stage in the process, which is either filling (tubs, pints, etc.), extrusion, or molding.

⊠ VANILLA COOKIES AND CREAM   Regular

Over the last fifteen years, cookies and cream has become immensely popular with kids and today is regarded as one of the most popular flavors in dipping stores. Most operators use either Oreo or Hydrox cookies to produce this flavor.

There are many ways to make this flavor depending on the color and texture you want the finished product to have. A dark cookie color is created by putting a lot of cookies into the batch freezer at the beginning; a lighter color by putting a lot in at the end. My favorite method is to put just enough in at the beginning to mildly flavor the cream, and because I like big chunks of everything, I save most of the cookies for the end. This procedure is difficult but worth the effort.

Batch		**Continuous**
2½ gallons	16% ice cream mix	100 gallons
4 ounces	two-fold vanilla extract	5 quarts
3 pounds	Oreo or Hydrox cookies	120 pounds

Batch Freezing Method

Pour all ingredients except cookies into batch freezer. Turn on dasher and refrigeration. Put ½ pound of cookies into batch at beginning and 1 pound in at end of run. When batch is complete, turn off refrigeration and swirl remaining 1½ pounds of cookies around in finished product as it is being extruded into tubs from batch freezer.

Decorate tops of tubs with cookie pieces.

Batch time: 8–10 minutes.

Continuous Freezing Method

Before you start the continuous freezing of this flavor, make sure the sanitizing solution or the previous flavor of mix has been pushed through the freezer. Pour the cookies into the fruit feeder and adjust the controls to the appropriate setting. Open the outlet valve of the aging tank and let the proper amount of ice cream mix flow into the flavor tank. Next, pour the vanilla extract into the flavor tank. The mix is then pumped to the inlet of the continuous freezer. Set the speed, viscosity (stiffness), and overrun settings according to the manufacturer's recommendations. Start the continuous freezing process. As the ice cream leaves the continuous freezer, it is then piped through the fruit feeder (ingredient feeder) so that the cookies can be discharged and mixed with the ice cream that has already become semifrozen. The ice cream is then piped to the next stage in the process, which is either filling (tubs, pints, etc.), extrusion, or molding.

⊠ VANILLA CHOCOLATE ALMOND   Regular

I love chocolate-covered almonds, so this has always been one of my favorite flavors. Like my other chip and nut flavors, I use only large pieces that can be seen easily by the customers.

Batch		**Continuous**
2½ gallons	16% ice cream mix	100 gallons
4 ounces	two-fold vanilla extract	5 quarts
½ pound	sliced almonds	20 pounds
2 pounds	chocolate-covered almonds (large)	80 pounds
	sliced and chocolate-covered almonds for garnish	

Batch Freezing Method

Pour all ingredients except chocolate-covered almonds into batch freezer. (Adding the sliced almonds at the beginning creates a nutty almond taste.) Turn on both dasher and refrigeration and begin batch. Add the chocolate-covered almonds at very end so they can be clearly seen by customers. After chocolate-covered almonds are put in the chamber, let refrigeration continue to run for about 1 minute longer to give the almonds a chance to circulate. Then turn off refrigeration and extrude finished product.

Decorate tops of tubs with sliced and chocolate-covered almonds.

Batch time: 8–10 minutes.

Continuous Freezing Method

Before you start the continuous freezing of this flavor, make sure the sanitizing solution or the previous flavor of mix has been pushed through the freezer. Mix, and then pour both the sliced and chocolate covered almonds into the fruit feeder and adjust the controls to the appropriate setting. Open the outlet valve of the aging tank and let the proper amount of ice cream mix flow into the flavor tank. Next, pour the vanilla extract into the flavor tank. The mix is then pumped to the inlet of the continuous freezer. Set the speed, viscosity (stiffness), and overrun settings according to the manufacturer's recommendations. Start the continuous freezing process. As the ice cream leaves the continuous freezer, it is then piped through the fruit feeder (ingredient feeder) so that the almonds can be discharged and mixed with the ice cream that has already become semifrozen. The ice cream is then piped to the next stage in the process, which is either filling (tubs, pints, etc.), extrusion, or molding.

⊠ HONEY VANILLA   Superpremium

Honey vanilla was a very popular flavor during the 1970s for health-conscious people. It is still popular in urban areas on both the East and West coasts. Because of the natural sweetness of honey, this flavor is tricky to produce. So be careful not to oversweeten. Be sure to purchase a good quality honey.

Batch		Continuous
2½ gallons	16% ice cream mix	100 gallons
2 ounces	two-fold vanilla extract	2½ quarts
1 pound	honey	20 pounds*
	honey for garnish	

*Note: In a continuous freezing operation, the amount of honey needs to be reduced because of the sweetness of the honey.

Batch Freezing Method

Pour ice cream mix and vanilla extract into batch freezer. Turn on dasher and slowly pour ¼ pound of honey to circulate. After 30 seconds, taste the mixture to make sure it is not oversweet. When you have reached the desired sweetness by adding honey as needed, turn on refrigeration and begin batch. When batch is complete, turn off refrigeration and swirl the remaining honey into the tubs as you extrude the finished product.

For decoration, swirl some honey on top of the packed tubs.

Batch time: 8–10 minutes.

Continuous Freezing Method

Before you start the continuous freezing of this flavor, make sure the sanitizing solution or the previous flavor of mix has been pushed through the freezer. Open the outlet valve of the mix storage tank and let the proper amount of ice cream mix flow into the flavor tank. Pour the honey into the flavor tank and mix the ingredients together. The mix is then pumped to the inlet of the continuous freezer. Set the speed, viscosity (stiffness), and overrun settings according to the manufacturer's recommendations. Start the continuous freezing process. As the ice cream leaves the continuous freezer, it is then piped to the next stage in the process, which is either filling (tubs, pints, etc.), extrusion, or molding.

⊠ MALTED VANILLA   Superpremium

Malted vanilla is popular with customers who love milk shakes. Because malt powder has a very distinct taste, be careful not to overpower the flavor with the taste of malt. For years, one of my pet projects to improve this flavor has been trying to create the ultimate taste of a malted milk shake in an ice cream.

Batch   **Continuous**

2½ gallons	16% ice cream mix	100 gallons
2 ounces	two-fold vanilla extract	2½ quarts
¾ pound	dry malt powder	30 pounds
½ pound	malt ball candy	20 pounds
	malt powder and malt	
	ball candy for garnish	

Batch Freezing Method

Pour all ingredients except malt ball candy into batch freezer. Turn on both dasher and refrigeration and begin batch. Halfway into batch, pour malt ball candy into batch so it can be broken up, resulting in a chunky malt flavor throughout product. When batch is complete, turn off refrigeration and extrude finished product.

For decoration, sprinkle some malt powder on tops of tubs along with some malt ball candy.

Batch time: 8–10 minutes.

Continuous Freezing Method

Before you start the continuous freezing of this flavor, make sure the sanitizing solution or the previous flavor of mix has been pushed through the freezer. Pour the malt ball candy into the fruit feeder and adjust the controls to the appropriate setting. Open the outlet valve of the aging tank and let the proper amount of ice cream mix flow into the flavor tank. Next, pour the vanilla extract and dry malt powder into the flavor tank. The mix is then pumped to the inlet of the continuous freezer. Set the speed, viscosity (stiffness), and overrun settings according to the manufacturer's recommendations. Start the continuous freezing process. As the ice cream leaves the continuous freezer, it is then piped through the fruit feeder (ingredient feeder) so that the malt ball candy can be discharged and mixed with the ice cream that has already become semifrozen. The ice cream is then piped to the next stage in the process, which is either filling (tubs, pints, etc.), extrusion, or molding.

⬚ BUTTERSCOTCH VANILLA   Regular

Butterscotch vanilla has all but disappeared from the supermarket shelves because of the decrease in flavors being offered by most large ice cream manufacturers. It can be found in dipping stores on a limited basis but is considered a difficult flavor to produce. Although the production procedure is similar to that for vanilla fudge, it demands more effort on your part to make this flavor look and taste great.

In the batch freezing method, do not use a variegate butterscotch ingredient because most variegates are weak in texture and are not suited for batch freezers. Swirl the butterscotch around the ice cream as it is being extruded and packed, and because it is messy to begin with, make sure you are organized to handle the swirling. Making this flavor properly is worth the effort and the public will seek you out if they know you have it.

Batch		Continuous	
2½ gallons	16% ice cream mix	100 gallons	
2 ounces	two-fold vanilla extract	2½ quarts	
2¼ quarts	quality butterscotch topping		
	butterscotch variegate	22½ gallons	
	butterscotch for garnish ·		

Batch Freezing Method
Pour all ingredients except butterscotch into batch freezer and turn on dasher. Slowly pour in 16 ounces of butterscotch then turn on refrigeration to begin batch. When batch is complete, turn off refrigeration and have the remaining butterscotch ready to use so that you can weave it around the finished product as it is being extruded from the chamber.

For decoration, swirl some butterscotch on tops of packed tubs.

Batch time: 8–10 minutes.

Continuous Freezing Method
Before you start the continuous freezing of this flavor, make sure the sanitizing solution or the previous flavor of mix has been pushed through the freezer. Pour the chilled (40 degrees Fahrenheit) butterscotch variegate into the ripple pump supply tank and adjust speed to inject at the rate as prescribed in the formula, or approximately 10–14 percent of the weight of the ice cream mix. Open the outlet valve of the aging tank and let the proper amount of ice cream mix flow into the flavor tank. Next, pour the vanilla extract into the flavor tank. The mix is then pumped to the inlet of the continuous freezer. Set the speed, viscosity (stiffness), and overrun settings according to the manufacturer's recommendations. Start the continuous freezing process. As the ice cream leaves the continuous freezer, it is then piped through the ripple injection unit so that the butterscotch variegating sauce can be injected into the stream of ice cream that has already become semifrozen. The ice cream is then piped to the next stage in the process, which is either filling (tubs, pints, etc.), extrusion, or molding.

⊠ VANILLA MARSHMALLOW   Regular

We all have our list of favorites, and my wife Barbara has this flavor at the top of her list. It is a wonderful habit-forming smooth-tasting flavor that melts in your mouth.

When producing this flavor using the continuous freezing method whereby both fruit feeder and ripple pump are both used, the variegating sauce is always injected just ahead of the filler.

Batch		Continuous
2½ gallons	16% ice cream mix	100 gallons
2 ounces	two-fold vanilla extract	2½ quarts
1 pound	mini marshmallows	40 pounds
3 quarts	marshmallow parfait (volume weight)	30 gallons
	mini marshmallows and marshmallow parfait for garnish	

Batch Freezing Method

Pour ice cream mix and vanilla extract into batch freezer. Turn on both dasher and refrigeration and begin batch. Halfway into batch as ice cream is beginning to freeze, add mini marshmallows. At very end of batch, add 1 quart of marshmallow parfait. Turn off refrigeration and, using a spatula, swirl in remaining marshmallow parfait as ice cream is being extruded into tubs.

Decorate tops of tubs with mini marshmallows and marshmallow parfait.

Batch time: 8–10 minutes.

Continuous Freezing Method

Before you start the continuous freezing of this flavor, make sure the sanitizing solution or the previous flavor of mix has been pushed through the freezer. Pour the marshmallow parfait variegate into the ripple pump (temperature of marshmallow variegate at time of usage should be 40 degrees Fahrenheit) and adjust the setting to inject the marshmallow at the rate of 10–14 percent of the weight of the ice cream. Next, pour the mini marshmallows (40 degrees Fahrenheit) into the fruit feeder and adjust the controls to the appropriate setting. Open the outlet valve of the aging tank and let the proper amount of ice cream mix flow into the flavor tank. Pour the vanilla extract into the flavor tank. The mix is then pumped to the inlet of the continuous freezer. Set the speed, viscosity (stiffness), and overrun settings according to the manufacturer's recommendations. Start the continuous freezing process. As the ice cream leaves the continuous freezer, it is then piped through the fruit feeder (ingredient feeder) so that the mini marshmallows can be discharged and mixed with the ice cream. The ice cream is then piped to the ripple pump so that the marshmallow parfait variegate can be injected into the stream of ice cream that has already become semifrozen. The ice cream is then piped to the next stage in the process, which is either filling (tubs, pints, etc.), extrusion, or molding.

Fruit and Berry Flavors

From raspberries and strawberries that are rich and intense in flavor, to tangy peaches and pineapple, fruits and berries are an ice cream maker's pot of gold because of their variety and abundance, especially during the summer when they are reasonably priced. Everyone enjoys fresh fruits in season and when used in the production of ice cream, sorbets, frozen yogurt, and other frozen desserts, they yield fantastic results.

To bring out the ultimate flavor of any fruit, it is important to use only ripe fruit, and plenty of it. Unripened fruit is hard and has no flavor. Almost any variety of fresh fruit can be used, but your success will depend on properly marinating it before use (see "Fruits" in Chapter 5). Briefly, marinating the fruit with sugar for up to 24 hours at 40 degrees Fahrenheit produces a fruit syrup. This syrup fortifies the fruit flavor and eliminates water as an icing agent in the finished product. The process takes time, effort, and money, and that is why many ice cream producers use processed fruits instead. Processed fruits have already been marinated and usually have a preservative added by the manufacturer before they are packed in 5-gallon pails or #10 cans.

For the following recipes I recommend the use of fresh fruits whenever possible, especially for a batch freezing operation. However, I do note the use of various combinations of fresh, frozen, or processed fruits when time or costs are prohibitive. In a continuous freezing operation, the use of frozen fruit, either whole or in puree form, as well as processed fruit purees makes a lot of sense and is highly recommended.

⊠ STRAWBERRY

Give me a bowl of fresh strawberries picked right off the vine and I am in heaven. Over the years, I have canned them, baked with them, and, I am sure you realize by now, made ice cream with them. They are simply my favorite fruit. Since strawberries are a full-bodied textured fruit, they are ideal for use in any frozen dessert. In all of my recipes using this fruit I have tried, and in most cases succeeded, to bring out the essence of the berry in the finished product.

Below are the recipes for making strawberry ice cream three different ways— using fresh, frozen, or processed strawberries.

Using Fresh Strawberries (Regular): Patience and time are needed to prepare the strawberries properly for this great flavor. Regardless of the frozen dessert you might be producing, fresh strawberries are certainly superior to frozen or processed, and their use is easily detected by the consumer.

Batch   **Continuous**

2½ gallons	16% ice cream mix	100 gallons
4 ounces	two-fold vanilla extract	5 quarts
1 (flat) 12 pints	ripe strawberries	60 gallons
2 pounds	sugar	80 pounds
	strawberry pieces for garnish	

Note: The easiest way to prepare the strawberry mixture is to start first thing in the morning so that by midafternoon, everything is ready. Do not refrigerate strawberries.

Batch Freezing Method

Let the flat of strawberries sit out overnight so that they continue to become very ripe. Wash and hull them and in a container and then mix them with 2 pounds of sugar. Allow to sit for 2 hours. Puree two-thirds of the strawberries and allow to sit for another 6 hours.

Pour all ingredients except remaining third of unpureed strawberries into batch freezer. Turn on dasher and refrigeration. Halfway into the batch, add remaining strawberries. When batch is complete, turn off refrigeration and extrude finished product from batch freezer.

Decorate tops of tubs with strawberry pieces.

Batch time: 8–10 minutes.

Continuous Freezing Method

Let the strawberries sit out overnight so that they continue to become very ripe. Wash and hull them. In a container mix them with 80 pounds of sugar. Allow to sit for 2 hours. Puree two-thirds of the strawberries, and marinate them for an additional 6 hours.

Before you start the continuous freezing of this flavor, make sure the sanitizing solution or the previous flavor of mix has been pushed through the freezer. Pour the remaining one-third of the strawberries into the fruit feeder and adjust the controls to the appropriate setting. Open the outlet valve of the aging tank and let the proper amount of ice cream mix flow into the flavor tank. Next, pour the vanilla extract and strawberry puree into the flavor tank. The mix is then pumped to the inlet of the continuous freezer. Set the speed, viscosity (stiffness), and overrun settings according to the manufacturer's recommendations. Start the continuous freezing process. As the ice cream leaves the continuous freezer, it is then piped through the fruit feeder (ingredient feeder) so that the strawberries can be discharged and mixed with the ice cream that has already become semifrozen. The ice cream is then piped to the next stage in the process, which is either filling (tubs, pints, etc.), extrusion, or molding.

Using Frozen Strawberries (Regular): Using a combination of fresh and frozen strawberries is not as expensive as using all fresh berries and produces results almost as good. Be sure to drain all the excess liquid from the defrosted frozen strawberries.

Batch		Continuous
2½ gallons	16% ice cream mix	100 gallons
3 ounces	two-fold vanilla extract	3¾ quarts
2 #10 cans	frozen strawberries	32½ gallons
(192 ounces)		
1 pound	sugar	40 pounds
	frozen strawberry puree	32½ gallons
3 pints	fresh strawberries*	
	strawberry pieces for garnish	

*Note: If you do not use any fresh strawberries, increase the amount of frozen strawberries proportionally.

Batch Freezing Method

Defrost two #10 cans of frozen strawberries, empty into a container, and add 3 pints of hulled fresh strawberries. Drain the juice and add 1 pound of sugar. Marinate mixture for approximately 8 hours. Puree half of this mixture and you are ready to begin the batch.

Pour all ingredients except remaining half of unpureed strawberries into batch freezer. Turn on dasher and refrigeration and begin batch. Halfway into batch, add remaining strawberries.

When batch is complete, turn off refrigeration and extrude finished product.

Batch time: 8–10 minutes.

Continuous Freezing Method

Defrost frozen strawberries and empty into a container. Drain the juice (either part or all of the juice can be used for added flavor by adding it to the flavor tank) and add 40 pounds of sugar. Marinate mixture for approximately 8 hours.

Before you start the continuous freezing of this flavor, make sure the sanitizing solution or the previous flavor of mix has been pushed through the freezer. Pour the strawberries into the fruit feeder and adjust the controls to the appropriate setting. Open the outlet valve of the aging tank and let the proper amount of ice cream mix flow into the flavor tank. Next, pour the vanilla extract and strawberry puree into the flavor tank. The mix is then pumped to the inlet of the continuous freezer. Set the speed, viscosity (stiffness), and overrun settings according to the manufacturer's recommendations. Start the continuous freezing process. As the ice cream leaves the continuous freezer, it is then piped through the fruit feeder (ingredient feeder) so that the strawberries can be discharged and mixed with the ice cream that has already become semifrozen. The ice cream is then piped to the next stage in the process, which is either filling (tubs, pints, etc.), extrusion, or molding.

Using Processed Strawberries (Regular): Using processed strawberries makes this the easiest of all the strawberry recipes to prepare. In the batch freezing method, adding the strawberries at the three different stages of the run creates the right balance between flavoring and having pieces of strawberries present in the finished product. If you use lots of processed strawberries, your finished product will be well received.

Batch		Continuous
2½ gallons	16% ice cream mix	100 gallons
3 ounces	two-fold vanilla extract	3¾ quarts
2¼ quarts	dry pack strawberries	20 gallons
1 quart	strawberry puree	10 gallons
	strawberry pieces for garnish	

Batch Freezing Method

Pour ice cream mix, vanilla extract, and 24 ounces of processed strawberries into batch freezer. Turn on dasher and refrigeration and begin batch. Halfway into batch, add another 24 ounces strawberries. At the very end, add remaining strawberries.

When batch is complete, turn off refrigeration and extrude finished product.

Batch time: 8–10 minutes.

Continuous Freezing Method

Before you start the continuous freezing of this flavor, make sure the sanitizing solution or the previous flavor of mix has been pushed through the freezer. Pour the strawberries into the fruit feeder and adjust the controls to the appropriate setting. Open the outlet valve of the aging tank and let the proper amount of ice cream mix flow into the flavor tank. Next, pour the vanilla extract and strawberry puree into the flavor tank. The mix is then pumped to the inlet of the continuous freezer. Set the speed, viscosity (stiffness), and overrun settings according to the manufacturer's recommendations. Start the continuous freezing process. As the ice cream leaves the continuous freezer, it is then piped through the fruit feeder (ingredient feeder) so that the strawberries can be discharged and mixed with the ice cream that has already become semifrozen. The ice cream is then piped to the next stage in the process, which is either filling (tubs, pints, etc.), extrusion, or molding.

⊠ STRAWBERRY BANANA   **Regular**

The combination of strawberries and banana is very refreshing and the ice cream is easy to prepare. In the batch recipe, because this is a strawberry base ice cream, it is important to add the strawberries at the beginning of the batch along with the ripe bananas. Use only 4 pounds of bananas so that the finished product is not overpowered by a banana taste.

Batch		Continuous
2½ gallons	16% ice cream mix	100 gallons
3 ounces	two-fold vanilla extract	3¾ quarts
½ #10 can	processed dry pack strawberries	15 gallons
(1½ quarts)		
5 pounds	fresh ripe bananas (4 pounds peeled)*	
	pasteurized banana puree	20 gallons
	pieces of strawberries and bananas	
	for garnish	

*Note: 5 pounds of whole bananas will yield approximately 4 pounds of peeled bananas because banana skin is approximately 20 percent of the weight of a banana.

Batch Freezing Method
Pour all ingredients into batch freezer. Turn on dasher and refrigeration. When batch is complete, turn off refrigeration and extrude finished product.

Batch time: 8–10 minutes.

Continuous Freezing Method
Before you start the continuous freezing of this flavor, make sure the sanitizing solution or the previous flavor of mix has been pushed through the freezer. Pour the strawberries into the fruit feeder and adjust the controls to the appropriate setting. Open the outlet valve of the aging tank and let the proper amount of ice cream mix flow into the flavor tank. Next, pour the vanilla extract and banana puree into the flavor tank. The mix is then pumped to the inlet of the continuous freezer. Set the speed, viscosity (stiffness), and overrun settings according to the manufacturer's recommendations. Start the continuous freezing process. As the ice cream leaves the continuous freezer, it is then piped through the fruit feeder (ingredient feeder) so that the strawberries can be discharged and mixed with the ice cream that has already become semifrozen. The ice cream is then piped to the next stage in the process, which is either filling (tubs, pints, etc.), extrusion, or molding.

⊠ BLACK RASPBERRY   Superpremium

A distinctive adult-oriented flavor, black raspberry is hard to find in supermarkets, and to some extent in ice cream stores as well because of the cost of black raspberry puree. I like this flavor because it is refreshing and during the summer months I like to feature a variety of fruit flavors.

Batch		Continuous
2½ gallons	16% ice cream mix	100 gallons
3 ounces	two-fold vanilla extract	3¾ quarts
1¼ quarts	black raspberry puree	12½ gallons
	raspberry puree for garnish	

Batch Freezing Method

Pour all ingredients into batch freezer. Turn on dasher and refrigeration and begin batch. Halfway into batch, sample to make sure there is a distinctive raspberry taste. If needed, add more puree.

When batch is complete, turn off refrigeration and extrude finished product. Swirl tops of tubs with raspberry puree.

Batch time: 8–10 minutes.

Continuous Freezing Method

Before you start the continuous freezing of this flavor, make sure the sanitizing solution or the previous flavor of mix has been pushed through the freezer. Open the outlet valve of the aging tank and let the proper amount of ice cream mix flow into the flavor tank. Pour the vanilla extract and black raspberry puree into the flavor tank. The mix is then pumped to the inlet of the continuous freezer. Set the speed, viscosity (stiffness), and overrun settings according to the manufacturer's recommendations. Start the continuous freezing process. As the ice cream leaves the continuous freezer, it is then piped to the next stage in the process, which is either filling (tubs, pints, etc.), extrusion, or molding.

⊠ BANANA   Regular

Banana is the easiest fresh fruit flavor you can make. I am continually amazed by how many ice cream makers using the batch freezing process use processed banana puree instead of fresh. A ripe banana has a natural sweetness that is missing in processed banana puree. Use ripe bananas and you will be very happy with the results.

In a continuous freezing operation, it does make sense to use a frozen pasteurized banana puree, which does have good flavor and is certainly easier to use than using fresh bananas.

Batch		Continuous
2½ gallons	16% ice cream mix	100 gallons
3 ounces	two-fold vanilla extract	3¾ quarts
10 pounds	fresh ripe bananas (8 pounds peeled)*	
	pasteurized banana puree	40 gallons
	pieces of banana for garnish	

*Note: 10 pounds of whole bananas will yield approximately 8 pounds of peeled bananas because banana skin is approximately 20 percent of the weight of a banana.

Batch Freezing Method
Peel bananas and put them into batch freezer along with 1 gallon of ice cream mix. Turn on dasher for about 5 minutes to puree bananas. Add remaining ingredients, turn on dasher and refrigeration, and begin batch.

When batch is complete, turn off refrigeration and extrude finished product. Because the bananas have so much weight, you will have a larger yield of finished product.

Batch time: 9–11 minutes.

Continuous Freezing Method
Before you start the continuous freezing of this flavor, make sure the sanitizing solution or the previous flavor of mix has been pushed through the freezer. Open the outlet valve of the aging tank and let the proper amount of ice cream mix flow into the flavor tank. Pour the vanilla extract and banana puree into the flavor tank. The mix is then pumped to the inlet of the continuous freezer. Set the speed, viscosity (stiffness), and overrun settings according to the manufacturer's recommendations. Start the continuous freezing process. As the ice cream leaves the continuous freezer, it is then piped to the next stage in the process, which is either filling (tubs, pints, etc.), extrusion, or molding.

⊠ BANANABERRY   Superpremium

A different version of the strawberry banana flavor, in this flavor the base is reversed so that banana becomes the dominant ingredient. Both flavors are great, but use only one on a regular basis, otherwise you will confuse your customers.

Batch   **Continuous**

2½ gallons	16% ice cream mix	100 gallons
3 ounces	two-fold vanilla extract	3¾ quarts
½ #10 can (1½ quarts)	processed dry pack strawberries	15 gallons
10 pounds	fresh ripe bananas (8 pounds peeled)	
	pasteurized banana puree	40 gallons
	pieces of bananas and strawberries for garnish	

*Note: 10 pounds of whole bananas will yield approximately 8 pounds of peeled bananas because banana skin is approximately 20 percent of the weight of a banana.

Batch Freezing Method

Pour all ingredients except the strawberries into batch freezer. Turn on dasher and refrigeration. Add 1 pound of strawberries at beginning and 1 pound at very end of run. When batch is complete, turn off refrigeration and swirl remaining 1 pound of strawberries into tubs as ice cream is being extruded from batch freezer.

Batch time: 8–10 minutes.

Continuous Freezing Method

Before you start the continuous freezing of this flavor, make sure the sanitizing solution or the previous flavor of mix has been pushed through the freezer. Pour the strawberries into the fruit feeder and adjust the controls to the appropriate setting. Open the outlet valve of the aging tank and let the proper amount of ice cream mix flow into the flavor tank. Next, pour the vanilla extract and banana puree into the flavor tank. The mix is then pumped to the inlet of the continuous freezer. Set the speed, viscosity (stiffness), and overrun settings according to the manufacturer's recommendations. Start the continuous freezing process. As the ice cream leaves the continuous freezer, it is then piped through the fruit feeder (ingredient feeder) so that the strawberries can be discharged and mixed with the ice cream that has already become semifrozen. The ice cream is then piped to the next stage in the process, which is either filling (tubs, pints, etc.), extrusion, or molding.

⊠ BANANA NUT FUDGE   **Superpremium**

A more sophisticated version of banana ice cream, this flavor includes nuts and fudge. It has visual appeal and sells well year round.

Batch		Continuous
2½ gallons	16% ice cream mix	100 gallons
3 ounces	two-fold vanilla extract	3¾ quarts
7½ pounds	very ripe bananas, peeled	
	pasteurized banana puree	30 gallons
1 pound	walnut pieces	40 pounds
1½ quarts	fudge	
	fudge variegate	15 gallons
	sliced pieces of banana, walnuts,	
	and fudge for garnish	

---

*Note: 7½ pounds of whole bananas will yield approximately 6 pounds of peeled bananas because banana skin is approximately 20 percent of the weight of a banana.

Batch Freezing Method

Pour all ingredients except fudge and walnut pieces into batch freezer. Turn on both dasher and refrigeration and begin batch. At end of batch, add nuts to batch freezer. When batch is complete, turn off refrigeration and, as the ice cream is being extruded, use a spatula to swirl the fudge around the finished product.*

Decorate tops of tubs with pieces of bananas and, using a spatula, swirl some fudge on top.

---

*Note: Lining the inside of the tubs with fudge beforehand, as done with the vanilla fudge recipe, will make it easier to prepare this flavor.

Batch time: 8–10 minutes.

Continuous Freezing Method

Before you start the continuous freezing of this flavor, make sure the sanitizing solution or the previous flavor of mix has been pushed through the freezer. Pour the chilled (40 degrees Fahrenheit) fudge variegate into the ripple pump supply tank and adjust speed to inject at the rate as prescribed in the formula, or approximately 10–14 percent of the weight of the ice cream mix. Pour the walnut pieces into the fruit feeder and adjust the controls to the appropriate setting. Open the outlet valve of the aging tank and let the proper amount of ice cream mix flow into the flavor tank. Next, pour the vanilla extract and banana puree into the flavor tank. The mix is then pumped to the inlet of the continuous freezer. Set the speed, viscosity (stiffness), and overrun settings according to the manufacturer's recommendations. Start the continuous freezing process. As the ice cream leaves the continuous freezer, it is then piped through the fruit feeder (ingredient feeder) so that the walnut pieces can be discharged and mixed with the ice cream. The ice cream is then piped through the ripple injection unit so that the fudge variegate can be injected into the stream of ice cream that has already become semifrozen. The ice cream is then piped to the next stage in the process, which is either filling (tubs, pints, etc.), extrusion, or molding.

⊠ CHERRY VANILLA   Regular

This old-fashioned flavor is still very popular and easy to prepare. I prefer to use Bordeaux black cherries because of their distinctive look and taste.

Batch		Continuous
2½ gallons	16% ice cream mix	100 gallons
3 ounces	two-fold vanilla extract	3¾ quarts
½ #10 can (1½ quarts)	cherry halves	15 gallons
	cherry halves or garnish	

Batch Freezing Method

Drain and discard half of juice from the cherry halves (too much juice makes the finished ice cream look artificial). Pour the ice cream mix, vanilla extract, and 24 ounces of cherry halves and remaining liquid into batch freezer. Turn on both dasher and refrigeration and begin batch. Add remaining cherries at end of batch. When batch is complete, turn off refrigeration and extrude finished product.

Decorate tops of tubs with cherry pieces.

Batch time: 8–10 minutes.

Continuous Freezing Method

Before you start the continuous freezing of this flavor, make sure the sanitizing solution or the previous flavor of mix has been pushed through the freezer. Pour the cherry halves into the fruit feeder and adjust the controls to the appropriate setting. Open the outlet valve of the aging tank and let the proper amount of ice cream mix flow into the flavor tank. Next, pour the vanilla extract into the flavor tank. The mix is then pumped to the inlet of the continuous freezer. Set the speed, viscosity (stiffness), and overrun settings according to the manufacturer's recommendations. Start the continuous freezing process. As the ice cream leaves the continuous freezer, it is then piped through the fruit feeder (ingredient feeder) so that the cherry halves can be discharged and mixed with the ice cream that has already become semifrozen. The ice cream is then piped to the next stage in the process, which is either filling (tubs, pints, etc.), extrusion, or molding.

⊠ RASPBERRY   **Regular**

A delicate flavor to make, raspberry is extremely popular. Of all the fruit flavors, it has a special sensual attraction about it. Customers tend to get very excited when they see it because they rarely do. In general, raspberries are quite expensive and ice cream producers often steer away from producing expensive flavors. Try it.

Batch		Continuous
½ quart (1 pint)	frozen raspberries	5 gallons
8 ounces	sugar	20 pounds
2½ gallons	16% ice cream mix	100 gallons
3 ounces	two-fold vanilla extract	3¾ quarts
1 quart	seedless red raspberry puree	10 gallons
	pieces of raspberries for garnish	

Batch Freezing Method

Defrost frozen raspberries with 8 ounces sugar and let sit for at least 4 hours before you begin this flavor. Next, puree mixture and strain it through a sieve to remove the seeds.

Pour all ingredients except the pureed raspberry mixture into batch freezer. Turn on both dasher and refrigeration and begin batch. Add raspberry mixture at the middle of batch as the ice cream begins to freeze. (This procedure will emphasize the taste of fruit in the finished product that your customers will find very satisfying.)

When batch is complete, turn off refrigeration and extrude finished product. Decorate tops of tubs with pieces of raspberries.

Batch time: 8–10 minutes.

Continuous Freezing Method

Defrost frozen raspberries with sugar and let sit for at least 4 hours before you begin this flavor. Next, puree mixture and strain it through a sieve to remove the seeds.

Before you start the continuous freezing of this flavor, make sure the sanitizing solution or the previous flavor of mix has been pushed through the freezer. Open the outlet valve of the aging tank and let the proper amount of ice cream mix flow into the flavor tank. Next, pour the vanilla extract and red raspberry puree into the flavor tank. The mix is then pumped to the inlet of the continuous freezer. Set the speed, viscosity (stiffness), and overrun settings according to the manufacturer's recommendations. Start the continuous freezing process. As the ice cream leaves the continuous freezer, it is then piped to the next stage in the process, which is either filling (tubs, pints, etc.), extrusion, or molding.

⊠ PEACH   **Regular**

This flavor has been very successful when made with fresh ripe Georgia peaches, and the best time of year to produce and sell this flavor is in June and July. When made with processed peaches, there always seems to be the aftertaste of an artificial ingredient. The recipe I use takes time, but is certainly worth the effort.

In a continuous freezing operation, the use of both frozen peaches and peach puree is definitely preferable over a processed peach.

Batch		Continuous
26–28 (yield 4 quarts puree)	fresh ripe peaches	1,120 (yield 40 gallons puree)
3½ pounds	sugar	140 pounds
	OR	
	peach puree	40 gallons
3 ounces	natural peach extract	4 quarts
2½ gallons	16% ice cream mix	100 gallons
3 ounces	two-fold vanilla extract	3¾ quarts

Batch Freezing Method

Blanch the peaches in boiling water for 30–45 seconds so that they peel easily. (You will quickly learn that the hardest part of this recipe is peeling the fruit.) Peel, then mix them with 3½ pounds of sugar. Marinate mixture for 8 hours until ready to use. Puree ¾ of this mixture, and cut remaining peaches into small pieces.

Pour pureed mixture into batch freezer along with remaining ingredients except small cut pieces of peaches. Turn on both dasher and refrigeration and begin batch. When batch is complete, pour in remaining small cut pieces of peaches, turn off refrigeration, and extrude finished product.

Decorate top of tubs with fresh peach slices.

Batch time: 8–10 minutes.

Continuous Freezing Method

Using fresh peaches: Blanch the peaches in boiling water for 30–45 seconds so that they peel easily. (You will quickly learn that the hardest part of this recipe is peeling the fruit.) Peel, then mix them with 140 pounds of sugar. Puree half of the peaches. Cut the remaining peaches into small pieces. Marinate both mixtures for 8 hours until ready to use.

Before you start the continuous freezing of this flavor, make sure the sanitizing solution or the previous flavor of mix has been pushed through the freezer. Pour the peach pieces into the fruit feeder and adjust the controls to the appropriate setting. Open the outlet valve of the aging tank and let the proper amount of ice cream mix flow into the flavor tank. Pour the vanilla extract, peach puree, and natural peach extract into the flavor tank. The mix is then pumped to the inlet of the continuous freezer. Set the speed, viscosity (stiffness), and overrun settings according to the manufacturer's recommendations. Start the continuous freezing process. As the ice cream leaves the continuous freezer, it is then piped through the fruit feeder (ingredient feeder) so that the peach pieces can be discharged and mixed with the ice cream that has already become semifrozen. It is then piped to the next stage in the process, which is either filling (tubs, pints, etc.), extrusion, or molding.

Using peach puree only: Pour the peach puree into the flavor tank and follow the foregoing recipe.

⊠ CHERRY VANILLA CHIP   Regular

This is a variation of the popular Cherry Vanilla flavor.

Batch		Continuous
2½ gallons	16% ice cream mix	100 gallons
3 ounces	two-fold vanilla extract	3¾ quarts
½ #10 can	Bordeaux cherry halves	15 gallons
(1½ quarts)		
1 pound	chocolate chips	40 pounds
	cherry halves and chocolate chips for garnish	

Batch Freezing Method

Drain and discard half of juice from the cherry halves (too much juice makes the finished ice cream look artificial). Pour the ice cream mix, vanilla extract, and 24 ounces of cherry halves and remaining liquid into batch freezer. Turn on both dasher and refrigeration and begin batch. Add remaining cherries and chocolate chips at end of batch. When batch is complete, turn off refrigeration and extrude finished product.

Decorate tops of tubs with cherry pieces and chocolate chips.

Batch time: 8–10 minutes.

Continuous Freezing Method
Before you start the continuous freezing of this flavor, make sure the sanitizing solution or the previous flavor of mix has been pushed through the freezer. Pour the cherry halves and chocolate chips into the fruit feeder and adjust the controls to the appropriate setting. Open the outlet valve of the aging tank and let the proper amount of ice cream mix flow into the flavor tank. Next, pour the vanilla extract into the flavor tank. The mix is then pumped to the inlet of the continuous freezer. Set the speed, viscosity (stiffness), and overrun settings according to the manufacturer's recommendations. Start the continuous freezing process. As the ice cream leaves the continuous freezer, it is then piped through the fruit feeder (ingredient feeder) so that the cherry halves and chocolate chips can be discharged and mixed with the ice cream that has already become semi-frozen. The ice cream is then piped to the next stage in the process, which is either filling (tubs, pints, etc.), extrusion, or molding.

⊠ BOYSENBERRY   Regular
Simply delicious!

Batch		Continuous
6 quarts	fresh boysenberries	240 quarts
2 pounds	sugar	80 pounds
	OR*	
	boysenberry puree	40 gallons
	frozen boysenberries	20 gallons
	sugar	40 pounds
2½ gallons	16% ice cream mix	100 gallons
3 ounces	two-fold vanilla extract	3¾ quarts
	boysenberry mixture for garnish	

*Note: If a processed boysenberry puree is used instead of fresh boysenberries, omit the sugar for the puree portion of this recipe.

Batch Freezing Method
Wash and drain boysenberries well. Puree 4 quarts of boysenberries with 2 pounds of sugar. Add remaining 2 quarts of boysenberries to this mixture and marinate for 8 hours.

Pour all ingredients into batch freezer. Turn on both the dasher and refrigeration and begin the batch. When batch is complete, turn off refrigeration and extrude the finished product.

Decorate the top of the tubs with boysenberry mixture.

Batch time: 8–10 minutes.

Continuous Freezing Method

Using fresh boysenberries: Wash and drain boysenberries well. Puree 160 quarts of boysenberries with 80 pounds of sugar. Add remaining 80 quarts of boysenberries to this mixture and marinate for 8 hours. Next, follow recipe for using processed boysenberry puree.

Using processed boysenberry puree: Before you start the continuous freezing of this flavor, make sure the sanitizing solution or the previous flavor of mix has been pushed through the freezer. Pour 80 quarts of the boysenberry–sugar mixture into the fruit feeder and adjust the controls to the appropriate setting. Open the outlet valve of the aging tank and let the proper amount of ice cream mix flow into the flavor tank. Next, pour the vanilla extract and boysenberry puree into the flavor tank. The mix is then pumped to the inlet of the continuous freezer. Set the speed, viscosity (stiffness), and overrun settings according to the manufacturer's recommendations. Start the continuous freezing process. As the ice cream leaves the continuous freezer, it is then piped through the fruit feeder (ingredient feeder) so that the boysenberries can be discharged and mixed with the ice cream that has already become semifrozen. The ice cream is then piped to the next stage in the process, which is either filling (tubs, pints, etc.), extrusion, or molding.

⊠ BERRY CRUNCH   Superpremium

A blend of fresh berries combined with a graham cracker crunch, this flavor is sure to attract attention.

Using fresh fruit

Batch		Continuous
1¼ quarts	fresh strawberries	12½ gallons
1¼ quarts	fresh raspberries	12½ gallons
1¼ quarts	fresh blueberries	12½ gallons
1¼ quarts	fresh blackberries	12½ gallons
3 pounds	sugar	120 pounds
2½ gallons	16% ice cream mix	100 gallons
3 ounces	two-fold vanilla extract	3¾ quarts
1½ pounds	graham crackers	60 pounds
	whole berries and graham crackers for garnish	

Batch Freezing Method

Wash and drain all berries. In one container combine ¾ quart each of strawberries, raspberries, blueberries, and blackberries with 2 pounds of sugar. Puree this mixture. In another container, combine the remaining whole berries with 1 pound sugar and set aside. Marinate both mixtures for 8 hours. Pour all ingredients except the whole berry–sugar mixture and graham crackers into batch freezer. Turn on both dasher and refrigeration and begin. Halfway into batch, as ice cream begins to freeze, add whole berries and graham crackers. When batch is complete, turn off refrigeration and extrude finished product.

Batch time: 8–10 minutes.

Continuous Freezing Method

Wash and drain all berries. In one container combine 8¾ gallons each of strawberries, raspberries, blueberries, and blackberries with 80 pounds of sugar. Puree this mixture. In another container, combine the remaining whole berries (3¾ gallons of each) with 40 pounds sugar and set aside. Marinate both mixtures for 8 hours.

Before you start the continuous freezing of this flavor, make sure the sanitizing solution or the previous flavor of mix has been pushed through the freezer. Pour the whole berry mixture into the fruit feeder and adjust the controls to the appropriate setting. Open the outlet valve of the aging tank and let the proper amount of ice cream mix flow into the flavor tank. Next, pour the vanilla extract and berry puree into the flavor tank. The mix is then pumped to the inlet of the continuous freezer. Set the speed, viscosity (stiffness), and overrun settings according to the manufacturer's recommendations. Start the continuous freezing process. As the ice cream leaves the continuous freezer, it is then piped through the fruit feeder (ingredient feeder) so that the whole berry mixture can be discharged and mixed with the ice cream that has already become semifrozen. The ice cream is then piped to the next stage in the process, which is either filling (tubs, pints, etc.), extrusion, or molding.

Using Processed Fruit Puree

Batch		Continuous
¾ quart	strawberry puree	7½ gallons
¾ quart	seedless raspberry puree	7½ gallons
¾ quart	blueberry puree	7½ gallons
¾ quart	blackberry puree	7½ gallons
12 ounces each	processed whole strawberries, raspberries, blueberries, and blackberries	3¾ gallons each
2½ gallons	16% ice cream mix	100 gallons
3 ounces	two-fold vanilla extract	3¾ quarts
1½ pounds	graham crackers	60 pounds
	whole berries and graham crackers for garnish	

Batch Freezing Method
Pour all ingredients except the whole berries and graham crackers into batch
freezer. Turn on both dasher and refrigeration and begin. Halfway into batch, as
ice cream begins to freeze, add whole berries and graham crackers. When batch
is complete, turn off refrigeration and extrude finished product.

Batch time: 8–10 minutes.

Continuous Freezing Method
Before you start the continuous freezing of this flavor, make sure the sanitizing solution or the previous flavor of mix has been pushed through the
freezer. Pour the whole berry mixture into the fruit feeder and adjust the
controls to the appropriate setting. Open the outlet valve of the aging tank
and let the proper amount of ice cream mix flow into the flavor tank. Next,
pour the vanilla extract and berry puree into the flavor tank. The mix is then
pumped to the inlet of the continuous freezer. Set the speed, viscosity (stiffness), and overrun settings according to the manufacturers recommendations. Start the continuous freezing process. As the ice cream leaves the continuous freezer, it is then piped through the fruit feeder (ingredient feeder)
so that the whole berry mixture can be discharged and mixed with the ice
cream that has already become semifrozen. The ice cream is then piped to the
next stage in the process, which is either filling (tubs, pints, etc.), extrusion,
or molding.

⊠ BANANA CHIP   Regular

*Banana is a very versatile fruit and its use in creating new ice cream flavors is al-
most limitless. Banana chip is a simple creation that not only looks good, but tastes
good. The freshness of banana combined with chocolate chips will bring raves from
your customers.*

Batch		Continuous
2½ gallons	16% ice cream mix	100 gallons
3 ounces	two-fold vanilla extract	3¾ quarts
10 pounds	ripe bananas (8 pounds peeled)*	
	pasteurized banana puree	40 gallons
1 pound	large chocolate chips	40 pounds
	pieces of banana and chocolate chips	
	for garnish	

*Note: 10 pounds of whole bananas will yield approximately 8 pounds of peeled bananas because
banana skin is approximately 20 percent of the weight of a banana.

Batch Freezing Method

Peel bananas and put them into batch freezer along with 1 gallon of ice cream mix. Turn on dasher for about 5 minutes to puree bananas and blend with ice cream mix. Pour remaining ingredients except chocolate chips into batch freezer. Turn on both dasher and refrigeration, and begin batch. At end of batch, pour in chocolate chips, turn off refrigeration and extrude finished product.

Batch time: 8–10 minutes.

Continuous Freezing Method

Before you start the continuous freezing of this flavor, make sure the sanitizing solution or the previous flavor of mix has been pushed through the freezer. Pour the chocolate chips into the fruit feeder and adjust the controls to the appropriate setting. Open the outlet valve of the aging tank and let the proper amount of ice cream mix flow into the flavor tank. Next, pour the vanilla extract and banana puree into the flavor tank. The mix is then pumped to the inlet of the continuous freezer. Set the speed, viscosity (stiffness), and overrun settings according to the manufacturer's recommendations. Start the continuous freezing process. As the ice cream leaves the continuous freezer, it is then piped through the fruit feeder (ingredient feeder) so that the chocolate chips can be discharged and mixed with the ice cream that has already become semifrozen. The ice cream is then piped to the next stage in the process, which is either filling (tubs, pints, etc.), extrusion, or molding.

⊠ BLUEBERRY   Superpremium

Blueberry is rarely found either on supermarket shelves or in shops, and I can't really explain why. It is a great tasting flavor and not difficult to prepare. For the summertime, blueberry fits in well with the rest of the fruit selections you should be presenting to your customers.

Although fresh blueberries are preferred, the water content of the berry makes using them difficult. Also, it takes too long to marinate the fresh berries for use in this flavor. The addition of a blueberry natural flavor extract is recommended to boost the flavor profile.

Batch		Continuous
2½ gallons	16% ice cream mix	100 gallons
3 ounces	two-fold vanilla extract	3¾ quarts
½ #10 can (1½ quarts)	processed blueberries	15 gallons
	processed blueberries for garnish	

Batch Freezing Method
Pour the ice cream mix, vanilla extract, and 32 ounces of blueberries into batch freezer. Turn on both dasher and refrigeration and begin batch. Add remaining blueberries at end of batch. When batch is complete, turn off refrigeration and extrude finished product.

Decorate tops of tubs with processed blueberries.

Batch time: 8–10 minutes.

Continuous Freezing Method
Before you start the continuous freezing of this flavor, make sure the sanitizing solution or the previous flavor of mix has been pushed through the freezer. Pour the blueberries into the fruit feeder and adjust the controls to the appropriate setting. Open the outlet valve of the aging tank and let the proper amount of ice cream mix flow into the flavor tank. Next, pour the vanilla extract into the flavor tank. The mix is then pumped to the inlet of the continuous freezer. Set the speed, viscosity (stiffness), and overrun settings according to the manufacturer's recommendations. Start the continuous freezing process. As the ice cream leaves the continuous freezer, it is then piped through the fruit feeder (ingredient feeder) so that the blueberries can be discharged and mixed with the ice cream that has already become semifrozen. The ice cream is then piped to the next stage in the process, which is either filling (tubs, pints, etc.), extrusion, or molding.

⊠ GOOSEBERRY   Superpremium

This is a seasonal summer flavor. If fresh gooseberries are not available, substitute frozen.

Batch		Continuous
9 dry fresh or frozen pints (yield 4 quarts puree)	gooseberries	
2 pounds	sugar	
	gooseberry puree	40 gallons
2½ gallons	16% ice cream mix	100 gallons
3 ounces	two-fold vanilla extract	3¾ quarts
	gooseberry pieces for garnish	

Batch Freezing Method
Wash and remove stems from fresh gooseberries. Puree and then pass gooseberry puree through a strainer to yield 4 quarts. Combine puree with 2 pounds of sugar and marinate for 8 hours.

Pour all ingredients into batch freezer. Turn on both dasher and refrigeration and begin batch. When batch is complete, turn off refrigeration and extrude finished product.

Batch time: 8–10 minutes.

Continuous Freezing Method

Before you start the continuous freezing of this flavor, make sure the sanitizing solution or the previous flavor of mix has been pushed through the freezer. Open the outlet valve of the aging tank and let the proper amount of ice cream mix flow into the flavor tank. Next, pour the vanilla extract and gooseberry puree into the flavor tank. The mix is then pumped to the inlet of the continuous freezer. Set the speed, viscosity (stiffness), and overrun settings according to the manufacturer's recommendations. Start the continuous freezing process. As the ice cream leaves the continuous freezer, it is then piped to the next stage in the process, which is either filling (tubs, pints, etc.), extrusion, or molding.

⊠ **CANTALOUPE**   **Superpremium**

All melons make great frozen desserts and cantaloupe is no exception. Use very ripe cantaloupes and you will be extremely pleased with the results.

Batch		Continuous
7–8	ripe cantaloupes	
3 pounds	sugar	
	cantaloupe puree	40 gallons
2 ounces	lemon juice	2½ quarts
2½ gallons	16% ice cream mix	100 gallons
3 ounces	two-fold vanilla extract	3¾ quarts

Batch Freezing Method

Peel, cut, and remove seeds from cantaloupes. Puree enough cantaloupes to yield 4 quarts of puree. Add 3 pounds of sugar and 2 ounces of lemon juice to puree. Marinate mixture for 8 hours.

Pour all ingredients into batch freezer. Turn on both dasher and refrigeration and begin batch. At end of batch, turn off refrigeration and extrude finished product.

Batch time: 8–10 minutes.

Continuous Freezing Method

Before you start the continuous freezing of this flavor, make sure the sanitizing solution or the previous flavor of mix has been pushed through the freezer. Open the outlet valve of the aging tank and let the proper amount of ice cream mix flow into the flavor tank. Next, pour the vanilla extract, lemon juice, and cantaloupe puree into the flavor tank. The mix is then pumped to the inlet of the continuous freezer. Set the speed, viscosity (stiffness), and overrun settings according to the manufacturer's recommendations. Start the continuous freezing process. As the ice cream leaves the continuous freezer, it is then piped to the next stage in the process, which is either filling (tubs, pints, etc.), extrusion, or molding.

⊠ **KIWI**   **Superpremium**

Other than peeling the kiwifruit, this flavor is easy to prepare. It looks and tastes great.

Batch		**Continuous**
32 (yield 3 quarts puree)	kiwifruit	
2 pounds	sugar	
	kiwi puree (processed)	30 gallons
2½ gallons	16% ice cream mix	100 gallons
3 ounces	two-fold vanilla extract	3¾ quarts
	thin slices of kiwifruit for garnish	

Batch Freezing Method

Peel and puree enough kiwifruit to yield 3 quarts of puree. Combine pureed fruit with 2 pounds sugar and marinate mixture for 8 hours. Pour all ingredients into batch freezer. Turn on both dasher and refrigeration and begin batch. When batch is complete, turn off refrigeration and extrude finished product.

Batch time: 8–10 minutes.

Continuous Freezing Method

Before you start the continuous freezing of this flavor, make sure the sanitizing solution or the previous flavor of mix has been pushed through the freezer. Open the outlet valve of the aging tank and let the proper amount of ice cream mix flow into the flavor tank. Next, pour the vanilla extract and kiwi puree into the flavor tank. The mix is then pumped to the inlet of the continuous freezer. Set the speed, viscosity (stiffness), and overrun settings according to the manufacturer's recommendations. Start the continuous freezing process. As the ice cream leaves the continuous freezer, it is then piped to the next stage in the process, which is either filling (tubs, pints, etc.), extrusion, or molding.

⊠ PEAR   Superpremium

This ice cream has to be slightly overflavored to bring out the delicate flavor of the pear in the finished product. Frozen pears are recommended over fresh to reduce the preparation time.

Batch		Continuous
30 (yield 5 quarts puree)	ripe Bartlett pears	
2 pounds	sugar	
	pear puree (processed)	37½ gallons
2 ounces	lemon juice	2½ quarts
2½ gallons	16% ice cream mix	100 gallons
3 ounces	two-fold vanilla extract	3¾ quarts
	small pieces of pear for garnish	

Batch Freezing Method

Peel, core, and cut up pears. Gently poach them with 1 quart water in an uncovered pot for approximately 10 minutes or until softened. Drain water and puree the pears to yield 5 quarts puree. Combine puree with 2 quarts of sugar and 2 ounces of lemon juice and marinate for 8 hours.

Pour all ingredients into batch freezer. Turn on both dasher and refrigeration and begin batch. When batch is complete, turn off refrigeration and extrude finished product.

Batch time: 8–10 minutes.

Continuous Freezing Method

Before you start the continuous freezing of this flavor, make sure the sanitizing solution or the previous flavor of mix has been pushed through the freezer. Open the outlet valve of the aging tank and let the proper amount of ice cream mix flow into the flavor tank. Next, pour the vanilla extract and pear puree into the flavor tank. The mix is then pumped to the inlet of the continuous freezer. Set the speed, viscosity (stiffness), and overrun settings according to the manufacturer's recommendations. Start the continuous freezing process. As the ice cream leaves the continuous freezer, it is then piped to the next stage in the process, which is either filling (tubs, pints, etc.), extrusion, or molding.

Coffee and Mocha Flavors

Americans have had a passion for coffee for generations. It wakes us up in the mornings, perks us up in the afternoons, and relaxes us in the evenings. Flavor preferences run from the mild, like the mocha java bean, or the strong, like the espresso bean. Regardless of the strength, coffee has a distinct flavor that has been and continues to be a popular flavor for ice cream.

There are as many methods and variations for producing coffee ice cream as there are ice cream producers. Personally, I prefer a strong coffee essence, so I use freeze-dried coffee in all my coffee flavors. I also like to mix in cocoa to smooth out some of the bitter aftertaste you sometimes notice in coffee ice cream. Besides, cocoa also adds a touch of class.

When preparing the coffee paste for the following recipes using freeze-dried coffee, use only a little hot water to avoid diluting the coffee flavor.

⊠ COFFEE   Regular

Because this is the base flavor for all the following coffee recipes, it is important to establish the taste of the finished product. This recipe can be adjusted slightly depending on how strong a coffee flavor you want. Cocoa is used to create a smoother tasting flavor and also helps to remove the bitter aftertaste that occurs in many coffee flavors produced.

Batch		Continuous
5 ounces	freeze-dried coffee	12½ pounds
½ ounce	cocoa (22–24% fat)	1¼ pounds
3 tablespoons	hot water	1¾ quarts
2½ gallons	16% ice cream mix	100 gallons
3 ounces	two-fold vanilla extract	3¾ quarts

Batch Freezing Method

Mix freeze-dried coffee with as little hot water as possible and add cocoa. The resulting paste should be smooth with no dry coffee or cocoa visible.

Pour all ingredients, including coffee paste, into batch freezer and let dasher run for approximately 2 minutes, allowing coffee paste to blend evenly with cream. Turn on refrigeration and begin batch. When batch is complete, turn off refrigeration and extrude finished product.

Batch time: 8–10 minutes.

Continuous Freezing Method
Before you start the continuous freezing of this flavor, make sure the sanitizing solution or the previous flavor of mix has been pushed through the freezer.

Mix freeze-dried coffee with as little hot water as possible and add cocoa. The resulting paste should be smooth with no dry coffee or cocoa visible. Open the outlet valve of the mix storage tank and let the proper amount of ice cream mix flow into the flavor tank. Pour the vanilla extract and prepared coffee base into the flavor tank and mix all the ingredients together. The mix is then pumped to the inlet of the continuous freezer. Set the speed, viscosity (stiffness), and overrun settings according to the manufacturer's recommendations. Start the continuous freezing operation. As the ice cream leaves the continuous freezer, it is then piped to the next stage in the process, which is either filling (tubs, pints, etc.), extrusion, or molding.

⊠ COFFEE CHIP   Regular

Coffee and chocolate are a winning combination and will become a real favorite with anyone who loves coffee, so this is a must-have flavor.

Batch		Continuous
5 ounces	freeze-dried coffee	12½ pounds
½ ounce	cocoa (22–24% fat)	1¼ pounds
3 tablespoons	hot water	1¾ quarts
2½ gallons	16% ice cream mix	100 gallons
3 ounces	two-fold vanilla extract	3¾ quarts
2 pounds	chocolate chips	80 pounds
	chocolate chips for garnish	

Batch Freezing Method
Mix freeze-dried coffee with as little hot water as possible and add cocoa. The resulting paste should be smooth with no dry coffee or cocoa visible.

Pour all ingredients, including coffee paste but excluding 1 pound of chocolate chips, into batch freezer. Turn on dasher for 2 minutes. Turn on refrigeration and begin batch. At end of batch, pour in remaining chips. When batch is complete, turn off refrigeration and extrude finished product.

Decorate tops of tubs with chocolate chips.

Batch time: 8–10 minutes.

Continuous Freezing Method
Before you start the continuous freezing of this flavor, make sure the sanitizing solution or the previous flavor of mix has been pushed through the freezer.

Mix freeze-dried coffee with as little hot water as possible and add cocoa. The resulting paste should be smooth with no dry coffee or cocoa visible. Pour the chocolate chips into the fruit feeder and adjust the controls to the appropriate setting. Open the outlet valve of the mix storage tank and let the proper amount of ice cream mix flow into the flavor tank. Pour the vanilla extract and prepared coffee base into the flavor tank and mix all the ingredients together. The mix is then pumped to the inlet of the continuous freezer. Set the speed, viscosity (stiffness), and overrun settings according to the manufacturer's recommendations. Start the continuous freezing operation. As the ice cream leaves the continuous freezer, it is then piped through the fruit feeder (ingredient feeder) so that the chocolate chips can be discharged and mixed with the ice cream that has already been semifrozen. The ice cream is then piped to the next stage in the process, which is either filling (tubs, pints, etc.), extrusion, or molding.

⊠ MUD PIE   Superpremium

This flavor was developed in New England and became very popular on the East Coast. Mud pie is really a sundae with hot fudge, but as you can see from this recipe, I have expanded on that idea.

Batch		Continuous
4 ounces	freeze-dried coffee	10 pounds
½ ounce	cocoa (22–24% fat)	1¼ pounds
3 tablespoons	hot water	1¾ quarts
2½ gallons	16% ice cream mix	100 gallons
2 ounces	two-fold vanilla extract	2½ quarts
1 pound	graham crackers	40 pounds
3 pounds	hot fudge	
	fudge variegate	120 pounds
	hot fudge and pieces of graham cracker for garnish	

Batch Freezing Method
Mix freeze-dried coffee with as little hot water as possible and add cocoa. The resulting paste should be smooth with no dry coffee or cocoa visible.

Pour ice cream mix, vanilla extract, coffee paste, and half the graham crackers into batch freezer. Turn on dasher for 2 minutes, and then refrigeration.

While batch is running, spread inner linings of tubs with fudge.

When batch is complete, turn off refrigeration and extrude finished product while using a spatula to swirl fudge from sides of tubs into ice cream.

Decorate tops of tubs with graham crackers and fudge.

Batch time: 8–10 minutes.

Continuous Freezing Method

Before you start the continuous freezing of this flavor, make sure the sanitizing solution or the previous flavor of mix has been pushed through the freezer.

Mix freeze-dried coffee with as little hot water as possible and add cocoa. The resulting paste should be smooth with no dry coffee or cocoa visible. Pour the chilled (40 degrees Fahrenheit) fudge variegate into the ripple pump supply tank and adjust speed to inject at the rate as prescribed in the formula, or approximately 10–14 percent of the weight of the ice cream mix. Next, pour the graham crackers into the fruit feeder and adjust the controls to the appropriate setting. Open the outlet valve of the mix storage tank and let the proper amount of ice cream mix flow into the flavor tank. Pour the vanilla extract and prepared coffee base into the flavor tank and mix all the ingredients together. The mix is then pumped to the inlet of the continuous freezer. Set the speed, viscosity (stiffness), and overrun settings according to the manufacturer's recommendations. Start the continuous freezing operation. As the ice cream leaves the continuous freezer, it is then piped through the fruit feeder (ingredient feeder) so that the graham crackers can be discharged and mixed with ice cream. The ice cream is then piped through the ripple injection unit so that the fudge variegate can be injected into the stream of ice cream that has already become semifrozen. The ice cream is then piped to the next stage in the process, which is either filling (tubs, pints, etc.), extrusion, or molding.

⊠ MOCHA ALMOND FUDGE   Superpremium

Whoever thought up this great flavor was a genius of sophistication and creativity. The addition of almonds and fudge to the mocha flavor is a terrific combination. It is similar to mud pie but uses almonds instead of graham crackers.

Batch		Continuous
4 ounces	freeze-dried coffee	10 pounds
½ ounce	cocoa (22–24% fat)	1¼ pounds
3 tablespoons	hot water	1¾ quarts
2½ gallons	16% ice cream mix	100 gallons
2 ounces	two-fold vanilla extract	2½ quarts
1 pound	sliced roasted almonds	40 pounds
3 pounds	hot fudge	
	fudge variegate	120 pounds
	hot fudge and pieces of sliced roasted almonds for garnish	

Batch Freezing Method

Mix freeze-dried coffee with as little hot water as possible and add cocoa. The resulting paste should be smooth with no dry coffee or cocoa visible.

Pour all ingredients, including coffee paste but excluding almonds and fudge, into batch freezer. Turn on dasher for 2 minutes so that ingredients mix thoroughly. Turn on refrigeration and begin batch. Halfway into batch, add almonds. When batch is complete, turn off refrigeration, and use a spatula to swirl fudge into tubs as ice cream as being extruded from batch freezer.

Decorate tops of tubs with almonds and fudge.

Batch time: 8–10 minutes.

Continuous Freezing Method

Before you start the continuous freezing of this flavor, make sure the sanitizing solution or the previous flavor of mix has been pushed through the freezer.

Mix freeze-dried coffee with as little hot water as possible and add cocoa. The resulting paste should be smooth with no dry coffee or cocoa visible. Pour the chilled (40 degrees Fahrenheit) fudge variegate into the ripple pump supply tank and adjust speed to inject at the rate as prescribed in the formula, or approximately 10–14 percent of the weight of the ice cream mix. Next, pour the sliced almonds into the fruit feeder and adjust the controls to the appropriate setting. Open the outlet valve of the mix storage tank and let the proper amount of ice cream mix flow into the flavor tank. Pour the vanilla extract and prepared coffee base into the flavor tank and mix all the ingredients together. The mix is then pumped to the inlet of the continuous freezer. Set the speed, viscosity (stiffness), and overrun settings according to the manufacturer's recommendations. Start the continuous freezing operation. As the ice cream leaves the continuous freezer, it is then piped through the fruit feeder (ingredient feeder) so that the sliced almonds can be discharged and mixed with the ice cream. The ice cream is then piped through the ripple injection unit so that the fudge variegate can be injected into the stream of ice cream that has already become semifrozen. The ice cream is then piped to the next stage in the process, which is either filling (tubs, pints, etc.), extrusion, or molding.

⊠ MOCHA CHIP   Regular

This mild flavor is a variation of coffee chip ice cream with an equal amount of chocolate flavor added to the coffee mixture.

Batch   **Continuous**

Batch		Continuous
4 ounces	freeze-dried coffee	10 pounds
4 ounces	cocoa (22–24% fat)	10 pounds
4 tablespoons	hot water	5 quarts
2½ gallons	16% ice cream mix	100 gallons
2 ounces	two-fold vanilla extract	2½ quarts
2 pounds	chocolate chips	80 pounds
	chocolate chips for garnish	

Batch Freezing Method

Mix freeze-dried coffee with as little hot water as possible and add cocoa. The resulting paste should be smooth with no dry coffee or cocoa visible.

Pour all ingredients, including coffee/cocoa paste but excluding half the chips, into batch freezer. Turn on dasher for approximately 2 minutes to mix all ingredients thoroughly. Turn on refrigeration and begin batch. At end of batch, add remaining chips. When batch is complete, turn off refrigeration and extrude finished product.

Decorate tops of tubs with chocolate chips.

Batch time: 8–10 minutes.

Continuous Freezing Method

Before you start the continuous freezing of this flavor, make sure the sanitizing solution or the previous flavor of mix has been pushed through the freezer.

Mix freeze-dried coffee and cocoa with as little hot water as possible. The resulting paste should be smooth with no dry coffee or cocoa visible. Pour the chocolate chips into the fruit feeder and adjust the controls to the appropriate setting. Open the outlet valve of the mix storage tank and let the proper amount of ice cream mix flow into the flavor tank. Pour the vanilla extract and prepared coffee base into the flavor tank and mix all the ingredients together. The mix is then pumped to the inlet of the continuous freezer. Set the speed, viscosity (stiffness), and overrun settings according to the manufacturer's recommendations. Start the continuous freezing operation. As the ice cream leaves the continuous freezer, it is then piped through the fruit feeder (ingredient feeder) so that the chocolate chips can be discharged and mixed with the ice cream that has already been semifrozen. The ice cream is then piped to the next stage in the process, which is either filling (tubs, pints, etc.), extrusion, or molding.

⊠ MOCHA FUDGE PIE   Regular

This recipe is a delectable combination of coffee and chocolate mixed with cookies and fudge.

Batch		Continuous
4 ounces	freeze-dried coffee	10 pounds
4 ounces	cocoa (22–24% fat)	10 pounds
4 tablespoons	hot water	2½ quarts
2½ gallons	16% ice cream mix	100 gallons
2 ounces	two-fold vanilla extract	2½ quarts
1 pound	chocolate chips	40 pounds
1 pound	chocolate chip cookies	40 pounds
4 pounds	hot fudge	
	fudge variegate	160 pounds
	chocolate chips, cookie pieces, and fudge for garnish	

Batch Freezing Method
Mix freeze-dried coffee with as little hot water as possible and add cocoa. The resulting paste should be smooth with no dry coffee or cocoa visible.

Pour ice cream mix, vanilla extract, and coffee/cocoa paste into batch freezer and turn on dasher for 2 minutes to allow paste to thoroughly blend into ice cream mix. Turn on refrigeration and begin batch. At end of batch, add chocolate chips and cookies. After they are completely fed into batch, turn off refrigeration and, using a spatula, swirl fudge into ice cream while extruding finished product.

Decorate tops of tubs with chocolate chips, cookies, and fudge.

Batch time: 8–10 minutes.

Continuous Freezing Method
Before you start the continuous freezing of this flavor, make sure the sanitizing solution or the previous flavor of mix has been pushed through the freezer.

Mix freeze-dried coffee with as little hot water as possible and add cocoa. The resulting paste should be smooth with no dry coffee or cocoa visible. Pour the chilled (40 degrees Fahrenheit) fudge variegate into the ripple supply tank and adjust speed to inject at the rate as prescribed in the formula, or approximately 10–14 percent of the weight of the ice cream mix. Next, mix together and then pour the chocolate chips and chocolate chip cookie pieces into the fruit feeder and adjust the controls to the appropriate setting. Open the outlet valve of the mix storage tank and let the proper amount of ice cream mix flow into the flavor tank. Pour the vanilla extract and prepared coffee base into the flavor tank and mix all the ingredients together. The mix is then pumped to the inlet of the continuous freezer. Set the speed, viscosity (stiffness), and overrun settings according to the manufacturer's recommendations. Start the continuous freezing operation. As the ice cream leaves the continuous freezer, it is then piped through the fruit feeder (ingredient feeder) so that the chocolate chip and chocolate chip cookie pieces can be discharged and mixed with the ice cream. The ice cream is then piped through the ripple injection unit so that the fudge variegate can be injected into the stream of ice cream that has already become semifrozen. The ice cream is then piped to the next stage in the process, which is either filling (tubs, pints, etc.), extrusion, or molding.

Nuts

As ice cream producers become more creative with their use of the many varieties of nuts, these ice cream flavors become more popular. Until the mid-1980s, butter pecan, maple walnut, burnt almond, and pistachio constituted the majority of nut-flavored ice creams produced in this country. Nearly 70 percent of the nut-flavor market was accounted for by the butter pecan and maple walnut flavors.

Recently, however, the success of peanut butter, pecan praline, and macadamia nut flavors has spurred the demand for more new and exciting flavors, resulting in increased sales of nutmeats to the ice cream industry. The following recipes feature both old and new favorites.

I recommend using roasted nuts with no added salt. I dislike salt for health reasons and I believe it acts as a melting agent during the hardening of the finished product. Be aware that nuts absorb the water in the mix, so it is easy to end up with an overprocessed product if your product run goes over the allowable time. To avoid overprocessing using the batch process, watch closely during the last 3 minutes of production.

Because the appearance of the product is as important as the product itself, always decorate the tops of the packed tubs with some of the nuts of the flavor being produced.

⊠ BUTTER PECAN   Regular

Most popular of all the nut flavors, butter pecan has been a standard for over 50 years and continues to be popular today. Use only large roasted pecan pieces.

Batch		Continuous
2½ gallons	16% ice cream mix	100 gallons
2 ounces	two-fold vanilla extract	2½ quarts
30 ounces	butter pecan base (liquid measure)	37½ quarts
1 ounce	butter flavor	1¼ quarts
2 pounds	roasted pecan pieces	80 pounds
	pieces of roasted pecans for garnish	

Batch Freezing Method
Pour all ingredients except 1 pound of roasted pecans into batch freezer. (Both
the butter flavor and half of the roasted pecans are entered at the beginning for
additional flavor in the product.) Turn on both dasher and refrigeration and begin batch. At end of batch, add remaining pecans. When batch is completed,
turn off refrigeration and extrude finished product.
   Decorate tops of tubs with pieces of roasted pecans.

Batch time: 8–10 minutes.

Continuous Freezing Method
Before you start the continuous freezing of this flavor, make sure the sanitizing
solution or the previous flavor of mix has been pushed through the freezer.
   Pour the pecans into the fruit feeder and adjust the controls to the appropriate setting. Open the outlet valve of the mix storage tank and let the proper
amount of ice cream mix flow into the flavor tank. Pour the vanilla extract, butter pecan base, and butter flavor into the flavor tank and mix all the ingredients
together. The mix is then pumped to the inlet of the continuous freezer. Set the
speed, viscosity (stiffness), and overrun settings according to the manufacturer's
recommendations. Start the continuous freezing operation. As the ice cream
leaves the continuous freezer, it is then piped through the fruit feeder (ingredient feeder) so that the pecans can be discharged and mixed with the ice cream
that has already been semifrozen. The ice cream is then piped to the next stage
in the process, which is either filling (tubs, pints, etc.), extrusion, or molding.

⊠ PECAN PRALINE   **Superpremium**

*It took northerners a long time to discover pecan praline. Its popularity has grown
continuously and it is now a must for any upscale operation. Purchase only large
pralines for the best flavor. Smaller size pralines are considered inferior quality.*

Batch   **Continuous**

2½ gallons	16% ice cream mix	100 gallons
2 ounces	two-fold vanilla extract	2½ quarts
1 ounce	praline flavor	1¼ quarts
2 pounds	pecan pralines pieces (large)	80 pounds
32 ounces	caramel variegate	10 gallons
	pieces of praline pecans for garnish	

Batch Freezing Method
Even though the praline flavor is adequate, the real secret to a great pecan praline ice cream is in how you put the pieces of pecan pralines into the batch
freezer. Split the 2 pounds in half and pour 1 pound into the batch at the very
beginning. The breaking up of the pralines by the dasher adds a crunchy praline
taste throughout the product.

Pour all ingredients except half the praline pieces into batch freezer. Turn on both dasher and refrigeration and begin batch. At end of batch, add remaining 1 pound of pralines. When batch is complete, turn off refrigeration, swirl the caramel around the tubs as the finished product is being extruded.

Decorate tops of tubs with pieces of pecan pralines and caramel.

Batch time: 8–10 minutes.

Continuous Freezing Method
Before you start the continuous freezing of this flavor, make sure the sanitizing solution or the previous flavor of mix has been pushed through the freezer.

Pour the pecan pralines into the fruit feeder and adjust the controls to the appropriate setting. Next, pour the chilled (40 degrees Fahrenheit) caramel variegate into the ripple pump supply tank and adjust speed to inject at the rate as prescribed in the formula, or approximately 10–14 percent of the weight of the ice cream mix. Open the outlet valve of the mix storage tank and let the proper amount of ice cream mix flow into the flavor tank. Pour the vanilla extract and praline flavor into the flavor tank and mix all the ingredients together. The mix is then pumped to the inlet of the continuous freezer. Set the speed, viscosity (stiffness), and overrun settings according to the manufacturer's recommendations. Start the continuous freezing operation. As the ice cream leaves the continuous freezer, it is then piped through the fruit feeder (ingredient feeder) so that the pecan pralines can be discharged and mixed with the ice cream that has already been semifrozen. The ice cream is then piped through the ripple injection unit so that the caramel variegate can be injected into the stream of ice cream. The ice cream is then piped to the next stage in the process, which is either filling (tubs, pints, etc.), extrusion, or molding.

⊠ MAPLE WALNUT   **Regular**
This flavor is not as popular as butter pecan but it is popular in general with adults. It is a delicate flavor that can sometimes be too sweet, so be careful with the maple syrup or flavoring that is used. A high quality maple syrup can be substituted for the maple flavoring.

Batch		**Continuous**
2½ gallons	16% ice cream mix	100 gallons
2 ounces	two-fold vanilla extract	2½ quarts
2 ounces	maple flavoring	2½ quarts
	OR	
16 ounces	maple syrup	40 pounds
2 pounds	walnut pieces	80 pounds
	walnut pieces for garnish	

Batch Freezing Method
Pour all ingredients except 1 pound of walnut pieces into batch freezer. Turn on both dasher and refrigeration and begin batch. At end of batch, pour in remaining 1 pound of walnut pieces. When batch is complete, turn off refrigeration and extrude finished product.
    Decorate tops of tubs with walnut pieces.

Batch time: 8–10 minutes.

Continuous Freezing Method
Before you start the continuous freezing of this flavor, make sure the sanitizing solution or the previous flavor of mix has been pushed through the freezer.
    Pour the walnut pieces into the fruit feeder and adjust the controls to the appropriate setting. Open the outlet valve of the mix storage tank and let the proper amount of ice cream mix flow into the flavor tank. Pour the vanilla extract and maple flavoring into the flavor tank and mix all the ingredients together. The mix is then pumped to the inlet of the continuous freezer. Set the speed, viscosity (stiffness), and overrun settings according to the manufacturer's recommendations. Start the continuous freezing operation. As the ice cream leaves the continuous freezer, it is then piped through the fruit feeder (ingredient feeder) so that the walnut pieces can be discharged and mixed with the ice cream that has already been semifrozen. The ice cream is then piped to the next stage in the process, which is either filling (tubs, pints, etc.), extrusion, or molding.

⊠ **PISTACHIO**   **Superpremium**

This flavor is a staple for any upscale retail ice cream operation or Chinese restaurant. Even though pistachios are expensive, it is worthwhile to feature this flavor. The following recipe uses all natural ingredients and no green coloring. It makes no sense to spend a lot of money for pistachios and then to add green coloring just so the ice cream looks like everybody else's.

In a batch freezer operation, you can really make an impression with this flavor because it is usually poorly flavored for the commercial market. Remember that a common complaint of customers eating this flavor is "Where are the pistachios?"

Batch		Continuous
2½ gallons	16% ice cream mix	100 gallons
2 ounces	two-fold vanilla extract	2½ quarts
2 ounces	pistachio flavoring	2½ quarts
1½ pounds	pistachio pieces	60 pounds
	pistachio pieces for garnish	

Batch Freezing Method

Pour all ingredients except half of pistachios into batch freezer. Turn on dasher and let it run for about 5 minutes to granulate the nuts. Turn on refrigeration and begin batch. At end of batch, add remaining nuts. When batch is complete, turn off refrigeration and extrude finished product.

Decorate tops of tubs with pistachio pieces.

Batch time: 8–10 minutes.

Continuous Freezing Method

Before you start the continuous freezing of this flavor, make sure the sanitizing solution or the previous flavor of mix has been pushed through the freezer.

Pour the pistachio pieces into the fruit feeder and adjust the controls to the appropriate setting. Open the outlet valve of the mix storage tank and let the proper amount of ice cream mix flow into the flavor tank. Pour the vanilla extract and pistachio flavoring into the flavor tank and mix all the ingredients together. The mix is then pumped to the inlet of the continuous freezer. Set the speed, viscosity (stiffness), and overrun settings according to the manufacturer's recommendations. Start the continuous freezing operation. As the ice cream leaves the continuous freezer, it is then piped through the fruit feeder (ingredient feeder) so that the pistachios can be discharged and mixed with the ice cream that has already been semifrozen. The ice cream is then piped to the next stage in the process, which is either filling (tubs, pints, etc.), extrusion, or molding.

▧ PEANUT BUTTER   Regular

The peanut butter craze of the early 1980s created a demand for a peanut butter flavored ice cream.

You can substitute a high quality peanut butter for the commercial peanut butter used for the production of ice cream if you so desire. Either way, watch out for overprocessing during the production run.

Batch		Continuous
2½ gallons	16% ice cream mix	100 gallons
2 ounces	two-fold vanilla extract	2½ quarts
24 ounces	peanut butter flavoring	60 pounds
	OR	
1 pound	creamy peanut butter	40 pounds
1 pound	granulated peanut pieces	40 pounds
2 quarts	peanut butter variegate	20 gallons
	peanut butter and pieces of peanuts for garnish	

Batch Freezing Method

Pour all ingredients except half of the peanuts into batch freezer. Let dasher run for 3 minutes to blend peanut butter into cream. Turn on refrigeration and begin batch.

Watch the batch very closely during the last 3 minutes to prevent overprocessing. At end of batch, pour remaining peanuts into the batch freezer. Then turn off refrigeration and swirl the peanut butter variegate into finished ice cream as it is being extruded from freezer.

Decorate tops of tubs with peanut butter and pieces of peanuts.

Batch time: 8–10 minutes.

Continuous Freezing Method

Before you start the continuous freezing of this flavor, make sure the sanitizing solution or the previous flavor of mix has been pushed through the freezer.

Pour the peanuts into the fruit feeder and adjust the controls to the appropriate setting. Next, pour the chilled peanut butter variegate (40 degrees Fahrenheit) into the ripple pump supply tank and adjust speed to inject at the rate as prescribed in the formula, or approximately 10–14 percent of the weight of the ice cream mix. Open the outlet valve of the mix storage tank and let the proper amount of ice cream mix flow into the flavor tank. Pour the vanilla extract and peanut butter flavoring into the flavor tank and mix all the ingredients together. The mix is then pumped to the inlet of the continuous freezer. Set the speed, viscosity (stiffness), and overrun settings according to the manufacturer's recommendations. Start the continuous freezing operation. As the ice cream leaves the continuous freezer, it is then piped through the fruit feeder (ingredient feeder) so that the peanuts can be discharged and mixed with the ice cream that has already been semifrozen. The ice cream is then piped through the ripple injection unit so that the peanut butter variegate can be injected into the stream of ice cream. The ice cream is then piped to the next stage in the process, which is either filling (tubs, pints, etc.), extrusion, or molding.

⊠ PEANUT BUTTER CHOCOLATE CHIP   Regular

Chocolate is the perfect mate for peanut butter. This rich flavor is very popular with peanut butter lovers of all ages.

Batch		Continuous
2½ gallons	16% ice cream mix	100 gallons
2 ounces	two-fold vanilla extract	2½ quarts
1 quart	peanut butter flavoring	10 gallons
½ pound	granulated peanut pieces	20 pounds
1 pound	chocolate chips	40 pounds
	chocolate chips and granulated peanut pieces for garnish	

Batch Freezing Method

Pour all ingredients except peanut pieces and chocolate chips into batch freezer. Turn on both dasher and refrigeration and begin batch. Halfway into batch, pour in nuts and chips.

During the last 3 minutes, watch the batch very closely to prevent overprocessing from occurring. When batch is complete, turn off refrigeration and extrude finished product.

Decorate tops of tubs with chocolate chips and granulated peanuts.

Batch time: 8–10 minutes.

Continuous Freezing Method

Before you start the continuous freezing of this flavor, make sure the sanitizing solution or the previous flavor of mix has been pushed through the freezer.

Pour the granulated peanuts and chocolate chips into the fruit feeder and adjust the controls to the appropriate setting. Open the outlet valve of the mix storage tank and let the proper amount of ice cream mix flow into the flavor tank. Pour the vanilla extract and peanut butter flavoring into the flavor tank and mix all the ingredients together. The mix is then pumped to the inlet of the continuous freezer. Set the speed, viscosity (stiffness), and overrun settings according to the manufacturer's recommendations. Start the continuous freezing operation. As the ice cream leaves the continuous freezer, it is then piped through the fruit feeder (ingredient feeder) so that the peanuts and chocolate chips can be discharged and mixed with the ice cream that has already been semifrozen. The ice cream is then piped to the next stage in the process, which is either filling (tubs, pints, etc.), extrusion, or molding.

▨ HAZELNUT   Superpremium

This flavor is adapted from the gelato line that is very popular in Italy. Hazelnuts are naturally rich in flavor and are great when used to create an ice cream flavor.

Quality hazelnut flavor as an ingredient is hard to find and it wasn't until gelato became popular that it became readily available in this country. The hazelnuts are used in this flavor for background. The real flavor is derived from the hazelnut paste.

Batch		Continuous
2½ gallons	16% ice cream mix	100 gallons
2 ounces	two-fold vanilla extract	2½ quarts
30 ounces	hazelnut paste, European preferred	75 pounds
1 pound	hazelnut pieces	40 pounds
	hazelnut pieces for garnish	

Batch Freezing Method

Pour all ingredients into batch freezer. Turn on dasher and let it run to mix thoroughly all ingredients. This process will take at least 3 minutes.

When hazelnut paste is completely blended with the ice cream mix, turn on refrigeration and begin batch. To prevent overprocessing, watch the batch closely during the last 3 minutes. When batch is complete, turn off refrigeration and extrude finished product.

Decorate tops of tubs with hazelnut pieces.

Batch time: 8–10 minutes.

Continuous Freezing Method

Before you start the continuous freezing of this flavor, make sure the sanitizing solution or the previous flavor of mix has been pushed through the freezer.

Pour the hazelnut pieces into the fruit feeder and adjust the controls to the appropriate setting. Open the outlet valve of the mix storage tank and let the proper amount of ice cream mix flow into the flavor tank. Pour the vanilla extract and hazelnut paste into the flavor tank and mix all the ingredients together. The mix is then pumped to the inlet of the continuous freezer. Set the speed, viscosity (stiffness), and overrun settings according to the manufacturer's recommendations. Start the continuous freezing operation. As the ice cream leaves the continuous freezer, it is then piped through the fruit feeder (ingredient feeder) so that the hazelnut pieces can be discharged and mixed with the ice cream that has already been semifrozen. The ice cream is then piped to the next stage in the process, which is either filling (tubs, pints, etc.), extrusion, or molding.

⊠ GIANDUJA   Superpremium

Of all the Italian flavors, Gianduja, the combination of chocolate and hazelnut, is the most sophisticated. It is extremely popular and a must for any upscale ice cream operation or restaurant.

Batch		Continuous
2½ gallons	16% ice cream mix	100 gallons
2 ounces	two-fold vanilla extract	2½ quarts
24 ounces	Gianduja paste, European preferred	60 pounds
½ pound	hazelnut pieces	20 pounds
½ pound	chocolate pieces	20 pounds
	hazelnut pieces and chocolate chips for garnish	

Batch Freezing Method

Pour all ingredients except hazelnuts and chocolate chips into batch freezer. Turn on dasher. The Gianduja paste must be mixed with the ice cream mix for at least 5 minutes so that paste and mix are well blended. Turn on refrigeration and begin batch.

Halfway into batch, add hazelnuts and chocolate chips. Watch out for overprocessing. When batch is complete, turn off refrigeration and extrude finished product.

Decorate tops of tubs with both pieces of hazelnuts and chocolate chips.

Batch time: 8–10 minutes.

Continuous Freezing Method

Before you start the continuous freezing of this flavor, make sure the sanitizing solution or the previous flavor of mix has been pushed through the freezer.

Pour the hazelnut pieces and chocolate chips into the fruit feeder and adjust the controls to the appropriate setting. Open the outlet valve of the mix storage tank and let the proper amount of ice cream mix flow into the flavor tank. Pour the vanilla extract and Gianduja paste into the flavor tank and mix all the ingredients together. The mix is then pumped to the inlet of the continuous freezer. Set the speed, viscosity (stiffness), and overrun settings according to the manufacturer's recommendations. Start the continuous freezing operation. As the ice cream leaves the continuous freezer, it is then piped through the fruit feeder (ingredient feeder) so that the hazelnut pieces and chocolate chips can be discharged and mixed with the ice cream that has already been semifrozen. The ice cream is then piped to the next stage in the process, which is either filling (tubs, pints, etc.), extrusion, or molding.

⊠ CRAZY ABOUT NUTS   Superpremium

Using a little imagination, I created this flavor that sells well for two reasons: one, it is very good, and two, it has a catchy name. Once the product itself is perfected, merchandising is the next step to success. Simply put, the name attracts attention. The nuts used in this recipe are my preference: You can alter this recipe to your tastes. Have fun.

Batch		Continuous
2½ gallons	16% ice cream mix	100 gallons
2 ounces	two-fold vanilla extract	2½ quarts
2 ounces	maple falvoring	2½ quarts
2 pounds	mixed peanuts, hazelnuts, pecans, walnuts, and almond pieces assorted nut pieces for garnish	80 pounds

Batch Freezing Method

Pour all ingredients except nut mixture into batch freezer. Turn on both dasher and refrigeration and begin batch. Halfway into batch add half the nut mixture, saving other half for the end. This procedure will result in a finished product with large pieces of nuts.

When batch is complete, turn off refrigeration and extrude finished product. Decorate tops of tubs with an assortment of nuts.

Batch time: 8–10 minutes.

Continuous Freezing Method

Before you start the continuous freezing of this flavor, make sure the sanitizing solution or the previous flavor of mix has been pushed through the freezer.

Mix together and pour all the nuts into the fruit feeder and adjust the controls to the appropriate setting. Open the outlet valve of the mix storage tank and let the proper amount of ice cream mix flow into the flavor tank. Pour the vanilla extract and maple flavoring into the flavor tank and mix all the ingredients together. The mix is then pumped to the inlet of the continuous freezer. Set the speed, viscosity (stiffness), and overrun settings according to the manufacturer's recommendations. Start the continuous freezing operation. As the ice cream leaves the continuous freezer, it is then piped through the fruit feeder (ingredient feeder) so that the mixed nuts can be discharged and mixed with the ice cream that has already been semifrozen. The ice cream is then piped to the next stage in the process, which is either filling (tubs, pints, etc.), extrusion, or molding.

⊠ MACADAMIA NUT   Superpremium

This is my favorite nut flavor. It has real upscale appeal.

Batch		Continuous
2½ gallons	16% ice cream mix	100 gallons
2 ounces	two-fold vanilla extract	2½ quarts
2 ounces	macadamia extract	2½ quarts
1½ pounds	macadamia nut pieces (halves)	60 pounds
	chopped macadamia nuts for garnish	

Batch Freezing Method

Using a blender, blend ¾ of a pound of nuts with 1 quart of ice cream mix so that nuts become granulated. Chop remaining ¾ pound nuts into small pieces.

Pour all ingredients except ¾ pound of macadamia nuts chopped into small pieces into batch freezer. Turn on both dasher and refrigeration and begin batch. Halfway into batch, add remaining macadamia nuts. When batch is complete, turn off refrigeration and extrude finished product.

Decorate tops of tubs with chopped macadamia nuts.

Batch time: 8–10 minutes.

Continuous Freezing Method

Before you start the continuous freezing of this flavor, make sure the sanitizing solution or the previous flavor of mix has been pushed through the freezer.

Pour the chopped (halves) macadamia nuts into the fruit feeder and adjust the controls to the appropriate setting. Open the outlet valve of the mix storage tank and let the proper amount of ice cream mix flow into the flavor tank. Pour the vanilla extract and macadamia flavor extract into the flavor tank and mix all the ingredients together. The mix is then pumped to the inlet of the continuous freezer. Set the speed, viscosity (stiffness), and overrun settings according to the manufacturer's recommendations. Start the continuous freezing operation. As the ice cream leaves the continuous freezer, it is then piped through the fruit feeder (ingredient feeder) so that the macadamia nuts can be discharged and mixed with the ice cream that has already been semifrozen. The ice cream is then piped to the next stage in the process, which is either filling (tubs, pints, etc.), extrusion, or molding.

The Chocolates

Glorious chocolate—today's obsession food. We cannot seem to get enough of it. No matter its form, we just love it!

For years, though chocolate ice cream lagged well behind vanilla in popularity. As recently as the mid-1970s, there was only one flavor in the chocolate family other than plain chocolate that sold well, chocolate chocolate-chip. But since the craze for chocolate candy of the mid-1980s, ice cream makers have learned to be inventive and produce many variations within the chocolate category.

As with coffee ice cream, there are numerous ways to make chocolate ice creams that all taste good. Once you understand how to use all the different cocoas, chocolate liquors, and chocolate chips, you will be able to make a good product too.

I prefer to use rich cocoa (22–24 percent fat) in my chocolate ice cream. For years I have used Van Leer's Dutch 22–24 percent cocoa because it is a consistently good product that is easy to work with (from Van Leer Chocolate Corporation of Jersey City, New Jersey). However, other companies such as The Johnston Company of Milwaukee, Wisconsin, and Forbes Chocolate of Cleveland, Ohio, produce an equally fine cocoa and chocolate flavor base.

A pasteurized chocolate ice cream mix is made in the same manner as the plain ice cream mix. It will contain about 3–4 percent cocoa and an additional 2 percent of sugar solids to provide the proper chocolate flavor and sweetness. When preparing your chocolate ice cream mix, incorporate the cocoa and sugar with dry ingredients.

If you do not use a pasteurized chocolate ice cream mix for your different chocolate ice creams, you will have to make a chocolate paste with cocoa at the time of your ice cream production. Preparing a paste is messy and time consuming, but it will help you make great ice cream. To make a chocolate paste, you should use a 5-quart electric mixer in which you will add approximately 6–8 cups of very hot water to 2 pounds of dry cocoa and 8 ounces of sugar. The hotter the water is, the less of it you will need to make the paste. Mix thoroughly until a paste has been formed.

Once the paste is ready, you will pour 1 gallon of ice cream mix into the batch freezer and then add the paste. Be sure to let the dasher run for at least 5 minutes before turning on the refrigeration to dissolve the paste into the mix. Then you follow the recipe by adding the rest of the ice cream mix and so on.

⊠ CHOCOLATE   Regular

In many parts of the United States, a semisweet chocolate flavor is preferred by consumers. While not as rich as the bittersweet chocolate recipe, it has plenty of chocolate flavor to suit almost anyone.

Batch		**Continuous**
1¼ pounds	cocoa (22–24% fat)	50 pounds
1¼ pounds	sugar	50 pounds
5 cups	hot water	12½ gallons
2½ gallons	16% ice cream mix	100 gallons
4 ounces	two-fold vanilla extract	5 quarts

Batch Freezing Method

Thoroughly mix cocoa and sugar with 5 cups of extremely hot water, adding more water as needed, until a smooth creamy paste has been created.

Pour 1 gallon of mix into batch freezer and turn on dasher. Add cocoa paste and continue to let dasher run until smoothly blended. Pour in remaining ingredients, turn on refrigeration, and begin batch. When batch is complete, turn off refrigeration and extrude finished product.

Batch time: 9–11 minutes. Chocolate needs an extra minute to freeze properly because of the weight of the cocoa and its fat content.

Continuous Freezing Method

Before you start the continuous freezing of this flavor, make sure the sanitizing solution or the previous flavor of mix has been pushed through the freezer. Open the outlet valve of the mix storage tank and let the proper amount of chocolate ice cream mix flow into the flavor tank.*

Next, pour the vanilla extract into the flavor tank. The mix is then pumped to the inlet of the continuous freezer. Set the speed, viscosity (stiffness), and overrun settings according to the manufacturer's recommendations. Start the continuous freezing process. As the ice cream leaves the continuous freezer, it is then piped to the next stage in the process, which is either filling (tubs, pints, etc.), extrusion, or molding.

---

*Note: If you do not use a pasteurized chocolate ice cream mix, thoroughly mix the cocoa and sugar with hot water in a large mixer, adding more water is needed, until a smooth creamy paste has been created.

▨ BITTERSWEET CHOCOLATE   Regular

Besides vanilla, the only other flavor that both your critics and customers will taste for quality is your basic chocolate ice cream. Because I prefer a more bitter taste in my chocolate ice cream, I use this recipe as the standard for all my chocolate recipes. It is very dark, heavy in weight, and not too sweet.

Batch		Continuous
2 pounds	cocoa (22–24% fat)	80 pounds
½ pound	sugar	20 pounds
6–8 cups	hot water	15 gallons
2½ gallons	16% ice cream mix	100 gallons
4 ounces	two-fold vanilla extract	5 quarts

Batch Freezing Method

Thoroughly mix cocoa and sugar with 6–8 cups of extremely hot water, adding more water as needed, until a smooth creamy paste has been created.

Pour 1 gallon of mix into batch freezer and turn on dasher. Add cocoa paste and continue to let dasher run until smoothly blended. Pour in remaining ingredients, turn on refrigeration, and begin batch. When batch is complete, turn off refrigeration and extrude finished product.

Batch time: 9–11 minutes. Chocolate needs an extra minute to freeze properly because of the weight of the cocoa and its fat content.

Continuous Freezing Method

Before you start the continuous freezing of this flavor, make sure the sanitizing solution or the previous flavor of mix has been pushed through the freezer. Open the outlet valve of the mix storage tank and let the proper amount of chocolate ice cream mix flow into the flavor tank.*

Next, pour the vanilla extract into the flavor tank. The mix is then pumped to the inlet of the continuous freezer. Set the speed, viscosity (stiffness), and overrun settings according to the manufacturer's recommendations. Start the continuous freezing process. As the ice cream leaves the continuous freezer, it is then piped to the next stage in the process, which is either filling (tubs, pints, etc.), extrusion, or molding.

---

*Note: If you do not use a pasteurized chocolate ice cream mix, thoroughly mix the cocoa and sugar with hot water in a large mixer, adding more water as needed, until a smooth creamy paste has been created.

▧ CHOCOLATE CHOCOLATE CHIP   **Regular**

Of all the chocolate ice cream flavors increasing in popularity since the mid-1980s, this flavor's popularity has increased the most. Large chocolate flakes are used to stimulate the customer's perception of quality.

Batch		Continuous
2 pounds	cocoa (22–24% fat)	80 pounds
½ pound	sugar	20 pounds
6–8 cups	hot water	15 gallons
2½ gallons	16% ice cream mix	100 gallons
4 ounces	two-fold vanilla extract	5 quarts
2 pounds	large chocolate chips	80 pounds
	chocolate chips for garnish	

Batch Freezing Method

Thoroughly mix cocoa and sugar with 6–8 cups of extremely hot water, adding more water as needed, until a smooth creamy paste has been created.

Pour ice cream mix, vanilla extract, cocoa paste, and 1 pound chocolate chips into batch freezer. Turn dasher on and let it run for 5 minutes. (The 1 pound of chips are entered at the beginning to create an even blend of chips with the mix.) Turn on refrigeration and begin batch.

At end of batch, add remaining chips. When batch is complete, turn off refrigeration and extrude finished product.

Decorate tops of tubs with ice cream chips.

Batch time: 9–11 minutes.

Continuous Freezing Method

Before you start the continuous freezing of this flavor, make sure the sanitizing solution or the previous flavor of mix has been pushed through the freezer. Pour the chocolate chips into the fruit feeder and adjust the controls to the appropriate setting. Open the outlet valve of the mix storage tank and let the proper amount of chocolate ice cream mix flow into the flavor tank.*

Next, pour the vanilla extract into the flavor tank. The mix is then pumped to the inlet of the continuous freezer. Set the speed, viscosity (stiffness), and overrun settings according to the manufacturer's recommendations. Start the continuous freezing process. As the ice cream leaves the continuous freezer, it is then piped through the fruit feeder (ingredient feeder) so that the chocolate chips can be discharged and mixed with the ice cream that has already become semifrozen. The ice cream is then piped to the next stage in the process, which is either filling (tubs, pints, etc.), extrusion, or molding.

---

*Note: If you do not use a pasteurized chocolate ice cream mix, thoroughly mix the cocoa and sugar with hot water in a large mixer, adding more water as needed, until a smooth creamy paste has been created.

⊠ CHOCOLATE MOUSSE   Superpremium

This ice cream has rich chocolate flavor that is very smooth in texture and taste. This richness results from using pasteurized egg yolks in a continuous freezing operation or a relatively large quantity of egg base in a batch freezing operation.

Batch

		Continuous
1¾ pounds	cocoa (22–24% fat)	70 pounds
⅓ pound	sugar	13⅓ pounds
6–8 cups	hot water	15 gallons
2½ gallons	16% ice cream mix	100 gallons
4 ounces	two-fold vanilla extract	5 quarts
24 ounces	egg base	
	pasteurized egg yolks	30 pounds

Batch Freezing Method

Thoroughly mix cocoa and sugar with 6–8 cups of extremely hot water, adding more water as needed, until a smooth creamy paste has been created.

Pour 1 gallon of ice cream mix into batch freezer and turn on dasher. Add cocoa paste and continue to let dasher run until the mix and paste are smoothly blended. Pour in remaining ingredients, turn on refrigeration, and begin batch. When batch is complete, turn off refrigeration and extrude finished product.

Batch time: 9–11 minutes.

Continuous Freezing Method

Before you start the continuous freezing of this flavor, make sure the sanitizing solution or the previous flavor of mix has been pushed through the freezer. Open the outlet valve of the mix storage tank and let the proper amount of chocolate ice cream mix flow into the flavor tank.*

Next, pour the vanilla extract and pasteurized egg yolks into the flavor tank. The mix is then pumped to the inlet of the continuous freezer. Set the speed, viscosity (stiffness), and overrun settings according to the manufacturer's recommendations. Start the continuous freezing process. As the ice cream leaves the continuous freezer, it is then piped to the next stage in the process, which is either filling (tubs, pints, etc.), extrusion, or molding.

---

*Note: If you do not use a pasteurized chocolate ice cream mix, thoroughly mix the cocoa and sugar with hot water in a large mixer, adding more water as needed, until a smooth creamy paste has been created.

⬚ CHOCOLATE FUDGE   **Superpremium**

This recipe produces an incredibly rich chocolate flavor. The secret to the success of this flavor is making sure your customers not only taste the fudge, but are also able to see it. They'll love it.

In this and many other chocolate flavors, the amount of vanilla extract has been reduced because the other ingredients such as fudge, cheesecake, and peanut butter tend to overpower the flavor and mask the taste of vanilla.

Batch		Continuous
2 pounds	cocoa (22–24% fat)	80 pounds
½ pound	sugar	20 pounds
6–8 cups	hot water	15 gallons
2½ gallons	16% ice cream mix	100 gallons
2 ounces	two-fold vanilla extract	2½ quarts
2 quarts	hot fudge	
	fudge variegate	20 gallons
	fudge for garnish	

Batch Freezing Method

Thoroughly mix cocoa and sugar with 6–8 cups of extremely hot water, adding more water as needed, until a smooth creamy paste has been created.

Pour 1 gallon of mix into batch freezer and turn on dasher. Add cocoa paste and continue to let dasher run until mix and paste are smoothly blended. Pour remaining ingredients except fudge into batch freezer, turn on refrigeration, and begin batch. At very end of batch, pour in 16 ounces of fudge and at the same time, line tubs with the remainder. When batch is complete, turn off refrigeration and extrude finished product using a spatula to scrape fudge from the sides of tubs.

Decorate tops of tubs with fudge.

Batch time: 9–11 minutes.

Continuous Freezing Method

Before you start the continuous freezing of this flavor, make sure the sanitizing solution or the previous flavor of mix has been pushed through the freezer. Pour the chilled (40 degrees Fahrenheit) fudge variegate into the ripple pump supply tank and adjust speed to inject at the rate as prescribed in the formula, or approximately 10–14 percent of the weight of the ice cream mix. Open the outlet valve of the mix storage tank and let the proper amount of chocolate ice cream mix flow into the flavor tank.*

Next, pour the vanilla extract into the flavor tank. The mix is then pumped to the inlet of the continuous freezer. Set the speed, viscosity (stiffness), and overrun settings according to the manufacturer's recommendations. Start the continuous freezing process. As the ice cream leaves the continuous freezer, it is then piped through the ripple injection unit so that the fudge variegating sauce can be injected into the stream of ice cream that has already become semifrozen. The ice cream is then piped to the next stage in the process, which is either filling (tubs, pints, etc.), extrusion, or molding.

---

*Note: If you do not use a pasteurized chocolate ice cream mix, thoroughly mix the cocoa and sugar with hot water in a large mixer, adding more water as needed, until a smooth creamy paste has been created.

⊠ CHOCOLATE CHOCOLATE ALMOND   Regular

This flavor results from an irresistible combination of chocolate-covered almonds with bittersweet chocolate ice cream.

In this and in other chocolate flavors, the amount of cocoa has been reduced to allow the other ingredients to stand out. In a batch freezing operation, the sliced almonds are used at the beginning to create a nutty taste with the mix while the chocolate-covered almonds are entered at the end in order to keep them whole and big.

Batch		Continuous
1½ pounds	cocoa (22–24% fat)	60 pounds
⅓ pound	sugar	13 pounds
5–7 cups	hot water	12½ gallons
2½ gallons	16% ice cream mix	100 gallons
2 ounces	two-fold vanilla extract	2½ quarts
1½ pounds	large chocolate covered almonds	60 pounds
½ pound	sliced or diced roasted almonds	20 pounds
	chocolate-covered almonds for garnish	

Batch Freezing Method

Thoroughly mix cocoa and sugar with 5–7 cups of extremely hot water, adding more as needed, until a smooth creamy paste has been created.

Pour 1 gallon of mix into batch freezer and turn on dasher. Add cocoa paste and continue to let dasher run until mix and paste are smoothly blended. Pour remaining ingredients except chocolate-covered almonds into batch freezer, turn on refrigeration and begin batch. At end of batch, add chocolate-covered almonds. When batch is complete, turn off refrigeration and extrude finished product.

Decorate tops of tubs with both sliced or diced almonds and chocolate-covered almonds.

Batch time: 9–11 minutes.

Continuous Freezing Method

Before you start the continuous freezing of this flavor, make sure the sanitizing solution or the previous flavor of mix has been pushed through the freezer. Pour and mix thoroughly both the chocolate-covered almonds and sliced or diced almonds into the fruit feeder and adjust the controls to the appropriate setting. Open the outlet valve of the mix storage tank and let the proper amount of chocolate ice cream mix flow into the flavor tank.*

Next, pour the vanilla extract into the flavor tank. The mix is then pumped to the inlet of the continuous freezer. Set the speed, viscosity (stiffness), and overrun settings according to the manufacturer's recommendations. Start the continuous freezing process. As the ice cream leaves the continuous freezer, it is then piped through the fruit feeder (ingredient feeder) so that the chocolate-covered almonds and sliced or diced almonds can be discharged and mixed with the ice cream that has already become semifrozen. The ice cream is then piped to the next stage in the process, which is either filling (tubs, pints, etc.), extrusion, or molding.

---

*Note: If you do not use a pasteurized chocolate ice cream mix, thoroughly mix the cocoa and sugar with hot water in a large mixer, adding more water as needed, until a smooth creamy paste has been created.

⊠ ROCKY ROAD   Regular

Being a favorite with kids, this flavor is a must, either packaged and sold in a supermarket or at an ice cream shop located in a residential neighborhood.

Batch		Continuous
1½ pounds	cocoa (22–24% fat)	60 pounds
⅓ pound	sugar	13 pounds
5–7 cups	hot water	12½ gallons
2½ gallons	16% ice cream mix	100 gallons
2 ounces	two-fold vanilla extract	2½ quarts
1 pound	mini marshmallows	40 pounds
1 pound	large walnut pieces	40 pounds
	mini marshmallows and	
	walnut pieces for garnish	

Batch Freezing Method

Thoroughly mix cocoa and sugar with 5–7 cups of extremely hot water, adding more water as needed, until a smooth creamy paste has been created.

Pour 1 gallon of mix into batch freezer and turn on dasher. Add cocoa paste and continue to let dasher run until mix and paste are smoothly blended. Pour all ingredients except mini marshmallows and walnuts into batch freezer. Turn on refrigeration and begin batch.

As mix begins to freeze, pour in 4 ounces of mini marshmallows. At very end of batch, add remaining marshmallows and walnuts. When batch is complete, turn off refrigeration and extrude finished product. If marshmallows and walnuts do not look evenly distributed in the batch, add more as necessary as ice cream is being packed into the tubs.

Decorate tops of tubs with both marshmallows and walnuts.

Batch time: 9–11 minutes.

Continuous Freezing Method
Before you start the continuous freezing of this flavor, make sure the sanitizing solution or the previous flavor of mix has been pushed through the freezer. Pour, and mix thoroughly both the mini marshmallows and walnut pieces into the fruit feeder and adjust the controls to the appropriate setting. Open the outlet valve of the mix storage tank and let the proper amount of chocolate ice cream mix flow into the flavor tank.*

Next, pour the vanilla extract into the flavor tank. The mix is then pumped to the inlet of the continuous freezer. Set the speed, viscosity (stiffness), and overrun settings according to the manufacturer's recommendations. Start the continuous freezing process. As the ice cream leaves the continuous freezer, it is then piped through the fruit feeder (ingredient feeder) so that the mini marshmallows and walnut pieces can be discharged and mixed with the ice cream that has already become semifrozen. The ice cream is then piped to the next stage in the process, which is either filling (tubs, pints, etc.), extrusion, or molding.

---

*Note: If you do not use a pasteurized chocolate ice cream mix, thoroughly mix the cocoa and sugar with hot water in a large mixer, adding more water as needed, until a smooth creamy paste has been created.

⊠ CHOCOLATE COOKIES AND CREAM　　　　　　　　　**Regular**

If you can make a cookies-and-cream flavor vanilla ice cream, why can't you make it with chocolate? The answer is, why not?

Batch		**Continuous**
1¾ pounds	cocoa (22–24% fat)	70 pounds
⅓–½ pound	sugar	16 pounds
5–7 cups	hot water	12½ gallons
2½ gallons	16% ice cream mix	100 gallons
2 ounces	two-fold vanilla extract	2½ quarts
3 pounds	Oreo or Hydrox cookies pieces (broken halves, not whole cookies) cookie pieces for garnish	120 pounds

Batch Freezing Method
Thoroughly mix cocoa and sugar with 5–7 cups extremely hot water, adding more water as needed, until a smooth creamy paste has been created.

Pour 1 gallon of mix into batch freezer and turn on dasher. Add paste and let dasher run until mix and paste are smoothly blended. Pour in remaining ice cream mix, vanilla extract, and half the cookies. Turn on refrigeration and begin batch.

At end of batch, turn off refrigeration, begin extruding finished product, and swirl remaining cookie pieces into tubs as they are being filled.

Decorate tops of tubs with cookie pieces.

Batch time: 9–11 minutes.

Continuous Freezing Method
Before you start the continuous freezing of this flavor, make sure the sanitizing solution or the previous flavor of mix has been pushed through the freezer. Pour the cookie pieces into the fruit feeder and adjust the controls to the appropriate setting. Open the outlet valve of the mix storage tank and let the proper amount of chocolate ice cream mix flow into the flavor tank.*

Next, pour the vanilla extract into the flavor tank. The mix is then pumped to the inlet of the continuous freezer. Set the speed, viscosity (stiffness), and overrun settings according to the manufacturer's recommendations. Start the continuous freezing process. As the ice cream leaves the continuous freezer, it is then piped through the fruit feeder (ingredient feeder) so that the cookie pieces can be discharged and mixed with the ice cream that has already become semifrozen. The ice cream is then piped to the next stage in the process, which is either filling (tubs, pints, etc.), extrusion, or molding.

---

*Note: If you do not use a pasteurized chocolate ice cream mix, thoroughly mix the cocoa and sugar with hot water in a large mixer, adding more water as needed, until a smooth creamy paste has been created.

⊠ CHOCOLATE TRUFFLE   Superpremium

The most seductive of all chocolates, this flavor can be a real signature item for any restaurant or shop.

Batch		Continuous
2 pounds	cocoa (22–24% fat)	80 pounds
½ pound	sugar	20 pounds
6–8 cups	hot water	15 gallons
2½ gallons	16% ice cream mix	100 gallons
2 ounces	two-fold vanilla extract	2½ quarts
3 pounds	chocolate truffles	120 pounds
2 quarts	milk chocolate fudge	
	milk chocolate fudge variegate	20 gallons
	truffles and fudge for garnish	

Batch Freezing Method

Thoroughly mix cocoa and sugar with 6–8 cups extremely hot water, adding more water as needed, until a smooth creamy paste has been created.

Pour 1 gallon of ice cream mix into batch freezer and turn on dasher. Add paste and let dasher run for at least 5 minutes until mix and paste are blended. Pour in remaining ingredients except fudge and truffles. Turn on refrigeration and begin batch.

At end of batch, pour in half of the truffles, turn off refrigeration, and extrude finished product. As product is being extruded, swirl fudge and remaining truffles around in tubs.

Decorate tops of tubs with fudge and truffles.

Batch time: 9–11 minutes.

Continuous Freezing Method

Before you start the continuous freezing of this flavor, make sure the sanitizing solution or the previous flavor of mix has been pushed through the freezer. Pour the chilled (40 degrees Fahrenheit) fudge variegate into the ripple pump supply tank and adjust speed to inject at the rate as prescribed in the formula, or approximately 10–14 percent of the weight of the ice cream mix. Next, pour the chocolate truffles (40 degrees Fahrenheit) into the fruit feeder and adjust the controls to the appropriate setting. Open the outlet valve of the mix storage tank and let the proper amount of chocolate ice cream mix flow into the flavor tank.*

Next, pour the vanilla extract into the flavor tank. The mix is then pumped to the inlet of the continuous freezer. Set the speed, viscosity (stiffness), and overrun settings according to the manufacturer's recommendations. Start the continuous freezing process. As the ice cream leaves the continuous freezer, it is then piped through the fruit feeder (ingredient feeder) so that the truffles can be discharged and mixed with the ice cream. The ice cream is then piped through the ripple injection unit so that the fudge variegating sauce can be injected into the stream of ice cream that has already become semifrozen. The ice cream is then piped to the next stage in the process, which is either filling (tubs, pints, etc.), extrusion, or molding.

---

*Note: If you do not use a pasteurized chocolate ice cream mix, thoroughly mix the cocoa and sugar with hot water in a large mixer, adding more water as needed, until a smooth creamy paste has been created.

⊠ CHOCOLATE AMARETTO   Superpremium

This ice cream is a very popular dinner dessert that is extremely rich in flavor, perfect for restaurant use.

Batch		Continuous
1¾ pounds	cocoa (22–24% fat)	70 pounds
⅓–½ pound	sugar	16 pounds
5–7 cups	hot water	12½ gallons
2½ gallons	16% ice cream mix	100 gallons
2 ounces	two-fold vanilla extract	2½ quarts
5 ounces	amaretto extract*	6¼ quarts
1 pound	chocolate chips	40 pounds
1 pound	toasted sliced almonds	40 pounds
	chocolate chips and sliced almonds for garnish	

*Note: Amount to use varies according to manufacturer's recommendations.

Batch Freezing Method

Thoroughly mix cocoa and sugar with 5–7 cups extremely hot water, adding more water as needed, until a smooth creamy paste has been created.

Pour 1 gallon of ice cream mix into batch freezer and turn on dasher. Add cocoa paste and let dasher run for 5 minutes until mix and paste are smoothly blended. Pour in remaining ingredients except chocolate chips and sliced almonds. Turn on refrigeration and begin batch.

Halfway into batch, as mix begins to freeze, add chocolate chips and sliced almonds. When batch is complete, turn off refrigeration and extrude finished product.

Decorate tops of tubs with some chocolate chips and sliced almonds.

Batch time: 9–11 minutes.

Continuous Freezing Method

Before you start the continuous freezing of this flavor, make sure the sanitizing solution or the previous flavor of mix has been pushed through the freezer. Pour the chocolate chips (40 degrees Fahrenheit) and sliced almonds into the fruit feeder and adjust the controls to the appropriate setting. Open the outlet valve of the mix storage tank and let the proper amount of chocolate ice cream mix flow into the flavor tank.*

Next, pour both the vanilla and amaretto extract into the flavor tank. The mix is then pumped to the inlet of the continuous freezer. Set the speed, viscosity (stiffness), and overrun settings according to the manufacturer's recommendations. Start the continuous freezing process. As the ice cream leaves the continuous freezer, it is then piped through the fruit feeder (ingredient feeder) so that the chocolate chips and sliced almonds can be discharged and mixed with the ice cream that has already become semifrozen. The ice cream is then piped to the next stage in the process, which is either filling (tubs, pints, etc.), extrusion, or molding.

---

*Note: If you do not use a pasteurized chocolate ice cream mix, thoroughly mix the cocoa and sugar with hot water in a large mixer, adding more water as needed, until a smooth creamy paste has been created.

⊠ CHOCOLATE BROWNIE   Superpremium

I have always been very proud of this creation. It is a well thought out flavor that not only tastes great, but looks great. It is super rich in chocolate.

Batch		Continuous
2 pounds	cocoa (22–24% fat)	80 pounds
½ pound	sugar	20 pounds
6–8 cups	hot water	15 gallons
2½ gallons	16% ice cream mix	100 gallons
2 ounces	two-fold vanilla extract	2½ quarts
2 pounds	chocolate brownie pieces	80 pounds
1 quart	chocolate fudge	
	chocolate fudge variegate	10 gallons
½ pound	chocolate chips	20 pounds
½ pound	walnut pieces	20 pounds
	chocolate chips and pieces of brownie, fudge, and walnuts for garnish	

Batch Freezing Method

Thoroughly mix cocoa and sugar with 6–8 cups extremely hot water, adding water as needed, until a smooth creamy paste has been created.

Pour 1 gallon of ice cream mix into batch freezer and turn on dasher. Add cocoa paste and let dasher run for 5 minutes until mix and paste are smoothly blended. Pour in remaining ice cream mix, vanilla extract, and half of the brownies (rich chocolate cake, cut into pieces, mixed with fudge can be substituted for brownies pieces). Turn on refrigeration and begin batch.

Halfway into batch, add walnuts and chocolate chips. At end of batch, add remaining brownies. When batch is complete, turn off refrigeration, extrude finished product, and swirl in chocolate fudge as the tubs are being filled.

Decorate tops of tubs with chocolate chips, pieces of brownies, fudge, and walnuts.

Batch time: 9–11 minutes.

Continuous Freezing Method

Before you start the continuous freezing of this flavor, make sure the sanitizing solution or the previous flavor of mix has been pushed through the freezer. Pour the chilled (40 degrees Fahrenheit) fudge variegate into the ripple pump supply tank and adjust speed to inject at the rate as prescribed in the formula, or approximately 10–14 percent of the weight of the ice cream mix. Next, thoroughly mix together, and then pour the chocolate brownies (40 degrees Fahrenheit), chocolate chips (40 degrees Fahrenheit), and walnuts into the fruit feeder and adjust the controls to the appropriate setting. Open the outlet valve of the mix storage tank and let the proper amount of chocolate ice cream mix flow into the flavor tank.*

Next, pour the vanilla extract into the flavor tank. The mix is then pumped to the inlet of the continuous freezer. Set the speed, viscosity (stiffness), and overrun settings according to the manufacturer's recommendations. Start the continuous freezing process. As the ice cream leaves the continuous freezer, it is then piped through the fruit feeder (ingredient feeder) so that the brownies, chocolate chips, and walnuts can be discharged and mixed with the ice cream. The ice cream is then piped through the ripple injection unit so that the fudge variegating sauce can be injected into the stream of ice cream that has already become semifrozen. The ice cream is then piped to the next stage in the process which will be either filling (tubs, pints, etc.), extrusion, or molding.

---

*Note: If you do not use a pasteurized chocolate ice cream mix, thoroughly mix the cocoa and sugar with hot water in a large mixer, adding more water as needed, until a smooth creamy paste has been created.

⊠ CHOCOLATE MARSHMALLOW CLUSTER   **Regular**

Gooey and great!

Batch		Continuous
1¾ pounds	cocoa (22–24% fat)	70 pounds
⅓–½ pound	sugar	11 pounds
5–7 cups	hot water	12½ gallons
2½ gallons	16% ice cream mix	100 gallons
2 ounces	two-fold vanilla extract	2½ quarts
1½ pounds	chocolate-covered peanuts	60 pounds
2 quarts	marshmallow parfait	20 gallons
	marshmallow parfait and chocolate-covered peanuts for garnish	

Batch Freezing Method

Thoroughly mix cocoa and sugar with 5–7 cups extremely hot water, adding more water as needed, until a smooth creamy paste has been created.

Pour 1 gallon of ice cream mix into batch freezer and turn on dasher. Add cocoa paste and let dasher run for 5 minutes until mix and paste are smoothly blended. Add remaining ingredients except marshmallow parfait and chocolate-covered peanuts to mixture, turn on refrigeration, and begin batch.

At end of batch, add chocolate-covered peanuts, turn off refrigeration, and extrude finished product. As product is being extruded, swirl marshmallow parfait into ice cream as it is entering tubs.

Decorate tops of tubs with marshmallow parfait and chocolate-covered peanuts.

Batch time: 9–11 minutes.

Continuous Freezing Method

Before you start the continuous freezing of this flavor, make sure the sanitizing solution or the previous flavor of mix has been pushed through the freezer. Pour the chilled (40 degrees Fahrenheit) marshmallow parfait into the ripple pump supply tank and adjust speed to inject at the rate as prescribed in the formula, or approximately 10–14 percent of the weight of the ice cream mix. Next, pour the chocolate-covered peanuts into the fruit feeder and adjust the controls to the appropriate setting. Open the outlet valve of the mix storage tank and let the proper amount of chocolate ice cream mix flow into the flavor tank.*

Next, pour the vanilla extract into the flavor tank. The mix is then pumped to the inlet of the continuous freezer. Set the speed, viscosity (stiffness), and overrun settings according to the manufacturer's recommendations. Start the continuous freezing process. As the ice cream leaves the continuous freezer, it is then piped through the fruit feeder (ingredient feeder) so that the chocolate-covered peanuts can be discharged and mixed with the ice cream. The ice cream is then piped through the ripple injection unit so that the marshmallow parfait can be injected into the stream of ice cream that has already become semifrozen. The ice cream is then piped to the next stage in the process, which is either filling (tubs, pints, etc.), extrusion, or molding.

---

*Note: If you do not use a pasteurized chocolate ice cream mix, thoroughly mix the cocoa and sugar with hot water in a large mixer, adding more water as needed, until a smooth creamy paste has been created.

⊠ HEAVENLY HASH   **Regular**

Youngsters love this flavor for its name, its appearance, and its flavor.

Batch		Continuous
1¾ pounds	cocoa (22–24% fat)	70 pounds
⅓–½ pound	sugar	11 pounds
5–7 cups	hot water	12½ gallons
2½ gallons	16% ice cream mix	100 gallons
2 ounces	two-fold vanilla extract	2½ quarts
1 pound	chocolate-covered almonds	40 pounds
2 quarts	marshmallow parfait	20 gallons
	marshmallow parfait and chocolate-covered almonds for garnish	

Batch Freezing Method

Thoroughly mix cocoa and sugar with 5–7 cups extremely hot water, adding more water as needed, until a smooth creamy paste has been created.

Pour 1 gallon of ice cream mix into batch freezer and turn on dasher. Add cocoa paste to mix and let dasher run for 5 minutes until mix and paste are smoothly blended. Add remaining ingredients except marshmallow parfait and chocolate-covered almonds, turn on refrigeration, and begin batch.

At end of batch, add chocolate-covered almonds. When batch is complete, turn off refrigeration and swirl marshmallow parfait into finished product as it fills tubs.

Decorate tops of tubs with marshmallow parfait and chocolate-covered almonds.

Batch time: 9–11 minutes.

Continuous Freezing Method

Before you start the continuous freezing of this flavor, make sure the sanitizing solution or the previous flavor of mix has been pushed through the freezer. Pour the chilled (40 degrees Fahrenheit) marshmallow parfait into the ripple pump supply tank and adjust speed to inject at the rate as prescribed in the formula, or approximately 10–14 percent of the weight of the ice cream mix. Next, pour the chocolate-covered almonds in the fruit feeder and adjust the controls to the appropriate setting. Open the outlet valve of the mix storage tank and let the proper amount of chocolate ice cream mix flow into the flavor tank.*

Next, pour the vanilla extract into the flavor tank. The mix is then pumped to the inlet of the continuous freezer. Set the speed, viscosity (stiffness), and overrun settings according to the manufacturer's recommendations. Start the continuous freezing process. As the ice cream leaves the continuous freezer, it is then piped through the fruit feeder (ingredient feeder) so that the chocolate-covered almonds can be discharged and mixed with the ice cream. The ice cream is then piped through the ripple injection unit so that the marshmallow parfait can be injected into the stream of ice cream that has already become semifrozen. The ice cream is then piped to the next stage in the process, which is either filling (tubs, pints, etc.), extrusion, or molding.

*Note: If you do not use a pasteurized chocolate ice cream mix, thoroughly mix the cocoa and sugar with hot water in a large mixer, adding more water as needed, until a smooth creamy paste has been created.

⊠ CHOCOLATE MARSHMALLOW   Regular

This old-fashioned ice cream flavor is still popular throughout the country.

Batch		Continuous
2 pounds	cocoa (22–24% fat)	80 pounds
½ pound	sugar	20 pounds
6–8 cups	hot water	15 gallons
2½ gallons	16% ice cream mix	100 gallons
2 ounces	two-fold vanilla extract	2½ quarts
½ pound	mini marshmallows	20 pounds
3 quarts	marshmallow parfait	30 gallons
	marshmallow parfait and mini marshmallows for garnish	

Batch Freezing Method
Thoroughly mix cocoa and sugar with 6–8 cups extremely hot water, adding more water as needed, until a smooth creamy paste has been created.

Pour 1 gallon of ice cream mix into batch freezer and turn on dasher. Add cocoa paste and let dasher run for 5 minutes until mix and paste are smoothly blended. Add remaining ingredients except marshmallow parfait and mini marshmallows. Turn on refrigeration and begin batch.

At end of batch, add mini marshmallows. When batch is complete, turn off refrigeration and extrude finished product. Using a spatula, swirl marshmallow parfait into ice cream as it is being poured into tubs.

Decorate tops of tubs with marshmallow parfait and mini marshmallows.

Batch time: 9–11 minutes.

Continuous Freezing Method

Before you start the continuous freezing of this flavor, make sure the sanitizing solution or the previous flavor of mix has been pushed through the freezer. Pour the chilled (40 degrees Fahrenheit) marshmallow parfait into the ripple pump supply tank and adjust speed to inject at the rate as prescribed in the formula, or approximately 10–14 percent of the weight of the ice cream mix. Next, pour the mini marshmallows into the fruit feeder and adjust the controls to the appropriate setting. Open the outlet valve of the mix storage tank and let the proper amount of chocolate ice cream mix flow into the flavor tank.*

Pour the vanilla extract into the flavor tank. The mix is then pumped to the inlet of the continuous freezer. Set the speed, viscosity (stiffness), and overrun settings according to the manufacturer's recommendations. Start the continuous freezing process. As the ice cream leaves the continuous freezer, it is then piped through the fruit feeder (ingredient feeder) so that the mini marshmallows can be discharged and mixed with the ice cream. The ice cream is then piped through the ripple injection unit so that the marshmallow parfait can be injected into the stream of ice cream that has already become semifrozen. The ice cream is then piped to the next stage in the process, which is either filling (tubs, pints, etc.), extrusion, or molding.

---

*Note: If you do not use a pasteurized chocolate ice cream mix, thoroughly mix the cocoa and sugar with hot water in a large mixer, adding more water as needed, until a smooth creamy paste has been created.

⊠ CHOCOLATE TAPIOCA   Superpremium

This is an unusual flavor. Try it, you'll love it.

Batch		Continuous
2 pounds	cocoa (22–24% fat)	80 pounds
½ pound	sugar	20 pounds
6–8 cups	hot water	15 gallons
2½ gallons	16% ice cream mix	100 gallons
2 ounces	two-fold vanilla extract	2½ quarts
1 pound	tapioca	40 pounds
	prepared tapioca for garnish	

Batch Freezing Method

Prepare tapioca following manufacturer's instructions. Refrigerate cooked tapioca until it is completely cool.

Thoroughly mix cocoa and sugar with 6–8 cups extremely hot water, adding more water as needed, until a smooth creamy paste has been created.

Pour 1 gallon of ice cream mix into batch freezer and turn on dasher. Add cocoa paste and let dasher run for 5 minutes until mix and paste are smoothly blended. Add remaining ingredients except tapioca. Turn on refrigeration and begin batch.

Halfway into batch, as the mix begins to freeze, add the cooled tapioca. When batch is completed, turn off refrigeration and extrude finished product.

Decorate tops of tubs with tapioca.

Batch time: 9–11 minutes.

Continuous Freezing Method

Before you start the continuous freezing of this flavor, make sure the sanitizing solution or the previous flavor of mix has been pushed through the freezer. Open the outlet valve of the mix storage tank and let the proper amount of chocolate ice cream mix flow into the flavor tank.*

Next, pour the vanilla extract and cooked tapioca into the flavor tank. The mix is then pumped to the inlet of the continuous freezer. Set the speed, viscosity (stiffness), and overrun settings according to the manufacturers recommendations. Start the continuous freezing process. The ice cream is then piped to the next stage in the process, which is either filling (tubs, pints, etc.), extrusion, or molding.

---

*Note: If you do not use a pasteurized chocolate ice cream mix, thoroughly mix the cocoa and sugar with hot water in a large mixer, adding more water as needed, until a smooth creamy paste has been created.

⊠ CHOCOLATE BANANA   Regular

A perfect match—bananas and chocolate. In this recipe, chocolate is the dominant ingredient with a fresh banana taste throughout the product. This flavor sells very well in all markets. It uses less cocoa and bananas than would ordinarily be used if making either chocolate or banana ice cream. Less is sometimes better and the combination of the two ingredients strikes a perfect balance.

Batch		Continuous
1½ pounds	cocoa (22–24% fat)	60 pounds
⅓ pound	sugar	13 pounds
5–7 cups	hot water	11½ gallons
2½ gallons	16% ice cream mix	100 gallons
2 ounces	two-fold vanilla extract	2½ quarts
5 pounds	ripe bananas (4 pounds peeled)*	
	pasteurized banana puree	160 pounds
	sliced banana for garnish	

---

*Note: 5 pounds of whole bananas will yield approximately 4 pounds of peeled bananas because banana skin is approximately 20 percent of the weight of a banana.

Batch Freezing Method

Thoroughly mix cocoa and sugar with 5–7 cups extremely hot water, adding more water as needed, until a smooth creamy paste has been created.

Pour 1 gallon of ice cream mix into batch freezer and turn on dasher. Add cocoa paste and let dasher run until mix and paste are smoothly blended. At this point, mix bananas with cocoa mixture and blend for about 3 minutes. When the bananas and cocoa have been completely blended, pour in remaining ingredients, turn on refrigeration, and begin batch. When batch is complete, turn off refrigeration and extrude finished product.

Decorate tops of tubs with slices of bananas.

Batch time: 9–11 minutes.

Continuous Freezing Method

Before you start the continuous freezing of this flavor, make sure the sanitizing solution or the previous flavor of mix has been pushed through the freezer. Open the outlet valve of the mix storage tank and let the proper amount of chocolate ice cream mix flow into the flavor tank.*

Next, pour the vanilla extract and pasteurized banana puree into the flavor tank. The mix is then pumped to the inlet of the continuous freezer. Set the speed, viscosity (stiffness), and overrun settings according to the manufacturer's recommendations. Start the continuous freezing process. The ice cream is then piped to the next stage in the process, which is either filling (tubs, pints, etc.), extrusion, or molding.

---

*Note: If you do not use a pasteurized chocolate ice cream mix, thoroughly mix the cocoa and sugar with hot water in a large mixer, adding more water as needed, until a smooth creamy paste has been created.

⊠ CHOCOLATE CHERRY   Superpremium

There are times when you are in an ice cream store trying to decide what flavor to purchase, and the name of a flavor strikes your fancy. When I think of the name Chocolate Cherry I immediately want the ice cream because I love chocolate-covered cherries. I don't even stop to think, how does it taste? Names sell flavors as much as what the flavor tastes or looks like.

Batch		Continuous
1½ pounds	cocoa (22–24% fat)	60 pounds
⅓ pound	sugar	13 pounds
5–7 cups	hot water	11½ gallons
2½ gallons	16% ice cream mix	100 gallons
2 ounces	two-fold vanilla extract	2½ quarts
1 pound	chocolate chips	40 pounds
1½ quarts	cherry halves	15 gallons
	cherry halves and chocolate chips for garnish	

Batch Freezing Method

Thoroughly mix cocoa and sugar with 5–7 cups extremely hot water, adding more water as needed, until a smooth creamy paste has been created.

Pour 1 gallon of ice cream mix into batch freezer and turn on dasher. Add cocoa paste and let dasher run until paste and mix are smoothly blended. Pour in remaining ingredients except half of cherries. (The cherries and the chips entered at the beginning of batch create the flavor of the chocolate-covered cherry). Turn on refrigeration and begin batch.

At end of batch, pour in remaining cherries. When batch is complete, turn off refrigeration and extrude finished product.

Decorate tops of tubs with cherry halves and chocolate chips.

Batch time: 9–11 minutes.

Continuous Freezing Method

Before you start the continuous freezing of this flavor, make sure the sanitizing solution or the previous flavor of mix has been pushed through the freezer. Pour the chilled chocolate chips (40 degrees Fahrenheit) and cherry halves (drained) into the fruit feeder and adjust the controls to the appropriate setting. Open the outlet valve of the mix storage tank and let the proper amount of chocolate ice cream mix flow into the flavor tank.*

Next, pour the vanilla extract into the flavor tank. The mix is then pumped to the inlet of the continuous freezer. Set the speed, viscosity (stiffness), and over-run settings according to the manufacturer's recommendations. Start the continuous freezing process. As the ice cream leaves the continuous freezer, it is then piped through the fruit feeder (ingredient feeder) so that the chocolate chips and cherry halves can be discharged and mixed with the ice cream. The ice cream is then piped to the next stage in the process, which is either filling (tubs, pints, etc.), extrusion, or molding.

---

*Note: If you do not use a pasteurized chocolate ice cream mix, thoroughly mix the cocoa and sugar with hot water in a large mixer, adding more water as needed, until a smooth creamy paste has been created.

⊠ CHOCOLATE STRAWBERRY   Superpremium

This is similar to the chocolate cherry recipe. Chocolate-covered strawberries are "in" and mixing strawberries and chocolate in an ice cream is delectable.

Batch		Continuous
1½ pounds	cocoa (22–24% fat)	60 pounds
⅓ pound	sugar	13 pounds
5–7 cups	hot water	11½ gallons
2½ gallons	16% ice cream mix	100 gallons
2 ounces	two-fold vanilla extract	2½ quarts
1 pound	chocolate chips	40 pounds
1½ quarts	processed strawberries	15 gallons
	processed strawberries and chocolate chips for garnish	

Batch Freezing Method

Thoroughly mix cocoa and sugar with 5–7 cups extremely hot water, adding more water as needed, until a smooth creamy paste has been created.

Pour 1 gallon of ice cream mix into batch freezer and turn on dasher. Add cocoa paste and let dasher run until mix and paste are smoothly blended. Pour in remaining ingredients except half of strawberries. Turn on refrigeration and begin batch.

At end of batch, pour in remaining strawberries. When batch is complete, turn off refrigeration and extrude finished product.

Decorate tops of tubs with strawberries and chocolate chips.

Batch time: 9–11 minutes.

Continuous Freezing Method

Before you start the continuous freezing of this flavor, make sure the sanitizing solution or the previous flavor of mix has been pushed through the freezer. Pour the chilled chocolate chips (40 degrees Fahrenheit) and strawberries (drained) into the fruit feeder and adjust the controls to the appropriate setting. Open the outlet valve of the mix storage tank and let the proper amount of chocolate ice cream mix flow into the flavor tank.*

Next, pour the vanilla extract into the flavor tank. The mix is then pumped to the inlet of the continuous freezer. Set the speed, viscosity (stiffness), and overrun settings according to the manufacturer's recommendations. Start the continuous freezing process. As the ice cream leaves the continuous freezer, it is then piped through the fruit feeder (ingredient feeder) so that the chocolate chips and strawberries can be discharged and mixed with the ice cream. The ice cream is then piped to the next stage in the process, which is either filling (tubs, pints, etc.), extrusion, or molding.

---

*Note: If you do not use a pasteurized chocolate ice cream mix, thoroughly mix the cocoa and sugar with hot water in a large mixer, adding more water as needed, until a smooth creamy paste has been created.

⊠ CHOCOLATE CHEESECAKE   Regular

This recipe makes an ice cream that tastes just like chocolate cheesecake—rich and delicious.

Batch		Continuous
1 pound	cocoa (22–24% fat)	40 pounds
¼ pound	sugar	10 pounds
4 cups	hot water	10 gallons
2½ gallons	16% ice cream mix	100 gallons
2 ounces	two-fold vanilla extract	2½ quarts
3 pounds	dry cheesecake powder	120 pounds
½ pound	chocolate chips	20 pounds
1 pound	graham crackers	40 pounds
½ quart	fudge	
	fudge variegate	5 gallons
	chocolate chips, graham crackers, and fudge for garnish	

Batch Freezing Method

Thoroughly mix cocoa and sugar with 4 cups extremely hot water, adding more water as needed, until a smooth creamy paste has been created.

Pour 1 gallon of ice cream mix into batch freezer and turn on dasher. Add cocoa paste and let dasher run until mix and paste are smoothly blended. Pour all remaining ingredients except graham crackers and fudge into batch freezer. Continue mixing until the cheesecake mix has been thoroughly dissolved. Turn on refrigeration and begin batch.

Halfway through batch, add graham crackers. At end of batch, pour in chocolate fudge. When batch is complete, turn off refrigeration and extrude finished product.

Decorate tops of tubs with chocolate chips, graham crackers, and fudge.

Batch time: 9–11 minutes.

Continuous Freezing Method

Before you start the continuous freezing of this flavor, make sure the sanitizing solution or the previous flavor of mix has been pushed through the freezer. Pour the chilled (40 degrees Fahrenheit) fudge variegate into the ripple pump supply tank and adjust speed to inject at the rate as prescribed in the formula, or approximately 10–14 percent of the weight of the ice cream mix. Thoroughly mix together the chocolate chips (40 degrees Fahrenheit) and graham crackers and then pour the mixture into the fruit feeder and adjust the controls to the appropriate setting. Open the outlet valve of the mix storage tank and let the proper amount of chocolate ice cream mix flow into the flavor tank.*

Next, pour the vanilla extract and dry cheesecake powder into the flavor tank and mix thoroughly. The mix is then pumped to the inlet of the continuous freezer. Set the speed, viscosity (stiffness), and overrun settings according to the manufacturer's recommendations. Start the continuous freezing process. As the ice cream leaves the continuous freezer, it is then piped through the fruit feeder (ingredient feeder) so that the chocolate chips and graham crackers can be discharged and mixed with the ice cream. The ice cream is then piped through the ripple injection unit so that the fudge variegating sauce can be injected into the stream of ice cream that has already become semifrozen. The ice cream is then piped to the next stage in the process, which is either filling (tubs, pints, etc.), extrusion, or molding.

---

*Note: If you do not use a pasteurized chocolate ice cream mix, thoroughly mix the cocoa and sugar with hot water in a large mixer, adding more water as needed, until a smooth creamy paste has been created.

Candy Flavors

This category of flavors is relatively new to the ice cream industry, becoming popular at about the same time as the craze for superpremium ice cream began in the early 1980s. These flavors were created to satisfy consumers who enjoyed chilled or frozen candy bars and ultimately craved their favorite candy in a frozen dairy creation.

For the most part, candy manufacturers are now producing for the ice cream industry bulk packaging of small broken pieces of their candies for inclusion into ice cream flavors. If you are using whole candy bars, break them into pieces that can be seen in the finished ice cream, but the pieces should not be larger than ⅜-inch square. Larger pieces are likely to jam the fruit feeder equipment. Temperature at time of usage should be 40 degrees Fahrenheit to keep the candy as individual pieces in the finished product. In using candies in a batch freezing operation, do not add the candy to the freezer all at once. Add it at frequent intervals during the freezing process to prevent the candy from sticking together and forming clumps.

This category lends itself to experimentation, so do not be afraid to ask yourself "What if?" and then try it and see!

� MILKY WAY®   Superpremium

For years before any ice cream maker ever thought of using the Milky Way® candy bar as an ice cream flavor, consumers were freezing them and eating them as a frozen dessert. Today, it is a very popular ice cream flavor for upscale operations and it is one of my "set-me-apart-from-the-competition" flavors. The malt powder and the chocolate chips are used for added flavor.

Batch		Continuous
2½ gallons	16% ice cream mix	100 gallons
2 ounces	two-fold vanilla extract	2½ quarts
6 ounces	dry malt powder	15 pounds
½ pound	chocolate chips	20 pounds
24	Milky Way® candy bars (2.15 ounces each) OR	
56 ounces	candy bar pieces (Pecan Deluxe)	140 pounds
	pieces of Milky Way® candy bars for garnish	

Batch Freezing Method

Cut candy bars into small pieces. Pour all ingredients except half of Milky Way® candy bars into batch freezer. Turn on dasher for 5 minutes so that pieces of candy bars blend into mix. Turn on refrigeration and begin batch.

At end of batch, add remaining pieces of candy bars, turn off refrigeration, and extrude finished product.

Decorate tops of tubs with pieces of candy.

Batch time: 8–10 minutes.

Continuous Freezing Method
Before you start the continuous freezing of this flavor, make sure the sanitizing solution or the previous flavor of mix has been pushed through the freezer. Pour the Milky Way® candy pieces and chocolate chips into the fruit feeder and adjust the controls to the appropriate setting. Open the outlet valve of the aging tank and let the proper amount of ice cream mix flow into the flavor tank. Next, pour the vanilla extract and dry malt powder into the flavor tank and mix all the ingredients thoroughly. The mix is then pumped to the inlet of the continuous freezer. Set the speed, viscosity (stiffness), and overrun settings according to the manufacturer's recommendations. Start the continuous freezing process. As the ice cream leaves the continuous freezer, it is then piped through the fruit feeder (ingredient feeder) so that the Milky Way® candy bar pieces and chocolate chips can be discharged and mixed (temperature of candy bar pieces at time of usage should be 40 degrees Fahrenheit) with the ice cream that has already become semifrozen. The ice cream is then piped to the next stage in the process, which is either filling (tubs, pints, etc.), extrusion, or molding.

⊠ SNICKERS®   Superpremium

This flavor is as popular as the Milky Way® flavor. It is a must flavor for any up-scale operation because of the popularity of the candy bar itself. The granulated peanuts and chocolate chips are used for added flavor.

Batch		Continuous
2½ gallons	16% ice cream mix	100 gallons
2 ounces	two-fold vanilla extract	2½ quarts
½ pound	granulated peanuts	20 pounds
½ pound	chocolate chips	20 pounds
24	Snickers® candy bars (2.07 ounces each)	
	OR	
50 ounces	Snickers® broken pieces	125 pounds
	pieces of Snickers® candy bars for garnish	

Batch Freezing Method
Cut Snickers® candy bars into small pieces (also comes packaged already broken into small pieces). Pour all ingredients except half of Snickers® candy bars into batch freezer. Turn on dasher for 5 minutes so that pieces of candy bars blend into mix. Turn on refrigeration and begin batch.

At end of batch, add remaining Snickers® candy, turn off refrigeration, and extrude finished product.

Decorate tops of tubs with pieces of candy.

Batch time: 8–10 minutes.

Continuous Freezing Method

Before you start the continuous freezing of this flavor, make sure the sanitizing solution or the previous flavor of mix has been pushed through the freezer. Pour the Snickers® candy pieces, chocolate chips, and granulated peanuts into the fruit feeder and adjust the controls to the appropriate setting. Open the outlet valve of the aging tank and let the proper amount of ice cream mix flow into the flavor tank. Pour the vanilla extract into the flavor tank. The mix is then pumped to the inlet of the continuous freezer. Set the speed, viscosity (stiffness), and overrun settings according to the manufacturer's recommendations. Start the continuous freezing process. As the ice cream leaves the continuous freezer, it is then piped through the fruit feeder (ingredient feeder) so that the Snickers® candy bar pieces, chocolate chips, and granulated peanuts can be discharged and mixed (temperature of candy bar pieces at time of usage should be 40 degrees Fahrenheit) with the ice cream that has already become semifrozen. The ice cream is then piped to the next stage in the process, which is either filling (tubs, pints, etc.), extrusion, or molding.

⊠ COCONUT ALMOND JOY®　　　　Superpremium

This ice cream flavor is one of my favorites. I love both the candy bar and chocolate coconut Easter eggs, so how could I resist such an ice cream flavor? The shredded coconut and the chocolate chips are used for added flavor.

Batch

		Continuous
2½ gallons	16% ice cream mix	100 gallons
2 ounces	two-fold vanilla extract	2½ quarts
½ pound	shredded coconut	20 pounds
½ pound	chocolate chips	20 pounds
24	Coconut Almond Joy® candy bars (2 ounces each)	120 pounds
	pieces of Coconut Almond Joy® candy bars for garnish	

Batch Freezing Method

Refrigerate or freeze Coconut Almond Joy candy bars for one hour. Remove from refrigeration and cut into small pieces. Pour all the ingredients except half the candy bars into batch freezer. Turn on dasher for 5 minutes so that pieces of candy bars blend into mix. Turn on refrigeration and begin batch.

At end of batch, add remaining pieces of candy bars, turn off refrigeration, and extrude finished product.

Decorate tops of tubs with pieces of candy.

Batch time: 8–10 minutes.

Continuous Freezing Method

Before you start the continuous freezing of this flavor, make sure the sanitizing solution or the previous flavor of mix has been pushed through the freezer. Mix thoroughly, then pour the Coconut Almond Joy® candy bar pieces, chocolate chips, and shredded coconut into the fruit feeder and adjust the controls to the appropriate setting. Open the outlet valve of the aging tank and let the proper amount of ice cream mix flow into the flavor tank. Pour the vanilla extract into the flavor tank. The mix is then pumped to the inlet of the continuous freezer. Set the speed, viscosity (stiffness), and overrun settings according to the manufacturer's recommendations. Start the continuous freezing process. As the ice cream leaves the continuous freezer, it is then piped through the fruit feeder (ingredient feeder) so that the Coconut Almond Joy® candy bar pieces, chocolate chips, and shredded coconut can be discharged and mixed (temperature of candy bar pieces at time of usage should be 40 degrees Fahrenheit) with the ice cream that has already become semifrozen. The ice cream is then piped to the next stage in the process, which is either filling (tubs, pints, etc.), extrusion, or molding.

⊠ ENGLISH TOFFEE   Regular

This flavor is very popular in the Midwest, but for some reason it has not caught on in the rest of the country. It tastes very good and it is not difficult to make.

Batch		Continuous
2 ounces	freeze-dried coffee	5 pounds
2 tablespoons	hot water	1¼ quarts
2½ gallons	16% ice cream mix	100 gallons
2 ounces	two-fold vanilla extract	2½ quarts
3 ounces	rum extract*	120 ounces
2½ pounds	English Toffee candy (Leaf)	100 pounds
	pieces of English Toffee candy pieces for garnish	

_____

*Note: Usage depends on manufacturer's recommendations.

Batch Freezing Method

With 2 tablespoons of hot water, create a paste with freeze-dried coffee. Pour all ingredients except half the English Toffee candy into batch freezer. Turn on dasher for 5 minutes to allow candy to blend into ice cream mix. Turn on refrigeration and begin batch. At end of batch, add remaining candy, turn off refrigeration, and extrude finished product.

Decorate tops of tubs with pieces of toffee candy.

Batch time: 8–10 minutes.

Continuous Freezing Method

Before you start the continuous freezing of this flavor, make sure the sanitizing solution or the previous flavor of mix has been pushed through the freezer. Pour the English Toffee candy pieces into the fruit feeder and adjust the controls to the appropriate setting. Open the outlet valve of the aging tank and let the proper amount of ice cream mix flow into the flavor tank. Pour both the vanilla and rum extract into the flavor tank. The mix is then pumped to the inlet of the continuous freezer. Set the speed, viscosity (stiffness), and overrun settings according to the manufacturer's recommendations. Start the continuous freezing process. As the ice cream leaves the continuous freezer, it is then piped through the fruit feeder (ingredient feeder) so that the English Toffee candy pieces can be discharged and mixed (temperature of candy pieces at time of usage should be 40 degrees Fahrenheit) with the ice cream that has already become semifrozen. The ice cream is then piped to the next stage in the process, which is either filling (tubs, pints, etc.), extrusion, or molding.

▨ BUTTER BRICKLE   Regular

Ever since I was young, I have been fond of this flavor and I enjoy tasting it right out of the batch freezer. This flavor has universal appeal whether produced in half gallons for supermarket consumption or for an ice cream shop in Des Moines, Iowa.

Batch		Continuous
2 ounces	freeze-dried coffee	5 pounds
2 tablespoons	hot water	1¼ quart
2½ gallons	16% ice cream mix	100 gallons
2 ounces	two-fold vanilla extract	2½ quarts
3 ounces	butter flavor*	3¾ quarts
2½ pounds	Butter Brickle candy	100 pounds
	pieces of Butter Brickle candy pieces for garnish	

*Note: Amount to use varies according to manufacturer's recommendations.

Batch Freezing Method

Pour all ingredients except half the Butter Brickle candy into batch freezer. Turn on dasher for 3 minutes to allow candy to blend into ice cream mix. Turn on refrigeration and begin batch. At end of batch, add remaining Butter Brickle candy, turn off refrigeration, and extrude finished product.

Decorate tops of tubs with pieces of Butter Brickle candy.

Batch time: 8–10 minutes.

Continuous Freezing Method

Before you start the continuous freezing of this flavor, make sure the sanitizing solution or the previous flavor of mix has been pushed through the freezer. Pour the Butter Brickle candy pieces into the fruit feeder and adjust the controls to the appropriate setting. Open the outlet valve of the aging tank and let the proper amount of ice cream mix flow into the flavor tank. Pour both the vanilla and butter flavor into the flavor tank. The mix is then pumped to the inlet of the continuous freezer. Set the speed, viscosity (stiffness), and overrun settings according to the manufacturer's recommendations. Start the continuous freezing process. As the ice cream leaves the continuous freezer, it is then piped through the fruit feeder (ingredient feeder) so that the Butter Brickle candy pieces can be discharged and mixed (temperature of candy pieces at time of usage should be 40 degrees Fahrenheit) with the ice cream that has already become semifrozen. The ice cream is then piped to the next stage in the process, which is either filling (tubs, pints, etc.), extrusion, or molding.

⊠ HEATH BAR®   Superpremium

Heath Bar is one of the best-selling candy flavors in the ice cream market because of its great taste and its ease of production.

Batch		Continuous
2 ounces	freeze-dried coffee	5 pounds
2 tablespoons	hot water	1¼ quart
2½ gallons	16% ice cream mix	100 gallons
2 ounces	two-fold vanilla extract	2½ quarts
2 pounds	Heath Bar candy pieces	80 pounds
	pieces of Heath Bar candy pieces for garnish	

Batch Freezing Method

Pour all ingredients except half the granulated Heath Bars® pieces into batch freezer. Turn on dasher for 3 minutes to allow candy to blend into ice cream mix. Turn on refrigeration and begin batch. At end of batch, add remaining candy, turn off refrigeration, and extrude finished product.

Decorate tops of tubs with pieces of Heath Bars®.

Batch time: 8–10 minutes.

Continuous Freezing Method

Before you start the continuous freezing of this flavor, make sure the sanitizing solution or the previous flavor of mix has been pushed through the freezer.

Mix freeze-dried coffee with as little hot water as possible and add cocoa. The resulting paste should be smooth with no dry coffee or cocoa visible. Pour the Heath Bar® candy pieces into the fruit feeder and adjust the controls to the appropriate setting. Open the outlet valve of the aging tank and let the proper amount of ice cream mix flow into the flavor tank. Pour the vanilla extract and prepared coffee base into the flavor tank. The mix is then pumped to the inlet of the continuous freezer. Set the speed, viscosity (stiffness), and overrun settings according to the manufacturer's recommendations. Start the continuous freezing process. As the ice cream leaves the continuous freezer, it is then piped through the fruit feeder (ingredient feeder) so that the Heath Bar® candy pieces can be discharged and mixed (temperature of candy pieces at time of usage should be 40 degrees Fahrenheit) with the ice cream that has already become semifrozen. The ice cream is then piped to the next stage in the process, which is either filling (tubs, pints, etc.), extrusion, or molding.

⊠ CREME CARAMEL   **Superpremium**

This smooth, sweet, delicate flavor is a real gourmet's delight.

Batch		Continuous
2½ gallons	16% ice cream mix	100 gallons
2 ounces	two-fold vanilla extract	2½ quarts
4 ounces	caramel extract*	3¾ quarts
3 quarts	caramel variegate	22½ gallons
	caramel for garnish	

*Note: Amount to use varies according to manufacturer's recommendations.

Batch Freezing Method

Pour ice cream mix, caramel, and vanilla extracts, and 16 ounces of caramel variegates into batch freezer. Turn on both dasher and refrigeration and begin batch.

Using a spatula, line the ice cream tubs with caramel and put empty tubs into freezer until you are ready to use them.

When batch is complete, turn off refrigeration and extrude finished product, scraping caramel off sides of tubs in a swirling action into ice cream. Add more caramel as needed.

Decorate tops of tubs with caramel.

Batch time: 8–10 minutes.

Continuous Freezing Method
Before you start the continuous freezing of this flavor, make sure the sanitizing solution or the previous flavor of mix has been pushed through the freezer. Pour the chilled (40 degrees Fahrenheit) caramel variegate into the ripple pump supply tank and adjust speed to inject at the rate as prescribed in the formula, or approximately 10–14 percent of the weight of the ice cream mix. Open the outlet valve of the aging tank and let the proper amount of ice cream mix flow into the flavor tank. Pour both the vanilla and caramel extract into the flavor tank. The mix is then pumped to the inlet of the continuous freezer. Set the speed, viscosity (stiffness), and overrun settings according to the manufacturer's recommendations. Start the continuous freezing process. As the ice cream leaves the continuous freezer, it is then piped through the ripple injection unit so that the caramel variegate can be injected into the stream of ice cream that has already been semifrozen. The ice cream is then piped to the next stage in the process, which is either filling (tubs, pints, etc.), extrusion, or molding.

⊠ CHOCOLATE RAISIN   **Regular**

The appeal of chocolate-covered raisins inspired this terrific creation.

Batch		Continuous
2 pounds	cocoa (22–24% fat)	80 pounds
6–8 cups	hot water	15 gallons
¼ pound	sugar	20 pounds
2½ gallons	16% ice cream mix	100 gallons
2 ounces	two-fold vanilla extract	2½ quarts
½ pound	raisins	20 pounds
1½ pounds	chocolate-covered raisins	60 pounds
	chocolate-covered raisins for garnish	

Batch Freezing Method
Thoroughly mix cocoa and sugar with 6–8 cups extremely hot water, adding more water as needed, until a smooth creamy paste has been created.

Pour 1 gallon of ice cream mix into batch freezer and turn on dasher. Add cocoa paste and let dasher run for 5 minutes until mix and paste are smoothly blended. Pour in remaining ingredients except chocolate-covered raisins. Turn on refrigeration and begin batch.

At end of batch, add chocolate-covered raisins, turn off refrigeration, and extrude finished product.

Decorate tops of tubs with chocolate-covered raisins.

Batch time: 9–11 minutes.

Continuous Freezing Method

Before you start the continuous freezing of this flavor, make sure the sanitizing solution or the previous flavor of mix has been pushed through the freezer. Pour the chocolate-covered raisins and plain raisins into the fruit feeder and adjust the controls to the appropriate setting. Open the outlet valve of the aging tank and let the proper amount of chocolate ice cream mix flow into the flavor tank.*

Next, pour the vanilla extract into the flavor tank. The mix is then pumped to the inlet of the continuous freezer. Set the speed, viscosity (stiffness), and overrun settings according to the manufacturer's recommendations. Start the continuous freezing process. As the ice cream leaves the continuous freezer, it is then piped through the fruit feeder (ingredient feeder) so that both the chocolate-covered and plain raisins can be discharged and mixed (temperature of candy pieces at time of usage should be 40 degrees Fahrenheit) with the ice cream that has already become semifrozen. The ice cream is then piped to the next stage in the process, which is either filling (tubs, pints, etc.), extrusion, or molding.

---

*Note: If you do not use a pasteurized chocolate ice cream mix, thoroughly mix the cocoa and sugar with hot water in a large mixer, adding more water is needed, until a smooth creamy paste has been created.

▨ M&M's®   Regular

Kids love M&M's® as either a candy to eat or as an ice cream topping, and they especially love them when used to create an ice cream flavor. If you want to create excitement in your shop, make this flavor. Some of the candy pieces are added at the beginning of the batch to add the candy flavor to the ice cream.

Batch		Continuous
2½ gallons	16% ice cream mix	100 gallons
2 ounces	two-fold vanilla extract	2½ quarts
2 pounds	M&M's® mini chocolate candies	80 pounds
½ pound	chocolate chips	20 pounds
	M&M's® chocolate candies for garnish	

Batch Freezing Method

Pour all ingredients except 1 pound of mini M&M's® into the batch freezer. Turn on both dasher and refrigeration and begin batch. At end of batch, pour in remaining M&M's®, turn off refrigeration, and extrude finished product.

Decorate tops of tubs with M&M's®.

Batch time: 8–10 minutes.

Continuous Freezing Method
Before you start the continuous freezing of this flavor, make sure the sanitizing solution or the previous flavor of mix has been pushed through the freezer. Pour the M&M's® chocolate candies into the fruit feeder and adjust the controls to the appropriate setting. Open the outlet valve of the aging tank and let the proper amount of ice cream mix flow into the flavor tank. Pour the vanilla extract into the flavor tank. The mix is then pumped to the inlet of the continuous freezer. Set the speed, viscosity (stiffness), and overrun settings according to the manufacturer's recommendations. Start the continuous freezing process. As the ice cream leaves the continuous freezer, it is then piped through the fruit feeder (ingredient feeder) so that the M&M's® chocolate candies can be discharged and mixed (temperature of candy pieces at time of usage should be 40 degrees Fahrenheit) with the ice cream that has already become semifrozen. The ice cream is then piped to the next stage in the process, which is either filling (tubs, pints, etc.), extrusion, or molding.

⊠ EXTRA TERRESTRIAL   Regular

The movie E.T. *made this flavor very popular with children. Its production flavor is similar to that of the M&M® ice cream. Some of the candy pieces are added at the beginning of the batch for extra candy flavor.*

Batch   **Continuous**

2½ gallons	16% ice cream mix	100 gallons
2 ounces	two-fold vanilla extract	2½ quarts
2 pounds	Reese's Pieces® candy	80 pounds
	Reese's Pieces candy for garnish	

Batch Freezing Method
Pour all ingredients except 1 pound of Reese's Pieces® candy into batch freezer. Turn on both dasher and refrigeration and begin batch. At end of batch, pour in remaining candy, turn off refrigeration, and extrude finished product.
    Decorate tops of tubs with Reese's Pieces® candy.

Batch time: 8–10 minutes.

Continuous Freezing Method
Before you start the continuous freezing of this flavor, make sure the sanitizing solution or the previous flavor of mix has been pushed through the freezer. Pour the Reese's Pieces® candy into the fruit feeder and adjust the controls to the appropriate setting. Open the outlet valve of the aging tank

and let the proper amount of ice cream mix flow into the flavor tank. Pour the vanilla extract into the flavor tank. The mix is then pumped to the inlet of the continuous freezer. Set the speed, viscosity (stiffness), and overrun settings according to the manufacturer's recommendations. Start the continuous freezing process. As the ice cream leaves the continuous freezer, it is then piped through the fruit feeder (ingredient feeder) so that the Reese's Pieces® chocolate candies can be discharged and mixed (temperature of candy pieces at time of usage should be 40 degrees Fahrenheit) with the ice cream that has already become semifrozen. The ice cream is then piped to the next stage in the process, which is either filling (tubs, pints, etc.), extrusion, or molding.

⊠ CHOCOLATE MINT PATTIE   **Superpremium**

This is another excellent candy flavor that is easy to make and will get raves. The taste of either Peppermint Pattie® candy or Andes® Chocolate Mints really stands out.

Batch		Continuous
1½ pounds	cocoa (22–24% fat)	60 pounds
5–6 cups	hot water	12 gallons
⅓ pound	sugar	13½ pounds
2½ gallons	16% ice cream mix	100 gallons
2 ounces	two-fold vanilla extract	2½ quarts
2 ounces	peppermint flavor*	2½ quarts
½ pound	chocolate chips	20 pounds
1½ pounds	Peppermint Patties® or Andes® Chocolate Mint candies	60 pounds

*Note: Amount to use varies according to manufacturer's recommendations.

Batch Freezing Method

Thoroughly mix cocoa and sugar with 5–6 cups extremely hot water, adding more water as needed, until a smooth creamy paste has been created.

Pour 1 gallon of mix into batch freezer and turn on dasher. Add cocoa paste and let dasher run for 5 minutes until mix and paste are smoothly blended.

Pour in remaining ingredients except Peppermint Pattie® candy. Turn on refrigeration and begin batch. Halfway into batch, add all candy to batch. When batch is complete, turn off refrigeration and extrude finished product.

Decorate tops of tubs with pieces of Peppermint Pattie® or Andes® candy.

Batch time: 9–11 minutes.

Continuous Freezing Method

Before you start the continuous freezing of this flavor, make sure the sanitizing solution or the previous flavor of mix has been pushed through the freezer. Pour either the Peppermint Pattie® or Andes® Chocolate Mint candies into the fruit feeder and adjust the controls to the appropriate setting. Open the outlet valve of the aging tank and let the proper amount of chocolate ice cream mix flow into the flavor tank.*

Next, mix and then pour the vanilla extract and peppermint flavor into the flavor tank. The mix is then pumped to the inlet of the continuous freezer. Set the speed, viscosity (stiffness), and overrun settings according to the manufacturer's recommendations. Start the continuous freezing process. As the ice cream leaves the continuous freezer, it is then piped through the fruit feeder (ingredient feeder) so that the peppermint mint chocolate candies can be discharged and mixed (temperature of candy pieces at time of usage should be 40 degrees Fahrenheit) with the ice cream that has already become semifrozen. The ice cream is then piped to the next stage in the process, which is either filling (tubs, pints, etc.), extrusion, or molding.

---

*Note: If you do not use a pasteurized chocolate ice cream mix, thoroughly mix the cocoa and sugar with hot water in a large mixer, adding more water as needed, until a smooth creamy paste has been created.

Tropical Tastes

Some fruit ingredients are not available year round or are expensive when they are available. If you want to tempt your customers with images of exotic getaways or reminders of past vacations, choose from the following flavors to glamorize your flavor product line.

⊠ COCONUT   Superpremium

This flavor is very rich and is a favorite in the South and on the West Coast where tropical flavors sell very well. Be careful that the finished product is not too sweet: Taste the product for sweetness during production.

Batch		Continuous
2½ gallons	16% ice cream mix	100 gallons
2 ounces	two-fold vanilla extract	2½ quarts
30–48 ounces	coconut fruit base	9 gallons
1 pound	shredded coconut	40 pounds
	shredded coconut for garnish	

Batch Freezing Method

Pour ice cream mix, vanilla extract, 30 ounces of coconut fruit base, and 4 ounces of shredded coconut into batch freezer. Turn on both dasher and refrigeration and begin batch. After approximately 4 minutes, check mix for sweetness and taste. If needed, add more coconut fruit base. At end of batch, add remaining shredded coconut, turn off refrigeration, and extrude finished product.

Decorate tops of tubs with shredded coconut.

Batch time: 8–10 minutes.

Continuous Freezing Method

Before you start the continuous freezing of this flavor, make sure the sanitizing solution or the previous flavor of mix has been pushed through the freezer. Pour the shredded coconut into the fruit feeder and adjust the controls to the appropriate setting. Open the outlet valve of the aging tank and let the proper amount of ice cream mix flow into the flavor tank. Next, pour the vanilla extract and coconut fruit base into the flavor tank. The mix is then pumped to the inlet of the continuous freezer. Set the speed, viscosity (stiffness), and overrun settings according to the manufacturer's recommendations. Start the continuous freezing process. As the ice cream leaves the continuous freezer, it is then piped through the fruit feeder (ingredient feeder) so that the shredded coconut can be discharged and mixed with the ice cream that has already become semifrozen. The ice cream is then piped to the next stage in the process, which is either filling (tubs, pints, etc.), extrusion, or molding.

⊠ PINEAPPLE   Regular

Becoming increasingly hard to find in a dipping shop, this sweet-tart summer flavor sells well.

Batch		Continuous
3	pineapples	
½ pound	sugar	
	pineapple puree*	30 gallons
	pineapple chunks*	30 gallons
2½ gallons	16% ice cream mix	100 gallons
2 ounces	two-fold vanilla extract	2½ quarts
	cooked pineapple pieces for garnish	

*Note: If you use fresh or frozen pineapples, marinate the fruit (7–1 ratio) with sugar for 8 hours.

Batch Freezing Method

Core and pare 3 pineapples. Cut into pieces and bake at 150 degrees Fahrenheit for 30 minutes. Add sugar to pineapple pieces, reserve half for end of batch and decoration, and puree the rest.

Pour all ingredients except pineapple puree into batch freezer. Turn on both dasher and refrigeration and begin batch. Halfway into batch, as ice cream begins to freeze, add pureed pineapple. When batch is complete, add most of remaining of pineapple pieces, turn off refrigeration and extrude finished product.

Decorate tops of tubs with cooked pineapple pieces.

Batch time: 8–10 minutes.

Continuous Freezing Method

Before you start the continuous freezing of this flavor, make sure the sanitizing solution or the previous flavor of mix has been pushed through the freezer. Pour the pineapple pieces into the fruit feeder and adjust the controls to the appropriate setting. Open the outlet valve of the aging tank and let the proper amount of ice cream mix flow into the flavor tank. Next, pour the vanilla extract and pineapple puree into the flavor tank. The mix is then pumped to the inlet of the continuous freezer. Set the speed, viscosity (stiffness), and overrun settings according to the manufacturer's recommendations. Start the continuous freezing process. As the ice cream leaves the continuous freezer, it is then piped through the fruit feeder (ingredient feeder) so that the pineapple pieces can be discharged and mixed with ice cream that has already become semifrozen. The ice cream is then piped to the next stage in the process, which is either filling (tubs, pints, etc.), extrusion, or molding.

⊠ ORANGE PINEAPPLE   Regular

This ice cream is as refreshing as the drink.

Batch		Continuous
1	pineapple	
	pineapple puree	80 pounds
½ pound	sugar	
1 quart	orange juice	5 gallons
2½ gallons	16% ice cream mix	100 gallons
2 ounces	two-fold vanilla extract	2½ quarts
2 quarts	orange-pineapple base	20 gallons
	cooked pineapple pieces for garnish	

Batch Freezing Method

Core and pare pineapple. Cut into pieces and bake for 30 minutes at 150 degrees Fahrenheit. Add sugar to pineapple and reserve some pieces for garnish. Puree remaining pineapple with orange juice and marinate for 6–8 hours.

Pour all ingredients into batch freezer except pureed pineapple. Turn on both dasher and refrigeration and begin batch. Halfway into batch, as ice cream begins to freeze, add pineapple puree. When batch is complete, turn off refrigeration and extrude finished product.

Decorate tops of tubs with reserved cooked pineapple pieces.

Batch time: 8–10 minutes.

Continuous Freezing Method

Before you start the continuous freezing of this flavor, make sure the sanitizing solution or the previous flavor of mix has been pushed through the freezer. Open the outlet valve of the aging tank and let the proper amount of ice cream mix flow into the flavor tank. Pour the vanilla extract, pineapple puree, and orange-pineapple base into the flavor tank. The mix is then pumped to the inlet of the continuous freezer. Set the speed, viscosity (stiffness), and overrun settings according to the manufacturer's recommendations. Start the continuous freezing process. As the ice cream leaves the continuous freezer, it is then piped to the next stage in the process, which is either filling (tubs, pints, etc.), extrusion, or molding.

⊠ TROPICAL PARADISE   Regular

This recipe combines the flavor of pineapple with banana and rum.

Batch		Continuous
4 pounds	bananas	160 pounds
2½ gallons	16% ice cream mix	100 gallons
2 ounces	two-fold vanilla extract	2½ quarts
1½ quarts	pineapple ice cream base	15 gallons
10 ounces	rum	
	rum extract*	40 ounces
	pineapple base and pieces of banana for garnish	

*Note: Amount to use varies according to manufacturer's recommendations.

Batch Freezing Method

Puree the bananas.

Pour all ingredients except rum into the batch freezer. Turn on both dasher and refrigeration and begin batch. Halfway into batch, as ice cream begins to freeze, add rum. When batch is complete, turn off refrigeration and extrude finished product.

Decorate tops of tubs with pineapple base and pieces of bananas.

Batch time: 8–10 minutes.

Continuous Freezing Method

Before you start the continuous freezing of this flavor, make sure the sanitizing solution or the previous flavor of mix has been pushed through the freezer. Open the outlet valve of the aging tank and let the proper amount of ice cream mix flow into the flavor tank. Pour the vanilla extract, rum extract, banana puree, and pineapple ice cream base into the flavor tank, and mix all the ingredients thoroughly. The mix is them pumped to the inlet of the continuous freezer. Set the speed, viscosity (stiffness), and overrun settings according to the manufacturer's recommendations. Start the continuous freezing process. As the ice cream leaves the continuous freezer, it is then piped to the next stage in the process, which is either filling (tubs, pints, etc.), extrusion, or molding.

⊠ ORANGE PINEAPPLE MACAROON   Superpremium

This recipe is a more upscale version of the Orange Pineapple flavor.

Batch		Continuous
1	pineapple	
	pineapple puree	80 pounds
½ pound	sugar	
1 quart	orange juice	5 gallons
2½ gallons	16% ice cream mix	100 gallons
2 ounces	two-fold vanilla extract	2½ quarts
2 quarts	orange-pineapple base	20 gallons
1½ pounds	macaroon pieces	60 pounds
	macaroons for garnish	

Batch Freezing Method

Core and pare pineapple. Cut into pieces and bake for 30 minutes at 150 degrees Fahrenheit. Add sugar to pineapple. Puree pineapple with orange juice and marinate for 2 hours.

Pour all ingredients except pineapple puree and macaroon pieces into batch freezer. Turn on both dasher and refrigeration and begin batch. Halfway into batch, as ice cream begins to freeze, add pineapple puree and macaroons. When the batch is complete, turn off refrigeration and extrude finished product.

Decorate tops of tubs with macaroons.

Batch time: 8–10 minutes.

Continuous Freezing Method

Before you start the continuous freezing of this flavor, make sure the sanitizing solution or the previous flavor of mix has been pushed through the freezer. Pour the macaroon pieces into the fruit feeder and adjust the controls to the appropriate setting. Open the outlet valve of the aging tank and let the proper amount of ice cream mix flow into the flavor tank. Next, pour the vanilla extract, orange-pineapple base, and pineapple puree into the flavor tank. The mix is then pumped to the inlet of the continuous freezer. Set the speed, viscosity (stiffness), and overrun settings according to the manufacturer's recommendations. Start the continuous freezing process. As the ice cream leaves the continuous freezer, it is then piped through the fruit feeder (ingredient feeder) so that the macaroon pieces can be discharged and mixed with the ice cream that has already become semifrozen. The ice cream is then piped to the next stage in the process, which is either filling (tubs, pints, etc.), extrusion, or molding.

MANGO   Superpremium

This is a very refreshing summertime flavor. Since fresh mangos are used, it will take time to prepare this flavor. Frozen mango puree can be used, but the flavor difference is significant.

Batch		Continuous
4 quarts	fresh mangoes, pureed	
	mango puree	40 gallons
1 pound (for use with fresh mangoes only)	sugar	
2½ gallons	16% ice cream mix	100 gallons
2 ounces	two-fold vanilla extract	2½ quarts
	mango pieces or puree for garnish	

Batch Freezing Method

Peel, seed, and puree mangoes. Mix 1 pound sugar with mango puree and marinate for 6 hours at room temperature. If frozen mango puree is used, no added sugar is necessary.

Pour all ingredients into batch freezer, turn on both dasher and refrigeration, and begin batch. When batch is complete, turn off refrigeration and extrude finished product.

Decorate tops of tubs with fresh mango pieces or puree.

Batch time: 8–10 minutes.

Continuous Freezing Method
Before you start the continuous freezing of this flavor, make sure the sanitizing solution or the previous flavor of mix has been pushed through the freezer. Open the outlet valve of the aging tank and let the proper amount of ice cream mix flow into the flavor tank. Pour the vanilla extract and mango puree into the flavor tank. The mix is then pumped to the inlet of the continuous freezer. Set the speed, viscosity (stiffness), and overrun settings according to the manufacturer's recommendations. Start the continuous freezing process. As the ice cream leaves the continuous freezer, it is then piped to the next stage in the process, which is either filling (tubs, pints, etc.), extrusion, or molding.

⊠ **BANANA DAIQUIRI**   **Superpremium**

Adults will love this sophisticated summer flavor that is as tasty and refreshing as the drink.

Batch		Continuous
2½ gallons	16% ice cream mix	100 gallons
2 ounces	two-fold vanilla extract	2½ quarts
16 ounces	rum flavoring*	5 gallons
6 pounds	fresh bananas (5 pounds peeled)†	
	pasteurized banana puree	25 gallons
2 ounces	pure lemon juice	2½ quarts
	pieces of banana for garnish	

*Note: Amount to use varies according to manufacturer's recommendations.
†Note: 6 pounds of whole bananas will yield approximately 5 pounds of peeled bananas because banana skin is approximately 20 percent of the weight of a banana.

Batch Freezing Method
Peel bananas. Pour all ingredients into batch freezer. Turn on both dasher and refrigeration and begin batch. When batch is complete, turn off refrigeration and extrude finished product.
    Decorate tops of tubs with banana pieces.

Batch time: 8–10 minutes.

Continuous Freezing Method
Before you start the continuous freezing of this flavor, make sure the sanitizing solution or the previous flavor of mix has been pushed through the freezer. Open the outlet valve of the aging tank and let the proper amount of ice cream mix flow into the flavor tank. Pour the vanilla extract, rum flavoring, banana puree, and lemon juice into the flavor tank, and mix all the ingre-

dients thoroughly. The mix is then pumped to the inlet of the continuous freezer. Set the speed, viscosity (stiffness), and overrun settings according to the manufacturer's recommendations. Start the continuous freezing process. As the ice cream leaves the continuous freezer, it is then piped to the next stage in the process, which is either filling (tubs, pints, etc.), extrusion, or molding.

⊠ PAPAYA   Superpremium

A delightful exotic summer dessert, this flavor is suitable for restaurant use.

Batch		Continuous
12 (yield 4 quarts of puree)	ripe papayas	
2 pounds	sugar	
2 ounces	lemon juice	2½ quarts
	papaya puree	40 gallons
2½ gallons	16% ice cream mix	100 gallons
2 ounces	two-fold vanilla extract	2½ quarts
	pieces of papaya for garnish	

Batch Freezing Method
Peel, remove seeds, and cut papayas into pieces. Cook papaya flesh for 10 minutes to deactivate enzymes. Puree cooked papaya to yield 4 quarts. Add sugar and lemon juice and marinate mixture for 3 hours.

Pour all ingredients into batch freezer. Turn on both dasher and refrigeration and begin batch. When batch is complete, turn off refrigeration and extrude finished product.

Decorate tops of tubs with papaya pieces.

Batch time: 8–10 minutes.

Continuous Freezing Method
Before you start the continuous freezing of this flavor, make sure the sanitizing solution or the previous flavor of mix has been pushed through the freezer. Open the outlet valve of the aging tank and let the proper amount of ice cream mix flow into the flavor tank. Pour the vanilla extract, papaya puree, and lemon juice into the flavor tank. The mix is then pumped to the inlet of the continuous freezer. Set the speed, viscosity (stiffness), and overrun settings according to the manufacturer's recommendations. Start the continuous freezing process. As the ice cream leaves the continuous freezer, it is then piped to the next stage in the process, which is either filling (tubs, pints, etc.), extrusion, or molding.

⊠ BANANA MACADAMIA NUT   Superpremium

Bananas and macadamia nuts together make a great flavor combination.

Batch		Continuous
2½ gallons	16% ice cream mix	100 gallons
2 ounces	two-fold vanilla extract	2½ quarts
6 pounds	fresh bananas (5 pounds peeled)*	
	pasteurized banana puree	25 gallons
1 pound	macadamia nut pieces	40 pounds
	pieces of banana and macadamia nuts for garnish	

*Note: 6 pounds of whole bananas will yield approximately 5 pounds of peeled bananas because banana skin is approximately 20 percent of the weight of a banana.

Batch Freezing Method

Pour all ingredients except macadamia nuts into batch freezer. Turn on both dasher and refrigeration and begin batch. Halfway into batch, as ice cream begins to freeze, add macadamia nuts. When batch is complete, turn off refrigeration and extrude finished product.

Decorate tops of tubs with pieces of bananas and macadamia nuts.

Batch time: 8–10 minutes.

Continuous Freezing Method

Before you start the continuous freezing of this flavor, make sure the sanitizing solution or the previous flavor of mix has been pushed through the freezer. Pour the macadamia nut pieces into the fruit feeder and adjust the controls to the appropriate setting. Open the outlet valve of the aging tank and let the proper amount of ice cream mix flow into the flavor tank. Next, pour the vanilla extract and banana puree into the flavor tank. The mix is then pumped to the inlet of the continuous freezer. Set the speed, viscosity (stiffness), and overrun settings according to the manufacturer's recommendations. Start the continuous freezing process. As the ice cream leaves the continuous freezer, it is then piped through the fruit feeder (ingredient feeder) so that the macadamia nut pieces can be discharged and mixed with the ice cream that has already become semifrozen. The ice cream is then piped to the next stage in the process, which is either filling (tubs, pints, etc.), extrusion, or molding.

Specialty Flavors

You will not necessarily find the flavors provided by the following recipes in supermarkets or in most ice cream shops. But that does not mean you should not produce them because selling and marketing these specialties will set you apart from your competition. You might even choose one as a signature item.

⊠ APPLE STRUDEL   Superpremium

A wonderful seasonal item to feature in the fall, this flavor is one of my "set-you-apart-from-the-competition" flavors. It is not easy to prepare, but is worth the effort.

Batch   **Continuous**
2½ gallons   16% ice cream mix   100 gallons
2 ounces   two-fold vanilla extract   2½ quarts
3 pounds   apple pie filling   120 pounds
1 ounce   cinnamon   1¼ quarts
1 pound   raisins   40 pounds
½ pound   graham crackers (broken)   20 pounds
              cinnamon, raisins, and pieces of
                graham crackers for garnish

Batch Freezing Method
Pour all ingredients except raisins and graham crackers into batch freezer. (Apple pie filling and cinnamon are entered at beginning of batch to create an apple flavor in the mix.) Turn on both dasher and refrigeration and begin batch.

To keep them in larger pieces and give more substance to the finished product, add the raisins and graham crackers after the run is more than half done. When batch is complete, turn off refrigeration and extrude finished product.

To decorate, sprinkle some cinnamon on top of packed tubs along with pieces of graham crackers and raisins.

Batch time: 8–10 minutes.

Continuous Freezing Method
Before you start the continuous freezing of this flavor, make sure the sanitizing solution or the previous flavor of mix has been pushed through the freezer. Pour the apple pie filling, raisins, and graham crackers into the fruit feeder and adjust the controls to the appropriate setting. Open the outlet valve of the aging tank and let the proper amount of ice cream mix flow into the flavor tank. Next, pour the vanilla extract and cinnamon into the flavor tank, and mix all the ingredients thoroughly. The mix is then pumped to the inlet of the continuous freezer. Set the speed, viscosity (stiffness), and overrun settings according to the manufacturer's recommendations. Start the continuous freezing process. As the ice cream leaves the continuous freezer, it is then piped through the fruit feeder (ingredient feeder) so that the apple pie filling, raisins, and graham crackers can be discharged and mixed with the ice cream that has already become semifrozen. The ice cream is then piped to the next stage in the process, which is either filling (tubs, pints, etc.), extrusion, or molding.

⊠ OLD-FASHIONED APPLE   **Regular**

This is an autumn flavor that can't miss.

Batch   **Continuous**

2½ gallons	16% ice cream mix	100 gallons
2 ounces	two-fold vanilla extract	2½ quarts
2 quarts	spiced apples	20 gallons
½ ounce	cinnamon	20 ounces
	cinnamon and spiced apples for garnish	

Batch Freezing Method
Pour all ingredients into batch freezer. Turn on both dasher and refrigeration
and begin batch. When batch is complete, turn off refrigeration and extrude finished product.
    Decorate tops of tubs with spiced apple and cinnamon.

Batch time: 8–10 minutes.

Continuous Freezing Method
Before you start the continuous freezing of this flavor, make sure the sanitizing
solution or the previous flavor of mix has been pushed through the freezer.
Pour the spiced apples into the fruit feeder and adjust the controls to the appropriate setting. Open the outlet valve of the aging tank and let the proper
amount of ice cream mix flow into the flavor tank. Next, pour the vanilla extract
and cinnamon into the flavor tank, and mix all the ingredients thoroughly. The
mix is then pumped to the inlet of the continuous freezer. Set the speed, viscosity (stiffness), and overrun settings according to the manufacturer's recommendations. Start the continuous freezing process. As the ice cream leaves the continuous freezer, it is then piped through the fruit feeder (ingredient feeder) so
that the spiced apples can be discharged and mixed with the ice cream that has
already become semifrozen. The ice cream is then piped to the next stage in the
process, which is either filling (tubs, pints, etc.), extrusion, or molding.

⊠ PEACH COBBLER

Regular

This is a first-rate variation of peach ice cream.

Batch		Continuous
18–20 (yields 3 quarts puree)	peaches (fresh)*	800 (yields 30 gallons puree)
3 pounds	sugar	120 pounds
2½ gallons	16% ice cream mix	100 gallons
2 ounces	two-fold vanilla extract	2½ quarts
1 ounce	cinnamon	20 ounces
1 pound	graham crackers	40 pounds
	peach puree, graham crackers, and cinnamon for garnish	

Batch Freezing Method

Wash, cut, and remove the pits from the peaches. Do not peel the fruit because the skins enhance the flavor we are trying to achieve in the cobbler. Puree the cut peaches with 3 pounds of sugar and marinate mixture for at least 6 hours.

Pour all ingredients except graham crackers into batch freezer. Turn on both dasher and refrigeration and begin batch. Halfway into batch, as ice cream begins to freeze, add graham crackers. When batch is complete, turn off refrigeration and extrude finished product.

Decorate tops of tubs with peach puree, graham crackers, and cinnamon.

Batch time: 8–10 minutes.

Continuous Freezing Method

Wash, cut, and remove the pits from the peaches. Do not peel the fruit because the skins enhance the flavor we are trying to achieve in the cobbler. Puree the cut peaches with sugar and marinate mixture for at least 6 hours.*

Before you start the continuous freezing of this flavor, make sure the sanitizing solution or the previous flavor of mix has been pushed through the freezer. Pour the graham cracker pieces into the fruit feeder and adjust the controls to the appropriate setting. Open the outlet valve of the aging tank and let the proper amount of ice cream mix flow into the flavor tank. Next, pour the peach puree, vanilla extract, and cinnamon into the flavor tank and mix all the ingredients thoroughly. The mix is then pumped to the inlet of the continuous freezer. Set the speed, viscosity (stiffness), and overrun settings according to the manufacturer's recommendations. Start the continuous freezing process. As the ice cream leaves the continuous freezer, it is then piped through the fruit feeder (ingredient feeder) so that the graham cracker pieces can be discharged and mixed with the ice cream that has already become semifrozen. The ice cream is then piped to the next stage in the process, which is either filling (tubs, pints, etc.), extrusion, or molding.

*Note: To achieve the same peach flavor using frozen peaches, defrost the peaches, add sugar, and puree the fruit. Next, marinate the fruit for 6 hours.

⊠ PUMPKIN   **Regular**

A seasonal flavor appropriate from October through December, pumpkin also makes a great dessert for Thanksgiving and Christmas dinners.

Batch		Continuous
2½ gallons	16% ice cream mix	100 gallons
2 ounces	two-fold vanilla extract	2½ quarts
2½ quarts	pumpkin puree	25 gallons
2 ounces	cinnamon	2½ quarts
	cinnamon for garnish	

Batch Freezing Method
Pour all ingredients into batch freezer. Turn on both dasher and refrigeration. When batch is complete, turn off refrigeration and extrude finished product.

Decorate tops of tubs with cinnamon.

Batch time: 8–10 minutes.

Continuous Freezing Method
Before you start the continuous freezing of this flavor, make sure the sanitizing solution or the previous flavor of mix has been pushed through the freezer. Open the outlet valve of the aging tank and let the proper amount of ice cream mix flow into the flavor tank. Next, pour the pumpkin puree, vanilla extract, and cinnamon into the flavor tank and mix all the ingredients thoroughly. The mix is then pumped to the inlet of the continuous freezer. Set the speed, viscosity (stiffness), and overrun settings according to the manufacturer's recommendations. Start the continuous freezing process. As the ice cream leaves the continuous freezer, it is then piped to the next stage in the process, which is either filling (tubs, pints, etc.), extrusion, or molding.

⊠ CRANBERRY   Regular

This is another fall item that has wonderful body and flavor. It makes a suitable finale for Thanksgiving and Christmas dinners.

Batch		Continuous
10 pounds (yields 6 quarts puree)	fresh cranberries*	400 pounds (yields 60 gallons puree)
2 quarts	water	20 gallons
7 pounds	sugar	280 pounds
2½ gallons	16% ice cream mix	100 gallons
2 ounces	two-fold vanilla extract	2½ quarts
6 ounces	Triple Sec liqueur	7½ quarts
2 quarts	whole cranberry sauce	20 gallons
	whole cranberry sauce for garnish	

Batch Freezing Method

Combine fresh cranberries, sugar, and water. Puree, then strain the mixture. You should have 6 quarts of cranberry puree. Pour all ingredients except the Triple Sec and whole cranberry sauce into batch freezer. Turn on both dasher and refrigeration and begin batch.

At end of batch, add the Triple Sec and half of the whole cranberry sauce, turn off refrigeration, and extrude finished product. Using a spatula, swirl remaining whole cranberry sauce throughout the product as it fills tubs.

Decorate tops of tubs with whole cranberry sauce.

Batch time: 8–10 minutes.

Continuous Freezing Method

Combine fresh cranberries, sugar, and water. Puree, then strain the mixture. This mixture should yield approximately 60 gallons of cranberry puree.*

Before you start the continuous freezing of this flavor, make sure the sanitizing solution or the previous flavor of mix has been pushed through the freezer. Pour the whole cranberry sauce into the fruit feeder and adjust the controls to the appropriate setting. Open the outlet valve of the aging tank and let the proper amount of ice cream mix flow into the flavor tank. Next, pour the cranberry puree, vanilla extract, and Triple Sec liqueur into the flavor tank and mix all the ingredients thoroughly. The mix is then pumped to the inlet of the continuous freezer. Set the speed, viscosity (stiffness), and overrun settings according to the manufacturer's recommendations. Start the continuous freezing process. As the ice cream leaves the continuous freezer, it is then piped through the fruit feeder (ingredient feeder) so that the whole cranberry sauce can be discharged and mixed with the ice cream that has already become semifrozen. The ice cream is then piped to the next stage in the process, which is either filling (tubs, pints, etc.), extrusion, or molding.

---

*Note: You can achieve the same cranberry flavor using frozen cranberries or a processed cranberry puree. When using frozen cranberries, defrost the cranberries, add sugar and water, and puree the fruit. Next, marinate the fruit for 6 hours.

⊠ EGGNOG   **Regular**

This flavor is perfect for the Christmas and New Year holiday season. It is excellent for restaurant use.

Batch   **Continuous**
2½ gallons   16% ice cream mix   100 gallons
2 ounces   two-fold vanilla extract   2½ quarts
1½ quarts   eggnog base   15 gallons
1 ounce   nutmeg   2½ pounds
                nutmeg for garnish

Batch Freezing Method
Pour all ingredients into batch freezer. Turn on both dasher and refrigeration and begin batch. When batch is complete, turn off refrigeration and extrude finished product.

For decoration, sprinkle tops of tubs with nutmeg.

Batch time: 8–10 minutes.

Continuous Freezing Method
Before you start the continuous freezing of this flavor, make sure the sanitizing solution or the previous flavor of mix has been pushed through the freezer. Open the outlet valve of the aging tank and let the proper amount of ice cream mix flow into the flavor tank. Pour the vanilla extract, eggnog base, and nutmeg into the flavor tank and mix all the ingredients thoroughly. The mix is then pumped to the inlet of the continuous freezer. Set the speed, viscosity (stiffness), and overrun settings according to the manufacturer's recommendations. Start the continuous freezing process. As the ice cream leaves the continuous freezer, it is then piped to the next stage in the process, which is either filling (tubs, pints, etc.), extrusion, or molding.

⊠ EGGNOG CHIP   **Regular**

Chocolate chips add a touch of class to this exceptional flavor.

Batch   **Continuous**
2½ gallons   16% ice cream mix   100 gallons
2 ounces   two-fold vanilla extract   2½ quarts
1½ quarts   eggnog base   15 gallons
1 ounce   nutmeg   2½ pounds
1½ pounds   chocolate chips   60 pounds
                chocolate chips and nutmeg for garnish

Batch Freezing Method

Pour all ingredients into batch freezer. Turn on both dasher and refrigeration and begin batch. When batch is complete, turn off refrigeration and extrude finished product.

For decoration, sprinkle tops of tubs with nutmeg and chocolate chips.

Batch time: 8–10 minutes.

Continuous Freezing Method

Before you start the continuous freezing of this flavor, make sure the sanitizing solution or the previous flavor of mix has been pushed through the freezer. Pour the chocolate chips (40 degrees Fahrenheit) into the fruit feeder and adjust the controls to the appropriate setting. Open the outlet valve of the aging tank and let the proper amount of ice cream mix flow into the flavor tank. Next, pour the vanilla extract, eggnog base, and nutmeg into the flavor tank and mix all the ingredients thoroughly. The mix is then pumped to the inlet of the continuous freezer. Set the speed, viscosity (stiffness), and overrun settings according to the manufacturer's recommendations. Start the continuous freezing process. As the ice cream leaves the continuous freezer, it is then piped through the fruit feeder (ingredient feeder) so that the chocolate chips can be discharged and mixed with the ice cream that has already become semifrozen. The ice cream is then piped to the next stage in the process, which is either filling (tubs, pints, etc.), extrusion, or molding.

▨ STRAWBERRY CHEESECAKE   Superpremium

People love cheesecake, so why not give them an ice cream version? It really works and sells very well.

Batch		Continuous
2½ gallons	16% ice cream mix	100 gallons
2 ounces	two-fold vanilla extract	2½ quarts
3 pounds	commercial dry cheesecake mix*	120 pounds
2 quarts	processed strawberries	20 gallons
½ pound	graham crackers (broken)	20 pounds
	processed strawberries and	
	graham cracker pieces for garnish	

*Note: If you use a liquid cheesecake base, usage depends on manufacturer's recommendations.

Batch Freezing Method

Pour 1 gallon of ice cream mix into batch freezer and add dry cheesecake mix and vanilla extract. Turn on dasher to blend ingredients. Turn on refrigeration and begin batch. Near end of batch, pour in the strawberries and graham crackers. When batch is complete, turn off refrigeration and extrude finished product.

Decorate tops of tubs with processed strawberries and pieces of graham crackers.

Batch time: 9–11 minutes.

Continuous Freezing Method

Before you start the continuous freezing of this flavor, make sure the sanitizing solution or the previous flavor of mix has been pushed through the freezer. Pour the processed strawberries and graham crackers into the fruit feeder and adjust the controls to the appropriate setting. Open the outlet valve of the aging tank and let the proper amount of ice cream mix flow into the flavor tank. Next, pour the vanilla extract and cheesecake base into the flavor tank and mix all the ingredients thoroughly. The mix is then pumped to the inlet of the continuous freezer. Set the speed, viscosity (stiffness), and overrun settings according to the manufacturer's recommendations. Start the continuous freezing process. As the ice cream leaves the continuous freezer, it is then piped through the fruit feeder (ingredient feeder) so that the strawberries and graham crackers can be discharged and mixed with the ice cream that has already become semifrozen. The ice cream is then piped to the next stage in the process, which is either filling (tubs, pints, etc.), extrusion, or molding.

⊠ BLUEBERRY CHEESECAKE   Superpremium

Alternate this very popular cheesecake ice cream recipe with the strawberry cheesecake flavor.

Batch		Continuous
2½ gallons	16% ice cream mix	100 gallons
2 ounces	two-fold vanilla extract	2½ quarts
3 pounds	commercial dry cheesecake mix*	120 pounds
1½ quarts	processed sliced blueberries	15 gallons
½ pound	graham crackers (broken)	20 pounds
	processed sliced blueberries and	
	graham cracker pieces of garnish	

*Note: If you use a liquid cheesecake base, usage depends on manufacturer's recommendations.

Batch Freezing Method

Pour 1 gallon of ice cream mix into batch freezer and add dry cheesecake mix. Turn on dasher to blend ingredients. Pour in remaining ingredients except blueberries and graham crackers. Turn on refrigeration and begin batch. At end of batch, pour in blueberries and graham crackers. When batch is complete, turn off refrigeration and extrude finished product.

Decorate tops of tubs with pieces of graham crackers and blueberries.

Batch time: 9–11 minutes.

Continuous Freezing Method

Before you start the continuous freezing of this flavor, make sure the sanitizing solution or the previous flavor of mix has been pushed through the freezer. Pour the processed sliced blueberries and graham crackers into the fruit feeder and adjust the controls to the appropriate setting. Open the outlet valve of the aging tank and let the proper amount of ice cream mix flow into the flavor tank. Next, pour the vanilla extract and cheesecake base into the flavor tank, and mix all the ingredients thoroughly. The mix is then pumped to the inlet of the continuous freezer. Set the speed, viscosity (stiffness), and overrun settings according to the manufacturer's recommendations. Start the continuous freezing process. As the ice cream leaves the continuous freezer, it is then piped through the fruit feeder (ingredient feeder) so that the blueberries and graham crackers can be discharged and mixed with the ice cream that has already become semi-frozen. The ice cream is then piped to the next stage in the process, which is either filling (tubs, pints, etc.), extrusion, or molding.

⊠ WHITE CHOCOLATE   Superpremium

This flavor is one of the first gourmet flavors that I created. My wife, Barbara, loves white chocolate. She mentioned the idea of white chocolate ice cream to me one day when we were making chocolate truffles with white chocolate. Her instincts are right about a lot of things, and she certainly was right about this flavor.

Batch		Continuous
2½ gallons	16% ice cream mix	100 gallons
2 ounces	two-fold vanilla extract	2½ quarts
3½ pounds	white chocolate chunks	70 pounds
	white chocolate base*	9 gallons
	chunks of white chocolate for garnish	

*Note: For high volume commercial use, a prepared white chocolate base is more practical and economical. Usage depends on manufacturer's recommendation.

Batch Freezing Method
Using a double boiler, melt 2 pounds of white chocolate with 1 gallon of ice cream mix until smooth and creamy. Watch the melting chocolate closely and stir often. Do not allow mixture to boil or let chocolate become dried out from overcooking. (Overcooked chocolate looks chalky and sticks to the pot.) Cut remaining white chocolate into small chunks for later use.

Pour remaining ingredients into batch freezer and turn on dasher. Slowly pour white chocolate mixture into batch freezer, letting dasher run for 3 minutes. Turn on refrigeration and begin batch. At end of batch, add remaining white chocolate chunks, turn off refrigeration, and extrude finished product.

Decorate tops of tubs with white chocolate chunks.

Batch time: 9–11 minutes.

Continuous Freezing Method
Before you start the continuous freezing of this flavor, make sure the sanitizing solution or the previous flavor of mix has been pushed through the freezer. Pour 70 pounds of chocolate chunks (40 degrees Fahrenheit) into the fruit feeder and adjust the controls to the appropriate setting. Open the outlet valve of the aging tank and let the proper amount of ice cream mix flow into the flavor tank. Next, pour 9 gallons of white chocolate base and vanilla extract into the flavor tank and mix all the ingredients thoroughly. The mix is then pumped to the inlet of the continuous freezer. Set the speed, viscosity (stiffness), and overrun settings according to the manufacturer's recommendations. Start the continuous freezing process. As the ice cream leaves the continuous freezer, it is then piped through the fruit feeder (ingredient feeder) so that the white chocolate chunks can be discharged and mixed with the ice cream that has already become semifrozen. The ice cream is then piped to the next stage in the process, which is either filling (tubs, pints, etc.), extrusion, or molding.

▧ CHOCOLATE COCONUT CHIP   Regular

This flavor is a good idea for a change of pace when thinking of new items to create.

Batch		Continuous
2 pounds	cocoa (22–24%)	80 pounds
½ pound	sugar	20 pounds
6–8 cups	hot water	15 gallons
2½ gallons	16% ice cream mix	100 gallons
2 ounces	two-fold vanilla extract	2½ quarts
1 pound	chocolate chips	40 pounds
1 pound	shredded coconut	40 pounds
	shredded coconut and chocolate chips for garnish	

Batch Freezing Method

Thoroughly mix cocoa and sugar with 6–8 cups extremely hot water, adding more water as needed, until a smooth creamy paste is created.

Pour 1 gallon of ice cream mix into batch freezer and turn on dasher. Add cocoa paste and let dasher run for 5 minutes until mix and paste are smoothly blended. Add remaining ingredients except the coconut and chocolate chips. Turn on refrigeration and begin batch. Halfway into batch, as ice cream mix begins to freeze, add shredded coconut and chocolate chips. When batch is complete, turn off refrigeration and extrude finished product.

Decorate tops of tubs with shredded coconut and chocolate chips.

Batch time: 9–11 minutes.

Continuous Freezing Method

Before you start the continuous freezing of this flavor, make sure the sanitizing solution or the previous flavor of mix has been pushed through the freezer. Pour chocolate chips (40 degrees Fahrenheit) and shredded coconut into the fruit feeder and adjust the controls to the appropriate setting. Open the outlet valve of the aging tank and let the proper amount of chocolate ice cream mix flow into the flavor tank.*

Next, pour vanilla extract into the flavor tank. The mix is then pumped to the inlet of the continuous freezer. Set the speed, viscosity (stiffness), and overrun settings according to the manufacturer's recommendations. Start the continuous freezing process. As the ice cream leaves the continuous freezer, it is then piped through the fruit feeder (ingredient feeder) so that the shredded coconut and chocolate chips can be discharged and mixed with the ice cream that has already become semifrozen. The ice cream is then piped to the next stage in the process, which is either filling (tubs, pints, etc.), extrusion, or molding.

---

*Note: If you do not use a pasteurized chocolate ice cream mix, thoroughly mix the cocoa and sugar with hot water, adding more water as needed, until a smooth creamy paste has been created.

⊠ AMBROSIA   Superpremium

This recipe produces a refreshing blend of pineapple ice cream combined with the flavors of orange, coconut, and cherries.

Batch		Continuous
2½ gallons	16% ice cream mix	100 gallons
2 ounces	two-fold vanilla extract	2½ quarts
1 quart	orange-pineapple base	10 gallons
1 quart	pineapple base	10 gallons
½ pound	shredded coconut	20 pounds
1 quart	Bordeaux cherry halves	10 gallons
	coconut, pineapple base, and cherry halves for garnish	

Batch Freezing Method

Pour all ingredients into batch freezer and turn on both dasher and refrigeration. When batch is complete, turn off refrigeration and extrude finished product.

Decorate tops of tubs with coconut, pineapple base, and cherry halves.

Batch time: 8–10 minutes.

Continuous Freezing Method

Before you start the continuous freezing of this flavor, make sure the sanitizing solution or the previous flavor of mix has been pushed through the freezer. Pour shredded coconut and cherry halves into the fruit feeder and adjust the controls to the appropriate setting. Open the outlet valve of the aging tank and let the proper amount of ice cream mix flow into the flavor tank. Next, pour orange-pineapple base, pineapple base, and vanilla extract into the flavor tank, and mix all the ingredients thoroughly. The mix is then pumped to the inlet of the continuous freezer. Set the speed, viscosity (stiffness), and overrun settings according to the manufacturer's recommendations. Start the continuous freezing process. As the ice cream leaves the continuous freezer, it is then piped through the fruit feeder (ingredient feeder) so that the shredded coconut and cherry halves can be discharged and mixed with the ice cream that has already become semifrozen. The ice cream is then piped to the next stage in the process, which is either filling (tubs, pints, etc.), extrusion, or molding.

⊠ BANANA SPLIT   Superpremium

This is just the kind of flavor kids like—banana ice cream mixed with other fruits and nuts.

Batch		Continuous
2½ gallons	16% ice cream mix	100 gallons
2 ounces	two-fold vanilla extract	2½ quarts
8 pounds	fresh bananas (6 pounds peeled)*	
	banana puree (pasteurized)	25 gallons
1 quart	processed strawberries	10 gallons
½ quart	Bordeaux cherry halves	5 gallons
½ pound	sliced almonds	20 pounds
½ pound	shredded coconut	20 pounds
	strawberries, coconut, bananas, and cherry halves for garnish	

*Note: 8 pounds of whole bananas will yield approximately 6 pounds of peeled bananas because banana skin is approximately 20 percent of the weight of a banana.

Batch Freezing Method

Pour ice cream mix, vanilla extract, and peeled bananas into batch freezer. Turn on both dasher and refrigeration. At end of batch, add strawberries, cherries, almonds, and shredded coconut. When batch is complete, turn off refrigeration and extrude finished product.

Decorate tops of tubs with strawberries, cherries, bananas, and shredded coconut.

Batch time: 8–10 minutes.

Continuous Freezing Method

Before you start the continuous freezing of this flavor, make sure the sanitizing solution or the previous flavor of mix has been pushed through the freezer. Pour strawberries, sliced almonds, shredded coconut, and cherry halves into the fruit feeder and adjust the controls to the appropriate setting. Open the outlet valve of the aging tank and let the proper amount of ice cream mix flow into the flavor tank. Next, pour banana puree and vanilla extract into the flavor tank and mix all the ingredients thoroughly. The mix is then pumped to the inlet of the continuous freezer. Set the speed, viscosity (stiffness), and overrun settings according to the manufacturer's recommendations. Start the continuous freezing process. As the ice cream leaves the continuous freezer, it is then piped through the fruit feeder (ingredient feeder) so that the strawberries, sliced almonds, shredded coconut, and cherry halves can be discharged and mixed with the ice cream that has already become semifrozen. The ice cream is then piped to the next stage in the process, which is either filling (tubs, pints, etc.), extrusion, or molding.

⊠ BLUEBERRY HONEY GRAHAM   Regular

This honey-flavored ice cream with a swirl of blueberry sauce and graham crackers is bound to attract attention. Be sure to use a quality honey to flavor the mix.

Batch		Continuous
2½ gallons	16% ice cream mix	100 gallons
2 ounces	two-fold vanilla extract	80 ounces
½ quart	honey	5 gallons
1 pound	graham crackers	40 pounds
2 quarts	sliced processed blueberries	20 gallons
	processed sliced blueberries and	
	graham crackers for garnish	

Batch Freezing Method
Pour all ingredients except the sliced blueberries and graham crackers into batch freezer. Turn on both dasher and refrigeration and begin batch. At end of batch, add graham crackers. When batch is complete, turn off refrigeration and, using a spatula, swirl processed sliced blueberries into finished product as it is being extruded into tubs.
      Decorate tops of tubs with blueberries and graham crackers.

Batch time: 8–10 minutes.

Continuous Freezing Method
Before you start the continuous freezing of this flavor, make sure the sanitizing solution or the previous flavor of mix has been pushed through the freezer. Pour sliced blueberries and graham crackers into the fruit feeder and adjust the controls to the appropriate setting. Open the outlet valve of the aging tank and let the proper amount of ice cream mix flow into the flavor tank. Next, pour honey and vanilla extract into the flavor tank and mix all the ingredients thoroughly. The mix is then pumped to the inlet of the continuous freezer. Set the speed, viscosity (stiffness), and overrun settings according to the manufacturer's recommendations. Start the continuous freezing process. As the ice cream leaves the continuous freezer, it is then piped through the fruit feeder (ingredient feeder) so that the sliced blueberries and graham crackers can be discharged and mixed with the ice cream that has already become semifrozen. The ice cream is then piped to the next stage in the process, which is either filling (tubs, pints, etc.), extrusion, or molding.

⊠ COCONUT FUDGE   Regular

This recipe produces a delicious coconut ice cream with a swirl of fudge.

Batch		**Continuous**
2½ gallons	16% ice cream mix	100 gallons
2 ounces	two-fold vanilla extract	80 ounces
1–1½ quarts	coconut fruit base*	13–15 gallons
½ pound	shredded coconut	20 pounds
1½ quarts	fudge	
	fudge variegate	15 gallons
	shredded coconut and fudge for garnish	

*Note: Amount to use depends on the strength of the flavor desired.

Batch Freezing Method
Pour all ingredients except fudge and half of shredded coconut into batch freezer. Turn on both dasher and refrigeration and begin batch. At end of

batch, add remaining shredded coconut. When batch is complete, turn off refrigeration and extrude finished product into tubs while using a spatula to swirl fudge into coconut ice cream.

Decorate tops of tubs with shredded coconut and fudge.

Batch time: 8–10 minutes.

Continuous Freezing Method

Before you start the continuous freezing of this flavor, make sure the sanitizing solution or the previous flavor of mix has been pushed through the freezer. Pour the chilled (40 degrees Fahrenheit) fudge variegate into the ripple pump supply tank and adjust speed to inject at the rate as prescribed in the formula, or approximately 10–14 percent of the weight of the ice cream mix. Pour shredded coconut into the fruit feeder and adjust the controls to the appropriate setting. Open the outlet valve of the aging tank and let the proper amount of ice cream mix flow into the flavor tank.

Next, pour coconut fruit base and vanilla extract into the flavor tank and mix all the ingredients thoroughly. The mix is then pumped to the inlet of the continuous freezer. Set the speed, viscosity (stiffness), and overrun settings according to the manufacturer's recommendations. Start the continuous freezing process. As the ice cream leaves the continuous freezer, it is then piped through the fruit feeder (ingredient feeder) so that the shredded coconut can be discharged and mixed with the ice cream. The ice cream is then piped through the ripple injection unit so that the fudge variegating sauce can be injected into the stream of ice cream that has already become semifrozen. The ice cream is then piped to the next stage in the process, which is either filling (tubs, pints, etc.), extrusion, or molding.

⬨ LEMON CUSTARD   Regular

Any form of lemon is considered a year-round refresher, and this ice cream flavor is right on the mark.

Batch		**Continuous**
2½ gallons	16% ice cream mix	100 gallons
2 ounces	two-fold vanilla extract	2½ quarts
¾ quart	lemon custard base	7½ gallons
1 ounce	fruit acid	1¼ quarts
	lemon slices for garnish	

Batch Freezing Method

Pour all ingredients except fruit acid into batch freezer. Turn on both dasher and refrigeration and begin batch. As ice cream begins to freeze, add fruit acid. When batch is complete, turn off refrigeration and extrude finished product.

Decorate tops of tubs with thin lemon slices.

Batch time: 8–10 minutes.

Continuous Freezing Method

Before you start the continuous freezing of this flavor, make sure the sanitizing solution or the previous flavor of mix has been pushed through the freezer. Open the outlet valve of the aging tank and let the proper amount of ice cream mix flow into the flavor tank. Pour lemon custard base, vanilla extract, and fruit acid into the flavor tank, and mix all the ingredients thoroughly. The mix is then pumped to the inlet of the continuous freezer. Set the speed, viscosity (stiffness), and overrun settings according to the manufacturer's recommendations. Start the continuous freezing process. As the ice cream leaves the continuous freezer, it is then piped to the next stage in the process, which is either filling (tubs, pints, etc.), extrusion, or molding.

⊠ CHERRIES JUBILEE   Superpremium

A festive dessert for any special occasion, the touch of brandy enhances the cherry flavor of this tasty ice cream.

Batch		Continuous
2½ gallons	16% ice cream mix	100 gallons
2 ounces	two-fold vanilla extract	2½ quarts
1½ quarts	Bordeaux cherry halves	15 gallons
10 ounces	brandy	
	brandy flavor*	3¼ quarts
	brandy-soaked cherry halves for garnish	

*Note: Amount to use varies according to manufacturer's recommendations.

Batch Freezing Method

Pour all ingredients except half the cherries and brandy into batch freezer. Turn on both dasher and refrigeration and begin batch. Halfway into batch, as ice cream begins to freeze, add brandy. At end of batch, add remaining cherry halves. When batch is complete, turn off refrigeration and extrude finished product.

Decorate tops of tubs with cherry halves that have been soaked in brandy. (Place cherries in a container and pour just enough brandy to barely cover the tops of cherries. Soak for 15 minutes.)

Batch time: 9–11 minutes.

Continuous Freezing Method

Before you start the continuous freezing of this flavor, make sure the sanitizing solution or the previous flavor of mix has been pushed through the freezer. Pour cherry halves into the fruit feeder and adjust the controls to the appropriate setting. Open the outlet valve of the aging tank and let the proper amount of ice cream flow mix into the flavor tank. Next, pour brandy flavor and vanilla extract into the flavor tank and mix all the ingredients thoroughly. The mix is then pumped to the inlet of the continuous freezer. Set the speed, viscosity (stiffness), and overrun settings according to the manufacturer's recommendations. Start the continuous freezing process. As the ice cream leaves the continuous freezer, it is then piped through the fruit feeder (ingredient feeder) so that the cherry halves can be discharged and mixed with the ice cream that has already become semifrozen. The ice cream is then piped to the next stage in the process, which is either filling (tubs, pints, etc.), extrusion, or molding.

⊠ BISCUIT TORTONI   Superpremium

With its unusual almond-tasting flavor, the addition of sweet sherry and almond cookies makes this flavor a hit in restaurants and upscale operations.

Batch		Continuous
2½ gallons	16% ice cream mix	100 gallons
2 ounces	two-fold vanilla extract	2½ quarts
1½ ounces	almond extract*	1¾ quarts
1 pound	sliced almonds	40 pounds
10 ounces	sweet sherry	
	sherry flavor* (1 ounce per gallon)	3¼ quarts
1½ pounds	crushed almond cookies	60 pounds
	almond cookies pieces and sliced almonds for garnish	

*Note: Amount to use varies according to manufacturer's recommendations.

Batch Freezing Method
Pour all ingredients except sweet sherry and almond cookies into batch freezer. Turn on both dasher and refrigeration and begin batch. Halfway into batch, as ice cream begins to freeze, add sweet sherry. At end of batch, add crushed almond cookies. When batch is complete, turn off refrigeration and extrude finished product.

Decorate tops of tubs with pieces of almond cookies and sliced almonds.

Batch time: 9–11 minutes.

Continuous Freezing Method

Before you start the continuous freezing of this flavor, make sure the sanitizing solution or the previous flavor of mix has been pushed through the freezer. Pour almond cookies and sliced almonds into the fruit feeder and adjust the controls to the appropriate setting. Open the outlet valve of the aging tank and let the proper amount of ice cream mix flow into the flavor tank. Next, pour sherry flavor and vanilla extract into the flavor tank and mix all the ingredients thoroughly. The mix is then pumped to the inlet of the continuous freezer. Set the speed, viscosity (stiffness), and overrun settings according to the manufacturer's recommendations. Start the continuous freezing process. As the ice cream leaves the continuous freezer, it is then piped through the fruit feeder (ingredient feeder) so that the almond cookies and sliced almonds can be discharged and mixed with the ice cream that has aleardy become semifrozen. The ice cream is then piped to the next stage in the process, which is either filling (tubs, pints, etc.), extrusion, or molding.

 TAPIOCA   **Superpremium**

I love tapioca pudding! What else can I say?

Batch		Continuous
1½ pounds	dry tapioca	60 pounds
2½ gallons	16% ice cream mix	100 gallons
2 ounces	two-fold vanilla extract	2½ quarts
1 ounce	nutmeg	1¼ quarts
	nutmeg for garnish	

Batch Freezing Method

Prepare tapioca following manufacturer's instructions. Refrigerate cooked tapioca until completely cooled.

Pour all ingredients into batch freezer. Turn on both dasher and refrigeration and begin batch. When batch is complete, turn off refrigeration and extrude finished product.

For decoration, sprinkle tops of tubs with nutmeg.

Batch time: 8–10 minutes.

Continuous Freezing Method

Before you start the continuous freezing of this flavor, make sure the sanitizing solution or the previous flavor of mix has been pushed through the freezer. Open the outlet valve of the aging tank and let the proper amount of ice cream flow into the flavor tank. Pour prepared tapioca, vanilla extract, and nutmeg into the flavor tank and mix all the ingredients thoroughly. The mix is then pumped to the inlet of the continuous freezer. Set the speed, viscosity (stiffness), and overrun settings according to the manufacturer's recommendations. Start the continuous freezing process. As the ice cream leaves the continuous freezer, it is then piped to the next stage in the process, which is either filling (tubs, pints, etc.), extrusion, or molding.

Liquor and Liqueur Flavors

What succeeds as a beverage often succeeds as an ice cream flavor, sometimes even better. Ice cream makers have experimented with nearly every liquor and liqueur flavor imaginable, and recipes for the most popular results are presented here.

Care should be taken when using liquors, wines, or liqueurs because the alcohol in them can inhibit the freezing process. The use of alcoholic ingredients in a batch freezing operation will increase the freezing time by about 2–3 minutes. Alcoholic ingredients are usually added to the ice cream in production in the middle or at the end of the freezing stage. Natural or artificial liquor or liqueur extracts or flavorings can be added any time during the freezing process.

⊠ RUM RAISIN   Superpremium

This savory flavor appeals to an older clientele. Use golden raisins and make sure the finished flavor has a distinct rum taste.

Batch		Continuous
2½ gallons	16% ice cream mix	100 gallons
2 ounces	two-fold vanilla extract	2½ quarts
½ quart	rum flavoring*	5 gallons
2 pounds	golden raisins	80 pounds
	raisins for garnish	

*Note: Amount to use varies according to manufacturer's recommendations.

Batch Freezing Method
Pour all ingredients except half the golden raisins into batch freezer. Turn on both dasher and refrigeration and begin batch. At end of batch, add remaining golden raisins, turn off refrigeration, and extrude finished product.

Decorate tops of tubs with raisins.

Batch time: 9–11 minutes.

Continuous Freezing Method

Before you start the continuous freezing of this flavor, make sure the sanitizing solution or the previous flavor of mix has been pushed through the freezer. Pour the raisins into the fruit feeder and adjust the controls to the appropriate setting. Open the outlet valve of the aging tank and let the proper amount of ice cream mix flow into the flavor tank. Next, pour vanilla extract and rum flavoring into the flavor tank and mix all the ingredients thoroughly. The mix is then pumped to the inlet of the continuous freezer. Set the speed, viscosity (stiffness), and overrun settings according to the manufacturer's recommendations. Start the continuous freezing process. As the ice cream leaves the continuous freezer, it is then piped through the fruit feeder (ingredient feeder) so that the raisins can be discharged and mixed with the ice cream that has already become semifrozen. The ice cream is then piped to the next stage in the process, which is either filling (tubs, pints, etc.), extrusion, or molding.

⊠ CREME DE MENTHE   Superpremium

Geared toward an adult market, this flavor sells very well in upscale operations and restaurants.

Batch		Continuous
2½ gallons	16% ice cream mix	100 gallons
2 ounces	two-fold vanilla extract	2½ quarts
15 ounces	creme de menthe liqueur	
	creme de menthe flavoring*	4½ gallons
1 pound	chocolate chips	40 pounds
	chocolate chips for garnish	

*Note: Amount to use varies according to manufacturer's recommendations.

Batch Freezing Method

Pour ice cream mix, vanilla extract, and half the chocolate chips into batch freezer. Turn on both dasher and refrigeration and begin batch. Halfway into batch, as mix begins to freeze, add creme de menthe liqueur. At end of batch, add remaining chocolate chips, turn off refrigeration, and extrude finished product.

Decorate tops of tubs with chocolate chips.

Batch time: 9–11 minutes.

Continuous Freezing Method

Before you start the continuous freezing of this flavor, make sure the sanitizing solution or the previous flavor of mix has been pushed through the freezer. Pour the chocolate chips (40 degrees Fahrenheit) into the fruit feeder and adjust the controls to the appropriate setting. Open the outlet valve of the aging tank and let the proper amount of ice cream mix flow into the flavor tank. Next, pour the vanilla extract and creme de menthe flavoring into the flavor tank and mix all the ingredients thoroughly. The mix is then pumped to the inlet of the continuous freezer. Set the speed, viscosity (stiffness), and overrun settings according to the manufacturer's recommendations. Start the continuous freezing process. As the ice cream leaves the continuous freezer, it is then piped through the fruit feeder (ingredient feeder) so that the chocolate chips can be discharged and mixed with the ice cream that has already become semifrozen. The ice cream is then piped to the next stage in the process, which is either filling (tubs, pints, etc.), extrusion, or molding.

⊠ CHOCOLATE CREME CAKE   Superpremium

This recipe produces a rich and flavorful ice cream that includes Bailey's Irish Cream liqueur.

Batch		**Continuous**
1¾ pounds	cocoa (22–24% fat)	70 pounds
5–7 cups	hot water	12½ gallons
⅓ pound	sugar	13¼ pounds
2½ gallons	16% ice cream mix	100 gallons
2 ounces	two-fold vanilla extract	2½ quarts
2 pounds	chocolate cake	80 pounds
13 ounces	Bailey's Irish Cream liqueur	
	Irish cream flavor*	
	chocolate cake pieces for garnish	

*Note: Amount to use varies according to manufacturer's recommendations.

Batch Freezing Method

Thoroughly mix the cocoa and sugar with 5–7 cups extremely hot water, adding more water as needed, until a smooth creamy paste is created.

Pour 1 gallon of ice cream mix into batch freezer and turn on dasher. Add cocoa paste and let dasher run for 5 minutes until mix and paste are smoothly blended. Add remaining ice cream mix, vanilla extract, and half the chocolate cake to batch and turn on refrigeration.

Halfway into batch, as ice cream mix is beginning to freeze, add Bailey's Irish Cream. At end of batch, add remaining chocolate cake, turn off refrigeration, and extrude finished product.

Decorate tops of tubs with chocolate cake.

Batch time: 9–11 minutes.

Continuous Freezing Method

Before you start the continuous freezing of this flavor, make sure the sanitizing solution or the previous flavor of mix has been pushed through the freezer. Pour the chocolate cake pieces into the fruit feeder and adjust the controls to the appropriate setting. Open the outlet valve of the aging tank and let the proper amount of chocolate ice cream mix flow into the flavor tank.*

Next, pour the vanilla extract and Irish creme flavoring into the flavor tank, and mix all the ingredients thoroughly. The mix is then pumped to the inlet of the continuous freezer. Set the speed, viscosity (stiffness), and overrun settings according to the manufacturer's recommendations. Start the continuous freezing process. As the ice cream leaves the continuous freezer, it is then piped through the fruit feeder (ingredient feeder) so that the chocolate cake pieces can be discharged and mixed with the ice cream that has already become semi-frozen. The ice cream is then piped to the next stage in the process, which is either filling (tubs, pints, etc.), extrusion, or molding.

---

*Note: If you do not use a pasteurized chocolate ice cream mix, thoroughly mix the cocoa and sugar with hot water in a large mixer, adding more water as needed, until a smooth creamy paste has been added.

⊠ GRAND MARNIER   Superpremium

In the liqueur category of flavors, Grand Marnier stands out for its sophisticated flavor. It is very popular in restaurants and upscale ice cream operations.

Batch		Continuous
2½ gallons	16% ice cream mix	100 gallons
2 ounces	two-fold vanilla extract	2½ quarts
16 ounces	Grand Marnier liqueur	
	Grand Marnier flavoring*	5 gallons

---

*Note: Amount to use varies according to manufacturer's recommendations.

Batch Freezing Method

Pour all ingredients except Grand Marnier liqueur into batch freezer. Turn on both dasher and refrigeration and begin batch. Halfway into batch, add Grand Marnier. (The liqueur inhibits the freezing process if entered earlier.) When batch is complete, turn off refrigeration and extrude finished product.

Batch time: 9–11 minutes.

Continuous Freezing Method

Before you start the continuous freezing of this flavor, make sure the sanitizing solution or the previous flavor of mix has been pushed through the freezer. Open the outlet valve of the aging tank and let the proper amount of ice cream mix flow into the flavor tank.

Next, pour the vanilla extract and Grand Marnier flavoring into the flavor tank and mix all the ingredients thoroughly. The mix is then pumped to the inlet of the continuous freezer. Set the speed, viscosity (stiffness), and overrun settings according to the manufacturer's recommendations. Start the continuous freezing process. As the ice cream leaves the continuous freezer, it is then piped to the next stage in the process, which is either filling (tubs, pints, etc.), extrusion, or molding.

⬚ PEACH COGNAC   Superpremium

I enjoy eating peaches and peach ice cream during the summer, so this flavor was a natural for me to create.

Batch		Continuous
2½ gallons	16% ice cream mix	100 gallons
2 ounces	two-fold vanilla extract	2½ quarts
2 ounces	peach ice cream flavor	2½ quarts
10 ounces	cognac	
	cognac flavoring*	3 gallons
2 pounds	processed peaches	80 pounds
	processed peaches for garnish	

*Note: Amount to use varies according to manufacturer's recommendations.

Batch Freezing Method

Pour all ingredients except cognac into batch freezer. Turn on both dasher and refrigeration. Halfway into batch, add cognac. When batch is complete, turn off refrigeration and extrude finished product.

Decorate tops of tubs with stabilized peaches.

Batch time: 9–11 minutes.

Continuous Freezing Method
Before you start the continuous freezing of this flavor, make sure the sanitizing solution or the previous flavor of mix has been pushed through the freezer. Pour the stabilized peaches into the fruit feeder and adjust the controls to the appropriate setting. Open the outlet valve of the aging tank and let the proper amount of ice cream mix flow into the flavor tank. Next, pour the vanilla extract and cognac flavoring into the flavor tank and mix all the ingredients thoroughly. The mix is then pumped to the inlet of the continuous freezer. Set the speed, viscosity (stiffness), and overrun settings according to the manufacturer's recommendations. Start the continuous freezing process. As the ice cream leaves the continuous freezer, it is then piped through the fruit feeder (ingredient feeder) so that the peaches can be discharged and mixed with the ice cream that has already become semifrozen. The ice cream is then piped to the next stage in the process, which is either filling (tubs, pints, etc.), extrusion, or molding.

⊠ CHERRY AMARETTO   Superpremium

This recipe is a variation of Amaretto ice cream. The flavor of cherries marries well with amaretto and this flavor is a good addition to any seasonal line.

Batch		Continuous
2½ gallons	16% ice cream mix	100 gallons
2 ounces	two-fold vanilla extract	2½ quarts
4 ounces	Amaretto flavor (extract)*	1¼ gallons
1 quart	Bordeaux cherry halves (with some juice)	10 gallons
½ pound	sliced almonds	20 pounds
	cherry halves and sliced almonds for garnish	

*Note: Amount to use varies according to manufacturer's recommendations.

Batch Freezing Method
Pour all ingredients except cherry halves and sliced almonds into batch freezer. Turn on both dasher and refrigeration. Halfway into batch, add cherry halves and sliced almonds. When batch is complete, turn off refrigeration and extrude finished product.
    Decorate tops of tubs with cherry halves and sliced almonds.

Batch time: 9–11 minutes.

Continuous Freezing Method
Before you start the continuous freezing of this flavor, make sure the sanitizing solution or the previous flavor of mix has been pushed through the freezer. Pour the cherry halves (drained) and sliced almonds into the fruit feeder and

adjust the controls to the appropriate setting. Open the outlet valve of the aging tank and let the proper amount of ice cream mix flow into the flavor tank. Next, pour the vanilla extract, amaretto flavoring, and the cherry juice (juice drained from the cherry halves) into the flavor tank and mix all the ingredients thoroughly. The mix is then pumped to the inlet of the continuous freezer. Set the speed, viscosity (stiffness), and overrun settings according to the manufacturer's recommendations. Start the continuous freezing process. As the ice cream leaves the continuous freezer, it is then piped through the fruit feeder (ingredient feeder) so that the cherry halves and sliced almonds can be discharged and mixed with the ice cream that has already become semifrozen. The ice cream is then piped to the next stage in the process, which is either filling (tubs, pints, etc.), extrusion, or molding.

⊠ KAHLUA   Superpremium

Kahlua coffee-flavored liqueur was one of the first liqueurs to become popular as a beverage, so it was only natural that it became one of the first liqueur flavors to be produced as an ice cream. Its popularity is still strong and I recommend it highly. Coffee candy adds a touch of class.

Batch		Continuous
4 ounces	freeze-dried coffee	10 pounds
½ ounce	cocoa (22–24% fat)	1¼ pounds
2 tablespoons	hot water	1¼ quarts
2½ gallons	16% ice cream mix	100 gallons
2 ounces	two-fold vanilla extract	2½ quarts
3 ounces	coffee liqueur flavor*	3¾ quarts
	OR	
18 ounces	Kahlua liqueur	
1 pound	hard coffee candy	40 pounds
	hard coffee candy for garnish	

*Note: Amount to use varies according to manufacturer's recommendations.

Batch Freezing Method

Mix freeze-dried coffee with as little hot water as possible and add cocoa. Mix thoroughly so that resulting paste is smooth, with no dry coffee or cocoa visible.

Pour all ingredients including coffee paste and coffee liqueur flavor, if used instead of Kahlua, into batch freezer and let dasher run for approximately 2 minutes to blend coffee paste evenly into the mix. Turn on refrigeration and begin batch. If Kahlua is used instead of coffee liqueur flavor, add it halfway into batch. When batch is complete, turn off refrigeration and extrude finished product.

Decorate tops of tubs with hard coffee candy.

Batch time: 9–11 minutes.

Continuous Freezing Method

Before you start the continuous freezing of this flavor, make sure the sanitizing solution or the previous flavor of mix has been pushed through the freezer.

Mix freeze-dried coffee with as little water as possible and add cocoa. The resulting paste should be smooth with no dry coffee or cocoa visible. Pour the coffee candy into the fruit feeder and adjust the controls to the appropriate setting. Open the outlet valve of the aging tank and let the proper amount of ice cream mix flow into the flavor tank. Next, pour the vanilla extract, prepared coffee base, and coffee liqueur flavoring into the flavor tank and mix all the ingredients thoroughly. The mix is then pumped to the inlet of the continuous freezer. Set the speed, viscosity (stiffness), and overrun settings according to the manufacturer's recommendations. Start the continuous freezing process. As the ice cream leaves the continuous freezer, it is then piped through the fruit feeder (ingredient feeder) so that the coffee candy pieces can be discharged and mixed with the ice cream that has already become semifrozen. The ice cream is then piped to the next stage in the process, which is either filling (tubs, pints, etc.), extrusion, or molding.

⊠ IRISH COFFEE   Superpremium

The name sells the flavor. It is excellent for use in restaurants because of the strong flavor of Irish whiskey.

Batch		Continuous
4 ounces	freeze-dried coffee	10 pounds
½ ounce	cocoa (22–24% fat)	1¼ pounds
2 tablespoons	hot water	1¼ quarts
2½ gallons	16% ice cream mix	100 gallons
2 ounces	two-fold vanilla extract	2½ quarts
15 ounces	Irish whiskey	
	Irish whiskey flavor*	4½ gallons

*Note: Amount to use varies according to manufacturer's recommendations.

Batch Freezing Method

Mix freeze-dried coffee with as little hot water as possible. Mix thoroughly so that the resulting paste is smooth, with no dry coffee visible. Pour all ingredients except Irish whiskey into batch freezer and let the dasher run for approximately 2 minutes to blend coffee mixture evenly into mix. Turn on refrigeration and begin batch. Halfway into batch, add Irish whiskey. When batch is complete, turn off refrigeration and extrude finished product.

Batch time: 9–11 minutes.

Continuous Freezing Method

Before you start the continuous freezing of this flavor, make sure the sanitizing solution or the previous flavor of mix has been pushed through the freezer.

Mix freeze-dried coffee with as little water as possible and add cocoa. The resulting paste should be smooth with no dry coffee or cocoa visible. Open the outlet valve of the aging tank and let the proper amount of ice cream mix flow into the flavor tank. Next, pour the vanilla extract, prepared coffee base, and Irish whiskey flavoring into the flavor tank and mix all the ingredients thoroughly. The mix is then pumped to the inlet of the continuous freezer. Set the speed, viscosity (stiffness), and overrun settings according to the manufacturer's recommendations. Start the continuous freezing process. As the ice cream leaves the continuous freezer, it is then piped to the next stage in the process, which is either filling (tubs, pints, etc.), extrusion, or molding.

⊠ CREME DE CACAO   Superpremium

With its smooth liqueur flavor, this ice cream can be advertised as "for adults only."

Batch		Continuous
2 tablespoons	hot water	1¼ quarts
2½ gallons	16% ice cream mix	100 gallons
2 ounces	two-fold vanilla extract	2½ quarts
16 ounces	creme de cacao	4 gallons
1½ pounds	chocolate chips	60 pounds
	chocolate chips for garnish	

Batch Freezing Method

Pour all ingredients except the creme de cacao and half the ice cream chips into batch freezer. Turn on both dasher and refrigeration and begin batch. Halfway into batch, as ice cream begins to freeze, add creme de cacao. At end of batch, add remaining chocolate chips, turn off refrigeration, and extrude finished product.

Decorate tops of tubs with chocolate chips.

Batch time: 9–11 minutes.

Continuous Freezing Method

Before you start the continuous freezing of this flavor, make sure the sanitizing solution or the previous flavor of mix has been pushed through the freezer. Pour the chocolate chips (40 degrees Fahrenheit) into the fruit feeder and adjust the controls to the appropriate setting. Open the outlet valve of the aging tank and let the proper amount of ice cream mix flow into the flavor tank. Next, pour the vanilla extract and creme de cacao flavoring into the flavor tank and mix all the ingredients thoroughly. The mix is then pumped to the inlet of the continuous freezer. Set the speed, viscosity (stiffness), and overrun settings according to the manufacturer's recommendations. Start the continuous freezing process. As the ice cream leaves the continuous freezer, it is then piped through the fruit feeder (ingredient feeder) so that the chocolate chips can be discharged and mixed with the ice cream that has already become semifrozen. The ice cream is then piped to the next stage in the process, which is either filling (tubs, pints, etc.), extrusion, or molding.

14 ▨▨▨▨▨▨▨▨▨▨▨▨▨▨▨▨▨▨▨▨▨▨▨▨▨▨

ITALIAN GELATO

ITS MYSTIQUE AND ALLURE

Every time I talk to someone who has just come back from Italy, I hear the same story: "Wow, was the gelato fantastic, I could have eaten it for breakfast, lunch, and supper." Gelato is indeed a great frozen dairy dessert because of its freshness, softness, flavor, and foreign mystique. While it is much more popular in Europe and South America than in the United States, gelato is slowly building a solid niche in different parts of the country (California, Florida, New York, and Illinois). The main reason for this slow growth has been the dominance that American-style ice cream has had in our eating patterns. Anything untraditional usually has a hard time gaining consumer acceptance.

Gelato is a creamy low-fat ice-cream style product. When made in Italy, it typically contains 5.7 percent butterfat and is produced at 20–30 percent overrun. In the United States, consumers prefer a creamier flavor and the gelato produced here has approximately 10 percent butterfat and a 30–35 percent overrun. The basic ingredients are milk, fresh cream, sugar, and egg-yolk solids. The low overrun allows the flavor to be absorbed by the cream, resulting in a unique smoothness and density of flavor.

And if there is one thing gelato is noted for, it is intensity of flavor—the main difference between American ice cream and gelato. American-style ice cream emphasizes body, texture, and particulates; gelato emphasizes flavor. Regardless of the flavor produced, gelato has a uniquely intense flavor.

The following is a broad list of gelato flavors:

Amarena: cherry
Amaretto: almonds, chocolate, and macaroons
Cassata: candied fruit in syrup (for spumoni)
Cacao: rich dark chocolate
Caffe: espresso

Croccantino: almond crunch and rum
Fragola: strawberry
Gianduja: chocolate and hazelnut
Lauretta: cherries with cream
Limone: lemon
Malaga: rum raisin
Marron Glace: chestnut
Melone: melon
Mirtillo: blueberry
Nocciola: hazelnut
Stracciatella: chocolate flake
Tartufo: chocolate with whole hazelnuts
Tartufo Bianco: white chocolate with whole hazelnuts
Tiramisu: coffee and Marsala wine
Torrone: honey, almonds, and nougat
Zabaione: egg, honey, and Marsala wine
Zuppa Inglesse: English trifle

The most popular flavors are hazelnut, Gianduja, Amaretto, and strawberry. When working with imported flavor ingredients, you have to be aware of the metric system and its application to the U.S. market. Since all Italian gelato recipes are described in grams, liters, and kilograms, following you will find a simple conversion to ounces, gallons, and pounds:

$$1 \text{ ounce } = 28.3 \text{ grams}$$
$$1 \text{ gallon } = 3.78 \text{ liters}$$
$$1 \text{ pound} = 2.2 \text{ kilograms}$$

Note: All measurements of flavor ingredients for the recipes in this chapter are stated in pounds for use in batch freezer operations. These ingredients, for the most part, are packed in 6-kilo (13.2 pound) cans and the usage level recommended by the manufacturers are usually stated for the American market by weight.

GELATO RECIPES

As with other frozen desserts, product presentation is extremely important. The gelato should be firm (14–18 degrees Fahrenheit) but not hard, and not so soft that it is melting by the time it reaches the customer. Before being sold, the gelato should be frozen for about 4 hours after production. It should not be stored for sale from one day to the next, but should be produced daily to maintain freshness and flavor. Serve each portion with a garnish that represents its flavor.

The recipes in this section are based on using 10 percent gelato mix, a French mix with 1.4 percent egg-yolk solids, and Italian manufactured ingredients from Pre Gel, Monte Bianco, Perugina, and Fabri. You will have no problem using these recipes in Coldelite, Emery Thompson, and Taylor batch freezers, as well as any kind of continuous freezer. If you have a batch freezer with high and low speeds, make sure you produce gelato only on the low speed to reduce overrun below 50 percent. The low speed helps to create the creamy dense texture that is desired.

These recipes are all prime sellers, but many other flavors can be produced. Let your imagination go!

⊠ VANILLA

Just like in ice cream, your vanilla gelato should be the benchmark of all your gelato flavors.

Batch		**Continuous**
2½ gallons	5–10% gelato mix	100 gallons
3½ ounces	two-fold vanilla extract	4⅓ quarts

Batch Freezing Method
Pour ingredients into batch freezer, turn on both dasher and refrigeration, and begin batch. When batch is complete, turn off refrigeration and extrude finished product.

Batch time: 8–9 minutes.

Continuous Freezing Method
Before you start the continuous freezing of this flavor, make sure the sanitizing solution or the previous flavor of gelato mix has been pushed through the freezer. Open the outlet valve of the mix storage tank and let the proper amount of gelato mix flow into the flavor tank. Pour the vanilla extract into the flavor tank and mix all the ingredients together. The mix is then pumped to the inlet of the continuous freezer. Set the speed, viscosity (stiffness), and overrun settings according to the manufacturer's recommendations. Start the continuous freezing process. As the gelato leaves the continuous freezer, it is then piped to the next stage in the process, which is either filling (pints, etc.), extrusion, or molding.

⊠ CHOCOLATE

Very dense, rich chocolate flavor.

Batch		Continuous
1¾ pounds	cocoa (22–24% fat)	70 pounds
7 ounces	sugar	17½ pounds
60 ounces	hot water	18¾ gallons
2½ gallons	10% gelato mix	100 gallons
3 ounces	two-fold vanilla extract	3¾ quarts

Batch Freezing Method
Thoroughly mix cocoa with extremely hot water to create a smooth paste. Pour all ingredients into batch freezer, turn on dasher and let it run for 5 minutes until cocoa is completely blended into mix. Turn on refrigeration and begin batch.
When batch is complete, turn off refrigeration and extrude finished product.

Batch time: 8–9 minutes.

Continuous Freezing Method
Before you start the continuous freezing of this flavor, make sure the sanitizing solution or the previous flavor of gelato mix has been pushed through the freezer. Open the outlet valve of the mix storage tank and let the proper amount of chocolate gelato mix flow into the flavor tank.*
Pour the vanilla extract into the flavor tank and mix all the ingredients together. The mix is then pumped to the inlet of the continuous freezer. Set the speed, viscosity (stiffness), and overrun settings according to the manufacturer's recommendations. Start the continuous freezing process. As the chocolate gelato leaves the continuous freezer, it is then piped to the next stage in the process, which is either filling (pints, etc.), extrusion, or molding.

---

*Note: If you do not use a pasteurized chocolate gelato mix, thoroughly mix the cocoa and sugar with hot water, adding more water as needed, until a smooth creamy paste has been created.

⊠ STRACCIATELLA (Vanilla Chocolate Chip)

A very popular vanilla-based flavor.

Batch		Continuous
2½ gallons	5 or 10% gelato mix	100 gallons
3½ ounces	two-fold vanilla extract	4⅓ quarts
2 pounds	chocolate chips or liquid stracciatella*	80 pounds
	chocolate chips for garnish	

---

*Note: Stracciatella liquid chocolate is poured into the batch freeze as the gelato is reaching a semifrozen state. The liquid chocolate reacts with the semifrozen gelato by solidifying into very thin chocolate flakes.

Batch Freezing Method

Pour all ingredients except 1 pound of chocolate chips into batch freezer. (Using chocolate chips at the beginning will create a speckled chocolate look in the finished product). Turn on both dasher and refrigeration and begin batch. At end of batch, add remaining chips. When batch is complete, turn off refrigeration and extrude finished product.

Garnish with chocolate chips.

Batch time: 8–9 minutes.

Continuous Freezing Method

Before you start the continuous freezing of this flavor, make sure the sanitizing solution or the previous flavor of gelato mix has been pushed through the freezer. Pour the chocolate chips into the fruit feeder and adjust the controls to the appropriate setting. Open the outlet valve of the mix storage tank and let the proper amount of gelato mix flow into the flavor tank. Pour the vanilla extract into the flavor tank and mix all the ingredients together. The mix is then pumped to the inlet of the continuous freezer. Set the speed, viscosity (stiffness), and overrun settings according to the manufacturer's recommendations. Start the continuous freezing process. As the stracciatella gelato leaves the continuous freezer, it is then piped through the fruit feeder (ingredient feeder) so that the chocolate chips can be discharged and mixed with the gelato that has already become semifrozen. The stracciatella gelato is then piped to the next stage in the process, which is either filling (pints, etc.), extrusion, or molding.

⊠ FRAGOLA (Strawberry)

Delicious and creamy with a strong strawberry taste.

Batch		Continuous
2½ gallons	5 or 10% gelato mix	100 gallons
2½ ounces	two-fold vanilla extract	3 quarts
3 pints	fresh strawberries (rinsed, drained, and hulled)	120 pints
18 ounces	sugar	4½ pounds
1 quart	solid pack strawberries or	10 gallons
26 ounces	gelato strawberry fruit paste (Pre Gel, Monte Bianco, or Fabri) sliced strawberries for garnish	8 gallons

Batch Freezing Method

Mix strawberries with sugar and puree mixture. Marinate for 2 hours.

Pour all ingredients into batch freezer, turn on both dasher and refrigeration, and begin batch. When batch is complete, turn off refrigeration and extrude finished product.

Garnish with slices of strawberries.

Batch time: 8–9 minutes.

Continuous Freezing Method

Mix strawberries with sugar and puree mixture. Marinates for 2 hours.

Before you start the continuous freezing of this flavor, make sure the sanitizing solution or the previous flavor of gelato mix has been pushed through the freezer. Open the outlet valve of the mix storage tank and let the proper amount of gelato mix flow into the flavor tank. Pour the vanilla extract, strawberry puree, and gelato strawberry fruit paste into the flavor tank and mix all the ingredients together. The mix is then pumped to the inlet of the continuous freezer. Set the speed, viscosity (stiffness), and overrun settings according to the manufacturer's recommendations. Start the continuous freezing process. As the fragola gelato leaves the continuous freezer, it is then piped to the next stage in the process, which is either filling (pints, etc.), extrusion, or molding.

▨ BANANA

Any frozen dessert using fresh bananas is going to taste terrific.

Batch		Continuous
2½ gallons	5 or 10% gelato mix	100 gallons
2½ ounces	two-fold vanilla extract	3 quarts
5 pounds	fresh bananas (4 pounds peeled)*	160 pounds
	or	
22½ ounces	gelato banana fruit paste†	7 gallons
	sliced bananas for garnish	

*Note: 5 pounds of whole bananas will yield approximately 4 pounds of peeled bananas because banana skin is approximately 20 percent of the weight of a banana.
†Note: If you use a banana fruit paste, delete the fresh bananas from the above recipe. If you want to add an extra boost to this flavor, use 2 pounds of peeled bananas (pureed) along with the gelato banana fruit paste.

Batch Freezing Method

Pour all ingredients into batch freezer, including peeled bananas. Turn on dasher and let it run for 3 minutes to blend bananas into mix. Turn on refrigeration and begin batch. When batch is complete, turn off refrigeration and extrude finished product.

Garnish with sliced banana.

Batch time: 8–9 minutes.

Continuous Freezing Method

Before you start the continuous freezing of this flavor, make sure the sanitizing solution or the previous flavor of gelato mix has been pushed through the freezer. Open the outlet valve of the mix storage tank and let the proper amount of gelato mix flow into the flavor tank. Pour the vanilla extract and pureed bananas (and/or banana fruit paste) into the flavor tank and mix all the ingredients together. The mix is then pumped to the inlet of the continuous freezer. Set the speed, viscosity (stiffness), and overrun settings according to the manufacturer's recommendations. Start the continuous freezing process. As the banana gelato leaves the continuous freezer, it is then piped to the next stage in the process, which is either filling (pints, etc.), extrusion, or molding.

⊠ LAURETTA (Cream with Cherries)

A cherry liqueur flavor produced with whole Italian Amarena cherries.

Batch		Continuous
2½ gallons	5 or 10% gelato mix	100 gallons
2½ ounces	two-fold vanilla extract	3 quarts
2½ pounds	Amarena cherries	12½ gallons
	Amarena cherries for garnish	

Batch Freezing Method

Pour ingredients into batch freezer, turn on both dasher and refrigeration, and begin batch. When batch is complete, turn off refrigeration and extrude finished product.

Garnish each serving with two Amarena cherries and some syrup.

Batch time: 8–9 minutes.

Continuous Freezing Method

Before you start the continuous freezing of this flavor, make sure the sanitizing solution or the previous flavor of gelato mix has been pushed through the freezer. Pour the Amarena cherries chips into the fruit feeder and adjust the controls to the appropriate setting. Open the outlet valve of the mix storage tank and let the proper amount of gelato mix flow into the flavor tank. Pour the vanilla extract into the flavor tank and mix all the ingredients together. The mix is then pumped to the inlet of the continuous freezer. Set the speed, viscosity (stiffness), and overrun settings according to the manufacturer's recommendations. Start the continuous freezing process. As the lauretta gelato leaves the continuous freezer, it is then piped through the fruit feeder (ingredient feeder) so that the Amarena cherries can be discharged and mixed with the gelato that has already become semifrozen. The lauretta gelato is then piped to the next stage in the process, which is either filling (pints, etc.), extrusion, or molding.

⊠ BLUEBERRY

Very intense flavor that is "terrifico."

Batch		Continuous
2½ gallons	5 or 10% gelato mix	100 gallons
2½ ounces	two-fold vanilla extract	3 quarts
3 pints	fresh or frozen blueberries	
18 ounces	sugar	
	blueberry puree	5½ gallons
2 pounds	gelato blueberry fruit paste	10 gallons
	fresh blueberries for garnish	

Batch Freezing Method

Mix fresh or frozen blueberries with sugar and puree mixture. Marinate for 4 hours.

Pour all ingredients into batch freezer, turn on both dasher and refrigeration, and begin batch. When batch is complete, turn off refrigeration and extrude finished product.

Garnish with fresh blueberries.

Batch time: 8–9 minutes.

Continuous Freezing Method

Before you start the continuous freezing of this flavor, make sure the sanitizing solution or the previous flavor of gelato mix has been pushed through the freezer. Open the outlet valve of the mix storage tank and let the proper amount of gelato mix flow into the flavor tank. Pour the vanilla extract, blueberry puree, and gelato blueberry fruit paste into the flavor tank and mix all the ingredients together. The mix is then pumped to the inlet of the continuous freezer. Set the speed, viscosity (stiffness), and overrun settings according to the manufacturer's recommendations. Start the continuous freezing process. As the Blueberry gelato leaves the continuous freezer, it is then piped to the next stage in the process, which is either filling (pints, etc.), extrusion, or molding.

RASPBERRY

Extremely creamy, very dense raspberry taste.

Batch		Continuous
2½ gallons	5 or 10% gelato mix	100 gallons
2½ ounces	two-fold vanilla extract	3 quarts
1½ pints	fresh or frozen raspberries	
18 ounces	sugar	
	raspberry puree	6¼ gallons
2 pounds	gelato raspberry fruit paste	6¾ gallons
	fresh raspberries for garnish	

Batch Freezing Method

Mix fresh or frozen raspberries with sugar and puree mixture. Strain juice and remove seeds through a sieve. Marinate remaining juice for 4 hours.

Pour all ingredients into batch freezer, turn on both dasher and refrigeration, and begin batch. When batch is complete, turn off refrigeration and extrude finished product.

Garnish with fresh raspberries.

Batch time: 8–9 minutes.

Continuous Freezing Method

Before you start the continuous freezing of this flavor, make sure the sanitizing solution or the previous flavor of gelato mix has been pushed through the freezer. Open the outlet valve of the mix storage tank and let the proper amount of gelato mix flow into the flavor tank. Pour the vanilla extract, raspberry puree, and gelato raspberry fruit paste into the flavor tank and mix all the ingredients together. The mix is then pumped to the inlet of the continuous freezer. Set the speed, viscosity (stiffness), and overrun settings according to the manufacturer's recommendations. Start the continuous freezing process. As the raspberry gelato leaves the continuous freezer, it is then piped to the next stage in the process, which is either filling (pints, etc.), extrusion, or molding.

CAPPUCCINO

Combining the softness of the gelato with the taste of coffee translates into a sublime dessert.

Batch		Continuous
2½ gallons	5 or 10% gelato mix	100 gallons
2½ ounces	two-fold vanilla extract	3 quarts
15 ounces	cappuccino (Pre Gel recommended)	4½ gallons

Batch Freezing Method

Pour ingredients into batch freezer, turn on dasher and let it run for 2 minutes to allow cappuccino flavor to blend properly with the mix. Turn on refrigeration and begin batch. When batch is complete, turn off refrigeration and extrude finished product.

Batch time: 8–9 minutes.

Continuous Freezing Method

Before you start the continuous freezing of this flavor, make sure the sanitizing solution or the previous flavor of gelato mix has been pushed through the freezer. Open the outlet valve of the mix storage tank and let the proper amount of gelato mix flow into the flavor tank. Pour the vanilla extract and gelato cappuccino paste into the flavor tank and mix all the ingredients together. The mix is then pumped to the inlet of the continuous freezer. Set the speed, viscosity (stiffness), and overrun settings according to the manufacturer's recommendations. Start the continuous freezing process. As the cappuccino gelato leaves the continuous freezer, it is then piped to the next stage in the process, which is either filling (pints, etc.), extrusion, or molding.

⊠ NOCCIOLA (Hazelnut)

A must for any gelato store and restaurant producing and selling gelato.

Batch		Continuous
2½ gallons	5 or 10% gelato mix	100 gallons
2½ ounces	two-fold vanilla extract	3 quarts
2 pounds	gelato hazelnut paste (Pre Gel recommended)	80 pounds
1½ pounds	broken hazelnuts	60 pounds
	hazelnut pieces for garnish	

Batch Freezing Method

Pour ingredients into batch freezer. Turn on dasher and let it run for 3 minutes to blend hazelnut paste into mix. Turn on refrigeration and begin batch. When batch is complete, turn off refrigeration and extrude finished product.

Garnish with pieces of hazelnuts.

Batch time: 8–9 minutes.

Continuous Freezing Method

Before you start the continuous freezing of this flavor, make sure the sanitizing solution or the previous flavor of gelato mix has been pushed through the freezer. Pour the hazelnut pieces into the fruit feeder and adjust the controls to the appropriate setting. Open the outlet valve of the mix storage tank and let the proper amount of gelato mix flow into the flavor tank. Pour the vanilla extract and gelato hazelnut paste into the flavor tank and mix all the ingredients together. The mix is then pumped to the inlet of the continuous freezer. Set the speed, viscosity (stiffness), and overrun settings according to the manufacturer's recommendations. Start the continuous freezing process. As the nocciola gelato leaves the continuous freezer, it is then piped through the fruit feeder (ingredient feeder) so that the hazelnut pieces can be discharged and mixed with the gelato that has already become semifrozen. The nocciola gelato is then piped to the next stage in the process, which is either filling (pints, etc.), extrusion, or molding.

⊠ GIANDUJA (Chocolate and Hazelnut)

One of my favorite gelato flavors and a bestseller wherever it is featured.

Batch		Continuous
2½ gallons	5 or 10% gelato mix	100 gallons
2½ ounces	two-fold vanilla extract	3 quarts
2 pounds	gelato gianduja paste (Pre Gel recommended)	80 pounds
1¼ pounds	chocolate chips	50 pounds
1¼ pounds	broken hazelnuts	50 pounds
	hazelnut pieces and chocolate chips for garnish	

Batch Freezing Method
Pour ingredients into batch freezer. Turn on dasher and let it run for 3 minutes to blend Gianduja paste into mix. Turn on refrigeration and begin batch. When batch is complete, turn off refrigeration and extrude finished product.

Garnish with pieces of hazelnuts.

Batch time: 8–9 minutes.

Continuous Freezing Method
Before you start the continuous freezing of this flavor, make sure the sanitizing solution or the previous flavor of gelato mix has been pushed through the freezer. Pour the hazelnut pieces and chocolate chips into the fruit feeder and adjust the controls to the appropriate setting. Open the outlet valve of the mix storage tank and let the proper amount of gelato mix flow into the flavor tank. Pour the vanilla extract and gelato Gianduja paste into the flavor tank and mix all the ingredients together. The mix is then pumped to the inlet of the continuous freezer. Set the speed, viscosity (stiffness), and overrun settings according to the manufacturer's recommendations. Start the continuous freezing process. As the Gianduja gelato leaves the continuous freezer, it is then piped through the fruit feeder (ingredient feeder) so that the hazelnut pieces and chocolate chips can be discharged and mixed with the gelato that has already become semifrozen. The Gianduja gelato is then piped to the next stage in the process, which is either filling (pints, etc.), extrusion, or molding.

⊠ AMARETTO

One of the more popular flavors that you should carry on a regular basis.

Batch		Continuous
2½ gallons	5 or 10% gelato mix	100 gallons
2½ ounces	two-fold vanilla extract	3 quarts
2 pounds	gelato Amaretto paste (Pre Gel recommended)	80 pounds
1½ pounds	sliced almonds	60 pounds
	sliced almonds for garnish	

Batch Freezing Method
Pour ingredients into batch freezer. Turn on dasher and let it run for 3 minutes to blend amaretto paste into mix. Turn on refrigeration and begin batch. When batch is complete, turn off refrigeration and extrude finished product.
    Garnish with sliced almonds.

Batch time: 8–9 minutes.

Continuous Freezing Method
Before you start the continuous freezing of this flavor, make sure the sanitizing solution or the previous flavor of gelato mix has been pushed through the freezer. Pour the almond slices into the fruit feeder and adjust the controls to the appropriate setting. Open the outlet valve of the mix storage tank and let the proper amount of gelato mix flow into the flavor tank. Pour the vanilla extract and gelato amaretto paste into the flavor tank and mix all the ingredients together. The mix is then pumped to the inlet of the continuous freezer. Set the speed, viscosity (stiffness), and overrun settings according to the manufacturer's recommendations. Start the continuous freezing process. As the Amaretto gelato leaves the continuous freezer, it is then piped through the fruit feeder (ingredient feeder) so that the almond slices can be discharged and mixed with the gelato that has already become semifrozen. The Amaretto gelato is then piped to the next stage in the process, which is either filling (pints, etc.), extrusion, or molding.

15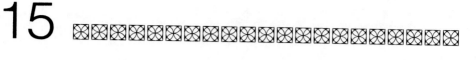

SORBET AND WATER ICE

INCREDIBLY REFRESHING, INCREDIBLY COOL

The ice age has arrived. Whether sorbet or water ice, U.S. consumers are discovering the glories of each. Everywhere you turn, in restaurants and retail ice cream shops, on supermarket freezer shelves, or at amusement parks, ices have become the dessert of the twenty-first century. Flavored ice has long been considered the first frozen dessert created, predating ice cream and other frozen dairy desserts. Alexander the Great supposedly indulged in a cache of flavored snow after a hard day of sacking Persia. In fact, an early form of granita is attributed to Nero who, during the first century A.D., had runners along the Appian Way pass buckets of snow hand over hand from the mountains to his banquet hall, where it was then mixed with fruit and honey.

Today's consumers have discovered something unique in sorbets: flavor, taste, and, except for the citrus flavors that have no fiber and are mostly water in content, excellent body texture. Water ices also have excellent taste and flavor but very little texture because most of the flavor comes from extracts, not from fresh, frozen, or processed fruit. Using no dairy products, both sorbets and water ices also pass the nutrition test of being cholesterol and fat free (except for chocolate), with an average of 110 calories per 4-ounce serving.

Differences Between Sorbet and Water Ice

Sorbets are a French version of Italian ice or granita, but, because of the fruit content, they are sweeter and more flavorful than the traditional Italian water ices available today. They should not be confused with sherbet, which contains some milkfat. Some confusion can arise because the word *sorbet* translates from the French to mean sherbet, which is occasionally used to describe ices that include a beaten egg white. But if you were to check the frozen food section of your supermarket for sherbet, what you would find is an Americanized version that replaces egg white with milk or cream.

A pure fruit sorbet contains only fruit (fresh, frozen, or processed) and some fresh citrus juice, sugar, water, and a stabilizer (if the sorbet is blast frozen), except for all citrus sorbets that must include a stabilizer to improve smoothness and prevent separation. Fruit sorbets are the highlight of any elegant dinner table, being served as a palate cleanser between courses or as a dessert to climax the meal. They mark a meal as something special with just the right hint of culinary glamour.

Water ices, sometimes called "Italian water ice" or simply "ices," are made up of water, fruit extract and/or fruit, sugar, and a stabilizer. The most popular flavors are lemon, cherry, orange, strawberry, and chocolate. They can be eaten before dinner as an aperitif, between courses as an intermezzo, or after dinner as a luscious dessert. Better yet, during the hot summer months, they are eaten day and night as a refreshing treat that can be purchased from a water ice vendor on some busy street corner or at your local pizza parlor.

While many people confuse one with the other, each product has its own attributes and flavor profile.

Sorbets
- Use only fruit puree and fruit pieces.
- Are more expensive to produce because fresh, frozen, or pureed fruit is used.
- Generally use less sugar than water ice.
- Are smoother than water ice.
- Are suitable for a wide array of flavors.
- Perceived by consumers as an upscale product.

Water Ice
- Fruit extract or fruit juice is the major flavor ingredient.
- Is a coarser, colder-tasting product than sorbet.
- Generally use more sugar than sorbet.
- Is considered a pedestrian dessert sold in pizza parlors, on street corners, and at supermarkets as a single-service product.

Actual or perceived differences aside, many retail water ice operations actually produce sorbets but call them water ices or Italian water ices. For this reason, all the sorbet recipes in this chapter can be used and marketed as water ices.

Basic Components of Sorbet and Water Ice

Sorbets and water ices are made up of water, sugar, fruit and/or fruit extracts, citrus juice, and a stabilizer.

Water Since water is such an important ingredient in the production of sorbets and water ices, it is important to know how it works when mixed with other ingredients. On its own water freezes into hard ice, but when it is churned and frozen in combination with the other ingredients, such as sugar, a frozen slush will result.

At around 17 degrees Fahrenheit, some 67 percent of the water has formed ice crystals, depending on the recipe.

If you have the means to get it, filtered water will greatly improve the mouthfeel of either the sorbet or water ice.

Sugar Sugar is used to add sweetness, to build up the body and give smoothness to the product, and to influence the freezing point. The more sugar used, the longer it will take for a product to freeze.

A sugar syrup is to sorbet and water ice as a stock is to a sauce. The syrup is the foundation that actually binds the final product together. And it is responsible for giving the product its snowlike texture. Surprisingly enough, the primary function of a syrup is not to sweeten the sorbet or water ice (which it does), but to aid in the freezing process. Here's how it works.

Sugar syrup, also known as simple syrup, is made up from granulated sugar mixed with very hot to boiling water just long enough to dissolve the sugar and create a clear syrup. The higher the sugar to water ratio, the heavier the syrup. The heavier the syrup, the longer it takes to freeze, and, in most cases, the smoother the product. The syrup lowers the freezing temperature of water or juices from 32 degrees Fahrenheit to 27 degrees Fahrenheit and keeps the product from turning into a solid ice block.

Simple syrup is best made in advance so it can cool down properly under refrigeration. Table 15-1 lists the ingredients for producing a small to large quantity of simple syrup.

The sugar content of both sorbet and water ice is approximately twice that of ice cream. Sugar is needed for desirable body, flavor, and texture. Too much

Table 15-1. Quantities for a Simple Syrup Mixture

Water	Sugar	Simple Syrup Mixture
32 ounces (1 quart)	38 ounces	51 ounces
64 ounces (2 quarts)	76 ounces	102 ounces
96 ounces (3 quarts)	114 ounces	153 ounces (approximately 5 quarts)
128 ounces (4 quarts)	152 ounces	204 ounces (approximately 10 quarts)

Note: All measurements are by fluid weight.

sugar results in the product being soft and sticky while too little results in one being hard and crumbly. Corn syrup, which can replace 20–25 percent of the sugar, is sometimes used to make the product smoother and easier to scoop.

Fruit   Use only fresh fully ripened fruit to create a sorbet product that tastes as close to the fruit itself. Ripe fruit, especially bananas, strawberries, and peaches, is naturally sweeter than fruit not fully ripened.

Frozen fruit is ideal for either sorbet or water ice production. For the most part, you can expect frozen fruit to have a consistent taste the same all year long because it is packed and frozen during the growing season. This consistency is a big advantage over fresh fruit that tastes differently depending on the time of the year. Keep in mind that most frozen fruit produced for commercial use has at least 10 percent sugar added.

Processed fruit is fruit that has been pasteurized (cooked) mainly to remove all forms of bacteria that might have been picked up from the growing fields. While it does not have the same fresh fruit characteristics as either fresh or frozen fruit, pasteurized fruit is used by all major daily manufacturers because of health concerns.

Fruit Extracts   Used mainly in water ice production because of cost concerns, fruit extracts are sometimes used in sorbet production as an added flavor booster to improve the fruit flavor, especially when any fresh fruit being used is not fully ripened.

Citrus Juice   A good sorbet or water ice, like a fine wine, should have a balance of flavors. To counteract the sweetness of the syrup without destroying texture, and to enhance the fruit used, fresh citrus juices—usually lemon, lime, or orange—are added. Citric acid will also work, but not as well as the juices. Of all the fruits, lemon is the most neutral and probably the best to use with a majority of sorbets and water ices. Lime, on the other hand, can tame the most strongly flavored ingredients and bring them down to a more palatable level, but it will add its own distinctive flavor. Orange is sweeter and more recognizable in flavor than lemon, but its flavor is less intense so it needs to be used in larger quantities.

Stabilizer   The best stabilizer to use in a sorbet or water ice is a pectin or guar gum stabilizer. Use guar gum at 0.20 percent and pectin at 0.18 percent for excellent results, but remember each flavor produced has its own stabilizing criterion that need to be addressed (see the recipes). Fruits that have a predominantly fiber or pulp (e.g., strawberry or mango) content need less stabilization than citrus fruits such as orange, lemon, grapefruit, and lime that are primarily water based (any water-based fruit used in sorbet production would freeze hard if stabilizer were not used). Pulp gives body to the product and the more body there is, the less the need for stabilization.

I highly recommend Continental Colloids CC917 cold-water stabilizer for batch freezer operations and CC427 for continuous freezing operations. The difference between the two is the CC917 is easy to use because it is cold-water soluble, while the CC427 needs to be heated to 180 degree Fahrenheit under agitation, so it takes a lot more care and skill to use. If you use any other brand of stabilizer for the following recipes, be sure to follow the manufacturer's directions to get the results you are after.

Following is an example of computing the amount of stabilizer to be used:

Batch Process		*Continuous Process*	
Stabilizer	CC917	Stabilizer	CC427
Size of batch	30 pounds	Size of run	900 pounds
Usage rate	1.5%	Usage rate	0.25%

Converted to Ounces

30 pounds $\times$ 1.5% = .045		900 pounds $\times$ 0.25% = 2.25 $\times$ 16	
.045 $\times$ 16	= 7.2 ounces	2.25 $\times$ 16	= 36 ounces

REFERENCES

International Ice Cream Association. 1995. *The Latest Scoop.* Washington, D.C.: IICA.
Liddell, Caroline, and Robin Weir. 1993. *ICES, The Definitive Guide.* London: Hodder & Stoughton.
Tarantino, Jim. 1988. *Sorbets.* Freedom, Calif.: The Crossing Press.

SORBET RECIPES

Fresh Fruit Puree Breakdown

Table 15-2 lists the specifics for obtaining approximately 1 quart of puree or juice when using fresh fruit. For example, one peach weighs about 5 ounces, so there will be about three peaches in a pound of them. Allowing for a 12 percent loss for removing the skin and stone from a peach means you need three and a half peaches to net a pound of fruit for pureeing. To obtain 1 quart (liquid measurement) of peach puree, you will need to use seven peaches.

Special Notes

Timing is critical during the production of any sorbet, especially in batch freezer operations. On average, most sorbets take 13–17 minutes to produce. After about 12 minutes, you should start watching for the product to begin thickening (looks like gravy) and getting fluffy, which indicates there is still plenty of air in the product. That is the time to turn off the refrigeration and extrude the product, because if you allow it to continue to freeze, the product will become too dense (overprocessed). The overrun of the batch as well as the yield will decrease. Denseness will result in a flaky, grainy finished product that will be unscoopable.

Table 15-2. Fresh Fruit Puree Breakdown

Fruit	Weight per Piece (oz.)	Piece per Amount/Pound	Loss (%)	Amount Need per Pound	Amount to Yield Quart
Peach	5	3	12	$3\frac{1}{2}$	7
Banana	$5\frac{1}{2}$	3	15	$3\frac{1}{2}$	7
Apples	8	2	10	$2\frac{1}{4}$	$4\frac{1}{2}$
Orange	4	10 oz. juice			14 juice
Grapefruit	2	10 oz. juice			7
Papaya	16	1	15	$1\frac{1}{4}$	$2\frac{1}{2}$
Pineapple	1	$3\frac{1}{2}$	20	$4\frac{1}{2}$	$1\frac{1}{2}$–2
Cantaloupe	1	3	20	$3\frac{1}{2}$	$1\frac{1}{4}$–$1\frac{1}{2}$
Kiwi	4	4	10	5	10
Tangerine	4	10 oz. juice			14
Lime	5	10 oz. juice			17
Pear	5	3	15	4	8

The batch freezer recipes in this chapter have been converted for continuous freezing production by multiplying the ingredients quantities by 30. In the conversion, all continuous freezing ingredients amounts have been rounded off to the nearest fraction of a unit.

In order to figure out the percentage of the stabilizer to be used, it is necessary to know the weight of the ingredients of the batch or run. That information appears in the list of ingredients for each recipe.

Finally, the yields given following the processing instructions are measured by volume, based on the overrun desired.

⊠ APPLE BRANDY

This is a perfect flavor for the fall season when apples are at their peak. This zesty flavor with a touch of apple brandy can also be merchandised as a winter holiday treat.

Batch		Continuous
10½ pounds (4 quarts puree)	apples (Matsu or other eating apple)	
	apple puree	30 gallons
4 quarts	unsweetened apple juice	30 gallons
1½ ounces	cinnamon	2¾ pounds
2 quarts	hot water	15 gallons
7¾ pounds	sugar	232½ pounds
8 ounces	apple brandy	
	apple brandy flavor*	3⅓ quarts
7 ounces	CC917 stabilizer* (1.0–1.5%)	
	CC427 stabilizer* (0.15–0.25%)	2¼ pounds
weight: 3½ gallons, 30 pounds		weight: 105 gallons, 900 pounds
	sliced apples and cinnamon for garnish	

*Note: Amount to use varies according to manufacturer's recommendations.

Great New Idea: Apple Cranberry Sorbet. Eliminate the apple brandy and unsweetened apple juice. Replace both with fresh or frozen cranberries. Marinate 4½ pounds fresh cranberries with 1 quart water and 3½ pounds sugar. Let mixture marinate for 3 hours. Puree mixture and strain thoroughly to yield approximately 3 quarts cranberry juice. Add this mixture to the batch recipe. For use in a continuous freezer, multiply these new additions by 30.

Batch Freezing Method
Peel, core, and seed apples. Puree apples with unsweetened apple juice. Add cinnamon to this mixture. Under good agitation (using a spatula), slowly sift the stabilizer into the apple puree. Allow the stabilizer to hydrate at least 30 minutes or more. Next, thoroughly mix sugar with 2 quarts of extremely hot water.

Pour apple puree and sugar-water solution into batch freezer. Turn on both dasher and refrigeration and begin batch. Halfway into batch, as mixture begins to freeze, add apple brandy. As mixture starts to firm up and look fluffy, turn off refrigeration and extrude finished product.

Decorate tops of tubs with slices of apple and cinnamon.

Batch time: 13–17 minutes, depending on amount of sugar used and liquid mix in the barrel.

Yield: 4¼ gallons, based on an overrun of approximately 20%.

Continuous Freezing Method

Before you start the continuous freezing of this sorbet flavor, make sure the sanitizing solution or the previous flavor has been pushed through the freezer. Combine the dry sugar and stabilizer, then dissolve this mixture in hot water until sugar-water solution becomes clear. Next, pour all the ingredients into the flavor tank and thoroughly mix them together. The mix is then pumped to the inlet of the continuous freezer. Set the speed, viscosity (stiffness), and overrun settings according to the manufacturer's recommendations. Start the continuous freezing process. As the sorbet flavor leaves the continuous freezer, it is then piped to the next stage in the process, which is either filling (tubs, pints, etc.), extrusion, or molding.

Yield: Approximately 126 gallons, based on an overrun of 20–30%.

⬡ APRICOT

This rich fruit has its own pronounced character that makes for an exquisite sorbet flavor. Fresh, frozen, or dried apricots can be used.

Batch		Continuous
7½ quarts	water	56¼ gallons
5½ pounds	sugar	165 pounds
5½ quarts	frozen apricot puree, thawed*	41¼ gallons
7½ ounces	CC917 stabilizer† (1.0–1.5%)	
	CC427 stabilizer† (0.15–0.25%)	2¼ pounds
weight:		weight:
3¾ gallons,		112½ gallons,
31¾ pounds		952½ pounds
	pieces of apricot for garnish	

---

*Note: 12 pounds of dried apricots cover with 4 quarts of water and cooked to soften, then drained and pureed may be substituted for the frozen puree.
†Note: Amount to use varies according to manufacturer's recommendations.

Great New Idea: Apricot Mango Sorbet. Combine 3 quarts mango puree with 12 ounces sugar dissolved in 2 ounces hot water. Add this mixture to the batch recipe. For use in a continuous freezer, multiply these new additions by 30.

Batch Freezing Method

Thaw frozen apricot puree. Under good agitation (using a spatula), slowly sift the stabilizer into the apricot puree. Allow the stabilizer to hydrate at least 30 minutes or more. Next, thoroughly mix sugar with 7½ quarts of hot water.

Pour apricot puree and sugar-water solution into batch freezer. Turn on both dasher and refrigeration, and begin batch. As mixture starts to firm up and look fluffy, turn off refrigeration and extrude finished product.

Decorate tops of tubs with apricot pieces.

Batch time: 13–17 minutes, depending on amount of sugar used and liquid mix in the barrel.

Yield: Approximately 4½ gallons, based on an overrun of 20%.

Continuous Freezing Method

Before you start the continuous freezing of this sorbet flavor, make sure the sanitizing solution or the previous flavor has been pushed through the freezer. Combine the dry sugar and stabilizer, then dissolve this mixture into hot water until sugar-water solution becomes clear. Next, pour all the ingredients into the flavor tank and thoroughly mix them together. The mix is then pumped to the inlet of the continuous freezer. Set the speed, viscosity (stiffness), and overrun settings according to the manufacturer's recommendations. Start the continuous freezing process. As the sorbet flavor leaves the continuous freezer, it is then piped to the next stage in the process, which is either filling (tubs, pints, etc.), extrusion, or molding.

Yield: Approximately 135 gallons, based on an overrun of 20–30%.

⊠ BANANA

This is another summer refresher. The year-round availability of bananas makes this recipe an outstanding choice to feature on any sorbet menu.

Batch		Continuous
22 pounds	bananas (18 pounds peeled)*	
	pasteurized banana puree	71¼ gallons
6 quarts	water	45 gallons
3 pounds	sugar	90 pounds
4 tablespoons	lemon juice	2 quarts
9 ounces	CC917 stabilizer† (1.0–1.5%)	
	CC427 stabilizer† (0.15–0.25%)	2¾ pounds
weight:		weight:
4¼ gallons,		127½ gallons,
37 pounds		1,110 pounds
	slices of banana for garnish	

*Note: 22 pounds of whole bananas will yield approximately 18 pounds of peeled bananas because banana skin is approximately 20 percent of the weight of a banana.
†Note: Amount to use varies according to manufacturer's recommendations.

Great New Idea: Banana Rum Sorbet. Tastes just like a banana daiquiri. Add 3 ounces of natural rum extract or 16 ounces rum (just before extrusion takes place) to the batch recipe. For use in a continuous freezer, multiply this new addition by 30.

Batch Freezing Method

Peel and puree bananas. Under good agitation (using a spatula), slowly sift the stabilizer into the banana puree. Allow the stabilizer to hydrate at least 30 minutes or more. Next, thoroughly mix sugar with 6 quarts of extremely hot water.

Pour all ingredients into batch freezer. Turn on both dasher and refrigeration and begin batch. As mixture starts to firm up and look fluffy, turn off refrigeration and extrude finished product.

Decorate tops of tubs with banana slices.

Batch time: 13–17 minutes, depending on amount of sugar used and liquid mix in the barrel.

Yield: Approximately 5 gallons, based on an overrun of 20%.

Continuous Freezing Method

Before you start the continuous freezing of this sorbet flavor, make sure the sanitizing solution or the previous flavor has been pushed through the freezer. Combine the dry sugar and stabilizer, then dissolve this mixture in hot water until sugar-water solution becomes clear. Next, pour all the ingredients into the flavor tank and thoroughly mix them together. The mix is then pumped to the inlet of the continuous freezer. Set the speed, viscosity (stiffness), and overrun settings according to the manufacturer's recommendations. Start the continuous freezing process. As the sorbet flavor leaves the continuous freezer, it is then piped to the next stage in the process, which is either filling (tubs, pints, etc.), extrusion, or molding.

Yield: Approximately 153 gallons, based on an overrun of 20–30%.

▨ BLACKBERRY

The blackberry looks like a raspberry, except for its color. While it is required to re-move the seeds from raspberries, the blackberry can be eaten whole. A delicious tast-ing sorbet.

Batch		Continuous
5 pounds	sugar	150 pounds
6 quarts	water	45 gallons
1¼ gallon	frozen blackberry puree	37½ gallons
7 ounces	CC917 stabilizer* (1.0–1.5%)	
	CC427 stabilizer* (0.15–0.25%)	34 ounces
weight:		weight:
3⅓ gallons,		100 gallons,
28½ pounds		855 pounds

*Note: Amount to use varies according to manufacturer's recommendations.

Great New Idea: Blackberry Brandy Sorbet. The addition of brandy sweetens the flavor and adds a little zing to the sorbet. Add 3 ounces blackberry flavored extract or 16 ounces blackberry brandy (just before extrusion takes place) to the batch recipe. For use in a continuous freezer, multiply this new addition by 30.

Batch Freezing Method

Thaw frozen blackberry puree. Under good agitation (using a spatula), slowly sift the stabilizer into the blackberry puree. Allow the stabilizer to hydrate at least 30 minutes or more. Thoroughly mix sugar with 3 quarts of extremely hot water, then add 3 quarts of cold water to this mixture.

Pour all ingredients into batch freezer. Turn on both dasher and refrigeration and begin batch. As mixture starts to firm up and look fluffy, turn off refrigera-tion and extrude finished product.

Batch time: 13–17 minutes, depending on amount of sugar used and liquid mix in the barrel.

Yield: 4 gallons, based on an overrun of 20%.

Continuous Freezing Method

Before you start the continuous freezing of this sorbet flavor, make sure the sanitiz-ing solution or the previous flavor has been pushed through the freezer. Combine the dry sugar and stabilizer, then dissolve this mixture in hot water until sugar-water solution becomes clear. Next, pour all the ingredients into the flavor tank and thoroughly mix them together. The mix is then pumped to the inlet of the con-tinuous freezer. Set the speed, viscosity (stiffness), and overrun settings ac-cording to the manufacturer's recommendations. Start the continuous freezing pro-cess. As the sorbet flavor leaves the continuous freezer, it is then piped to the next stage in the process, which is either filling (tubs, pints, etc.), extrusion, or molding.

Yield: Approximately 120 gallons, depending on an overrun of 20–30%.

▧ BLACK CURRANT

Black currants have a natural intense flavor that makes a delicious sorbet flavor. If fresh black currants are used, they must be strained.

Batch		Continuous
2½ pounds	sugar	7¼ pounds
1¼ gallons	water	35½ gallons
2 gallons	frozen black currant puree	60 gallons
2 ounces	lemon juice	1¾ quarts
8 ounces	creme de cassis liqueur	
	cassis flavor*	3¼ quarts
7 ounces	CC917 stabilizer* (1.0–1.5%)	
	CC427 stabilizer* (0.15–0.25%)	2¼ pounds
weight:		weight:
3½ gallons,		105 gallons,
30 pounds		900 pounds

*Note: Amount to use varies according to manufacturer's recommendations.

Batch Freezing Method

Thaw frozen black currant puree. Under good agitation (using a spatula), slowly sift the stabilizer into the black currant puree. Allow the stabilizer to hydrate at least 30 minutes or more. Thoroughly mix sugar with 2 quarts of extremely hot water, then add 2¾ quarts of cold water to this mixture.

Pour all ingredients except creme de cassis liqueur into batch freezer. Turn on both dasher and refrigeration and begin batch. Halfway into batch, as mixture begins to freeze, pour in creme de cassis. As mixture starts to firm up and look fluffy, turn off refrigeration and extrude finished product.

Batch time: 13–17 minutes, depending on amount of sugar used and liquid mix in the barrel.

Yield: 4¼ gallons, based on an overrun of 20%.

Continuous Freezing Method

Before you start the continuous freezing of this sorbet flavor, make sure the sanitizing solution or the previous flavor has been pushed through the freezer. Combine the dry sugar and stabilizer, then dissolve this mixture into hot water until sugar-water solution becomes clear. Next, pour all the ingredients into the flavor tank and thoroughly mix them together. The mix is then pumped to the inlet of the continuous freezer. Set the speed, viscosity (stiffness), and overrun settings according to the manufacturer's recommendations. Start the continuous freezing process. As the sorbet flavor leaves the continuous freezer, it is then piped to the next stage in the process, which is either filling (tubs, pints, etc.), extrusion, or molding.

Yield: Approximately 126 gallons, depending on an overrun of 20–30%.

⊠ BLUEBERRY

The flavor of the blueberry is intense. These plump, juicy fruits make a flavorful fresh sorbet. During the summer, especially in July, I recommend using only fresh blueberries because of availability and price. The rest of the year, use frozen blueberries that are properly thawed and pureed at least twice.

Batch		Continuous
17 pints	fresh blueberries	
or		
8½ quarts	frozen blueberries	63¾ gallons
4¼ quarts	water	32 gallons
4¼ pounds	sugar	32 gallons
7½ ounces	CC917 stabilizer* (1.0–1.5%)	
	CC427 stabilizer* (0.15–0.25%)	2¼ pounds
weight:		weight:
3¾ gallons,		112½ gallons,
32 pounds		960 pounds
	blueberries for garnish	

*Note: Amount to use varies according to manufacturer's recommendations.

Great New Idea: Blueberry Mint Sorbet. The addition of mint makes this a cool sorbet. Add 1½–2 ounces natural mint flavor to the batch recipe. For use in a continuous freezer, multiply this new addition by 30.

Batch Freezing Method

Puree blueberries twice. Under good agitation (using a spatula), slowly sift the stabilizer into the blueberry puree. Allow the stabilizer to hydrate at least 30 minutes or more. Dissolve sugar in 2 quarts of hot water and mix thoroughly. Add 2¼ quarts of cold water to this mixture.

Pour blueberry puree and sugar-water solution into batch freezer, turn on both dasher and refrigeration, and begin batch. As mixture starts to firm up and look fluffy, turn off refrigeration and extrude finished product.

Decorate tops of tubs with blueberries.

Batch time: 13–17 minutes, depending on amount of sugar used and liquid mix in the barrel.

Yield: 4½ gallons, based on an overrun of 20%.

Continuous Freezing Method
Thaw and then puree frozen blueberries. Next, strain the blueberry puree
through a sieve to remove all of the outer skin.*

Before you start the continuous freezing of this sorbet flavor, make sure the sanitizing solution or the previous flavor has been pushed through the freezer. Combine the dry sugar and stabilizer, then dissolve this mixture in hot water until
sugar-water solution becomes clear. Next, pour all ingredients into the flavor tank
and thoroughly mix them together. The mix is then pumped to the inlet of the
continuous freezer. Set the speed, viscosity (stiffness), and overrun settings according to the manufacturer's recommendations. Start the continuous freezing process.
As the sorbet flavor leaves the continuous freezer, it is then piped to the next stage
in the process, which is either filling (tubs, pints, etc.), extrusion, or molding.

*Note: Straining the blueberry puree through a sieve is required because the outer blueberry skins
will not pump properly from the flavor tank to the continuous freezer.

Yield: Approximately 135 gallons, based on an overrun of 20–30%.

⊠ CANTALOUPE

Cantaloupes at the peak of their season and fully ripened are wonderful for use as a
sorbet flavor. The delicious aroma that the sorbet exudes make this an easy flavor to
merchandise.

Batch		Continuous
16–18 (yield 8½ quarts puree)	cantaloupes	
	cantaloupe puree	63¾ gallons
4¼ quarts	water	32 gallons
6½ pounds	sugar	195 pounds
3 ounces	lemon juice	2¾ quarts
8 ounces	CC917 stabilizer* (1.0–1.5%)	
	CC427 stabilizer* (0.15–0.25%)	2½ pounds
weight:		weight:
4 gallons, 35 pounds		120 gallons, 1,050 pounds
	slices of cantaloupe for garnish	

*Note: Amount to use varies according to manufacturer's recommendations.

Great New Idea: Cantaloupe Champagne Sorbet. An incredible tasting summer sorbet that tops off a meal with a bang. Add 26 ounces champagne to the
batch recipe (just before extrusion takes place). For use in a continuous freezer,
multiply this new addition by 30.

Batch Freezing Method

Cut cantaloupes in half. Peel and remove all seeds, then puree melons. Under good agitation (using a spatula), slowly sift the stabilizer into the cantaloupe puree. Allow the stabilizer to hydrate at least 30 minutes or more. Thoroughly mix sugar with 2 quarts of hot water, then add 2¼ quarts of cold water and lemon juice to this mixture.

Pour cantaloupe puree and sugar-water solution into batch freezer. Turn on both dasher and refrigeration and begin batch. As mixture starts to firm up and look fluffy, turn off refrigeration and extrude finished product.

Decorate tops of tubs with cantaloupe slices.

Batch time: 13–17 minutes, depending on amount of sugar used and liquid mix in the barrel.

Yield: 4¾ gallons, based on an overrun of 20%.

Continuous Freezing Method

Before you start the continuous freezing of this sorbet flavor, make sure the sanitizing solution or the previous flavor has been pushed through the freezer. Combine the dry sugar and stabilizer, then dissolve this mixture into hot water until sugar-water solution becomes clear. Next, pour all the ingredients into the flavor tank and thoroughly mix them together. The mix is then pumped to the inlet of the continuous freezer. Set the speed, viscosity (stiffness), and overrun settings according to the manufacturer's recommendations. Start the continuous freezing process. As the sorbet flavor leaves the continuous freezer, it is then piped to the next stage in the process, which is either filling (tubs, pints, etc.), extrusion, or molding.

Yield: Approximately 144 gallons, based on an overrun of 20–30%.

⊠ CHAMPAGNE

For that special celebration, this extraordinary sorbet is a festive touch. It is well suited for restaurants and caterers to use as a dessert.

Batch		Continuous
4 pounds	sugar	120 pounds
2¼ quarts	water	17 gallons
12 bottles	champagne	360 bottles
		(73 gallons)
2 ounces	lemon juice	2 quarts
7 ounces	CC917 stabilizer* (1.0–1.5%)	
	CC427 stabilizer* (0.15–0.25%)	2 pounds
weight:		weight:
3½ gallons,		105 gallons,
28 pounds		854 pounds

*Note: Amount to use varies according to manufacturer's recommendations.

Great New Idea: Champagne Peach Sorbet. Combine 2 quarts peach puree with 1 pound sugar dissolved in 2 ounces hot water. Add this mixture to the batch recipe. For use in a continuous freezer, multiply these new additions by 30.

Batch Freezing Method

Under good agitation (using a spatula), slowly sift the stabilizer into the champagne. Allow the stabilizer to hydrate at least 30 minutes or more. Thoroughly mix sugar with 16 ounces of extremely hot water, then add 16 ounces of cold water to this mixture. Pour all ingredients into batch freezer, turn on both dasher and refrigeration, and begin batch. As mixture starts to firm up and look fluffy, turn off refrigeration and extrude finished product.

Batch time: 13–17 minutes, depending on amount of sugar used and liquid mix in the barrel.

Yield: 4¼ gallons, based on an overrun of 20%.

Continuous Freezing Method

Before you start the continuous freezing of this sorbet flavor, make sure the sanitizing solution or the previous flavor has been pushed through the freezer. Combine the dry sugar and stabilizer, then dissolve this mixture in hot water until sugar-water solution becomes clear. Next, pour all the ingredients into the flavor tank and thoroughly mix them together. The mix is then pumped to the inlet of the continuous freezer. Set the speed, viscosity (stiffness), and overrun settings according to the manufacturer's recommendations. Start the continuous freezing process. As the sorbet flavor leaves the continuous freezer, it is then piped to the next stage in the process, which is either filling (tubs, pints, etc.), extrusion, or molding.

Yield: Approximately 126 gallons, based on an overrun of 20–30%.

▨ CHOCOLATE

Creating quality in a specific product depends on the standards of the producer. I have always thought of my chocolate sorbet as the finest sorbet flavor I have ever produced. The time spent creating that ultimate chocolate flavor in a sorbet was long and difficult.

I have tasted and eaten many different versions over the years, and most chocolate sorbets I have tried are weak in flavor. Part of this problem stems from the difficulty in processing dry cocoa with water and sugar to end up with a smooth, rich-tasting product. Most operators use too much water, which dilutes the flavor. This chocolate sorbet recipe is smooth, rich in flavor, and quite scoopable. Without a doubt, the use of vanilla extract really helps bring out the full flavor of chocolate in the finished product.

Batch		**Continuous**
1 pound	cocoa (22–24% fat)	30 pounds
5 pounds	sugar	150 pounds
2 ounces	vanilla extract	2 quarts
2 gallons	hot water	60 gallons
1 pound	fudge	30 pounds
5½ ounces	CC917 stabilizer* (1.0–1.5%)	
	CC427 stabilizer* (0.15–0.25%)	1¾ pounds
weight:		weight:
3 gallons,		90 gallons,
24 pounds		720 pounds

*Note: Amount to use varies according to manufacturer's recommendations.

Great New Idea: Chocolate Coconut Sorbet. Even since I was a child, I loved chocolate coconut Easter eggs. Thanks to my friend Art Sherman who owned Zitners of Philadelphia (the very best ever), he kept me supplied year after year with coconut Easter eggs. I even used them to make my coconut almond fudge ice cream. Try this new version as a sorbet, it's just great! Combine 2 quarts coconut fruit base with ½ pound shredded coconut. Add this mixture to the batch recipe. For use in a continuous freezer, multiply these new additions by 30.

Batch Freezing Method

Combine the sugar, cocoa, and stabilizer. Mix these ingredients thoroughly using either a spatula or a 5-quart electric mixer and add 1 gallon of extremely hot water until a smooth chocolate paste is created. Allow the stabilizer to hydrate in the cocoa mixture for at least 30 minutes before you begin production.

Next, pour the cocoa mixture, vanilla extract, and 1 gallon of cold water into the batch freezer. Turn on dasher for 3 minutes, then turn on refrigeration to begin batch. Add fudge slowly to batch after 2 more minutes. As mixture starts to firm up and look fluffy, turn off refrigeration and extrude finished product.

Batch time: 13–17 minutes, depending on amount of sugar used and liquid mix in the barrel.

Yield: 3½ gallons, based on an overrun of 20%.

Continuous Freezing Method

Before you start the continuous freezing of this sorbet flavor, make sure the sanitizing solution or the previous flavor has been pushed through the freezer. Combine the dry sugar and stabilizer, then dissolve this mixture in hot water until sugar-water solution becomes clear. Next, pour all the ingredients into the flavor tank and thoroughly mix them together. The mix is the pumped to the inlet of the continuous freezer. Set the speed, viscosity (stiffness), and overrun settings according to the manufacturer's recommendations. Start the continuous freezing process. As the sorbet flavor leaves the continuous freezer, it is then piped to the next stage in the process, which is either filling (tubs, pints, etc.), extrusion, or molding.

Yield: Approximately 108 gallons, based on an overrun of 20–30%.

⊠ CHOCOLATE BANANA

Creating different and unusual sorbet flavors is not difficult. It just takes time to think out the process. Let your mind wander. This variation of chocolate is not only refreshing, but extremely rich in flavor. Use just enough cocoa and banana so that the taste of each is evident in the finished product.

Batch		Continuous
½ pound	cocoa (22–24% fat)	15 pounds
6 pounds	very ripe bananas (5 pounds peeled)*	
	pasteurized banana puree	11¾ gallons
2 gallons	hot water	60 gallons
5 pounds	sugar	150 pounds
2 ounces	vanilla extract	2 quarts
1 pound	fudge	30 pounds
6½ ounces	CC917 stabilizer† (1.0–1.5%)	
	CC427 stabilizer† (0.15–0.25%)	2 pounds
weight:		weight:
3½ gallons,		105 gallons,
28 pounds		840 pounds
	pieces of banana for garnish	

---

*Note: 6 pounds of whole bananas will yield approximately 5 pounds of peeled bananas because banana skin is approximately 20 percent of the weight of a banana.

†Note: Amount to use varies according to manufacturer's recommendations.

Batch Freezing Method

Thoroughly mix 1 gallon of extremely hot water with cocoa, using a spatula or mixer so that the dry cocoa is completely dissolved. Pour sugar into the other gallon of hot water and mix until both are completely dissolved. Using a blender, blend bananas with just enough water so that no pieces of bananas remain. Under good agitation (using a spatula), slowly sift in the stabilizer into the banana puree. Allow the stabilizer to hydrate at least 30 minutes or more.

Pour all ingredients into batch freezer, turn on dasher for 3 minutes, then turn on refrigeration to begin batch. After 2 more minutes slowly add fudge to batch. As mixture starts to firm up and look fluffy, turn off refrigeration and extrude finished product.

Decorate tops of tubs with pieces of bananas.

Batch time: 13–17 minutes, depending on amount of sugar used and liquid mix in the barrel.

Yield: 4¼ gallons, based on an overrun of 20%.

Continuous Freezing Method

Before you start the continuous freezing of this sorbet flavor, make sure the sanitizing solution or the previous flavor has been pushed through the freezer. Combine the dry sugar and stabilizer, then dissolve this mixture in hot water until sugar-water solution becomes clear. Next, pour all the ingredients into the flavor tank and thoroughly mix them together. The mix is then pumped to the inlet of the continuous freezer. Set the speed, viscosity (stiffness), and overrun settings according to the manufacturer's recommendations. Start the continuous freezing process. As the sorbet flavor leaves the continuous freezer, it is then piped to the next stage in the process, which is either filling (tubs, pints, etc.), extrusion, or molding.

Yield: Approximately 126 gallons, based on an overrun of 20–30%.

▧ COCONUT

A luscious tropical sorbet flavor, this product is received very well by consumers. Be careful of the amount of sugar used because coconut is naturally sweet.

Batch		Continuous
32 ounces	coconut fruit base	60 pounds
5 small cans (15-ounce size)	Coco Lopez coconut base	141 pounds
10 ounces	shredded coconut	18¾ pounds
10 quarts	water	75 gallons
2¾ pounds	sugar	82½ pounds
7¼ ounces	CC917 stabilizer* (1.0–1.5%)	
	CC427 stabilizer* (0.15–0.25%)	2¼ pounds
weight:		weight:
3¾ gallons,		112½ gallons,
30½ pounds		917 pounds
	shredded coconut for garnish	

*Note: Amount to use varies according to manufacturer's recommendations.

Great New Idea: Coconut Galliano Sorbet. Galliano adds a vanilla flavor burst to this very refreshing sorbet. Add 16 ounces of Galliano and 4 ounces of fresh lime juice (just before extrusion takes place) to the batch recipe. For use in a continuous freezer, multiply these new additions by 30.

Batch Freezing Method

Mix together coconut fruit base, Coco Lopez, and shredded coconut. Thoroughly mix sugar with 5 quarts of hot water, then add 5 quarts of cold water to this mixture. Combine all the ingredients and under good agitation (using a spatula), slowly sift the stabilizer into the coconut mixture. Allow the stabilizer to hydrate at least 30 minutes or more.

Pour coconut mixture and sugar-water solution into batch freezer. Turn on both dasher and refrigeration and begin batch. As mixture starts to firm up and look fluffy, turn off refrigeration and extrude finished product.

Decorate tops of tubs with shredded coconut.

Batch time: 13–17 minutes, depending on amount of sugar used and liquid mix in the barrel.

Yield: 4½ gallons, based on an overrun of 20%.

Continuous Freezing Method

Before you start the continuous freezing of this sorbet flavor, make sure the sanitizing solution or the previous flavor has been pushed through the freezer. Combine the sugar and stabilizer, then dissolve this mixture in hot water until sugar-water solution becomes clear. Next, pour all the ingredients except the shredded coconut into the flavor tank and thoroughly mix them together. Pour the shredded coconut into the fruit feeder. The mix is then pumped to the inlet of the continuous freezer. Set the speed, viscosity (stiffness), and overrun settings according to the manufacturer's recommendations. Start the continuous freezing process. As the sorbet flavor leaves the continuous freezer, it is then piped through the fruit feeder (ingredient feeder) so that the shredded coconut can be discharged and mixed with the sorbet that has already become semi-frozen. The sorbet is then piped to the next stage in the process, which is either filling (tubs, pints, etc.), extrusion, or molding.

Yield: Approximately 135 gallons, based on an overrun of 20–30%.

⊠ CRANBERRY

This fall seasonal flavor sells very well around Thanksgiving and Christmas.

Batch		Continuous
3¾ quarts	water	
14¼ pounds	sugar	
18¾ pounds (above mixture yields 11¼ quarts juice)	fresh or frozen cranberries	
	cranberry puree	84⅓ gallons
3¾ quarts	water	28 gallons
10 ounces	Triple Sec liqueur	
	Triple Sec flavor*	1¾ quarts
7½ ounces	CC917 stabilizer* (1.0–1.5%)	
	CC427 stabilizer* (0.15–0.25%)	2½ pounds
weight:		weight:
3¾ gallons, 32 pounds		112½ gallons, 960 pounds

*Note: Amount to use varies according to manufacturer's recommendations.

Batch Freezing Method
Mix together 3¾ quarts of water, 14¼ pounds of sugar, and cranberries. Puree mixture and strain thoroughly to yield 11¼ quarts of cranberry juice. Under good agitation (using a spatula), slowly sift the stabilizer into the cranberry juice. Allow the stabilizer to hydrate at least 30 minutes or more.

Pour cranberry juice and 3¾ more quarts of water into batch freezer. Turn on both dasher and refrigeration and begin batch. Halfway into batch, as sorbet begins to freeze, add Triple Sec. As mixture starts to firm up and look fluffy, turn off refrigeration and extrude finished product.

Batch time: 13–17 minutes, depending on amount of sugar used and liquid mix in the barrel.

Yield: 4½ gallons, based on an overrun of 20%.

Continuous Freezing Method

Before you start the continuous freezing of this sorbet flavor, make sure the sanitizing solution or the previous flavor has been pushed through the freezer. Combine the sugar and stabilizer, then dissolve this mixture in hot water until sugar-water solution becomes clear. Next, pour all the ingredients into the flavor tank and thoroughly mix them together. The mix is then pumped to the inlet of the continuous freezer. Set the speed, viscosity (stiffness), and overrun settings according to the manufacturer's recommendations. Start the continuous freezing process. As the sorbet flavor leaves the continuous freezer, it is then piped to the next stage in the process, which is either filling (tubs, pints, etc.), extrusion, or molding.

Yield: Approximately 135 gallons, based on an overrun of 20–30%.

⊠ ESPRESSO

This sophisticated flavor is served in many Italian-style cafes and restaurants.

Batch		**Continuous**
12 ounces	espresso flavor (liquid, Weber 21-85-1346)	3 gallons
¾ ounce	cocoa (22–24% fat)	22½ ounces
3 gallons	water	90 gallons
4½ pounds	sugar	135 pounds
12 ounces	Kahlua liqueur	
	Kahlua flavor*	5 quarts
3 ounces	CC917 stabilizer* (1.0–1.5%)	
	CC427 stabilizer* (0.15–0.25%)	2½ pounds
weight:		weight:
3 gallons, 24 pounds		112½ gallons, 1,017 pounds

*Note: Amount to use varies according to manufacturer's recommendations.

Batch Freezing Method

Mix the liquid espresso flavor and cocoa with 3 ounces of extremely hot water to create a smooth creamy paste. Thoroughly mix sugar with 1 gallon of extremely hot water, then add 2 gallons of cold water to this mixture. Under good agitation (using a spatula), slowly sift the stabilizer into the espresso mixture. Allow the stabilizer to hydrate at least 30 minutes or more.

Pour coffee and sugar-water mixture into batch freezer. Turn on both dasher and refrigeration and begin batch. Halfway into batch, as sorbet begins to freeze, pour in Kahlua. As mixture starts to firm up and look fluffy, turn off refrigeration and extrude finished product.

Batch time: 13–17 minutes, depending on amount of sugar used and liquid mix in the barrel.

Yield: 4½ gallons, based on an overrun of 20%.

Continuous Freezing Method

Before you start the continuous freezing of this sorbet flavor, make sure the sanitizing solution or the previous flavor has been pushed through the freezer. Combine the sugar and stabilizer, then dissolve this mixture in hot water until sugar-water solution becomes clear. Next, pour all the ingredients into the flavor tank and thoroughly mix them together. The mix is then pumped to the inlet of the continuous freezer. Set the speed, viscosity (stiffness), and overrun settings according to the manufacturer's recommendations. Start the continuous freezing process. As the sorbet flavor leaves the continuous freezer, it is then piped to the next stage in the process, which is either filling (tubs, pints, etc.), extrusion, or molding.

Yield: Approximately 108 gallons, based on an overrun of 20–30%.

▩ GRAPE

This wonderful Concord grape sorbet brings back lots of memories of Popsicles that we all ate as kids.

Batch		Continuous
20 pounds (yields 16 pounds skinless grape juice)	Concord grapes	
	grape puree	60 gallons
1 gallon	water	30 gallons
1½ pounds	sugar	45 pounds
5 ounces	lemon juice	4½ quarts
8½ ounces	CC917 stabilizer* (1.0–1.5%)	
	CC427 stabilizer* (0.15–0.25%)	2½ pounds
weight:		weight:
3½ gallons, 34 pounds		105 gallons, 1,020 pounds
	grapes for garnish	

*Note: Amount to use varies according to manufacturer's recommendations.

Great New Idea: Green Grape Sorbet. Simply substitute green seedless grapes for the Concord grapes.

Batch Freezing Method

Puree grapes in blender, then strain grapes through a fine sieve to remove the skins. (For a deeper and richer color, leave the puree in the refrigerator overnight before straining out the grape skins. Under good agitation (using a spatula), slowly sift the stabilizer into the grape puree. Allow the stabilizer to hydrate at least 30 minutes or more. Dissolve sugar in 2 quarts of hot water and mix thoroughly. Add 2¼ quarts of cold water to this mixture.

Pour lemon juice, grape puree, and sugar-water solution into batch freezer, turn on both dasher and refrigeration, and begin batch. As mixture starts to firm up and look fluffy, turn off refrigeration and extrude finished product.

Decorate tops of tubs with grapes.

Batch time: 13–17 minutes, depending on amount of sugar used and liquid mix in the barrel.

Yield: 4¼ gallons, based on an overrun of 20%.

Continuous Freezing Method

Thaw and then puree the frozen grapes. Next, strain the grape puree through a sieve to remove all the outer skin.*

Before you start the continuous freezing of this sorbet flavor, make sure the sanitizing solution or the previous flavor has been pushed through the freezer. Combine the sugar and stabilizer, then dissolve this mixture in hot water until sugar-water solution becomes clear. Next, pour all the ingredients into the flavor tank and thoroughly mix them together. The mix is then pumped to the inlet of the continuous freezer. Set the speed, viscosity (stiffness), and overrun settings according to the manufacturer's recommendations. Start the continuous freezing process. As the sorbet flavor leaves the continuous freezer, it is then piped to the next stage in the process, which is either filling (tubs, pints, etc.), extrusion, or molding.

---

*Note: Straining the grape puree through a sieve is required because the outer grape skins will not pump properly from the flavor tank to the continuous freezer.

Yield: Approximately 126 gallons, based on an overrun of 20–30%.

⊠ GRAPEFRUIT

Of all the citrus fruits used for producing sorbets, grapefruit is my favorite. Grapefruit sorbet is extremely refreshing and the retention of the fresh grapefruit flavor is remarkable. Use large ripe fruit for best results as this size usually has the most juice. This sorbet flavor is a must for upscale operations.

Batch		Continuous
36–40 (yield 8 quarts juice)	grapefruits	
	fresh grapefruit juice	60 gallons
1 gallon	water	30 gallons
7½ pounds	sugar	225 pounds
8 ounces	CC917 stabilizer* (1.0–1.5%)	
	CC427 stabilizer* (0.15–0.25%)	2½ pounds
weight:		weight:
3¾ gallons, 34½ pounds		112½ gallons, 1,035 pounds
	grapefruit slices for garnish	

*Note: Amount to use varies according to manufacturer's recommendations.

Batch Freezing Method

Squeeze grapefruits to obtain 8 quarts of juice. Strain juice and remove seeds. Save half of pulp and discard rest. (The pulp adds body and texture to the finished product.) Thoroughly mix sugar with 2 quarts of extremely hot water, then add 2 quarts of cold water to this mixture. Under good agitation (using a spatula), slowly sift the stabilizer into the grapefruit juice. Allow the stabilizer to hydrate at least 30 minutes or more.

Pour juice and pulp mixture into batch freezer. Turn on both dasher and refrigeration and begin batch. As mixture starts to firm up and look fluffy, turn off refrigeration and extrude finished product.

Decorate tops of tubs with fresh grapefruit slices.

Batch time: 13–17 minutes, depending on amount of sugar used and liquid mix in the barrel.

Yield: 4½ gallons, based on an overrun of 20%.

Continuous Freezing Method

Before you start the continuous freezing of this sorbet flavor, make sure the sanitizing solution or the previous flavor has been pushed through the freezer. Combine the sugar and stabilizer, then dissolve this mixture in hot water until sugar-water solution becomes clear. Next, pour all the ingredients into the flavor tank and thoroughly mix them together. The mix is then pumped to the inlet of the continuous freezer. Set the speed, viscosity (stiffness), and overrun settings according to the manufacturer's recommendations. Start the continuous freezing process. As the sorbet flavor leaves the continuous freezer, it is then piped to the next stage in the process, which is either filling (tubs, pints, etc.), extrusion, or molding.

Yield: Approximately 135 gallons, based on an overrun of 20–30%.

⊠ GRAPEFRUIT CAMPARI

This elegant flavor has a fresh tangy taste that comes from the Campari. This sorbet is excellent for restaurant use.

Batch		Continuous
36–40 (yields 8 quarts juice)	grapefruits	
	fresh grapefruit juice	60 gallons
1 gallon	water	30 gallons
7½ pounds	sugar	225 pounds
26 ounces	Campari	6 gallons
8 ounces	CC917 stabilizer* (1.0–1.5%)	
	CC427 stabilizer* (0.15–0.25%)	2½ pounds
weight:		weight:
4¼ gallons, 34½ pounds		127½ gallons, 1,035 pounds
	thin grapefruit slices for garnish	

*Note: Amount to use varies according to manufacturer's recommendations.

Great New Idea: Grapefruit Vermouth Sorbet. The addition of vermouth brings out a more assertive flavor to this sorbet. Replace the Campari with 13 ounces of very dry vermouth (pour in to batch just prior to extrusion). For use in a continuous freezer, multiply these new additions by 30.

Batch Freezing Method

Squeeze grapefruits to obtain 8 quarts of juice. Strain juice and remove seeds. Save half of pulp and discard rest. (The pulp adds body and texture to the finished product.) Thoroughly mix sugar with 2 quarts of extremely hot water, then add 2 quarts of cold water to this mixture. Under good agitation (using a spatula), slowly sift the stabilizer into the grapefruit juice. Allow the stabilizer to hydrate at least 30 minutes or more.

Pour sugar mixture, juice, and pulp into batch freezer. Turn on both dasher and refrigeration and begin batch. Halfway into batch, as sorbet begins to freeze, pour in Campari. As mixture starts to firm up and look fluffy, turn off refrigeration and extrude finished product.

Decorate tops of tubs with fresh grapefruit slices.

Batch time: 13–17 minutes. (Freezing takes slightly longer because of the alcohol in the Campari.)

Yield: 5 gallons, based on an overrun of 20–30%.

Continuous Freezing Method

Before you start the continuous freezing of this sorbet flavor, make sure the sanitizing solution or the previous flavor has been pushed through the freezer. Combine the sugar and stabilizer, then dissolve this mixture in hot water until sugar-water solution becomes clear. Next, pour all the ingredients into the flavor tank and thoroughly mix them together. The mix is then pumped to the inlet of the continuous freezer. Set the speed, viscosity (stiffness), and overrun settings according to the manufacturer's recommendations. Start the continuous freezing process. As the sorbet flavor leaves the continuous freezer, it is then piped to the next stage in the process, which is either filling (tubs, pints, etc.), extrusion, or molding.

Yield: Approximately 153 gallons, based on an overrun of 20–30%.

⊠ GUAVA

The taste of guava is acid, but sweet. Guavas are best used when fully ripened.

Batch		Continuous
4⅓ pounds	sugar	130 pounds
4⅓ quarts	water	3¼ gallons
8⅔ quarts	frozen guava puree	6½ gallons
8 ounces	CC917 stabilizer* (1.0–1.5%)	
	CC427 stabilizer* (0.15–0.25%)	2½ pounds
weight:		weight:
3¾ gallons,		112½ gallons,
32½ pounds		975 pounds

*Note: Amount to use varies according to manufacturer's recommendations.

Batch Freezing Method

Thaw frozen guava puree. Under good agitation (using a spatula), slowly sift the stabilizer into the guava puree. Allow the stabilizer to hydrate at least 30 minutes or more. Thoroughly mix sugar with 2 quarts of extremely hot water, then add 2⅓ quarts of cold water to this mixture.

Pour all ingredients into the batch freezer. Turn on both dasher and refrigeration and begin batch. As mixture starts to firm up and look fluffy, turn off refrigeration and extrude finished product.

Batch time: 13–17 minutes, depending on amount of sugar used and liquid mix in the barrel.

Yield: 4½ gallons, based on an overrun of 20%.

Continuous Freezing Method

Before you start the continuous freezing of this sorbet flavor, make sure the sanitizing solution or the previous flavor has been pushed through the freezer. Combine the sugar and stabilizer, then dissolve this mixture in hot water until sugar-water solution becomes clear. Next, pour all the ingredients into the flavor tank and thoroughly mix them together. The mix is then pumped to the inlet of the continuous freezer. Set the speed, viscosity (stiffness), and overrun settings according to the manufacturer's recommendations. Start the continuous freezing process. As the sorbet flavor leaves the continuous freezer, it is then piped to the next stage in the process, which is either filling (tubs, pints, etc.), extrusion, or molding.

Yield: Approximately 135 gallons, depending on an overrun of 20–30%.

⊠ KEY LIME

This is truly a wonderful summer refresher that was made popular in Key West, Florida, where key limes are plentiful. Be careful that the finished product is not too tart.

Batch		Continuous
50–55 (yields 3 quarts fresh juice)	limes	
	fresh lime juice	22½ gallons
7½ quarts	water	56¼ gallons
7 pounds	sugar	210 pounds
6¾ ounces	CC917 stabilizer* (1.0–1.5%)	
	CC427 stabilizer* (0.15–0.25%)	2 pounds
weight:		weight:
3½ gallons, 28½ pounds		105 gallons, 855 pounds
	Key lime slices for garnish	

*Note: Amount to use varies according to manufacturer's recommendations.

Batch Freezing Method

Squeeze enough limes to obtain 3 quarts of juice (or use bottled juice). Strain fresh juice and retain half the pulp. (The pulp adds body and texture to the finished product.) Thoroughly mix sugar with 4 quarts of extremely hot water, then add 3½ quarts of cold water to this mixture. Under good agitation (using a spatula), slowly sift the stabilizer into the lime juice. Allow the stabilizer to hydrate at least 30 minutes or more.

Pour sugar mixture, juice, and pulp into batch freezer. Turn on both dasher and refrigeration and begin batch. As mixture starts to firm up and look fluffy, turn off refrigeration and extrude finished product.

Decorate tops of tubs with fresh key lime slices.

Batch time: 13–17 minutes, depending on amount of sugar used and liquid mix in the barrel.

Yield: 4¼ gallons, based on an overrun of 20%.

Continuous Freezing Method

Before you start the continuous freezing of this sorbet flavor, make sure the sanitizing solution or the previous flavor has been pushed through the freezer. Combine the sugar and stabilizer, then dissolve this mixture into hot water until sugar-water solution becomes clear. Next, pour all the ingredients into the flavor tank and thoroughly mix them together. The mix is then pumped to the inlet of the continuous freezer. Set the speed, viscosity (stiffness), and overrun settings according to the manufacturer's recommendations. Start the continuous freezing process. As the sorbet flavor leaves the continuous freezer, it is then piped to the next stage in the process, which is either filling (tubs, pints, etc.), extrusion, or molding.

Yield: Approximately 126 gallons, based on an overrun of 20–30%.

⬚ KIWI

This is an exotic flavor. If you have the patience to peel the kiwifruit, you'll be very happy with the results.

Batch		Continuous
75–80 (yields 9 quarts puree)	kiwifruit	
	kiwi puree	67½ gallons
3 quarts	water	22½ gallons
5 pounds	sugar	150 pounds
3 ounces	fresh lime juice	2¾ quarts
7¼ ounces	CC917 stabilizer* (1.0–1.5%)	
	CC427 stabilizer* (0.15–0.25%)	2¼ pounds
weight:		weight:
3½ gallons,		105 gallons,
31½ pounds		915 pounds
	kiwifruit slices for garnish	

*Note: Amount to use varies according to manufacturer's recommendations.

Great New Idea: Strawberry Kiwi Sorbet. A subtle smooth strawberry-kiwi flavor that is not overbearing either from the kiwis or strawberries. Combine 4 quarts strawberry puree with 1½ pounds sugar dissolved in 4 ounces hot water. Add this mixture to the above batch recipe. For use in a continuous freezer, multiply these new additions by 30.

Batch Freezing Method

Peel and puree the kiwifruit. Thoroughly mix sugar with 1 quart of extremely hot water, then add 2 quarts of cold water and lime juice to this mixture. Under good agitation (using a spatula), slowly sift the stabilizer into the kiwi puree. Allow the stabilizer to hydrate at least 30 minutes or more.

Pour kiwifruit puree and sugar-water solution into batch freezer. Turn on both dasher and refrigeration and begin batch. As mixture starts to firm up and look fluffy, turn off refrigeration and extrude finished product.

Decorate tops of tubs with kiwifruit slices.

Batch time: 13–17 minutes, depending on amount of sugar used and liquid mix in the barrel.

Yield: 4¼ gallons, based on an overrun of 20%.

Continuous Freezing Method

Before you start the continuous freezing of this sorbet flavor, make sure the sanitizing solution or the previous flavor has been pushed through the freezer. Combine the sugar and stabilizer, then dissolve this mixture in hot water until sugar-water solution becomes clear. Next, pour all the ingredients into the flavor tank and thoroughly mix them together. The mix is then pumped to the inlet of the continuous freezer. Set the speed, viscosity (stiffness), and overrun settings according to the manufacturer's recommendations. Start the continuous freezing process. As the sorbet flavor leaves the continuous freezer, it is then piped to the next stage in the process, which is either filling (tubs, pints, etc.), extrusion, or molding.

Yield: Approximately 126 gallons, based on an overrun of 20–30%.

⊠ LEMON

Lemon sorbet is undoubtedly the most difficult sorbet to produce. Usually the finished product is either too sweet or too tart. The ripeness of the lemons used determines how much sugar is needed.

I prefer lemon sorbet on the sweet side rather than tart, because most consumers choose the flavor seeking something refreshing to cool them off on a hot summer day. Creating the right balance is difficult. Don't be fooled by the taste of the product right after it has been extruded from the batch freezer. In the soft state, most fruit sorbets are very sweet. This sweetness will dissipate after the product has been hardened.

Use only fresh lemons, no concentrate or reconstituted lemon juice. The process takes time but is worth the effort.

Batch		Continuous
70 (yields 3½ quarts juice)	lemons	
	fresh lemon juice	26¼ gallons
16 ounces	fresh orange juice	3¾ gallons
1¼ gallons	hot water	37½ gallons
5½ pounds	sugar	165 pounds
6 ounces	CC917 stabilizer* (1.0–1.5%)	
	CC427 stabilizer* (0.15–0.25%)	2 pounds
weight:		weight:
3 gallons, 25 pounds		90 gallons, 750 pounds
	lemon slices for garnish	

*Note: Amount to use varies according to manufacturer's recommendations.

Great New Idea: Lemon Strawberry Sorbet. Truly delicious! Combine 1 quart fresh or frozen strawberry puree with 8 ounces sugar dissolved in 1 ounce hot water. Add this mixture to the above batch recipe. For use in a continuous freezer, multiply these new additions by 30.

Batch Freezing Method
Using an electric juicer, squeeze lemons. Strain juice and remove seeds. Save half of pulp and discard rest. (The pulp adds body and texture to the finished product.) Mix 5 quarts hot water with sugar until the sugar is completely dissolved. Under good agitation (using a spatula), slowly sift the stabilizer into the lemon juice. Allow the stabilizer to hydrate at least 30 minutes or more.

Pour juice and pulp mixture into batch freezer. Turn on dasher and refrigeration and begin batch. As mixture starts to firm up and look fluffy, turn off refrigeration and extrude finished product.

Decorate tops of tubs with slices of lemons.

Batch time: 13–17 minutes, depending on amount of sugar used and liquid mix in the barrel.

Yield: 3½–3¾ gallons, based on an overrun of 20%.

Continuous Freezing Method

Before you start the continuous freezing of this sorbet flavor, make sure the sanitizing solution or the previous flavor has been pushed through the freezer. Combine the sugar and stabilizer, then dissolve this mixture in hot water until sugar-water solution becomes clear. Next, pour all the ingredients into the flavor tank and thoroughly mix them together. The mix is then pumped to the inlet of the continuous freezer. Set the speed, viscosity (stiffness), and overrun settings according to the manufacturer's recommendations. Start the continuous freezing process. As the sorbet flavor leaves the continuous freezer, it is then piped to the next stage in the process, which is either filling (tubs, pints, etc.), extrusion, or molding.

Yield: Approximately 108 gallons, based on an overrun of 20–30%.

 MANGO

Mangoes are a delicious fruit to use in creating a sorbet. They must be fully ripe and peeled before use.

Mango sorbet can be prepared using fresh or frozen mangoes and both ways are recommended. Using frozen mangoes will give you a slightly sweeter product, so watch the use of sugar closely.

Using Fresh Fruit

Batch		Continuous
27 (yields 9 quarts puree)	mangoes	
	mango puree	67½ gallons
4½ quarts	water	33¾ gallons
5¼ pounds	sugar	157½ pounds
8¼ ounces	CC917 stabilizer* (1.0–1.5%)	
	CC427 stabilizer* (0.15–0.25%)	2½ pounds
weight:		weight:
4 gallons, 35 pounds		120 gallons, 1,050 pounds
	fresh mango slices for garnish	

*Note: Amount to use varies according to manufacturer's recommendations.

Great New Idea: Mango Coconut Sorbet. Combine 2 quarts coconut fruit base with ½ pound shredded coconut. Add this mixture to the above batch recipe. For use in a continuous freezer, multiply these new additions by 30.

Batch Freezing Method
Peel, seed, and puree enough fully ripened mangoes to yield 9 quarts of mango puree. Mix sugar thoroughly with 2 quarts of hot water, then add 2½ quarts of cold water to this mixture. Under good agitation (using a spatula), slowly sift the stabilizer into the mango puree. Allow the stabilizer to hydrate at least 30 minutes or more.

Pour mango puree and sugar-water solution into batch freezer. Turn on both dasher and refrigeration and begin batch. As mixture starts to firm up and look fluffy, turn off refrigeration and extrude finished product.

Decorate tops of tubs with fresh mango slices.

Batch time: 13–17 minutes, depending on amount of sugar used and liquid mix in the barrel.

Yield: 4¾ gallons, based on an overrun of 20%.

Using Frozen Puree

Batch		Continuous
5 quarts	water	39¾ gallons
3½ pounds	sugar	105 pounds
2¼ gallons	frozen mango puree, thawed	67½ gallons
8 ounces	CC917 stabilizer* (1.0–1.5%)	
	CC427 stabilizer* (0.15–0.25%)	2½ pounds
weight:		weight:
4 gallons,		120 gallons,
34 pounds		1,020 pounds
	mango puree for garnish	

---

*Note: Amount to use varies according to manufacturer's recommendations.

Batch Freezing Method
Completely thaw mango puree. Thoroughly mix sugar with 3 quarts of hot water, then add 2 quarts of cold water to this mixture.

Pour mango puree and sugar-water solution into batch freezer. Turn on both dasher and refrigeration and begin batch. As mixture starts to firm up and look fluffy, turn off refrigeration and extrude finished product.

Decorate tops of tubs with a decorative swirl of mango puree.

Batch time: 13–17 minutes, depending on amount of sugar used and liquid mix in the barrel.

Yield: 4¾ gallons, based on an overrun of 20%.

Continuous Freezing Method
Before you start the continuous freezing of this sorbet flavor, make sure the sanitizing solution or the previous flavor has been pushed through the freezer. Combine the sugar and stabilizer, then dissolve this mixture in hot water until sugar-

water solution becomes clear. Next, pour all the ingredients into the flavor tank and thoroughly mix them together. The mix is then pumped to the inlet of the continuous freezer. Set the speed, viscosity (stiffness), and overrun settings according to the manufacturer's recommendations. Start the continuous freezing process. As the sorbet flavor leaves the continuous freezer, it is then piped to the next stage in the process, which is either filling (tubs, pints, etc.), extrusion, or molding.

Yield: Approximately 144 gallons, based on an overrun of 20–30%.

⊠ MARGARITA

Can't get much more refreshing than this. Great for use in a Mexican or tropical theme restaurant.

Batch		Continuous
1½ quarts	fresh lime juice	11¼ gallons
6 quarts	water	45 gallons
6 pounds	sugar	180 pounds
3 quarts	Tequila	
1½ quarts	Triple Sec	
	Tequila flavor	2 quarts
	Triple Sec flavor	1 quart
7½ ounces	CC917 stabilizer* (1.0–1.5%)	
	CC427 stabilizer* (0.15–0.25%)	2½ pounds
weight:		weight:
3¾ gallons,		79½ gallons,
31½ pounds		658 pounds
	Key limes slices for garnish	

*Note: Amount to use varies according to manufacturer's recommendations.

Batch Freezing Method
Squeeze enough limes to obtain 1½ quarts of juice (or use bottled juice). Strain fresh juice and retain half the pulp. (The pulp adds body and texture to the finished product.) Thoroughly mix sugar with 3 quarts of extremely hot water, then add 3 quarts of cold water to this mixture. Under good agitation (using a spatula), slowly sift the stabilizer into the lime juice. Allow the stabilizer to hydrate at least 30 minutes or more.

Pour juice and pulp into batch freezer. Turn on both dasher and refrigeration and begin batch. As mixture starts to firm up and look fluffy, pour Tequila and Triple Sec into the batch freezer. Next, turn off refrigeration and extrude finished product.

Decorate tops of tubs with fresh key lime slices.

Batch time: 13–17 minutes, depending on amount of sugar used and liquid mix in the barrel.

Yield: 4½ gallons, based on an overrun of 20%.

Continuous Freezing Method

Before you start the continuous freezing of this sorbet flavor, make sure the sanitizing solution or the previous flavor has been pushed through the freezer. Combine the sugar and stabilizer, then dissolve this mixture in hot water until sugar-water solution becomes clear. Next, pour all the ingredients into the flavor tank and thoroughly mix them together. The mix is then pumped to the inlet of the continuous freezer. Set the speed, viscosity (stiffness), and overrun settings according to the manufacturer's recommendations. Start the continuous freezing process. As the sorbet flavor leaves the continuous freezer, it is then piped to the next stage in the process, which is either filling (tubs, pints, etc.), extrusion, or molding.

Yield: Approximately 95 gallons, based on an overrun of 20–30%.

⊠ ORANGE

Orange has always been a popular ice, and since oranges have a natural sweetness to them, producing orange sorbet is not difficult. Use only fresh-squeezed orange juice and don't use too much sugar as oversweetening will hide the natural flavor of the orange.

Batch		Continuous
85–90 (yields 8 quarts juice)	oranges	
	fresh orange juice	60 gallons
1 gallon	water	30 gallons
7½ pounds	sugar	225 pounds
7½ ounces	CC917 stabilizer* (1.0–1.5%)	
	CC427 stabilizer* (0.15–0.25%)	2½ pounds
weight:		weight:
4 gallons, 32 pounds		120 gallons, 960 pounds
	orange slices for garnish	

*Note: Amount to use varies according to manufacturer's recommendations.

Great New Idea: Tequila Sunrise Sorbet. This recipe was the creation of two outstanding individuals. Shipen Lebzelter and Guido Magnaguagno, the owners of New York Ice. When it came to pure creativity, they were clearly the best sorbet and ice cream makers I have even known. Add 1 quart of tequila (just before extrusion takes place) to the batch recipe. For use in a continuous freezer, multiply this new addition by 30.

Batch Freezing Method

Using an orange juicer, squeeze enough ripe oranges to obtain 8 quarts of juice. Strain juice and remove seeds. Save half of pulp and discard rest. (The pulp adds body and texture to the finished product.)

Thoroughly mix sugar with 2½ quarts of hot water, then add 1½ quarts of cold water to this mixture. Under good agitation (using a spatula), slowly sift the stabilizer into the lemon juice. Allow the stabilizer to hydrate at least 30 minutes or more.

Pour sugar mixture, juice, and pulp into batch freezer. Turn on dasher and refrigeration and begin batch. As mixture starts to firm up and look fluffy, turn off refrigeration and extrude finished product.

Decorate tops of tubs with fresh orange slices.

Batch time: 13–17 minutes, depending on amount of sugar used and liquid mix in the barrel.

Yield: 4¾ gallons, based on an overrun of 20%.

Continuous Freezing Method

Before you start the continuous freezing of this sorbet flavor, make sure the sanitizing solution or the previous flavor has been pushed through the freezer. Combine the sugar and stabilizer, then dissolve this mixture in hot water until sugar-water solution becomes clear. Next, pour all the ingredients into the flavor tank and thoroughly mix them together. The mix is then pumped to the inlet of the continuous freezer. Set the speed, viscosity (stiffness), and overrun settings according to the manufacturer's recommendations. Start the continuous freezing process. As the sorbet flavor leaves the continuous freezer, it is then piped to the next stage in the process, which is either filling (tubs, pints, etc.), extrusion, or molding.

Yield: Approximately 144 gallons, based on an overrun of 20–30%.

⊠ **PAPAYA**

Papaya is a very refreshing summertime fruit that is excellent as a sorbet flavor.

Batch		Continuous
17–19 (yields 7½ quarts puree)	papaya	
	papaya puree	56¼ gallons
1¼ gallons	water	37½ gallons
4⅓ pounds	sugar	130 pounds
8 ounces	CC917 stabilizer* (1.0–1.5%)	
	CC427 stabilizer* (0.15–0.25%)	2½ pounds
weight:		weight:
3¾ gallons, 32 pounds		112½ gallons, 960 pounds
	fresh papaya pieces for garnish	

*Note: Amount to use varies according to manufacturer's recommendations.

Great New Idea: Coconut Papaya Sorbet. Welcome to the Caribbean! Subtract 2 quarts of papaya puree from this batch recipe. Add 1 quart fresh orange juice, 1½ quarts coconut fruit base, and 16 ounce of fresh lime juice to the puree. For use in a continuous freezer, multiply these new additions by 30.

Batch Freezing Method
Peel papayas, scrape out seeds, and puree flesh. Thoroughly mix sugar with 2 quarts of hot water, then add 3 quarts of cold water to this mixture. Under good agitation (using a spatula), slowly sift the stabilizer into the papaya puree. Allow the stabilizer to hydrate at least 30 minutes or more. Pour all ingredients into batch freezer. Turn on both dasher and refrigeration and begin batch. As mixture starts to firm up and look fluffy, turn off refrigeration and extrude finished product.

Decorate tops of tubs with fresh papaya pieces.

Batch time: 13–17 minutes, depending on amount of sugar used and liquid mix in the barrel.

Yield: 4½ gallons, based on an overrun of 20%.

Continuous Freezing Method
Before you start the continuous freezing of this sorbet flavor, make sure the sanitizing solution or the previous flavor has been pushed through the freezer. Combine the sugar and stabilizer, then dissolve this mixture in hot water until sugar-water solution becomes clear. Next, pour all the ingredients into the flavor tank and thoroughly mix them together. The mix is then pumped to the inlet of the continuous freezer. Set the speed, viscosity (stiffness), and overrun settings according to the manufacturer's recommendations. Start the continuous freez-

ing process. As the sorbet flavor leaves the continuous freezer, it is then piped to the next stage in the process, which is either filling (tubs, pints, etc.), extrusion, or molding.

Yield: Approximately 135 gallons, based on an overrun of 20–30%.

⊠ PASSION FRUIT

This exotic fruit sorbet adds excitement to any dinner table, especially in restaurants.

Batch		Continuous
20 pounds (strained to yield 6¾ quarts of juice and pulp)	passion fruit	
	frozen passion fruit puree	50¾ gallons
1½ gallons	water	45 gallons
3½ pounds	sugar	65 pounds
4 ounces	fresh lemon juice and peel	3¾ quarts
7¼ ounces	CC917 stabilizer* (1.0–1.5%)	
	CC427 stabilizer* (0.15–0.25%)	2½ pounds
weight:		weight:
3½ gallons, 30¾ pounds		105 gallons, 923 pounds
	passion fruit pulp for garnish	

*Note: Amount to use varies according to manufacturer's recommendations.

Great New Idea: Passion Fruit Mango Sorbet. Combine 3 quarts mango puree with 12 ounces sugar dissolved in 2 ounces hot water. Add this mixture to the batch recipe. For use in a continuous freezer, multiply these new additions by 30.

Batch Freezing Method

Cut passion fruit in half and scoop the pulp out into a strainer over a bowl. Press pulp through strainer to extract as much juice as possible. Discard seeds, but retain some pulp for body and texture. Thoroughly mix sugar with 4 quarts of extremely hot water, then add 2 quarts of cold water and the lemon juice to this mixture. Under good agitation (using a spatula), slowly sift the stabilizer into the passion fruit puree. Allow the stabilizer to hydrate at least 30 minutes or more.

Pour juice, pulp, and sugar-water solutions into batch freezer. Turn on both dasher and refrigeration and begin batch. As mixture starts to firm up and look fluffy, turn off refrigeration and extrude finished product.

Decorate tops of tubs with passion fruit pulp.

Batch time: 13–17 minutes, depending on amount of sugar used and liquid mix in the barrel.

Yield: 4¼ gallons, based on an overrun of 20%.

Continuous Freezing Method
Before you start the continuous freezing of this sorbet flavor, make sure the sanitizing solution or the previous flavor has been pushed through the freezer. Combine the sugar and stabilizer, then dissolve this mixture in hot water until sugar-water solution becomes clear. Next, pour all the ingredients into the flavor tank and thoroughly mix them together. The mix is then pumped to the inlet of the continuous freezer. Set the speed, viscosity (stiffness), and overrun settings according to the manufacturer's recommendations. Start the continuous freezing process. As the sorbet flavor leaves the continuous freezer, it is then piped to the next stage in the process, which is either filling (tubs, pints, etc.), extrusion, or molding.

Yield: Approximately 126 gallons, based on an overrun of 20–30%.

⊠ PEACH

This is a great summer flavor when southern and eastern peaches are in season. It is extremely important to use only ripened peaches, otherwise it will be difficult to achieve the desired flavor.

Batch		Continuous
75 (yields 8¾ quarts puree)	peaches	
	peach puree	65½ gallons
4½ pounds	sugar	135 pounds
3¼ quarts	water	24½ gallons
3 ounces	fresh lemon juice	2¾ quarts
1¼ quart	peach fruit base	9½ gallons
7½ ounces	CC917 stabilizer* (1.0–1.5%)	
	CC427 stabilizer* (0.15–0.25%)	2½ pounds
weight:		weight:
3½ gallons, 32 pounds		105 gallons, 960 pounds
	pieces of peach for garnish	

*Note: Amount to use varies according to manufacturer's recommendations.

Great New Idea: Peach Schnapps Sorbet. Ever so good, ever so refreshing, especially when you taste the peach schnapps, and see how it brings out the true flavor of the peaches. Add 26 ounces of peach schnapps (just before extrusion takes place) to the batch recipe. For use in a continuous freezer, multiply this new addition by 30.

Batch Freezing Method

Wash peaches thoroughly, then cut them in half, remove stones, and puree. Thoroughly mix sugar with 2¼ quarts of extremely hot water, then add 1 quart of cold water to this mixture. Under good agitation (using a spatula), slowly sift the stabilizer into the peach puree. Allow the stabilizer to hydrate at least 30 minutes or more.

Pour all ingredients into batch freezer, turn on both dasher and refrigeration, and begin batch. As mixture starts to firm up and look fluffy, turn off refrigeration and extrude finished product.

Decorate tops of tubs with fresh peach pieces.

Batch time: 13–17 minutes, depending on amount of sugar used and liquid mix in the barrel.

Yield: 4¼ gallons, based on an overrun of 20%.

Continuous Freezing Method

Before you start the continuous freezing of this sorbet flavor, make sure the sanitizing solution or the previous flavor has been pushed through the freezer. Combine the sugar and stabilizer, then dissolve this mixture in hot water until sugar-water solution becomes clear. Next, pour all the ingredients into the flavor tank and thoroughly mix them together. The mix is then pumped to the inlet of the continuous freezer. Set the speed, viscosity (stiffness), and overrun settings according to the manufacturer's recommendations. Start the continuous freezing process. As the sorbet flavor leaves the continuous freezer, it is then piped to the next stage in the process, which is either filling (tubs, pints, etc.), extrusion, or molding.

Yield: Approximately 126 gallons, based on an overrun of 20–30%.

PEAR

Pears make a delicious tasting sorbet, but this is one of the few recipes in this book that doesn't use fresh or frozen ingredients in production. It is difficult to find frozen pears on the commercial market and using fresh pears entails a tremendous amount of peeling, seeding, and cooking.

Batch		Continuous
3 #10 cans (9 quarts)	pears in heavy syrup	
	pear puree	67½ gallons
2 quarts	water	15 gallons
3½ pounds	sugar	105 pounds
1 quart	pear nectar	7½ gallons
2 ounces	lemon juice	2 quarts
7 ounces	CC917 stabilizer* (1.0–1.5%)	
	CC427 stabilizer* (0.15–0.25%)	2 pounds
weight:		weight:
3½ gallons, 29¼ pounds		105 gallons, 877½ pounds
	pieces of pear for garnish	

*Note: Amount to use varies according to manufacturer's recommendations.

Great New Idea: Poire William Sorbet. An elegant, intensely flavored sorbet. Just right as the dessert du jour after that great meal. Add 26 ounces of Poire William or pear schnapps (just before extrusion takes place) to the batch recipe. For use in a continuous freezer, multiply this new addition by 30.

Batch Freezing Method
Drain and puree pears and retain heavy syrup. Thoroughly mix sugar with 1 quart of extremely hot water, then add 1 quart of cold water to this mixture. Under good agitation (using a spatula), slowly sift the stabilizer into the pear puree. Allow the stabilizer to hydrate at least 30 minutes or more.

Pour all ingredients into batch freezer. Turn on both dasher and refrigeration and begin batch. As mixture starts to firm up and look fluffy, turn off refrigeration and extrude finished product.

Decorate tops of tubs with pieces of pear.

Batch time: 13–17 minutes, depending on amount of sugar used and liquid mix in the barrel.

Yield: 4¼ gallons, based on an overrun of 20%.

Continuous Freezing Method
Before you start the continuous freezing of this sorbet flavor, make sure the sanitizing solution or the previous flavor has been pushed through the freezer. Com-

bine the sugar and stabilizer, then dissolve this mixture in hot water until sugar-water solution becomes clear. Next, pour all the ingredients into the flavor tank and thoroughly mix them together. The mix is then pumped to the inlet of the continuous freezer. Set the speed, viscosity (stiffness), and overrun settings according to the manufacturer's recommendations. Start the continuous freezing process. As the sorbet flavor leaves the continuous freezer, it is then piped to the next stage in the process, which is either filling (tubs, pints, etc.), extrusion, or molding.

Yield: Approximately 126 gallons, based on an overrun of 20–30%.

⊠ PEAR PERNOD

This sorbet is an elegant restaurant dessert menu item. The Pernod liqueur intensifies the pear flavor.

Batch		Continuous
3 #10 cans (288 ounces)	pears in heavy syrup	
	pear puree	67½ gallons
2 quarts	water	15 gallons
3½ pounds	sugar	105 pounds
1 quart	pear nectar	7½ gallons
1 ounce	lemon juice	2 quarts
10 ounces	Pernod liqueur	
	Pernod flavor	1¾ gallons
7 ounces	CC917 stabilizer* (1.0–1.5%)	
	CC427 stabilizer* (0.15–0.25%)	2¼ pounds
weight: 3¾ gallons, 29¾ pounds		weight: 112½ gallons, 892½ pounds
	sliced pears for garnish	

*Note: Amount to use varies according to manufacturer's recommendations.

Batch Freezing Method
Drain and puree pears; retain heavy syrup. Thoroughly mix sugar with 1 quart of extremely hot water, then add 1 quart of cold water to this mixture. Under good agitation (using a spatula), slowly sift the stabilizer into the pear puree. Allow the stabilizer to hydrate at least 30 minutes or more.

Pour all ingredients except Pernod into batch freezer. Turn on both dasher and refrigeration and begin batch. Halfway into batch, as mixture begins to freeze, add Pernod. As mixture starts to firm up and look fluffy, turn off refrigeration and extrude finished product.

Decorate tops of tubs with pear slices.

Batch time: 13–17 minutes, depending on amount of sugar used and liquid mix in the barrel.

Yield: 4½ gallons, based on an overrun of 20%.

Continuous Freezing Method

Before you start the continuous freezing of this sorbet flavor, make sure the sanitizing solution or the previous flavor has been pushed through the freezer. Combine the sugar and stabilizer, then dissolve this mixture in hot water until sugar-water solution becomes clear. Next, pour all the ingredients into the flavor tank and thoroughly mix them together. The mix is then pumped to the inlet of the continuous freezer. Set the speed, viscosity (stiffness), and overrun settings according to the manufacturer's recommendations. Start the continuous freezing process. As the sorbet flavor leaves the continuous freezer, it is then piped to the next stage in the process, which is either filling (tubs, pints, etc.), extrusion, or molding.

Yield: Approximately 135 gallons, depending on an overrun of 20–30%.

⧖ PIÑA COLADA

The flavor combination of pineapple and coconut is a perfect match that tastes wonderful. The name alone sells this flavor.

Batch		Continuous
2½ quarts	fresh (2–3) or frozen pineapple cubes	18¾ gallons
1 quart	coconut fruit base	7½ gallons
2 quarts	Coco Lopez	15 gallons
½ pound	shredded coconut	15 pounds
7½ quarts	water	56¼ gallons
2½ pounds	sugar	75 pounds
4 ounces	rum flavor	3¾ gallons
7½ ounces	CC917 stabilizer* (1.0–1.5%)	
	CC427 stabilizer* (0.15–0.25%)	2¼ pounds
weight:		weight:
3¾ gallons,		112½ gallons,
31½ pounds		945 pounds
	shredded coconut and pineapple pieces for garnish	

*Note: Amount to use varies according to manufacturer's recommendations.

Batch Freezing Method

Puree pineapple cubes. Mix together coconut fruit base, Coco Lopez, shredded coconut, and pureed pineapple. Thoroughly mix sugar with 3½ quarts of extremely hot water, then add 4 quarts of cold water to this mixture. Combine both mixtures. Under good agitation (using a spatula), slowly sift the stabilizer into the fruit puree. Allow the stabilizer to hydrate at least 30 minutes or more.

Pour pineapple puree/coconut mixture into batch freezer. Turn on both dasher and refrigeration and begin batch. As mixture starts to firm up and look fluffy, turn off refrigeration and extrude finished product.

Decorate tops of tubs with shredded coconut and pineapple.

Batch time: 13–17 minutes, depending on amount of sugar used and liquid mix in the barrel.

Yield: 4½ gallons, based on an overrun of 20%.

Continuous Freezing Method

Before you start the continuous freezing of this sorbet flavor, make sure the sanitizing solution or the previous flavor has been pushed through the freezer. Combine the sugar and stabilizer, then dissolve this mixture in hot water until sugar-water solution becomes clear. Next, pour all the ingredients into the flavor tank and thoroughly mix them together. The mix is then pumped to the inlet of the continuous freezer. Set the speed, viscosity (stiffness), and overrun settings according to the manufacturer's recommendations. Start the continuous freezing process. As the sorbet flavor leaves the continuous freezer, it is then piped to the next stage in the process, which is either filling (tubs, pints, etc.), extrusion, or molding.

Yield: Approximately 135 gallons, depending on an overrun of 20–30%.

▨ PINEAPPLE

This popular fruit will make a delicious sorbet flavor and should be a success on any menu.

Batch		Continuous
9–11 (yields 10 quarts puree)	pineapples	
	pineapple puree	75 gallons
1 gallon	water	30 gallons
3 pounds	sugar	90 pounds
8 ounces	CC917 stabilizer* (1.0–1.5%)	
	CC427 stabilizer* (0.15–0.25%)	2½ pounds
weight:		weight:
4 gallons, 33½ pounds		120 gallons, 1,005 pounds
	fresh pineapple pieces for garnish	

*Note: Amount to use varies according to manufacturer's recommendations.

Batch Freezing Method
Core, pare, and cut pineapples into pieces, then puree. Thoroughly mix sugar with 2 quarts of extremely hot water, then add 2 quarts of cold water. Combine puree and sugar syrup. Under good agitation (using a spatula), slowly sift the stabilizer into the pineapple mixture. Allow the stabilizer to hydrate at least 30 minutes or more.

Pour pineapple puree mixture into batch freezer. Turn on both dasher and refrigeration and begin batch. As mixture starts to firm up and look fluffy, turn off refrigeration and extrude finished product.

Decorate tops of tubs with fresh pineapple pieces.

Batch time: 13–17 minutes, depending on amount of sugar used and liquid mix in the barrel.

Yield: 4¾ gallons, based on an overrun of 20%.

Continuous Freezing Method
Before you start the continuous freezing of this sorbet flavor, make sure the sanitizing solution or the previous flavor has been pushed through the freezer. Combine the sugar and stabilizer, then dissolve this mixture in hot water until sugar-water solution becomes clear. Next, pour all the ingredients into the flavor tank and thoroughly mix them together. The mix is then pumped to the inlet of the continuous freezer. Set the speed, viscosity (stiffness), and overrun settings according to the manufacturer's recommendations. Start the continuous freezing process. As the sorbet flavor leaves the continuous freezer, it is then piped to the next stage in the process, which is either filling (tubs, pints, etc.), extrusion, or molding.

Yield: Approximately 144 gallons, based on an overrun of 20–30%.

⬚ RASPBERRY

Of all the upscale sorbet flavors, raspberry is the leading sorbet flavor sold in pints at the supermarket level. The intense rich flavor of the raspberry has always been appealing to the palate of the serious food purchaser. Be careful not to use too much sugar as this will mask the taste of the fruit.

Batch		Continuous
2½ gallons	water	75 gallons
9 pounds	sugar	270 pounds
3 #10 cans	frozen raspberries (9 quarts)	
(288 ounces)	raspberry puree	41¼ gallons
(yields 5½ quarts seedless puree)		
9 ounces	CC917 stabilizer* (1.0–1.5%)	
	CC427 stabilizer* (0.15–0.25%)	3 pounds
weight:		weight:
4¼ gallons,		127½ gallons,
39 pounds		1,170 pounds
	pieces of frozen raspberries for garnish	

*Note: Amount to use varies according to manufacturer's recommendations.

Batch Freezing Method

Thoroughly mix 1 gallon of extremely hot water with sugar until sugar is completely dissolved. Add one gallon of cold water to this mixture. Using a sieve, strain and remove all seeds from the raspberries. Add raspberries and their juice to sugar-water mixture. Under good agitation (using a spatula), slowly sift the stabilizer into the raspberry puree. Allow the stabilizer to hydrate at least 30 minutes or more.

Pour mixture into batch freezer, turn on both dasher and refrigeration, and begin batch. As mixture starts to firm up and look fluffy, turn off refrigeration and extrude finished product.

Decorate tops of tubs with pieces of frozen raspberries.

Batch time: 13–17 minutes, depending on amount of sugar used and liquid mix in the barrel.

Yield: 5 gallons, based on an overrun of 20%.

Continuous Freezing Method

Before you start the continuous freezing of this sorbet flavor, make sure the sanitizing solution or the previous flavor has been pushed through the freezer. Combine the sugar and stabilizer, then dissolve this mixture in hot water until sugar-water solution becomes clear. Next, pour all the ingredients into the flavor tank and thoroughly mix them together. The mix is then pumped to the inlet of the continuous freezer. Set the speed, viscosity (stiffness), and overrun settings according to the manufacturer's recommendations. Start the continuous freezing process. As the sorbet flavor leaves the continuous freezer, it is then piped to the next stage in the process, which is either filling (tubs, pints, etc.), extrusion, or molding.

Yield: Approximately 153 gallons, based on an overrun of 20–30%.

⊠ STRAWBERRY

Extremely refreshing, popular, and easy to produce, strawberry is the leading sorbet sold in retail frozen dessert shops in the United States. There is no comparison between the strawberry sorbet produced with the following recipe and the commercial sorbets sold in supermarkets. This recipe uses the whole strawberry whereas the commercial sorbets generally use only the juice that is obtained from straining the berry to remove the pulp and the seeds.

If you use fresh strawberries, you will have to overflavor the batch with extra strawberries to obtain the full flavor.

These two recipes produce an excellent sorbet and are highly recommended.

Using Fresh Fruit

Batch		Continuous
24 pints (yields 11 quarts of puree)	strawberries, rinsed and hulled	82½ gallons
3 quarts	water	22½ gallons
3 pounds	sugar	90 pounds
8 ounces	CC917 stabilizer* (1.0–1.5%)	
	CC427 stabilizer* (0.15–0.25%)	2½ pounds
weight:		weight:
4 gallons, 34 pounds		120 gallons, 1,020 pounds
	fresh strawberries for garnish	

*Note: Amount to use varies according to manufacturer's recommendations.

Batch Freezing Method

Thoroughly mix 1 quart of extremely hot water with sugar to create a sugar-water solution. Add 2 quarts of cold water to this mixture. Using some of the water from this mixture, puree strawberries in a blender. Under good agitation (using a spatula), slowly sift the stabilizer into the strawberry puree. Allow the stabilizer to hydrate at least 30 minutes or more.

Pour strawberry puree and sugar-water solution into batch freezer, turn on both dasher and refrigeration, and begin batch. As the mixture begins to firm up and look fluffy, turn off refrigeration and extrude finished product.

Decorate tops of tubs with fresh strawberries.

Batch time: 13–17 minutes, depending on amount of sugar used and liquid mix in the barrel.

Yield: 4¾–5 gallons, based on an overrun of 20%.

Continuous Freezing Method

Before you start the continuous freezing of this sorbet flavor, make sure the sanitizing solution or the previous flavor has been pushed through the freezer. Combine the sugar and stabilizer, then dissolve this mixture in hot water until sugar-water solution becomes clear. Puree the strawberries and pass them through a sieve to remove any seeds. Next, pour all the ingredients into the flavor tank and thoroughly mix them together. The mix is then pumped to the inlet of the continuous freezer. Set the speed, viscosity (stiffness), and overrun settings according to the manufacturer's recommendations. Start the continuous freezing process. As the sorbet flavor leaves the continuous freezer, it is then piped to the next stage in the process, which is either filling (tubs, pints, etc.), extrusion, or molding.

Yield: Approximately 144 gallons, depending on an overrun of 20–30%.

Using Frozen Fruit

Batch		Continuous
3 #10 cans (288 ounces)	frozen strawberries, thawed	82½ gallons
4 pints	fresh strawberries, pureed	
3½ quarts	water	20¼ gallons
2½ pounds	sugar	75 pounds
8 ounces	CC917 stabilizer* (1.0–1.5%)	
	CC427 stabilizer* (0.15–0.25%)	2½ pounds
weight:		weight:
4 gallons, 33 pounds		120 gallons, 990 pounds
	fresh strawberries for garnish	

*Note: Amount to use varies according to manufacturer's recommendations.

Great New Idea: Strawberry Champagne Sorbet. Replace 1½ quarts of strawberry puree with an equal amount of a good quality champagne (just before extrusion takes place) to the batch recipe. For use in a continuous freezer, multiply this new addition by 30.

Batch Freezing Method

Puree fresh strawberries in 1½ quarts of water and combine with thawed frozen strawberries. Mix sugar thoroughly with 1 quart of extremely hot water, then add 1 quart of cold water to this mixture. Under good agitation (using a spatula), slowly sift the stabilizer into the strawberry puree. Allow the stabilizer to hydrate at least 30 minutes or more.

Pour strawberry puree and sugar-water solution into batch freezer, turn on both dasher and refrigeration, and begin batch. As mixture starts to firm up and look fluffy, turn off refrigeration and extrude finished product.

Decorate tops of tubs with fresh strawberries.

Batch time: 13–17 minutes, depending on amount of sugar used and liquid mix in the barrel.

Yield: 4¾–5 gallons, based on an overrun of 20%.

Continuous Freezing Method

Before you start the continuous freezing of this sorbet flavor, make sure the sanitizing solution or the previous flavor has been pushed through the freezer. Combine the sugar and stabilizer, then dissolve this mixture in hot water until sugar-water solution becomes clear. Next, pour all the ingredients into the flavor tank and thoroughly mix them together. The mix is then pumped to the inlet of the continuous freezer. Set the speed, viscosity (stiffness), and overrun settings according to the manufacturer's recommendations. Start the continuous freezing process. As the sorbet flavor leaves the continuous freezer, it is then piped to the next stage in the process, which is either filling (tubs, pints, etc.), extrusion, or molding.

Yield: Approximately 144 gallons, depending on an overrun of 20–30%.

⊠ STRAWBERRY BANANA

The combination of banana and strawberry is very enticing and sells well in restaurants and ice cream parlors.

Batch		Continuous
3 #10 cans (2¼ gallons)	frozen strawberries	67½ gallons
5 pounds	ripe bananas (4 pounds peeled)*	
	banana puree	120 pounds
3 quarts	water	22½ gallons
3 pounds	sugar	90 pounds
7½ ounces	CC917 stabilizer† (1.0–1.5%)	
	CC427 stabilizer† (0.15–0.25%)	2¼ pounds
weight:		weight:
3¾ gallons, 31 pounds		112½ gallons, 930 pounds
	sliced bananas for garnish	

*Note: 5 pounds of whole bananas will yield approximately 4 pounds of peeled bananas because banana skin is approximately 20 percent of the weight of a banana.
†Note: Amount to use varies according to manufacturer's recommendations.

Great New Idea: A Taste of the Tropics Sorbet. Add 3 ounces of rum flavor (just before extrusion takes place) to the batch recipe. For use in a continuous freezer, multiply this new addition by 30.

Batch Freezing Method

Completely thaw frozen strawberries. Peel and puree bananas and add to strawberries. Thoroughly mix sugar with 2 quarts of extremely hot water, then add 1 quart of cold water to this mixture. Under good agitation (using a spatula), slowly sift the stabilizer into the strawberry-banana puree. Allow the stabilizer to hydrate at least 30 minutes or more.

Pour banana/strawberry puree and sugar-water solution into batch freezer. Turn on both dasher and refrigeration and begin batch. As mixture starts to firm up and look fluffy, turn off refrigeration and extrude finished product.

Decorate tops of tubs with bananas and strawberries.

Batch time: 13–17 minutes, depending on amount of sugar used and liquid mix in the barrel.

Yield: 4½–4¾ gallons, based on an overrun of 20%.

Continuous Freezing Method
Before you start the continuous freezing of this sorbet flavor, make sure the sanitizing solution or the previous flavor has been pushed through the freezer. Combine the sugar and stabilizer, then dissolve this mixture in hot water until sugar-water solution becomes clear. Puree the strawberries, and then pass them through a sieve to remove the seeds. Next, pour all the ingredients into the flavor tank and thoroughly mix them together. The mix is then pumped to the inlet of the continuous freezer. Set the speed, viscosity (stiffness), and overrun settings according to the manufacturer's recommendations. Start the continuous freezing process. As the sorbet flavor leaves the continuous freezer, it is then piped to the next stage in the process, which is either filling (tubs, pints, etc.), extrusion, or molding.

Yield: Approximately 135 gallons, depending on an overrun of 20–30%.

▨ TANGERINE

Tangerines have a more intense, subtle favor than oranges. This creative flavor will arouse interest from your customers and should sell well during the summer.

Batch		Continuous
100 (yields 7½ quarts juice)	tangerine	
	fresh tangerine juice	56¼ gallons
1¼ gallon	water	37½ gallons
2½ pounds	sugar	75 pounds
7 ounces	CC917 stabilizer* (1.0–1.5%)	
	CC427 stabilizer* (0.15–0.25%)	2 pounds
weight:		weight:
3½ gallons, 28¾ pounds		105 gallons, 862½ pounds
	tangerine slices for garnish	

*Note: Amount to use varies according to manufacturer's recommendations.

Great New Idea: Tangerine Mango Sorbet. Combine 3 quarts mango puree with 12 ounces sugar dissolved in 2 ounces hot water. Add this mixture to the batch recipe. For use in a continuous freezer, multiply these new additions by 30.

Batch Freezing Method
Squeeze tangerines, strain juice, and remove seeds. Save half of pulp and discard rest. Thoroughly mix sugar with 2 quarts of extremely hot water, then add 3 quarts of cold water to this mixture. Under good agitation (using a spatula),

slowly sift the stabilizer into the tangerine juice. Allow the stabilizer to hydrate at least 30 minutes or more.

Pour juice, pulp, and sugar-water solution into batch freezer. Turn on both dasher and refrigeration and begin batch. As mixture starts to firm up and look fluffy, turn off refrigeration and extrude finished product.

Decorate tops of tubs with tangerine slices.

Batch time: 13–17 minutes, depending on amount of sugar used and liquid mix in the barrel.

Yield: 4¼ gallons, based on an overrun of 20%.

Continuous Freezing Method

Before you start the continuous freezing of this sorbet flavor, make sure the sanitizing solution or the previous flavor has been pushed through the freezer. Combine the dry sugar and stabilizer, then dissolve this mixture in hot water until sugar-water solution becomes clear. Next, pour all the ingredients into the flavor tank and thoroughly mix them together. The mix is then pumped to the inlet of the continuous freezer. Set the speed, viscosity (stiffness), and overrun settings according to the manufacturer's recommendations. Start the continuous freezing process. As the sorbet flavor leaves the continuous freezer, it is then piped to the next stage in the process, which is either filling (tubs, pints, etc.), extrusion, or molding.

Yield: Approximately 126 gallons, depending on an overrun of 20–30%.

⊠ WATERMELON

This is strictly a summertime sorbet flavor—a very refreshing flavor to have on the menu on a hot day. Sugar is critical in this recipe because of the large water content of the watermelon. For this reason, very little water is added to the recipe.

Batch		Continuous
2 average size (yields 8 quarts seedless watermelon flesh)	watermelon (25–30 pounds each)	60 gallons
6 pounds	sugar	180 pounds
24 ounces	hot water	2¼ quarts
8 ounces	lemon juice	1¾ gallons
6 ounces	CC917 stabilizer* (1.0–1.5%)	
	CC427 stabilizer* (0.15–0.25%)	2 pounds
weight:		weight:
3¼ gallons, 27 pounds		105 gallons, 810 pounds
	thin slices of watermelon for garnish	

*Note: Amount to use varies according to manufacturer's recommendations.

Great New Idea: Watermelon Mango Sorbet. Combine 3 quarts mango puree with 12 ounces sugar dissolved in 2 ounces hot water. Add this mixture to the batch recipe. For use in a continuous freezer, multiply these new additions by 30.

Batch Freezing Method

Cut watermelon in quarters. Remove rind and seeds. Puree remaining melon. Thoroughly mix sugar with 3 cups of extremely hot water, then add lemon juice to this mixture. Under good agitation (using a spatula), slowly sift the stabilizer into the watermelon puree. Allow the stabilizer to hydrate at least 30 minutes or more.

Pour watermelon puree and sugar syrup solution into batch freezer. Turn on both dasher and refrigeration and begin batch. As mixture starts to firm up and look fluffy, turn off refrigeration and extrude finished product.

Decorate tops of tubs with watermelon slices.

Batch time: 13–17 minutes, depending on amount of sugar used and liquid mix in the barrel.

Yield: 3¾–4 gallons, based on an overrun of 20%.

Continuous Freezing Method

Before you start the continuous freezing of this sorbet flavor, make sure the sanitizing solution or the previous flavor has been pushed through the freezer.

Combine the sugar and stabilizer, then dissolve this mixture in hot water until sugar-water solution becomes clear. Next, pour all the ingredients into the flavor tank and thoroughly mix them together. The mix is then pumped to the inlet of the continuous freezer. Set the speed, viscosity (stiffness), and overrun settings according to the manufacturer's recommendations. Start the continuous freezing process. As the sorbet flavor leaves the continuous freezer, it is then piped to the next stage in the process, which is either filling (tubs, pints, etc.), extrusion, or molding.

Yield: Approximately 126 gallons, based on an overrun of 20–30%.

WATER ICE RECIPES

Basic Water Ice Formula

The proportions of the ingredients used to make water ice can vary depending on the flavor ingredient used and the supplier. For the most part, water ices use the following percentages of ingredients:

Cane sugar	23.00%
Corn syrup	7.00%
Stabilizer	0.30%
Fruit flavor	5.00%
Water	64.70%

To obtain a more tart flavor or to bring out the flavor of the fruit, citric acid is added at the rate of 4–10 ounces per 100 pounds of finished weight of product.

Tips for Preparing Water Ices

Water ices are basically prepared the same way as ice cream, whether by the batch or continuous freezing method. Product should be removed at a temperature of 22 degrees Fahrenheit. The finished product should have a clean fruit flavor. If the taste of a chemical in the finished product is noticeable it is because too much fruit extract, either natural or artificial, has been used. If the product is too coarse, it is because not enough sugar has been used or the product has been overprocessed.

Overrun should be kept at a minimum of 25 percent regardless of the freezing method used. In the batch method, this is accomplished by using 6–8 gallons of mixture in a 40-quart batch freezer. To achieve 25 percent overrun using the continuous method, simply make an adjustment to the overrun button on the main control panel.

The acidic level of the water ice mixture results in a high rate of wear and tear of the scraper blades because of the lack of cream (fat) that would otherwise constantly lubricate all the metal surfaces. For this reason, the blades should be sharpened on a regular basis to maintain the capability of producing small ice particles.

The following points will ensure an excellent product being produced:

- The ratio of sugar to water should be approximately 6–8 pounds of sugar to 14 quarts of water. Depending on the water ice flavor, this ratio can go either up or down, but the more sugar used, the longer it will take for the product to freeze. More sugar is used in water ices than in sorbets to give body texture because water ices, in most cases, do not use real fruit that do add texture, body, and sweetness to the product.
- Corn syrup can replace one-fourth of the sugar to give a smoother dipping product.
- The stabilizer being used should be one that is proven to work.
- Too much critic acid will give an aftertaste at the back of the throat.
- Extrude product at a firm, but not overprocessed state, and blast freeze immediately.
- Protect the product from temperature fluctuations.

To produce water ices using a continuous freezer, multiply ingredient quantities of batch freezer recipes by 30.

Sample Water Ice Flavor Recipe

Lemon water ice is the biggest seller you will have for your entire water ice business. It is to water ice as vanilla is to ice cream—the benchmark flavor that consumers will judge you by.

▧ LEMON WATER ICE

Ingredients
4–5 ounces natural lemon flavor
2–3 ounces citric acid
6–7 pounds sugar
2 ounces stabilizer
5 gallons water

Preparation
To make a 20-quart batch, mix 6–7 pounds sugar with 2 ounces of stabilizer. Pour this mixture into 2 gallons of very hot water to dissolve the sugar–stabilizer mixture. Next, pour all the remaining ingredients plus 3 gallons cold water into

Table 15-3. Recommended Flavor Recipes and Ingredients Used

Flavor	Amount (fluid ounces)	Citric Acid (fluid ounces)	Stabilizer (fluid ounces)
Cantaloupe	3	$\frac{1}{2}$	2
Cherry	3	2	2
Grape	3	2	2
Key lime	4	2–3	2
Orange	3	2	2
Piña colada	3	1	2
Pink grapefruit	3	2	2
Pineapple	3	2	2
Strawberry	3	2	2
Watermelon	2	0	2

the batch freezer. Turn on the dasher for one minute, and then the refrigeration. When the batch is semifrozen, soft, slightly firm, extrude out the product.

Batch time is approximately 16 minutes.

Other Water Ice Flavor Recipes

Table 15-3 lists the most popular flavors produced and sold along with recommended flavor usage for each. Each batch requires 5 gallons of water and should be prepared following the directions given for the lemon water ice.

16 ⊠⊠⊠⊠⊠⊠⊠⊠⊠⊠⊠⊠⊠⊠⊠⊠⊠⊠⊠⊠⊠⊠⊠⊠⊠⊠⊠

HARDPACK
FROZEN YOGURT

SMOOTH, DELICIOUS, AND LOW-FAT

Hardpack frozen yogurt has become popular because of its large variety of flavors, body and texture being similar to ice cream, and potential appeal to male customers who would rather eat a hardpack product that was similar to ice cream than a soft serve product. The late 1980s saw a tremendous growth in the sales of soft frozen yogurt, and, based on its sales growth, dairy processors dramatically increased production of hardpack frozen yogurt products for sale in supermarkets. Consumers looking for lower fat products gravitated to this product segment after becoming aware of hard frozen yogurt's attributes via promotion and supermarket exposure. Today, it is being sold in pints, quarts, and various forms of novelty bars. National companies such as Häagen-Dazs, Ben & Jerry's, Dreyer's, Breyers, and Colombo have introduced many new hardpack frozen yogurt products and have succeeded in getting shelf space for them. Along with these national companies, regional chains such as AE Farms and Blue Bell have been very successful with hardpack frozen yogurt.

THE RECIPES

Note: As for hardpack ice cream, to convert a batch recipe to use for continuous freezing production, multiply all ingredients by 40.

⊠ VANILLA

The most popular flavor of frozen yogurt sold. Prepared with natural vanilla extract, it will become an instant success.

Batch		Continuous
2½ gallons	lowfat or nonfat frozen yogurt	25 gallons
1½ ounces	Madagascar Bourbon and Tahitian pure vanilla extract* (two-fold)	1¾ quarts

*Note: A blend of Madagascar Bourbon and Tahitian pure vanilla extract is used for frozen yogurt applications in order to provide a sweet, fruity, and creamy flavor. Madagascar Bourbon vanilla smoothes and mellows the acid bite of the frozen yogurt, while the Tahitian vanilla component lifts and enhances the fruit flavor.

Batch Freezing Method

Pour all ingredients into batch freezer, turn on dasher and refrigeration, and begin batch. When batch is complete, turn off refrigeration and extrude finished product.

Batch time: 8–9 minutes.

Continuous Freezing Method

Before you start the continuous freezing of this flavor, make sure the sanitizing solution or the previous flavor of mix has been pushed through the freezer. Open the outlet valve of the mix storage tank and let the proper amount of frozen yogurt mix flow into the flavor tank. Pour the vanilla extract into the flavor tank and mix all the ingredients together. The mix is then pumped to the inlet of the continuous freezer. Set the speed, viscosity (stiffness), and overrun settings according to the manufacturer's recommendations. Start the continuous freezing process. As the frozen yogurt leaves the continuous freezer, it is then piped to the next stage in the process, which is either filling (tubs, pints, etc.), extrusion, or molding.

⊠ VANILLA CHOCOLATE CHIP

A delightful variation of the vanilla flavor.

Batch		Continuous
2½ gallons	lowfat or nonfat frozen yogurt	25 gallons
1½ ounces	Madagascar Bourbon and Tahitian pure vanilla extract (two-fold)	1¾ quarts
2 pounds	chocolate chunks or chips chocolate chunks or chips for garnish	80 pounds

Batch Freezing Method
Pour the frozen yogurt mix, vanilla extract, and 1 pound of chocolate chunks into batch freezer, turn on dasher and refrigeration, and begin batch. Just before batch is complete, pour in remaining chocolate chunks. Turn off refrigeration and extrude finished product.

Garnish with chocolate chunks or chips.

Batch time: 8–9 minutes.

Continuous Freezing Method
Before you start the continuous freezing of this flavor, make sure the sanitizing solution or the previous flavor of mix has been pushed through the freezer. Pour the chocolate chunks or chips into the fruit feeder and adjust the controls to the appropriate setting. Open the outlet valve of the mix storage tank and let the proper amount of frozen yogurt mix flow into the flavor tank. Pour the vanilla extract into the flavor tank and mix all the ingredients together. The mix is then pumped to the inlet of the continuous freezer. Set the speed, viscosity (stiffness), and overrun settings according to the manufacturer's recommendations. Start the continuous freezing process. As the frozen yogurt leaves the continuous freezer, it is then piped through the fruit feeder (ingredient feeder) so that the chocolate chunks or chips can be discharged and mixed with the frozen yogurt that has already become semifrozen. The frozen yogurt is then piped to the next stage in the process, which is either filling (tubs, pints, etc.), extrusion, or molding.

APPLE PIE

A wonderful fall and holiday (Thanksgiving) flavor.

Batch		Continuous
2½ gallons	lowfat or nonfat frozen yogurt	25 gallons
1½ ounces	Madagascar Bourbon and Tahitian pure vanilla extract (two-fold)	1¾ quarts
2 quarts	apple pie filling	20 gallons
1 ounce	cinnamon	2½ pounds
1 pound	dark raisins	40 pounds
½ pound	graham crackers	20 pounds
	graham crackers and raisins for garnish	

Batch Freezing Method
Pour the frozen yogurt mix, vanilla extract, cinnamon, and apple pie filling into batch freezer, turn on dasher and refrigeration, and begin batch. Just before batch is complete, pour in raisins and graham crackers. Turn off refrigeration and extrude finished product.

Garnish with raisins and graham crackers.

Batch time: 8–9 minutes.

Continuous Freezing Method

Before you start the continuous freezing of this flavor, make sure the sanitizing solution or the previous flavor of mix has been pushed through the freezer. Pour the raisins and graham crackers into the fruit feeder and adjust the controls to the appropriate setting. Open the outlet valve of the mix storage tank and let the proper amount of frozen yogurt mix flow into the flavor tank. Pour the vanilla extract, cinnamon, and pureed apple pie filling into the flavor tank and mix all the ingredients together. The mix is then pumped to the inlet of the continuous freezer. Set the speed, viscosity (stiffness), and overrun settings according to the manufacturer's recommendations. Start the continuous freezing process. As the frozen yogurt leaves the continuous freezer, it is then piped through the fruit feeder (ingredient feeder) so that the raisins and graham crackers can be discharged and mixed with the frozen yogurt that has already become semifrozen. The frozen yogurt is then piped to the next stage in the process, which is either filling (tubs, pints, etc.), extrusion, or molding.

⊠ COOKIE DOUGH

The rage of the 90s. In this lowfat version, you not only taste the cookie dough, but get to taste lots of chips and fudge as well.

Batch		Continuous
2½ gallons	lowfat or nonfat frozen yogurt	25 gallons
1½ ounces	Madagascar Bourbon and Tahitian pure vanilla extract (two-fold)	1¾ quarts
2 pounds	cookie dough pieces	80 pounds
1 pound	chocolate chunks or chips	40 pounds
2 quarts	fudge	
	fudge variegate	20 gallons
	cookie dough pieces, chocolate chunks, and fudge for garnish	

Batch Freezing Method

Pour the frozen yogurt mix, vanilla extract, chocolate chunks, and 1 pound of the cookie dough pieces into the batch freezer. Turn on dasher and refrigeration, and begin batch. Just before batch is complete, pour in remaining cookie dough pieces. Turn off refrigeration and extrude finished product swirling in fudge as the tubs are being filled.

Batch time: 8–9 minutes.

Continuous Freezing Method
Before you start the continuous freezing of this flavor, make sure the sanitizing solution or the previous flavor of mix has been pushed through the freezer. Pour the fudge variegate into the ripple pump (temperature of fudge variegate at the time of usage should be 40 degrees Fahrenheit) and adjust the setting to inject the fudge at the rate of 10–14 percent of the weight of the ice cream. Next, pour the cookie dough pieces and chocolate chunks or chips into the fruit feeder and adjust the controls to the appropriate setting. Open the outlet valve of the mix storage tank and let the proper amount of frozen yogurt mix flow into the flavor tank. Pour the vanilla extract into the flavor tank and mix all the ingredients together. The mix is then pumped to the inlet of the continuous freezer. Set the speed, viscosity (stiffness), and overrun settings according to the manufacturer's recommendations. Start the continuous freezing process. As the frozen yogurt leaves the continuous freezer, it is then piped through the fruit feeder (ingredient feeder) so that the cookie dough pieces and chocolate chunks or chips can be discharged and mixed with the frozen yogurt. The frozen yogurt is then piped to the ripple pump so that the fudge variegate can be injected into the stream of frozen yogurt that has already become semifrozen. The frozen yogurt is then piped to the next stage in the process, which is either filling (tubs, pints, etc.), extrusion, or molding.

▧ COOKIES AND CREAM

Simply a great flavor, any way you make it.

Batch		Continuous
2½ gallons	lowfat or nonfat frozen yogurt	100 gallons
1½ ounces	Madagascar Bourbon and Tahitian pure vanilla extract (two-fold)	1¾ quarts
2½ pounds	Oreo or Hydrox cookie (broken)	100 pounds
	Oreo or Hydrox cookies for garnish	

Batch Freezing Method
Combine frozen yogurt mix, vanilla extract, and half of the Oreos and pour into batch freezer. Turn on dasher and refrigeration and begin batch. Just before batch is complete, pour in remaining Oreos. Turn off refrigeration and extrude finished product.

Garnish with pieces of Oreo cookies.

Batch time: 8–9 minutes.

Continuous Freezing Method
Before you start the continuous freezing of this flavor, make sure the sanitizing solution or the previous flavor of mix has been pushed through the freezer.

Pour the Oreo or Hydrox cookies into the fruit feeder and adjust the controls to the appropriate setting. Open the outlet valve of the mix storage tank and let the proper amount of frozen yogurt mix flow into the flavor tank. Pour the vanilla extract into the flavor tank and mix all the ingredients together. The mix is then pumped to the inlet of the continuous freezer. Set the speed, viscosity (stiffness), and overrun settings according to the manufacturer's recommendations. Start the continuous freezing process. As the frozen yogurt leaves the continuous freezer, it is then piped through the fruit feeder (ingredient feeder) so that the Oreo or Hydrox cookies can be discharged and mixed with the frozen yogurt that has already become semifrozen. The frozen yogurt is then piped to the next stage in the process, which is either filling (tubs, pints, etc.), extrusion, or molding.

⊠ BANANABERRY

A very refreshing summer flavor with a strong fresh banana flavor.

Batch		Continuous
2½ gallons	lowfat or nonfat frozen yogurt	100 gallons
1½ ounces	Madagascar Bourbon and Tahitian pure vanilla extract (two-fold)	1¾ quarts
6 pounds	fresh bananas (5 pounds peeled)*	
	pasteurized banana puree	240 pounds
48 ounces	solid pack strawberries	120 pounds
	sliced bananas and strawberries for garnish	

*Note: 6 pounds of bananas will yield approximately 5 pounds of peeled bananas because banana skin is approximately 20 percent of the weight of a banana.

Batch Freezing Method

Chill the strawberries to 40 degrees Fahrenheit prior to use. Combine frozen yogurt mix, vanilla extract, and bananas and pour into batch freezer. Turn on dasher for approximately 3 minutes to puree bananas. Turn on refrigeration and begin batch. When batch is complete, turn off refrigeration and extrude finished product. Gently fold in chilled strawberries rotating tub as needed to distribute fruit evenly.

Garnish with sliced bananas and strawberries.

Batch time: 8–9 minutes.

Continuous Freezing Method
Before you start the continuous freezing of this flavor, make sure the sanitizing solution or the previous flavor of mix has been pushed through the freezer. Pour the strawberries into the fruit feeder and adjust the controls to the appropriate settings. Open the outlet valve of the mix storage tank and let the proper amount of frozen yogurt mix flow into the flavor tank. Pour the vanilla extract and banana puree into the flavor tank and mix all the ingredients together. The mix is then pumped to the inlet of the continuous freezer. Set the speed, viscosity (stiffness), and overrun settings according to the manufacturer's recommendations. Start the continuous freezing process. As the frozen yogurt leaves the continuous freezer, it is then piped through the fruit feeder (ingredient feeder) so that the strawberries can be discharged and mixed with the frozen yogurt that has already become semifrozen. The frozen yogurt is then piped to the next stage in the process, which is either filling (tubs, pints, etc.), extrusion, or molding.

BLACK CHERRY

Black cherry frozen yogurt is made with Bordeaux cherry halves, creating a very delightful fruity flavor.

Batch		Continuous
2½ gallons	lowfat or nonfat frozen yogurt	100 gallons
1½ ounces	Madagascar Bourbon and Tahitian pure vanilla extract (two-fold)	1¾ quarts
1½ quarts	Bordeaux cherry halves cherry halves for garnish	15 gallons

Batch Freezing Method
Chill Bordeaux cherry halves prior to use. Drain juice from cherry halves and add ½ of juice to the mix and discard the rest. Pour the mix and ¾ quart of cherries into batch freezer, turn on dasher and refrigeration, and begin batch. Just before batch is complete, add remaining cherry halves to batch. Turn off refrigeration and extrude finished product.

Garnish with cherry halves.

Batch time: 8–9 minutes.

Continuous Freezing Method
Before you start the continuous freezing of this flavor, make sure the sanitizing solution or the previous flavor of mix has been pushed through the freezer. Using a sieve, drain cherry halves and reserve juice. Pour the Bordeaux cherry halves into the fruit feeder and adjust the controls to the appropriate setting. Open the outlet valve of the mix storage tank and let the proper amount of frozen yogurt mix flow into the flavor tank. Pour the vanilla extract and half of the juice (discard remaining

half) from the cherry halves into the flavor tank and mix all the ingredients together. The mix is then pumped to the inlet of the continuous freezer. Set the speed, viscosity (stiffness), and overrun settings according to the manufacturer's recommendations. Start the continuous freezing process. As the frozen yogurt leaves the continuous freezer, it is then piped through the fruit feeder (ingredient feeder) so that the cherry halves can be discharged and mixed with the frozen yogurt that has already become semifrozen. The frozen yogurt is then piped to the next stage in the process, which is either filling (tubs, pints, etc.), extrusion, or molding.

⊠ BLUEBERRY

Dense appealing flavor that is an excellent seller.

Batch		Continuous
2½ gallons	lowfat or nonfat frozen yogurt	100 gallons
1½ ounces	Madagascar Bourbon and Tahitian pure vanilla extract (two-fold)	1¾ quarts
1½ quarts	solid pack blueberries	15 gallons
	blueberries for garnish	

Batch Freezing Method

Chill blueberries to 40 degrees Fahrenheit prior to use. Combine the frozen yogurt mix, vanilla extract, and ½ quart of blueberries and pour into batch freezer. Turn on dasher and refrigeration and begin batch. Just before batch is complete, pour in remaining blueberries. Turn off refrigeration and extrude finished product.

Garnish with blueberries.

Batch time: 8–9 minutes.

Continuous Freezing Method

Before you start the continuous freezing of this flavor, make sure the sanitizing solution or the previous flavor of mix has been pushed through the freezer. Pour the blueberries into the fruit feeder and adjust the controls to the appropriate setting. Open the outlet valve of the mix storage tank and let the proper amount of frozen yogurt mix flow into the flavor tank. Pour the vanilla extract into the flavor tank and mix all the ingredients together. The mix is then pumped to the inlet of the continuous freezer. Set the speed, viscosity (stiffness), and overrun settings according to the manufacturer's recommendations. Start the continuous freezing process. As the frozen yogurt leaves the continuous freezer, it is then piped through the fruit feeder (ingredient feeder) so that the blueberries can be discharged and mixed with the frozen yogurt that has already become semifrozen. The frozen yogurt is then piped to the next stage in the process, which is either filling (tubs, pints, etc.), extrusion, or molding.

PEACH

I have always liked peach ice cream since I was a child, so making this flavor right has always been a challenge for me.

Batch		Continuous
2½ gallons	lowfat or nonfat frozen yogurt	100 gallons
1½ ounces	Madagascar Bourbon and Tahitian pure vanilla extract (two-fold)	1¾ quarts
3 ounces	natural peach extract*	3¾ quarts
2 quarts	stabilized peaches	20 gallons
	sliced peaches for garnish	

*Note: Amount to use varies according to manufacturer's recommendations.

Batch Freezing Method

Pour the frozen yogurt mix, vanilla extract, and peach extract into batch freezer. Turn on dasher and refrigeration and begin batch. Just before batch is complete, add peaches. Turn off refrigeration and extrude finished product.

Garnish with sliced peaches.

Batch time: 8–9 minutes.

Continuous Freezing Method

Before you start the continuous freezing of this flavor, make sure the sanitizing solution or the previous flavor of mix has been pushed through the freezer. Pour the peaches into the fruit feeder and adjust the controls to the appropriate setting. Open the outlet valve of the mix storage tank and let the proper amount of frozen yogurt mix flow into the flavor tank. Pour the vanilla extract and peach extract into the flavor tank and mix all the ingredients together. The mix is then pumped to the inlet of the continuous freezer. Set the speed, viscosity (stiffness), and overrun settings according to the manufacturer's recommendations. Start the continuous freezing process. As the frozen yogurt leaves the continuous freezer, it is then piped through the fruit feeder (ingredient feeder) so that the peaches can be discharged and mixed with the frozen yogurt that has already become semifrozen. The frozen yogurt is then piped to the next stage in the process, which is either filling (tubs, pints, etc.), extrusion, or molding.

MANGO

The taste of mango stands out in this frozen yogurt flavor.

Batch		Continuous
2½ gallons	lowfat or nonfat frozen yogurt	100 gallons
1½ ounces	Madagascar Bourbon and Tahitian pure vanilla extract (two-fold)	1¾ quarts
2½ quarts	frozen mango puree* mango puree for garnish	25 gallons

---

*Note: If frozen mango puree comes with 10% sugar, no additional sugar is needed to inhibit crystallization.

Batch Freezing Method

Defrost mango puree. Pour all ingredients into batch freezer, turn on dasher and refrigeration, and begin batch. When the batch is complete, turn off refrigeration and extrude finished product.

Garnish with mango puree.

Batch time: 8–9 minutes.

Continuous Freezing Method

Before you start the continuous freezing of this flavor, make sure the sanitizing solution or the previous flavor of mix has been pushed through the freezer. Open the outlet valve of the mix storage tank and let the proper amount of frozen yogurt mix flow into the flavor tank. Pour the vanilla extract and mango puree into the flavor tank and mix all the ingredients together. The mix is then pumped to the inlet of the continuous freezer. Set the speed, viscosity (stiffness), and overrun settings according to the manufacturer's recommendations. Start the continuous freezing process. As the frozen yogurt leaves the continuous freezer, it is then piped to the next stage in the process, which is either filling (tubs, pints, etc.), extrusion, or molding.

 RASPBERRY

A very popular flavor that certainly ranks with the top sellers.

Batch		Continuous
2½ gallons	lowfat or nonfat frozen yogurt	100 gallons
1½ ounces	Madagascar Bourbon and Tahitian pure vanilla extract (two-fold)	1¾ quarts
2 quarts	red raspberry seedless puree	22½ gallons
8 ounces	frozen raspberries fresh or frozen raspberries for garnish	

Batch Freezing Method
Set aside 8 ounces of raspberry puree for garnish. Press 8 ounces of defrosted frozen raspberries through a sieve. Next, pour all ingredients into batch freezer, turn on dasher and refrigeration, and begin batch. When batch is complete, turn off refrigeration and extrude finished product.

Garnish with raspberry puree.

Batch time: 8–9 minutes.

Continuous Freezing Method
Before you start the continuous freezing of this flavor, make sure the sanitizing solution or the previous flavor of mix has been pushed through the freezer. Open the outlet valve of the mix storage tank and let the proper amount of frozen yogurt mix flow into the flavor tank. Pour the vanilla extract and raspberry puree into the flavor tank and mix all the ingredients together. The mix is then pumped to the inlet of the continuous freezer. Set the speed, viscosity (stiffness), and overrun settings according to the manufacturer's recommendations. Start the continuous freezing process. As the frozen yogurt leaves the continuous freezer, it is then piped to the next stage in the process, which is either filling (tubs, pints, etc.), extrusion, or molding.

STRAWBERRY

The generous amount of strawberries used in this flavor is very evident in the taste of the finished product.

Batch		Continuous
2½ gallons	lowfat or nonfat frozen yogurt	100 gallons
1½ ounces	Madagascar Bourbon and Tahitian pure vanilla extract (two-fold)	1¾ quarts
1½ quarts	solid pack strawberries	15 gallons
1½ quarts	frozen strawberries, juice drained and discarded	15 gallons
10 ounces	sugar	25 pounds
	strawberries for garnish	

Batch Freezing Method
Set aside 8 ounces of solid pack strawberries for garnish. Combine sugar with defrosted frozen strawberries, mix thoroughly and marinate for 8 hours. Drain juice off and set it aside. Also, set aside half of the drained strawberry mixture for use at end of batch. Combine all remaining ingredients and pour them into batch freezer. Turn on dasher and refrigeration and begin batch. Just before batch is complete, pour in remaining strawberries, turn off refrigeration, and extrude finished product.

Garnish with strawberries.

Batch time: 8–9 minutes.

Continuous Freezing Method

Combine sugar with defrosted frozen strawberries. Thoroughly mix this mixture and marinate for 8 hours. Before you start the continuous freezing of this flavor, make sure the sanitizing solution or the previous flavor of mix has been pushed through the freezer. Pour all the strawberries into the fruit feeder and adjust the controls to the appropriate setting. Open the outlet valve of the mix storage tank and let the proper amount of frozen yogurt mix flow into the flavor tank. Pour the vanilla extract into the flavor tank and mix all the ingredients together. The mix is then pumped to the inlet of the continuous freezer. Set the speed, viscosity (stiffness), and overrun settings according to the manufacturer's recommendations. Start the continuous freezing process. As the frozen yogurt leaves the continuous freezer, it is then piped through the fruit feeder (ingredient feeder) so that the strawberries can be discharged and mixed with the frozen yogurt that has already become semifrozen. The frozen yogurt is then piped to the next stage in the process, which is either filling (tubs, pints, etc.), extrusion, or molding.

⊠ STRAWBERRY CHEESECAKE

This flavor tastes great, period!

Batch		Continuous
2½ gallons	lowfat or nonfat frozen yogurt	100 gallons
1½ ounces	Madagascar Bourbon and Tahitian pure vanilla extract (two-fold)	1¾ quarts
3 pounds	dry cheesecake mix	120 pounds
1 pound	broken pieces of graham crackers	40 pounds
2 quarts	solid pack strawberries	20 gallons

Batch Freezing Method

Chill solid pack strawberries at 40 degrees Fahrenheit prior to use and set aside. Thoroughly mix dry cheesecake mix with the frozen yogurt. Pour mixture and vanilla extract into batch freezer, turn on dasher and refrigeration, and begin batch. Just before batch is complete, pour in pieces of graham crackers, turn off refrigeration, and extrude finished product into tubs, swirling chilled strawberries as tubs are being rotated.

Batch time: 8–9 minutes.

Continuous Freezing Method
Before you start the continuous freezing of this flavor, make sure the sanitizing solution or the previous flavor of mix has been pushed through the freezer. Pour the strawberries and graham crackers into the fruit feeder and adjust the controls to the appropriate setting. Open the outlet valve of the mix storage tank and let the proper amount of frozen yogurt mix flow into the flavor tank. Pour the vanilla extract and dry cheesecake mix into the flavor tank and mix all the ingredients together. The mix is then pumped to the inlet of the continuous freezer. Set the speed, viscosity (stiffness), and overrun settings according to the manufacturer's recommendations. Start the continuous freezing process. As the frozen yogurt leaves the continuous freezer, it is then piped through the fruit feeder (ingredient feeder) so that the strawberries and graham crackers can be discharged and mixed with the frozen yogurt that has already become semi-frozen. The frozen yogurt is then piped to the next stage in the process, which is either filling (tubs, pints, etc.), extrusion, or molding.

⊠ BUTTER PECAN

The best-selling nut flavor ice cream is a winner when produced as a frozen yogurt.

Batch		Continuous
2½ gallons	lowfat or nonfat frozen yogurt	100 gallons
1½ ounces	Madagascar Bourbon and Tahitian pure vanilla extract (two-fold)	1¾ quarts
24 ounces	butter pecan base	7½ gallons
2 pounds	large roasted pecan pieces pecans for garnish	80 pounds

Batch Freezing Method
Set aside 4 ounces of pecans for garnish. Pour frozen yogurt mix, butter pecan base, vanilla extract, and 1 pound of roasted pecans, and pour mixture into batch freezer. Turn on dasher and refrigeration, and begin batch. Just before batch is complete, add remaining pecans, turn off refrigeration, and extrude finished product.
    Garnish with pecans.

Batch time: 8–9 minutes.

Continuous Freezing Method
Before you start the continuous freezing of this flavor, make sure the sanitizing solution or the previous flavor of mix has been pushed through the freezer. Pour the large pecan pieces into the fruit feeder and adjust the controls to the appropriate setting. Open the outlet valve of the mix storage tank and let the

proper amount of frozen yogurt mix flow into the flavor tank. Pour the vanilla extract and butter pecan base into the flavor tank and mix all the ingredients together. The mix is then pumped to the inlet of the continuous freezer. Set the speed, viscosity (stiffness), and overrun settings according to the manufacturer's recommendations. Start the continuous freezing process. As the frozen yogurt leaves the continuous freezer, it is then piped through the fruit feeder (ingredient feeder) so that the pecan pieces can be discharged and mixed with the frozen yogurt that has already been semifrozen. The frozen yogurt is then piped to the next stage in the process, which is either filling (tubs, pints, etc.), extrusion, or molding.

⊠ COFFEE

Strong coffee flavor for those coffee addicts.

Batch		Continuous
2½ gallons	lowfat or nonfat frozen yogurt	100 gallons
1½ ounces	Madagascar Bourbon and Tahitian pure vanilla extract (two-fold)	1¾ quarts
4 ounces	freeze-dried coffee	10 pounds
½ ounce	cocoa (10–12% or 22–24% fat)	1¼ pounds
1 ounce	hot water	1¼ quarts

Batch Freezing Method
Using a few drops of hot water, create a paste with the freeze-dried coffee and cocoa. Combine the frozen yogurt mix, vanilla extract, and coffee mixture. Pour all the ingredients into batch freezer, turn on dasher and refrigeration, and begin batch. When batch is complete, turn off refrigeration and extrude finished product.

Batch time: 8–9 minutes.

Continuous Freezing Method
Using hot water, create a paste with the freeze-dried coffee and cocoa. Before you start the continuous freezing of this flavor, make sure the sanitizing solution or the previous flavor of mix has been pushed through the freezer. Open the outlet valve of the mix storage tank and let the proper amount of frozen yogurt mix flow into the flavor tank. Pour the vanilla extract and coffee mixture into the flavor tank and mix all the ingredients together. The mix is then pumped to the inlet of the continuous freezer. Set the speed, viscosity (stiffness), and overrun settings according to the manufacturer's recommendations. Start the continuous freezing process. As the frozen yogurt leaves the continuous freezer, it is then piped to the next stage in the process, which is either filling (tubs, pints, etc.), extrusion, or molding.

⊠ MOCHA CHIP

A chocolate-coffee combination that has a wonderful smooth taste.

Batch		Continuous
2½ gallons	lowfat or nonfat frozen yogurt	100 gallons
1 ounce	Madagascar Bourbon and Tahitian pure vanilla extract (two-fold)	1¼ quarts
3 ounces	freeze-dried coffee	7½ pounds
10 ounces	cocoa (10–12% or 22–24% fat)	2¼ pounds
4 ounces	hot water	5 quarts
2 pounds	chocolate chunks or chips	80 pounds
	chocolate chunks or chips for garnish	

Batch Freezing Method

Set aside 4 ounces of chocolate chunks for garnish. Using as little hot water as possible, create a paste with cocoa and freeze-dried coffee. Combine the frozen yogurt mix, cocoa/coffee mixture and ½ pound of chocolate chunks or chips and pour into batch freezer. Turn on dasher and refrigeration and begin batch. Just before batch is complete, add remaining chocolate chunks, turn off refrigeration, and extrude finished product.

   Garnish with chocolate chunks or chips.

Batch time: 8–9 minutes.

Continuous Freezing Method

Using hot water, create a paste with the freeze-dried coffee and cocoa. Before you start the continuous freezing of this flavor, make sure the sanitizing solution or the previous flavor of mix has been pushed through the freezer. Pour the chocolate chunks or chips into the fruit feeder and adjust the controls to the appropriate setting. Open the outlet valve of the mix storage tank and let the proper amount of frozen yogurt mix into the flavor tank. Pour the vanilla extract and coffee/cocoa mixture into the flavor tank and mix all the ingredients together. The mix is then pumped to the inlet of the continuous freezer. Set the speed, viscosity (stiffness), and overrun settings according to the manufacturer's recommendations. Start the continuous freezing process. As the frozen yogurt leaves the continuous freezer, it is then piped through the fruit feeder (ingredient feeder) so that the chocolate chunks or chips can be discharged and mixed with the frozen yogurt that has already become semifrozen. The frozen yogurt is then piped to the next stage in the process, which is either filling (tubs, pints, etc.), extrusion, or molding.

⊠ CHOCOLATE

The number two best-selling frozen yogurt.

Batch		Continuous
2½ gallons	lowfat or nonfat frozen yogurt	100 gallons
1½ ounces	Madagascar Bourbon and Tahitian pure vanilla extract (two-fold)	1¾ quarts
1¼ pounds	cocoa (10–12 or 22–24% fat)	50 pounds*
⅓ pound	sugar	12½ pounds*
48 ounces	hot water	15 gallons*

Batch Freezing Method
Combine cocoa and sugar, add hot water, and thoroughly mix to create a very smooth paste. Combine cocoa paste with frozen yogurt mix and vanilla extract. Pour mixture into batch freezer, turn on dasher for 5 minutes to allow cocoa paste to blend into the mix. Next, turn on the refrigeration and begin batch. When batch is complete, turn off refrigeration and extrude finished product.

Batch time: 8–9 minutes.

Great New Idea: Add 1 pound of chocolate chunks at beginning of batch and 1 pound at end (before turning off refrigeration) to create Chocolate Chocolate Chip frozen yogurt.

Continuous Freezing Method
Before you start the continuous freezing of this flavor, make sure the sanitizing solution or the previous flavor of mix has been pushed through the freezer. Open the outlet valve of the mix storage tank and let the proper amount of chocolate frozen yogurt mix flow into the flavor tank.*

Pour the vanilla extract into the flavor tank and mix all the ingredients together. The mix is then pumped to the inlet of the continuous freezer. Set the speed, viscosity (stiffness), and overrun settings according to the manufacturer's recommendations. Start the continuous freezing process. As the frozen yogurt leaves the continuous freezer, it is then piped to the next stage in the process, which is either filling (tubs, pints, etc.), extrusion, or molding.

---

*Note: If you do not use a pasteurized chocolate frozen yogurt mix, thoroughly mix the cocoa and sugar with hot water in a large mixer, adding more water as needed, until a smooth creamy paste has been created.

Appendix ⊠⊠⊠⊠⊠⊠⊠⊠⊠⊠⊠⊠⊠⊠⊠⊠⊠⊠⊠⊠⊠⊠

SOURCES OF SUPPLIES AND INFORMATION

SUPPLIERS

Equipment

Continuous Freezing and Filling Equipment

APV HOMOGENIZER
500 Research Center
Wilmington, DE 01887
508-988-9300
Gaulin homogenizing equipment

APV ICE CREAM
100 South CP Avenue
Lake Mills, WI 53551
414-648-8311
Ice cream continuous freezing and filling equipment

AUTOPROD
5355 115th Avenue North
Clearwater, FL 34620
813-572-7753
Ice cream continuous freezing and filling equipment

CATTA 27
40056 Crespellano
Bologna, Italy
051-960038
Continuous ice cream freezing, novelty, and filling equipment

CHERRY-BURRELL/WAUKESHA
611 Sugar Creek Road
Delavan, WI 53115
414-728-1900
Continuous freezing equipment

FRIGOMAT
Via 1 Maggio
20070 Guardamiglio (MI)
Milan, Italy
0377-451170
Gelato pasteurizing equipment

GRAM EQUIPMENT OF AMERICA
1212 North 39th St., Suite 438
Tampa, FL 33605
813-248-1978
Ice cream continuous freezing and filling equipment

NORTHFIELD FREEZING SYSTEMS
719 Cannon Road
Northfield, MN 55057
507-645-9546
Ice cream freezing systems (tunnels)

PROCESSING MACHINERY & SUPPLY
1108 Frankford Avenue
Philadelphia, PA 19125
215-425-4320
*New and reconditioned ice cream
continuous freezing equipment.
(U.S. agent for Sidam and
Technogel continuous freezing
equipment)*

PROMAG
Via Romagna 12
20098 S. Giulano Milanese
Milan, Italy
02-98296-1
Gelato continuous freezing equipment

SEPARATORS, INC.
747 East Sumner Avenue
Indianapolis, IN 46227
800-233-9022
Separators

SILVERSON MACHINES
P.O. Box 589
East Longmeadow, MA 01028
413-525-4825
Batch and shear mixers

T.D. SAWVEL CO., INC.
5775 Highway 12
Maple Plain, MN 55359
612-479-4322
Ice cream filling equipment

TETRA LAVAL FOOD (HOYER)
Søren Nymarks Vej 13
DK-8270
Aarhus-Hejbjerg
Denmark
45 89 39 39 39

7711 95th Street
Box 0902
Pleasant Prairie, WI 53158
414-947-9100
*Ice cream continuous freezing and
filling equipment*

TINDALL PACKAGING
1150 East U Street
Vicksburg, MI 49097
616-649-1163
*Ice cream filling and packaging
equipment*

TRI-CLOVER, INC.
9201 Wilmont Road
Kenosha, WI 53141
414-694-5511
Batch mixers

WALKER STAINLESS EQUIPMENT
COMPANY
625 State Street
New Lisbon, WI 53950
608-562-3151
Processing tanks

Batch Freezing Equipment

CARPIGIANI
Via Emilia 45
Anzola Emilia
Bologna, Italy
051-6505111
*Gelato batch freezers and soft serve
equipment*

COLDELITE CORPORATION OF
    AMERICA
P.O. Box 4069
Winston Salem, NC 27115
910-661-9893
*Soft serve freezers, batch freezers,
    display showcases*

ELECTRO-FREEZE
2116 8th Avenue
East Moline, IL 61244
800-755-4545
*Soft serve freezers, batch freezers,
    blend-in machines*

EMERY THOMPSON MACHINE AND
    SUPPLY CO.
1349 Inwood Avenue
Bronx, NY 10452
718-588-7300
Batch freezers

TAYLOR COMPANY
88 Executive Avenue
Edison, NJ 08817
908-287-4350 or 800-255-0626
*Soft serve freezers, batch freezers,
    frozen drink machines*

Refrigeration

BEVERAGE AIR
P.O. Box 5932
Spartansburg, SC 29304
800-845-9800
*Refrigerators and freezers: stand-up
    and undercounter*

BIG APPLE EQUIPMENT COMPANY
Industrial Park
P.O. Box 408
Yonkers, New York 10705
*Refrigeration distributors for Master-
    Bilt and Beverage Air*

DELFIELD, INC.
P.O. Box 470
Mt. Pleasant, MI 48804
517-773-7981
*Refrigeration and freezing
    equipment*

EXCELLENCE COMMERCIAL PRODUCTS
P.O. Box 770127
Coral Springs, FL 33077
800-441-4014
*Freezer dipping cabinets and
    merchandising equipment*

HUSSMANN CORPORATION
Convenience and Special Store Group
Gloversville, NY 12078
518-725-0644
Dipping cabinets

ISA
06083 Bastia Umbra
Perugia, Italy
075-8001441
Gelato dipping cabinets

KELVINATOR COMMERCIAL PRODUCTS
707 Robins Street
Conway, AR 72032
501-327-8945
*Dipping cabinets, storage refrigerators
    and freezers, ice cream cake display
    cases*

MASTER-BILT
Highway 15N
New Albany, MS 38652
601-534-9061
*Dipping cabinets, storage refrigerators
    and freezers, ice cream cake display
    cases*

MCCRAY REFRIGERATOR
Grant Avenue and Blue Grass Road

Philadelphia, PA 19114
215-464-6800
Dipping cabinets, storage refrigerators and freezers, ice cream cake display cases

C. NELSON MANUFACTURING CO.
132 Railroad Street
Oak Harbor, OH 43449
419-898-2821
Ice cream storage chest and hardening chests

SILVER KING COMPANY
1600 Xenium Lane North
Minneapolis Industrial Park
Minneapolis, MN 55441
612-553-1881
Refrigerators and freezers: stand-up and undercounter; countertop novelty merchandising cases

TRAULSEN & COMPANY, INC.
114-02 15th Avenue
College Point, NY 11356
718-463-9000
Refrigeration equipment

Trucks and Mobile Vending Carts

ALL STAR CARTS
1565D Fifth Industrial Court
Bayshore, NY 11706
516-666-5252
Mobile vending carts

CARTS OF COLORADO, INC.
5750 Holly Street
P.O. Box 16249
Denver, CO 80022
303-288-1000
Mobile ice cream carts

CUSTOM SALES AND SERVICE
11th Street and Second Road

Hammonton, NJ 08037
609-561-6900
Ice cream vans

HACKNEY BROTHERS INC.
P.O. Box 2728
Wilson, NC 27894
919-237-8171
Mobile carts

JOHNSON TRUCK BODIES
215 East Allen Street
Rice Lake, WI 54868
800-922-8360
Refrigerator and freezer truck bodies

WORKMAN TRADING CORPORATION
94-15 100th Street
Ozone Park, NY 11416
718-322-2000
Mobile vending carts

Sanitation Equipment and Supplies

HAYNES MANUFACTURING COMPANY
4180 Lorain Avenue
Cleveland, OH 44113
800-992-2166
Food-grade lubricants

McGLAUGHLIN OIL COMPANY
3750 East Livingston Avenue
Columbus, OH 43277
614-231-2518
Lubricating oil (Petro Gel) for processing equipment

NELSON-JAMESON
2400 East 5th Street
Marshfield, WI 54449
800-472-0840
Sanitation and lab equipment and supplies

PURDY PRODUCTS
379 Hollow Hill Drive
Wauconda, IL 60084
800-726-4849
Sanitation supplies

REFRIGIWEAR, INC.
Breakstone Drive
P.O. Box 39
Dahlonega, GA 30533
706-864-5457
*Refrigerator and freezer plant
clothing*

WEBER SCIENTIFIC
2732 Kuser Road
Hamilton, NJ 08691
609-584-7677
Lab equipment and supplies

Miscellaneous Equipment

CAL-MIL PLASTIC PRODUCTS
4079 Calle Platino
Oceanside, CA 92056
619-630-5100
Coneholders

CRC
3218 Nebraska Avenue
Council Bluffs, IA 51501
712-323-9477
Mix-in shake machines

DIAMOND BRANDS
1660 South Highway 100, Suite 590
Minneapolis, MN 55416
612-541-1500
Ice cream novelty sticks

FLURRY INTERNATIONAL INC.
1100 West 9th Street
Cleveland, OH 44113
216-696-1133
Blend-in machines

FROZEN DESSERT MACHINE
CLEANING
P.O. Box 554
Jericho, NY 11753
516-731-8617
Soft serve cleaning maintenance

GELTECNICA MACHINE
Salita Al Molinello, 32
Rapallo, Italy
0185-230339
Italian novelty bar machines

HAMILTON BEACH COMMERCIAL
4421 Waterfront Drive
Glen Allen, VA 23060
800-527-7174
Milk shake blenders and ice cream scoops

INNOVATIVE MARKETING
9909 South Shore Drive
Plymouth, MN 55441
612-525-8686
Five gallon pail opener

ISI NORTH AMERICA, INC.
30 Chapin Road
Pine Brook, NJ 07058
201-227-2426
Whipped cream dispensers

KOPYCAKE ENTERPRISES
3701 West 240th Street
Torrance, CA 90505
800-999-5253
Cake decorating equipment

LLOYD DISHER COMPANY
5 Powers Lane Place
Decatur, IL 62522
217-423-2611
Ice cream scoops

LUCKS FOOD DECORATING COMPANY
303 South Pine Street

Tacoma, WA 98409
800-426-9778
Cake decorating equipment and edible images

NEGUS CONTAINER COMPANY
110 North Bedford Street
Madison, WI 53703
608-251-2533
Plastic containers

NOVELTY BASKETS
1132 Heather Lane
Carrillton, TX 75007
214-492-4738
Wire trays to hold novelties

PELOUZE SCALE COMPANY
7560 West 100th Place
Bridgeview, IL 60455
800-654-8330
Weight scales

ROPAK CORPORATION
20024 87th Avenue South
Building F
Kent, WA 98031
800-426-9040
Plastic containers

SERVER PRODUCTS
P.O. Box 249
Menomonee Falls, WI 53051
800-558-8722
Hot fudge machines, syrup dispensers and warmers

SOLON MANUFACTURING COMPANY
P.O. Box 285
Solon, ME 04979
207-643-2210
Ice cream novelty sticks

SWIRL FREEZE CORPORATION
2474 Directors Row

Salt Lake City, UT 84104
801-972-0109
Blend-in machines

T.J'S RACKS
1141 W. Swain Road, #132
Stockton, CA 95207
800-532-3917
Ice cream can collars

WILCH MANUFACTURING
1345 SW 42nd Street
Topeka, KS 66609
913-267-2762
Frozen slush machines

THE ZEROLL COMPANY
P.O. Box 999
Fort Pierce, FL 34954
800-872-5000
Ice cream scoops

Flavoring Ingredients

Chocolates

AMBROSIA/GRACE COCOA
12500 West Carmen Avenue
Milwaukee, WI 53225
800-558-9958
Cocoa, chocolate chips, chocolate coatings, etc.

CALLEBAUT
Asistersestraat 124
B-9280 Lebbeke
Wieze, Belgium
053-73-02-11
Chocolates and novelty bar coatings

FORBES CHOCOLATE
15620 Industrial Parkway
Cleveland, OH 44135
216-433-1090
Cocoa and chocolate chips

GERTRUDE HAWK CHOCOLATES
9 Keystone Industrial Park
Dunmore, PA 18512
717-342-7556
*Chocolate inclusions for ice cream
    production*

HOOTON CHOCOLATE COMPANY
364 North 5th Street
Newark, NJ 07107
201-485-5385
Cocoa and chocolate coatings

THE MASTERSON COMPANY
P.O. Box 691
Milwaukee, WI 53201
414-647-1132
Cocoa, fudges, chocolate chips, etc.

SHADE FOODS
400 Prairie Village Drive
New Century, KS 66031
800-255-6312
*Chocolates, candies, and novelty
    coatings*

VAN HOUTEN
Industrial Park
St. Albans, VT 05478
802-524-9711
*Cocoa, chocolate chips, chocolate
    coatings*

VAN LEER CHOCOLATE CORPORATION
110 Hoboken Avenue
Jersey City, NJ 07302
201-798-8080
Cocoa, chocolate coatings

W.L.W. BENSDORP CO.
1800 Westpark Drive #305
Westborough, MA 01581
800-772-6210
Cocoa

Fruit (Processed)

BUNGE FOODS
3582 McCall Place NE
Atlanta, GA 30340
800-241-9485
Ice cream flavor ingredients

CHIQUITA BRANDS
250 East Fifth Street
Cincinnati, OH 45202
800-438-0015
*Banana ingredients, various sizes and
    shapes*

COCO LOPEZ
180 East Broad Street
Columbus, OH 43215
800-341-2242
Coconut cream

FANTASY FLAVORS/BLANKE BEAR, INC.
611 North 10th Street
St. Louis, MO 63101
800-886-3476
*Ice cream and yogurt bases, fruits,
    candies, fudges, coated nuts, etc.*

LIMPERT BROTHERS, INC.
P.O. Box 520
Vineland, NJ 08360
800-691-1353
*Ice cream and yogurt flavor bases,
    fruits, fudges, syrups, etc.*

LYONS-MAGNUS
1636 South Second Street
Fresno, CA 93702
209-268-5966
Ice cream flavor ingredients

MILNE FRUIT PRODUCTS
P.O. Box 111
Prosser, WA 99350
509-786-2611
Fruit purees

RAMSEY/SIAS
6850 Southpointe Parkway
Brecksville, OH 44141
216-546-1199
Fruit preparations and purees

I. RICE & COMPANY
Adams Avenue and Leiper Street
Philadelphia, PA 19124
800-232-6022
Ice cream and Italian ice flavorings

SBI SYSTEMS
8 Neshaminy Interplex, Suite 213
Trevose, PA 19053
215-638-7801
Ice cream flavorings and purees

STAR KAY WHITE
85 Brenner Drive
Congers, NY 10920
914-268-2600
*Ice cream bases, fruits, chocolates,
    coated nuts, etc.*

Fruit (Frozen)

CLERMONT FRUIT PACKERS
P.O. Box 604
Hillsboro, OR 97123
503-648-8544
Fruit purees

FLAVORLAND MARKETING
P.O. Box 2240
Orinda, CA 94563
415-253-1920
Fruit purees

GLOBAL TRADING COMPANY
P.O. Box 26809
Greenville, SC 29616
800-849-9990
Fruits from all over U.S. and Mexico

ITI, INC.
3371 Route 1
Lawrenceville, NJ 08648
609-987-0550
Fruit ingredients

J.R. BROOKS & SON, INC.
P.O. Drawer 9
18400 SW 256th Street
Homestead, FL 33090
305-247-3544
Fruit purees

OREGON CHERRY GROWERS
P.O. Box 7357
Salem, OR 97303
800-367-2536
Cherries, various kinds and sizes

PRIMA FOODS INTERNATIONAL
1604 Esex Avenue
Deland, FL 32724
904-736-9138
Fruit purees

RAVIFRUIT-FRENCH FOOD EXPORTS
100 Manhattan Avenue
Union City, NJ 07087
201-867-2151
Fruit purees from France

WAWONA FROZEN FRUIT
100 West Alluvial
Clovis, CA 93612
209-299-2901
Frozen fruits

Nuts

ACE PECAN COMPANY
900 Morse Village
Elk Grove Village, IL 60007
312-364-3250
Nuts

BOYER BROTHERS, INC.
821 17th Street
Altoona, PA 16603
814-944-9401
Peanut butter pastes and variegates

NAVARRO PECAN COMPANY
Highway 31 East
P.O. Box 147
Corsicana, TX 75151
903-874-7143
Pecan nuts

PEANUT CORPORATION OF AMERICA
P.O. Box 10037
Lynchburg, VA 24506
800-446-0998
Peanuts: all sizes and varieties

PECAN DELUXE CANDY COMPANY
2570 Lone Star Drive
Dallas, TX 75212
214-631-3669
Candy-coated nuts

SNA NUT COMPANY
1348-54 West Grand Avenue
Chicago, IL 60622
800-544-NUTS
Pecan nuts

SUPERIOR NUT COMPANY
225 Monsignor O'Brien Highway
Cambridge, MA 02141
617-876-3808
Peanut butter variegate

TRACY-LUCKEY
110 North Hicks Street
Harlem, GA 30814
800-476-4796
Pecan nuts

YOUNG PECAN SHELLING COMPANY
1200 Pecan Street

Florence, SC 29501
800-845-4364
Pecan nuts

WESTCOTT NUT PRODUCTS
93-97 Colt Street
Irvington, NJ 07111
201-373-1866
Variety of nuts

Flavor Extracts

BECK FLAVORS
411 East Gano
St. Louis, MO 63147
800-851-8100
Flavor extracts and vanilla

DAVID MICHAEL & COMPANY
10801 Decatur Road
Philadelphia, PA 19154
215-632-3100
Extracts and fruit flavors

EDGAR A. WEBER & COMPANY
549 Palwaukee Drive
Whelling, IL 60090
800-558-9078
Vanilla and coffee flavor ingredients

NIELSEN-MASSEY VANILLAS
1550 Shields Drive
Waukegan, IL 60085
800-525-7873
Natural vanilla extracts

OSF
121 South Street
Elmwood, CT 06110
203-953-6015
Fruit flavor extracts

VIRGINIA DARE EXTRACT COMPANY,
    INC.
882 Third Avenue

Brooklyn, NY 11232
800-847-4500
Extracts and flavors

Miscellaneous Flavor Ingredient Companies

CAKE-D COR
P.O. Box 402
Lebanon, NJ 08333
908-236-9570
Ice cream cake ingredients

CTL
514 Main Street
P.O. Box 526
Colfax, WI 54730
800-962-5227
Malt powder, serving merchandisers

GUERNSEY-BELL, INC.
4300 South Morgan Street
Chicago, IL 60609
800-621-0271
Fruits, coated nuts, fudges, etc.

HERSHEY FOODSERVICE
14 East Chocolate Street
Hershey, PA 17033
717-534-6397
Chocolate candies for ice cream production and toppings

INSTANTWHIP FOODS
2200 Cardigan Avenue
Columbus, OH 43215
800-544-9447
Whipped cream and toppings

KRAUS & COMPANY/BATTLE CREEK FLAVORS
21070 Coolidge Highway
Oak Park, MI 48237
800-662-5871
Ice cream ingredient flavorings

LAKELAND CONFECTIONERY COMPANY
48 Lincoln Road
P.O. Box 867
Butler, NJ 07405
800-447-0043
Distributes ice cream production and toppings ingredients

LEAF INC.
500 North Field Drive
Lake Forest, IL 60045
708-735-7500
Candy ingredients

M&M/MARS
Division of Mars, Incorporated
High Street
Hackettstown, NJ 07840
908-852-1000
Candies

NABISCO BRANDS, INC.
P.O. Box 720
Hudson, WI 54016
800-852-9393
Oreo cookies and candy ingredients for ice cream production and toppings

NESTLE FOODSERVICE
800 North Bland Boulevard
Glendale, CA 91203
800-288-8682
Candy ingredients for ice cream production and toppings

A. PANZA & SONS, LTD.
60 Parkway Place
Raritan Center
Edison, NJ 08837
800-ICE-CREAM
Distributor of ice cream production, cake, and serving ingredients

PARKER BROTHERS
2737 Tillar Street
P.O. Box 9335
Fort Worth, TX 76107
817-336-7441
Ice cream ingredients

PARRISH'S
225 West 146th Street
Gardenia, CA 90248
800-736-8443
Ice cream cake-making supplies

SETHNESS-GREENLEAF
1826 North Lorel Avenue
Chicago, IL 60639
312-889-1400
*Ice cream and yogurt bases, fruits,
    nuts, and extracts*

SUNSHINE BISCUITS, INC.
Foodservice and Ingredient Products
100 Woodbridge Center Drive
Woodbridge, NJ 07974
800-423-6546
Hydrox cookies

WILTON INDUSTRIES
2240 West 75th Street
Woodridge, IL 60517
708-963-7100
*Ice cream cake equipment and
    supplies*

Gelato Flavor Ingredients

COLAVITA USA
2537 Brunswick Avenue
Linden, NJ 07036
908-862-5454
*Gelato flavorings (Monte Bianco and
    Perugina)*

FABRI (DE CHOIX SPECIALTY FOODS)
58-25 52nd Avenue
Woodside, NJ 11377

800-332-4649
Gelato flavorings

INTER-CONTINENTAL IMPORTS
149 Louis Street
Newington, CT 06111
800-424-4221
Gelato flavorings

PRE GEL GRANDE ISLE INC.
28-F Hunter Road
Hilton Head, SC 29926
803-681-7255
Gelato flavorings

Stabilizers

CONTINENTAL COLLOIDS
246 West Roosevelt Road
West Chicago, IL 60185
708-231-8650
Stabilizers

GERMANTOWN USA
505 Parkway
Broomall, PA 19008
800-345-8209
Stabilizers

CHARLES HANSEN
9015 West Maple Street
Milwaukee, WI 53214
414-476-3630
Frozen yogurt cultures

HERCULES, INC.
500 Hercules Road
Research Center
Wilmington, DE 19808
302-995-4578
Stabilizers

Ice Cream Cones

ACE BAKING COMPANY
P.O. Box 2476
Green Bay, WI 54306
800-279-2331
Waffle, sugar, and wafer cones: all sizes and varieties

COBATCO INC.
1327 NE Adams Street
Peoria, IL 61603
309-676-2663
Waffle cone batter and machines

CREAM CONE
P.O. Box 1819
Columbus, OH 43216
614-294-4931
Waffle, sugar, and wafer cones: all sizes and varieties

DANISH CONES
9703 NE 2d Avenue
Miami Shores, FL 33138
305-756-9500
Waffle cones

KEEBLER FOODSERVICE
One Hollow Tree Lane
Elmhurst, IL 60126
708-833-2900
Waffle, sugar, and wafer cones: all sizes and varieties

NOVELTY CONE COMPANY
807 Sherman Avenue
Pennsauken, NJ 08110
609-665-9525
Wafer and cake cones

PDI CONE COMPANY
69 Leddy Street
Buffalo, NY 14210
716-825-8750
Ice cream cones and sprinkles

SWEETHEART CUP COMPANY
10100 Reisertown Road
Owings Mill, MD 21117
800-800-0300
Waffle, sugar, and wafer cones: all sizes and varieties

Menu Boards

FUTURA 2000 CORPORATION
39-06 Crescent Street
Long Island City, NY 11101
800-783-6368
Menu boards, flavor identifiers and point-of-purchase signs

GREAT AMERICAN STOCK
521 Quantum Road, NE
Rio Rancho, NM 87124
1-800-624-5834
Food photography

MAINSTREET MENU SYSTEMS
1375 North Barker Road
Brookfield, WI 53005
800-782-6222
Menu boards

Mixes: Ice Cream, Frozen Yogurt, Soft Serve, and Nondairy

AE FARMS
2420 East University Avenue
Des Moines, IA 50317
800-234-6455
Ice cream mixes

BISON FOODS
196 Scott Street
Buffalo, NY 14204
716-854-8400
Soft serve ice cream and frozen yogurt mixes

COLOMBO/GENERAL MILLS
P.O. Box 1113
Minneapolis, MN 55440
800-874-1451
Soft serve frozen yogurt mix

GISE CREME GLACE
6064 Corte Del Cedro
Carlsbad, CA 92009
800-448-4473
Nondairy frozen dessert mix

KOHLER MIX SPECIALTIES
4041 Highway 61
White Bear Lake, MN 55110
800-231-1167
Ice cream mixes

WELSH FARM
55 Fairview Avenue
Long Valley, NJ 07853
908-876-3131
Hard ice cream mix

Packaging

AIRLITE PLASTICS
914 North 18th Street
Omaha, NE 68102
402-341-7300
Plastic cups, all sizes and varieties

ANDERSON PACKAGING
P.O. Box 510
Oak Ridge, NJ 07438
201-697-8888
Cup and aluminum seal packaging

CARDINAL PACKAGING
1275 Ethan Avenue
Streetsboro, OH 44241
800-544-9573
Plastic cup packaging

DOUGLAS STEPHANS PLASTICS
22-36 Green Street
Paterson, NJ 07509
201-523-3030
Plastic lids

DRISCOLL LABEL COMPANY, INC.
1275 Bloomfield Avenue
Fairfield, NJ 07004
201-575-8492
*Product labels for paper or plastic
packaging*

GEN PAK CANADA
260 Rexdale Boulevard
Rexdale, Ontario M9W 1R2
Canada
800-387-7452
Plastic containers

POLAR PLASTICS
7132 Daniels Drive
Allentown, PA 18106
215-398-7400
Plastic cups and spoons

SEALRIGHT COMPANY
7101 College Boulevard
Overland Park, MO 66210
913-344-9000
Paper cups, all sizes and varieties

SHERRI CUP INC.
245 Old Brickyard Lane
Kensington, CT 06037
860-828-6338
*Paper cup packaging, all sizes and
varieties*

SWEETHEART PACKAGING
10100 Reisertown Road
Owings Mill, MD 21117
800-800-0300
Paper and plastic cups and lids

Packaging and Storage Containers

BUCKHORN
55 West Techecenter Drive
Milford, OH 45150
800-543-4454
*Shipping and storage handling
   containers*

POLAR TECH INDUSTRIES
415 East Railroad Avenue
Genoa, IL 60135
800-423-2749
Insulated boxes for shipping

POLYFOAM PACKERS
2320 Foster Avenue
Wheeling, IL 60090
800-323-7442
Insulated boxes for shipping

Promotional Supplies

ANTHONY ENTERPRISES
28425 South Cole Grade Road
Valley Center, CA 92082
800-647-8372
Ice cream promotional clothing

ASSOCIATIONS

Domestic Organizations

AMERICAN DAIRY ASSOCIATION
Dairy Management, Inc.
P.O. Box 2018
Brownsdale, MN 55918
800-454-COWS

CALIFORNIA INDEPENDENT ALMOND
   GROWERS
13000 Newport Road
Ballico, CA 95303
209-667-4856

DAIRY AND FOOD INDUSTRIES SUPPLY
   ASSOCIATION
1451 Dolley Madison Boulevard
McClean, VA 22101
703-761-2600

GEORGIA PEANUT COMMISSION
P.O. Box 967
Tifton, GA 31794
912-386-3470

HAZELNUT MARKETING BOARD
P.O. Box 23126
Portland, OR 97281
503-639-3118

INTERNATIONAL ICE CREAM
   ASSOCIATION
(formerly the International
   Association of Ice Cream
   Manufacturers)
1250 H Street NW, Suite 900
Washington, DC 20005
202-737-4332
Annual source book: The Latest Scoop

NATIONAL ICE CREAM MIX
   ASSOCIATION
P.O. Box 0503
Fulton, MD 20759
301-369-3050

NATIONAL ICE CREAM & YOGURT
   RETAILERS ASSOCIATION
1429 King Avenue
Columbus, OH 43212
614-486-1444

NATIONAL PECAN MARKETING
   COUNCIL
Knapp Hall
Louisiana State University
Baton Rouge, LA 70803
504-388-2222

NATIONAL SOFT SERVE AND FAST
FOOD ASSOCIATION
9614 Tomstown Road
Waynesboro, PA 17268
800-535-7748

NATIONAL YOGURT ASSOCIATION
1764 Old Meadow Lane, Suite 350
McClean, VA 22102
703-821-0770

NEW ENGLAND ASSOCIATION OF ICE
CREAM MANUFACTURERS
500 Rutherford Avenue
Boston, MA 02129
617-734-6750

NEW JERSEY BLUEBERRY INDUSTRY
ADVISORY COUNCIL
548 Pleasant Mills Road
Hammonton, NJ 08037
609-561-3661

NORTH AMERICAN BLUEBERRY
COUNCIL
4995 Golden Foothill Parkway,
Suite #2
El Dorado Hills, CA 95762
916-933-9399

NORTHEAST ICE CREAM ASSOCIATION
P.O. Box 0503
Fulton, MD 20759
301-369-3050

UNDERWRITERS LABORATORIES
333 Pfingsten Road
Northbrook, IL 60062
847-272-8800
UL approval for equipment

WALNUT MARKETING BOARD
1540 River Park Drive, Suite 101
Sacramento, CA 95815
916-922-5888

International Organizations

DEUTSCHE LANDWIRTSCHAFTS-
GESELLSCHAFT V.
Michael Boehm
Zimmerweg 16 D-6000
Frankfurt aM. 1
Germany
069-71680

PRINTED INFORMATION

BATCH FREEZER NEWS
41 Tudor Lane
Scarsdale, NY 10583
914-472-7255

CORRESPONDENCE COURSE 102: ICE
CREAM MANUFACTURE
The Pennsylvania State University
Department of Independent Living
128 AG-Mitchell Building
P.O. Box 3207
University Park, PA 16802
814-865-7371

DAIRY FIELD Magazine
Stagnito Publishing Company
1935 Shermer Road, Suite 100
Northbrook, IL 60062
708-205-5660

DAIRY FOODS Magazine
Cahners Publishing Company
8773 South Ridgeline Blvd.
Highlands Ranch, CO 80216
303-470-4445

EUROPEAN DAIRY MAGAZINE
Verlag Mann
Nordring 10
D-45894 Gelsenkirchen
Postfach 20-02-54

Germany
02-09-93040

FOOD FORMULATING
One Chilton Way
Radnor, PA 19089
610-964-4447

FOOD PRODUCTION MANAGEMENT
2619 Maryland Avenue
Baltimore, MD 21218
410-467-3338

ICE CREAM, FIFTH EDITION
Chapman & Hall
115 Fifth Avenue
New York, NY 10003
212-254-3232

ICE CREAM UNIVERSITY
41 Tudor Lane
Scarsdale, NY 10583
914-472-7255
*Seminars on batch freezer and ice
cream cake production and
marketing*

THE NATIONAL DIPPER
1480 Renaissance Drive, Suite 101
Park Ridge, IL 60068
847-390-6550

SCANDINAVIAN DAIRY MAGAZINE
Frederiks Alle 22
DK-8000 Arhus C
Denmark
45-86-13-26-93

RECIPE INDEX

SUBJECT INDEX

Page numbers in italics refer to illustrations.

Mixes, ice cream, *(cont'd)*
  manual calculation of formulas for, 95–99
  measuring of ingredients for, 99
  mixing ingredients for, 99–100
  pasteurization with, 91, 100–101
  software programs for, 95
  stabilizers/emulsifiers in, 93–94
  storing, 103
  sweeteners in, 93
Mobile merchandising, 273–280
  carts, 273–279, *277–279*
  concession trailers, 280
  vans, 279–280
Monoglycerides, 94
Montezuma, 106
Monthly cleaning procedures, 86
Monthly operating statement, 225–226
Montmorency cherry, 123
MSNF, 92
Mud, 16

Name, choosing a business, 206
*National Food Processors Association
    Sanitation Report Form,* 79
Natural flavors/extracts, 107
Neapolitan, 13
Negus Square Pak, 36, *37*
Neighborhood marketing, 269–273
Nelson, C. K., 4–5
C. Nelson Manufacturing Company, 196
Networking, 270
Nielsen-Massey, 108, 109
NLEA, 147
No cow, 16
Nonfat ice cream, 10
Novelties, ice cream, 129–137
  for adults, 131–132
  and brand identity, 130
  for children, 130–131
  equipment manufacturers, 135–137
  innovation in, 129–130
  licensing of, 132
  market for, 10–11
  merchandising of, 133
  packaging of, 132–133
  production of, 133–135
  and value, 129

Nuts, 113–118
  almonds, 117
  coatings for, 113, 115
  hazelnuts, 118
  macadamias, 118
  and overrun, 35
  peanuts, 116–117
  pecans, 117
  pistachios, 118
  pralines, 117–118
  suppliers of, 114
  walnuts, 115–116
Nutrition Facts label, 147–149, *148*
Nutrition Labeling and Education Act of 1990 (NLEA), 147

O.J., 16
One on the City, 16
Opening a retail establishment, 161–213
  action plan for, 167–171
  advantages/disadvantages of, 162
  and business conditions, 163
  construction/remodeling of premises, 179–182
  employees, hiring/training, 207–210
  equipment requirements, *See* Equipment
  financing, start-up, 172–174
  finishing touches, 212–213
  grand opening, 212
  hours of operation, 211–212
  ideas, refining, 163–164
  leasing, 176–179
  and making vs. buying product, 164–166
  market surveys, using, 168–169
  permits/inspections, 210–211
  pro forma statement, preparing, 169, *170–171*
  signage, 204, 206–207
  space, locating, 175–179
  telephone listing, 212
Operating a retail establishment, 215–237
  cash management, *See* Cash management
  employees, 215–219
  sanitary conditions, 232–237
  security/emergency procedures, 219
Operating hours, 211–212

Operating statement, monthly, 225–226
Ordering, of ingredients, 126
Origins of ice cream, 1–2
Outerwear clothing, *70*
Overpricing, 157–158
Overrun, 14, 34–35
Overscooping, 218–219, 240
Owner-employee relations, 215–217

Packaging:
    bottom-up filling systems, 50
    continuous freezing process, 50–52, 61–68
    design of, 144–145
    of ice cream novelties, 132–133
    and merchandising, 144–146
    printing on, 145–146
Paper containers, 51
Parker, I. C., 5
Parker, Jewel, 5
Partnerships, 172
Pasteurization, 88–89, 91, 100–101
Pasteurizing vat, 100, 101
Payroll records, 224–225
Peaches, 122–123
Peanuts, 116–117
Pearson's Square, 97–98, *98*
Pecans, 117
Permits, 210–211
Personal hygiene, 236–237
Personnel, *See* Employees
Pest control, 236
Philadelphia ice cream, 14
Pies, ice cream, *See* Cakes/pies, ice cream
Pilferage, by employees, 218
Pineapple, 124
Pink Stick, 16
Pints, serving, 243–244
Pistachios, 118
Plan of action, developing, 167–171
PMS Company, 60–61
Point-of-purchase (POP) displays, 155–156
Polysorbates, 94
Popsicle, 5
PP film, 133
Pralines, 117–118
Premium ice cream, 13
Pricing, 28, 149–150

and merchandising, 263
and overpricing, 157–158
Pro forma statement, 169, *170–171*
Prohibition, 7–8
Promotion, *See* Merchandising
Purchasing:
    for batch freezing operations, 27–28
    of ingredients, 126
    and product costs, 226–227
Pure Food, Drug, and Cosmetic Act, 78

Quality control, 26–27, 29–30. *See also* Sanitary conditions
Quality-Pak, 36
Quality standards, decline of, 9
Quarts, serving, 243–244

Raspberries, 122
Recipe cost sheet, *228*
Recipes, 30, 34
    first printed, 1
Recycling, 51
Reduced-fat ice cream, 10, 14
Reed's, 7, *7*
Refrigerants, 183
Refrigeration:
    for mobile carts, 275–276
    walk-in, 68–72
Refrigerator/freezer bases, 197, 199
Rejecting ingredients, 80–81
Rent, as expense, 228–229
Retail establishments:
    first, 2
    marketing for, *See* Marketing (by retail establishments)
    in novelty market, 10
    opening, *See* Opening a retail establishment
    operating, *See* Operating a retail establishment
    serving customers in, *See* Serving customers
Rinsing, of equipment, 82–83
Ripple pump, 50
Roach control, 236
Rodent control, 236
Ropak Corporation, 36, *36*, 51
Roussel, Eugene, 3
Russia, 9, 11